SEARS LIST OF SUBJECT HEADINGS

Sears List
of
Subject
Headings

10th Edition

Edited by

BARBARA M. WESTBY

Chief, Catalog Management Division
Processing Department
Library of Congress

NEW YORK

The H. W. Wilson Company

1972

First Edition, 1923, ed. by Minnie Earl Sears
Second Edition, 1926, ed. by Minnie Earl Sears
Third Edition, 1933, ed. by Minnie Earl Sears
Fourth Edition, 1939, ed. by Isabel Stevenson Monro
Fifth Edition, 1944, ed. by Isabel Stevenson Monro
Sixth Edition, 1950, ed. by Bertha Margaret Frick
Seventh Edition, 1954, ed. by Bertha Margaret Frick
Eighth Edition, 1959, ed. by Bertha Margaret Frick
Ninth Edition, 1965, ed. by Barbara M. Westby
Tenth Edition, 1972, ed. by Barbara M. Westby

Copyright © 1972
By The H. W. Wilson Company

Printed in the United States of America

Library of Congress Cataloging in Publication Data

Sears, Minnie Earl, 1873-1933.
    Sears List of subject headings.

    "First-fifth editions had title: List of subject head-
ings for small libraries."
    1. Subject headings. I. Westby, Barbara Marietta,
ed. II. Title. III. Title: List of subject headings.
Z695.S43 1972   025.33   79-38376
    ISBN 0-8242-0445-X

Preface to the Tenth Edition

Minnie Earl Sears prepared the first edition of this work in response to demands for a list of subject headings that was more suitable to the needs of the small library than the A.L.A. and the Library of Congress lists. Published in 1923 the *List of Subject Headings for Small Libraries* was based on the headings used by nine small libraries that were known to be well cataloged. However, Miss Sears early recognized the need for uniformity, and she followed the form of the Library of Congress subject headings with few exceptions. This decision was important and foresighted because it allowed a library to add Library of Congress headings as needed when not provided by the Sears List and to graduate to the full use of Library of Congress headings when collections grew too large for a limited subject heading list.

Miss Sears used only *See* and "refer from" references in the first edition. In the second (1926) edition she added *See also* references at the request of teachers of cataloging who were using the List as a textbook. To make the List more useful as a textbook she wrote a chapter on "Practical Suggestions for the Beginner in Subject Heading Work" for the third edition.

Isabel Stevenson Monro edited the fourth (1939) and fifth (1944) editions. A new feature of the fourth edition was the inclusion of Dewey Decimal Classification numbers as adapted for the *Standard Catalog for Public Libraries*. The new subjects added to the List were based on those used in the Standard Catalog Series and on the catalog cards issued by The H. W. Wilson Company. Therefore, the original subtitle "Compiled from Lists used in Nine Representative Small Libraries" was dropped. Another new feature was the printing in italics of those subdivisions that had a more general application.

The sixth (1950), seventh (1954), and eighth (1959) editions were prepared by Bertha M. Frick. In recognition of the pioneering and fundamental contributions made by Miss Sears the title was changed to *Sears List of Subject Headings* with the sixth edition. Since the List was being used by medium sized libraries as well as small ones, the phrase "for Small Libraries" was deleted from the title. The symbols *x* and *xx* were substituted for the *See* and "refer from" phrases to conform to the format adopted by the Library of Congress.

The ninth edition, the first to be prepared by the present editor, continued the policies of the earlier editions, with one major exception. The Dewey Decimal Classification numbers were dropped. Many users of Sears had called to the attention of the publisher the inconsistency of including classification numbers and at the same time instructing the cataloger to consult the *Dewey Decimal Classification* for numbers. Moreover, it was the expressed opinion of these users that the inclusion of numbers often led to a misuse of the publication due to a misunderstanding of the relationship between subject headings and classification. In view of these important professional considerations, the publisher decided to omit the numbers from the ninth edition.

Protests were forthcoming but their number, in relation to the number who purchased Sears, was small. Previously, librarians using Sears had been urging that all possible Dewey numbers for a heading be listed. This was never practicable but is now almost impossible with the interdisciplinary relationships of subjects and the increasing complexity of subject heading work. The publisher has, therefore, reaffirmed its decision to omit the classification numbers in the tenth edition. The reader may be interested in the fact that in the Library of Congress list of subject headings there are classification numbers for only 8-10 per cent of the headings.

The "Practical Suggestions for the Beginner in Subject Heading Work" has been a continuing feature since it was written by Miss Sears. The chapter as revised by Miss Frick for her editions was reprinted in the ninth edition. For this edition the present editor has revised and retitled the introduction. Her indebtedness is obvious and is gratefully acknowledged.

New headings added to this tenth edition were suggested by librarians representing various sizes and types of libraries and by the catalogers at The H. W. Wilson Company who are responsible for the headings used on Wilson cards and in the Standard Catalog Series. In addition, selections were made by the editor from *Subject Headings used in the Dictionary Catalogs of the Library of Congress,* 7th edition and supplements, 1966—November 1971. While the new headings added to the ninth edition were chiefly from the fields of science and technology, those suggested and selected for this edition reflect the current interest in social and environmental problems. The swift developments in knowledge, the interrelationships of subjects, and the fluctuating popularity of interests increase the difficulty of the selection and wording of headings. The interdisciplinary interaction between subjects affects the books written about them. Biology, psychology, and mathematics, for example, are being applied to almost every subject. No list can hope to keep completely abreast of the present knowledge explosion, nor can it provide for every idea, object, process, and relationship. However, with patterns established and examples provided, the cataloger can supply new headings as needed. Guides for the wording of new headings may be found in the books themselves as well as in periodical literature and indexes. Although the daily newspaper may employ terms too colloquial for use as headings, it does provide a clue to the way in which a patron may ask for materials and suggest terms to be used as cross references.

The successive editors of the Sears List have followed the policy established by Miss Sears to use the Library of Congress form of subject headings with some modifications for current terminology and spelling. These modifications to meet the needs of smaller collections have been the simplification of phrasing (e.g. **City planning** rather than Cities and towns—Planning) and, in some cases, a broader level of specificity. Thus, closely related headings have been combined to create one heading for Sears from two Library of Congress headings. For example, Bacteria and Bacteriology were combined into **Bacteriology.** Similarly, Cotton manufacture and Cotton trade became **Cotton manufacture and trade.** Current spelling is illustrated by the use of **Airplanes** rather than Aeroplanes. The fickleness of terminology is shown by the Library of Congress heading Boots and shoes which was changed to **Shoes and shoe industry** in Sears and has remained good phraseology. However, the current vogue for boots has lent new validity to the Library of Congress form of the heading.

The Cataloging of Children's Materials Committee of the Cataloging and Classification Section of the Resources and Technical Services Division of A.L.A. requested that for the tenth edition these modifications of Library of Congress headings be kept to a minimum or eliminated entirely. Therefore, few changes in Library of Congress headings were made in this edition. However, the publisher and editor would appreciate comment on this policy from a wider spectrum of the library community, especially from the users of Sears. The policy is important because it affects the formulation of new headings and the modernization of old ones. Library of Congress subject headings, devised for the largest collection in the country, are not always practicable for a small collection. On the other hand, the increase of centralized, cooperative, and commercial cataloging and processing services make standardization not only desirable but virtually mandatory.

The question of modification in the Sears List is particularly pertinent at this time. Deliberations are underway at the Library of Congress on the methodology and timing of the modernization of its subject headings. The decisions to be made will affect the catalogs of all libraries and will influence the future of the *Sears List of Subject Headings*. For this reason the editor decided that a thorough and drastic revision of the Sears List was not appropriate or timely.

In response to a further suggestion made by the Cataloging of Children's Materials Committee the editor incorporated into the Sears List the headings from the *Subject Headings for Children's Literature* issued by the Library of Congress. Those that were not added were omitted for the following reasons: 1) they were already standard Sears headings; 2) they fall into the category of headings that can be added to Sears as needed; 3) they already existed in Sears in a slightly different form. The cataloger should be aware that some of the headings designated for juvenile books by the Library of Congress are modifications of headings assigned to adult books on the same subject. When such conflicts arose, the editor made an arbitrary choice.

When books are written from a particular point of view, specific headings are created for them. Thus, subject headings on the Negro were developed as the need arose. Today, the terminology of these headings is under review. Should a library change Negro to Black? The pressure for this change is great from some sectors of the population and in certain sections of the country. For this edition the change was deliberated long and thoughtfully and discussed with librarians of both races here and abroad. The meeting of the International Federation of Library Associations in 1971 afforded a unique opportunity to speak to librarians from Europe and Africa.

In the United States youth prefers and demands to be called Black while their parents and the older generation still prefer Negro. European librarians prefer Negro. African librarians accept Negro but reject Black, and refer to themselves as Africans, or more specifically Nigerians, etc. In the newspapers and the more popular publications the term Black is favored while in other materials both terms are being used. A further consideration is the fact that the word Negro is an exclusive term and so is very specific. On the other hand, the word Black is inclusive and is applied to many words having no relation to race. Because the use of Sears is international, because the terminology depends on the age of the speaker and the type of media, and because the preferred terminology has not stabilized, the editor decided to continue to use the Negro headings as previously established. However, an alternate list of Black subject headings has been provided in an Appendix for those libraries that wish to make the change. This compromise will perhaps satisfy both sides of the semantic question.

Physical characteristics. Webster's *Third New International Dictionary, Unabridged* (1961) was consulted for spelling, hyphenization, and definition. Capitalization and the forms of corporate entries used as examples are based on the *Anglo-American Cataloging Rules* (1967).

Filing of entries in Sears continues to follow Rule 35, subject arrangement 2, in the *A.L.A. Rules for Filing Catalog Cards* (1942) with a slight modification for parenthetical qualifiers. The straight alphabetical arrangement of the revised edition (1965), which disregards all punctuation, would have separated the subdivisions under a particular heading with the interspersion of other subject headings. The editor felt that a list of subject headings serves a different purpose from a dictionary catalog. In using a list of headings the cataloger is concentrating on one subject and its subdivisions, and would be distracted by extraneous topics not germane to the problem in hand. The two columns below illustrate the old and new A.L.A. filing rules. The reader will note that the Sears List has certain cross references that are no longer needed in the card catalog according to the revised filing rules, (e.g. Christmas—Poetry and Christmas—Stories). The editor suggests that libraries using the new filing rules cancel these unnecessary references in their copy of Sears and remove the cards from their catalogs.

Old	*New*
Christmas	**Christmas**
Christmas—Drama	Christmas cards
Christmas—Poetry	Christmas carols
Christmas—Stories	**Christmas decorations**
Christmas—U.S.	Christmas—Drama
Christmas cards	**Christmas entertainments**
Christmas carols	**Christmas plays**
Christmas decorations	Christmas—Poetry
Christmas entertainments	**Christmas poetry**
Christmas plays	Christmas—Stories
Christmas poetry	**Christmas stories**
Christmas stories	**Christmas—U.S.**

Old	*New*
Art	**Art**
Art, Abstract	**Art, Abstract**
Art, American	**Art, American**
Art—Analysis . . .	Art—Analysis . . .
Art, Ancient	Art anatomy
Art, Applied	**Art, Ancient**
Art, Arabic	**Art and mythology**
Art—Study and teaching	**Art and religion**
Art anatomy	**Art and society**
Art and mythology	Art, Applied
Art and religion	**Art appreciation**
Art and society	Art, Arabic
Art appreciation	**Art as a profession**
Art as a profession	**Art—Study and teaching**

A common criticism of any list concerns the degree of specificity in its headings. Specificity is relative and depends on the size of a library, its function, the nature of its collection, and its patrons. Practicality rather than theory should determine the degree of specificity, and a balanced blend of theory and practice has been the philosophy of Sears. In a small collection the use of too many specific headings can result in the scattering of like materials. Sears, by example, or instruction, suggests approximately 200 classes of headings that may be added by the cataloger when more specific subject headings are needed. Combinations of related materials under one heading and the use or nonuse of subdivisions also affect specificity.

"Key" headings with subdivisions applicable to a similar class of headings were provided in the first edition (**English language** and **U.S.**). Their number has steadily increased. The "key" for individual presidents, provided in the ninth edition, has been deleted in favor of an expansion of the subdivisions applicable to presidents individually and collectively under **Presidents—U.S.** Most of the subdivisions under **European War, 1914-1918** were omitted because they also appear under **World War, 1939-1945.** The latter heading was made a "key" for all wars.

Every heading in the List that may be used as a subject heading is printed in boldface type whether it is in the main file, in a *See also* paragraph, in a "refer from" reference, or an example for an explanation. That is, a boldface term is a used term, and conversely, if a term is not printed in boldface, then it is not a heading to be used for entering books.

The "refer from" references are listed in the format followed by the Library of Congress:

> **Arena theater**
> > *x* Round stage; Theater-in-the-round
> > *x x* **Theater**

A single *x* means a "refer from (*See* ref.)", and doubled *xx* indicates a "refer from (*See also* ref.)". (Consult the "Directions for Use" on the front flyleaf). These references are traced, i.e. recorded, under each subject to which reference is made. If a heading is mentioned only as an example in an explanatory note it is not traced.

Under subject headings representing broad fields of knowledge there are many *See also* references. No catalog will need all of these but in the List they are intended to aid the cataloger in comprehending the scope of the heading under which they are placed.

Scope. In compiling an abridged list of headings it is difficult to decide on the number of specific names to include for special classes of subjects. The needs of libraries are varied and this kind of heading can be supplied by the cataloger. Therefore, the specific names of some classes are omitted. Even in classes where specific names are included, other names in the same category may have to be supplied as the List is far from exhaustive. This edition follows its predecessors in types of headings included and omitted.

Classes of Headings Included in the List

1. Names of the *most common*

   a. Animals

   b. Chemical and mineral substances

   c. Diseases

   d. Games

    e. Musical instruments

    f. Organs and regions of the body

    g. Scientific and technical subjects

2. Names of the principal languages and literatures

3. Names of the most prominent church denominations

N.B. Specific names for representatives of these classes that are not in the List are to be added by the cataloger as needed.

*Classes of Headings Omitted from the List
for which the cataloger must supply specific names as needed*

1. Names of persons, except:

    a. Jesus Christ (included because of unique subdivisions)

    b. Shakespeare (included to show subdivisions which may be used under the name of any voluminous author)

2. Names of places, except:

    a. to serve as example of use of subdivisions under geographic names (e.g. **United States; Ohio; Chicago**)

    b. to list historical period divisions (e.g. **France**)

    c. to indicate the scope of the heading (e.g. **Northwest, Old**)

3. Names of corporate bodies such as associations, institutions, government bodies *except* names of prominent church denominations

4. Names of buildings, parks, ships, etc.

5. Names of tribes of North American Indians

6. Names of individual:

Battles	Fruits	Treaties
Birds	Nuts	Trees
Fishes	Tools	Vegetables
Flowers		

Directions for adding individual names are in the main List under these headings

Acknowledgments. As editor I wish to express my gratitude and heartfelt thanks to the catalogers who responded to my request for suggestions for additional headings for the tenth edition. I wish to express special appreciation to William J. Welsh, Director of the Processing Department, Library of Congress, for permitting me to continue my editorship of Sears and for his interest in the project. Individual thanks are due to many of my colleagues at the Library of Congress for their generous response to requests for information, suggestions, and criticism, and for allowing me to avail myself of their expertise. Two of these must be accorded special mention: Dr. Edith Scott, who read the introductory chapter on subject headings and gave generously of her valuable advice and counsel; and Eugene Frosio for advice and suggestions for the alternate list of Black subject headings. In addition, I must mention my secretary, Olivia Lucas, for assisting me with the typing copy. Last, but not least, my thanks to The H. W. Wilson Company, especially Estelle A. Fidell, Editor of the Standard Catalog Series, Lillian Clarke, and Thomas E. Sullivan, Assistant Director of Indexing Services, for specific suggestions, constructive criticism, and editorial assistance.

This edition is submitted with the editor's hope that it will prove helpful and practical. Continued consumer reaction will aid in its improvement. An invitation is hereby extended to users and readers to submit requests at any time for new or revised headings and to forward constructive criticism. All suggestions will be received with gratitude and will receive serious consideration and study.

Barbara M. Westby

November 1971

TABLE OF CONTENTS

SUBJECT HEADINGS
Principles and Applications of the Sears List

This chapter considers some principles and practices of subject cataloging that must be understood before an attempt is made to assign subject headings to books. Most of the illustrations refer to the *Sears List of Subject Headings* but the principles are applicable to other lists of subject headings as well, particularly the one issued by the Library of Congress on which the headings in this List are based.

Purpose of Subject Cataloging. The purpose of subject cataloging is to list under one uniform word or phrase all the books on a given subject that a library has in its collection. A subject is the theme or topic treated by the author in his book. A subject heading is the word or phrase used in the library catalog to express this theme or topic. A subject entry is the catalog card with the subject heading placed at the top as the filing medium.

Books are given subject entries in the catalog in order to show what books the library has on a given subject, just as author entries are made to show what books the library has by a given author. Properly made, the subject entry is a very important supplement to the reference tools in the library because it may enable the reader or librarian to find quickly and surely the material needed to answer a question on a subject. Subject entries are sometimes also the fastest way of finding a particular book. Ordinarily one consults the author entry for a specific book, but, if there is uncertainty about the author's name, one may find the individual book more rapidly under a subject entry. Smith's *History of Mathematics* would be difficult to find quickly if one did not know the author's first name and had to consult all the cards in the catalog under Smith. What if the author's name were really spelled Smyth? In either case, the book could be found readily under the subject **Mathematics.**

The Subject of the Book. The first step in subject cataloging is to ascertain the real subject of the book and the author's purpose in writing it. Sometimes this is readily determined, e.g. **Butterflies** is obviously the subject of the book titled *Butterfly Book.* In other cases, the subject is not so easy to ascertain because it may be a complex one or the author may not express it in a manner clear to someone unfamiliar with the subject. The subject of a book cannot be determined from the title page alone. The title page is often misleading and undue dependence on it can result in errors. A book entitled *Men of Art* immediately suggests the subject **Artists** but closer examination reveals the book to be about painters specifically, not artists in general. Therefore, the more exact subject is **Painters, not Artists.** Another illustration is "Fundamentals of Instrumentation," part 1 of a *Manual of Instrumentation.* This title may suggest a treatise on musical instruments or music, but actually it is a book on engineering instruments.

The steps to follow in determining the subject of a book are the same whether one is considering its value for a reader, classifying it, or assigning subject headings. After reading the title page of the book to be cataloged, examine the table of contents, and read the preface. Then, if the theme of the book is still not clear, examine the text carefully and read parts of it, if necessary. The cataloger will be in a position to determine the subject of the book in hand *only* after this preliminary work has been done. If the meaning of a subject is not clearly understood, one should consult reference books, not only an unabridged dictionary and general encyclopedias, but also specialized reference books as well. Only when the cataloger has decided on the subject content of the book and *identified it with explicit words,* can the List of subject headings be used to advantage. The cataloger must adapt his own phrasing of the subject of the book to the terminology of the List. The library catalog will be more useful if the cataloger considers books from the reader's point of view. The reader's profile depends on his age, background, education, occupation, and geographical location as well as the type of library he is using—school, public, university, or special. When examining a book the cataloger should ask "If I wanted material on this subject, under what words would I look in the catalog?" In choosing these words, that is, assigning the proper subject headings, there are certain principles that should be followed.

Specific Entry. Appreciation of the principle of specific entry is fundamental both in using and in making a modern subject catalog. The rule of specific entry is to enter a book under the most specific term, i.e. subject heading, which accurately and precisely represents the content of the book. This word serves as a succinct abstract of the book. If a reader wants a book about bridges, the direct approach is to consult the catalog under the heading **Bridges,** not under the large topic **Engineering,** or even the more restricted field, **Civil engineering.** Or, consider the principle of specific entry from the cataloger's point of view. If one is examining a book about penguins, it is not sufficient to dismiss it as a book belonging under the subject **Birds,** or even under **Water birds.** It must be entered under the most specific heading that expresses the book's content, that is **Penguins.** If entered under **Birds** a reader would have to look through many entries in order to find the few books on penguins. Having found the most specific entry that will fit the book do not then make subject entries under both the specific and the general subject headings. A book with the title *Birds of the Ocean* should not be entered under both **Birds** and **Water birds** but only under **Water birds.** To eliminate this duplication, a network of *See also* references directs the reader from the general subject headings to the more specific ones, e.g. **Birds.** *See also . . .* **Water birds;** and names of birds . . . In many cases the most specific entry may be a general subject, e.g. the book *Song Birds of the World* will have the subject heading **Birds.** The specific term, as can be seen, refers to the exact word that summarizes the subject of the book for the user of the catalog. Specificity is relative and depends on the size of the library, the nature of its collection, its function, and its patrons.

The heading should be as specific as the topic it is intended to cover. On the other hand, the heading should not be broader than the topic.

Books should be considered in categories. The word or phrase chosen as a subject must fit not only the books being cataloged but also apply to a group of books on the same subject. The cataloger must consider not only the one book in hand but also the other books that discuss the same subject, albeit under different titles, in order to select a subject heading that will serve the entire group of books in the catalog with relation to other groups. In cataloging *Everybody's Cook Book* the inexperienced cataloger might think first of Cook Books as the heading that will best describe this book. But there are two other books that belong in the same group: *How's and Why's of Cooking* and *Cooking for Profit.* These contain not only recipes but also other material on cooking. **Cookery** fits the three closely related books better than Cook Books and it also fits well with the related subject **Cookery for the sick.**

Common Usage. The word or words used to express a subject must represent common usage. In American libraries this means current American spelling and terminology: **Labor** not Labour; **Color** not Colour; **Elevator** not Lift. Foreign terms are not used unless they have been incorporated into the English language, e.g. Laissez faire. By the same token contemporary words are to be used: **Home economics** not Domestic economy. Today a more current term might be Homemaking, or Household management, but changing a heading is not always possible or advisable. There may be too many cards to change or, as in the case of **Home economics,** the term is still being used and newer usage may not have stabilized.

A general rule is to use a popular, or common, rather than a scientific, or technical, name where there is a choice. Subject headings are chosen to fit the needs of the people who are likely to use the catalog. A reader in a small public library will look under **Birds,** not Ornithology, or **Cancer,** not Carcinoma. After deciding on the common name as entry word, the scientific name should be taken care of by a reference to the form used. Such references will be discussed later. A term in common usage and expressed in the language of the user will be understood by him and will pass the test of comprehensibility.

A decision must be made whether the form of the heading is to be in a singular or plural form. Plural is the most prevalent but in practice both are used. Abstract ideas are usually stated in the singular. A concept is singular **(Drawing)** whereas objects and things are plural **(Drawings).** The names of fruit trees are stated in the singular so that they can stand for either the fruit or the tree. In this case, singular is more inclusive than the plural. In other cases, plural will have the broader coverage **(Art; The arts).** In still other cases, both singular and plural are used because they have different meanings, e.g. **Play** which refers to games and Plays (a *See* reference in Sears) which refers to drama.

Some descriptive phrases also carry different connotations, e.g. Arab, Arabian, and Arabic. Their use in headings appears to be inconsistent, but they are used in the following ways: Arab meaning of the Arabs; Arabian referring to Arabia, the geographical area; and Arabic for the language or writing or literature. These subject headings should be consistent, with distinction being made between ethnic, geographical, and linguistic terms.

Uniformity. Another factor to be considered is that of uniformity. One uniform term must be selected from several synonyms and this term must be applied consistently to all books on the topic. China, Chinaware, and Porcelain are all entered under **Porcelain**. This example also illustrates the fact that the subject heading must be inclusive and cover the topic. The heading chosen must be unambiguous. If several meanings attach to one word it must be qualified: **Masks (for the face)**; **Masks (Plays)**; **Masks (Sculpture)**. When variant spellings are in use, one must be selected and uniformly applied: **Rhyme**, not Rime.

Value of a List of Subject Headings. A printed list of subject headings, such as the Sears List, incorporates the thought and experience of many minds in various types of libraries. By using the List as a base, the cataloger has a source on which to rely. Consistency in both the specificity and the form of subject headings for the present and for the future is attained by working from an accepted list of subject headings where the choice among possible wordings has been made and recorded.

Form Headings. In addition to the subject headings that stand for subject matter found in the book, there are headings of another kind, usually known as form headings, or form subject headings, that have the same appearance as regular subject headings but refer to the literary or artistic form of a book and not to its subject matter, e.g. **Essays, Poetry, Fiction, Hymns, Songs**, etc. Literary form headings are used for collections rather than works of an individual. For example, the form heading **Essays** is used not for works of an individual author but for collections of essays by authors of different nationalities. If the collection includes essays only by American authors, then the more specific heading **American essays** would be used. While the use of form entries for works of individual authors might be helpful, the result in most libraries would not be worth the effort because such entries usually duplicate subject approaches already available in reference books in the library. The proliferation of entries would be an extra cost and would increase the size of the catalog unnecessarily. Books of this type are generally classified and arranged on the shelves according to their literary forms and the reader often has access to the shelves or to the shelf list. Ordinarily individual works of literature are remembered in association with an author, and a reader consults the author or title entry in the catalog for such works.

For a book about the essay as a literary form, e.g. the appreciation of the essay or how to write it, the heading **Essay** represents a true subject and not a form heading. The distinction between form headings and subject headings can sometimes be made by using the singular form for the true subject heading and the plural for the form heading, e.g. **Short story; Short stories**. But the peculiarities of our language do not always permit this. For example, the heading **English poetry** is used for a book about English poetry but in order to show that a book is a collection of poetry by several English authors the subdivision *Collections* must be added, i.e. **English poetry—Collections**.

In addition to the literary form headings there are some other useful form headings that are determined by the general format of the material and the purpose of the book, e.g. **Almanacs; Encyclopedias and dictionaries; Yearbooks**.

Classification and Subject Headings. The cataloger should now recognize a fundamental difference between classification and subject headings for the dictionary catalog. In a system of classification, which determines the arrangement of books on the shelves and groups together books on one subject, a book can obviously be in only one place. But in the catalog, cards representing the book can appear, if necessary, under more than one subject. The cataloger does not have to decide on one subject to the exclusion of all others, but can make the book useful with cards for as many different points of view as there are distinct subjects in the book (usually, however, not more than three).

Theoretically, there is no limit to the number of subject cards that could be made for one book, but practically such a policy not only would be expensive but also inefficient for the user of the catalog. For many books, one subject heading will represent the book accurately. A book such as *Guide to the Trees* is fully and specifically covered by the subject heading **Trees**. Frequently two are necessary as in the title *Field Book of American Trees and Shrubs* to which one would assign both **Trees** and **Shrubs**. Occasionally three are required to do justice to the book. More than three should be considered very carefully. The need for more than three may be due to the cataloger's inability to identify precisely the single heading that would cover all the topics in the book.

The practice may be stated as follows: As many as three specific subject headings in a given area may be assigned, but if the book treats of more than three, then the next larger inclusive heading is adopted and the specific headings are omitted. A book about lemons and limes would be entered under **Lemon** and **Lime**. If the book also included material on oranges, a third card with the heading **Orange** would be made for the catalog. But if the work discusses grapefruit and citron as well, the only subject heading assigned would be **Citrus fruit**.

Do not assign both a general heading and one of its specific aspects to the same book. In the example cited above, the book may have discussed the orange in more detail than the other fruits, but **Citrus fruit** and **Orange** would not be assigned simultaneously.

The following statistics give a practical demonstration of the proportion of books requiring more than one subject entry. Miss Sears in one of her early editions reported on books cataloged for a high school library, the books having the same characteristics as those in the collections of small public libraries. Of 1241 titles belonging in the first seven classes of the Dewey Decimal Classification, 788, or 63 per cent, required only one subject heading; 358, or 29 per cent, required two subjects; 76, or 6 per cent, received three subjects, and the remaining 2 per cent had received four or five headings. This study showed that the average number of subject cards for each title was 1.46. An interesting comparison may be made with a similar study made by the Technical Processes Research Office at the Library of Congress which revealed that 1.2 subject headings are assigned to each title cataloged.

The cataloger is now aware of another difference between classification and subject cataloging, one particularly significant for small libraries where the classification is by broader subjects and so is not as closely subdivided as the subject entries for the catalog. Books on birds, water birds, and all the special kinds of water birds are classed together in 598.2. Another example to emphasize this point is found in the treatment of fruit. A book on fruits in general, one on citrus fruits, and one on oranges will all three be classified in one number in a library, while in the catalog each book will have its own specific subject heading: **Fruit**; **Citrus fruit**; **Orange**.

It is well to remember this essential difference in the two processes; otherwise, the rule for classifying by broad subject in a small library (large libraries are not considered here) may cause confusion when the librarian attempts to assign subject headings which must be specific in order to achieve maximum usefulness.

The cataloger has learned that subject headings are used for books that have definite, definable subjects. However, there are a few books in which the subject is so indefinite that it is better not to assign a heading. If a cataloger cannot find a definite subject, the reader may not find the book under a makeshift or general heading. Do not use vague terms. They are a disservice to the reader. A book titled *Appreciation* received the heading **Behavior** from one cataloger while another assigned the word **Happiness**. In reality neither was correct. The book was a personal account of one source of the author's pleasure in life.

Now that certain principles of subject headings have been considered, the cataloger should understand the structure of subject headings.

Grammar of Subject Headings. (1) *Single Noun.* The simplest form of subject heading consists of a single noun and is the ideal type when the language supplies it. Such terms are not only the simplest in form but often the easiest to comprehend. Most of the large fields of knowledge can be expressed by single words (**Art; Agriculture; Education; Religion;** etc.) as can many concrete objects (**Apple; Chairs; Pottery; Trees; Violin;** etc.). But many words have synonyms from which a choice has to be made, and conversely a word may have two or more quite different meanings; for others there is a choice in spelling; another consideration is the use of the singular or plural form.

For example, in the case of **Pottery,** other words that might be used are: Crockery; Dishes; Earthenware; Faïence; Fayency; Stoneware. In the Sears List, the term chosen is **Pottery** and references are made from other terms.

On the other hand, the word Date may mean a fruit, an historical period, or a social engagement; Files may refer to an arrangement of material or a tool; Forging may mean counterfeiting or metalwork; Bridge may refer among other things to a game or an engineering structure. In the latter case, using the plural removes the possibility of the game but the singular form has to be qualified: **Bridge (Game).** Also the plural **Bridges (Dentistry)** must be distinguished from the engineering structure.

Whenever identical words with different meanings are used in the catalog one of them must be qualified, that is defined more specifically. In the example of the book on lemons and limes, neither heading is listed in Sears but may be added when needed, as instructed under both **Fruit** or **Citrus fruit.** However, in adding Lime to the List the cataloger finds **Lime** used in relation to **Cement.** The plural Limes cannot be used because Sears states that the name of all fruit should be in the singular form. The cataloger would therefore add a qualifier to Lime, i.e. **Lime (Fruit).**

Whether to use the singular or the plural or both sometimes depends on the peculiarities of the language since the two forms may express quite different concepts. In many cases, the singular connotes the general, and the plural the specific aspects. Or stated another way, the singular expresses abstract ideas and the plural refers to things. Thus, **Painting** means the art while **Paintings** refers to the objects. (According to the latest Library of Congress policy **Paintings** will be used for both the art and the objects, but Sears will continue to make the distinction.) The same parallel exists in the terms, **Essay** and **Essays, Short story** and **Short stories.** In all these cases, both forms are necessary, but in general if only one form is required, the plural has been adopted. However, the singular form has been chosen for the names of most fruits and nuts so that the more general term (**Apple; Pecan;** etc.) can be used to include books that consider the fruit or the tree or both.

(2) *Compound Headings.* Using two nouns joined by "and" usually groups together under one heading closely related material which cannot be separated easily in concept and which is usually treated together in books (**Boats and boating; Cities and towns; Crime and criminals; Publishers and publishing**); or two different subjects are treated in their relation to each other (**Aeronautics and civilization; Religion and science; Television and children**); or two subjects that are opposites but are usually discussed together (**Belief and doubt; Good and evil; Joy and sorrow**).

The problem in forming such headings is word order. There is no rule to cover all situations although catalogers have been prone to follow the alphabetic when there is no common usage. Whichever order is chosen, reference must be made from the opposite order.

(3) *Adjective with Noun.* Often a specific concept is best expressed by qualifying the noun with an adjective (**American literature; Electric engineering; Tropical fish**). Sometimes the expression is inverted (**Flies, Artificial; Philosophy, Modern**). The reasons for inversion are twofold: 1) an assumption is made that the reader will think first of the noun; or, 2) the noun is placed first in order to keep all aspects of a broad subject together when that result is deemed desirable. Inversion can be made when the first element qualifies the second and the second is an independent unit.

Art, Abstract	Education, Elementary	Insurance, Accident
Art, American	Education, Higher	Insurance, Fire
Art, Decorative	Education, Secondary	Insurance, Health

In formulating this kind of heading it is difficult to decide whether to use the normal order followed in speaking and writing or the inverted order; some users of the catalog will think of it one way, others in the opposite. (The current tendency of the Library of Congress is to use normal word order.) A reference is usually required from the order not chosen for the subject heading.

It should be noted that some adjective noun phrases could never be inverted because the noun has no significance without the adjective, e.g. **International relations.**

(4) *Phrase Heading.* Some concepts which involve two areas of knowledge can be expressed only by more or less complex phrases. These are the least satisfactory headings as they offer the greatest variation in wording, are often the longest, and may not be thought of readily by either the maker or the user of the catalog— but the English language seems to offer no more compact terminology. Examples are: **Freedom of information; Geographical distribution of animals and plants; Information storage and retrieval systems.** Some phrase headings have been standardized to serve as types for many situations: **Medicine as a profession** (the same form is used for other professions and occupations); **Italians in Africa** (the same form is used for other nationalities and other countries); **Women as physicians** (the same form is used for women in other professions and capacities).

Sometimes the phrase is inverted to place the important word first, or to facilitate the filing of related subjects together, although this results in an awkward appearance: **Cities and towns, Ruined, extinct, etc.**

Subdivisions of Subjects. There are other means by which the scope of the List can be enlarged far beyond the actual headings printed. This is through the use of subdivisions of headings.

The principle of specific entry can be achieved in some cases only by subdividing a general subject by words or phrases which indicate special aspects.

Birds	**Music**	**Water**
Birds—Eggs and nests	**Music—Acoustics and**	**Water—Analysis**
Birds—Migration	**physics**	**Water—Pollution**
Birds—Protection	**Music—Theory**	**Water—Purification**

In each of these fields, the subdivisions are characteristic of it and those used under one are not applicable to the other two listed here. However, the subdivision *Analysis* would be applicable to a number of other topics besides **Water**; such as **Air**; **Blood**; **Food**; etc.

Some terms or phrases used as subdivisions are applicable to so many different topics that the subdivisions are not printed under all possible headings but are referred to in their alphabetic places with directions for their use. They vary in kind and in value to an individual library.

(1) *Subdivisions by Physical Form.* Some books present material on a subject not in expository or narrative form but arranged in lists, outlines, or tables; or, graphically as maps or pictures. The work may be a directory of chemists, a bibliography of children's literature, a dictionary of psychology, a collection of geological maps, a Bible picture book. In such cases, it is important to show the user of the catalog that they are not books *about* chemists, or children's literature, or psychology, or geology, or the Bible, respectively. If the reader wants a bibliography or dictionary or maps or pictures, etc., it is equally important for him to be able to locate this directly without having to read through all the cards under the main heading. Standard terms known as "form divisions" are the most common subdivisions and may be used whenever appropriate. Since they show what the book *is,* rather than what it is *about,* they are as necessary for a small collection of books as for a large library. These terms are:

Bibliography	*Gazetteers*	*Portraits*
Catalogs	*Indexes*	*Registers*
Dictionaries	*Maps*	*Statistics*
Directories	*Pictorial works*	*Terminology*

Some of these terms are used alone as actual subject headings, but as subdivisions they are usually form headings. In either case, each term is listed in its alphabetic place in the List with directions for use; for example (entry shortened):

Bibliography
> *See also* **Archives** . . . also names of persons, places and subjects with
> the subdivision *Bibliography,* e.g. **U.S.—Bibliography; Agriculture**
> **—Bibliography;** etc.

Comparable statements are included under each of the other **form headings.** Applying these directions to the types of books cited above, the headings would be:

Chemists—Directories   Geology—Maps
Children's literature—Bibliography   Bible—Pictorial works
Psychology—Dictionaries

None of these headings appears in this form in the List, unless it has been cited as an example. Therefore, the *See* or *See also* under the name of the form is to be interpreted as directions for use. Only when a heading has been formulated and added can the words *See* or *See also* be interpreted literally.

(2) *Subdivisions that show Noncomprehensive Treatment.* Some books though literary in composition and general in subject are not comprehensive in scope. Random essays on a topic, if they do not present a connected and extensive review; yearbooks on a subject; or periodicals in a particular field are representative of this type of treatment. The standard terms for such noncomprehensive material, which may be used as subdivisions of general subject headings, are:

Addresses and essays   *Periodicals*
Handbooks, manuals, etc.   *Societies*
Laboratory manuals   *Yearbooks*

By following directions under these terms, subject headings such as those listed below could be formulated:

Architecture—Addresses and essays
Radio—Handbooks, manuals, etc.
Engineering—Periodicals
Commerce—Yearbooks

This kind of subdivision is particularly valuable under headings for the large fields of knowledge which are represented by many cards in the catalog. The cataloger must be guided by the character of the book's content, not by its title. Many books whose titles begin with such expressions as "Outlines of," "Handbook of," "Manual of" are in fact comprehensive works. For example, Wells' *Outline of History,* Locke's *Essay Concerning Human Understanding,* and Rose's *Handbook of Latin Literature* are comprehensive, lengthy treatises and to use the form divisions that the titles suggest would be inaccurate and ridiculous! Other so-titled "Outlines" or "Manuals" or "Handbooks" may prove to be bibliographies, dictionaries, or statistics of the subject.

(3) *Subdivisions that show Special Aspects.* Authors often treat a general subject from a particular point of view. The work may be a history of the subject, the most common of the special aspects; or it may deal with the philosophy of the subject, or of research in the field, or the laws about it, or how to study and teach it. These concepts applied to general subjects are expressed by such headings as:

Education—History   Radio—Laws and regulations
Religion—Philosophy   Mathematics—Study and teaching
Aeronautics—Research

(4) *Subdivisions that show Chronology.* In any catalog, large or small, there will be many books on American history. If they are all entered under the general heading, the library patron must look through many cards to find the specific era that he wants. However, with chronological subdivisions corresponding to gen-

erally accepted periods of a country's history or to the spans of time most frequently treated in books, he can pinpoint his search to **U.S.—History—1945-1953,** etc. If a chronological era has been given a specific name, this has been included in the heading with or without dates, e.g., **U.S.—History—Revolution.** The current trend is to use dates in preference to names.

The List includes period subdivisions only for those countries for which a library is apt to acquire so many books about their history (Great Britain, France, Germany, Italy and a few others) that it is necessary to separate them into groups according to the period treated. Although some countries have a longer history than any of these, period subdivisions of history are not needed because the library acquires so few books about them. Regardless of the period treated all the books would be assigned the general headings, e.g. **India—History.**

The subject and form subdivisions that are applicable to a considerable number of subjects are listed in their alphabetic places in the List and are also gathered together in one list on p. xlii. There the cataloger can see readily what possibilities of subdivision are available. History subdivisions, however, are different for each country and so cannot be listed in one place.

Geographic Names in Subject Headings. Many authors limit the discussion of an otherwise general subject to a specific country, state, city, or other region. This is such a common method of treatment that the List has provided directions for many subjects that may be so treated.

(1) *Subject Subdivided by Place.* Various subject headings, especially in the fields of science, technology, and economics are followed by a parenthetic statement giving permission to subdivide the heading geographically, such as: "**Agriculture** (May subdiv. geog.)." In application this means that if the work in hand deals with agriculture in general, only the heading **Agriculture** is used; but if the book deals with agriculture in Iowa or in France, for example, then the cataloger may assign the heading **Agriculture—Iowa** or **Agriculture—France.**

The unit may be the name of a country, state, city, or other political or geographic area, depending on the nature of the subject and its treatment in the book. There are, however, some topics which would not apply to cities, in which case the note will read: "(May subdiv. geog. country or state)."

If the subject is in the field of art or music, then the wording varies slightly since we think of Spanish art, for example (rather than art in Spain), or German music (rather than music in Germany). The List reads "**Art** (May subdiv. geog. adjective form, e.g. **Art, French**)" and "**Music** (May subdiv. geog. adjective form, e.g. **Music, American**)." From these directions the work on Spanish art would be assigned the heading **Art, Spanish** and that on German music, **Music, German.**

It is to be observed that the parenthetic note is permissive not mandatory. If the library has only a few books on a subject for which geographic treatment is suggested, perhaps it would be easier for the user of the catalog to find these under the main heading without geographic subdivision. Some small libraries limit the use of geographic subdivision to countries other than the United States and to nationalities other than American since most of their material, general or special, will be concerned with the United States. The Sears List historically has never distinguished between French art or Art in France (which is not necessarily French). Should a library have sufficient material to warrant such a distinction, **Art—France** could be established in addition to **Art, French** which is suggested.

One of the fundamentals of cataloging is to use one's judgment based on the materials on hand and the purpose and/or needs of the library.

(2) *Names of Places Subdivided by Subject.* A different procedure is followed for most topics in the fields of history, geography, politics and social sciences, which are treated from a regional point of view. In such works as a history of California, a census of Peru, the government of Italy, the boundaries of Bolivia, the population of Paris, or the climate of Alaska, the area treated is the unique factor and its name is the most specific heading for the book, with the particular subject as a subdivision.

Directions for formulating the headings are given under the general subjects in the same way that subject subdivisions are indicated, for example:

> **Census**
>> *See also* **Statistics;** also names of countries, cities, etc. with the subdivision *Census,* e.g. **U.S.—Census;** etc.

Again, the *See also* must be interpreted as a direction for formulating a heading for the specific area needed. Similar directions appear under **Boundaries; Climate; Population;** etc, which, applied to the topics cited above, would result in the headings:

California—History	**Bolivia—Boundaries**
Peru—Census	**Paris—Population**
Italy—Politics and government	**Alaska—Climate**

The name of any country, state, city, or other area could have been used if needed. However, some topics are applicable to countries only (e.g. *Commercial policy; Diplomatic and consular service*); others are used only under names of cities (e.g. *Harbor; Streets; Suburbs and environs*). The subdivision *Description and travel* is used for countries, states, and other large areas but is modified to the single word *Description* when applied to cities; therefore, **New Orleans— Description,** but **Louisiana—Description and travel.**

Headings that represent classes of institutions, such as hospitals, libraries and public schools, are used as subdivisions of names of cities but if the discussion covers a larger area, then the order is reversed. That is:

> **Chicago—Churches** but **Churches—U.S.**
> **Cleveland—Hospitals** but **Hospitals—Ohio**
> **Baltimore—Libraries** but **Libraries—Maryland.**

In such cases, the general heading will limit the subdivision to country and state while the *See also* directions will indicate its use for cities:

> **Hospitals** (May subdiv. geog. country or state)
>> *See also* . . . names of cities with the subdivision *Hospitals,* e.g. **Chicago— Hospitals;** etc.

In addition, a complete list of the subject subdivisions which may be used under the name of any city is given in the List under **Chicago;** those that may be used under the name of any state are listed under **Ohio;** while under the **United States** are those that may be used under the name of any country or region, except the subdivisions of history. Since each country's history is unique, its periods of history are individual.

Local materials are an exception to these rules if the library wishes to keep all of the home town or area materials together. Then (1) and (2) above are ignored and all books are listed under the name of the locality with all aspects as subdivisions.

There are no definite rules on subdividing by place or by subject. In general, subject headings in the field of science, technology, economics and the arts are subdivided by place, while history, geography, politics, and the social sciences are made subdivisions under place. But there are exceptions. That aspect of the subject that is most important or has the primary interest is the criteria for decision. When one reads about social life and customs, one asks where the social life exists, e.g. **U.S.— Social life and customs.** However, one aspect of social life is the **Family.** This is the subject of importance and one asks secondarily where the family is located. (Note that **Family** is not subdivided by place in Sears as it is in the Library of Congress but if a library has many books on the subject it might be advisable and permissible to do so).

In general the cataloger would enter under place and subdivide by subject those topics whose predominant interest is focused on area or people as history, geography, or government. One would enter under subject and subdivide by place those topics that are primarily of interest for the subject matter regardless of place. In the field of the social sciences the decision must be made in each instance on the element of predominance because no general rule applies.

Some headings in the subject areas of biography, language, and literature require subdivisions relevant to their areas, but others do not. Since knowing when not to subdivide is as important as when to use subdivisions, these areas will be treated in some detail.

Biography. Works in the field of biography are of two different categories: books in which biography as a form of writing is discussed, a relatively small class covered adequately by the subject heading **Biography (as a literary form);** and lives of persons, a very large class which must be considered in two groups—individual biography and collective biography.

(1) *Individual Biography.* Usually the only subject heading needed for the life of an individual is the name of the person treated, established in the same way as an author entry. If the work is an autobiography, some catalogers do not make a subject card for it since the author and the subject are the same. However, since readers have been trained to look under subject entries it seems reasonable to make both an author and a subject card, especially if there are many other entries as author or if there are subject entries by other authors, or if the library has a divided catalog.

Occasionally a biography will include so much material about the field in which the individual was concerned that a second subject heading is required in addition to the personal name. A life of Mary Baker Eddy, for example, may include a valuable account of the development of Christian Science that would require the subject heading, **Christian Science—History.** It must be emphasized that such second subject headings should be used only when there is a substantial amount of material included and when the book tells more about a person's work than his personal life. It is not used just because the biographee was prominent in the field.

There are a few individuals about whom there is a large amount of material that is other than biographical, such as works about their writings or other activities. In such cases, subdivisions are added to the individual's name to separate various aspects treated, among which is *Biography*. The two outstanding individuals are Jesus Christ and William Shakespeare. The List includes these names with subdivisions appropriate to material written about them. The subdivisions listed under Shakespeare may be used, if needed, under the names of other authors about whom there is a large amount of varied literature, notably Dante and Goethe. Subdivisions listed under **Presidents—U.S.** are to be used where appropriate under the name of any president. It must be noted that this represents the exceptional, not the usual treatment. For most individual biographies only the name is needed. That is, do not use the subdivision *Biography*.

(2) *Collective Biography*. This term refers usually to works containing more than three biographies, for if there are no more than three, each subject will be given a heading, consisting of his name, as in individual biography. (Some catalogers will treat even larger collections as a group of individual biographies). There are several varieties of collective biography, each requiring separate kind of treatment.

General. Collections of biographies not limited to any area or to any class of people are assigned the heading **Biography.** Sometimes the work includes many individuals, such as *International Who's Who;* sometimes a small group, such as *Ten Biographies of Famous Men and Women.*

Local Biography. Very common are the biographies devoted to persons of a particular area, such as *Who's Who in Asia, Who's Who in Latin America, Dictionary of American Biography, Eminent Californians, Leaders in London;* or to ethnic groups, such as *Prominent Jews.* In such works the subject heading is the name of the area or ethnic group with the subdivision *Biography:*

Asia—Biography	California—Biography
Latin America—Biography	London—Biography
U.S.—Biography	Jews—Biography

If there are many cards under any such heading, the literary works (that is, those designed for continuous reading) may be separated from the reference books which list a large number of names in alphabetic order, by adding to the heading for the latter, the subdivision *Dictionaries.* The heading for such a work as *Who's Who in America* may be, therefore, **U.S.—Biography—Dictionaries.**

Classes of Persons. Collective biographies that are devoted to lives of persons of a particular occupation or profession are entered under the term applied to its members, such as **Artists; Authors; Engineers; Librarians; Physicians; Poets; Radiologists; Scientists.** These terms are used alone, without subdivision.

In a field where there is no adequate term to express its members, or when the name of the class or group refers to the subject in general not to individuals, the heading used for the specific field is subdivided by the term *Biography:*

Catholic Church—Biography	U.S.—History—Civil War—
Religions—Biography	Biography
	Woman—Biography

N.B. The headings for areas, classes and groups are used for collective biographies only and not for the life of an individual American, artist, author, Jew, woman, etc.

However, reference to names of individuals should be made under the class names, for example: "Artists. See also names of individual artists."

Language and Literature. These two fields are closely related but they differ considerably in the number of books published and in their treatment in the subject catalog. Any general library has proportionately a large number of books in literature, often its largest field of interest, and a comparatively small number of books in language. In both areas, but more particularly in language, the major interest is not in the general treatment but in the national aspect, that is, French language or English literature, German grammar or Italian drama, Spanish dictionary or Hebrew poetry, etc.

Language. The subject heading for a general book about a specific language is the direct expression: **English language; French language; German language.** If the work deals with a particular aspect or form of that language, terms representing them are used as subdivisions of the name of the language. Examples are:

English language—Etymology	**Spanish language—Conversation**
French language—Dictionaries	**and phrase books**
German language—Grammar	

Some of the general form and subject subdivisions will be needed also under names of languages, for example, **Italian language—History.**

Names of some languages are included in this List (and others are to be added as needed) but no subdivisions are listed except under **English language.** This serves as a guide or "key" to the subdivisions that may be used under the name of any language.

Literature. The field of literature includes two classes of material which must be distinguished carefully: (1) Works about literature, a relatively small class; (2) examples of literature, that is *belles-lettres,* or the literature itself, a very large class. In the first group we are dealing with actual subjects; in the second with literary forms, not subjects.

(1) *Works about Literature.* The subject headings for books about the various literary forms are their specific names, e.g. **Drama; Essay; Fiction; Poetry.** Works about the major literary forms of national literatures are entered also under the direct phrase, not, as in language, as subdivisions; e.g. **Irish drama; Italian poetry; Russian fiction.** Specific aspects are expressed by subdivisions, as for other subjects; e.g. **Drama—Technique; English literature—Dictionaries; Poetry—Indexes; German literature—History and criticism.** It should be noted that the subdivision *History and criticism* is always used in its entirety and corresponds to the subdivision *History* used with other than literature and music subjects.

Names of some national literatures are included in the List (and others are to be added as needed) but the full list of subdivisions which may be used under them are listed only under **English literature** which thus serves as the "key" to subdivisions that may be used under the name of any national literature. The major literary forms may be used for any national literature by substituting its name for the word "English."

(2) *Examples of Literature, i.e. Belles-lettres.* This large class of material must be separated into two categories whose treatment is entirely different.

Individual Authors. In general, the literary works of individual authors receive no subject entry. Literature is known by author and title and readers usually want a specific novel, or a certain play, or poetry by a specific author—material which can be located in the catalog by author and title entries.

Collections of Several Authors. Because collections containing works of several authors are entered in the catalog under the name of the compiler or editor a device has been adopted to locate such works in the subject catalog by giving them a heading representing the form of literature in the collection. Since such headings are used also for actual subjects, distinction must be made between the headings for works *describing* a particular literary form and *examples* of it. (C.f. paragraph on form headings).

The singular form is used as an actual subject heading. If it has an acceptable plural, that is used to represent collections, but if there is no true plural then the subdivision *Collections* is added to the name of the literary form:

Subject Heading	*Form Heading for Collections*
Essay	Essays; American essays; etc.
Parody	Parodies
Short story	Short stories
Drama	Drama—Collections
French drama	French drama—Collections
Fiction	Fiction—Collections
Russian fiction	Russian fiction—Collections
Literature	Literature—Collections
German literature	German literature—Collections
Poetry	Poetry—Collections
Japanese poetry	Japanese poetry—Collections

Minor literary forms, such as parodies, satire, and short stories, are not listed under the national adjective. If national treatment is needed, the adjective is added after the name of the form, e.g. **Satire, English.** These headings are used not only for collections by several authors but also for works of individual authors and for works about such forms. This departure in treatment from that given to the major literary forms is due to the small number of books involved. If the number of books for any of them is large the heading may be subdivided to separate the works about them from the literature itself, e.g. **Satire, English—History and criticism.**

Literary Forms used as Subdivisions. Catalogers frequently give novels, poems and plays based on historical events or lives of famous persons a subject entry. Such headings must be distinguished from the headings which are assigned to factual accounts by adding the subdivision *Drama; Fiction;* or *Poetry,* as the case may be:

> **Slavery in the U.S.—Drama**
> **Lincoln, Abraham—Fiction**
> **Bunker Hill, Battle of, 1775—Poetry**

Popular libraries often give subject headings to classes of stories in which their readers are interested, such as **College stories; Mystery and detective stories; Science fiction; Vocational stories.** Names of animals, birds, flowers, holidays, etc. are subdivided by the term *Stories,* e.g. **Dogs—Stories** (Consult the references in the List under *Fiction* and *Stories*).

Scope of the Sears List. It is essential that the cataloger be aware not only of the kinds and forms of headings included in the List but also of kinds of headings which are not in the List but which will be needed for the catalog. These are summarized on p. x under "Classes of Headings Omitted from the List" and expanded on p. xliv under "Headings to be Added by the Cataloger." These types of headings were omitted not only because of limitations of space but also because of the widely variant needs of libraries and the fact that it is not difficult for the cataloger to supply the ones needed. Throughout the List directions for their addition are supplied.

(1) *Proper Names.* Perhaps the most used subject headings in a library's catalog are names of persons and names of places, only a few of which are included in the List, mainly as examples. The form of name is determined by means of the *Anglo-American Cataloging Rules* and reference books in the same way that author entries are established. The same form is used as subject heading with a change only in position on the card and perhaps in typography. (Many libraries use red for subject headings). The names of societies, institutions, and other corporate bodies, of individual battles and treaties, and of Indian tribes are established in the same way except that different kinds of reference books may be needed.

(2) *Common Names.* In quite another category are the names of animals, birds, fishes, flowers, fruits, etc. and of some other concrete objects whose common names can be verified in an ordinary dictionary. (Scientific names are seldom used in the kind of general library for which this List was compiled). Let us consider specific material in one of these areas. Suppose the cataloger has a book that discusses elm and ash trees and thinks, of course, of these two simple concrete words as subject headings. But shall the singular or plural form be used? On consulting the List, neither term is found so the cataloger must turn to the larger subject, **Trees.** In this case, the heading will give the direction the cataloger needs: "Names of trees are not included in this list but are to be added as needed, in the singular form." The cataloger thus has the authority for using the two headings, **Elm** and **Ash,** and writes them in their alphabetical places.

The procedure may be stated in this way: If the name of a specific object is not found in the List, consult the name of the class to which it belongs for directions for adding it.

Comprehension of the Terminology of the List. The subject headings for the general fields of knowledge and for concrete objects are simple to comprehend, but terms for abstract ideas may offer some difficulty. By looking through the *See also* references under a given heading, or noting the *See* references to it, a cataloger may often find how the term is used.

Sometimes two or more terms may seem to cover the same subject, unless the exact meaning and limitations of each is appreciated. Some headings in the List are accompanied by a scope note explaining their limitations as an aid to differentiating between overlapping subjects. For example, the headings **Alcoholism; Liquor problem; Liquor traffic; Prohibition; Temperance** overlap to a certain degree, but because of doubt in their distinctions one should not use all of them for any one book. By means of the scope notes included with these terms, it is understood that **Alcoholism** is used for medical works and works on drunkenness; **Liquor problem** includes works of an administrative or local character; **Liquor traffic** is used for works on the liquor industry; **Prohibition** for works dealing with the legal prohibition of liquor traffic and liquor manufacture; and **Temperance** is used for general works on the temperance question and the temperance movement.

A cataloger must consult the library's own catalog in order to see how a subject heading has been used. Printed subject catalogs such as the *Cumulative Book Index* and the "Standard Catalog Series" are also of value in order to see what kind of books are included under a given subject. Other cataloging aids are the *Publishers' Weekly, Subject Guide to Books in Print,* and the *Library of Congress Catalog—Books: Subjects.* Aid in interpreting the scope and meaning of a subject heading may be found by looking up its classification number or numbers in the *Dewey Decimal Classification.* There the topic can be studied in its relation to other topics, a development usually impossible to see directly in an alphabetic arrangement.

The individual cataloger will have individual problems in interpretation of subjects. Having decided on the scope of a term where there has been doubt, a definition or explanation should be recorded for future use. Such notes are a necessity for catalogers and they may be helpful also to users of the catalog. Whenever it is felt that such an explanation would be of general value, it may be typed on a card and filed in the catalog preceding the entries under the subject heading. Of course, the wording may have to be adapted slightly from that in the List which is addressed to catalogers.

References in the Catalog. After a book has been assigned a subject heading, attention must be directed to insuring that the reader who is searching for this book will not fail to find it because of insufficient guidance by means of references to the proper heading. The matter of references has been mentioned before in this text and attention has been called to them in the "Directions for Use" on the front flyleaf. The following is a summary of their types, methods of formulation, and use.

(1) *Specific "See" References.* These refer the reader from terms or phrases not used as subject headings to terms or phrases that are used. They are, therefore, absolutely essential to the success of the catalog. The reader must be directed from variant spellings and terminology to the one word or phrase that has been selected to represent the subject. While a subject heading may be used on as many cards as the library has books on the subject, the *See* reference is made on one card only. For example, the first time the heading **Agriculture** is used for a book, the cataloger (following the suggestion in the *x* paragraph under **Agriculture** in the List) will make a card for the catalog that reads: "Farming. See Agriculture." This will not be made again, no matter how many times the heading **Agriculture** is used, and no book will ever be assigned the word Farming as a heading.

See references to headings used are made:

(1) from synonyms or from terms so nearly synonymous that they would cover the same kind of material

(2) from the second part of a compound heading, e.g. **Prejudices and antipathies** requires a reference from Antipathies

(3) from the second part of an inverted heading, e.g. **Chemistry, Technical** requires a reference from Technical chemistry

(4) sometimes from an inverted heading to normal order, e.g. **Adult education** requires a reference from Education, Adult. (Note the number of used headings that begin with the word Education)

(5) from variant spellings to the spelling used, e.g. **Esthetics** requires a reference from Aesthetics

(6) from opposites when they are included without being specifically mentioned, e.g. **Temperance** requires a reference from Intemperance

(7) from the singular to the plural when the two forms would not file together in the catalog, e.g. **Mice** requires a reference from Mouse; **Cats** requires a reference from Cat. (Note the long list of headings between the singular and the plural of each of these two words)

It is not always necessary to make every *See* reference indicated in the List; for example, under the heading **Prisons**, a *See* reference from Dungeons is indicated but this should not be made unless the books listed under **Prisons** contain something about ancient prisons, that is, Dungeons. On the other hand, the cataloger may need to make additions to the *See* references in order to include local terminology.

(2) *Specific "See also" References.* The *See* references are concerned mainly with terminology, guiding the reader from words he may think of to those actually used for subject headings. But the *See also* references are concerned entirely with guiding the reader from headings where he has found books listed to other headings which list books on related or more specific aspects of the subject. Consequently such references cannot be made without knowing whether the library has material under the subjects concerned.

In general, *See also* references are made from the general subject to more specific parts of it, and not ordinarily from the specific to the general. For example, "Science. See also Mathematics," but not the other way around. Proceeding one step at a time to the next more specific topic would result in: "Mathematics. See also Arithmetic"; and "Arithmetic. See also Business arithmetic." *See also* references are also made between related subjects of more or less equal specificity, for example, "Drawing. See also Painting."

See also references are much more difficult than *See* references both to make and to understand, and their value is not so unquestioned. They have been included freely under headings (in the *xx* paragraph) in the List but only knowledge of the library's collection can determine whether any of these suggestions should be followed. For example, a book that discusses both inventions and patents will be entered in the catalog under **Inventions** and under **Patents.** The List suggests the reference, "Inventions. See also Patents," but it must not be made if all that is to be found in the catalog under **Patents** is this book which is already listed under **Inventions.** If there is a choice between two headings, the predominant one should be chosen.

(3) *General References.* In addition to specific references, there are general *See* and *See also* references which, instead of referring to many individual headings, serve as blanket references to all headings of a particular class. Some references are

a combination of specific and general. It is the general references which give the cataloger directions for supplying specific headings omitted from the List, as explained previously. Their use and value in the public catalog are somewhat different. The most common types of general references are to refer to:

(1) Common names of different species of a class, e.g.
>   **Flowers**
>> *See also* **Annuals (Plants)** . . . also names of flowers, e.g. **Roses;** etc.

(2) Names of individual persons, e.g.
>   **Artists**
>> *See also* **Architects** . . . also names of individual artists

(3) Names of particular institutions, buildings, societies, etc., e.g.
>   **Abbeys**
>> *See also* **Cathedrals** . . . also names of individual abbeys, e.g. **Westminster Abbey;** etc.
>
>   **Labor unions**
>> *See also* **Arbitration, Industrial** . . . also names of individual labor unions, e.g. **United Steelworkers of America;** etc.

(4) Names of particular geographic features, e.g.
>   **Mountains**
>> *See also* **Mountaineering** . . . also names of mountain ranges (e.g. **Rocky Mountains;** etc.) ; and names of mountains, e.g. **Elk Mountain, Wyo.;** etc.

(5) Geographic treatment of a general subject, e.g.
>   **Population**
>> *See also* **Birth control** . . . also names of countries, cities, etc. with the subdivision *Population,* e.g. **U.S.—Population; Chicago—Population;** etc.

(6) Form divisions, e.g.
>   Glossaries. *See* name of language or subject with the subdivision *Dictionaries, e.g.* **English language—Dictionaries; Chemistry—Dictionaries;** etc.

(7) National literatures, e.g.
>   **Poetry**
>> *See also* **Ballads** . . . also **American poetry; English poetry;** etc.

It is apparent that the general references in the List save an enormous amount of space both in the List and the library catalog. If all the headings for which directions are given were formulated they would be almost innumerable. In an individual library relatively few of these headings are used so that it may be preferable to formulate specific references when specific headings are added, particularly if there are only a few in the class. That is, if the cataloger uses the headings **Azaleas; Parakeets; Pineapple** (none of which is in the printed List), these names would be added to the *See also* references under the respective classes represented. For example, assuming that the headings **Fruits; Berries;** and **Citrus**

fruit had been used for books, the reference in the List and in the catalog would now read: "Fruit. See also Berries; Citrus fruit; Pineapple."

However, if there should be a long list of specific headings, catalogers disagree on the policy of adding them to the reference. For example, the heading **Artists** in the List, reads: "*See also* . . . names of individual artists." Some catalogers, in preparing this reference for the catalog, would omit the phrase, "names of individual artists," and instead, add the names of all the artists that have been used as subject headings in the library's catalog; other catalogers expect the reader to think of possible names himself and the reference is left as printed. Each library must determine this on the basis of the number of specific references that would be needed. But under classes where the individual names may not be numerous or well-known, it is feasible for the cataloger and useful to the reader to list the names rather than to rely on the general reference. However, in the example in the preceding paragraph the cataloger would be advised to make the reference as follows: "Fruit. See also Berries, Citrus fruit; also names of fruit, e.g., Pineapple, etc."

The cataloger should note that under a *See* reference there is never a subject entry for a book, while under *See also* references there are always entries. Reading the reference structure in the List always poses a problem for beginners as does the making of the references for the library catalog. Below is a heading from the List and its reading:

> **Birds** (May subdiv. geog.)
>> Names of birds are not included in this list but are to be added as needed, in the plural form, e.g. **Canaries**; etc.
>> *See also* **Birds of prey; Cage birds; Game and game birds; State birds; Water birds;** and names of birds, e.g. **Canaries;** etc.
>> *x* Bird; Bird watching; Ornithology
>> *xx* **Animals; Vertebrates; Zoology**

Note that the *See also* references read in direct order from top to bottom: **Birds.** *See also* **Birds of prey; Cage birds; Game and game birds;** . . .
The *See* references read in the reverse order, from bottom to top, that is, from the word opposite the *x* up to the heading: Bird. *See* **Birds. Bird watching.** *See* **Birds.** Ornithology. *See* **Birds.** "*See also* from" references also read from the bottom to the top, that is, from the word opposite the *xx* up to the heading: **Animals.** *See also* **Birds. Vertebrates.** *See also* **Birds. Zoology.** *See also* **Birds.**

To maintain a subject authority on cards rather than checking in the book as described on p. xli the cataloger would make cards as illustrated opposite but would not include on the card all the instructions and scope notes printed in the List.

Birds

    See also

Birds of prey
Cage birds
Game and game birds
State birds
    and names of birds, e.g. Canaries; etc.

Bird

    See

Birds

Bird watching

    See

Birds

Ornithology

    See

Birds

Animals

    See also

Birds

Vertebrates

    See also

Birds

Zoology

    See also

Birds

The directions and scope notes printed in the List for the guidance of the cataloger should be modified for the card catalog if the cataloger feels that a note is needed for the patron. Following is an example of a rewording:

As it appears in the List for the cataloger:

> **Air lines**
>> Use for works dealing with systems of aerial transportation and with companies engaged in this business. Works dealing with the routes along which the planes are flown are entered under **Airways**
>> *See also* **Airways**
>> *x* Airlines
>> *xx* **Aeronautics, Commercial; Airways**

As it appears in the card catalog for the reader:

Air lines

   Here are listed books dealing with the systems of aerial transportation and with companies engaged in this business

   Books on the routes along which the planes are flown are entered under Airways

New Terminology for Old Subjects. The English language is changing constantly so that from time to time new terms appear for subjects which are not new. Through the years many changes have had to be made: **Child welfare** was formerly *Children—Charities, protection, etc.;* **Radio advertising** started out as *Radio broadcasting—Business applications; House decoration* was in use before the present **Interior decoration,** and *Profession, Choice of* before **Vocational guidance.**

It is impossible for the subject headings to reflect all the newest language styles, particularly in fields whose terminology fluctuates frequently, for a term current today may soon be superseded by others or a term considered passé may return to favor. But at least new terms must be represented in the catalog by *See* references to the heading used.

Of course, if a heading is found to be incorrect or is no longer in common usage, changes must be made. The adoption of a new term means changing not only all the old entries to the new form but also the various references to and from it.

It is impossible to state at what stage in the development of the language such changes should be made. Each heading must be considered individually. The Library of Congress makes changes from time to time but because of its huge catalog it cannot always make as many as would be desirable—the expense is prohibitive. Changes in terminology are included in quarterly supplements to its list of subject headings.

If change is desirable but the number of cards to be changed is prohibitive, one can accomplish the change by *See also* reference cards. Using one of the aforementioned changes as an example, the cataloger would make the following cards substituting for (date) the calendar year in which the change is made:

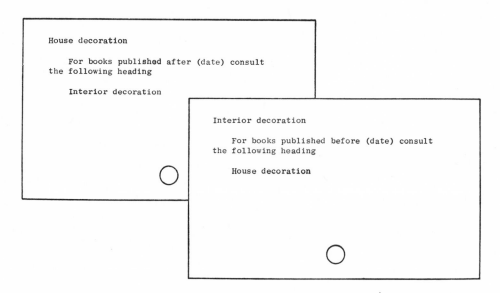

New subjects. No printed list of subject headings can be entirely up to date. There are constantly new ideas, new inventions, or new countries being created. Headings for these new topics of current interest will have to be added as needed. They should be constructed in the same way as headings for related topics and as the cataloger has been shown in this text.

First aid is supplied by the periodical indexes, such as the *Readers' Guide to Periodical Literature, Applied Science & Technology Index,* etc., since their editors must assign subject headings to material as soon as it is published. As the new subject develops, some change in the heading may be made in succeeding issues of the index. By the time a book is written about a new subject, the terminology may have changed and become stabilized since the first periodical index article appeared. Therefore, the catalogs of new books, such as *The Booklist, Cumulative Book Index,* and *Book Review Digest* are valuable aids. The Library of Congress includes headings for new subjects in the quarterly supplements to its list of subject headings. *Publishers' Weekly* publishes the Library of Congress cataloging information in its "Weekly Record," which are then cumulated in the *Book Publishers Record.* Cataloging in Publication, a revival of the Cataloging in Source program, will print the Library of Congress cataloging information on the verso of the title pages in the books of those publishers cooperating in the program.

It is not always possible to decide at once on the permanent form for a new subject heading but the cataloger cannot wait for the subject to develop before giving headings to new material. Tentative headings can be assigned, perhaps written in pencil on the cards, to be used until the terminology becomes standardized. A list of these tentative headings should be kept (it will never be long) so that they can be reconsidered later and either adopted permanently or changed, as the case may be, and added to the List. One must be sure that the new term is not merely a new name or a colloquialism for a subject already in the catalog.

Recording Headings and References Used. The cataloger should keep a list of subject headings used and references made for them. This may be kept on cards and filed in the catalog department or a copy of the List may be checked whenever a heading is used for the first time. Additions to the List will be written in as well as references needed. Detailed directions for checking the List and a Sample Page illustrating them will be found on p. xli.

Aids to Subject Cataloging

Akers, Susan Grey
    Simple library cataloging. 5th ed. Metuchen, N.Y., Scarecrow Press, 1969.
    (Chapter 2)

Canadian Library Association. Committee on Canadian Subject Headings
    A list of Canadian subject headings. Ottawa, CLA, 1968.

Dewey, Harry
    An introduction to library cataloging and classification. 4th ed. rev. and enl.
    Madison, Wis., Capital Press ₍c1957₎ (Chapters 10-13 and 15)

Dunkin, Paul S.
    Cataloging USA. Chicago, ALA, 1969. (Chapter 5)

Eaton, Thelma
    Cataloging and classification; an introductory manual. 4th ed. Ann Arbor,
    Mich., Edwards, 1967. (Chapters 5-6)

Foskett, A. C.
    The subject approach to information. Hamden, Conn., Archon Books, 1969.
    (Chapters 3-4, 16-17)
      Chiefly a study on classification but the above chapters are pertinent

Frarey, Carlyle James
    Subject headings. New Brunswick, N.J., Graduate School of Library Service,
    Rutgers University, 1960. (The State of the library art, v. 1, pt. 2)
      A review and evaluation of the literature on subject headings

Harris, Jessica L.
    Subject analysis; computer implications of rigorous definition. Metuchen,
    N.Y., Scarecrow Press, 1970

Haykin, David Judson
    Subject headings; a practical guide. Washington, U.S. Govt. Print. Off., 1951

Library literature; a bimonthly index to books, periodicals and theses on library
    science and librarianship. New York, The H. W. Wilson Co.
      Refers to many articles on subject headings

Mann, Margaret
    Introduction to cataloging and the classification of books. 2d ed. Chicago,
    American Library Association, 1943 (Chapters 9-10)

Pettee, Julia
    Subject headings; the history and theory of the alphabetical subject approach
    to books. New York, The H. W. Wilson Co., 1946 (Out-of-print)

Piercy, Esther J.
    Commonsense cataloging; a manual for the organization of books and other
    materials in school and small public libraries. New York, The H. W.
    Wilson Co., 1965 (Chapter 7) (New edition in preparation)

Tauber, Maurice Falcolm
    Technical services in libraries; acquisitions, cataloging, classification, binding,
    photographic reproduction, and circulation operations. New York, Co-
    lumbia University Press, 1954 (Chapter 10)

Wynar, Bohdan S.
    Introduction to cataloging and classification. 3d ed. Rochester, N.Y., Libraries
    Unlimited, 1967. (Chapter 8)

CHECKING HEADINGS AND REFERENCES IN THE LIST AND ADDING HEADINGS TO IT

See Sample Page opposite

1. *Check the subject heading used.* When the subject heading **Birds** is used for the first time, a check mark is placed in front of it.

2. *Make and check "See" references to the heading.* The *x* terms under **Birds** are considered and the cataloger decides to make a reference from Bird and from Ornithology as suggested. Cards are made for the catalog reading: "Bird. See Birds" and "Ornithology. See Birds." The terms Bird and Ornithology are checked both in their alphabetic places in the List and in the *x* references under **Birds.** The reference from Bird watching is not made until a book on this subject is received by the library. When such a book is filed under **Birds,** then Bird watching is checked and a card for the reference made for the catalog.

3. *Make and check "See also" references to the heading.* The *xx* headings given under **Birds** are examined to see whether they have been used in the catalog. The heading **Vertebrates** has a check mark beside it showing that it has been used. The cataloger decides to place a reference card in the catalog reading: "Vertebrates. See also Birds." It is recorded in the List:

> under **Birds,** in the *xx* paragraph, **Vertebrates** is checked
> under **Vertebrates,** in the *See also* paragraph, **Birds** is checked

For purposes of this explanation assumption is made that **Zoology** has not been used yet.

4. *Adding headings to the List.* The library acquires a book about ostriches. The term is not in the List but the directions given in the note under **Birds** tell the cataloger that the heading **Ostriches** may be added. It is written in the margin in its alphabetic place and checked. To the public catalog is added the reference card: "Birds. See also Ostriches." It is recorded in the List:

> under **Birds,** to the *See also* paragraph is added, **Ostriches,** and checked
> under **Ostriches,** is added, *xx* **Birds,** and checked

The library acquires a book on birds of the Gaspé Peninsula. Following the permission given with the heading **Birds,** "(May subdiv. geog.)," the cataloger uses the heading, **Birds—Gaspé Peninsula,** writing it in the margin in its alphabetic place and checking it. Since the library has very little material about this region, it is decided to make a reference for the catalog reading, "Gaspé Peninsula—Birds. See Birds—Gaspé Peninsula." This reference is added also to the List and traced under the new heading by adding, *x* Gaspé Peninsula—Birds.

5. *Canceled subjects.* If all cards for a subject are withdrawn from the catalog, turn to the subject heading in the List, find what references have been made and remove the cards (if they are individual references) or cancel the heading (if other references are on the card). At the same time, erase or cross off the check marks in the List to show that the subject and its references are not now used.

SAMPLE PAGE OF CHECKING

Abbreviated entries taken from various pages of the Sears List
A check (∨) indicates that the heading or reference
has been used in the library's catalog

✓Birds (May subdiv. geog.)
    Names of birds are not included in this
       list but are to be added as needed,
       in the plural form, e.g. **Canaries;** etc.
    See also **Birds of prey; Cage birds;** and
       names of birds, e.g. **Canaries;** etc.
    x Bird; Bird watching; Ornithology
    xx **Animals; Vertebrates; Zoology**
Birds—Flight. *See* **Flight**
Birds—Habits and behavior
    xx Animals—Habits and behavior

    ✓ Ostriches;

    Birds - Gaspé Peninsula
    x ✓ Gaspé Peninsula - Birds

Gasoline engines. *See* **Gas and oil engines**

    ✓ Gaspé Peninsula - Birds. See
    ✓ Birds - Gaspé Peninsula

Gastronomy. *See* **Cookery; Dinners and din-**
    ing; Food; Menus

Ornamental plants. *See* **Plants, Ornamental**

✓Ornithology. *See* **Birds**

Orphans and orphans' homes
    See also **Child Welfare**
    x Charitable institutions; Dependent chil-
       dren; Foundlings; Homes (Institu-
       tions)
    xx **Charities; Child welfare; Children—In-**
       stitutional care; Institutional care;
       Public welfare

Osteopathy
    See also **Massage**
    xx **Massage; Medicine; Medicine—Prac-**
       tice

Ostrogoths. *See* **Teutonic race**

    ✓ Ostriches
    xx ✓ Birds

Versification
    See also **Poetry; Rhyme**
    x English language—Versification; Meter;
       Prosody
✓ *xx* **Authorship; Poetics; Rhythm**
Vertebrates
    See also **Amphibians;** ✓ **Birds; Fishes;**
       Mammals; Reptiles
    xx **Zoology**

LIST OF SUBDIVISIONS

Which May Be Used under Subject Headings

The subdivisions which may be used under the names of countries, states, and cities; under names of language and names of literature; under names of voluminous authors; under names of presidents; and under names of wars are not listed below but are to be found under the following Key names in the List:

Key country: **United States**   Key literature: **English literature**
Key state: **Ohio**   Key author: **Shakespeare, William**
Key city: **Chicago**   Key president: **Presidents—U.S.**
Key language: **English language**   Key war: **World War, 1939-1945**

The following subdivisions may be used under general subject headings as needed.

Addresses and essays
Anecdotes, facetiae, satire, etc.
Automation
Bibliography
Bio-bibliography
Biography
Cartoons and caricatures
Case studies
Catalogs
Collections
Dictionaries
Directories
Discography
Encyclopedias
Exhibitions

Handbooks, manuals, etc.
History (for all works except literature and music)
History and criticism (for literature and music)
Indexes
Outlines, syllabi, etc.
Periodicals
Philosophy
Pictorial works
Psychology
Research
Societies
Statistics
Study and teaching
Yearbooks

The subdivisions listed below are not as general in application as those listed above but may be used under classes of subjects. They are to be used where applicable. This is not an all-inclusive list but these subdivisions are recorded here for convenient and rapid reference.

Accidents
Accounting
Air conditioning
Analysis
Anatomy
Assassination
Attitude
Audio-visual aids
Care and treatment
Censorship
Civil rights
Collection and preservation
Collectors and collecting
Colonies
Computer programs
Conservation and restoration
Diseases
Diseases and pests
Documentation
Drama
Dwellings
Economic aspects
Education
Employment

Entrance requirements
Equipment and supplies
Estimates
Examination, questions, etc.
Experiments
Fiction
Finance
Habits and behavior
Institutional care
Laboratory manuals
Laws and regulations
Maps
Marketing
Medical care
Migration
Models
Personal narratives
Physiological effect
Poetry
Political activity
Portraits
Programmed instruction
Psychological aspects
Recruiting

Rehabilitation
Religious life
Repairing
Safety appliances
Safety measures
Sexual behavior
Songs and music
Sources

Stories
Stories, plots, etc.
Suffrage
Surgery
Terminology
Tropics
Vocational guidance

HEADINGS TO BE ADDED BY THE CATALOGER

Classes of Headings for Which the Cataloger Must Supply the Specific Names if not Included in the List

N.B. Names are to be found in reference books in the library

A. PROPER NAMES

1. Names of persons
2. Names of families
3. Names of places
   a. Political units: countries, states, cities, provinces, counties, etc.
   b. Groups of states or countries: e.g. **Atlantic States; Baltic States;** etc.
   c. Geographic features: Mountain ranges and individual mountains
   Island groups and individual islands
   River valleys and individual rivers
   Regions, oceans, lakes, etc.
4. Names of nationalities
5. Names of national languages and literatures
6. Names of battles
7. Names of treaties
8. Names of Indian tribes

B. CORPORATE NAMES

1. Names of societies, clubs, etc.
2. Names of institutions: colleges, libraries, hospitals, etc.
3. Names of government bodies
4. Names of buildings, parks, ships, etc.

C. COMMON NAMES

1. Names of

animals	flowers	tools
birds	games	trees
fishes	nuts	vegetables

2. Names of diseases
3. Names of organs and other parts of the body
4. Names of chemicals
5. Names of minerals

D. GENERAL INSTRUCTIONS

Wherever the List cites, "*See also* [or *See*] names of . . . ," the specific name wanted for the class may be added even though not included in the List

DIRECTIONS FOR USE

BOLDFACE TYPE is used for all terms which may be used as subject headings:
> **Gifts**

LIGHTFACE TYPE is used for terms which are *not* to be used as subject headings, but are only *references* to subject headings that may be used:
> Bequests. *See* **Gifts; Inheritance and succession; Wills**

See also means to also consider using the subject headings listed. They are always related to the heading under which they are placed and are usually more specific. They show the scope of the larger, more inclusive subject under which they appear:
> **Clubs**
>> *See also* **Boys' Clubs; Girls' clubs; Social group work; Societies; Women's clubs**

x before a term or terms means that a "see reference" may be made (if needed) *from* each such term *to* the heading under which it is placed

xx before a term or terms means that a "see also reference" may be made (if needed) *from* each such term *to* the heading under which it is placed
> **Algae**
>> *x* Sea mosses; Seaweeds
>> *xx* **Marine plants**

That is:

> Sea mosses. *See* **Algae**
> Seaweeds. *See* **Algae**
> **Marine plants**
>> *See also* **Algae**

"May subdiv. geog." Any heading followed by this phrase may be subdivided by the name of a country, state, city, or other area

"May subdiv. geog. country or state." Any heading followed by this phrase may be subdivided by the name of a country or state, but *not* by the name of a city

"May subdiv. geog. adjective form." Any heading followed by this phrase may be used with the national adjective, in inverted form, e.g. **Art, French**

Under headings:

> "*See also* (or *See*) names of countries, cities, etc. . . ." means that the name of any country, state, city or other area may be used followed by the heading cited

> "*See also* (or *See*) names of countries, states, etc. . . ." means that the name of any country, state or other large area (but *not* cities) may be used followed by the heading cited, e.g. **Maine—Constitutional history**

KEY HEADINGS for which subdivisions are printed in full and so serve as examples for other localities, nationalities, voluminous authors, presidents, and wars

Key country: **United States** (or **U.S.**)	Key literature: **English literature**
Key state: **Ohio**	Key author: **Shakespeare, William**
Key city: **Chicago**	Key president: **Presidents—U.S.**
Key language: **English language**	Key war: **World War, 1939-1945**

SEARS LIST OF SUBJECT HEADINGS

ABC books. *See* **Alphabet books**

ABM. *See* **Antimissile missiles**

A.D.C. *See* **Child welfare**

Abacus

Abandoned towns. *See* **Cities and towns, Ruined, extinct, etc.**

Abbeys

    See also **Cathedrals; Convents; Monasteries;** also names of individual abbeys, e.g. **Westminster Abbey;** etc.

    xx **Church architecture; Church history; Convents; Monasteries**

Abbreviations

    See also **Acronyms; Ciphers; Shorthand; Signs and symbols**

    x Contractions; Symbols

    xx **Ciphers; Shorthand; Signs and symbols; Writing**

Ability

    See also **Executive ability; Leadership; Musical ability;** also similar headings describing specific kinds of ability

    xx **Success**

Ability—Testing

    x Aptitude testing

    xx **Educational tests and measurements; Mental tests**

Ability grouping in education

    See also **Nongraded schools**

    x Grouping by ability

    xx **Grading and marking (Students)**

Abnormal children. *See* **Exceptional children; Handicapped children**

Abnormal psychology. *See* **Psychology, Pathological**

Abolition of slavery. *See* **Abolitionists; Slavery**

Abolitionists

    x Abolition of slavery

    xx **Slavery in the U.S.**

Aborigines. *See* **Ethnology; Native races;** and names of native races, e.g. **Indians of North America;** etc.

Abortion

    x Fetal death; Miscarriage

    xx **Birth control**

Abrasives

Absence from school. *See* **School attendance**

Absenteeism (Labor)

    x Employee absenteeism; Labor absenteeism

1

Absenteeism (Labor)—*Continued*

  xx Labor and laboring classes; Personnel management

Abstinence. *See* **Fasting; Temperance**

Abstract art. *See* **Art, Abstract**

Academic degrees. *See* **Degrees, Academic**

Academic dissertations. *See* **Dissertations, Academic**

Academic freedom

  See also **Church and education**

  x Freedom of teaching; Teaching, Freedom of

  xx **Church and education; Civil rights; Intellectual freedom; Toleration**

Accelerated reading. *See* **Rapid reading**

Accident insurance. *See* **Insurance, Accident**

Accidents

  See also

Disasters	Occupations, Dangerous
Explosions	
Fires	Poisons
First aid	Shipwrecks
	Traffic accidents

  also subjects with the subdivision *Accidents, e.g.* **Aeronautics—Accidents; Railroads—Accidents;** etc.

  x Emergencies; Injuries

  xx **Disasters; First aid**

Accidents—Prevention

  See also **Safety appliances; Safety education;** also subjects with the subdivision *Safety appliances* or *Safety measures, e.g.* **Aeronautics—Safety measures; Railroads—Safety appliances;** etc.

  x Prevention of accidents; Safety measures

  xx **Safety appliances; Safety education**

Accidents, Space craft. *See* **Astronautics—Accidents**

Acclimatization. *See* **Adaptation (Biology); Man — Influence of environment; Plant introduction**

Accompaniment, Musical. *See* **Musical accompaniment**

Accountants

  x Bookkeepers; Certified public accountants

Accounting

  See also **Auditing; Bookkeeping; Cost accounting;** also names of industries, professions, etc. with the subdivision *Accounting, e.g.* **Corporations—Accounting;** etc.

  xx **Auditing; Bookkeeping; Business; Business arithmetic; Business education**

Accounting machines. *See* **Calculating machines**

Accounts, Collecting of. *See* **Collecting of accounts**

Acculturation

See also **East and West; Intercultural education**

xx **Anthropology; Civilization; Culture;
East and West; Ethnology; Race
problems**

Acetate silk. *See* **Rayon**

Achievement tests. *See* **Examinations**

Acids

Names of acids are not included in this
list but are to be added as needed, e.g.
Carbolic acid; etc.

See also names of acids, e.g. **Carbolic acid;**
etc.

xx **Chemicals; Chemistry**

Acne

xx **Skin—Diseases**

Acoustics. *See* **Architectural acoustics; Hearing; Music—Acoustics and physics;
Sound**

Acquisitions (Libraries)

See also **Book selection**

x Libraries—Order department; Library
acquisitions

xx **Processing (Libraries)**

Acrobats and acrobatics

See also **Gymnastics;** also names of acro-
batic feats, e.g. **Tumbling;** etc.

xx **Circus; Gymnastics**

Acronyms

x Code names; English language—Acronyms; Initialisms

xx **Abbreviations**

Acting

Use for general works on the art and technique of acting in any medium (stage,
television, etc.), in the presentation of
plays, and on acting as a profession.
Works limited to presentation of plays
are entered under **Amateur theatricals**
or, if professional actors are involved,
under **Theater—Production and direction.** Works about members of the
profession are entered under **Actors
and actresses**

See also **Actors and actresses; Drama in
education; Pageants; Pantomimes;
Theater**

x Dramatic art; Histrionics; Stage

xx **Actors and actresses; Amateur theatricals; Drama; Drama in education;
Public speaking; Theater**

Acting—Costume. *See* **Costume**

Acting as a profession

xx **Actors and actresses; Moving pictures
as a profession**

Activity schools. *See* **Education—Experimental methods**

3

Actors and actresses (May subdiv. geog. adjective form, e.g. **Actors and actresses, American**)

Use for works about several actors or actresses

See also **Acting; Acting as a profession; Comedians; Moving pictures—Biography; Negro actors; Theater;** also names of individual actors and actresses

x Actresses ; Stage

xx **Acting; Entertainers; Theater**

Actors and actresses, American

x American actors and actresses ; U.S.—Actors and actresses

Actresses. *See* **Actors and actresses**

Adages. *See* **Proverbs**

Adaptability (Psychology). *See* **Adjustment (Psychology)**

Adaptation (Biology)

See also **Man—Influence of environment**

x Acclimatization ; Environment

xx **Biology; Ecology; Evolution; Genetics; Variation (Biology)**

Adaptation (Psychology). *See* **Adjustment (Psychology)**

Adding machines. *See* **Calculating machines**

Additives, Food. *See* **Food additives**

Addresses. *See* **Lectures and lecturing; Orations; Speeches, addresses, etc.;** and general subjects with the subdivision *Addresses and essays,* e.g. **Agriculture —Addresses and essays; U.S.—History—Addresses and essays;** etc.

Adhesives

See also names of adhesives, e.g. **Cement; Glue; Mortar;** etc.

Adjustment (Psychology)

x Adaptability (Psychology) ; Adaptation (Psychology) ; Maladjustment (Psychology)

xx **Psychology**

Adjustment, Social. *See* **Social adjustment**

Administration. *See* **Civil service; Management; Political science; Public administration; The State;** and names of countries, cities, etc. with the subdivision *Politics and government,* e.g. **U.S.—Politics and government;** etc.

Administration of justice. *See* **Justice, Administration of**

Administrative ability. *See* **Executive ability**

Administrative law

See also **Civil service; Constitutional law; Local government; Municipal corporations; Public administration**

x Law, Administrative

xx **Constitutional law; Law; Public administration**

Administrators and executors. *See* **Executors and administrators**

4

Admirals

    xx Naval biography

Adolescence

    x Teen age

    xx **Child study; Youth**

Adolescent psychiatry

    x Psychiatry, Adolescent

    xx **Child psychiatry; Psychiatry**

Adoption

    See also **Foster home care**

    x Children—Adoption

    xx **Foster home care**

Adult education

    See also **Agricultural extension work; Education of prisoners; Evening and continuation schools; Social group work**

    x Education, Adult; Education of adults

    xx **Education; Education, Higher; Education, Secondary; Evening and continuation schools; University extension**

Adventure and adventurers

    See also **Discoveries (in geography); Escapes; Explorers; Frontier and pioneer life; Heroes; Sea stories; Seafaring life; Shipwrecks; Underwater exploration; Voyages and travels**

    xx **Voyages and travels**

Advertisement writing. *See* **Advertising copy**

Advertising

    May be subdivided by topic, e.g. **Advertising—Libraries**; etc.

    See also

Commercial art	**Radio advertising**
Electric signs	**Salesmen and salesmanship**
Mail-order business	
Marketing	**Show windows**
Packaging	**Sign painting**
Posters	**Signs and signboards**
Printing—Specimens	
Propaganda	**Television advertising**
Public relations	
Publicity	

    xx **Business; Propaganda; Public relations; Publicity; Retail trade; Salesmen and salesmanship**

Advertising, Art in. *See* **Commercial art**

Advertising, Fraudulent

    x False advertising; Truth in advertising

Advertising—Libraries

    x Libraries—Advertising; Library advertising

Advertising, Pictorial. *See* **Commercial art; Posters**

Advertising, Radio. *See* **Radio advertising**

Advertising, Television. *See* **Television advertising**

Advertising copy

    x Advertisement writing; Copy writing

    xx **Authorship**

5

Advertising layout and typography

    xx **Printing; Type and type founding**

Aerial bombs. *See* **Bombs**

Aerial navigation. *See* **Navigation (Aeronautics)**

Aerial photography. *See* **Photography, Aerial**

Aerial rockets. *See* **Rockets (Aeronautics)**

Aerodromes. *See* **Airports**

Aerodynamics

    See also **Aeronautics; Ground cushion phenomena**

    x Streamlining

    xx **Aeronautics; Air; Dynamics; Pneumatics**

Aerodynamics, Supersonic

    See also **Aerothermodynamics**

    x High speed aerodynamics; Speed, Supersonic; Supersonic aerodynamics

    xx **High speed aeronautics**

Aeronautical instruments

    See also **Airplanes—Electric equipment;** also names of specific instruments, e.g. **Gyroscope;** etc.

    x Airplanes — Instruments; Instruments, Aeronautical

    xx **Scientific apparatus and instruments**

Aeronautical sports

    See also names of specific sports, e.g. **Airplane racing; Skydiving;** etc.

    xx **Aeronautics; Sports**

Aeronautics

    Use for works on the scientific aspects of aircraft and their construction and operation; or for works that treat collectively various types of aircraft

    See also

Aerodynamics	High speed aeronautics
Aeronautical sports	Kites
Airplanes	Meteorology in aeronautics
Airships	
Astronautics	Navigation (Aeronautics)
Balloons	
Flight	Parachutes
Flying saucers	Radio in aeronautics
Gliders (Aeronautics)	Rocketry
	Rockets (Aeronautics)
Helicopters	

    x Aviation; Locomotion

    xx **Aerodynamics; Airplanes; Airships; Balloons; Engineering; Flight**

Aeronautics—Accidents

    See also **Survival (after airplane accidents, shipwrecks, etc.)**

    x Air crashes; Airplane accidents; Airplanes—Accidents

    xx **Accidents**

Aeronautics—Biography

    See also **Air pilots; Women in aeronautics**

Aeronautics, Commercial
>*See also* **Air lines; Air mail service; Airplane industry and trade**
>
>*x* Air cargo; Air freight; Air transport; Commercial aeronautics; Commercial aviation
>
>*xx* **Freight and freightage; Transportation**

Aeronautics, Commercial—Hijacking. *See* **Hijacking of airplanes**

Aeronautics—Flights
>*See also* **Space flight**
>
>*x* Aeronautics—Voyages; Flights around the world; Transatlantic flights
>
>*xx* **Voyages and travels**

Aeronautics, High speed. *See* **High speed aeronautics**

Aeronautics—Medical aspects. *See* **Aviation medicine**

Aeronautics, Meteorology in. *See* **Meteorology in aeronautics**

Aeronautics, Military
>*See also* **Air bases; Air defenses; Air power; Air raid shelters; Aircraft carriers; Aiplanes, Military; Parachute troops;** also names of wars with the subdivision *Aerial operations,* e.g. **World War, 1939-1945—Aerial operations;** etc.
>
>*x* Aeronautics, Naval; Air raids—Protective measures; Air warfare; Military aeronautics; Naval aeronautics
>
>*xx* **Military art and science; War**

Aeronautics, Naval. *See* **Aeronautics, Military**

Aeronautics—Navigation. *See* **Navigation (Aeronautics)**

Aeronautics—Piloting. *See* **Airplanes—Piloting**

Aeronautics, Radio in. *See* **Radio in aeronautics**

Aeronautics—Safety measures
>*x* Safety measures
>
>*xx* **Accidents—Prevention**

Aeronautics—Songs and music
>*xx* **Songs**

Aeronautics—Study and teaching
>*See also* **Airplanes—Piloting**
>
>*x* Flight training

Aeronautics — Voyages. *See* **Aeronautics — Flights**

Aeronautics and civilization
>*See also* **Astronautics and civilization**
>
>*x* Civilization and aeronautics
>
>*xx* **Civilization**

Aeronautics as a profession
>*See also* **Air lines—Hostesses; Air pilots; Women in aeronautics**

Aeronautics in agriculture

    x Airplanes in agriculture; Crop dusting

    xx **Agricultural pests; Agriculture; Insects, Injurious and beneficial; Spraying and dusting**

Aeronautics in literature

Aeroplanes. *See* **Airplanes**

Aerospace (Law). *See* **Space law**

Aerospace industries

    See also **Airplane industry and trade**

    x Aircraft production

Aerospace medicine. *See* **Aviation medicine; Space medicine**

Aerothermodynamics

    x Thermoaerodynamics

    xx **Aerodynamics, Supersonic; Astronautics; High speed aeronautics; Thermodynamics**

Aesthetics. *See* **Esthetics**

Affection. *See* **Friendship; Love**

Affliction. *See* **Joy and sorrow**

Africa

    See also **Pan-Africanism**

Africa—History

Africa—History—1960-

Africa, Central

    A general term covering the area 17°N-17°S (Chad to Angola): from Nigeria and the Atlantic on the West to Sudan and the Lake plateau on the East

    x Central Africa

Africa, East

    A general term covering roughly Uganda, Kenya and Tanzania

    x East Africa

Africa—Native races

    See note under **Native races**

    See also **Negroes in Africa**

    xx **Native races**

Africa, North

    A general term for the area north of the Sahara

    x Barbary States; North Africa

Africa, South

    x South Africa; Union of South Africa

Africa, South—History

    See also **South African War, 1899-1902**

Africa, Southern

    Here are entered works on the area south of the countries of the Congo (Democratic Republic) and Tanzania. Works on the Republic of South Africa are entered under **Africa, South**

    x Southern Africa

Africa, West

    A general term covering the area South of the Sahara from Senegal to Nigeria

    x West Africa

African-Americans. *See* **Negroes**

African relations. *See* **Pan-Africanism**

Afro-American studies
>   *x* Black studies
>   *xx* **Area studies; Negroes—Education;
>   Negroes—Race identity**

Afro-Americans. *See* **Negroes**

After-dinner speeches
>   *See also* **Speeches, addresses, etc.; Toasts**
>   *xx* **Orations; Speeches, addresses, etc.;
>   Toasts**

Age. *See* **Middle age; Old age; Youth**

Age and employment
>   *See also* **Child labor**
>   *x* Employment and age
>   *xx* **Discrimination in employment; Middle
>   age; Old age**

Aged (May subdiv. geog.)
>   *x* Gerontology; Senior citizens
>   *xx* **Old age**

Aged—Care and hygiene

Aged—Diseases
>   *x* Geriatrics

Aged—Dwellings
>   *x* Dwellings; Homes for the aged; Hous-
>   ing for the aged; Old age homes

Aged—Library service. *See* **Libraries and the
        aged**

Aged—Medical care
>   *x* Medicare; Medical care for the aged
>   *xx* **Medical care**

Aged—Recreation
>   *xx* **Recreation**

Aged—Societies and clubs

Aged—U.S.
>   *x* U.S.—Aged

Agents. *See* **Salesmen and salesmanship**

Aggregates. *See* **Set theory**

Aggressiveness (Psychology)
>   *See also* **Violence**

Agnosticism
>   *See also* **Atheism; Belief and doubt; Posi-
>   tivism; Rationalism; Skepticism**
>   *xx* **Atheism; Belief and doubt; Faith; Free
>   thought; God; Positivism; Rational-
>   ism; Religion; Skepticism; Truth**

Agrarian question. *See* **Agriculture—Eco-
        nomic aspects; Agriculture and state;
        Land tenure**

Agreements. *See* **Contracts**

Agricultural bacteriology. *See* **Bacteriology,
        Agricultural**

Agricultural banks. *See* **Agricultural credit;
        Banks and banking**

Agricultural botany. *See* **Botany, Economic**

Agricultural chemistry
>   *See also* **Chemurgy; Fertilizers and ma-
>   nures; Pesticides; Soils**
>   *x* Chemistry, Agricultural
>   *xx* **Chemistry; Fertilizers and manures;
>   Soils**

Agricultural clubs. *See* **Agriculture—Societies**

Agricultural cooperation. *See* **Agriculture, Co-operative**

Agricultural credit

  x Agricultural banks; Credit, Agricultural; Farm credit; Rural credit

  xx **Agriculture—Economic aspects; Banks and banking; Credit; Mortgages**

Agricultural economics. *See* **Agriculture—Economic aspects**

Agricultural education. *See* **Agriculture—Study and teaching**

Agricultural engineering

  See also **Drainage; Electricity in agriculture; Irrigation**

  x Farm mechanics

  xx **Agricultural machinery; Engineering; Farm engines**

Agricultural experiment stations

  See also **Agricultural extension work**

  x Experimental farms; Farms, Experimental

  xx **Agriculture—Research; Agriculture — Study and teaching; Agriculture and state**

Agricultural extension work (May subdiv. geog. by state)

  Use for general works and for agricultural extension work in the U.S. Works dealing with agricultural extension work in particular states or localities are entered under this heading with local subdivision, e.g. **Agricultural extension work—Ohio;** etc.

  See also **Agriculture—Study and teaching; County agricultural agents**

  x Extension work, Agricultural

  xx **Adult education; Agricultural experiment stations; Agriculture—Study and teaching; Agriculture and state**

Agricultural laborers

  See also **Migrant labor; Peasantry**

  x Farm laborers; Laborers

  xx **Labor and laboring classes; Peasantry**

Agricultural machinery

  See also **Agricultural engineering; Electricity in agriculture; Farm engines;** also names of farm machinery, e.g. **Harvesting machinery; Plows; Tractors;** etc.

  x Agricultural tools; Farm implements; Farm machinery; Farm mechanics; Implements, utensils, etc.

  xx **Machinery; Tools**

Agricultural pests

  See also **Aeronautics in agriculture; Fungi; Insects, Injurious and beneficial; Pest control; Plants—Diseases; Spraying and dusting; Weeds;** also names of crops, etc. with the subdivi-

Agricultural pests—*Continued*
　　sion *Diseases and pests,* e.g. **Fruit—Diseases and pests;** etc.
　　x Diseases and pests; Garden pests; Pests
　　xx **Insects, Injurious and beneficial; Zoology, Economic**

Agricultural pests—Biological control. *See* **Pest control—Biological control**

Agricultural policy. *See* **Agriculture and state**

Agricultural products. *See* **Farm produce**

Agricultural research. *See* **Agriculture—Research**

Agricultural societies. *See* **Agriculture—Societies**

Agricultural tools. *See* **Agricultural machinery**

Agriculture (May subdiv. geog.)
　　See also

Aeronautics in agriculture	**Land**
	Land tenure
Botany, Economic	**Livestock**
Dairying	**Organiculture**
Domestic animals	**Pastures**
Dry farming	**Plant breeding**
Farms	**Reclamation of land**
Forests and forestry	**Rotation of crops**
Fruit culture	**Soils**
Gardening	

　　also names of agricultural products (e.g. **Corn;** etc.); and headings beginning with the words **Agricultural** and **Farm**
　　x Agronomy; Farming; Planting
　　xx **Land**

Agriculture—Addresses and essays
　　x Addresses
　　xx **Essays; Lectures and lecturing; Speeches, addresses, etc.**

Agriculture—Bibliography
　　xx **Bibliography**

Agriculture, Cooperative
　　Use for works dealing with cooperation in the production and disposal of agricultural products
　　See also **Agriculture—Societies**
　　x Agricultural cooperation; Collective farms; Cooperative agriculture; Farmers' cooperatives
　　xx **Cooperation**

Agriculture—Documentation
　　xx **Documentation**

Agriculture—Economic aspects
　　See also **Agricultural credit; Farm management; Farm produce—Marketing; Land tenure**
　　x Agrarian question; Agricultural economics
　　xx **Economics; Farm management; Farm produce—Marketing; Land**

agricultural prices

11

Agriculture—Research
>*See also* **Agricultural experiment stations**
>*x* Agricultural research
>*xx* **Research**

Agriculture—Societies
>*See also* names of agricultural societies, e.g.
>**4-H clubs; Grange;** etc.
>*x* Agricultural clubs; Agricultural soci-
>eties; Boys' agricultural clubs; Girls'
>agricultural clubs
>*xx* **Agricultural, Cooperative; Country life;**
>**Societies**

Agriculture, Soilless. *See* **Plants—Soilless cul-**
ture

Agriculture—Statistics
>*x* Crop reports
>*xx* **Food supply; Statistics**

Agriculture—Study and teaching
>*See also* **Agricultural experiment stations;**
>**Agricultural extension work; County**
>**agricultural agents**
>*x* Agricultural education
>*xx* **Agricultural extension work; Voca-**
>**tional education**

Agriculture—Tenant farming. *See* **Farm ten-**
ancy

Agriculture—Tropics
>*xx* **Tropics**

Agriculture—U.S.
>*x* U.S.—Agriculture

Agriculture and state
>*See also* **Agricultural experiment stations;**
>**Agricultural extension work**
>*x* Agrarian question; Agricultural policy;
>State and agriculture
>*xx* **Industry and state**

Agronomy. *See* **Agriculture**

Ague. *See* **Malaria**

Aid to dependent children. *See* **Child welfare**

Aid to developing areas. *See* **Economic assis-**
tance; Technical assistance

Air
>Use for works treating of air as an ele-
>ment and of its chemical and physical
>properties. Works treating of the body
>of air surrounding the earth are en-
>tered under **Atmosphere**
>*See also* **Aerodynamics; Atmosphere;**
>**Ventilation**
>*xx* **Atmosphere; Hygiene; Meteorology**

Air, Compressed. *See* **Compressed air**

Air—Microbiology
>*xx* **Microbiology**

Air—Pollution (May subdiv. geog.)
>*x* Air pollution; Atmosphere—Pollution;
>Pollution of air
>*xx* **Pollution**

Air—Pollution—U.S.
>*x* U.S.—Air—Pollution

Air bases

  x Air stations, Military; Air stations, Naval; Military air bases; Naval air bases

  xx **Aeronautics, Military; Airports**

Air bearing lift. *See* **Ground cushion phenomena**

Air bearing vehicles. *See* **Ground effect machines**

Air cargo. *See* **Aeronautics, Commercial**

Air conditioning

  See also **Refrigeration and refrigerating machinery; Ventilation;** also subjects with the subdivision *Air conditioning,* e.g. **Automobiles—Air conditioning;** etc.

  xx **Refrigeration and refrigerating machinery; Ventilation**

Air crashes. *See* **Aeronautics—Accidents**

Air cushion vehicles. *See* **Ground effect machines**

Air defenses

  Use for works on civilian defense against air attack. Works on military defense against air raids are entered under **Aeronautics, Military.** General works on civilian defense are entered under **Civil defense**

  See also **Air raid shelters; Ballistic missile early warning system; Radar defense networks**

  x Air raids—Protective measures; Air warfare; Defenses, Air

  xx **Aeronautics, Military; Civil defense**

Air engines. *See* **Heat engines**

Air freight. *See* **Aeronautics, Commercial**

Air hostesses. *See* **Air lines—Hostesses**

Air lines

  Use for works dealing with systems of aerial transportation and with companies engaged in this business. Works dealing with the routes along which the planes are flown are entered under **Airways**

  See also **Airways**

  x Airlines

  xx **Aeronautics, Commercial; Airways**

Air lines—Hijacking. *See* **Hijacking of airplanes**

Air lines—Hostesses

  x Air hostesses; Air stewardesses; Airplane hostesses; Hostesses, Air line; Stewardesses, Air line

  xx **Aeronautics as a profession; Women in aeronautics**

Air mail service

  xx **Aeronautics, Commercial; Postal service**

Air navigation. *See* **Navigation (Aeronautics)**

13

Air pilots

    See also **Astronauts; Women in aeronautics**

    x Airplanes—Pilots; Aviators; Pilots, Airplane; Test pilots

    xx **Aeronautics—Biography; Aeronautics as a profession**

Air pilots—Diseases and hygiene. *See* **Aviation medicine**

Air piracy. *See* **Hijacking of airplanes**

Air planes. *See* **Airplanes**

Air pollution. *See* **Air—Pollution**

Air ports. *See* **Airports**

Air power

    xx **Aeronautics, Military**

Air raid shelters

    x Bomb shelters; Fallout shelters; Shelters, Air raid

    xx **Aeronautics, Military; Air defenses; Civil defense**

Air raids—Protective measures. *See* **Aeronautics, Military; Air defenses**

Air routes. *See* **Airways**

Air-ships. *See* **Airships**

Air space law. *See* **Space law**

Air stations, Military. *See* **Air bases**

Air stations, Naval. *See* **Air bases**

Air stewardesses. *See* **Air lines—Hostesses**

Air transport. *See* **Aeronautics, Commercial**

Air warfare. *See* **Aeronautics, Military; Air defenses; Airplanes, Military; Chemical warfare;** and names of wars with the subdivision *Aerial operations,* e.g. **World War, 1939-1945—Aerial operations;** etc.

Aircraft. *See* **Airplanes; Airships; Gliders (Aeronautics); Helicopters**

Aircraft carriers

    x Airplane carriers; Carriers, Aircraft

    xx **Aeronautics, Military; Warships**

Aircraft production. *See* **Airplane industry and trade; Aerospace industries**

Airdromes. *See* **Airports**

Airlines. *See* **Air lines**

Airplane accidents. *See* **Aeroanutics—Accidents**

Airplane carriers. *See* **Aircraft carriers**

Airplane engines. *See* **Airplanes—Engines**

Airplane hostesses. *See* **Air lines—Hostesses**

Airplane industry and trade

    x Aircraft production

    xx **Aeronautics, Commercial; Aerospace industries**

Airplane racing

    x Airplanes—Racing

    xx **Aeronautical sports**

Airplane spotting. *See* **Airplanes—Identification**

Airplanes

> *See also* **Aeronautics; Gliders (Aeronautics); Propellers, Aerial;** also types of airplanes, e.g. **Bombers; Vertically rising airplanes;** etc.
>
> *x* Aeroplanes; Air planes; Aircraft; Biplanes; Monoplanes
>
> *xx* **Aeronautics**

Airplanes—Accidents. *See* **Aeronautics—Accidents**

Airplanes—Design and construction

Airplanes—Electric equipment

> *x* Airplanes—Instruments
>
> *xx* **Aeronautical instruments**

Airplanes—Engines

> *See also* **Jet propulsion**
>
> *x* Airplane engines; Airplanes—Motors
>
> *xx* **Engines; Gas and oil engines**

Airplanes—Flight testing. *See* **Airplanes—Testing**

Airplanes—Hijacking. *See* **Hijacking of airplanes**

Airplanes—Identification

> *x* Airplane spotting; Airplanes—Recognition
>
> *xx* **Identification**

Airplanes—Inspection

Airplanes—Instruments. *See* **Aeronautical instruments; Airplanes—Electric equipment**

Airplanes, Jet propelled. *See* **Jet planes**

Airplanes—Maintenance and repair

> *x* Airplanes—Repair

Airplanes—Materials

Airplanes, Military

> *See also* types of military airplanes, e.g. **Bombers;** etc.
>
> *x* Air warfare; Airplanes, Naval; Military airplanes; Naval airplanes
>
> *xx* **Aeronautics, Military**

Airplanes—Models

> *x* Miniature objects; Model airplanes; Models
>
> *xx* **Machinery—Models; Models and model making**

Airplanes—Motors. *See* **Airplanes—Engines**

Airplanes, Naval. *See* **Airplanes, Military**

Airplanes—Noise ·

> *xx* **Noise; Noise—Pollution**

Airplanes—Operation. *See* **Airplanes—Piloting**

Airplanes—Piloting

> Use for manuals of instruction in the mechanics of flying
>
> *x* Aeronautics—Piloting; Airplanes—Operation; Flight training; Piloting (Aeronautics)
>
> *xx* **Aeronautics—Study and teaching; Navigation (Aeronautics)**

Airplanes—Pilots. *See* **Air pilots**

Airplanes—Propellers. *See* **Propellers, Aerial**

Airplanes—Racing. *See* **Airplane racing**

Airplanes—Recognition. *See* **Airplanes—Identification**

Airplanes—Repair. *See* **Airplanes—Maintenance and repair**

Airplanes, Rocket propelled. *See* **Rocket planes**

Airplanes—Testing
> *x* Airplanes—Flight testing; Test pilots

Airplanes, Vertically rising. *See* **Vertically rising airplanes**

Airplanes in agriculture. *See* **Aeronautics in agriculture**

⌐ **Airports**
> *See also* **Air bases; Heliports**
> *x* Aerodromes; Air ports; Airdromes

Airships
> Use for works on lighter-than-air craft, mechanically driven
> *See also* **Aeronautics; Balloons**
> *x* Air-ships; Aircraft; Balloons, Dirigible; Dirigible balloons; Zeppelins
> *xx* **Aeronautics**

Airspace (Law). *See* **Space law**

Airways
> Use for works dealing with routes along which planes are flown and where aids to navigation are maintained such as landing fields, beacons, etc. Works dealing with the companies engaged in aerial transportation are entered under **Air lines**
> *See also* **Air lines**
> *x* Air routes
> *xx* **Air lines**

Alaska Highway

Alchemy
> Use for works on the medieval chemical science which sought to transmute baser metals into gold. Modern works on the transmutation of metals are entered under **Transmutation (Chemistry)**
> *See also* **Transmutation (Chemistry)**
> *x* Hermetic art and philosophy; Metals, Transmutation of; Philosophers' stone; Transmutation of metals
> *xx* **Chemistry; Occult sciences; Superstition**

Alcohol
> *See also* **Alcoholism; Distillation; Liquor problem; Liquor traffic; Liquors; Temperance**
> *x* Intoxicants
> *xx* **Distillation; Stimulants**

Alcohol, Denatured
> *x* Alcohol, Industrial; Denatured alcohol; Industrial alcohol

Alcohol, Industrial. *See* **Alcohol, Denatured**

16

Alcohol—Physiological effect
> *x* Physiological effect
> *xx* **Alcoholism; Temperance**

Alcoholics. *See* **Alcoholism**

✓ **Alcoholism**
> Use chiefly for medical works; includes works on drunkenness, dipsomania, etc.
>
> *See also* **Alcohol—Physiological effect; Liquor problem; Temperance**
> *x* Alcoholics; Dipsomania; Drunkenness; Inebriates; Intemperance; Intoxication
> *xx* **Alcohol; Drug abuse; Liquor problem; Temperance**

Alfalfa
> *xx* **Hay**

Algae
> *x* Sea mosses; Seaweeds
> *xx* **Marine plants**

Algebra
> *See also* **Logarithms; Number theory; Probabilities**
> *xx* **Mathematics**

Algebra, Boolean
> *x* Boolean algebra
> *xx* **Logic, Symbolic and mathematical; Set theory**

Alienation (Social psychology)
> *x* Estrangement (Social psychology); Social alienation
> *xx* **Social psychology**

Aliens
> *See also* **Citizenship; Naturalization; Refugees;** also **Italians in the U.S.** and similar headings
> *x* Enemy aliens; Foreigners
> *xx* **Citizenship; Immigration and emigration; International law; Naturalization**

Alkoran. *See* **Koran**

All Fools' Day. *See* **April Fools' Day**

All Hallows' Eve. *See* **Halloween**

Allegories
> *See also* **Fables; Parables**
> *xx* **Fiction; Parables; Symbolism in literature**

Allergy
> *xx* **Immunity**

Alleys. *See* **Streets**

Alligators
> Use for works on the American crocodile. General works are entered under **Crocodiles**
> *xx* **Crocodiles**

Alloys
> *See also* **Brass; Metallurgy; Pewter;** also names of alloys, e.g. **Aluminum alloys;** etc.
> *xx* **Brass; Chemistry, Technical; Metallurgy; Metals; Solder and soldering**

Allusions
Almanacs
 See also **Calendars; Nautical almanacs;
  Yearbooks**
 x Annuals
 xx **Astronomy; Calendars; Yearbooks**
Alphabet
 Use for works dealing with the series of
  characters which form the elements
  of a written language. Works dealing
  with the styles of alphabets used by
  artists, etc. are entered under **Alphabets**
 See also **Alphabets; Writing**
 x Letters of the alphabet
 xx **Writing**
Alphabet books
 Use for ABC books
 x ABC books
 xx **Primers**
Alphabeting. *See* **Files and filing**
Alphabets
 See note under **Alphabet**
 See also **Illumination of books and manu-
  scripts; Initials; Lettering; Monograms**
 xx **Alphabet; Decoration and ornament;
  Initials; Lettering; Sign painting**
Alpine plants
 x Mountain plants
 xx **Geographical distribution of animals
  and plants; Plants**
Alternating current machinery. *See* **Electric
 machinery—Alternating current**
Alternating currents. *See* **Electric currents,
 Alternating**
Alternative life style. *See* **Counter culture**
Alternative press. *See* **Underground press**
Alternative schools. *See* **Free schools**
Alternative universities. *See* **Free universities**
Altitude, Influence of. *See* **Man—Influence of
 environment**
Aluminum
Aluminum alloys
 xx **Alloys**
Ama. *See* **Pearl diving and divers**
Amateur radio stations
 x Radio stations, Amateur
 xx **Radio, Short wave**
Amateur theatricals
 Use for works on the production of plays
  by non-professional groups. Collec-
  tions of plays for such groups are
  entered under **Drama—Collections;
  American drama—Collections;** and
  similar subjects
 See also **Acting; Charades; Children's
  plays; College and school drama;
  Drama in education; Make-up, Theatrical; One-act plays; Pantomimes;**

18

Amateur theatricals—*Continued*
> Shadow pantomimes and plays; The-
> ater—Production and direction
>
> *x* Play production; Private theatricals;
> Theatricals, Amateur
>
> *xx* Amusements; Drama in education;
> Theater—Production and direction

Ambassadors. *See* **Diplomats**

Ambition

America
> Use for general works on the western hemi-
> sphere or the two Americas
>
> *See also* **Central America; Latin America;
> North America; South America;** and
> names of separate countries of these
> areas

America—Antiquities

America—Discovery and exploration
> *See also* **Explorers; Northwest Passage;
> U.S.—Exploring expeditions**
>
> *x* Canada—Discovery and exploration;
> Conquistadores; Explorations; North
> America—Discovery and exploration;
> South America—Discovery and explo-
> ration; U.S.—Discovery and explora-
> tion
>
> *xx* **Discoveries (in geography); Explorers**

America—History
> *x* American history

America—Politics
> Use for general works on politics and
> government in the western hemisphere
> or in three or more countries of the
> two Americas
>
> *See also* **Pan-Americanism**
>
> *xx* **Pan-Americanism**

American aborigines. *See* **Indians of North
America; Indians of South America;**
etc.

American actors and actresses. *See* **Actors and
actresses, American**

American architecture. *See* **Architecture,
American**

American art. *See* **Art, American**

American artificial satellites. *See* **Artificial
satellites, American**

American artists. *See* **Artists, American**

American arts. *See* **The Arts, American**

American authors. *See* **Authors, American**

American ballads. *See* **Ballads, American**

American bison. *See* **Bison**

American characteristics. *See* **National characteristics, American**

American Civil War. *See* **U.S.—History—
Civil War**

American civilization. *See* **Civilization, American; U.S.—Civilization**

American colleges. *See* **Colleges and universities—U.S.**

American colonies. *See* **U.S.—History—Colonial period**

American color prints. *See* **Color prints, American**

American composers. *See* **Composers, American**

American decoration and ornament. *See* **Decoration and ornament, American**

American drama
 xx **Drama**

American drama—Collections
 xx **Drama—Collections**

American drama—History and criticism
 xx **Drama—History and criticism**

American dramatists. *See* **Dramatists, American**

American drawings. *See* **Drawings, American**

American engraving. *See* **Engraving, American**

American engravings. *See* **Engravings, American**

American environmental policy. *See* **Environmental policy—U.S.**

American espionage. *See* **Espionage, American**

American essays
 Use for collections of literary essays by several American authors
 xx **Essays**

American ethics. *See* **Ethics, American**

American fiction
 x Fiction, American
 xx **Fiction**

American flag. *See* **Flags—U.S.**

American folk art. *See* **Folk art, American**

American folk dancing. *See* **Folk dancing, American**

American folk songs. *See* **Folk songs—U.S.**

American furniture. *See* **Furniture, American**

American graphic arts. *See* **Graphic arts, American**

American historians. *See* **Historians, American**

American history. *See* **America—History; U.S.—History**

American illustrators. *See* **Illustrators, American**

American Indians. *See* **Indians; Indians of North America; Indians of South America;** etc.

American letters
 xx **Letters**

American literature
 May be subdivided by the name of a state or region, e.g. **American literature—Massachusetts; American literature—Southern States**
 May use same subdivisions and literary forms as for **English literature**
 See also **Authors, American; Ballads, American; Canadian literature; Latin**

20

American literature—*Continued*
>American literature; Negro literature
>*x* U.S.—Literature

American literature—Biography. *See* **Authors, American**

American literature—Collections
>Use for collections of both poetry and prose by several American authors. Collections consisting of prose only are entered under **American prose literature**; collections of poetry are entered under **American poetry—Collections**

American Loyalists
>*x* Loyalists, American; Tories, American
>*xx* U.S.—History—Revolution

American military assistance. *See* **Military assistance, American**

American missions. *See* **Missions**

American music. *See* **Music, American**

American musicians. *See* **Musicians, American**

American names. *See* **Names, Personal—U.S.**

American national characteristics. *See* **National characteristics, American**

American national songs. *See* **National songs, American**

American newspapers
>*xx* Newspapers

American novelists. *See* **Novelists, American**

American orations
>Use for collections of orations by several authors
>*xx* Orations

American painters. *See* **Painters, American**

American painting. *See* **Painting, American**

American paintings. *See* **Paintings, American**

American periodicals
>*xx* Periodicals

American philosophers. *See* **Philosophers, American**

American philosophy. *See* **Philosophy, American**

American poetry
>*See also* Negro poetry
>*xx* Poetry

American poetry—Collections
>*xx* Poetry—Collections

American poetry—History and criticism
>*xx* Poetry—History and criticism

American poets. *See* **Poets, American**

American pottery. *See* **Pottery, American**

American prints. *See* **Prints, American**

American propaganda. *See* **Propaganda, American**

American prose literature
>Use for collections of prose writings by several American authors which may include a variety of literary forms such as essays, fiction, orations, etc.
>*x* Prose literature, American

American refugees. *See* **Refugees, American**

✓ American party

21

American Revolution. *See* **U.S.—History—Revolution**

American satire. *See* **Satire, American**

American science. *See* **Science—U.S.**

American sculptors. *See* **Sculptors, American**

American sculpture. *See* **Sculpture, American**

American songs. *See* **Songs, American**

American-Spanish War, 1898. *See* **U.S.—History—War of 1898**

American statesmen. *See* **Statesmen, American**

American travelers. *See* **Travelers, American**

American wit and humor
> Use for collections of several authors. May be used also for works about American wit and humor
> *x* Tall tales
> *xx* **Wit and humor**

American youth. *See* **Youth—U.S.**

Americanisms
> Use for works dealing with usage of words and expressions peculiar to the United States
> *x* English language—Americanisms
> *xx* **English language—Dialects**

Americanization
> *See also* **Naturalization; U.S.—Foreign population; U.S.—Immigration and emigration**

Americans in foreign countries
> *See also* **Americans in Greece**; and similar headings

Americans in Greece
> Use same form for Americans in other countries, states, etc. e.g. **Americans in Europe**; etc.
> *xx* **Americans in foreign countries**

Amish
> *xx* **Mennonites**

✓ amnesty

Ammunition
> *See also* names of ammunition, e.g. **Bombs; Gunpowder**; etc.
> *xx* **Explosives; Gunpowder; Projectiles**

Amphibians
> *See also* names of amphibians, e.g. **Frogs; Salamanders**; etc.
> *x* Batrachia
> *xx* **Vertebrates**

Amplifiers, Vacuum tube
> *x* Loud speakers
> *xx* **Radio—Apparatus and supplies; Vacuum tubes**

✓ amtrak

✓ **Amusement parks**
> *See also* names of specific parks, e.g. **Disneyland**; etc.
> *x* Carnivals (Circus)
> *xx* **Parks**

22

Amusements

Use for works that include material about various kinds of entertainment and pastimes

See also

Amateur theatricals
Charades
Church entertainments
Circus
Concerts
Dancing
Entertaining
Fortune telling
Games
Hobbies
Indoor games
Magic
Mathematical recreations
Moving pictures
Play
Puzzles
Recreation
Riddles
Scientific recreations
Sports
Theater
Toys
Vaudeville
Ventriloquism

x Entertainments; Pastimes

xx **Entertaining; Games; Indoor games; Play; Recreation; Sports**

Anaesthetics. *See* **Anesthetics**

Analysis (Chemistry). *See* **Chemistry, Analytic;** and names of substances with the subdivision *Analysis,* e.g. **Food—Analysis;** etc.

Analysis (Mathematics). *See* **Calculus**

Analysis, Microscopic. *See* **Metallography; Microscope and microscopy**

Analysis, Spectrum. *See* **Spectrum**

Analysis of food. *See* **Food—Analysis; Food adulteration and inspection**

Analytical chemistry. *See* **Chemistry, Analytic**

Analytical geometry. *See* **Geometry, Analytic**

Anarchism and anarchists

xx **Crime and criminals; Liberty; Political crimes and offenses; Political science; Syndicalism**

Anatomy

Use for general treatises and for works on human anatomy. General works on animal anatomy are entered under **Anatomy, Comparative**

See also **Anatomy, Comparative; Bones; Nervous system; Physiology;** also subjects with the subdivision *Anatomy,* e.g. **Birds—Anatomy; Botany—Anatomy;** etc.; and names of organs and regions of the body, e.g. **Heart; Throat;** etc.

x Body, Human; Histology; Human body; Morphology

xx **Biology; Medicine; Physiology**

Anatomy, Artistic

See also **Figure drawing; Figure painting**

Anatomy, Artistic—*Continued*

    x Art anatomy; Artistic anatomy; Human figure in art

  xx **Art; Drawing**

Anatomy, Comparative

    See note under **Anatomy**

    See also **Man—Origin and antiquity**

    x Animals—Anatomy; Comparative anatomy; Histology; Morphology; Zoology—Anatomy

  xx **Anatomy; Evolution; Man—Origin and antiquity; Zoology**

Anatomy, Dental. *See* **Teeth**

Anatomy, Vegetable. *See* **Botany—Anatomy**

Anatomy of plants. *See* **Botany—Anatomy**

Ancestor worship

    x The dead, Worship of

  xx **Funeral rites and ceremonies; Mythology; Religion, Primitive; Shinto; Worship**

Ancestry. *See* **Genealogy; Heredity**

Ancient architecture. *See* **Architecture, Ancient**

Ancient art. *See* **Art, Ancient**

Ancient civilization. *See* **Civilization, Ancient**

Ancient geography. *See* **Geography, Ancient**

Ancient history. *See* **History, Ancient**

Ancient philosophy. *See* **Philosophy, Ancient**

Anecdotes

    See also subjects with the subdivision *Anecdotes, facetiae, satire, etc.,* e.g. **Music—Anecdotes, facetiae, satire, etc.**; etc.

    x Facetiae; Stories

  xx **Wit and humor**

Anesthetics

    x Anaesthetics

  xx **Materia medica; Pain; Surgery**

Angina pectoris. *See* **Heart—Diseases**

Anglican Church. *See* **Church of England**

Angling. *See* **Fishing**

Anglo-French intervention in Egypt, 1956. *See* **Sinai Campaign, 1956**

Anglo-Saxon language

    May be subdivided like **English language**

    x English language—Old English; Old English language

Anglo-Saxon literature

    May use same subdivisions and names of literary forms as for **English literature**

    x English literature—Old English; Old English literature

Anglo-Saxons

    x Saxons

  xx **Gt. Brit.—History—To 1066; Teutonic race**

Animal babies. *See* **Animals—Infancy**

Animal behavior. *See* **Animals—Habits and behavior**

Animal chemistry. *See* **Physiological chemistry**

Animal coloration. *See* **Color of animals**

Animal communication

    x Animal language; Animals—Language; Communication among animals

Animal drawing. *See* **Animal painting and illustration**

Animal homes. *See* **Animals—Habitations**

Animal husbandry. *See* **Livestock**

Animal industry. *See* **Domestic animals; Livestock**

Animal instinct. *See* **Instinct**

Animal intelligence

    See also **Animals—Habits and behavior; Instinct; Learning, Psychology of; Psychology, Comparative**

    x Animal psychology; Intelligence of animals

    xx **Animals—Habits and behavior; Instinct; Psychology, Comparative**

Animal kingdom. *See* **Zoology**

Animal language. *See* **Animal communication**

Animal light. *See* **Bioluminescence**

Animal locomotion

    x Animals—Movements; Locomotion; Movements of animals

Animal lore. *See* **Animals, Mythical; Animals—Stories; Animals in literature; Natural history**

Animal magnetism. *See* **Hypnotism**

Animal migration. *See* **Animals—Migration**

Animal oils. *See* **Oils and fats**

Animal painting and illustration

    Use for works on the art and methods of painting and drawing animals. Books about representations of animals in works of art (painting, sculpture, etc.), or reproductions of them, are entered under **Animals in art.** Works consisting of photographs or illustrations of animals are entered under **Animals—Pictorial works**

    See also **Animals—Pictorial works; Animals in art; Photography of animals**

    x Animal drawing

    xx **Animals—Pictorial works; Animals in art; Painting; Photography of animals**

Animal parasites. *See* **Parasites**

Animal photography. *See* **Photography of animals**

Animal physiology. *See* **Zoology**

Animal pictures. *See* **Animals — Pictorial works**

Animal products. *See* **Dairy products;** and names of special products, e.g. **Hides and skins; Ivory; Wool;** etc.

Animal psychology. *See* **Animal intelligence; Psychology, Comparative**

Animal stories. *See* **Animals—Stories**

Animal training. *See* **Animals—Training**

Animals (May subdiv. geog.)

Use for descriptive and non-systematic or non-technical material

See also **Color of animals; Desert animals; Domestic animals; Fresh-water animals; Fur-bearing animals; Game and game birds; Geographical distribution of animals and plants; Marine animals; Natural history; Pets; Zoological gardens; Zoology;** also names of orders and classes of the animal kingdom (e.g. **Birds; Insects;** etc.) ; and names of animals, e.g. **Dogs; Bears;** etc.

x Beasts; Fauna; Wild animals

xx **Zoology**

Animals—Anatomy. *See* **Anatomy, Comparative**

Animals, Aquatic. *See* **Fresh-water animals; Marine animals**

Animals—Color. *See* **Color of animals**

Animals—Courtship

x Courtship of animals

Animals, Cruelty to. *See* **Animals—Treatment**

Animals—Diseases. *See* **Veterinary medicine**

Animals, Domestic. *See* **Domestic animals**

Animals, Extinct. *See* **Extinct animals**

Animals, Fictitious. *See* **Animals, Mythical**

Animals, Fossil. *See* **Fossils**

Animals, Fresh-water. *See* **Fresh-water animals**

Animals—Geographical distribution. *See* **Geographical distribution of animals and plants**

Animals—Habitations

x Animal homes; Habitations of animals; Houses of animals

Animals—Habits and behavior

Use for factual books whose aim is to describe and instruct. Fictional or legendary tales about animals are entered under **Animals—Stories**

See also **Animal intelligence; Animals—Migration; Animals—Stories; Instinct; Nature study; Tracking and trailing;** also names of animals with the subdivision *Habits and behavior,* e.g. **Birds—Habits and behavior;** etc.

x Animal behavior; Habits of animals

xx **Animal intelligence; Animals—Stories; Nature study**

Animals—Hibernation

Animals, Imaginary. *See* **Animals, Mythical**

Animals—Infancy

x Animal babies; Baby animals

Animals—Language. *See* **Animal communication**

Animals—Legends. *See* **Animals—Stories**

Animals, Marine. *See* **Marine animals**

Animals—Migration

> *See also* names of animals with the subdivision *Migration,* e.g. **Birds—Migration;** etc.
>
> *x* Animal migration; Migration of animals
>
> *xx* **Animals—Habits and behavior; Geographical distribution of animals and plants**

Animals—Movements. *See* **Animal locomotion**

Animals, Mythical

> *See also* names of mythical animals, e.g. **Unicorn;** etc.
>
> *x* Animal lore; Animals, Fictitious; Animals, Imaginary; Fictitious animals; Imaginary animals; Mythical animals
>
> *xx* **Mythology**

Animals—Photography. *See* **Photography of animals**

Animals—Pictorial works

> See note under **Animal painting and illustration**
>
> *See also* **Animal painting and illustration; Animals in art; Photography of animals**
>
> *x* Animal pictures; Illustrations; Pictorial works
>
> *xx* **Animal painting and illustration; Animals in art; Photography of animals; Pictures**

Animals—Poetry

> *See also* **Animals in literature**
>
> *xx* **Animals in literature; Poetry**

Animals, Prehistoric. *See* **Fossils**

Animals—Protection. *See* **Animals—Treatment**

Animals, Rare. *See* **Rare animals**

Animals, Sea. *See* **Marine animals**

Animals—Stories

> See note under **Animals—Habits and behavior**
>
> *See also* **Animals—Habits and behavior; Animals in literature; Fables;** also names of animals with the subdivision *Stories,* e.g. **Dogs—Stories;** etc.
>
> *x* Animal lore; Animal stories; Animals—Legends; Legends and stories of animals; Stories
>
> *xx* **Animals—Habits and behavior; Animals in literature; Fables; Fiction**

Animals—Training

> *See also* names of animals with the subdivision *Training,* e.g., **Dogs—Training; Horses—Training;** etc.
>
> *x* Animal training; Training of animals
>
> *xx* **Circus**

Animals—Treatment
   See also **Vivisection**
   x Animals, Cruelty to; Animals—Protection; Cruelty to animals; Kindness to animals; Prevention of cruelty to animals; Protection of animals
   xx **Domestic animals; Vivisection**
Animals—U.S.
   x U.S.—Animals
Animals, Useful and harmful. *See* **Zoology, Economic**
Animals, War use of
   See also **Dogs, War use of**
Animals in art
   See note under **Animal painting and illustration**
   See also **Animal painting and illustration; Animals—Pictorial works**
   xx **Animal painting and illustration; Animals—Pictorial works; Art**
Animals in literature
   Use for works that discuss animals in literature. Poems or stories about animals are entered under **Animals—Poetry; Animals—Stories**
   See also **Animals—Poetry; Animals—Stories; Bible—Natural history**; also **Birds in literature**; and similar headings
   x Animal lore
   xx **Animals—Poetry; Animals—Stories; Nature in literature**
Animated cartoons. *See* **Moving picture cartoons**
Annapolis Naval Academy. *See* **U.S. Naval Academy, Annapolis**
Anniversaries. *See* **Holidays**; and names of special days, e.g. **Fourth of July**; etc.
Annual income guarantee. *See* **Guaranteed annual income**
Annual wage plans. *See* **Wages—Annual wage**
Annuals. *See* **Almanacs; Calendars; Yearbooks**; and general subjects and names of organizations with the subdivision *Yearbooks,* e.g. **Literature—Yearbooks; United Nations—Yearbooks**; etc.
Annuals (Plants)
   xx **Flower gardening; Flowers; Plants, Cultivated**
Annuities
   See also **Insurance, Life; Pensions**
   x Retirement income
   xx **Insurance, Life; Investments**
Annulment of marriage. *See* **Divorce**
Anonyms. *See* **Pseudonyms**
Answers to questions. *See* **Questions and answers**
Ant. *See* **Ants**

annexation (municipal government

Antarctic expeditions. *See* **Antarctic regions;** and names of expeditions, e.g. **Byrd Antarctic Expedition, 1st, 1928-1930;** etc.

Antarctic regions

See also **Scientific expeditions; South Pole;** also names of explorers

x Antarctic expeditions; Expeditions, Antarctic and Arctic; Polar expeditions

xx **Discoveries (in geography); Earth; Polar regions; Scientific expeditions; South Pole; Voyages and travels**

Anthracite coal. *See* **Coal**

Anthropogeography

See also **Geopolitics; Man—Influence of environment**

x Biogeography; Environment; Geographical distribution of man; Geography, Social

xx **Anthropology; Ethnology; Geography; Geopolitics; History; Human ecology; Immigration and emigration**

Anthropology

See also

Acculturation	**Language and languages**
Anthropogeography	
Anthropometry	**Man**
Archeology	**National characteristics**
Civilization	
Color of man	**Race psychology**
Ethnology	**Social change**
Eugenics	**Somatology**
	Woman

also names of races and tribes (e.g. **Semitic race; Cherokee Indians;** etc.); and names of countries, cities, etc. with the subdivision *Race relations,* e.g. **U.S.—Race relations**

x Human race

xx **Civilization; Ethnology; Man**

Anthropology, Physical. *See* **Somatology**

Anthropometry

See also **Fingerprints**

xx **Anthropology; Ethnology; Man**

Anti-Americanism. *See* **U.S.—Foreign opinion**

Antiballistic missiles. *See* **Antimissile missiles**

Antibiotics

See also names of specific antibiotics, e.g. **Penicillin;** etc.

xx **Chemotherapy**

Anti-Communist movements

x Underground, Anti-communist

xx **Communism**

Anticorrosive paint. *See* **Corrosion and anticorrosives**

Antidotes. *See* **Poisons;** and names of poisons

Antimissile missiles

x ABM; Antiballistic missiles

xx **Guided missiles**

Antipathies. *See* **Prejudices and antipathies**

Antipoverty programs. *See* **Economic assistance, Domestic**

Antiques

    See also **Art objects; Collectors and collecting**

Antiquities. *See* **Archeology; Bible—Antiquities; Christian antiquities; Classical antiquities; Indians of North America—Antiquities; Jews—Antiquities; Man—Origin and antiquity; Man, Prehistoric;** and names of countries, cities, etc. with the subdivision *Antiquities,* e.g. **U.S.—Antiquities;** etc.

Antiquities, Biblical. *See* **Bible—Antiquities**

Antiquities, Christian. *See* **Christian antiquities**

Antiquities, Classical. *See* **Classical antiquities**

Antiquities, Ecclesiastical. *See* **Christian antiquities**

Anti-Reformation. *See* **Reformation**

Antisemitism. *See* **Jewish question**

Antiseptics

    See also **Disinfection and disinfectants**

    xx **Disinfection and disinfectants; Surgery; Therapeutics**

Antislavery. *See* **Slavery**

Antivivisection. *See* **Vivisection**

Antonyms. *See* names of languages with the subdivision *Synonyms and antonyms,* e.g. **English language—Synonyms and antonyms;** etc.

Ants

    x Ant; Hymenoptera

Anxiety. *See* **Fear; Worry**

Apartheid. *See* **Segregation**

Apartment houses

    See also **Housing**

    x Condominiums; Flats

    xx **Architecture, Domestic; Houses; Housing; Landlord and tenant**

Apiculture. *See* **Bees**

Apollo project

    See also headings beginning with **Lunar** and **Moon**

    x Project Apollo

    xx **Life support systems (Space environment); Orbital rendezvous (Space flight); Space flight to the moon**

Apologetics

    See also **Natural theology; Religion and science**

    x Christianity—Apologetic works; Christianity—Evidences; Evidences of Christianity; Fundamental theology

Apostles

    x Disciples, Twelve

    xx **Bible—Biography; Christian biography; Christianity; Church history—Primitive and early church; Saints**

Apostles' Creed

    xx **Creeds**

Apostolic Church. *See* **Church history—Primitive and early church**

Apparatus, Chemical. *See* **Chemical apparatus**

Apparatus, Electric. *See* **Electric apparatus and appliances**

Apparatus, Electronic. *See* **Electronic apparatus and appliances**

Apparatus, Scientific. *See* **Scientific apparatus and instruments**

Apparitions

    See also **Demonology; Ghosts; Hallucinations and illusions; Miracles; Spiritualism; Visions**

    x Phantoms; Specters; Spirits

    xx **Demonology; Ghosts; Hallucinations and illusions; Psychical research; Spiritualism; Superstition; Visions**

Apperception

    See also **Attention; Consciousness; Knowledge, Theory of; Perception**

    xx **Educational psychology; Knowledge, Theory of; Perception; Psychology**

Apple

    xx **Fruit**

Appliances, Electric. *See* **Electric apparatus and appliances; Household appliances, Electric**

Appliances, Electronic. *See* **Electronic apparatus and appliances**

Applications for positions

    See also **Interviewing**

    x Employment references; Job resumés; Letters of recommendation; Recommendations for positions; Resumés (Employment)

    xx **Personnel management**

Applied art. *See* **Art industries and trade**

Applied mechanics. *See* **Mechanics, Applied**

Applied psychology. *See* **Psychology, Applied**

Applied science. *See* **Technology**

Apportionment (Election law)

    x Legislative reapportionment; Reapportionment (Election law)

    xx **Representative government and representation**

Appraisal. *See* **Assessment; Valuation**

Appraisal of books. *See* **Book reviews; Books and reading; Books and reading—Best books; Criticism; Literature—History and criticism**

Appreciation of art. *See* **Art appreciation**

Appreciation of music. *See* **Music—Analysis, appreciation**

Apprentices

    See also **Employees—Training**

    xx **Child labor; Employees—Training; Labor and laboring classes; Technical education**

April Fools' Day
> *x* All Fools' Day

Aptitude testing. *See* **Ability—Testing**

Aquanauts
> *xx* **Manned undersea research stations; Underwater exploration**

Aquariums
> *See also* **Fish culture; Goldfish; Marine aquariums**
>
> *xx* **Fishes; Fresh-water animals; Fresh-water biology; Fresh-water plants; Natural history**

Aquariums, Saltwater. *See* **Marine aquariums**

Aquatic animals. *See* **Fresh-water animals; Marine animals**

Aquatic birds. *See* **Water birds**

Aquatic plants. *See* **Fresh-water plants; Marine plants**

Aquatic sports. *See* **Water sports**

Aquatint
> *xx* **Engraving; Etching**

Aqueducts
> *x* Conduits; Water conduits
>
> *xx* **Civil engineering; Hydraulic structures; Water supply**

Arab civilization. *See* **Civilization, Arab**

Arab countries

Arab-Israel War, 1967. *See* **Israel-Arab War, 1967**

Arab-Jewish relations. *See* **Jewish-Arab relations**

Arabic art. *See* **Art, Islamic**

Arabs
> *See also* **Bedouins; Moors**

Arabs in Isreal
> Use same form for Arabs in other countries

Arachnida. *See* **Spiders**

Arbitration, Industrial
> *See also* **Collective bargaining; Strikes and lockouts**
>
> *x* Conciliation, Industrial; Industrial arbitration; Industrial conciliation; Labor disputes; Mediation, Industrial; Trade agreements (Labor)
>
> *xx* **Collective bargaining; Industrial relations; Labor and laboring classes; Labor unions; Strikes and lockouts**

Arbitration, International
> *See also* **Disarmament; League of Nations; Peace; United Nations**
>
> *x* International arbitration
>
> *xx* **Disarmament; International cooperation; International law; International relations; Peace; Security, International; Treaties**

Arboriculture. *See* **Forests and forestry; Fruit culture; Trees**

Arc light. *See* **Electric lighting**

Arc welding. *See* **Electric welding**

Archaeology. *See* **Archeology**
Archeologists
  xx **Historians**
✓ **Archeology**
  See also

Architecture, Ancient
Arms and armor
Art, Primitive
Bible—Antiquities
Brasses
Bronze age
Bronzes
Christian antiquities
Christian art and symbolism
Cities and towns, Ruined, extinct, etc.
Classical antiquities
Cliff dwellers and cliff dwellings
Ethnology
Excavations (Archeology)
Funeral rites and ceremonies
Gems
Heraldry
Indians of North America—Antiquities
Inscriptions
Iron age
Man, Prehistoric
Mounds and mound builders
Mummies
Numismatics
Obelisks
Pottery
Pyramids
Radiocarbon dating
Stone age
Stone implements
Temples
Tombs

  also names of countries, cities, etc. with the subdivision *Antiquities,* e.g. **U.S.—Antiquities;** etc.
  x Antiquities; Archaeology; Prehistory; Ruins
  xx **Anthropology; Art; Bronze age; Civilization; Classical antiquities; Ethnology; History; History, Ancient; Iron age**
Archeology, Biblical. *See* **Bible—Antiquities**
Archeology, Christian. *See* **Christian antiquities**
Archeology, Classical. *See* **Classical antiquities**
Archery
  See also **Bow and arrow**
  xx **Bow and arrow; Shooting**
Architects
  See also **Architecture as a profession**
  xx **Artists**
Architectural acoustics
  See also **Soundproofing**
  x Acoustics
  xx **Sound**
Architectural decoration and ornament. *See* **Decoration and ornament, Architectural**
Architectural design. *See* **Architecture—Details**
Architectural designs. *See* **Architecture—Designs and plans**
Architectural details. *See* **Architecture—Details**

Architectural drawing

    See also **Architecture—Designs and plans;
Architecture—Details**

    x Drawings, Architectural; Plans

    xx **Drawing; Mechanical drawing**

Architectural engineering. *See* **Building;
Building, Iron and steel; Strains and
stresses; Strength of materials;
Structures, Theory of**

Architectural metalwork

    x Metalwork, Architectural

    xx **Metalwork**

Architectural orders. *See* **Architecture—Orders**

Architectural perspective. *See* **Perspective**

Architecture (May subdiv. geog. adjective
form, e.g. **Architecture, Greek;** etc.)

    See also

Building	**Obelisks**
Building materials	**Palaces**
Castles	**Public buildings**
Cathedrals	**School buildings**
Church architecture	**Skyscrapers**
Concrete construc-	**Spires**
tion	**Strains and stresses**
Decoration and or-	**Strength of materi-**
nament, Architec-	**als**
tural	**Structural en-**
Farm buildings	**gineering**
Industrial buildings	**Synagogues**
Library architecture	**Temples**
Monuments	**Theaters**
Mosques	**Tombs**
Naval architecture	

    also headings beginning with the word
Architectural

    x Construction

    xx **Art; Building**

Architecture, American

    x American architecture; U.S.—Architecture

Architecture, Ancient

    See also **Architecture, Greek; Architecture, Roman; Pyramids; Temples**

    x Ancient architecture

    xx **Archeology**

Architecture, Baroque

    x Baroque architecture

Architecture, Byzantine

    x Byzantine architecture

Architecture, Church. *See* **Church architecture**

Architecture, Colonial

    See also names of countries, cities, etc.
with the subdivision *Historic houses,
etc.,* e.g. **Chicago—Historic houses,
etc.;** etc.

    x Colonial architecture

Architecture—Composition, proportion, etc.
 x Architecture—Proportion; Proportion (Architecture)
 xx **Composition (Art)**
Architecture—Conservation and restoration
 See also **Building—Repair and reconstruction**
 x Architecture—Restoration; Buildings, Restoration of; Conservation of buildings; Preservation of buildings; Restoration of buildings
 xx **Building—Repair and reconstruction**
Architecture—Decoration and ornament. *See* **Decoration and ornament, Architectural**
Architecture—Designs and plans
 See also **Architecture, Domestic—Designs and plans**
 x Architectural designs; Architecture—Plans; Designs, Architectural
 xx **Architectural drawing**
Architecture—Details
 See also **Chimneys; Doors; Fireplaces; Floors; Foundations; Roofs; Windows; Woodwork**
 x Architectural design; Architectural details; Design, Architectural; Details, Architectural
 xx **Architectural drawing**
Architecture, Domestic
 See also **Apartment houses; Farm buildings; Houses; Prefabricated houses**
 x Architecture, Rural; Country houses; Domestic architecture; Dwellings; Habitations, Human; Residences; Rural architecture; Suburban homes; Summer homes; Villas
Architecture, Domestic—Designs and plans
 x House plans
 xx **Architecture—Designs and plans**
Architecture, Ecclesiastical. *See* **Church architecture**
Architecture, Gothic
 See also **Cathedrals; Church architecture**
 x Gothic architecture
 xx **Cathedrals; Christian antiquities; Church architecture**
Architecture, Greek
 x Greek architecture
 xx **Architecture, Ancient**
Architecture, Medieval
 See also **Architecture, Romanesque; Castles; Cathedrals**
 x Medieval architecture
 xx **Middle Ages**
Architecture, Modern—20th century
 x Modern architecture
Architecture, Naval. *See* **Naval architecture; Shipbuilding**

Architecture—Orders
>*x* Architectural orders; Orders, Architectural

Architecture, Oriental
>*See also* **Mosques**
>*x* Oriental architecture

Architecture—Plans. *See* **Architecture—Designs and plans**

Architecture—Proportion. *See* **Architecture—Composition, proportion, etc.**

Architecture, Renaissance
>*xx* **Renaissance**

Architecture—Restoration. *See* **Architecture—Conservation and restoration**

Architecture, Roman
>*x* Roman architecture
>*xx* **Architecture, Ancient**

Architecture, Romanesque
>*x* Romanesque architecture
>*xx* **Architecture, Medieval**

Architecture, Rural. *See* **Architecture, Domestic; Farm buildings**

Architecture as a profession
>*xx* **Architects**

Archives (May subdiv. geog.)
>*See also* **Charters; Manuscripts**
>*x* Documents; Government records—Preservation; Historical records—Preservation; Preservation of historical records; Public records—Preservation; Records—Preservation
>*xx* **Bibliography; Charters; Documentation; History—Sources**

Archives—U.S.
>*x* U.S.—Archives

Arctic expeditions. *See* **Arctic regions;** and names of special expeditions

Arctic regions
>*See also* **North Pole; Northeast Passage; Northwest Passage; Scientific expeditions;** also names of explorers
>*x* Arctic expeditions; Expeditions, Antarctic and Arctic; Polar expeditions
>*xx* **Discoveries (in geography); Earth; North Pole; Polar regions; Scientific expeditions**

Ardennes, Battle of the, 1944-1945
>*x* Battle of the Bulge; Bulge, Battle of the
>*xx* **Battles; World War, 1939-1945; World War, 1939-1945—Campaigns and battles**

Area studies
>*See also* names of specific area studies, e.g. **Afro-American studies;** etc.
>*x* Foreign area studies
>*xx* **Education**

Arena theater
>*x* Round stage; Theater-in-the-round
>*xx* **Theater**

Argentine rummy. *See* **Canasta (Game)**

Argumentation. *See* **Debates and debating;**
　　Logic
Aristocracy
　　See also **Democracy; Nobility; Upper**
　　　　classes
　　xx **Democracy; Equality; Nobility; Po-**
　　　　litical science; Social classes; Soci-
　　　　ology
Arithmetic
　　See also **Business arithmetic**
　　xx **Mathematics; Set theory; Textbooks**
Arithmetic, Commercial. *See* **Business arith-**
　　　　metic
Arithmetic—Study and teaching
　　See also **Counting books; Number games**
Armada, 1588
　　x Spanish Armada
　　xx **Gt. Brit.—History—Tudors, 1485-1603**
Armaments. *See* **Armies; Disarmament; In-**
　　　　dustrial mobilization; Munitions;
　　　　Navies
Armed forces. *See* **Armies; Navies; Seamen;**
　　　　Soldiers; and names of countries
　　　　and international organizations with the
　　　　subdivision *Armed Forces,* e.g. **U.S.—**
　　　　Armed Forces; etc.
Armies
　　See also **Disarmament; Military art and**
　　　　science; Military service, Compul-
　　　　sory; Navies; Soldiers; War; World
　　　　War, 1939-1945—Manpower; also
　　　　names of countries with the subhead
　　　　Army (e.g. **U.S. Army;** etc.); and
　　　　headings beginning with the word
　　　　Military
　　x Armaments; Armed forces; Army;
　　　　Military forces; Military power
　　xx **Military art and science; Navies; Sol-**
　　　　diers; Strategy; War
Armies—Medical and sanitary affairs
　　See also **Medicine, Military; Military hy-**
　　　　giene; also names of wars with the
　　　　subdivision *Medical and sanitary af-*
　　　　fairs, e.g. **World War, 1939-1945—**
　　　　Medical and sanitary affairs; etc.
　　xx **Medicine, Military; Military hygiene**
Armistice Day. *See* **Veterans Day**
Armor. *See* **Arms and armor**
Armored cars (Tanks). *See* **Tanks (Military**
　　　　science)
Arms, Coats of. *See* **Heraldry**
Arms and armor
　　See also **Firearms; Ordnance; Rifles**
　　x Armor; Weapons
　　xx **Archeology; Costume; Military art and**
　　　　science
Arms control. *See* **Disarmament**
Army. *See* **Armies; Military art and science;**
　　　　and names of countries with the sub-
　　　　head *Army,* e.g. **U.S. Army;** etc.

Army desertion. *See* **Desertion, Military**

Army life. *See* **Soldiers;** and names of countries with the subdivision *Army—Military life,* e.g. **U.S. Army—Military life;** etc.

Army posts. *See* **Military posts**

Army schools. *See* **Military education**

Army tests. *See* **U.S. Army—Examinations**

Army vehicles. *See* **Vehicles, Military**

Aromatic plant products. *See* **Essences and essential oils**

Arrow. *See* **Bow and arrow**

⌐ **Art** (May subdiv. geog. adjective form, e.g. **Art, French;** etc.)

Subdivisions listed under this heading may be used under other art media where applicable

See also

Anatomy, Artistic	**Forgery of works of**
Animals in art	**art**
Archeology	**Futurism (Art)**
Architecture	**Gems**
Art objects	**Graphic arts**
Arts and crafts	**Illumination of**
Brasses	**books and manu-**
Bronzes	**scripts**
Children in litera-	**Illustration of books**
ture and art	**Negroes in litera-**
Christian art and	**ture and art**
symbolism	**Painting**
Collage	**Photography, Artis-**
Collectors and col-	**tic**
lecting	**Pictures**
Commercial art	**Plants in art**
Composition (Art)	**Portraits**
Design, Decorative	**Sculpture**
Drawing	**Surrealism**
Engraving	**Symbolism**
Etching	**Women in literature**
Folk art	**and art**

x Iconography

xx **Civilization; Esthetics; Humanities**

Art, Abstract

See also **Kinetic art**

x Abstract art; Art, Nonobjective; Nonobjective art; Paintings, Abstract

xx **Art, Modern—20th century**

Art, American

x American art; U.S.—Art

Art—Analysis, interpretation, appreciation. *See* **Art appreciation; Art—Study and teaching; Art criticism**

Art, Ancient

See also **Art, Primitive; Classical antiquities**

x Ancient art

Art, Applied. *See* **Art industries and trade; Design, Industrial**

Art, Arabic. *See* **Art, Islamic**

Art, Baroque

   x Baroque art

Art, Buddhist

   x Buddhist art

Art, Byzantine

   x Byzantine art

   xx **Art, Medieval**

Art, Christian. *See* **Christian art and symbolism**

Art, Classical. *See* **Art, Greek; Art, Roman**

Art, Commercial. *See* **Commercial art**

Art—Composition. *See* **Composition (Art)**

Art—Criticism. *See* **Art criticism**

Art, Decorative

   Use for general works on the decoration and use of artistic objects. Works limited to the line or form that these objects may take are entered under **Design.** Works limited to the external ornamentation of objects are entered under **Design, Decorative**

   See also

Bronzes	**Illustration of**
Decoration and or-	**books**
nament	**Mosaics**
Design, Decorative	**Mural painting and**
Enamel and enamel-	**decoration**
ing	**Needlework**
Furniture	**Pottery**

   x Decorative art; Decorative arts

   xx **Decoration and ornament; Design, Decorative**

Art, Ecclesiastical. *See* **Christian art and symbolism**

Art—Education. *See* **Art—Study and teaching**

Art—Exhibitions

   x Art exhibitions

   xx **Exhibitions**

Art—Forgeries. *See* **Forgery of works of art**

Art—Galleries and museums

   Use for general works only

   See also names of countries, cities, etc. with the subdivision *Galleries and museums* (e.g. **U.S.—Galleries and museums; Chicago—Galleries and museums;** etc.) ; and names of particular galleries and museums, e.g. **Boston. Museum of Fine Arts;** etc.

   x Art galleries; Art museums; Galleries (Art) ; Picture galleries

   xx **Museums**

Art, Graphic. *See* **Graphic arts**

Art, Greek

   x Art, Classical; Classical art; Greek art

   xx **Classical antiquities**

Art—History

   xx **History**

Art, Immoral. *See* **Pornography**

Art, Indian. *See* **Indians of North America—
Art**
Art, Islamic
    x Arabic art; Art, Arabic; Art, Moham-
medan; Art, Moorish; Mohammedan
art; Moorish art; Moslem art
Art, Kinetic. *See* **Kinetic art**
Art, Medieval
    See also **Art, Byzantine; Illumination of
books and manuscripts**
    x Medieval art; Religious art
    xx **Civilization, Medieval; Middle Ages**
Art, Modern
    x Modern art
Art, Modern—19th century
    See also **Postimpressionism (Art)**
Art, Modern—20th century
    See also names of modern art, e.g. **Art, Ab-
stract; Kinetic art;** etc.
    x Contemporary art
Art, Mohammedan. *See* **Art, Islamic**
Art, Moorish. *See* **Art, Islamic**
Art, Municipal
    See also **City planning; Public buildings**
    x Civic art; Municipal art; Municipal im-
provement
    xx **Cities and towns; City planning**
Art, Negro. *See* **Negro art**
Art, Nonobjective. *See* **Art, Abstract**
Art, Oriental
    x Oriental art
Art—Prices
    xx **Prices**
Art, Primitive
    See also **Cave drawings; Folk art; Indians
of North America—Art;** also names
of countries, cities, etc. with the sub-
division *Antiquities,* e.g. **U.S.—Antiq-
uities;** etc.
    x Prehistoric art; Primitive art
    xx **Archeology; Art, Ancient; Folk art;
Society, Primitive**
Art, Renaissance
    xx **Renaissance**
Art, Roman
    x Art, Classical; Classical art; Roman art
    xx **Classical antiquities**
Art, Romanesque
    See also **Painting, Romanesque**
    x Romanesque art
Art—Study and teaching
    x Art—Analysis, interpretation, apprecia-
tion; Art—Education; Art education;
Art schools
    xx **Study, Method of**
Art—Technique
Art anatomy. *See* **Anatomy, Artistic**
Art and mythology
    x Mythology in art
    xx **Art and religion; Mythology**

Art and religion

    See also **Art and mythology; Christian art and symbolism**

    x Religion and art

    xx **Art and society; Christian art and symbolism**

Art and society

    See also **Art and religion; Art and state; Art industries and trade; Folk art**

    x Society and art

Art and state

    x State and the arts; State encouragement of the arts

    xx **Art and society**

Art appreciation

    x Appreciation of art; Art—Analysis, interpretation, appreciation

    xx **Art criticism; Esthetics**

Art as a profession

    xx **Artists**

Art criticism

    See also **Art appreciation**

    x Art—Analysis interpretation, appreciation; Art—Criticism

    xx **Criticism**

Art education. *See* **Art—Study and teaching**

Art exhibitions. *See* **Art—Exhibitions**

Art forgeries. *See* **Forgery of works of art**

Art galleries. *See* **Art—Galleries and museums**

Art in advertising. *See* **Commercial art**

Art in motion. *See* **Kinetic art**

Art industries and trade. (May subdiv. geog.)

    Use for works dealing with decorative art in industry, peasant art, etc. and the production for commercial purposes of handicrafts and objects having an artistic value or interest

    See also **Arts and crafts; Commercial art; Design, Industrial; Folk art**; also special industries, trades, etc., e.g. **Glass painting and staining; Leather work;** etc.

    x Applied art; Art, Applied; Decorative arts; Industry and art; Peasant art

    xx **Art and society; Folk art; Industrial arts**

Art industries and trade—U.S.

    x U.S.—Art industries and trade

Art metalwork

    See also kinds of art metalwork, e.g. **Bronzes; Jewelry;** etc.

    x Decorative metalwork; Metalwork, Art

    xx **Metalwork**

Art museums. *See* **Art—Galleries and museums**

Art objects

    Use for general works about articles of artistic merit such as snuff boxes,

Art objects—*Continued*
>> brasses, pottery, needlework, glassware, etc.

> *See also* classes of art objects, e.g. **Furniture; Pottery;** etc.

> *xx* **Antiques; Art**

Art objects, Forgery of. *See* **Forgery of works of art**

Art schools. *See* **Art—Study and teaching**

Artesian wells. *See* **Wells**

Arthritis
> *xx* **Gout; Rheumatism**

Arthur, King
> *See also* **Grail**

> *x* Arthurian romances; Knights of the Round Table; Round Table

> *xx* **Chivalry; Grail**

Arthurian romances. *See* **Arthur, King**

Articles of war. *See* **Military law**

Articulation (Education)
> Use for works that discuss the integration of various elements of the school system so as to provide for continuous progress by the student. This may be the adjustments and relationships between different levels (e.g. elementary and secondary schools, high school and college); the integration between subjects (e.g. humanities and social studies); or the relationship between the school's program and outside factors (e.g. church, scouts, welfare agencies)

> *x* Integration in education

> *xx* **Education—Curricula; School administration and organization**

Artificial flies. *See* **Flies, Artificial**

Artificial flowers
> *x* Flowers, Artificial

Artificial heart
> *xx* **Artificial organs**

Artificial insemination
> *x* Impregnation, Artificial; Insemination, Artificial

Artificial intelligence
> *x* Brain, Electronic; Electronic brains; Intelligence, Artificial; Machine intelligence

> *xx* **Bionics**

Artificial organs
> *See also* names of artificial organs, e.g. **Artificial heart;** etc.

> *x* Organs, Artificial; Prosthesis

Artificial respiration
> *x* Respiration, Artificial

> *xx* **First aid**

Artificial rubber. *See* **Rubber, Artificial**

Artificial satellites (May subdiv. geog. adjective form)

    See also **Meteorological satellites; Space stations; Space vehicles;** also names of specific satellites, e.g., **Explorer (Artificial satellite)**; etc.

    x Orbiting vehicles; Satellites, Artificial

    xx **Astronautics; Space vehicles**

Artificial satellites, American

    x American artificial satellites; U.S.—Artificial satellites

Artificial satellites—Control systems

Artificial satellites—Launching

    x Launching of satellites

    xx **Rockets (Aeronautics)**

Artificial satellites—Laws and regulations. *See* **Space law**

Artificial satellites—Orbits

Artificial satellites, Russian

    x Russian artificial satellites; Sputniks

Artificial satellites—Tracking

    x Tracking of satellites

Artificial satellites in telecommunication

    See also names of specific satellites or projects, e.g., **Telstar project**; etc.

    x Communications relay satellites; Global satellite communications systems

    xx **Telecommunication**

Artificial silk. *See* **Rayon**

Artificial weather control. *See* **Weather control**

Artillery

    See also **Ordnance**

Artistic anatomy. *See* **Anatomy, Artistic**

Artistic photography. *See* **Photography, Artistic**

Artists (May subdiv. geog. adjective form, e.g. **Artists, French**; etc.)

    See also

Architects	**Negro artists**
Art as a profession	**Painters**
Children as artists	**Potters**
Engravers	**Sculptors**
Etchers	**Women as artists**
Illustrators	

    also names of individual artists

    xx **Biography; Painters**

Artists, American

    x American artists; U.S.—Artists

Artists, Negro. *See* **Negro artists**

Artists' materials

    x Drawing materials; Painters' materials

The arts (May subdiv. geog. adjective form)

    Use for works on the arts in general, including the visual arts, literature, and the performing arts. For works on the visual arts only (architecture, painting, etc.) use **Art**

    x Arts, Fine; Fine arts

The arts, American

    x American arts

43

Arts, Fine. *See* **The arts**

Arts, Graphic. *See* **Graphic arts**

Arts, Useful. *See* **Industrial arts; Technology**

Arts and crafts

See also

Basket making	Industrial arts education
Beadwork	Jewelry
Bookbinding	Lacquer and lacquering
China painting	Leather work
Decoration and ornament	Metalwork
Design, Decorative	Modeling
Enamel and enameling	Mosaics
Folk art	Mural painting and decoration
Glass painting and staining	Needlework
Handicraft	Pottery
Illumination of books and manuscripts	Rugs
	Stencil work
	Weaving
	Wood carving

x Crafts; Decorative arts

xx **Art; Art industries and trade; Folk art; Industrial arts; Industrial arts education**

Asbestos

xx **Geology, Economic**

Asceticism

See also **Monasticism and religious orders**

xx **Christian life; Fasting; Monasticism and religious orders**

Asia

See also **Asia, Southeastern**

x Middle East

xx **East**

Asia—Politics

x Politics

Asia, Southeastern

Use for works on Southeast Asia including Burma, Thailand, Malaysia, Singapore, Indonesia, North and South Vietnam, Cambodia, Laos, and the Philippine Islands

x Indochina; Southeast Asia

xx **Asia**

Asphalt

xx **Concrete; Pavements**

Asphyxiating gases. *See* **Gases, Asphyxiating and poisonous**

Assassination

See also **Murder**; also names of persons and groups of persons with the subdivision *Assassination,* e.g. **Presidents—U.S.—Assassination**

xx **Crime and criminals; Murder; Offenses against the person; Political crimes and offenses**

Assembly, Right of. *See* **Freedom of assembly**

Assembly programs, School. *See* **School assembly programs**

✓ **Assessment**

Use for general works only. Works on the assessment of a given locality are entered under **Taxation** followed by the appropriate geographical division

See also **Taxation; Valuation**

x Appraisal

xx **Taxation**

Assessments, Political. *See* **Campaign funds**

Assistance to developing areas. *See* **Economic assistance; Technical assistance**

Associations

See also **Clubs; Community life; Cooperation; Societies;** also names of types of associations, e.g. **Trade and professional associations;** etc.; and subjects with the subdivision *Societies,* e.g. **Agriculture—Societies;** etc.

x Organizations; Voluntary associations

xx **Societies**

Assyro-Babylonian inscriptions. *See* **Cuneiform inscriptions**

Astrobiology. *See* **Space biology**

Astrodynamics

See also **Astronautics; Navigation (Astronautics); Space flight**

xx **Astronautics; Dynamics; Space flight**

Astrology

See also **Occult sciences**

x Hermetic art and philosophy; Horoscope

xx **Astronomy; Divination; Fortune telling; Occult sciences; Prophecies; Stars; Superstition**

Astronautical accidents. *See* **Astronautics—Accidents**

Astronautical communication systems. *See* **Astronautics—Communication systems**

Astronautical instruments

See also **Astronautics—Communication systems**

x Instruments, Astronautical; Space vehicles—Instruments

xx **Astronautics — Communication systems; Navigation (Astronautics)**

Astronautics (May subdiv. geog.)

See also **Aerothermodynamics; Artificial satellites; Astrodynamics; Interplanetary voyages; Manned space flight; Navigation (Astronautics); Outer space; Rocketry; Space flight; Space flight to the moon; Space sciences; Space ships; Space stations; Space vehicles**

xx **Aeronautics; Astrodynamics; Space sciences; Space vehicles**

45

Astronautics—Accidents
> *x* Accidents, Spacecraft; Astronautical accidents; Space ships—Accidents; Space vehicles—Accidents

Astronautics—Communication systems
> *See also* **Astronautical instruments; Radio in astronautics; Television in astronautics**
> *x* Astronautical communication systems; Space communication
> *xx* **Astronautical instruments; Interstellar communication; Telecommunication**

Astronautics—International cooperation
> *x* International space cooperation

Astronautics—Laws and regulations. *See* **Space law**

Astronautics, Photography in. *See* **Space photography**

Astronautics—U.S.
> *x* U.S.—Astronautics

Astronautics and civilization
> *See also* **Religion and astronautics; Space law**
> *x* Civilization and astronautics; Outer space and civilization; Space power
> *xx* **Aeronautics and civilization; Civilization**

Astronautics and religion. *See* **Relgion and astronautics**

Astronauts
> *See also* **Space vehicles—Piloting**
> *x* Cosmonauts; Space ships—Pilots
> *xx* **Manned space flight**

Astronauts—Clothing
> *x* Pressure suits; Space suits
> *xx* **Life support systems (Space environment)**

Astronauts—Nutrition
> *x* Meals for astronauts; Menus for astronauts; Nutrition of astronauts; Space nutrition

Astronavigation. *See* **Navigation (Astronautics)**

Astronomers
> *xx* **Scientists**

Astronomical instruments
> *See also* **Astronomical photography; Telescope**
> *x* Instruments, Astronomical
> *xx* **Scientific apparatus and instruments**

Astronomical observatories
> *x* Observatories, Astronomical

Astronomical photography
> *x* Photography, Astronomical
> *xx* **Astronomical instruments; Photography**

Astronomical physics. *See* **Astrophysics**

Astronomical spectroscopy. *See* **Astrophysics; Spectrum**

Astronomy

    See also

Almanacs	**Planets,** and names
Astrology	of planets
Astrophysics	**Quasars**
Bible—Astronomy	Radio astronomy
Comets	**Seasons**
Eclipses, Lunar	Solar system
Eclipses, Solar	Space environment
Life on other planets	Space sciences
Meteorites	Spectrum
Meteors	**Stars**
Moon	**Sun**
Nautical astronomy	**Tides**
Outer space	**Zodiac**

    also headings beginning with the word **Astronomical**

    x Constellations

    xx **Science; Space sciences; Stars; Universe**

Astronomy—Atlases. *See* **Stars—Atlases**

Astronomy, Nautical. *See* **Nautical astronomy**

Astrophysics

    x Astronomical physics; Astronomical spectroscopy; Physics, Astronomical

    xx **Astronomy; Physics; Stars**

Astros. *See* **Houston Astros**

Asylums. *See* **Institutional care;** also classes of people with the subdivision *Institutional care;* e.g. **Blind—Institutional care; Deaf—Institutional care; Mentally ill—Institutional care;** etc.

Atheism

    See also **Agnosticism; Deism; Rationalism; Skepticism; Theism**

    xx **Agnosticism; Deism; Faith; God; Rationalism; Religion; Theism; Theology**

Athletes

Athletes, Negro. *See* **Negro athletes**

Athletics

    See also

Coaching (Athletics)	Physical education and training
Gymnastics	**Sports**
Olympic games	Track athletics

    also names of specific athletic activities, e.g. **Boxing; Rowing;** etc.

    x College athletics; Intercollegiate athletics

    xx **Physical education and training; Sports**

Atlantic cable. *See* **Cables, Submarine**

Atlantic Ocean

    xx **Ocean**

Atlantic States

    x Eastern Seaboard; Middle Atlantic States; South Atlantic States

    xx **United States**

Atlas (Missile)

    xx **Ballistic missiles; Intercontinental ballistic missiles**

Atlases

    See also **Bible—Geography;** also names of countries, cities, etc. with the subdivision *Maps,* e.g. **U.S.—Maps;** etc.

    x Geographical atlases

    xx **Geography; Maps**

Atlases, Astronomical. *See* **Stars—Atlases**

Atlases, Historical

    x Geography, Historical—Maps; Historical atlases; Historical geography; History—Atlases; Maps, Historical

Atmosphere

    Use for works treating of the body of air surrounding the earth as distinguished from the upper rarefied air. Works dealing with air as an element and of its chemical and physical properties are entered under **Air**

    See also **Air; Meteorology**

    xx **Air; Earth; Meteorology**

Atmosphere—Pollution. *See* **Air—Pollution**

Atmosphere, Upper

    See also **Stratosphere**

    x Upper atmosphere

Atolls. *See* **Coral reefs and islands**

Atom smashing. *See* **Cyclotron**

Atomic bomb

    See also **Hydrogen bomb; Radioactive fallout**

    xx **Atomic energy; Atomic warfare; Atomic weapons; Bombs; Hydrogen bomb**

Atomic bomb—Physiological effect

    See also **Radiation—Physiological effect**

    xx **Radiation—Physiological effect**

Atomic bomb—Testing

Atomic energy

    See also **Atomic bomb; Nuclear engineering; Nuclear propulsion; Nuclear reactors**

    x Atomic power; Nuclear energy

    xx **Atomic theory; Nuclear physics**

Atomic energy—Economic aspects

Atomic medicine

    x Medicine, Atomic

    xx **Radiation—Physiological effect**

Atomic nuclei. *See* **Nuclear physics**

Atomic piles. *See* **Nuclear reactors**

Atomic power. *See* **Atomic energy**

Atomic power plants

    x Power plants, Atomic

    xx **Power plants**

Atomic powered vehicles. *See* **Nuclear propulsion**

Atomic submarines

    x Submarines, Atomic

    xx **Nuclear propulsion**

Atomic theory

See also **Atomic energy; Quantum theory**

xx **Chemistry, Physical and theoretical; Quantum theory**

Atomic warfare

See also **Atomic bomb; Atomic weapons; Hydrogen bomb**

x Nuclear warfare

Atomic weapons

See also **Atomic bomb; Ballistic missiles; Intercontinental ballistic missiles; Hydrogen bomb**

x Nuclear weapons; Weapons, Atomic

xx **Atomic warfare; Ordnance**

Atomic weapons and disarmament. *See* **Disarmament**

Atoms

See also **Cyclotron; Electrons; Nuclear physics; Transmutation (Chemistry)**

xx **Chemistry, Physical and theoretical; Neutrons; Protons**

Atonement

x Jesus Christ—Atonement; Redemption

xx **Jesus Christ; Sacrifice; Salvation; Sin; Theology**

Atrocities

See also **Persecution**; also names of wars with the subdivision *Atrocities,* e.g. **World War, 1939-1945—Atrocities;** etc.

xx **Crime and criminals; Cruelty**

Attendance, School. *See* **School attendance**

Attention

See also **Listening**

x Concentration

xx **Apperception; Educational psychology; Listening; Memory; Psychology; Thought and thinking**

Attitude (Psychology)

See also **Conformity; Public opinion**; also names of groups of individuals with the subdivision *Attitudes,* e.g. **Youth—Attitudes;** etc.

x Frustration

xx **Emotions; Psychology; Public opinion; Social psychology**

Attorneys. *See* **Lawyers**

Auction bridge. *See* **Bridge (Game)**

Auctions

x Sales, Auction

Audio-visual education

See also **Audio-visual materials; Moving pictures in education; Phonograph records; Radio in education; Television in education**; also subjects with the subdivision *Audio-visual aids,* e.g. **Library education — Audio-visual aids;** etc.

x Visual instruction

xx **Education**

Audio-visual materials

See also subjects with the subdivision *Audio-visual aids,* e.g. **Library education—Audio-visual aids;** etc.; also names of specific materials, e.g. **Filmstrips; Motion pictures; Phonograph records;** etc.

xx **Audio-visual education; Teaching—Aids and devices**

Audio-visual materials centers. *See* **Instructional materials centers**

Auditing

See also **Accounting**

xx **Accounting; Bookkeeping**

Aurora borealis. *See* **Auroras**

Auroras

x Aurora borealis; Northern lights; Polar lights

xx **Geophysics; Meteorology**

Austria—History

See also **Holy Roman Empire; Seven Years' War, 1756-1763**

Austria—History—Allied occupation, 1945-1955

Author and publisher. *See* **Authors and publishers**

Authoritarianism. *See* **Fascism; Totalitarianism**

Authors (May subdiv. geog. adjective form, e.g. **Authors, English;** etc.)

Use for works dealing with the personal lives of several authors. Books dealing with their literary works are entered under **Literature—History and criticism.** Works in which the two aspects are combined are entered under **Literature—Bio-bibliography**

See also **Literature—Bio-bibliography; Literature—History and criticism;** also **Children as authors; Negro authors; Pseudonyms; Women as authors;** also classes of writers (e.g. **Dramatists; Novelists; Poets;** etc.); and names of individual authors

x Bio-bibliography; Literature — Biography; Literature as a profession; Writers

xx **Biography; Books; Literature—Bio-bibliography; Literature — History and criticism**

Authors, American

x American authors; American literature —Biography; U.S.—Authors

xx **American literature**

Authors, English

See also **English literature—Bio-bibliography**

x English authors; English literature—Biography

xx **English literature**

Authors—Homes and haunts. *See* **Literary landmarks**

Authors, Negro. *See* **Negro authors**

Authors and publishers

Use for works on the legal relations between author and publisher

See also **Copyright**

x Author and publisher; Publishers and authors

xx **Authorship; Contracts; Copyright; Publishers and publishing**

Authorship

Use for general works treating of the means of becoming an author. Works concerning the composition of special types of literature are entered under more specific headings such as **Fiction—Technique; Short story;** etc.

See also

Advertising copy	Plots (Drama, fiction, etc.)
Authors and publishers	Radio authorship
Biography (as a literary form)	Report writing
Copyright	Short story
Drama—Technique	Technical writing
Fiction—Technique	Television authorship
Journalism	Versification

x Literature as a profession; Writing (Authorship)

xx **Literature**

Authorship—Handbooks, manuals, etc.

See also **Printing—Style manuals**

x Copyreading

xx **Printing—Style manuals**

Auto courts. *See* **Hotels, motels, etc.**

Autobiographies

Use for collections of autobiographies

x Diaries; Memoirs

xx **Biography**

Autocodes. *See* **Programming languages (Electronic computers)**

Autographs

See also **Manuscripts**

x Handwriting

xx **Biography; Manuscripts; Writing**

Automata

Use for works on robots in non-human form. Works on automata in human form are entered under **Robots**

See also **Robots**

xx **Mechanical movements; Robots**

Automatic computers. *See* **Computers**

Automatic control. *See* **Automation; Cybernetics; Electric controllers; Servomechanisms**

Automatic data processing. *See* **Electronic data processing**

Automatic information retrieval. *See* **Information storage and retrieval systems**

51

Automatic program languages. *See* **Programming languages** (Electronic computers)

Automatic teaching. *See* **Teaching machines**

Automation

> *See also* **Servomechanisms; Systems engineering;** also subjects with the subdivision *Automation,* e.g. **Libraries—Automation;** etc.
>
> *x* Automatic control; Computer control; Machinery, Automatic
>
> *xx* **Machinery in industry**

Automobile accidents. *See* **Traffic accidents**

Automobile driver education. *See* **Automobile drivers—Education**

Automobile drivers

> *x* Automobile driving; Automobiles—Driving; Drivers, Automobile

Automobile drivers—Education

> *x* Automobile driver education; Driver education
>
> *xx* **Education**

Automobile driving. *See* **Automobile drivers**

Automobile engines. *See* **Automobiles—Engines**

Automobile guides. *See* **Automobiles—Road guides**

Automobile industry and trade

Automobile insurance. *See* **Insurance, Automobile**

Automobile racing

> *See also* **Karts and karting;** also names of types of automobile races and names of specific races
>
> *x* Automobiles—Racing; Racing

Automobile touring. *See* **Automobiles—Touring**

Automobile trailers. *See* **Automobiles—Trailers**

Automobile transmission. *See* **Automobiles—Transmission devices**

Automobile trucks. *See* **Trucks**

Automobiles

> *See also* **Buses; Sports cars; Trucks;** also names of automobiles, e.g. **Ford automobile;** etc.
>
> *x* Cars (Automobiles); Jeeps; Locomotion; Motor cars
>
> *xx* **Transportation; Transportation, Highway**

Automobiles—Accidents. *See* **Traffic accidents**

Automobiles—Air conditioning

> *xx* **Air conditioning**

Automobiles—Brakes

> *xx* **Brakes**

Automobiles—Design and construction

Automobiles—Driving. *See* **Automobile drivers**

Automobiles, Electric

> *x* Electric automobiles

Automobiles & Collectors and collecting

automobiles, Racing

Automobiles—Electric equipment
  x Electric equipment of automobiles
Automobiles—Engines
  x Automobile engines; Automobiles—Motors
  xx **Engines; Gas and oil engines**
Automobiles, Foreign
  x Foreign automobiles
Automobiles—Gearing. *See* **Automobiles—Transmission devices**
Automobiles—Laws and regulations
  See also **Traffic regulations**
  x Laws
  xx **Law; Legislation; Traffic regulations**
Automobiles—Models
  x Model cars
  xx **Machinery—Models**
Automobiles—Motors. *See* **Automobiles—Engines**
Automobiles—Pollution control devices
  x Pollution control devices (Motor vehicles)
Automobiles—Racing. *See* **Automobile racing**
Automobiles—Repairing
Automobiles—Road guides
  x Automobile guides; Maps, Road; Road maps; Roads—Maps
  xx **Maps**
Automobiles—Service stations
  x Filling stations; Gas stations; Service stations, Automobile
Automobiles—Touring
  x Automobile touring; Motoring
  xx **Travel**
Automobiles—Trailers
  See also **Travel trailers and campers**
  x Automobile trailers; Recreational vehicles; Trailers
Automobiles—Transmission devices
  x Automobile transmission; Automobiles—Gearing; Transmissions, Automobile
  xx **Gearing**
Autosuggestion. *See* **Hypnotism; Mental suggestion**
Autumn
  x Fall
  xx **Seasons**
Avant-garde churches. *See* **Noninstitutional churches**
Avant-garde films. *See* **Experimental films**
Avant-garde theater. *See* **Experimental theater**
Avesta
  See also **Zoroastrianism**
  x Zend-Avesta
  xx **Sacred books; Zoroastrianism**
Aviation. *See* **Aeronautics**
Aviation medicine
  See also **Space medicine**
  x Aeronautics—Medical aspects; Aero-

Aviation medicine—*Continued*
> space medicine; Air pilots—Diseases
> and hygiene; Medicine, Aviation

    xx **Medicine**

Aviators. *See* **Air pilots**

✓ Awards. *See* **Rewards (Prizes, etc.)**; and
> names of awards

Aztecs

    xx **Indians of Mexico**

BMEWS. *See* **Ballistic missile early warning
system**

B-36 bomber

    xx **Bombers**

Babies. *See* **Infants**

Baby animals. *See* **Animals—Infancy**

Baby sitters

    xx **Children—Care and hygiene; Children
—Management; Infants—Care and
hygiene**

Babylonian inscriptions. *See* **Cuneiform inscriptions**

Bacilli. *See* **Bacteriology; Germ theory of
disease**

Back packing. *See* **Backpacking**

Backpacking

    x Back packing; Pack transportation

    xx **Camping; Hiking**

Backward areas. *See* **Underdeveloped areas**

Backward children. *See* **Mentally handicapped
children; Slow learning children**

Bacon-Shakespeare controversy. *See* **Shakespeare, William—Authorship**

Bacon's Rebellion, 1676

    xx **U.S.—History—Colonial period**

Bacteria. *See* **Bacteriology**

Bacterial warfare. *See* **Biological warfare**

Bacteriology

    See also **Disinfection and disinfectants;
Fermentation; Germ theory of disease; Immunity; Microorganisms;**
also subjects with the subdivision *Bacteriology,* e.g. **Cheese—Bacteriology;**
etc.

    x Bacilli; Bacteria; Disease germs;
Germs; Medicine, Preventive; Microbes; Preventive medicine

    xx **Communicable diseases; Fermentation;
Fungi; Germ theory of disease; Medicine; Microorganisms; Microbiology; Parasites; Pathology; Science**

Bacteriology, Agricultural

    See also **Soils—Bacteriology;** also names
of crops, etc. with the subdivision *Diseases and pests,* e.g. **Fruit—Diseases
and pests;** etc.

    x Agricultural bacteriology; Diseases and
pests

    xx **Soils—Bacteriology**

Badges of honor. *See* **Decorations of honor;
Insignia; Medals**

Bahaism
   xx Islam; Religions
Baking
   See also Bread; Cake; Pastry
   xx Bread; Cookery
Balance of nature. *See* Ecology
Balance of payments
   xx International economic relations
Balance of power
   x Power politics
Ball bearings. *See* Bearings (Machinery)
Ball games. *See* names of games, e.g. Baseball;
      Soccer; etc.
Ballads (May subdiv. geog. adjective form)
      Use for collections of ballads, and for
         works about ballads. Works treating
         of the folk tunes associated with these
         ballads, and collections which include
         both words and music, are entered un-
         der Folk songs
   See also Folk songs
   xx Literature; Folk songs; Poetry; Songs
Ballads, American
   x American ballads; U.S.—Ballads
   xx American literature
Ballet
   See also Pantomimes
   x Choreography
   xx Dancing; Drama; Opera; Performing
      arts; Theater
Ballet, Water. *See* Synchronized swimming
Ballet dancers. *See* Dancers
Ballets—Stories, plots, etc.
   x Stories
   xx Plots (Drama, fiction, etc.)
Ballistic missile early warning system
   x BMEWS; Early warning system, Bal-
      listic missile
   xx Air defenses; Radar defense networks
Ballistic missiles
   See also types of ballistic missiles, e.g. In-
      tercontinental ballistic missiles; etc.;
      also names of missiles, e.g. Atlas (Mis-
      sile); etc.
   x Missiles, Ballistic
   xx Atomic weapons; Guided missiles;
      Rocketry; Rockets (Aeronautics)
Balloons
   See also Aeronautics
   xx Aeronautics; Airships
Balloons, Dirigible. *See* Airships
Ballot. *See* Elections
Band music. *See* Bands (Music)
Bandages and bandaging
   xx First aid
Bandits. *See* Robbers and outlaws
Bandmasters. *See* Conductors (Music)
Bands (Music)
   See also Conducting; Drum majoring;
      Instrumentation and orchestration;

55

Bands (Music)—*Continued*

      Military music; Orchestra; Wind instruments

   x Band music

   xx **Conducting; Instrumental music; Military music; Orchestra; Wind instruments**

Banking. *See* **Banks and banking**

Bankruptcy

   x Business failures; Failure (in business); Insolvency

   xx **Commercial law; Debtor and creditor; Finance**

Banks and banking (May subdiv. geog.)

   See also

Agricultural credit	Foreign exchange
Bills of exchange	Interest and usury
Building and loan	Investment trusts
associations	Investments
Clearing house	Money
Consumer credit	Negotiable instru-
Credit	ments
Federal Reserve	Savings banks
banks	Trust companies

   x Agricultural banks; Banking

   xx **Business; Capital; Clearing house; Commerce; Credit; Finance; Money; Trust companies**

Banks and banking, Cooperative

   x Cooperative banks; Credit unions; People's banks

   xx **Cooperation; Cooperative societies**

Banks and banking—U.S.

   x U.S.—Banks and banking

Banned books. *See* **Books—Censorship**

Banners. *See* **Flags**

Banquets. *See* **Dinners and dining**

Baptism

   x Christening; Immersion, Baptismal

   xx **Rites and ceremonies; Sacraments; Theology**

Baptists

   See also **Church of the Brethren; Mennonites**

Bar. *See* **Lawyers**

Barbary corsairs. *See* **Pirates**

Barbary States. *See* **Africa, North**

Barbecue cooking. *See* **Outdoor cookery**

Barns. *See* **Farm buildings**

Barometer

   xx **Meteorological instruments**

Baronage. *See* **Nobility**

Baroque architecture. *See* **Architecture, Baroque**

Baroque art. *See* **Art, Baroque**

Barristers. *See* **Lawyers**

Barrows. *See* **Mounds and mound builders**

Bars and restaurants. *See* **Restaurants, bars, etc.**

Baseball

    See also **Little league baseball; Softball**

    x Ball games

    xx **College sports; Sports**

Baseball—Anecdotes, facetiae, satire, etc.

Baseball clubs

    See also names of individual clubs, e.g.
        Houston Astros; etc.

Basements

    x Cellars

    xx **Foundations**

Bashfulness

    x Shyness

    xx **Emotions**

Basket making

    xx **Arts and crafts; Industrial arts educa-
        tion; Weaving**

Bastardy. *See* **Illegitimacy**

Bat. *See* **Bats**

Baths

    See also **Hydrotherapy**

    x Cleanliness

    xx **Hydrotherapy;   Hygiene;   Physical
        therapy**

Bathyscaphe

    x Diving, Submarine

    xx **Oceanography—Research**

Batik

    xx **Dyes and dyeing**

Baton twirling

    See also **Drum majoring**

    xx **Drum majoring**

Batrachia. *See* **Amphibians**

Bats

    x Bat

    xx **Mammals**

Battered child syndrome. *See* **Cruelty to chil-
    dren**

Batteries, Electric. *See* **Electric batteries;
    Storage batteries**

Battle of the Bulge. *See* **Ardennes, Battle of
    the, 1944-1945**

Battle ships. *See* **Warships**

Battle songs. *See* **War songs**

Battles

    Names of battles are not included in this
        list but are to be added as needed, e.g.
        Ardennes, Battle of the, 1944-1945;
        etc.

    See also **Naval battles;** also names of wars
        with the subdivision *Campaigns and
        battles* (e.g. **U.S.—History—Civil
        War—Campaigns and battles; World
        War, 1939-1945—Campaigns and bat-
        tles;** etc.) and names of individual
        battles, e.g. **Ardennes, Battle of the,
        1944-1945;** etc.

    x Fighting; Sieges

    xx **Military art and science; Military his-
        tory; Naval battles; War**

✓ Basketball

Battleships. *See* **Warships**

Bay of Pigs invasion. *See* **Cuba—History—Invasion, 1961**

Bazaars. *See* **Fairs**

Beaches. *See* **Seashore**

Beadwork
  xx **Arts and crafts; Crocheting; Embroidery; Weaving**

Bearings (Machinery)
  See also **Lubrication and lubricants**
  x Ball bearings; Journals (Machinery)
  xx **Lubrication and lubricants; Machinery**

Bears
  xx **Animals**

Beasts. *See* **Animals**

Beat generation. *See* **Bohemianism**

Beatniks. *See* **Bohemianism**

Beautification of the landscape. *See* **Landscape protection**

Beauty. *See* **Esthetics**

Beauty, Personal
  See also **Cosmetics; Costume; Hair**
  x Complexion; Good grooming; Grooming, Personal; Grooming for women; Personal appearance; Personal grooming; Toilet
  xx **Beauty shops; Hygiene**

Beauty shops
  See also **Beauty, Personal; Cosmetics**

Beavers
  xx **Fresh-water animals; Fur-bearing animals**

Bedouins
  xx **Arabs**

Bedspreads. *See* **Coverlets**

Bee. *See* **Bees**

Beef
  xx **Meat**

Beef cattle. *See* **Cattle**

Bees
  See also **Honey**
  x Apiculture; Bee; Hymenoptera
  xx **Honey; Insects**

Beets and beet sugar
  x Sugar beets
  xx **Sugar**

Begging
  See also **Charity; Tramps**
  x Mendicancy; Vagrancy
  xx **Tramps**

Behavior
  See also

Charity	**Family life**
Christian life	**education**
Courage	**Friendship**
Courtesy	**Habit**
Duty	**Honesty**
Ethics	**Human relations**
Etiquette	**Justice**

Behavior—*Continued*

Love

Loyalty

Obedience

Patriotism

Self-control

Self-culture

Social adjustment

Spiritual life

Sympathy

Temperance

Truthfulness and

falsehood

x Conduct of life; Morals

xx **Behaviorism (Psychology); Character; Courtesy; Ethics; Human relations**

Behavior problems (Children). *See* **Problem children**

Behaviorism (Psychology)

See also **Behavior**

xx **Psychology**

Being. *See* **Ontology**

Belief and doubt

Use for works treating the subject from the philosophical standpoint. Works on religious belief are entered under **Faith**

See also **Agnosticism; Rationalism; Skepticism; Truth**

x Certainty; Doubt; Religious belief

xx **Agnosticism; Emotions; Knowledge, Theory of; Philosophy; Rationalism; Religion; Skepticism**

Bell System Telstar satellite. *See* **Telstar project**

Belles-lettres. *See* **Literature**

Bells

x Carillons; Chimes; Church bells

Belts and belting

See also **Power transmission**

x Chain belting

xx **Machinery; Power transmission**

Benevolence. *See* **Charity**

Benevolent institutions. *See* **Institutional care**

Bequests. *See* **Gifts; Inheritance and succession; Wills**

Berries

Names of berries are not included in this list but are to be added as needed, in the plural form, e.g. **Strawberries**

See also names of berries, e.g. **Strawberries**; etc.

xx **Fruit; Fruit culture**

Best books. *See* **Books and reading—Best books**

Best sellers

x Books—Best sellers

xx **Books and reading**

Betting. *See* **Gambling**

Bevel gearing. *See* **Gearing**

Beverages

See also **Liquors**; also names of beverages, e.g. **Cocoa; Coffee**; etc.

x Drinks

xx **Diet; Food**

Bible

The subject subdivisions under **Bible** may be used also for any part of the Bible, under the same form of entry as for the texts of such parts, e.g. **Bible. O.T.—Biography; Bible. O.T. Pentateuch—Commentaries; Bible. O.T. Psalms—History; Bible. N.T. Gospels—Inspiration;** etc.

x Holy Scriptures; Scriptures, Holy

xx **Hebrew literature; History, Ancient; Jewish literature; Sacred books**

Bible—Animals. *See* **Bible—Natural history**

Bible—Antiquities

See also **Christian antiquities**

x Antiquities; Antiquities, Biblical; Archeology, Biblical; Biblical archeology

xx **Archeology**

Bible—Astronomy

xx **Astronomy**

Bible—Biography

See also **Apostles; Christian biography; Prophets; Women in the Bible**

x Biblical characters

Bible—Birds. *See* **Bible—Natural history**

Bible—Botany. *See* **Bible—Natural history**

Bible—Catechisms, question books

x Bible—Question books

xx **Bible—Study; Catechisms**

Bible—Chronology

x Chronology, Biblical

Bible—Commentaries

x Bible — Interpretation; Commentaries, Biblical

Bible—Concordances

x Bible—Indexes; Concordances

xx **Bible—Dictionaries**

Bible—Criticism, interpretaton, etc.

x Bible—Exegesis; Bible—Hermeneutics; Bible—Interpretation; Exegesis, Biblical; Hermeneutics, Biblical; Higher criticism

xx **Bible as literature; Criticism**

Bible—Dictionaries

See also **Bible—Concordances**

x Bible—Indexes

Bible—Drama. *See* **Bible as literature; Mysteries and miracle plays; Religious drama**

Bible—Evidences, authority, etc.

See also **Miracles**

x Evidences of the Bible

xx **Free thought**

Bible—Exegesis. *See* **Bible—Criticism, interpretation, etc.**

Bible—Festivals. *See* **Fasts and feasts**

Bible—Fiction. *See* **Bible—History of Biblical events—Fiction**

Bible—Flowers. *See* **Bible—Natural history**

Bible—Gardens. *See* **Bible—Natural history**

Bible—Geography

   x Bible—Maps; Geography, Biblical

   xx **Atlases**

Bible—Hermeneutics. *See* **Bible—Criticism, interpretation, etc.**

Bible—History

   Use for works on the origin, authorship and composition of the Bible as a book. Works dealing with historical events as described in the Bible are entered under **Bible—History of Biblical events**

Bible—History of Biblical events

   See note under **Bible—History**

   x History, Biblical

Bible—History of Biblical events—Fiction

   See note under **Bible—Stories**

   x Bible—Fiction

Bible—Illustrations. *See* **Bible — Pictorial works**

Bible—Indexes. *See* **Bible—Concordances; Bible—Dictionaries**

Bible—Inspiration

   See also **Revelation**

   x Inspiration, Biblical

Bible—Interpretation. *See* **Bible—Commentaries; Bible—Criticism, interpretation, etc.**

Bible—Introductions. *See* **Bible—Study**

Bible—Language, style, etc. *See* **Bible as literature**

Bible—Literary character. *See* **Bible as literature**

Bible—Maps. *See* **Bible—Geography**

Bible—Miracles. *See* **Miracles**

Bible—Natural history

   x Bible—Animals; Bible—Birds; Bible—Botany; Bible—Flowers; Bible—Gardens; Bible—Plants; Bible—Zoology; Botany of the Bible; Natural history, Biblical; Zoology of the Bible

   xx **Animals in literature; Birds in literature**

Bible—Parables. *See* **Jesus Christ—Parables**

Bible—Pictorial works

   x Bible—Illustrations

   xx **Christian art and symbolism; Jesus Christ—Art**

Bible—Plants. *See* **Bible—Natural history**

Bible—Prophecies

   xx **Prophecies**

Bible—Psychology

   x Psychology, Biblical

Bible—Question books. *See* **Bible—Catechisms, question books**

Bible—Reading

Bible—Science. *See* **Bible and science**

Bible—Stories

   Use for works which retell or adapt stories from the Bible. Not to be used for fic-

Bible—Stories—*Continued*

    tion in which characters and settings are taken from the Bible; such works are entered under **Bible—History of Biblical events—Fiction**

    x Bible stories; Stories

Bible—Study

    See also **Bible — Catechisms, question books**

    x Bible — Introductions; Bible classes; Bible study

    xx **Religious education; Sunday schools**

Bible—Theology. *See* **Theology**

Bible—Use

    Use for works that show how the Bible is used as a guide to living, to cultivation of a spiritual life, and to problems of doctrine

Bible—Versions

    Use for history of versions, including works on both the Old Testament and the New Testament

Bible—Women. *See* **Women in the Bible**

Bible—Zoology. *See* **Bible—Natural history**

Bible. Old Testament

    Use same subject subdivisions as those given under **Bible**. They may be used also for groups of books (e.g. **Bible. O.T. Pentateuch;** etc. and for single books (e.g. **Bible. O.T. Psalms;** etc.)

    x Old Testament

Bible. New Testament

    Use same subject subdivisions as those given under **Bible**. They may be used also for groups of books (e.g. **Bible. N.T. Gospels;** etc.) and for single books (e.g. **Bible. N.T. Matthew;** etc.)

    x New Testament

Bible and science

    x Bible—Science; Science and the Bible

    xx **Religion and science**

Bible as literature

    See also **Bible—Criticism, interpretation, etc.; Religious literature**

    x Bible—Drama; Bible—Language, style, etc.; Bible—Literary character

    xx **Religious literature**

Bible classes. *See* **Bible—Study; Sunday schools; Vacation schools, Religious**

Bible in literature

    Use for works that discuss the effect of the Bible on literature in general, on a national literature or on an individual author. A second subject heading is necessary for the name of the literature or the name of the author discussed

    See also **Religion in literature**

    xx **Literature; Religion in literature**

Bible in the schools. *See* **Religion in the public schools**

Bible plays. *See* **Mysteries and miracle plays; Religious drama**

Bible stories. *See* **Bible—Stories**

Bible study. *See* **Bible—Study**

Biblical archeology. *See* **Bible—Antiquities**

Biblical characters. *See* **Bible—Biography**

Bibliography
> *See also*

Archives	Indexing
Bookbinding	Information storage
Books	and retrieval
Cataloging	systems
Classification—	Library science
Books	Manuscripts
Indexes	Printing

> *also* names of persons, places and subjects with the subdivision *Bibliography,* e.g. Shakespeare, William—Bibliography; U.S.—Bibliography; Agriculture—Bibliography; etc.
>
> *xx* **Books; Cataloging; Documentation; Library science**

Bibliography—Best books. *See* **Books and reading—Best books**

Bibliography—Editions
> *See also* **Paperback books**
>
> *x* Bibliography—Reprints; Editions; Reprints

Bibliography—First editions
> *x* Books—First editions; First editions

Bibliography—Paperback editions. *See* **Paperback books**

Bibliography—Rare books. *See* **Rare books**

Bibliography—Reference books. *See* **Reference books**

Bibliography—Reprints. *See* **Bibliography—Editions**

Bibliomania. *See* **Book collecting**

Bibliophily. *See* **Book collecting**

Biculturalism (May subdivide geog. except U.S.)
> *xx* **Civilization; Culture**

Biculturalism—Canada
> *x* Canada—Biculturalism
>
> *xx* **Canada—English-French relations**

Bicycle racing
> *x* Racing
>
> *xx* **Bicycles and bicycling**

Bicycles and bicycling
> *See also* **Bicycle racing; Motorcycles**
>
> *x* Cycling; Tricycles

Bigotry. *See* **Toleration**

Bilingual books (May subdivide by languages)

Bilingualism (May subdivide geog. except U.S.)
> *xx* **Language and languages**

Bilingualism—Canada
> *x* Canada—Bilingualism

(handwritten margin note) ✓ Bicentennial events

(handwritten margin note) ✓ Big brothers

Bill of rights. *See* **U.S. Constitution—Amendments**

Billboards. *See* **Signs and signboards**

Bills and notes. *See* **Negotiable instruments**

Bills of credit. *See* **Credit; Negotiable instruments; Paper money**

Bills of exchange
> *See also* **Negotiable instruments**
> *x* Exchange, Bills of
> *xx* **Banks and banking; Credit; Foreign exchange; Money; Negotiable instruments**

Bills of fare. *See* **Menus**

Bimetallism. *See* **Currency question; Gold; Silver**

Binary system (Mathematics)
> *x* Pair system
> *xx* **Mathematics**

Binding of books. *See* **Bookbinding**

Bioastronautics. *See* **Space biology; Space medicine**

Bio-bibliography. *See* **Authors;** names of persons with the subdivision *Bibliography;* and general subjects and names of countries, cities, etc. with the subdivision *Bio-bibliography,* e.g. **English literature — Bio-bibliography; U.S.— Bio-bibliography;** etc.

Biochemistry
> *See also* **Metabolism; Molecular biology; Physiological chemistry**
> *x* Biological chemistry; Chemistry, Biological
> *xx* **Chemistry; Physiological chemistry**

Biogeography. *See* **Anthropogeography; Geographical distribution of animals and plants**

Biography
> Use for collections of biographies which are not limited to one country or to one class of people. Works that deal with the writing of biography are entered under **Biography (as a literary form)**
> *See also*

Anecdotes	**Genealogy**
Autobiographies	**Heraldry**
Autographs	**Naval biography**
Christian biography	**Obituaries**
Epitaphs	**Portraits**

> *also* names of classes of persons (e.g. **Artists; Authors; Musicians;** etc.); names of countries, cities, etc. and special subjects with the subdivision *Biography* (e.g. **U.S.—Biography; Negroes —Biography; Religions—Biography; Woman—Biography;** etc.) and names of persons for biographies of individuals

Biography—*Continued*

    x Memoirs

    xx **Genealogy; History**

Biography—Dictionaries

    Use for collections of biographies, which are not limited to one country or to one class of people, that are arranged in dictionary form

Biography (as a literary form)

    Use for works that deal with the writing of biography

    xx **Authorship; Literature**

Biological chemistry. *See* **Biochemistry**

Biological control of pests. *See* **Pest control— Biological control**

Biological physics. *See* **Biophysics**

Biological warfare

    x Bacterial warfare; Germ warfare

    xx **Communicable diseases; Military art and science; Tactics**

Biologists

    xx **Naturalists**

Biology

    See also

Adaptation (Biology)	**Life (Biology)**
Anatomy	**Marine biology**
Botany	**Microbiology**
Cells	**Natural history**
Color of animals	**Physiology**
Cryobiology	**Protoplasm**
Death	**Radiobiology**
Embryology	**Reproduction**
Evolution	**Sex**
Fresh-water biology	**Space biology**
Genetics	**Variation (Biology)**
Heredity	**Zoology**

    x Morphology

    xx **Evolution; Life (Biology); Natural history; Science**

Biology—Ecology. *See* **Ecology**

Biology, Economic. *See* **Botany, Economic; Zoology, Economic**

Biology, Marine. *See* **Marine biology**

Biology, Molecular. *See* **Molecular biology**

Bioluminescence

    x Animal light; Luminescence, Animal

    xx **Phosphorescence**

Biomechanics. *See* **Human engineering**

Bionics

    Use for works on the science of technological systems which function in the manner of living systems

    See also **Artificial intelligence; Optical data processing**

    x Biotechnology

    xx **Biophysics; Cybernetics; Systems engineering**

Biophysics

> *See also* **Bionics; Cells; Molecular biology; Radiobiology**
>
> *x* Biological physics; Molecular physiology; Physiology, Molecular; Physics, Biological
>
> *xx* **Physics**

Biotechnology. *See* **Bionics**

Biplanes. *See* **Airplanes**

Bird. *See* **Birds**

Bird houses

Bird photography. *See* **Photography of birds**

Bird song

> *x* Birds—Song

Bird watching. *See* **Birds**

Birdbanding

> *x* Birds—Banding; Birds—Marking

Birds (May subdiv. geog.)

> Names of birds are not included in this list but are to be added as needed, in the plural form, e.g. **Canaries;** etc.
>
> *See also* **Birds of prey; Cage birds; Game and game birds; State birds; Water birds;** and names of birds, e.g. **Canaries;** etc.
>
> *x* Bird; Bird watching; Ornithology
>
> *xx* **Animals; Vertebrates; Zoology**

Birds—Anatomy

> *xx* **Anatomy**

Birds, Aquatic. *See* **Water birds**

Birds—Banding. *See* **Birdbanding**

Birds—Collection and preservation

> *x* Collections of natural specimens; Specimens, Preservation of
>
> *xx* **Collectors and collecting; Taxidermy; Zoological specimens—Collection and preservation**

Birds—Eggs and nests

> *x* Birds' eggs; Birds' nests; Nests
>
> *xx* **Eggs**

Birds—Flight. *See* **Flight**

Birds—Habits and behavior

> *xx* **Animals—Habits and behavior**

Birds—Marking. *See* **Birdbanding**

Birds—Migration

> *x* Migration of birds
>
> *xx* **Animals — Migration; Geographical distribution of animals and plants**

Birds—Photography. *See* **Photography of birds**

Birds—Protection

> *See also* **Game protection**
>
> *x* Protection of birds
>
> *xx* **Game protection; Wildlife—Conservation**

Birds, Rare. *See* **Rare birds**

Birds—Song. *See* **Bird song**

Birds—Stories

> *x* Stories

Birds—U.S.

   x U.S.—Birds

Birds' eggs. *See* **Birds—Eggs and nests**

Birds in literature

   See also **Bible—Natural history**

   xx **Animals in literature; Nature in literature**

Birds' nests. *See* **Birds—Eggs and nests**

Birds of prey

   See also names of birds of prey, e.g. **Eagles**; etc.

   xx **Birds**

Birth. *See* **Childbirth**

Birth control

   See also **Birth rate**; also methods of birth control, e.g. **Abortion; Sterilization (Birth control)**; etc.

   x Conception—Prevention; Contraception; Family planning; Planned parenthood

   xx **Birth rate; Eugenics; Population; Sexual ethics; Sexual hygiene**

Birth control—Religious aspects

Birth rate

   See also **Birth control; Population**

   xx **Birth control; Children; Population**

Birth records. *See* **Registers of births, etc.**

Birthdays

   x Days

Births, Registers of. *See* **Registers of births, etc.**

Bison

   x American bison; Buffalo, American

Bituminous coal. *See* **Coal**

Black

   xx **Color**

Black Americans. *See* **Negroes**

Black death. *See* **Plague**

Black friars. *See* **Dominicans**

Black Hawk War, 1832

   xx **Indians of North America—Wars; U.S.—History—1815-1861**

Black lead. *See* **Graphite**

Black literature. *See* **Negro literature**

Black magic. *See* **Witchcraft**

Black Muslims

   x Nation of Islam; Muslims, Black; Negro nationalism

   xx **Black nationalism; Negroes—Religion; U.S.—Race relations**

Black nationalism

   See also **Black Muslims**

   x Black separatism; Nationalism, Negro; Negro nationalism; Separatism, Black

   xx **Negroes—Political activity; Negroes—Race identity**

Black power

   xx **Negroes—Civil rights; Negroes—Economic conditions; Negroes—Political activity**

Black separatism. *See* **Black nationalism**

Black studies. *See* **Afro-American studies**

Blackboard drawing. *See* **Chalk talks; Crayon drawings**

Blackouts, Electric power. *See* **Electric power failures**

Blackouts in war. *See* **Civil defense**

Blacks (U.S.). *See* **Negroes**

✓ **Blacksmithing**

    See also **Forging; Welding**

    x Horseshoeing

    xx **Forging; Ironwork**

Blast furnaces

    xx **Furnaces; Smelting**

Bleaching

    See also **Dyes and dyeing**

    xx **Chemistry, Technical; Cleaning; Dyes and dyeing; Textile industry and fabrics**

Blind

    xx **Physically handicapped; Vision**

Blind, Books for the

    See also **Large print books; Talking books**

    x Books for the blind; Braille system

Blind, Dogs for the. *See* **Guide dogs**

Blind—Education

    x Blind—Rehabilitation; Education of the blind

    xx **Vocational education; Vocational guidance**

Blind—Institutional care

    x Asylums; Charitable institutions; Homes (Institutions)

    xx **Institutional care**

Blind—Rehabilitation. *See* **Blind—Education**

Blizzards

    xx **Storms**

Block printing. *See* **Color prints; Linoleum block printing; Textile printing; Wood engraving**

Block signal systems. *See* **Railroads—Signaling**

Blood

    xx **Physiology**

Blood—Circulation

    See also **Blood pressure**

    x Circulation of the blood

    xx **Blood pressure; Heart**

Blood—Diseases

    See also names of blood diseases, e.g. **Leukemia**; etc.

    x Diseases of the blood

Blood—Groups. *See* **Blood groups**

Blood—Pressure. *See* **Blood pressure**

Blood—Transfusion

    xx **Blood groups**

Blood groups

    See also **Blood—Transfusion**

    x Blood—Groups; Rh factor

    xx **Heredity**

Blood pressure
> *See also* **Blood—Circulation**
> *x* Blood—Pressure
> *xx* **Blood—Circulation**

Blue prints. *See* **Blueprints**

Blueprints
> *x* Blue prints

Blues (Songs, etc.)
> *x* Soul music
> *xx* **Jazz music; Music, Popular (Songs, etc.); Negro songs; Negro spirituals**

Boarding houses. *See* **Hotels, motels, etc.**

Boarding schools. *See* **Private schools**

Boards of education. *See* **School boards**

Boards of health. *See* **Health boards**

Boards of trade. *See* **Chambers of commerce**

Boat building. *See* **Boatbuilding**

Boat racing
> *See also* names of races
> *x* Motorboat racing; Racing; Yacht racing
> *xx* **Boats and boating**

Boatbuilding
> *See also* **Shipbuilding; Yachts and yachting**
> *x* Boat building
> *xx* **Boats and boating; Naval architecture; Shipbuilding**

Boating. *See* **Boats and boating**

Boats, Submarine. *See* **Submarine boats; Submarines**

Boats and boating
> *See also*

Boat racing	**Motorboats**
Boatbuilding	**Rowing**
Canoes and canoeing	**Sailing**
Catamarans	**Ships**
Houseboats	**Steamboats**
Iceboats	**Submarines**
	Yachts and yachting

> *x* Boating; Locomotion
> *xx* **Sailing; Ships; Water sports**

Body, Human. *See* **Anatomy; Physiology**

Body and mind. *See* **Mind and body**

Body weight control. *See* **Weight control**

Boer War, 1899-1902. *See* **South African War, 1899-1902**

Bogs. *See* **Marshes**

Bohemianism
> *See also* **Hippies**
> *x* Beat generation; Beatniks
> *xx* **Collective settlements; Manners and customs**

Bohemians. *See* **Czechs**

Boilers
> *x* Steam boilers
> *xx* **Heating; Steam engines**

Boilers, Marine
> *x* Marine boilers; Marine steam boilers; Naval boilers
> *xx* **Marine engines; Steam navigation**

Bolshevism. *See* **Communism**
Bomb shelters. *See* **Air raid shelters**
Bombers
>*See also* names of bombers, e.g. **B-36 bomber**; etc.
>*xx* **Airplanes; Airplanes, Military**

Bombs
>Use for works on bombs in general and those to be launched from aircraft.
>*See also* **Atomic bomb; Guided missiles; Hydrogen bomb; Incendiary bombs**
>*x* Aerial bombs
>*xx* **Ammunition; Ordnance; Projectiles**

Bombs, Flying. *See* **Guided missiles**
Bombs, Incendiary. *See* **Incendiary bombs**
Bonds
>*See also* **Debts, Public; Investments; Securities; Stocks**
>*xx* **Debts, Public; Finance; Investments; Negotiable instruments; Securities; Stock exchange; Stocks**

Bones
>*See also* **Fractures**
>*x* Osteology
>*xx* **Anatomy; Physiology**

Bonsai. *See* **Dwarf trees**
Bonus, Soldiers'. *See* **Pensions, Military**
Book awards. *See* **Literary prizes**, and names of awards, e.g. **Caldecott Medal books**; etc.
Book catalogs. *See* **Catalogs, Book**
Book collecting
>*x* Bibliomania; Bibliophily
>*xx* **Book selection; Collectors and collecting**

Book fairs. *See* **Book industries and trade—Exhibitions**
Book illustration. *See* **Illustration of books**
Book industries and trade
>*See also* **Bookbinding; Booksellers and bookselling; Paper making and trade; Printing; Publishers and publishing**
>*x* Book trade
>*xx* **Booksellers and bookselling; Paper making and trade; Publishers and publishing**

Book industries and trade—Exhibitions
>*See also* **Printing—Exhibitions**
>*x* Book fairs; Books—Exhibitions
>*xx* **Printing—Exhibitions**

Book lending. *See* **Libraries—Circulation, loans**
Book numbers, Publishers' standard. *See* **Publishers' standard book numbers**
Book-plates. *See* **Bookplates**
Book prices. *See* **Books—Prices**
Book prizes. *See* **Literary prizes**; and names of prizes, e.g. **Caldecott Medal books**; etc.
Book rarities. *See* **Rare books**

√Bonanzaville Pioneer Villg.

Book reviews

    x Appraisal of books; Books—Appraisal; Books—Reviews; Evaluation of literature; Literature—Evaluation; Reviews

    xx **Books and reading; Criticism**

Book sales. *See* **Books—Prices**

Book selection

    Use for works that discuss the principles of book appraisal, and how to select books for libraries. Lists of recommended books are entered under **Books and reading—Best books**

    See also **Book collecting; Books and reading—Best books**

    x Books — Appraisal; Books—Selection; Choice of books

    xx **Acquisitions (Libraries); Books and reading—Best books**

Book trade. *See* **Book industries and trade; Booksellers and bookselling; Publishers and publishing**

Book Week

Bookbinding

    x Binding of books

    xx **Arts and crafts; Bibliography; Book industries and trade; Industrial arts; Leather industry and trade**

Bookkeepers. *See* **Accountants**

Bookkeeping

    See also **Accounting; Auditing; Cost accounting; Office equipment and supplies;** also names of industries, professions, etc. with the subdivision *Accounting,* e.g. **Corporations—Accounting;** etc.

    xx **Accounting; Business; Business arithmetic; Business education**

Bookmobiles

    xx **Library extension**

Bookplates

    x Book-plates; Ex libris

Books

    See also

Authors	**Illustration of books**
Bibliography	**Libraries**
Cataloging	**Literature**
Classification— Books	**Manuscripts**
	Paperback books
Copyright	**Printing**
Illumination of books and manuscripts	**Publishers and publishing**

    also headings beginning with the word **Book**

    xx **Bibliography; Copyright; Literature; Printing; Publishers and publishing**

71

Books—Appraisal. *See* **Book reviews; Book selection; Books and reading; Books and reading—Best books; Criticism; Literature—History and criticism**

Books—Best sellers. *See* **Best sellers**

Books—Catalogs. *See* **Catalogs, Book; Catalogs, Booksellers'; Catalogs, Publishers'; Library catalogs**

Books—Censorship
    x Banned books; Index librorum prohibitorum; Prohibited books
    xx **Censorship; Freedom of the press**

Books—Exhibitions. *See* **Book industries and trade—Exhibitions; Printing—Exhibitions**

Books—First editions. *See* **Bibliography—First editions**

Books—Large print. *See* **Large print books**

Books, Paperback. *See* **Paperback books**

Books—Prices
    x Book prices; Book sales; Manuscripts—Prices
    xx **Booksellers and bookselling; Prices**

Books, Rare. *See* **Rare books**

Books—Reviews. *See* **Book reviews**

Books, Sacred. *See* **Sacred books**

Books—Selection. *See* **Book selection**

Books, Talking. *See* **Talking books**

Books and reading
    Use for general works on reading for information and culture, advice to readers, and surveys of reading habits
    See also **Best sellers; Book reviews; Children's literature; Libraries; Literature; Readability (Literary style); Reference books**
    x Appraisal of books; Books—Appraisal; Choice of books; Evaluation of literature; Literature—Evaluation; Reading interests
    xx **Communication; Education; Reading; Self-culture**

Books and reading—Best books
    Use for lists of recommended books
    See also **Book selection**
    x Appraisal of books; Best books; Bibliography—Best books; Books—Appraisal; Choice of books; Evaluation of literature; Literature—Evaluation
    xx **Book selection; Reference books**

Books for children. *See* **Children's literature**

Books for sight saving. *See* **Large print books**

Books for the blind. *See* **Blind, Books for the**

Booksellers and bookselling
    See also **Book industries and trade; Books—Prices; Catalogs, Booksellers'; Publishers and publishing**
    x Book trade
    xx **Book industries and trade; Publishers**

72

Booksellers and bookselling—*Continued*
      and publishing; Salesmen and salesmanship

Booksellers' catalogs. *See* **Catalogs, Booksellers'**

Boolean algebra. *See* **Algebra, Boolean**

Boots. *See* **Shoes and shoe industry**

Border life. *See* **Frontier and pioneer life**

Boring
      Use for works on the operation of cutting holes in earth or rock. Works dealing with workshop operations in metal, wood, etc. are entered under **Drilling and boring**
      See also **Wells**
      x Drilling and boring (Earth and rocks); Shaft sinking; Well boring
      xx **Gas, Natural; Hydraulic engineering; Mining engineering; Petroleum; Tunnels; Water supply engineering; Wells**

Boring (Metal, wood, etc.). *See* **Drilling and boring**

Boss rule. *See* **Corruption (in politics)**

Boston. Museum of Fine Arts
      xx **Art—Galleries and museums; Museums**

Botanical chemistry
      See also **Plants—Chemical analysis**
      x Chemistry, Botanical; Plant chemistry
      xx **Chemistry; Plants—Chemical analysis**

Botanical gardens
      See also names of botanical gardens, e.g. **Brooklyn. Botanic Garden**; etc.
      xx **Gardens; Parks**

Botanical specimens—Collection and preservation. *See* **Plants—Collection and preservation**

Botanists
      xx **Naturalists**

Botany (May subdiv. geog.)
      See also

Bulbs	**Plants, Fossil**
Flower gardening	**Seeds**
Flowers	**Shrubs**
Fruit	**Trees**
Grafting	**Variation (Biology)**
Leaves	**Vegetables**
Plant physiology	**Weeds**
Plants	

      x Flora; Vegetable kingdom
      xx **Biology; Natural history; Nature study; Science**

Botany, Agricultural. *See* **Botany, Economic**

Botany—Anatomy
      x Anatomy, Vegetable; Anatomy of plants; Botany—Structure; Histology; Morphology; Plant anatomy; Plants—Anatomy; Structural botany; Vegetable anatomy
      xx **Anatomy**

Botany—Ecology
> *See also* **Desert plants**
> *x* Plants—Ecology; Symbiosis
> *xx* **Ecology; Forest influences**

Botany, Economic
> *See also* **Cotton; Forest products; Grain; Grasses; Plant introduction; Plants, Edible; Poisonous plants; Weeds**
> *x* Agricultural botany; Biology, Economic; Botany, Agricultural; Economic botany; Plants, Useful
> *xx* **Agriculture**

Botany, Fossil. *See* **Plants, Fossil**

Botany—Geographical distribution. *See* **Geographical distribution of animals and plants**

Botany, Medical
> *x* Herbals; Herbs, Medical; Medical botany; Medicinal plants; Plants, Medicinal
> *xx* **Medicine; Pharmacy**

Botany—Nomenclature. *See* **Botany—Terminology; Plant names, Popular**

Botany—Pathology. *See* **Plants—Diseases**

Botany—Physiology. *See* **Plant physiology**

Botany—Structure. *See* **Botany—Anatomy**

Botany—Terminology
> Use for works on scientific names of plants, etc. Works on popular names are entered under **Plant names, Popular**
> *See also* **Plant names, Popular**
> *x* Botany—Nomenclature; Nomenclature; Plant names, Scientific; Terminology
> *xx* **Plant names, Popular**

Botany—U.S.
> *x* U.S.—Botany

Botany of the Bible. *See* **Bible—Natural history**

Boulder Dam. *See* **Hoover Dam**

Boundaries
> *See also* **Geopolitics;** also names of wars with the subdivision *Territorial questions* (e.g. **World War, 1939-1945—Territorial questions;** etc.) and names of countries, cities etc. with the subdivision *Boundaries,* e.g. **U.S.—Boundaries;** etc.
> *x* Frontiers; Geography, Political; Political geography
> *xx* **Geography; Geopolitics; International law; International relations**

Bounties. *See* **Subsidies**

Bounty (Ship)
> *xx* **Ships; Voyages and travels**

Bourgeoisie. *See* **Middle classes**

Bow and arrow
> *See also* **Archery**
> *x* Arrow
> *xx* **Archery**

Bowed instruments. *See* **Stringed instruments**
Bowling
    x Tenpins
Boxing
    x Fighting; Prize fighting; Pugilism;
        Sparring
    xx **Athletics; Self-defense**
Boy choir training. *See* **Choirboy training**
Boy Scouts
    x Cub Scouts
    xx **Boys; Boys' clubs; Scouts and scout-
        ing**
~~Boycott. *See* Passive resistance; Strikes and
        lockouts~~   *Boycott*
Boys
    See also **Boy Scouts; Children; News-
        boys; Young men; Youth**
    xx **Children; Young men; Youth**
Boys—Clubs. *See* **Boys' clubs**
Boys—Employment. *See* **Child labor**
Boys—Societies. *See* **Boys' clubs**
Boys' agricultural clubs. *See* **Agriculture—So-
    cieties; Boys' clubs; 4-H clubs**
Boys' clubs
    See also **Boy Scouts; 4-H clubs**
    x Boys' agricultural clubs; Boys—Clubs;
        Boys—Societies
    xx **Clubs; Social settlements; Societies**
Boys' towns. *See* **Children—Institutional care**
Brahmanism
    See also **Caste; Hinduism**
    xx **Buddha and Buddhism; Hinduism; Re-
        ligions**
Braille system. *See* **Blind, Books for the**
Brain
    See also **Dreams; Head; Memory; Mind
        and body; Nervous system; Phrenol-
        ogy; Psychology; Sleep**
    x Skull
    xx **Head; Nervous system**
Brain—Diseases
    See also **Cerebral palsy; Insanity**
Brain, Electronic. *See* **Artificial intelligence;
    Computers**
Brainwashing
    x Will
    xx **Mental suggestion**
Brakes
    See also **Railroads—Safety appliances;**
        also subjects with the subdivision
        Brakes, e.g. **Automobiles—Brakes;**
        etc.
    xx **Railroads—Safety appliances**
Branch stores. *See* **Chain stores**
Brand names. *See* **Trade-marks**
Brass
    See also **Alloys; Brasses**
    xx **Alloys; Founding; Zinc**
Brass instruments. *See* **Wind instruments**

Brasses

    x Monumental brasses; Sepulchral brasses

    xx **Archeology; Art; Brass; Inscriptions; Sculpture; Tombs**

Bravery. *See* **Courage**

Brazilian literature

    May use same subdivisions and names of literary forms as for **English literature**

    See also **Portuguese literature**

    xx **Latin American literature; Portuguese literature**

Brazing. *See* **Solder and soldering**

Bread

    See also **Baking**

    xx **Baking; Cookery; Food**

Breadstuffs. *See* **Flour and flour mills; Grain; Wheat**

Breakfast foods. *See* **Cereals, Prepared**

Breathing. *See* **Respiration**

Breeding. *See* **Livestock; Plant breeding**

Bricklaying

    See also **Masonry**

    xx **Bricks; Building; Masonry**

Bricks

    See also **Bricklaying; Tiles**

    x Ceramics

    xx **Building materials; Clay; Clay industries**

Bridal customs. *See* **Marriage customs and rites**

Bridge (Game)

    x Auction bridge; Contract bridge; Duplicate bridge

    xx **Cards**

Bridges

    See also names of cities and rivers with the subdivision *Bridges* (e.g. **Chicago—Bridges; Hudson River—Bridges;** etc.) also names of bridges, e.g. **Golden Gate Bridge;** etc.

    x Suspension bridges; Viaducts

    xx **Building, Iron and steel; Civil engineering; Masonry; Transportation**

Brigands. *See* **Robbers and outlaws**

Bright children. *See* **Gifted children**

British Commonwealth of Nations. *See* **Commonwealth of Nations**

British Dominions. *See* **Commonwealth of Nations**

British in India

    Use same form for British in other countries, states, etc., e.g. **British in France;** etc.

    x English in India

Broadcasting. *See* **Radio broadcasting; Television broadcasting**

Bronze age
>*See also* **Archeology; Iron age**
>*x* Prehistory
>*xx* **Archeology; Iron age; Man, Prehistoric**

Bronzes
>*xx* **Archeology; Art; Art, Decorative; Art metalwork; Decoration and ornament; Metalwork; Sculpture**

Brooklyn. Botanic Garden
>*xx* **Botanical gardens**

Brownouts. *See* **Electric power failures**

Brutality. *See* **Cruelty**

Bubonic plague. *See* **Plague**

Buccaneers. *See* **Pirates**

Buddha and Buddhism
>*See also* **Brahmanism; Theosophy; Zen Buddhism**
>*xx* **Religions; Theosophy**

Buddhist art. *See* **Art, Buddhist**

Budget (May subdiv. geog.) , 𝑛.𝒩
>Use for works on the budget or reports on the appropriations and expenditures of a government
>*See also* **Finance**
>*xx* **Finance**

Budget—U.S.
>*See also* **U.S.—Appropriations and expenditures**
>*x* Federal budget; U.S.—Budget

Budgets, Business
>*x* Business—Budget
>*xx* **Business**

Budgets, Household
>*x* Domestic finance; Family budget; Home economics—Accounting;   Household expenses
>*xx* **Cost and standard of living; Finance, Personal**

Budgets, Personal. *See* **Finance, Personal**

Buffalo, American. *See* **Bison**

Bugs. *See* **Insects**

Building
>*See also*

Architecture	**Foundations**
Bricklaying	**Masonry**
Carpentry	**Roofs**
Chimneys	**Sanitary engineering**
Concrete construction	**Strength of materials**
Doors	**Walls**
Engineering	**Windows**
Floors	

>*x* Architectural engineering; Construction
>*xx* **Architecture;   Carpentry;   Houses; Structural engineering; Structures, Theory of; Technology**

Building, Concrete. *See* **Concrete construction**

✓Building, Construction

Building—Contracts and specifications
> *x* Buildings—Specifications; Building contracts
>
> *xx* **Contracts**

Building—Estimates
> *x* Estimates

Building, Iron and steel
> *See also* **Bridges; Roofs; Skyscrapers; Steel, Structural; Strains and stresses; Strength of materials; Structures, Theory of**
>
> *x* Architectural engineering; Iron and steel building; Steel construction
>
> *xx* **Iron; Steel; Steel, Structural**

Building—Materials. *See* **Building materials**

Building—Repair and reconstruction
> *See also* **Architecture—Conservation and restoration**
>
> *x* Building repair; Buildings—Maintenance and repair; Buildings—Remodeling; Remodeling of buildings
>
> *xx* **Architecture—Conservation and restoration; Houses; Repairing**

Building—Specifications. *See* **Building—Contracts and specifications**

Building and loan associations
> *x* Cooperative building associations; Loan associations; Savings and loan associations
>
> *xx* **Banks and banking; Cooperation; Cooperative societies; Investments; Loans; Saving and thrift; Savings banks**

Building contracts. *See* **Building—Contracts and specifications**

Building materials
> *See also*

Bricks	**Strength of materials**
Cement	**terials**
Concrete	**Structural engineering**
Concrete, Reinforced	**neering**
	Stucco
Glass construction	**Terra cotta**
Steel, Structural	**Tiles**
Stone	**Wood**

> *x* Building—Materials; Structural materials
>
> *xx* **Architecture; Materials; Strength of materials**

Building repair. *See* **Building—Repair and reconstruction**

Buildings
> *See also* names of types of buildings and construction, e.g. **Buildings, Prefabricated; Farm buildings; School buildings;** etc.; also names of cities and names of institutions with the subdivision *Buildings*, e.g. **Chicago—Buildings; Colleges and universities—Buildings;** etc.

Buildings, College. *See* **Colleges and univer-
sities—Buildings**
Buildings, Farm. *See* **Farm buildings**
Buildings, Industrial. *See* **Industrial buildings**
Buildings, Library. *See* **Library architecture**
Buildings—Maintenance and repair. *See* **Build-
ing—Repair and reconstruction**
Buildings, Office. *See* **Office buildings**
Buildings, Prefabricated
See also **Prefabricated houses**
xx **Buildings**
Buildings, Public. *See* **Public buildings;** and
names of countries, cities, etc. with
the subdivision *Public buildings,* e.g.
Chicago—Public buildings; etc.
Buildings—Remodeling. *See* **Building—Repair
and reconstruction**
Buildings, Restoration of. *See* **Architecture—
Conservation and restoration**
Buildings, School. *See* **School buildings**
Built-in furniture
x Furniture, Built-in
xx **Furniture**
Bulbs
xx **Botany; Flower gardening; Gardening**
Bulge, Battle of the. *See* **Ardennes, Battle of
the, 1944-1945**
Bullets. *See* **Projectiles**
Bullfights
x Fighting
Bullion. *See* **Gold; Money; Silver**
Bunker Hill, Battle of, 1775—Poetry
xx **Poetry**
Burglar alarms
xx **Burglary protection; Electric apparatus
and appliances**
Burglary protection
See also types of protective devices, e.g.
Burglar alarms; Locks and keys; etc.
x Protection against burglary
Burglars. *See* **Robbers and outlaws**
Burial. *See* **Catacombs; Cemeteries; Cremation; Cryonics; Epitaphs; Funeral
rites and ceremonies; Mounds and
mound builders; Mummies; Tombs**
Burial statistics. *See* **Mortality; Registers of
births, etc.; Vital statistics** and names
of countries, cities, etc. with the subdivision *Statistics,* e.g. **U.S.—Statistics;** etc.
Buried cities. *See* **Cities and towns, Ruined,
extinct, etc.**
Buried treasure
x Treasure-trove; Sunken treasure
Burying grounds. *See* **Cemeteries**
Buses ✓ *Bus driving* See   ✓ *Motor bus driving*
x Motor buses
xx **Automobiles; Local transit; Transportation; Transportation, Highway**
Bush survival. *See* **Wilderness survival**

79

Business

See also

Accounting	Instalment plan
Advertising	Mail-order business
Banks and banking	Manufactures
Bookkeeping	Marketing
Budgets, Business	Markets
Commercial law	Merchants
Competition	Occupations
Corporations	Office management
Credit	Profit
Department stores	Real estate business
Economic conditions	Salesmen and sales-
Efficiency, Industrial	manship
Industrial manage-	Small business
ment	Trust companies

x Trade

xx Commerce; Economics; Industrial management; Salesmen and salesmanship; Success

Business—Budget. *See* Budgets, Business

Business, Choice of. *See* Vocational guidance

Business, Small. *See* Small business

Business and government. *See* Industry and state

Business arithmetic

See also Accounting; Bookkeeping; Interest and usury

x Arithmetic, Commercial; Commercial arithmetic

xx Arithmetic

Business colleges. *See* Business education

Business combinations. *See* Railroads—Consolidation; Trusts, Industrial

Business correspondence. *See* Business letters

Business cycles

See also Depressions

x Business depressions; Economic cycles; Stabilization in industry

xx Economic conditions

Business depressions. *See* Business cycles; Depressions; Economic conditions

Business education

Use for works on how to teach business and for description of business operations

See also Accounting; Bookkeeping; Commercial law; Penmanship; Secretaries; Shorthand; Typewriting

x Business colleges; Business schools; Clerical work—Training; Commercial education; Commercial schools; Education, Business; Office work—Training; Schools, Commercial

xx Education

Business English. *See* English language—Business English

Business ethics

See also Competition; Honesty; Success

xx Ethics; Honesty; Professional ethics

Business failures. *See* **Bankruptcy**
Business forecasting
    x Forecasting, Business
Business law. *See* **Commercial law**
Business letters
    See also **English language—Business English**
    x Business correspondence; Commercial correspondence; Correspondence
    xx **English language—Business English; Letter writing**
Business libraries
    x Libraries, Business
    xx **Libraries; Libraries, Special**
Business machines. *See* **Office equipment and supplies**
Business schools. *See* **Business education**
Busing (School integration) (May subdiv. geog. state or city)
    x Racial balance in schools; School busing; School integration
    xx **Segregation in education**
Butter
    See also **Margarine**
    xx **Dairy products; Dairying; Milk**
Butter, Artificial. *See* **Margarine**
Butterflies
    See also **Caterpillars; Moths**
    x Cocoons; Lepidoptera
    xx **Caterpillars; Insects; Moths**
Buttons
    xx **Clothing and dress**
Buyers' guides. *See* **Consumer education; Shopping**
Buying
    Use for works on buying by government agencies and commercial and industrial enterprises. Works on buying by the consumer are entered under **Consumer education; Shopping.** See notes under these headings
    See also **Consumer education; Instalment plan; Shopping**
    x Purchasing
    xx **Consumer education; Industrial management; Shopping**
By-products. *See* **Waste products**
Byrd Antarctic Expedition, 1st, 1928-1930
    x Antarctic expeditions; Expeditions, Antarctic and Arctic
Byzantine architecture. *See* **Architecture, Byzantine**
Byzantine art. *See* **Art, Byzantine**
Byzantine Empire
    x Eastern Empire; Greece, Medieval, 323-1453
CATV. *See* **Community antenna television**
Cabinet officers
    x Ministers of state; Secretaries of state

[handwritten in right margin:] ✓ Busing of school children. See School children – Transportation

81

Cabinet work
> See note under **Carpentry**
>
> *See also* **Veneers and veneering; Wood-work**
>
> *xx* **Carpentry; Furniture; Woodwork**

Cabins. *See* **Log cabins**

Cable codes. *See* **Cipher and telegraph codes**

Cable television. *See* **Community antenna television**

Cables
> *xx* **Power transmission; Rope**

Cables, Submarine
> *x* Atlantic cable; Ocean cables; Pacific cable; Submarine cables; Submarine telegraph; Telegraph, Submarine
>
> *xx* **Telecommunicaton; Telegraph**

Cafeterias. *See* **Restaurants, bars, etc.**

Cage birds
> *See also* names of cage birds, e.g. **Canaries;** etc.
>
> *xx* **Birds**

Cake
> *xx* **Baking; Cookery**

Cake decorating
> *x* Icings, Cake
>
> *xx* **Confectionery**

Calculating machines
> *See also* **Cybernetics; Computers; Slide rule**
>
> *x* Accounting machines; Adding machines
>
> *xx* **Computers; Office equipment and supplies**

Calculus
> *x* Analysis (Mathematics); Integral calculus
>
> *xx* **Mathematics**

Caldecott Medal books
> *x* Book awards; Book prizes; Literary awards; Literature—Prizes
>
> *xx* **Children's literature; Illustration of books; Literary prizes**

Calendars
> *See also* **Almanacs**
>
> *x* Annuals; Chronology
>
> *xx* **Almanacs; Time; Yearbooks**

California—Gold discoveries
> *x* Gold rush

Calisthenics. *See* **Gymnastics; Physical education and training**

Calligraphy. *See* **Writing**

Calvinism
> *See also* **Congregationalism; Predestination; Puritans**
>
> *xx* **Congregationalism; Puritans; Reformation**

Cambistry. *See* **Foreign exchange; Weights and measures**

Camels
> *x* Dromedaries
>
> *xx* **Desert animals; Domestic animals**

Cameras

See also names of individual makes of cameras, e.g. **Kodak camera**; etc.

x Miniature cameras; Moving picture cameras

xx Photography; Photography—Equipment and supplies

Camouflage

xx **Military art and science; Naval art and science**

Camp cooking. *See* **Outdoor cookery**

Camp Fire Girls

xx **Girls' clubs**

Camp sites. *See* **Campgrounds**

Campaign funds

x Assessments, Political; Political assessments; Political parties—Finance

xx **Corruption (in politics); Elections; Politics, Practical**

Campaign literature (May subdivide by date and party)

xx **Politics, Practical**

Campaigns, Political. *See* **Politics, Practical**

Campaigns, Presidential. *See* **Presidents—U.S. —Election**

Campbellites. *See* **Disciples of Christ**

Campers and trailers. *See* **Travel trailers and campers**

Campgrounds

See also **Trailer parks**

x Camp sites

Camping

See note under **Camps**

See also **Backpacking; Outdoor cookery; Outdoor life; Tents; Travel trailers and campers; Wilderness areas**

xx **Outdoor life; Outdoor recreation**

Camps

Use for works on camps with a definite program of activities. Works on the technique of camping are entered under **Camping**

x Summer camps

Camps (Military)

See also **Concentration camps**

x Military camps

xx **Military art and science**

Campus disorders. *See* **College students—Political activity; Youth**

Canada

See also **Northwest, Canadian**; also names of individual provinces

Canada—Biculturalism. *See* **Biculturalism—Canada**

Canada—Bilingualism. *See* **Bilingualism—Canada**

Canada—Discovery and exploraton. *See* **America—Discovery and exploration**

Canada—English-French relations
>   *See also* Biculturalism—Canada; Quebec
>   (Province)—History—Autonomy
>   and independence movements
>   *x* Canada—French-English relations

Canada—French-English relations. *See* **Canada
     —English-French relations**

Canada—History—To 1763 (New France)
>   *x* New France—History

Canada—History—1763-1791

Canada—History—19th century

Canada—History—1914-1945

Canada—History—1945-

Canada, Northwest. *See* **Northwest, Canadian**

Canadian Indians. *See* **Indians of North Amer-
     ica—Canada**

Canadian Invasion, 1775-1776
>   *xx* U.S.—History—Revolution

Canadian literature
>   May use same subdivisions and names of
>   literary forms as for **English litera-
>   ture**
>   *See also* **French Canadian literature**
>   *xx* **American literature**

Canadian literature, French. *See* **French Cana-
     dian literature**

Canadian Northwest. *See* **Northwest, Cana-
     dian**

Canadians
>   *See also* **French Canadians**

Canals
>   *See also* **Inland navigation**; also names of
>   canals, e.g. **Panama Canal**; etc.
>   *xx* **Civil engineering; Hydraulic struc-
>   tures; Inland navigation; Transporta-
>   tion; Waterways**

Canaries
>   *xx* **Birds; Cage birds**

Canasta (Game)
>   *x* Argentine rummy
>   *xx* **Cards**

Cancer
>   *x* Carcinoma
>   *xx* **Tumors**

Candles
>   *xx* **Lighting**

Candy. *See* **Confectionery**

Caning of chairs. *See* **Chair caning**

Canned goods. *See* **Canning and preserving**

Cannibalism
>   *xx* **Ethnology; Society, Primitive**

Canning and preserving
>   *x* Canned goods; Food, Canned; Fruit—
>   Canning; Pickling; Preserving; Vege-
>   tables—Canning
>   *xx* **Chemistry, Technical; Cookery; Food
>   —Preservation**

Cannon. *See* **Ordnance**

Canoes and canoeing
  xx **Boats and boating; Water sports**
Canon law. *See* **Ecclesiastical law**
Cantata. *See* **Choral music**
Capital
  See also **Banks and banking; Capitalism; Interest and usury; Investments; Labor and laboring classes; Monopolies; Profit; Trusts, Industrial; Wealth**
  xx **Capitalism; Economics; Finance; Income; Money; Wealth**
Capital and labor. *See* **Industrial relations**
Capital punishment
  x Death penalty; Executions; Hanging
  xx **Crime and criminals; Criminal law; Murder; Punishment**
Capitalism
  See also **Capital; Socialism**
  xx **Capital; Economics; Labor and laboring classes; Monopolies; Profit; Socialism; Trusts, Industrial**
Capitalists and financiers
  See also **Millionaires**
  x Financiers
  xx **Wealth**
Capitalization (Finance). *See* **Corporations—Finance; Railroads—Finance; Securities; Valuation**
Capitals (Cities)
  Use for works on the capital cities of several countries or states
Capitols
Car wheels. *See* **Wheels**
Carbines. *See* **Rifles**
Carbolic acid
  xx **Acids; Chemicals**
Carbon
  See also **Charcoal; Coal; Diamonds; Graphite**
Carbon 14 dating. *See* **Radiocarbon dating**
Carburetors
  xx **Gas and oil engines**
Carcinoma. *See* **Cancer**
Card catalogs. *See* **Catalogs, Card**
Card games. *See* **Cards**
Card tricks
  See also **Fortune telling**
  xx **Cards; Magic; Tricks**
Cardiac diseases. *See* **Heart—Diseases**
Cardinals
  xx **Christian biography**
Cards
  See also **Card tricks; Fortune telling;** also names of card games, e.g. **Bridge (Game); Canasta (Game);** etc.
  x Card games; Playing cards
  xx **Fortune telling; Gambling; Games**
Cards, Greeting. *See* **Greeting cards**
Career stories. *See* **Vocational stories**

85

Careers. *See* **Occupations; Professions; Vocational guidance**

Caricatures. *See* **Cartoons and caricatures**

Carillons. *See* **Bells**

Carnivals. *See* **Festivals**

Carnivals (Circus). *See* **Amusement parks**

Carols

    See also names of individual carols

    x Christmas carols

    xx **Christmas poetry; Church music; Folk songs; Hymns; Religious poetry; Songs; Vocal music**

Carpentry

    Use for works dealing with the constructing of a wooden building or the wooden portion of any building. Works that treat of the making and finishing of fine woodwork, such as furniture or interior details, are entered under **Cabinet work**

    See also **Building; Cabinet work; Doors; Floors; Roofs; Turning; Walls; Woodwork**

    xx **Building; Industrial arts education; Woodwork**

Carpentry—Tools

    See also names of tools, e.g. **Saws**; etc.

    xx **Tools**

Carpetbag rule. *See* **Reconstruction**

Carpets

    See also **Rugs; Weaving**

    xx **Decoration and ornament; Interior decoration; Rugs; Textile industry and fabrics; Weaving**

Carriages and carts

    x Carts; Coaches; Wagons

    xx **Transportation**

Carriers, Aircraft. *See* **Aircraft carriers**

Cars (Automobiles). *See* **Automobiles**

Cars, Armored (Tanks). *See* **Tanks (Military science)**

Cartels. *See* **Trusts, Industrial**

Cartography. *See* **Charts; Map drawing; Maps**

Cartoons and caricatures

    Use for general collections of, and works about, caricatures and cartoons

    See also **Comic books, strips, etc.; Moving picture cartoons;** also subjects with the subdivision *Cartoons and caricatures,* e.g. **Computers—Cartoons and caricatures;** and names of wars with the subdivision *Humor, caricatures, etc.,* e.g. **World War, 1939-1945—Humor, caricatures, etc.;** etc.

    x Caricatures; Humorous pictures; Illustrations, Humorous; Pictures, Humorous

    xx **Comic books, strips, etc.; Pictures; Portraits**

Carts. *See* **Carriages and carts**

86

Carving (Meat, etc.)

  xx **Dinners and dining; Meat; Table**

Carving, Wood. *See* **Wood carving**

Case studies. *See* subjects with the subdivision
  Case studies, e.g. **Juvenile delinquency
  —Case studies**; etc.

Case work, Social. *See* **Social case work**

Castaways. *See* **Survival (after airplane accidents, shipwrecks, etc.)**

Caste

  xx **Brahmanism; Hinduism; Manners and
  customs; Social classes**

Casting. *See* **Founding; Plaster casts**

Castles

  x Chateaux

  xx **Architecture; Architecture, Medieval**

Casts, Plaster. *See* **Plaster casts**

Casualty insurance. *See* **Insurance, Casualty**

Cat. *See* **Cats**

Catacombs

  See also **Church history—Primitive and
  early church**

  x Burial

  xx **Cemeteries; Christian antiquities;
  Christian art and symbolism; Church
  history—Primitive and early church;
  Tombs**

Cataloging

  See also **Bibliography; Classification—
  Books; Indexing; Subject headings**

  x Cataloguing

  xx **Bibliography; Books; Documentation;
  Indexing; Library science; Processing (Libraries)**

Cataloging—Music

  Use same form for the cataloging of other
  types of materials

  x Music—Cataloging

Catalogs. *See* **Catalogs, Booksellers'; Catalogs, Publishers'; Library catalogs;**
  and subjects with the subdivision *Catalogs,* e.g. **Moving pictures—Catalogs;**
  etc.

Catalogs, Book

  x Book catalogs; Books—Catalogs; Catalogs in book form

  xx **Library catalogs**

Catalogs, Booksellers'

  x Books—Catalogs; Booksellers' catalogs;
  Catalogs

  xx **Booksellers and bookselling**

Catalogs, Card

  x Card catalogs

  xx **Library catalogs**

Catalogs, Classified

  See also **Classification—Books**

  x Catalogs, Systematic; Classed catalogs;
  Classified catalogs

  xx **Classification—Books; Library catalogs**

Catalogs, Library. *See* **Library catalogs**

87

Catalogs, Publishers'

    x Books—Catalogs; Catalogs; Publishers' catalogs

  xx Publishers and publishing

Catalogs, Subject

    See also **Subject headings**

  xx **Library catalogs**

Catalogs, Systematic. *See* **Catalogs, Classified**

Catalogs in book form. *See* **Catalogs, Book**

Cataloguing. *See* **Cataloging**

Catalysis

  xx **Chemistry, Physical and theoretical**

Catamarans

  xx **Boats and boating**

Catastrophes. *See* **Disasters**

Catechisms

    See also **Bible—Catechisms, question books; Creeds**

  xx **Creeds; Religious education; Theology —Study and teaching**

Caterers and catering

    See also **Desserts; Dinners and dining; Luncheons; Menus**

  xx **Cookery; Menus**

Caterpillars

    See also **Butterflies; Moths**

    x Cocoons

  xx **Butterflies; Moths**

Cathedrals (May subdiv. geog.)

    See also **Architecture, Gothic;** also names of individual cathedrals

  xx **Abbeys; Architecture; Architecture, Gothic; Architecture, Medieval; Christian art and symbolism; Church architecture; Churches**

Cathedrals—U.S.

    x U.S.—Cathedrals

Cathode ray tubes

  xx **Vacuum tubes**

Catholic Church

    See also subjects with the subdivision *Catholic Church,* e.g. **Church and state— Catholic Church;** etc.

    x Holy See; Roman Catholic Church

  xx **Christianity; Papacy**

Catholic Church—Clergy

    See also **Ex-priests; Priests**

  xx **Clergy**

Catholic Church—Converts. *See* **Converts, Catholic**

Catholic Church—Doctrinal and controversial works

    See also **Encyclicals, Papal**

Catholic Church—Foreign relations. *See* **Catholic Church—Relations (Diplomatic)**

Catholic Church—Missions

  xx **Missions**

Catholic Church—Relations

Use for works on relations between the Catholic Church and other churches and religions

Catholic Church—Relations (Diplomatic)

x Catholic Church—Foreign relations

xx **International relations**

Catholic Church in the U.S.

Use same form for Catholic Church, and for other churches, in other countries, states, etc., e.g. **Catholic Church in France; Methodist Church in California;** etc.

Catholic converts. *See* **Converts, Catholic**

Catholic ex-priests. *See* **Ex-priests**

Catholic literature

x Index librorum prohibitorum

xx **Literature; Religious literature**

Catholics in the U.S.

Use same form for Catholics in other countries, cities, etc., e.g. **Catholics in Boston;** etc.

Cats

x Cat

xx **Domestic animals; Pets**

Cattle

Use for general works and for works on beef cattle. Works limited to dairy cattle are entered under **Cows**

See also **Cows; Dairying; Livestock; Pastures; Veterinary medicine**

x Beef cattle

xx **Dairying; Domestic animals; Livestock**

Cattle—Diseases

x Cows—Diseases

xx **Diseases; Veterinary medicine**

Cattle brands

Cave drawings

xx **Art, Primitive; Mural painting and decoration; Picture writing**

Cave dwellers

xx **Man, Prehistoric**

Caves

x Grottoes; Speleology

Celery

xx **Vegetables**

Celibacy

xx **Marriage; Monasticism and religious orders**

Cellars. *See* **Basements**

Cello. *See* **Violoncello**

Cells

See also **DNA; Embryology; Protoplasm; Protozoa**

x Cytology; Histology

xx **Biology; Biophysics; Embryology; Physiological chemistry; Physiology; Protoplasm; Reproduction**

Cells, Electric. *See* **Electric batteries**

Cellulose

Celtic legends. *See* **Legends, Celtic**

Celts

> *See also* **Druids and Druidism**
>
> *x* Gaels
>
> *xx* **France—History—To 1328; Gt. Brit. —History—To 1066**

Cement

> *See also* **Concrete; Pavements**
>
> *x* Hydraulic cement; Portland cement
>
> *xx* **Adhesives; Building materials; Ceramics; Concrete; Lime; Masonry; Plaster and plastering**

✓ **Cemeteries**

> *See also* **Catacombs; Epitaphs; Tombs;** also names of cities with the subdivision *Cemeteries* (e.g. **Chicago—Cemeteries;** etc.) ; and names of cemeteries, e.g. **Hampton, Va. National Cemetery;** etc.
>
> *x* Burial; Burying grounds; Churchyards; Graves; Graveyards
>
> *xx* **Landscape architecture; Public health; Sanitation; Tombs**

Censorship

> Use for general works on freedom of expression in various fields
>
> *See also* **Free speech; Freedom of the press;** also subjects with the subdivision *Censorship,* e.g. **Books—Censorship; Moving pictures—Censorship;** etc.
>
> *xx* **Intellectual freedom**

Census

> *See also* **Statistics;** also names of countries, cities, etc. with the subdivision *Census,* e.g. **U.S.—Census;** etc.
>
> *xx* **Population; Statistics; Vital statistics**

Centers for the performing arts

> *See also* **Theaters;** also names of individual centers
>
> *xx* **Performing arts**

Central Africa. *See* **Africa, Central**

Central America

> *xx* **America**

Central Europe

> Use for works on the area included in the basins of the Danube, Elbe and Rhine rivers
>
> *x* Europe, Central

Central States. *See* **Middle West**

Centralized processing (Libraries). *See* **Processing (Libraries)**

Ceramic materials

> *See also* names of individual materials, e.g. **Clay,** etc.

Ceramics

> Use for works on the technology of fired earth products or clay products intended for industrial use. Earthenware, china-

Ceramics—*Continued*
>> ware, porcelain are entered under **Pottery** and **Porcelain**
>> *See also* **Cement; Glass; Glazes; Pottery; Tiles**
>> *x* Keramics

Cereals. *See* **Cereals, Prepared; Grain**
Cereals, Prepared
>> *x* Breakfast foods; Cereals

Cerebral palsy
>> *x* Palsy, Cerebral; Paralysis, Cerebral; Paralysis, Spastic; Spastic paralysis
>> *xx* **Brain—Diseases**

Ceremonies. *See* **Etiquette; Manners and customs; Rites and ceremonies**
Certainty. *See* **Belief and doubt; Probabilities; Truth**
Certified public accountants. *See* **Accountants**
Chain belting. *See* **Belts and belting**
Chain stores
>> *x* Branch stores; Stores
>> *xx* **Retail trade**

Chair caning
>> *x* Caning of chairs

Chairs
>> *xx* **Furniture**

Chalk talks
>> *x* Blackboard drawing

Chamber music
>> *xx* **Instrumental music; Music; Orchestral music**

Chambers of commerce
>> *x* Boards of trade; Trade, Boards of
>> *xx* **Commerce**

Change, Social. *See* **Social change**
Change of life in women. *See* **Menopause**
Chanties. *See* **Sea songs**
Chants (Plain, Gregorian, etc.)
>> *x* Gregorian chant; Plain chant; Plainsong
>> *xx* **Church music**

Chaplains
>> *See also* names of bodies or institutions having chaplains, with the subdivision *Chaplains,* e.g. **U.S. Army—Chaplains;** etc.
>> *xx* **Clergy**

Character
>> *See also* **Behavior; Temperament**
>> *xx* **Christian life; Personality; Temperament**

Character education
>> *x* Education, Character; Education, Ethical; Education, Moral; Ethical education; Moral education
>> *xx* **Children — Management; Education; Ethics; Religious education**

Characteristics, National. *See* **National characteristics**

[handwritten in margin: ✓ Chaplains, Hospital]

91

Characters and characteristics in literature

> *See also* **Children in literature and art; Children in poetry; Drama—Technique; Negroes in literature and art; Plots (Drama, fiction, etc.); Women in literature and art;** also names of prominent authors with the subdivision *Characters,* e.g. **Shakespeare, William —Characters;** etc.
>
> *x* Literary characters
>
> *xx* **Literature**

Charades

> *xx* **Amateur theatricals; Amusements; Riddles**

Charcoal

> *xx* **Carbon; Fuel**

Charitable institutions. *See* **Charities; Institutional care; Orphans and orphans' homes;** also classes of people with the subdivision *Institutional care,* e.g. **Blind—Institutional care; Deaf—Institutional care; Mentally ill—Institutional care;** etc.

Charities

> Use for works on privately supported welfare activities. Works on tax supported welfare activities are entered under **Public welfare.** Works on the methods employed in welfare work, public or private, are entered under **Social work**
>
> *See also*

Charities, Medical	**Orphans and**
Charity organiza-	**orphans' homes**
tion	**Public welfare**
Child welfare	**Red Cross**
Day nurseries	**Social settlements**
Endowments	**Unemployed**
Institutional care	

> *also* names of cities with the subdivision *Charities* (e.g. **Chicago—Charities;** etc.) ; and names of wars with the subdivision *Civilian relief,* e.g. **World War, 1939-1945—Civilian relief;** etc.
>
> *x* Charitable institutions; Endowed charities; Homes (Institutions) ; Institutions, Charitable and philanthropic; Philanthropy; Poor relief; Social welfare; Welfare agencies; Welfare work
>
> *xx* **Charity organization; Endowments; Poverty; Public welfare; Social problems; Social work**

Charities, Legal. *See* **Legal aid**

Charities, Medical

> *See also* **Institutional care; Hospitals**
>
> *x* Medical charities; Socialized medicine
>
> *xx* **Charities; Medical care; Medicine, State; Public health**

Charities, Public. *See* **Public welfare**

Charity

    x Benevolence

    xx **Begging; Behavior; Ethics**

Charity organization

    See also **Charities**

    x Philanthropy

    xx **Charities**

Charms

    x Spells; Talismans

    xx **Demonology; Folklore; Superstition; Witchraft**

Charters

    See also **Archives; Manuscripts; Municipal corporations**

    x Documents

    xx **Archives; History—Sources; Manuscripts**

Chartography. *See* **Charts; Map drawing; Maps**

Charts

    See also **Maps**

    x Cartography; Chartography

    xx **Maps**

The chase. *See* **Hunting**

Chateaux. *See* **Castles**

Chattel mortgages. *See* **Mortgages**

Checkers

    x Draughts

Cheers and cheerleading

Cheese

    xx **Dairy products; Milk**

Cheese—Bacteriology

    xx **Bacteriology**

Chemical analysis. *See* **Chemistry, -Analytic;** and names of substances with the subdivision *Analysis,* e.g. **Water—Analysis;** etc.

Chemical apparatus

    x Apparatus, Chemical; Chemistry—Apparatus

    xx **Scientific apparatus and instruments**

Chemical elements

    See also **Periodic law;** also names of elements, e.g. **Hydrogen;** etc.

    x Elements, Chemical

Chemical engineering

    See also **Chemistry, Technical; Metallurgy**

    x Chemistry, Industrial; Industrial chemistry

    xx **Chemistry, Technical; Engineering; Metallurgy**

Chemical geology. *See* **Geochemistry**

Chemical industries

    Use for works about industries based mainly on chemical processes. Works on the manufacture of chemicals as such are entered under **Chemicals**

    See also names of industries, e.g. **Paper making and trade;** etc.

Chemical industries—*Continued*

 x Chemistry, Industrial; Industrial chemistry; Industries, Chemical

 xx **Chemicals; Chemistry, Technical**

Chemical societies. *See* **Chemistry—Societies**

Chemical technology. *See* **Chemistry, Technical**

Chemical warfare

 See also **Gases, Asphyxiating and poisonous—War use**

 x Air warfare

 xx **Military art and science; War**

Chemicals

 Use for general works on chemicals, including their manufacture. See note under **Chemical industries**

 See also **Chemical industries; Chemistry, Technical;** also names of groups of chemicals (e.g. **Acids;** etc.); and names of individual chemicals, e.g. **Carbolic acid;** etc.

 xx **Chemistry, Technical**

Chemiculture. *See* **Plants—Soilless culture**

Chemistry

 See also

Acids	Fire
Agricultural chemistry	Geochemistry
	Microchemistry
Alchemy	Pharmacy
Biochemistry	Photographic chemistry
Botanical chemistry	
Color	Physiological chemistry
Combustion	
Explosives	Poisons
Fermentation	Spectrum

 also headings beginning with the word **Chemical**

 xx **Science**

Chemistry, Agricultural. *See* **Agricultural chemistry**

Chemistry, Analytic

 See also names of substances with the subdivision *Analysis,* e.g. **Water—Analysis;** etc.

 x Analysis (Chemistry); Analytical chemistry; Chemical analysis; Qualitative analysis; Quantitative analysis

Chemistry, Animal. *See* **Physiological chemistry**

Chemistry—Apparatus. *See* **Chemical apparatus**

Chemistry, Biological. *See* **Biochemistry**

Chemistry, Botanical. *See* **Botanical chemistry**

Chemistry—Dictionaries

 x Dictionaries; Glossaries

 xx **Encyclopedias and dictionaries**

Chemistry—Experiments

 x Experiments, Scientific; Scientific experiments

 xx **Science—Experiments**

Chemistry, Industrial. *See* **Chemical engineering; Chemical industries; Chemistry, Technical**

Chemistry, Inorganic
> *See also* **Metals**
> *x* Inorganic chemistry

Chemistry—Laboratory manuals
> *x* Laboratory manuals

Chemistry, Medical and pharmaceutical
> *See also* **Disinfection and disinfectants; Drugs; Materia medica; Pharmacy; Poisonous plants; Poisons**
> *x* Chemistry, Pathological; Chemistry, Pharmaceutical; Medical chemistry; Pathological chemistry; Pharmaceutical chemistry
> *xx* **Medicine; Pharmacy; Physiological chemistry; Therapeutics**

Chemistry, Organic
> *x* Organic chemistry
> *xx* **Physiological chemistry**

Chemistry, Organic—Synthesis
> *See also* **Plastics; Polymers and polymerization; Synthetic products**
> *x* Chemistry, Synthetic; Synthetic chemistry
> *xx* **Plastics**

Chemistry, Pathological. *See* **Chemistry, Medical and pharmaceutical; Physiological chemistry**

Chemistry, Pharmaceutical. *See* **Chemistry, Medical and pharmaceutical**

Chemistry, Photographic. *See* **Photographic chemistry**

Chemistry, Physical and theoretical
> *See also*

Atomic theory	**Nuclear physics**
Atoms	**Periodic law**
Catalysis	**Polymers and**
Colloids	**polymerization**
Crystallography	**Quantum theory**
Electrochemistry	**Radiochemistry**
Molecules	**Thermodynamics**

> *x* Physical chemistry; Theoretical chemistry
> *xx* **Nuclear physics; Physics; Quantum theory**

Chemistry, Physiological. *See* **Physiological chemistry**

Chemistry—Societies
> *x* Chemical societies

Chemistry, Synthetic. *See* **Chemistry, Organic —Synthesis**

Chemistry, Technical
> *See also*

Alloys	**Chemical engineer-**
Bleaching	**ing**
Canning and pre-	**Chemical industries**
serving	**Chemicals**

Chemistry, Technical—*Continued*

Chemurgy
Corrosion and anti-
corrosives
Electrochemistry
Food—Analysis
Gums and resins
Synthetic products
Tanning
Textile chemistry
Waste products

also names of specific industries and products, e.g. **Clay industries; Dyes and
dyeing;** etc.

x Chemical technology; Chemistry, Industrial; Industrial chemistry; Technical
chemistry

xx **Chemical engineering; Chemicals;
Metallurgy; Technology**

Chemistry, Textile. *See* **Textile chemistry**

Chemistry as a profession
xx **Chemists**

Chemistry of food. *See* **Food—Analysis**

Chemists
See also **Chemistry as a profession**
xx **Scientists**

Chemotherapy
See also **Antibiotics**

Chemurgy
Use for books that deal with the advancement of the industrial use of farm
products by means of applied science

xx **Agricultural chemistry; Chemistry,
Technical; Synthetic products**

Cherokee Indians
xx **Anthropology; Indians of North
America**

Chess
xx **Games**

Chicago
Subdivisions have been given under this
subject to serve as a guide to the subdivisions that may be used under the
name of any city. They are examples
of the application of directions given
in the general references under various
headings throughout the list. References are given only for those headings
that are cited specifically under the general references. The subdivisions under
United States may be consulted as a
guide for formulating other references
that may be needed

Chicago—Antiquities
Chicago—Bibliography
Chicago—Bio-bibliography
Chicago—Biography
Chicago—Biography—Portraits
Chicago—Boundaries
Chicago—Bridges
xx **Bridges**
Chicago—Buildings
xx **Buildings**
Chicago—Cemeteries
xx **Cemeteries**

Chicago—Census
Chicago—Charities
 xx **Charities**
Chicago—Churches
 xx **Churches**
Chicago—Climate
Chicago—Commerce
Chicago—Demonstrations
 xx **Demonstrations**
Chicago—Description
 x Description
Chicago—Description—Guide books
 x Chicago—Guide books; Guide books
Chicago—Description—Maps. *See* **Chicago—
  Maps**
Chicago—Description—Views
 x Chicago—Pictures; Chicago—Views;
  Scenery
 xx **Pictures; Views**
Chicago—Directories
 Use for lists of names and addresses. Lists
  of names without addresses are entered
  under **Chicago—Registers**
 See also **Chicago—Registers**
 xx **Chicago—Registers**
Chicago—Economic conditions
Chicago—Fires and fire prevention
 xx **Fire prevention; Fires**
Chicago—Floods
 xx **Floods**
Chicago—Foreign population
 x Foreign population; Population, Foreign
Chicago—Galleries and museums
 xx **Art—Galleries and museums**
Chicago—Government. *See* **Chicago—Politics
  and government**
Chicago—Government publications
Chicago—Guide books. *See* **Chicago—Descrip-
  tion—Guide books**
Chicago—Harbor
 xx **Harbors**
Chicago—Historic houses, etc.
 xx **Architecture, Colonial**
Chicago—History
Chicago—History—Societies
Chicago—Hospitals
 xx **Hospitals**
Chicago—Hotels, motels, etc.
 xx **Hotels, motels, etc.**
Chicago—Industries
 x Chicago—Manufactures
 xx **Manufactures**
Chicago—Intellectual life
Chicago—Libraries
 xx **Libraries**
Chicago—Lighting
 xx **Lighting; Street lighting**
Chicago—Manufactures. *See* **Chicago—Indus-
  tries**

97

Chicago—Maps
  x Chicago—Description—Maps
  xx **Chicago—Streets; Maps**
Chicago—Moral conditions
Chicago—Occupations
  xx **Occupations**
Chicago—Office buildings
  xx **Office buildings**
Chicago—Officials and employees
  x Employees and officials; Municipal employees; Officials
  xx **Civil service**
Chicago—Parks
  xx **Parks**
Chicago—Pictures. *See* **Chicago—Description —Views**
Chicago—Poetry
  xx **Poetry**
Chicago—Police
  xx **Police**
Chicago—Politics and government
  x Chicago—Government; Politics
  xx **Municipal government**
Chicago—Poor
  x Poor
  xx **Poverty**
Chicago—Population
  xx **Population**
Chicago—Public buildings
  x Buildings, Public
  xx **City planning; Public buildings**
Chicago—Public schools
  x Chicago—Schools
  xx **High schools; Public schools; Schools**
Chicago—Public works
  x Municipal improvements
  xx **City planning; Public works**
Chicago—Race relations
  xx **Race problems**
Chicago—Registers
  Use for lists of names without addresses. Lists of names that include addresses are entered under **Chicago—Directories**
  See also **Chicago—Directories**
  xx **Chicago—Directories**
Chicago—Riots
  xx **Riots**
Chicago—Schools. *See* **Chicago—Public schools**
Chicago—Social conditions
  xx **Social conditions**
Chicago—Social life and customs
Chicago—Social policy
Chicago—Statistics
  xx **Statistics**
Chicago—Streets
  See also **Chicago—Maps**
  xx **Streets**

Chicago—Suburbs and environs
 See also Chicago metropolitan area
 xx Suburban life
Chicago—Synagogues
 xx Synagogues
Chicago—Transit systems
 x Transit systems
 xx Local transit
Chicago—Urban renewal. *See* Urban renewal
  —Chicago
Chicago—Views. *See* Chicago—Description—
  Views
Chicago—Water supply
 xx Water supply
Chicago metropolitan area
 xx Chicago—Suburbs and environs; Met-
  ropolitan areas
Chicago metropolitan area—Politics and gov-
  ernment
 xx Metropolitan government
Chicago metropolitan area—Transit systems
 x Transit systems
 xx Local transit
Chief justices. *See* Judges
Child abuse. *See* Cruelty to children
Child and parent. *See* Parent and child
Child birth. *See* Childbirth
Child development. *See* Child study; Children
  —Growth
Child labor (May subdiv. geog.)
 See also Apprentices; Hours of labor;
  Newsboys
 x Boys—Employment; Children—Employ-
  ment; Employment of children; Girls
  —Employment; Working girls
 xx Age and employment; Child welfare;
  Education, Compulsory; Hours of
  labor; Labor and laboring classes;
  Labor supply; School attendance;
  Social problems
Child labor—U.S.
 x U.S.—Child labor
Child psychiatry
 See also Adolescent psychiatry; Mentally
  handicapped children
 x Pediatric psychiatry; Psychiatry, Child
 xx Psychiatry
Child psychology. *See* Child study
Child study
 Use for works on the psychology, person-
  ality, habits, mental development, etc.,
  of the child
 See also Adolescence; Educational psy-
  chology; Exceptional children;
  Handicapped children; Kindergarten;
  Mental tests; Parent and child; Par-
  ents' and teachers' associations;
  Play; Problem children

Child study—*Continued*

> *x* Child development; Child psychology; Children — Psychology; Psychology, Child
>
> *xx* **Children; Education; Educational psychology; Kindergarten; Teaching**

Child welfare

> Use for works on the aid, support, and protection of children, by the state or by private welfare organizations
>
> *See also*

Child labor	Day nurseries
Children—Care and hygiene	Foster home care
Children—Hospitals	Juvenile delinquency
Children—Institutional care	Mothers' pensions
Cruelty to children	Orphans and orphans' homes
	Playgrounds

> *x* A.D.C.; Aid to dependent children; Children—Charities, protection, etc.; Dependent children; Protection of children
>
> *xx* **Charities; Children—Hospitals; Juvenile delinquency; Mothers' pensions; Orphans and orphans' homes; Public welfare**

Childbirth

> *See also* **Pregnancy**
>
> *x* Birth; Child birth; Labor (Obstetrics); Midwifery; Obstetrics
>
> *xx* **Medicine—Practice; Pregnancy**

Children

> The term is popularly applied to any age up to fifteen or even later. Works limited to the first two years of a child's life are entered under **Infants**
>
> *See also*

Birth rate	Infants
Boys	Kindergarten
Child study	Moving pictures and children
Education, Elementary	Play
Exceptional children	Playgrounds
Girls	Runaways
Heredity	Television and children
Indians of North America—Children	World War, 1939-1945—Children
	Youth

> *xx* **Boys; Family; Girls; Infants; Youth**

Children, Abnormal. *See* **Exceptional children; Handicapped children**

Children—Adoption. *See* **Adoption**

Children, Backward. *See* **Mentally handicapped children; Slow learning children**

Children—Care and hygiene

> Use for general works on the physical care of children. Works limited to their

Children—Care and hygiene—*Continued*

physical care in school are entered under **School hygiene**

See also **Baby sitters; Children—Diseases; Children—Hospitals; Children—Nutrition; Health education; Infants—Care and hygiene; Nurses and nursing; School children—Food; School hygiene; School nurses**

x Children—Health; Health of children; Pediatrics

xx **Child welfare; Hygiene; Nurses and nursing**

Children—Charities, protection, etc. *See* **Child welfare**

Children—Clothing. *See* **Children's clothing**

Children—Costume

Use for descriptive and historical works on children's costume among various nations and at different periods. Works dealing with children's clothing from a practical standpoint are entered under **Children's clothing**

xx **Costume**

Children, Crippled. *See* **Physically handicapped children**

Children, Cruelty to. *See* **Cruelty to children**

Children, Delinquent. *See* **Juvenile delinquency**

Children—Discipline. *See* **Children—Management**

Children—Diseases

See also **Children—Hospitals;** also names of diseases, e.g. **Diphtheria;** etc.

x Children's diseases; Diseases of children; Infants—Diseases; Medicine, Pediatric; Pediatrics

xx **Children—Care and hygiene; Children Hospitals; Diseases; Medicine—Practice**

Children—Education. *See* **Education, Elementary**

Children, Emotionally disturbed. *See* **Problem children**

Children—Employment. *See* **Child labor**

Children, Exceptional. *See* **Exceptional children**

Children, Gifted. *See* **Gifted children**

Children—Growth

x Child development

xx **Growth**

Children—Health. *See* **Children—Care and hygiene; School hygiene**

Children—Hospitals

See also **Child welfare; Children—Diseases**

x Children's hospitals

xx **Charities, Medical; Child welfare; Children—Care and hygiene; Children—Diseases; Hospitals; Public welfare**

Children, Illegitimate. *See* **Illegitimacy**

Children—Institutional care

    See also **Day nurseries; Foster home care; Orphans and orphans' homes; Reformatories**

    x Boys' towns; Children's homes; Homes (Institutions); Institutions, Charitable and philanthropic

    xx **Child welfare; Foster home care; Institutional care**

Children—Language

    xx **Language and languages**

Children—Management

    Use for books on child training and discipline. These books may include psychological matter such as is entered under **Child study,** but their content and purpose are more practical. Books on management of children in school are entered under **School discipline**

    See also **Baby sitters; Character education; Cruelty to children; Problem children; School discipline**

    x Children—Discipline; Children—Training; Discipline of children; Management of children; Training of children

    xx **Parent and child**

Children—Nutrition

    See also **School children—Food**

    x Infants—Nutrition; Nutrition of children

    xx **Children—Care and hygiene**

Children—Placing out. *See* **Foster home care**

Children—Psychology. *See* **Child study**

Children—Religious life

    xx **Christian life; Religious life**

Children, Retarded. *See* **Mentally handicapped children; Slow learning children**

Children, Runaway. *See* **Runaways**

Children—Training. *See* **Children—Management**

Children and moving pictures. *See* **Moving pictures and children**

Children and television. *See* **Television and children**

Children as artists

    Use for books about children as artists and for works of art by children

    See also **Finger painting**

    xx **Artists; Gifted children**

Children as authors

    Use for books written by children and for books about children as authors

    xx **Authors; Gifted children**

Children as consumers. *See* **Youth as consumers**

Children in art. *See* **Children in literature and art**

Children in literature and art

Use for works treating of children in literature, and children depicted in works of art. Books about children as authors and books written by children are entered under **Children as authors.** Books about child artists are entered under **Children as artists**

See also **Children in poetry**

x Children in art

xx **Art; Characters and characteristics in literature; Children in poetry; Literature**

Children in poetry

See also **Children in literature and art**

xx **Characters and characteristics in literature; Children in literature and art; Poetry**

Children in the U.S.

Use same form for children in other countries, e.g. **Children in India;** etc.

Children's books. *See* **Children's literature**

Children's clothing

See note under **Children—Costume**

x Children—Clothing; Infants—Clothing

xx **Clothing and dress**

Children's courts. *See* **Juvenile courts**

Children's diseases. *See* **Children—Diseases**

Children's homes. *See* **Children—Institutional care**

Children's hospitals. *See* **Children—Hospitals**

Children's libraries. *See* **Libraries, Children's; School libraries**

Children's literature

Use for books on the development of juvenile literature, discussions of good books for children, etc. Books written by children and books about children as authors are entered under **Children as authors**

See also **Caldecott Medal books; Children's plays; Children's poetry; Fairy tales; Libraries, Children's; Libraries and schools; Readers; Storytelling**

x Books for children; Children's books; Children's reading; Children's stories; Juvenile literature

xx **Books and reading; Libraries, Children's; Libraries and schools; Literature; School libraries**

Children's plays

Use for collections of plays for children by one or more authors

x Plays for children; School plays

xx **Amateur theatricals; Children's literature; Drama—Collections; Theater**

Children's poetry

Use for collections of poetry for children by one or more authors. Books of poe-

Children's poetry—*Continued*
>> try written by children are entered under **Children as authors**
>> *See also* **Children's songs; Lullabies; Nursery rhymes**
>> *x* Poetry for children
>> *xx* **Children's literature; Poetry—Collections**

Children's reading. *See* **Children's literature; Reading**

Children's songs
>> *See also* **Lullabies; Nursery rhymes**
>> *xx* **Children's poetry; School songbooks; Songs**

Children's stories. *See* **Children's literature; Fairy tales**

Chills and fever. *See* **Malaria**

Chimes. *See* **Bells**

Chimneys
>> *x* Smoke stacks
>> *xx* **Architecture—Details; Building; Fireplaces; Heating; Ventilation**

China

China—History

China—History—Republic, 1912-1949

China—History—1949- . *See* **China (People's Republic of China, 1949-   )—History; Formosa—History—1949-**

China (People's Republic of China, 1949-   )
>> *x* Communist China; People's Republic of China; Red China

China (People's Republic of China, 1949-   )—History
>> *x* China—History—1949-

China (Porcelain). *See* **Porcelain**

China painting
>> *x* Porcelain painting
>> *xx* **Arts and crafts; Painting; Porcelain**

Chinaware. *See* **Porcelain**

Chinese in the U.S.
>> Use same form for Chinese in other countries, states, etc., e.g. **Chinese in Russia**; etc.

Chipmunks
>> *xx* **Squirrels**

Chiropody
>> *x* Foot—Care and hygiene

Chivalry
>> *See also* **Arthur, King; Civilization, Medieval; Crusades; Feudalism; Heraldry; Knights and knighthood; Romances**
>> *xx* **Civilization, Medieval; Crusades; Feudalism; Heraldry; Knights and knighthood; Manners and customs; Middle Ages**

Chocolate
>> *See also* **Cocoa**
>> *xx* **Cocoa**

Choice, Freedom of. *See* **Free will and determinism**

Choice of books. *See* **Book selection; Books and reading; Books and reading— Best books**

Choice of profession. *See* **Vocational guidance**

Choirboy training

　x Boy choir training

Choirs (Music)

　See also **Choral music; Choral societies; Conducting, Choral; Singing**

　xx **Choral music; Choral societies; Church music; Conducting, Choral; Singing**

Choral conducting. *See* **Conducting, Choral**

Choral music

　See also **Choirs (Music); Choral societies; Conducting, Choral**

　x Cantata; Music, Choral

　xx **Choirs (Music); Choral societies; Church music; Conducting, Choral; Vocal music**

Choral societies

　See also **Choirs (Music); Choral music; Community music**

　x Singing societies

　xx **Choirs (Music); Choral music; Societies**

Choral speaking

　x Unison speaking

Choreography. *See* **Ballet; Dancing**

Christ. *See* **Jesus Christ**

Christening. *See* **Baptism**

Christian antiquities

　See also **Architecture, Gothic; Catacombs; Christian art and symbolism; Church architecture; Church furniture; Fasts and feasts**

　x Antiquities; Antiquities, Christian; Antiquities, Ecclesiastical; Archeology, Christian; Church antiquities; Ecclesiastical antiquities

　xx **Archeology; Bible—Antiquities; Christian art and symbolism**

Christian art and symbolism

　See also

Art and religion	**Church furniture**
Bible—Pictorial works	**Illumination of books and manuscripts**
Catacombs	**scripts**
Cathedrals	**Jesus Christ—Art**
Christian antiquities	**Mary, Virgin—Art**
Church architecture	

　x Art, Christian; Art, Ecclesiastical; Christian symbolism; Ecclesiastical art; Iconography; Painting, Religious; Religious art; Religious painting; Religious symbolism; Sacred art; Sculpture, Religious

　xx **Archeology; Art; Art and religion; Christian antiquities; Jesus Christ—Art; Mysticism; Symbolism**

105

Christian biography

See also

Apostles	Missionaries
Cardinals	Monasticism and
Clergy	religious orders
Fathers of the	Pilgrim Fathers
church	Popes
Hermits	Puritans
Martyrs	Saints

    x Church biography; Ecclesiastical biography; Religious biography

    xx Bible—Biography; Biography; Martyrs; Religions—Biography

Christian Church (Disciples). *See* **Disciples of Christ**

Christian civilization. *See* **Civilization, Christian**

Christian doctrine. *See* **Theology**

Christian education. *See* **Religious education**

Christian ethics

    See also **Christian life; Christianity and economics; Conscience; Psychology, Pastoral; Sin; Social ethics**

    x Ethics, Christian

    xx **Christian life; Ethics; Social ethics**

Christian life

See also

Asceticism	Love (Theology)
Character	Prayer
Children—Religious	Religious education
life	Religious life
Christian ethics	Revivals
Conversion	Sanctification
Devotional exercises	Spiritual life
Faith	

    x Life, Christian

    xx **Behavior; Christian ethics; Religious life; Spiritual life**

Christian literature, Early

    Use for works about the writings of Christian authors to the time of Gregory the Great in the West and John of Damascus in the East. Collections of such writings are entered under this heading with subdivision *Collections*

    See also **Church history—Primitive and early church; Fathers of the church**

    x Early Christian literature

    xx **Latin literature; Literature; Literature, Medieval; Religious literature**

Christian names. *See* **Names, Personal**

Christian Science

    See also **Faith cure; Mental healing**

    x Church of Christ, Scientist; Divine healing; Mind cure

    xx **Faith cure; Medicine and religion; Mental healing**

Christian socialism. *See* **Socialism, Christian**

Christian sociology. *See* **Sociology, Christian**

Christian symbolism. *See* **Christian art and symbolism**

Christian unity
> Use for works on the worldwide movement towards bringing all Christian faiths into cooperation, fellowship and eventually one organization
> *See also* **Community churches**
> *x* Church unity; Ecumenical movement
> *xx* **Church**

Christianity
> *See also*

Apostles	Miracles
Church	Missions
Civilization, Christian	Protestantism
Councils and synods	Reformation
Deism	Socialism, Christian
God	Theism
Jesus Christ	Theology

> *also* names of Christian churches and sects (e.g. **Catholic Church; Huguenots;** etc.) and headings beginning with the words **Christian** and **Church**
> *xx* **Church; Deism; God; Jesus Christ; Religions; Theism; Theology**

Christianity—Apologetic works. *See* **Apologetics**

Christianity—Evidences. *See* **Apologetics**

Christianity—History. *See* **Church history**

Christianity—Origin. *See* **Church history— Primitive and early church**

Christianity—Philosophy
> *x* Theology—Philosophy

Christianity and economics
> *See also* **Church and labor**
> *x* Economics and Christianity
> *xx* **Christian ethics; Church and labor; Communism and religion; Economics; Socialism, Christian; Sociology, Christian**

Christianity and other religions
> *See also* **Paganism**
> *x* Comparative religion

Christianity and politics
> *x* Politics and Christianity
> *xx* **Church and state**

Christianity and science. *See* **Religion and science**

Christianity and war. *See* **War and religion**

Christmas (May subdiv. geog.)
> *See also* **Christmas entertainments; Christmas plays; Christmas poetry; Christmas stories; Jesus Christ—Nativity; Santa Claus**
> *x* Days; Religious festivals
> *xx* **Fasts and feasts; Jesus Christ—Nativity**

Christmas—Drama. *See* **Christmas plays**

Christmas—Poetry. *See* **Christmas poetry**

Christmas—Stories. *See* **Christmas stories**

Christmas—U.S.
> *x* U.S.—Christmas

Christmas cards. *See* **Greeting cards**

Christmas carols. *See* **Carols**

Christmas decorations

Christmas entertainments
> *See also* **Christmas plays**
> *x* Entertainments
> *xx* **Christmas**

Christmas plays
> *x* Christmas—Drama; Plays, Christmas
> *xx* **Christmas; Christmas entertainments; Drama—Collections; Religious drama**

Christmas poetry
> *See also* **Carols**
> *x* Christmas—Poetry
> *xx* **Christmas; Poetry—Collections**

Christmas stories
> *x* Christmas—Stories; Stories
> *xx* **Christmas**

Christology. *See* **Jesus Christ**

Chromosomes
> *See also* **Genetics**
> *xx* **Genetics**

Chronology. *See* **Calendars; Time**

Chronology, Biblical. *See* **Bible—Chronology**

Chronology, Historical
> Use for works in which events are arranged by date
> *x* Dates; Historical chronology; History—Chronology; U.S.—History—Chronology

Church
> *See also* **Christian unity; Christianity**
> *xx* **Christianity; Theology**

Church, Apostolic. *See* **Church history—Primitive and early church**

Church and education
> Use for works on the relation of the church to education in general, and for works on the history of the part that the church has taken in secular education. Works on church supported and controlled elementary and secondary schools are entered under **Church schools.** Works on the history and theory of religious education are entered under **Religious education**
> *See also* **Academic freedom; Religion in the public schools; Theology—Study and teaching**
> *x* Education and church; Education and religion; Religion and education
> *xx* **Academic freedom; Church and state; Education; Religious education; Theology—Study and teaching**

Church and labor

    See also **Christianity and economics**

    x Labor and the church

    xx **Christianity and economics; Labor and laboring classes**

Church and race problems

    x Integrated churches; Race problems and the church

Church and social problems

    Use for works dealing with the practical treatment of social problems from the point of view of the church. For works on social theory from a Christian point of view use **Sociology, Christian**

    See also **Church work; Socialism, Christian**

    x Religion and social problems; Social problems and the church

    xx **Church work; Socialism, Christian**

Church and state

    See also **Christianity and politics; Church and education; Ecclesiastical law; Freedom of conscience; Popes—Temporal power; Religion in the public schools; Religious liberty**

    x Religion and state; State and church; State church

    xx **Church history; Political science; Popes—Temporal power; Religious liberty**

Church and state—Catholic Church

    xx **Catholic Church**

Church and state in Latin America

    Use same form for church and state in other countries, e.g. **Church and state in France**; etc.

Church and war. *See* **War and religion**

Church antiquities. *See* **Christian antiquities**

Church architecture

    See also **Abbeys; Architecture, Gothic; Cathedrals; Churches; Mosques; Spires; Temples**

    x Architecture, Church; Architecture, Ecclesiastical; Ecclesiastical architecture; Religious art

    xx **Architecture; Architecture, Gothic; Christian antiquities; Christian art and symbolism; Churches**

Church attendance. *See* **Public worship**

Church bells. *See* **Bells**

Church biography. *See* **Christian biography**

Church councils. *See* **Councils and synods**

Church denominations. *See* **Sects;** and names of particular denominations and sects

Church entertainments

    x Church sociables; Entertainments; Socials

    xx **Amusements; Church work**

Church fathers. *See* **Fathers of the church**

Church festivals. *See* **Fasts and feasts**

Church finance
> *See also* **Tithes**
> *x* Finance, Church
> *xx* **Finance**

Church furniture
> *x* Ecclesiastical furniture
> *xx* **Christian antiquities; Christian art and symbolism; Furniture**

Church history
> Use for works treating of the development of Christianity and church organization
>
> *See also*

Abbeys	**Monasticism and religious orders**
Church and state	
Convents	**Papacy**
Councils and synods	**Persecution**
Creeds	**Popes**
Fathers of the church	**Protestant churches**
	Protestantism
Jews	**Reformation**
Martyrs	**Revivals**
Miracles	**Sects**
Missions	

> *also* names of countries, states, etc. with the subdivision *Church history* (e.g. **U.S. —Church history;** etc.); names of denominations, sects, churches, etc.; and headings beginning with the word **Christian**
>
> *x* Christianity—History; Ecclesiastical history; History, Church; Religious history
>
> *xx* **History**

Church history—Middle Ages
> *See also* **Crusades; Papacy; Popes—Temporal power**
> *xx* **Middle Ages**

Church history—Modern period

Church history—Primitive and early church
> *See also* **Apostles; Catacombs; Fathers of the church; Gnosticism; Neoplatonism; Persecution**
> *x* Apostolic Church; Christianity—Origin; Church, Apostolic; Primitive Christianity
> *xx* **Catacombs; Christian literature, Early; Fathers of the church**

Church history—Reformation. *See* **Reformation**

Church law. *See* **Ecclesiastical law**

Church libraries. *See* **Libraries, Church**

Church music
> *See also* **Carols; Chants (Plain, Gregorian, etc.); Choirs (Music); Choral music; Hymns; Liturgies; Oratorio; Organ music**
> *x* Music, Sacred; Psalmody; Religious music; Sacred music
> *xx* **Devotional exercises; Hymns; Music**

Church of Christ (Disciples). *See* **Disciples of Christ**

Church of Christ, Scientist. *See* **Christian Science**

Church of Christ of Latter-Day Saints. *See* ✔**Mormons and Mormonism**

Church of England

    See also **Puritans**

    x Anglican Church; England, Church of; Episcopal Church

  xx **Puritans**

Church of the Brethren

    x Dunkards; Dunkers; German Baptist Brethren

  xx **Baptists**

Church of the New Jerusalem. *See* **New Jerusalem Church**

Church schools

    See note under **Church and education**

    x Denominational schools; Nonpublic schools; Parochial schools; School, Parochial

  xx **Private schools; Schools**

Church service books. *See* **Liturgies**

Church settlements. *See* **Social settlements**

Church sociables. *See* **Church entertainments**

Church unity. *See* **Christian unity**

Church work

    See also

Church and social problems	**Psychology, Pastoral**
Church entertainments	**Revivals**
Evangelistic work	**Rural churches**
Missions	**Sunday schools**

  xx **Church and social problems; Pastoral work**

Church work, Rural. *See* **Rural churches**

Church work with children. *See* **Church work with youth**

Church work with the sick

    Use same form for church work with other groups of people

Church work with youth

    x Church work with children

  xx **Youth**

Churches (May subdiv. geog. country or state)

    Use for general descriptive and historical works on churches which cannot be entered under **Church architecture.** Works relating to the churches of a city are entered under the name of the city with the subdivision *Churches*

    See also **Cathedrals; Church architecture;** also names of cities with the subdivision *Churches* (e.g. **Chicago—Churches;** etc.) ; and names of individual churches

  xx **Church architecture**

Churches, Avant-garde. *See* **Noninstitutional churches**

Churches, Community. *See* **Community churches**

Churches, Country. *See* **Rural churches**

Churches, Noninstitutional. *See* **Noninstitutional churches**

Churches, Rural. *See* **Rural churches**

Churches, Undenominational. *See* **Community churches**

Churches—U.S.
> *x* U.S.—Churches

Churchyards. *See* **Cemeteries**

Cicadas
> *See also* **Locusts**
> *x* Locusts, Seventeen-year; Seventeen-year locusts

Cigarettes
> *xx* **Smoking**

Cigars
> *xx* **Smoking**

Cinema. *See* **Moving pictures**

Cipher and telegraph codes
> *x* Cable codes; Codes, Telegraph; Morse code; Telegraph codes
> *xx* **Telegraph**

Ciphers
> *See also* **Abbreviations; Cryptography; Writing**
> *x* Code names; Contractions
> *xx* **Abbreviations; Cryptography; Signs and symbols; Writing**

Ciphers (Lettering). *See* **Monograms**

Circuits, Electric. *See* **Electric circuits**

Circulation of the blood. *See* **Blood—Circulation**

Circumnavigation. *See* **Voyages around the world**

Circus
> *See also* **Acrobats and acrobatics; Animals—Training; Clowns**
> *xx* **Amusements**

Cities and towns (May subdiv. geog.)
> Use for general works on cities and towns. For works on large cities and their surrounding areas use **Metropolitan areas.** General works on the government of cities are entered under **Municipal government;** general works on local government other than that of cities are entered under **Local government**
> *See also* **Art, Municipal; Markets; Parks; Sociology, Urban; Streets; Tenement houses; Villages;** also headings beginning with the word **Municipal;** and names of individual cities and towns
> *x* City life; Municipalities; Towns
> *xx* **Community life; Local government; Metropolitan areas; Municipal cor-**

Cities and towns—*Continued*
  porations; **Municipal government;
  Sociology; Sociology, Urban**
Cities and towns—Civic improvement
  See also **City planning; Community cen-
  ters**
  x Civic improvement; Municipal improve-
  ments
Cities and towns—Lighting. *See* **Street lighting**
Cities and towns—Planning. *See* **City planning**
Cities and towns, Ruined, extinct, etc.
  See also **Excavations (Archeology)**
  x Abandoned towns; Buried cities; Extinct cities; Ghost towns; Ruins;
  Sunken cities
  xx **Archeology**
Cities and towns—U.S.
  x U.S.—Cities and towns
Citizen's defender. *See* **Ombudsman**
Citizens radio service (Class D) *omit*
  x Personal radio-telephone; Radio-telephone, Private
  xx **Microwave communication systems**
Citizenship
  See also **Aliens; Naturalization; Patriotism; Suffrage**
  x Civics; Foreigners; Franchise; Nationality (Citizenship)
  xx **Aliens; Constitutional law; Naturalization; Political ethics; Political science; Social ethics**
Citrus fruit
  Names of fruits are not included in this list
  but are to be added as needed, in the
  singular form, e.g. **Orange**; etc.
  See also names of citrus fruits, e.g.
  Orange; etc.
  xx **Fruit**
City government. *See* **Municipal government**
City life. *See* **Cities and towns**
City manager. *See* **Municipal government by
  city manager**
City planning (May subdiv. geog.)
  See also **Art, Municipal; Housing; Social
  surveys; Urban renewal; Zoning;** also
  names of cities with the subdivisions
  Public buildings and *Public works*, e.g.
  **Chicago—Public buildings; Chicago
  —Public works;** etc.
  x Cities and towns—Planning; Planning,
  City; Town planning
  xx **Art, Municipal; Cities and towns—
  Civic improvement; Housing; Re-
  gional planning; Tenement houses;
  Urban renewal**
City planning—U.S.
  x U.S.—City planning
City planning—Zone system. *See* **Zoning**

*City planning. See also
Metropolitan council of
governments*

113

City traffic
> x Street traffic; Traffic, City; Urban traffic
> xx **Streets; Traffic engineering**

City transit. *See* **Local transit**

Civic art. *See* **Art, Municipal**

Civic improvement. *See* **Cities and towns—Civic improvement**

Civics. *See* **Citizenship; Political science; U.S.—Politics and government**

Civil defense
> See note under **Air defenses**
> *See also* **Air defenses; Air raid shelters; Disaster relief; Rescue work; World War, 1939-1945—Evacuation of civilians**
> x Blackouts in war; Civilian defense; Defense, Civil; World War, 1939-1945—Civilian defense
> xx **Disaster relief; Military art and science**

Civil disobedience. *See* **Government, Resistance to; Passive resistance**

Civil disorders. *See* **Riots**

Civil engineering
> *See also*

Aqueducts	Mining engineering
Bridges	Public works
Canals	Railroad engineering
Dams	Reclamation of land
Drainage	Rivers
Dredging	Roads
Excavation	Sanitary engineering
Foundations	
Harbors	Steel, Structural
Highway engineering	Streets
Hydraulic engineering	Strength of materials
Irrigation	Structural engineering
Marine engineering	Subways
Masonry	Surveying
Mechanical engineering	Tunnels
	Walls
Military engineering	Water supply

> xx **Engineering**

Civil engineering as a profession. *See* **Engineering as a profession**

Civil government. *See* **Political science; U.S.—Politics and government**

Civil liberty. *See* **Liberty**

Civil rights
> *See also* **Academic freedom; Free speech; Freedom of assembly; Freedom of information; Freedom of movement; Freedom of the press; Liberty; Religious liberty;** also names of groups of people with the subdivision *Civil rights,* e.g. **Negroes—Civil rights; Woman—Civil rights;** etc.
> x Human rights; Natural law; Rights, Civil

114

Civil rights—*Continued*

    xx **Constitutional law; Discrimination; Liberty; Political science**

Civil rights demonstrations. *See* **Negroes—Civil rights**

Civil service (May subdiv. geog.)

    Use for general works on the history and development of public service. Works on public personnel administration, including the duties of civil service employees, their salaries, pensions, etc., are entered under the name of the country, state or city with the subdivision *Officials and employees*

    See also names of countries, cities, etc. with the subdivision *Officials and employees,* **e.g. Chicago—Officials and employees**; etc.

    x Administration; Employees and officials; Government employees; Government service; Municipal employees; Office, Tenure of; Officials; Tenure of office

    xx **Administrative law; Political science; Public administration**

Civil service—Examinations

    xx **Examinations**

Civil service—U.S.

    See also **U.S.—Officials and employees**

    x U.S.—Civil service

    xx **U.S.—Officials and employees**

Civil War—England. *See* **Gt. Brit.—History—Civil War and Commonwealth, 1642-1660**

Civil War—U.S. *See* **U.S.—History—Civil War**

Civilian defense. *See* **Civil defense**

Civilian evacuation. *See* **World War, 1939-1945—Evacuation of civilians**

Civilization

    Use for works dealing with civilization in general and with the development of social customs, art, industry, religion, etc. of several countries or races. Books confined to the civilization of one country are entered under the name of the country with the subdivision *Civilization.* Works on peoples or races whose culture spread beyond their own boundaries are entered under such headings as **Civilization, Greek; Civilization, Occidental; Civilization, Oriental; Civilization, Scandinavian**; etc.

    See also

Acculturation	**Astronautics and civilization**
Aeronautics and civilization	
	Biculturalism
Anthropology	**Culture**
Archeology	**Education**
Art	**Ethics**

Civilization—*Continued*

Ethnology
Industry
Inventions
Learning and scholarship
Manners and customs
Progress
Religions
Science and civilization
Social problems
Society, Primitive
Technology and civilization
War and civilization

also names of countries, states, etc. with the subdivision *Civilization,* e.g. **U.S.—Civilization**; etc.

xx Anthropology; Culture; Ethnology; History; History—Philosophy; Progress; Sociology

Civilization, American

Use for general works on the civilization of the western hemisphere or of Latin America, and for works on ancient American civilization, including that of the Mayas, Aztecs, etc. Works limited to the civilization of the United States are entered under **U.S.—Civilization**

x American civilization

Civilization, Ancient

See also **Man, Prehistoric**

x Ancient civilization

xx **History, Ancient**

Civilization, Arab

x Arab civilization

Civilization, Christian

x Christian civilization

xx **Christianity**

Civilization, Greek

Use same form for works dealing with the culture of races and people not confined to one country, e.g. **Civilization, Arab; Civilization, Oriental**; etc.

See also **Hellenism**

x Greece—Civilization; Greek civilization

Civilization, Jewish. *See* **Jews—Civilization**

Civilization, Medieval

See also **Art, Medieval; Chivalry; Feudalism; Middle Ages; Monasticism and religious orders**

x Medieval civilization

xx **Chivalry; Middle Ages; Middle Ages—History; Renaissance**

Civilization, Modern

Use for works covering the period after 1453

See also **History, Modern; Renaissance**

x Modern civilization

xx **History, Modern**

Civilization, Modern, 1950-

Civilization, Occidental

x Occidental civilization; Western civilization

xx **East and West**

Civilization, Oriental
> *x* Oriental civilization
> *xx* **East and West**

Civilization, Scandinavian
> *x* Scandinavian civilization

Civilization and aeronautics. *See* **Aeronautics and civilization**

Civilization and astronautics. *See* **Astronautics and civilization**

Civilization and science. *See* **Science and civilization**

Civilization and technology. *See* **Technology and civilization**

Civilization and war. *See* **War and civilization**

Clairoyance
> *See also* **Divination; Extrasensory perception; Fortune telling; Hypnotism; Mind reading; Thought transference**
> *xx* **Divination; Fortune telling; Mind reading; Occult sciences; Psychical research; Spiritualism; Thought transference**

Clans and clan system
> *See also* **Tartans**
> *x* Highland clans; Scottish clans
> *xx* **Family; Feudalism; Society, Primitive**

Class conflict. *See* **Social conflict**

Class distinction. *See* **Social classes**

Class struggle. *See* **Social conflict**

Classed catalogs. *See* **Catalogs, Classified**

Classes (Mathematics). *See* **Set Theory**

Classical antiquities
> *See also* **Archeology; Art, Greek; Art, Roman; Mythology, Classical;** also names of countries, cities, etc. with the subdivision *Antiquities,* e.g. **Greece— Antiquities;** etc.
> *x* Antiquities; Antiquities, Classical; Archeology, Classical; Classical archeology; Greek antiquities; Roman antiquities
> *xx* **Archeology; Art, Ancient**

Classical archeology. *See* **Classical antiquities**

Classical art. *See* **Art, Greek; Art, Roman**

Classical biography. *See* **Greece—Biography; Rome—Biography**

Classical dictionaries
> *x* Dictionaries, Classical
> *xx* **History, Ancient**

Classical education
> *See also* **Colleges and universities; Humanism; Humanities**
> *x* Education, Classical
> *xx* **Colleges and universities; Education; Education, Higher; Humanism; Humanities**

Classical geography. *See* **Geography, Ancient**

Classical languages. *See* **Greek language; Latin language**

Classical literature

    See also **Greek literature; Latin literature**

    x Literature, Classical

    xx **Greek literature; Latin literature; Literature**

Classical mythology. *See* **Mythology, Classical**

Classification—Books

    See also **Catalogs, Classified; Classification, Dewey Decimal**

    x Libraries—Classification; Library classification

    xx **Bibliography; Books; Cataloging; Catalogs, Classified; Documentation; Library science; Processing (Libraries); Subject headings**

Classification, Dewey Decimal

    x Dewey Decimal Classification

    xx **Classification—Books**

Classified catalogs. *See* **Catalogs, Classified**

Classroom management

    xx **School discipline; Teaching**

Clay

    See also **Bricks; Modeling**

    xx **Ceramic materials; Soils**

Clay industries

    See also **Bricks; Pottery; Tiles**

    x Ceramic industries

    xx **Chemistry, Technical**

Clay modeling. *See* **Modeling**

Cleaning

    See also **Bleaching; Cleaning compounds; Dry cleaning; Dyes and dyeing; House cleaning; Laundry; Soap; Street cleaning**

Cleaning compounds

    See also **Detergents, Synthetic; Soap**

    xx **Cleaning**

Cleanliness. *See* **Baths; Hygiene; Sanitation**

Clearing house

    See also **Banks and banking; Trust companies**

    xx **Banks and banking**

Clearing of land. *See* **Reclamation of land**

Clergy

    See also **Chaplains; Monasticism and religious orders; Priests;** also church denominations with the subdivision *Clergy,* e.g. **Catholic Church—Clergy;** etc.

    x Curates; Ministers of the gospel; Pastors; Preachers; Rectors

    xx **Christian biography; Pastoral work**

Clergymen's wives

    x Pastors' wives; Preachers' wives; Wives of clergymen

Clerical employees. *See* **Clerks**

Clerical work—Training. *See* **Business education**

Clerks

    x Clerical employees; Commercial employees; Employees, Clerical; Office employees

    xx **Salesmen and salesmanship**

Clerks (Salesmen). *See* **Salesmen and salesmanship**

Cliff dwellers and cliff dwellings

    See also **Mounds and mound builders**

    xx **Archeology; Indians of North America**

Climate

    Use for works on climate as it relates to man and to plant and animal life, including the effects of changes of climate. Works limited to the climate of a particular region are entered under the name of the place with the subdivision *Climate*. Works on the state of the atmosphere at a given time and place with respect to heat or cold, wetness or dryness, calm or storm, are entered under **Weather.** Scientific works on the atmosphere, especially weather factors, are entered under **Meteorology**

    See also **Forest influences; Meteorology; Rain and rainfall; Seasons; Weather;** also names of countries, cities, etc. with the subdivision *Climate,* e.g. **U.S. —Climate;** etc.

    x Climatology

    xx **Meteorology; Physical geography; Weather**

Climate and forests. *See* **Forest influences**

Climatology. *See* **Climate**

Climbing plants

    x Vines

    xx **Gardening; Plants**

Clipper ships

    xx **Ships**

Clippings (Books, newspapers, etc.)

    x Newspaper clippings; Press clippings

    xx **Newspapers**

Clocks and watches

    See also **Sundials**

    x Horology; Watches

    xx **Time**

Clocks and watches—Repairing

Clog dancing. *See* **Folk dancing; Tap dancing**

Cloisters. *See* **Convents; Monasteries**

Closed-circuit television

    See also **Television in education**

    x Television, Closed-circuit

    xx **Intercommunication systems; Microwave communication systems; Television; Television in education**

Closed shop. *See* **Open and closed shop**

Cloth. *See* **Textile industry and fabrics**

Clothiers. *See* **Clothing trade**

Clothing, Leather. *See* **Leather garments**

Clothing, Men's. *See* **Men's clothing**

Clothing and dress

> Use for works dealing with clothing from a practical standpoint including the art of dress. Descriptive and historical works on the costume of particular countries or periods are entered under **Costume**

> *See also* **Buttons; Children's clothing; Costume; Costume design; Dress accessories; Dressmaking; Fashion; Hats; Hosiery; Leather garments; Men's clothing; Shoes and shoe industry; Tailoring**

> *x* Dress; Woman—Clothing; Woman—Dress; Women's clothing

> *xx* **Costume; Fashion; Hygiene; Manners and customs; Woman—Health and hygiene**

Clothing and dress—Cleaning. *See* **Dry cleaning**

Clothing and dress—Repairing

Clothing trade

> *See also* **Tailoring**

> *x* Clothiers

Cloud seeding. *See* **Weather control**

Clouds

> *xx* **Meteorology**

Clowns

> *xx* **Circus; Entertainers**

Clubs

> *See also* **Boys' clubs; Girls' clubs; Social group work; Societies; Women's clubs**

> *xx* **Associations; Societies**

Coaches. *See* **Carriages and carts**

Coaching (Athletics)

> For the coaching of individual sports see the name of the sport in the phrase **Football coaching** and similar phrases

> *xx* **Athletics; College sports; Physical education and training; School sports; Sports**

Coal

> *See also* **Coal mines and mining**

> *x* Anthracite coal; Bituminous coal

> *xx* **Carbon; Fuel; Geology, Economic**

Coal gas. *See* **Gas**

Coal miners. *See* **Miners**

Coal mines and mining

> *See also* **Mining engineering**

> *xx* **Coal; Mines and mineral resources**

Coal mines and mining—Safety appliances

Coal oil. *See* **Petroleum**

Coal-tar products

> *See also* **Gas; Oils and fats**

> *xx* **Gas; Petroleum**

Coast pilot guides. *See* **Pilot guides**

Coastal signals. *See* **Signals and signaling**

Coats of arms. *See* **Heraldry**

Coal gasification

120

Cocoa

See also **Chocolate**

xx **Beverages; Chocolate**

Cocoons. *See* **Butterflies; Caterpillars; Moths; Silkworms**

Code names. *See* **Acronyms; Ciphers**

Codes, Telegraph. *See* **Cipher and telegraph codes**

Coeducation

See also **Education; Education of women**

x Girls—Education

xx **Colleges and universities; Education; Education of women**

Coffee

xx **Beverages; Cookery**

Coffee houses

xx **Restaurants, bars, etc.**

Cog wheels. *See* **Gearing**

Cognition. *See* **Knowledge, Theory of**

Coin collecting. *See* **Coins**

Coinage

Use for works on the processing and history of metal money. Lists of coins and works about coins and coin collecting are entered under **Coins**

See also **Counterfeits and counterfeiting; Currency question; Gold; Mints; Money; Silver**

xx **Gold; Mints; Money; Silver**

Coinage of words. *See* **Words, New**

Coins

Use for lists of coins, works about coins and coin collecting. Works on coins from the point of view of art and archeology are entered under **Numismatics**; works on the processing of metal money are entered under **Coinage**

See also **Numismatics**

x Coin collecting

xx **Money; Numismatics**

Cold

See also **Cryobiology; Ice; Low temperatures**

xx **Low temperatures**

Cold—Physiological effect

xx **Cryobiology**

Cold—Therapeutic effect

xx **Cryosurgery**

Cold (Disease)

See also **Influenza**

x Common cold

Cold storage

See also **Compressed air; Refrigeration and refrigerating machiney**

xx **Food—Preservation; Meat industry and trade; Refrigeration and refrigerating machinery**

Cold war. *See* **Psychological warfare; World politics—1945-1965**

121

Collaborationists. *See* **Treason**

Collage
  x Fabric pictures
  xx **Art**

Collecting. *See* **Collectors and collecting**

Collecting of accounts
  x Accounts, Collecting of
  xx **Commercial law; Credit; Debtor and creditor**

Collections of literature. *See* **Essays; Short stories;** etc.; and names of literatures and literary forms with the subdivision *Collections,* e.g. **English literature —Collections; Poetry—Collections;** etc.

Collections of natural specimens. *See* **Zoological specimens—Collection and preservation;** and names of specimens with the subdivision *Collection and preservation,* e.g. **Birds—Collection and preservations;** etc.

Collections of objects. *See* **Collectors and collecting;** and names of objects collected with the subdivision *Collectors and collecting,* e.g. **Postage stamps—Collectors and collecting;** etc.

Collective bargaining
  See also **Arbitration, Industrial; Employees' representation in management; Labor contract; Labor unions; Strikes and lockouts**
  x Labor disputes
  xx **Arbitration, Industrial; Employees' representation in management; Industrial relations; Labor and labor-classes; Labor contract; Labor unions; Strikes and lockouts**

Collective farms. *See* **Agriculture, Cooperative**

Collective labor agreements. *See* **Labor contract**

Collective settlements (May subdiv. geog.)
  See also **Counter culture;** also names of individual communes
  x Communal living; Communes; Group living; Kibbutz
  xx **Counter culture**

Collective settlements—U.S.
  x U.S.—Collective settlements

Collectivism. *See* **Communism; Socialism**

Collectors and collecting
  See also **Book collecting;** also names of objects collected with the subdivision *Collectors and collecting,* e.g. **Postage stamps—Collectors and collecting;** etc.; and names of natural specimens with the subdivision *Collection and preservation,* e.g. **Birds—Collection and preservation; Zoological speci-**

Collectors and collecting—*Continued*
>   mens—**Collection and preservation;**
>   etc.
>
>   *x* Collecting; Collections of objects
>
> *xx* **Antiques; Art; Hobbies**

Collects. *See* **Prayers**

College and school drama
>   Use for works about college and school
>   drama. Collections of plays for produc-
>   tion in colleges and schools are entered
>   under **College and school drama—
>   Collections**
>
>   *See also* **Drama in education**
>
>   *x* College drama; School drama; Theatri-
>   cals, College
>
> *xx* **Amateur theatricals; Drama; Drama
>   in education; Student activities**

College and school drama—Collections
>   *x* College plays; Plays, College; School
>   plays
>
> *xx* **Drama—Collections**

College and school journalism
>   *x* College journalism; College periodicals;
>   School journalism; School newspapers
>
> *xx* **Journalism; Student activities**

College athletics. *See* **Athletics; College sports**

College costs
>   *x* Tuition
>
> *xx* **Colleges and universities—Finance**

College degrees. *See* **Degrees, Academic**

College drama. *See* **College and school drama**

College education, Value of
> *xx* **Education, Higher**

College entrance requirements. *See* **Colleges
and universities—Entrance requirements;** and names of individual colleges and universities with the subdivision *Entrance requirements*

College fraternities. *See* **Fraternities and sororities; Students' societies**

College journalism. *See* **College and school
journalism**

College libraries. *See* **Libraries, College and
university**

College life. *See* **College students**

College periodicals. *See* **College and school
journalism**

College plays. *See* **College and school drama
—Collections**

College songs. *See* **Students' songs**

College sports
>   *See also* **Coaching (Athletics);** also names
>   of individual sports, e.g. **Baseball;
>   Football; Rowing; Soccer; Track
>   athletics;** etc.
>
>   *x* College athletics; Intercollegiate ath-
>   letics
>
> *xx* **School sports; Sports**

123

College stories

  See also **School stories**

  x Stories

  xx **Fiction; School stories**

College students

  x College life; Colleges and universities—Students; Undergraduates; University students

  xx **Students**

College students—Political activity

  x Campus disorders

  xx **Politics, Practical**

College students—Sexual behavior

  xx **Sex**

College teachers. *See* **Colleges and universities—Faculty; Educators; Teachers**

Colleges and universities (May subdiv. geog.)

  See also

Classical education	Junior colleges
Coeducation	Libraries, College
Commencements	and university
Degrees, Academic	Scholarships, fel-
Dissertations, Aca-	lowships, etc.
demic	Students
Education, Higher	Teachers colleges
Fraternities and so-	University exten-
rorities	sion

  also headings beginning with the word **College** and names of individual institutions

  x Universities

  xx **Classical education; Education; Education, Higher; Professional education; Schools**

Colleges and universities—Buildings

  x Buildings, College

  xx **Buildings**

Colleges and universities—Curricula

  x Core curriculum; Courses of study; Curriculum (Courses of study); Schools—Curricula; Study, Courses of

  xx **Education—Curricula**

Colleges and universities—Entrance requirements

  See also names of individual colleges and universities with the subdivision *Entrance requirements*

  x College entrance requirements; Entrance requirements for colleges and universities

  xx **Examinations; Free universities**

Colleges and universities—Faculty

  x College teachers; Faculty (Education)

Colleges and universities—Finance

  See also **College costs; Federal aid to education**

  x Tuition

College and universities—Students. *See* **College students**

Colleges and universities—U.S.

   x American colleges; U.S.—Colleges and universities

Collies

   xx **Dogs**

Collisions, Railroad. *See* **Railroads—Accidents**

Colloids

   xx **Chemistry, Physical and theoretical**

Colonial architecture. *See* **Architecture, Colonial**

Colonial furniture. *See* **Furniture, American**

Colonial history (U.S.) *See* **U.S.—History—Colonial period**

Colonial life and customs (U.S.). *See* **U.S.—History—Colonial period; U.S.—Social life and customs—Colonial period**

Colonialism. *See* **Colonies; Imperialism**

Colonies

   Use for works on general colonial policy Works on the policy of settling immigrants or nationals in unoccupied areas are entered under **Colonization.** Works on migration from one country to another are entered under **Immigration and emigration.** Works on the movement of population within a country for permanent settlement are entered under **Migration, Internal**

   See also **Colonization; Immigration and emigration; Penal colonies; U.S.—Territories and possessions;** also names of countries other than the U.S. with the subdivision *Colonies,* e.g. **Gt. Brit.—Colonies;** etc.

   x Colonialism; Dependencies

   xx **Colonization**

Colonization

   See note under **Colonies**

   See also **Colonies; Immigration and emigration; Jews—Colonization; Migration, Internal; Penal colonies;** also names of countries with the subdivision *Immigration and emigration,* e.g. **U.S.—Immigration and emigration;** etc.

   x Dependencies; Land settlement

   xx **Colonies; History; Immigration and emigration**

Color

   See also **Dyes and dyeing;** also names of individual colors, e.g. **Black; Red;** etc.

   x Colour

   xx **Chemistry; Esthetics; Light; Optics; Painting; Photometry**

Color—Psychology

   x Pychology of color

   xx **Color sense; Psychology**

Color blindness

   xx **Color sense; Vision**

Color etchings. *See* **Color prints**

Color of animals

    x Animal coloration; Animals—Color; Pigmentation

    xx **Animals; Biology; Evolution; Variation (Biology)**

Color of man

    x Man—Color; Pigmentation; Skin, Color of

    xx **Anthropology; Ethnology; Evolution; Man—Influence of environment; Somatology**

Color photography

    x Color slides; Photography, Color

    xx **Photography**

Color printing

    Use for works on typographic printing in color. Works on pictures printed in color from engraved metal, wood or stone are entered under **Color prints**

    See also **Illustration of books; Lithography; Silk screen printing**

    xx **Printing**

Color prints (May subdiv. geog. adjective form)

    See note under **Color printing**

    See also **Linoleum block printing**

    x Block printing; Color etchings; Paintings—Color reproductions

    xx **Engravings**

Color prints, American

    x American color prints

Color prints, Japanese

    x Japanese color prints; Japanese prints

Color sense

    See also **Color blindness; Color—Psychology**

    xx **Psychology, Physiological; Senses and sensation; Vision**

Color slides. *See* **Color photography; Slides (Photography)**

Color television

    x Television, Color

    xx **Television**

Colorado River—Hoover Dam. *See* **Hoover Dam**

Colored people (U.S.). *See* **Negroes**

Colour. *See* **Color**

Columnists. *See* **Journalists**

Combinations, Industrial. *See* **Trusts, Industrial**

Combustion

    See also **Fire; Fuel; Heat**

    x Spontaneous combustion

    xx **Chemistry; Fire; Heat**

Comedians

    xx **Actors and actresses; Entertainers**

Comedy

    x Comic literature

    xx **Drama; Wit and humor**

✓ Combines (agricultural machinery)

Comets

xx **Astronomy; Solar system**

Comic books, strips, etc.

See also **Cartoons and caricatures**

x Comic strips; Funnies; Humorous pictures

xx **Cartoons and caricatures**

Comic literature. See **Comedy; Parody; Satire**

Comic opera. See **Opera; Operetta**

Comic strips. See **Comic books, strips, etc.**

Commandments, Ten. See **Ten commandments**

Commencements

x Graduation

xx **Colleges and universities; High schools; School assembly programs**

Commentaries, Biblical. See **Bible—Commentaries**

Commerce

Use for general works on foreign and domestic commerce. Works limited to commerce between states are entered under **Interstate commerce**

See also

Banks and banking	Markets
Business	Merchants
Chambers of commerce	Monopolies
	Prices
Competition	Profit sharing
Contracts	Retail trade
Cooperation	Statistics
Exchange	Stock exchange
Free trade and protection	Stocks
Geography, Commercial	Tariff
	Trade-marks
Insurance, Marine	Trade routes
Interstate commerce	Transportation
	Trusts, Industrial

also names of countries, cities, etc. with the subdivision *Commerce* (e.g. **U.S.— Commerce**; etc.) ; names of articles of commerce (e.g. **Cotton**; etc.) ; and headings beginning with the word **Commercial**

x Distribution (Economics) ; Exports; Foreign trade; Imports; International trade; Trade

xx **Economics; Exchange; Finance; Transportation**

Commerce, Interstate. See **Interstate commerce**

Commercial aeronautics. See **Aeronautics, Commercial**

Commercial arithmetic. See **Business arithmetic**

Commercial art

Use for general works on the application of art to business, i.e. in advertising layout, fashion design, lettering, etc.

Commercial art—*Continued*

See also **Costume design; Posters; Textile design**

x Advertising, Art in; Advertising, Pictorial; Art, Commercial; Art in advertising

xx **Advertising; Art; Art industries and trade; Drawing**

Commercial aviation. *See* **Aeronautics, Commercial**

Commercial correspondence. *See* **Business letters**

Commercial education. *See* **Business education**

Commercial employees. *See* **Clerks**

Commercial geography. *See* **Geography, Commercial**

Commercial law

See also

Bankruptcy	**Landlord and tenant**
Collecting of accounts	**Maritime law**
Contracts	**Mortgages**
Corporation law	**Negotiable instruments**
Debtor and creditor	

x Business law; Law, Business; Law, Commercial; Mercantile law

xx **Business; Business education; Law; Maritime law**

Commercial paper. *See* **Negotiable instruments**

Commercial photography. *See* **Photography, Commercial**

Commercial policy

Use for general works on the various regulations by which governments seek to protect and increase the commerce of a country such as subsidies, tariffs, free ports, etc.

See also **Free trade and protection; International economic relations; Subsidies; Tariff;** also names of countries with the subdivision *Commercial policy,* e.g. **U.S.—Commercial policy;** etc.

x Government regulation of commerce; Reciprocity; Trade barriers; World economics

xx **Economic policy**

Commercial products

See also **Forest products; Geography, Commercial; Manufactures; Marine resources; Raw materials;** also names of individual products

x Merchandise; Products, Commercial

Commercial schools. *See* **Business education**

Commercial travelers. *See* **Salesmen and salesmanship**

Commercials, Radio. *See* **Radio advertising**

Commercials, Television. *See* **Television advertising**

Commission government. *See* **Municipal government by commission**

Commission government with city manager. *See* **Municipal government by city manager**

Common cold. *See* **Cold (Disease)**

Common market. *See* **European Economic Community**

Common schools. *See* **Public schools**

The Commonwealth. *See* **Political science; Republics; The State**

Commonwealth of England. *See* **Gt. Brit.—History—Civil War and Commonwealth, 1642-1660**

Commonwealth of Nations

Use for works that deal collectively with Great Britain and the self-governing dominions

See also **Gt. Brit.—Colonies**

x British Commonwealth of Nations; British Dominions

xx **Great Britain**

Communal living. *See* **Collective settlements**

Communes. *See* **Collective settlements**

Communicable diseases

See also **Bacteriology; Biological warfare; Disinfection and disinfectants; Epidemics; Fumigation; Germ theory of disease; Immunity; Insects as carriers of disease; Vaccination;** also names of communicable diseases, e.g. **Smallpox;** etc.

x Contagious diseases; Diseases, Communicable; Diseases, Contagious; Diseases, Infectious; Infection and infectious diseases; Quarantine

xx **Diseases; Epidemics; Immunity; Medicine—Practice; Public health**

Communicable diseases—Prevention

Communication

Use for general works on communication in its broadest sense, including the spoken and written word

See also

Books and reading	**Newspapers**
Cybernetics	**Nonverbal commu-**
Information sciences	**nication**
Language and lan-	**Postal service**
guages	**Telecommunication**
Mass media	**Writing**

x Language arts; Mass communication

Communication among animals. *See* **Animal communication**

Communications relay satellites. *See* **Artificial satellites in telecommunication**

Communion. *See* **Lord's Supper**

Communism (May subdiv. geog.)

See also **Anti-Communist movements; Individualism; Social conflict; Socialism**

Communism—*Continued*

   x Bolshevism; Collectivism; Marxism

   xx **Cooperation; Individualism; Labor and laboring classes; Political science; Socialism; Sociology; Syndicalism; Totalitarianism**

Communism—Russia

   x Russia—Communism; Russian communism

Communism—U.S.

   x U.S.—Communism

Communism and literature

   Use same form for Communism and other subjects, e.g. **Communism and religion;** etc.

   x Literature and communism

Communism and religion

   See also **Christianity and economics**

   x Religion and communism

Communist China. *See* **China (People's Republic of China, 1949-   )**

Communist countries

   x Iron curtain countries; People's democracies; Russian satellite countries; Soviet bloc

Community and libraries. *See* **Libraries and community**

Community and school

   Use for works on ways in which the community at large, as distinct from government, may aid the school program

   See also **Parents' and teachers' associations**

   x School and community

   xx **Community life**

Community antenna television

   x CATV; Cable television; Television, Cable

   xx **Television broadcasting**

Community centers

   See also **Playgrounds**

   x Play centers; Recreation centers; School buildings as recreation centers; Schools as social centers; Social centers

   xx **Cities and towns—Civic improvement; Community life; Playgrounds; Recreation; Social problems; Social settlements**

Community chests. *See* **Fund raising**

Community churches

   Use for works on local churches that have no denominational affiliations

   x Churches, Community; Churches, Undenominational; Undenominational churches; Union churches

   xx **Christian unity**

Community colleges. *See* **Junior colleges**

Community life
    See also **Cities and towns; Community and school; Community centers**
    x Neighborhood
    xx **Associations**
Community music
    x Music, Community
    xx **Choral societies**
Community plays
    x Plays, Community
Community schools. *See* **Schools**
Community songbooks. *See* **Songbooks**
Community surveys. *See* **Social surveys**
Companies. *See* **Corporations**
Companies, Stock. *See* **Stock companies**
Companies, Trust. *See* **Trust companies**
Company unions. *See* **Employees' representation in management**
Comparative anatomy. *See* **Anatomy, Comparative**
Comparative librarianship
    x Librarianship, Comparative
    xx **International education; Library science**
Comparative linguistics. *See* **Language and languages**
Comparative literature. *See* **Literature, Comparative**
Comparative philology. *See* **Philology, Comparative**
Comparative physiology. *See* **Physiology, Comparative**
Comparative psychology. *See* **Psychology, Comparative**
Comparative religion. *See* **Christianity and other religions; Religions**
Compass
    x Magnetic needle; Mariner's compass
    xx **Magnetism; Navigation**
Compassion. *See* **Sympathy**
Compensation. *See* **Pensions; Wages; Workmen's compensation**
Competition
    See also **Monopolies; Trusts, Industrial**
    xx **Business; Business ethics; Commerce; Monopolies; Trusts, Industrial**
Competition, Unfair
    x Fair trade; Unfair competition
Competitions. *See* **Literature—Competitions; Rewards (Prizes, etc.)**
Complexion. *See* **Beauty, Personal; Cosmetics**
Composers (May subdiv. geog. adjective form)
    xx **Musicians**
Composers, American
    x American composers; U.S.—Composers
Composition (Art)
    See also **Architecture—Composition, proportion, etc.; Painting**
    x Art—Composition
    xx **Art; Painting**

131

Composition (Music)

See also **Counterpoint; Fugue; Harmony; Instrumentation and orchestration; Music, Popular (Songs, etc.)—Writing and publishing; Musical accompaniment**

x Music—Composition; Musical composition; Song writing

xx **Music; Music—Study and teaching; Music—Theory**

Composition (Printing). *See* **Typesetting**

Composition (Rhetoric). *See* **Rhetoric;** and names of languages with the subdivision *Composition and exercises,* e.g. **English language—Composition and exercises;** etc.

Compost. *See* **Fertilizers and manures**

Compressed air

x Air, Compressed; Pneumatic transmission

xx **Cold storage; Foundations; Pneumatics; Power (Mechanics)**

Compulsory education. *See* **Education, Compulsory**

Compulsory labor. *See* **Convict labor; Peonage; Slavery**

Compulsory military service. *See* **Military service, Compulsory**

Compulsory school attendance. *See* **Education, Compulsory; School attendance**

Computer control. *See* **Automation**

Computer program languages. *See* **Programming languages (Electronic computers)**

Computer programming. *See* **Programming (Electronic computers)**

Computer programs

See also subjects with the subdivision *Computer programs,* e.g. **Oceanography—Computer programs;** etc.

x Computer software; Programs, Computer; Software, Computer

xx **Programming (Electronic computers)**

Computer software. See **Computer programs; Programming (Electronic computers); Programming languages (Electronic computers)**

Computers

Use for works on modern electronic computers developed after 1945. Works on calculating machines and mechanical computers made before 1945 are entered under **Calculating machines**

See also **Calculating machines; Electronic data processing; Information storage and retrieval systems;** also names of specific computers, e.g. **IBM 7090 (Computer);** etc.

x Automatic computers; Brain, Electronic; Computers, Electronic; Computing ma-

132

Computers—*Continued*

chines (Electronic) ; Electronic brains ;
Electronic calculating machines ; Electronic computers ; Mechanical brains

xx **Calculating machines; Cybernetics;
Electronic apparatus and appliances**

Computers—Cartoons and caricatures

xx **Cartoons and caricatures**

Computers, Electronic. *See* **Computers**

Computers—Programming. *See* **Programming
(Electronic computers)**

Computing machines (Electronic). *See* **Computers**

Concentration. *See* **Attention**

Concentration camps

See also **Prisoners of war**

x Internment camps

xx **Camps, Military; Political crimes and
offenses; World War, 1939-1945—
Prisoners and prisons**

Conception—Prevention. *See* **Birth control**

Concerto

xx **Musical form**

Concerts

See also **Music festivals**

xx **Amusements; Music**

Conchology. *See* **Mollusks; Shells**

Conciliation, Industrial. *See* **Arbitration, Industrial**

Concordances. *See* **Bible—Concordances;** and
names of authors with the subdivision
Concordances, e.g. **Shakespeare, William—Concordances;** etc.

(handwritten) Concordia College, Mn

Concrete

See also **Asphalt; Cement; Pavements**

xx **Building materials; Cement; Foundations; Masonry; Plaster and plastering**

Concrete—Testing

xx **Strength of materials**

Concrete, Reinforced

x Reinforced concrete

xx **Building materials**

Concrete construction

x Building, Concrete; Construction, Concrete

xx **Architecture; Building**

Condemnation of land. *See* **Eminent domain**

Condensers (Electricity)

x Electric condensers

xx **Electric apparatus and appliances; Induction coils**

Condensers (Steam)

xx **Steam engines**

Condominiums. *See* **Apartment houses**

(handwritten) ✓ Condominium (Housing)

Conduct of life. *See* **Behavior**

Conducting

Use for works on orchestral conducting or
a combination of orchestral and choral
conducting. Works limited to choral

133

Conducting—*Continued*

conducting are entered under **Conducting, Choral**

See also Bands (Music); Conducting, Choral; Conductors (Music); Orchestra

xx Bands (Music); Conductors (Music); Music—Study and teaching; Orchestra

Conducting, Choral

See note under **Conducting**

See also Choirs (Music); Choral music; Conductors (Music)

x Choral conducting

xx Choirs (Music); Choral music; Conducting; Conductors (Music)

Conductors (Music)

See also Conducting; Conducting, Choral

x Bandmasters; Music conductors

xx Conducting; Conducting, Choral; Musicians; Orchestra

Conductors, Electric. *See* **Electric conductors**

Conduits. *See* **Aqueducts**

Confectionery

See also Cake decorating

x Candy

xx Cookery; Ice cream, ices, etc.

Confederacies. *See* **Federal government**

Confederate States of America

xx U.S.—History—Civil War

Confederation of American colonies. *See* **U.S.—History—1783-1809**

Conferences. *See* **Congresses and conventions**

Confessions of faith. *See* **Creeds**

Configuration (Psychology). *See* **Gestalt psychology**

Conflict, Social. *See* **Social conflict**

Conflict of generations

See also **Parent and child**

x Generation gap

xx Human relations; Parent and child; Social conflict

Conflict of interests

See also Corruption (in politics)

Conformity

See also Dissent; Individuality

x Nonconformity; Social conformity

xx Attitude (Psychology); Individuality

Confucius and Confucianism

xx Religions

Conglomerate corporations

x Corporations, Conglomerate; Mergers, Conglomerate

xx Corporations

Congregationalism

See also Calvinism; Friends, Society of; Puritans; Unitarianism

xx Calvinism; Puritans

Congress—U.S. *See* **U.S. Congress**

Congresses and conventions

   See also **International organization; Treaties;** also names of special congresses

   x Conferences; Conventions (Congresses); International conferences

   xx **Intellectual cooperation; International cooperation**

Congressional investigations. *See* **Governmental investigations**

Conjuring. *See* **Magic**

Conquistadores. *See* **America—Discovery and exploration**

Conscience

   See also **Freedom of conscience**

   xx **Christian ethics; Duty; Ethics**

Conscientious objectors

   See also **Pacifism;** also names of wars with the subdivision *Conscientious objectors,* e.g. **World War, 1939-1945—Conscientious objectors;** etc.

   xx **Freedom of conscience; Military service, Compulsory; Pacifism; War and religion**

Consciousness

   See also **Gestalt psychology; Individuality; Knowledge, Theory of; Personality; Self; Subconsciousness**

   xx **Apperception; Mind and body; Perception; Psychology; Subconsciousness**

Consciousness, Multiple. *See* **Personality disorders**

Conscription, Military. *See* **Military service, Compulsory**

Conservation of buildings. *See* **Architecture—Conservation and restoration**

Conservation of energy. *See* **Force and energy**

Conservation of forests. *See* **Forests and forestry**

Conservation of natural resources

   See also **Nature conservation**

   x Preservation of natural resources

   xx **Environmental policy; Natural resources**

Conservation of nature. *See* **Nature conservation**

Conservation of the soil. *See* **Soil conservation**

Conservation of water. *See* **Water conservation**

Conservation of wildlife. *See* **Wildlife—Conservation**

Conservation of works of art, books, etc. *See* subjects with the subdivision *Conservation and restoration,* e.g. **Paintings—Conservation and restoration;** etc.

Conservatism

   See also **Right and left (Political science)**

   xx **Right and left (Political science)**

Consolation. *See* **Sympathy**

Consolidation of schools. *See* **Schools—Centralization**

Constellations. *See* **Astronomy; Stars**

Constitution. *See* names of countries and states with the subhead *Constitution,* e.g. **U.S. Constitution;** etc.

Constitutional amendments—U.S. *See* **U.S. Constitution—Amendments**

Constitutional history

   See also **Democracy; Monarchy; Political science; Representative government and representation; Republics;** also names of countries, states, etc. with the subdivision *Constitutional history,* e.g. **U.S.—Constitutional history;** etc.

   x Constitutional law—History; History, Constitutional

   xx **Constitutions; History; Political science**

Constitutional law

   See also

Administrative law	Monarchy
Citizenship	Political science
Civil rights	Proportional repre-
Constitutions	sentation
Democracy	Referendum
Eminent domain	Representative gov-
Executive power	ernment and rep-
Federal government	resentation
Injunctions	Republics
Legislation	Suffrage
Legislative bodies	

   also names of countries with the subdivision *Constitutional law,* e.g. **U.S.—Constitutional law;** etc.

   x Law, Constitutional

   xx **Administrative law; Constitutions; Law; Political science**

Constitutional law—History. *See* **Constitutional history**

Constitutions

   See also **Constitutional history; Constitutional law; Representative government and representation;** also names of countries, states, etc. with the subhead *Constitution,* e.g. **U.S. Constitution;** etc.

   xx **Constitutional law; Political science; Representative government and representation**

Constitutions, State

   See also **State governments;** also names of states with the subhead *Constitution,* e.g. **Ohio. Constitution;** etc.

   x State constitutions

   xx **Political science; State governments**

Construction. *See* **Architecture; Building; Engineering**

Construction, Concrete. *See* **Concrete construction**

Construction of roads. *See* **Roads**

Consulates. *See* **Diplomatic and consular service**

Consuls. *See* **Diplomats**

Consumer behavior. *See* **Consumers**

Consumer credit
    See also **Instalment plan**
    x Credit, Consumer
    xx **Banks and banking; Credit; Finance, Personal**

Consumer education
    Use for works on the selection and most efficient use of consumer goods and services, including methods of educating the consumer. Works on the economic theory of consumption are entered under **Consumption (Economics)**
    See also **Buying; Shopping**
    x Buyers' guides; Consumers' guides; Shoppers' guides
    xx **Buying; Home economics; Shopping**

Consumer goods. *See* **Manufactures**

Consumer organizations. *See* **Cooperative societies**

Consumer price index. *See* **Cost and standard of living**

Consumer protection
    Use for works on governmental and private activities which guard the consumer against dangers to his health, safety, or economic well-being
    See also **Drugs—Adulteration and analysis; Food adulteration and inspection**

Consumers
    Use for works on consumer behavior
    See also **Youth as consumers**
    x Consumer behavior
    xx **Shopping**

Consumers' cooperative societies. *See* **Cooperative societies**

Consumers' guides. *See* **Consumer education**

Consumption (Economics)
    See note under **Consumer education**
    See also **Prices**
    xx **Economics**

Contact lenses. *See* **Eyeglasses**

Contagion and contagious diseases. *See* **Communicable diseases**

Contagious diseases. *See* **Communicable diseases**

Contaminated food. *See* **Food contamination**

Contamination of environment. *See* **Pollution**

Contemporary art. *See* **Art, Modern—20th century**

Continuation schools. *See* **Evening and continuation schools**

Contraception. *See* **Birth control**

Contract bridge. *See* **Bridge (Game)**

Contract labor

   See also **Convict labor; Peonage; Slavery**

   xx **Labor and laboring classes; Peonage**

Contractions. *See* **Abbreviations; Ciphers**

Contracts

   See also **Authors and publishers; Building—Contracts and specifications;
Labor contract; Mortgages; Negotiable instruments**

   x Agreements; Options

   xx **Commerce; Commercial law**

Control of pests. *See* **Pest control**

Conundrums. *See* **Riddles**

Conventions (Congresses). *See* **Congresses
and conventions**

Conventions, Political. *See* **Political conventions**

Convents

   See also **Abbeys; Monasteries; Monasticism and religious orders for
women**

   x Cloisters; Nunneries

   xx **Abbeys; Church history; Monasteries;
Monasticism and religious orders for
women**

Conversation

   x Discussion; Table talk; Talking

   xx **Language and languages**

Conversation in foreign languages. *See* **Languages, Modern—Conversation and
phrase books;** and names of foreign
languages with the subdivision *Conversation and phrase books,* e.g. **French
language—Conversation and phrase
books;** etc.

Conversion

   See also **Converts, Catholic; Grace (Theology); Salvation**

   xx **Christian life; Evangelistic work; Theology**

Converts

   Use for works on converts from one religion or denomination to another. For
persons affiliating with a particular denomination or religion use adjective
form, e.g. **Converts, Catholic;** etc.

Converts, Catholic

   x Catholic Church—Converts; Catholic
converts

   xx **Conversion; Converts**

Conveying machinery

   See also **Hoisting machinery**

   xx **Hoisting machinery**

Convict labor

   See also **Peonage; Prisons**

   x Compulsory labor; Convicts; Forced
labor; Prison labor

   xx **Contract labor; Crime and criminals;
Labor and laboring classes; Peon-
age; Prisons**

Convicts. *See* **Convict labor; Crime and criminals; Penal colonies; Prisons**

Cook books. *See* **Cookery**

Cookery

Use for general works on cookery, including American cookery. If limited to a particular area in the U.S. may use geog. subdiv., e.g. **Cookery—Maine; Cookery—Southern States;** etc. For works on foreign cookery, use geog. subdiv. adjective form, e.g. **Cookery, French;** etc.

See also

Baking	Desserts
Bread	Diet
Cake	Dinners and dining
Canning and preserving	Flavoring essences
	Food
Caterers and catering	Luncheons
	Menus
Coffee	Outdoor cookery
Confectionery	Pastry
Cookery for institutions, etc.	Salads
	Sandwiches
Cookery for the sick	Soups

x Cook books; Cooking; Gastronomy; Recipes

xx **Diet; Dinners and dining; Food; Home economics**

Cookery, Microwave. *See* **Microwave cookery**

Cookery—Vegetables

Use same form for the cooking of other foods

x Vegetarian cooking

xx **Vegetables**

Cookery for institutions, etc.

x Quantity cookery

xx **Cookery**

Cookery for the sick

See also names of diets, e.g. **Salt free diet;** etc.

x Food for invalids; Invalid cookery

xx **Cookery; Diet in disease; Nurses and nursing; Sick**

Cooking. *See* **Cookery**

Cooking, Outdoor. *See* **Outdoor cookery**

Cooking utensils. *See* **Household equipment and supplies**

Cooling appliances. *See* **Refrigeration and refrigerating machinery**

Cooperation

Use for general works on the theory and history of cooperation and the cooperative movement. Works dealing specifically with cooperative enterprises are entered under **Cooperative societies**

Cooperation—*Continued*

See also

Agriculture, Co-operative	Cooperative so-cieties
Banks and bank-ing, Cooperative	International co-operation
Building and loan associations	Labor unions
	Profit sharing
Communism	Savings banks
	Socialism

x Cooperative distribution; Distribution, Cooperative; Rochdale system

xx Associations; Commerce; Economics; Profit sharing

Cooperation, Intellectual. *See* **Intellectual cooperation**

Cooperation, International. *See* **International cooperation**

Cooperation, Library. *See* **Library cooperation**

Cooperative agriculture. *See* **Agriculture, Cooperative**

Cooperative banks. *See* **Banks and banking, Cooperative**

Cooperative building associations. *See* **Building and loan associations**

Cooperative distribution. *See* **Cooperation; Cooperative societies**

Cooperative societies

See note under **Cooperation**

See also **Banks and banking, Cooperative; Building and loan associations**

x Consumer organizations; Consumers' cooperative societies; Cooperative distribution; Cooperative stores; Distribution, Cooperative; Societies, Cooperative; Stores

xx **Cooperation; Corporation law; Corporations; Societies**

Cooperative stores. *See* **Cooperative societies**

Copper

Copper engraving. *See* **Engraving**

Coppersmithing

xx **Metalwork**

Copy writing. *See* **Advertising copy**

Copybooks. *See* **Penmanship**

Copying processes and machines

See also names of specific processes, e.g. **Xerography;** etc.

x Duplicating processes; Photocopying machines; Reproduction processes; Reprography

Copyreading. *See* **Authorship—Handbooks, manuals, etc.**

Copyright

See also **Authors and publishers; Books; Fair use (Copyright); Publishers and publishing**

x Intellectual property; International copyright; Literary property; Property, Literary

Copyright—*Continued*

    xx Authors and publishers; Authorship; Books; Publishers and publishing

Coral reefs and islands

    x Atolls

    xx Geology; Islands

Corals

    xx Invertebrates; Marine animals

Core curriculum. *See* Education—Curricula; also types of education and schools with the subdivision *Curricula*, e.g. Library education—Curricula; Colleges and universities—Curricula; etc.

Corn

    x Maize

    xx Agriculture; Forage plants; Grain

Coronary heart diseases. *See* Heart—Diseases

Corporation law

    See also Cooperative societies; Public service commissions; Public utilities; Trusts, Industrial

    x Law, Corporation

    xx Commercial law; Corporations; Law; Monopolies; Public utilities

Corporations

    See also

Conglomerate corporations	Municipal corporations
Cooperative societies	Municipal ownership
Corporation law	Public service commissions
Government ownership	Public utilities
Guilds	Stock companies
Holding companies	Trust companies
	Trusts, Industrial

    x Companies

    xx Business; Public utilities; Stock companies; Stocks; Trusts, Industrial

Corporations—Accounting

    xx Accounting; Bookkeeping

Corporations, Conglomerate. *See* Conglomerate corporations

Corporations—Finance

    x Capitalization (Finance)

Corpulence. *See* Weight control

Correctional institutions. *See* Prisons; Reformatories

Correspondence. *See* Business letters; Letter writing; Letters

Correspondence schools and courses

    x Home education; Home study courses; Self-instruction

    xx Education; Schools; Technical education; University extension

Corrosion and anticorrosives

    See also Paint

    x Anticorrosive paint; Rust; Rustless coatings

    xx Chemistry, Technical; Paint

141

Corruption (in politics)

    See also **Campaign funds; Lobbying**

    x Boss rule; Graft (in politics); Political corruption; Politics, Corruption in; Spoils system

    xx **Conflict of interests; Lobbying; Political crimes and offenses; Political ethics; Politics, Practical**

Corsairs. *See* **Pirates**

Cosmetics

    See also **Perfumes**

    x Complexion; Make-up (Cosmetics); Toilet preparations

    xx **Beauty, Personal; Beauty shops; Costume**

Cosmic rays

    x Millikan rays

    xx **Nuclear physics; Radiation; Radioactivity; Space environment**

Cosmobiology. *See* **Space biology**

Cosmogony. *See* **Universe**

Cosmogony, Biblical. *See* **Creation**

Cosmography. *See* **Universe**

Cosmology. *See* **Universe**

Cosmology, Biblical. *See* **Creation**

Cosmonauts. *See* **Astronauts**

Cost accounting

    See also **Efficiency, Industrial**

    xx **Accounting; Bookkeeping**

Cost and standard of living

    See also **Budgets, Household; Prices; Saving and thrift; Wages**

    x Consumer price index; Food, Cost of; Household expenses; Living, Cost of; Living, Standard of; Standard of living

    xx **Economics; Home economics; Labor and laboring classes; Prices; Saving and thrift; Social conditions; Social problems; Wages; Wealth**

Cost of medical care. *See* **Medical care—Costs**

Costume

    Use for descriptive and historical works on the costume of particular countries or periods and for works on fancy costume. Works dealing with clothing from a practical standpoint, including the art of dress, are entered under **Clothing and dress.** Works describing the prevailing mode or style in dress are entered under **Fashion**

    See also

Arms and armor	**Indians of North**
Children—Costume	**America—Cos-**
Clothing and dress	**tume and adorn-**
Cosmetics	**ment**
Dressmaking	**Jewelry**
Fans	**Make-up, Theatrical**
Fashion	**Men's clothing**
Hats	**Millinery**

Costume—*Continued*

Uniforms, Military   **Wigs**

    x Acting—Costume; Fancy dress; Style in dress; Theatrical costume; Woman—Dress

    xx Beauty, Personal; Clothing and dress; Ethnology; Fashion; Manners and customs

Costume, Military. *See* **Uniforms, Military**

Costume design

    xx Commercial art; Clothing and dress; Design

Cottages. *See* **Houses**

Cotton

    See also **Fibers**

    xx Botany, Economic; Commerce; Fibers; Yarn

Cotton manufacture and trade

    xx Textile industry and fabrics

Councils and synods

    See also names of special councils and synods, e.g. **Vatican Council, 2d**; etc.

    x Church councils; Ecumenical councils; Synods

    xx **Christianity; Church history**

Counseling

    Use for works that treat of principles or practices used in various types of guidance work—students, employment, veterans, personnel

    See also **Interviewing; Personnel service in education; Psychology, Pastoral; Social case work; Vocational guidance**

    x Guidance

    xx **Family life education; Interviewing; Personnel management; Personnel service in education; Psychology, Applied; Psychology, Pastoral; Social case work; Vocational guidance; Welfare work in industry**

Counter culture

    See also **Bohemianism; Collective settlements**

    x Alternative life style; Counterculture; Escape life style

    xx **Collective settlements; Social conditions**

Counter-Reformation. *See* **Reformation**

Counterculture. *See* **Counter culture**

Counterfeits and counterfeiting

    xx Coinage; Crime and criminals; Forgery; Impostors and imposture; Money; Swindlers and swindling

Counterpoint

    See also **Fugue**

    xx Composition (Music); Music—Theory

Counting books

    See also **Number games**

    xx Arithmetic—Study and teaching

Country churches. *See* **Rural churches**

Country houses. *See* **Architecture, Domestic**

Country life (May subdiv. geog.)

>Use for descriptive, popular and literary works on living in the country. Works dealing with social organization and conditions in rural communities are entered under **Sociology, Rural**
>
>*See also* **Agriculture—Societies; Farm life; Outdoor life; Sociology, Rural**
>
>*x* Rural life
>
>*xx* **Farm life; Outdoor life; Sociology, Rural**

Country life—U.S.

>*x* U.S.—Country life

Country schools. *See* **Rural schools**

County agricultural agents

>*xx* **Agricultural extension work; Agriculture—Study and teaching**

County government

>*x* County officers
>
>*xx* **Local government**

County libraries. *See* **Libraries, County**

County officers. *See* **County government**

County planning. *See* **Regional planning**

Coups d'état. *See* **Revolutions**

Courage

>*See also* **Fear; Heroes; Morale**
>
>*x* Bravery; Heroism
>
>*xx* **Behavior; Fear; Heroes**

Courses of study. *See* **Education—Curricula;** also types of education and schools with the subdivision *Curricula,* e.g. **Library education—Curricula; Colleges and universities—Curricula;** etc.

Court life. *See* **Courts and courtiers**

Court martial. *See* **Courts martial and courts of inquiry**

Courtesy

>*See also* **Behavior; Etiquette**
>
>*x* Manners; Politeness
>
>*xx* **Behavior; Etiquette**

Courtiers. *See* **Courts and courtiers**

Courting. *See* **Dating (Social customs)**

Courts (May subdiv. geog.)

>*See also* **Courts martial and courts of inquiry; Judges; Jury; Justice, Administration of; Juvenile courts**
>
>*xx* **Judges; Justice, Administration of; Law**

Courts—U.S.

>*x* Federal courts; U.S.—Courts

Courts and courtiers

>*See also* **Kings and rulers; Queens**
>
>*x* Court life; Courtiers
>
>*xx* **Kings and rulers; Manners and customs; Queens**

144

Courts martial and courts of inquiry

 See also **Military law**

 x Court martial

 xx **Courts; Military law; Trials**

Courtship. *See* **Dating (Social customs)**

Courtship of animals. *See* **Animals—Courtship**

Coverlets

 x Bedspreads; Quilts

 xx **Interior decoration**

Cow. *See* **Cows**

Cowboys

 See also **Rodeos**

 x Gauchos

 xx **Frontier and pioneer life; Ranch life**

Cowboys—Songs and music

 xx **Songs**

Cows

 See also **Dairying; Milk**

 x Cow; Dairy cattle

 xx **Cattle; Dairying; Domestic animals; Livestock**

Cows—Diseases. *See* **Cattle—Diseases**

Crabs

 xx **Crustacea**

Cradle songs. *See* **Lullabies**

Crafts. *See* **Arts and crafts; Handicraft**

Cranes, derricks, etc.

 x Derricks

 xx **Hoisting machinery**

Crayfish

 xx **Crustacea**

Crayon drawing

 See also **Pastel drawing**

 x Blackboard drawing

 xx **Drawing; Pastel drawing; Portrait painting**

Creation

 See also **Earth; Evolution; Geology; God; Man; Mythology; Theology; Universe**

 x Cosmogony, Biblical; Cosmology, Biblical

 xx **Earth; Evolution; Geology; God; Man; Natural theology; Religion and science; Universe**

Creation (Literary, artistic, etc.)

 x Creativeness; Inspiration

 xx **Genius; Imagination; Intellect; Inventions**

Creativeness. *See* **Creation (Literary, artistic, etc.)**

Credibility. *See* **Truthfulness and falsehood**

Credit

 See also **Agricultural credit; Banks and banking; Bills of exchange; Collecting of accounts; Consumer credit; Debtor and creditor; Debts, Public; Instalment plan; Loans; Negotiable instruments**

 x Bills of credit; Letters of credit

Credit—*Continued*

 xx Banks and banking; Business; Debtor and creditor; Economics; Finance; Money

Credit, Agricultural. *See* **Agricultural credit**

Credit, Consumer. *See* **Consumer credit**

Credit unions. *See* **Banks and banking, Cooperative**

Creeds

 See also **Apostles' Creed; Catechisms; Nicene Creed**

 x Confessions of faith; Faith, Confessions of

 xx Catechisms; Church history; Theology

Cremation

 See also **Funeral rites and ceremonies**

 x Burial; Incineration; Mortuary customs

 xx Funeral rites and ceremonies; Public health; Sanitation

Creoles

Crests. *See* **Heraldry**

Crewelwork

 xx **Embroidery**

Crime and criminals (May subdiv. geog.)

 See also

Anarchism and anarchists	Pirates
Assassination	Police
Atrocities	Prisons
Capital punishment	Prostitution
Convict labor	Punishment
Counterfeits and counterfeiting	Racketeering
	Reformatories
Crime prevention	Riots
Criminal law	Robbers and outlaws
Detectives	Rogues and vagabonds
Education of prisoners	Smuggling
Forgery	Swindlers and swindling
Justice, Administration of	Treason
	Trials
Juvenile delinquency	U.S. Federal Bureau of Investigation
Lynching	
Murder	Vigilance committees
Parole	
Penal colonies	

 x Convicts; Criminals; Criminology; Delinquents; Felony; Gangs; Prevention of crime; Reform of criminals; Vice

 xx **Justice, Administration of; Police; Prisons; Punishment; Social ethics; Social problems; Trials**

Crime and criminals—Identification

 Use for methods of identifying offenders by means of chemistry, photography, fingerprints, measurements, etc.

 See also **Fingerprints**

 xx **Criminal investigation; Identification**

Crime and criminals—U.S.

    x U.S.—Crime and Criminals

Crime prevention

    See also **Criminal psychology**

    x Prevention of crime

    xx **Crime and criminals**

Crimean War, 1853-1856

    x Gt. Brit.—History—Crimean War, 1853-1856; Russo-Turkish War, 1853-1856

Crimes, Military. *See* **Military offenses**

Crimes, Political. *See* **Political crimes and offenses**

Crimes against public safety. *See* **Offenses against public safety**

Crimes against the person. *See* **Offenses against the person**

Criminal investigation

    See also **Crime and criminals—Identification; Detectives; Eavesdropping; Fingerprints; Medical jurisprudence; Police; Wire tapping**

    xx **Detectives; Police**

Criminal law

    See also **Capital punishment; Crimes against public safety; Crimes against the person; Jury; Medical jurisprudence; Military offenses; Probation; Punishment; Trials; Vigilance committees;** also names of crimes, e.g. **Murder;** etc.

    x Law, Criminal; Misdemeanors (Law); Penal codes; Penal law

    xx **Crime and criminals; Law; Prisons; Punishment**

Criminal psychology

    See also **Psychology, Pathological**

    x Psychology, Criminal

    xx **Crime prevention; Psychology, Pathological**

Criminals. *See* **Crime and criminals**

Criminology. *See* **Crime and criminals**

Crippled children. *See* **Physically handicapped children**

Cripples. *See* **Physically handicapped**

Criticism

    Use for works on the history, principles, methods, etc. of criticism in general and of literary criticism in particular. Criticism in a specific field is entered under the subject in variant forms as listed below. Criticism of the work of an individual author, artist, composer, etc. is entered under his name as subject; only in the case of voluminous authors is it necessary to add the subdivision *Criticism, interpretation, etc.* Criticism of a single work is entered under the author's name followed by the title of the work

    See also **Art criticism; Bible—Criticism,**

147

Criticism—*Continued*

interpretation, etc.; **Book reviews;
Dramatic criticism; Shakespeare,
William — Criticism, interpretation,
etc.; Style, Literary;** also literature
and music subjects with the subdivision *History and criticism,* e.g. **English
literature—History and criticism;
English poetry—History and criticism; Music—History and criticism;**
etc.

x Appraisal of books; Books—Appraisal;
Evaluation of literature; Literary criticism; Literature—Evaluation

xx **Esthetics; Literature; Literature—History and criticism; Rhetoric; Style,
Literary**

Crocheting

See also **Beadwork; Lace and lace making**

Crockery. *See* **Pottery**

Crocodiles

For the American crocodiles use **Alligators**

See also **Alligators**

xx **Reptiles**

Crop dusting. *See* **Aeronautics in agriculture**

Crop reports. *See* **Agriculture—Statistics**

Crops. *See* **Farm produce**

Crops, Rotation of. *See* **Rotation of crops**

Cross-country running. *See* **Track athletics**

Cross-examination. *See* **Witnesses**

Crossword puzzles

xx **Puzzles; Word games**

Crowds

See also **Demonstrations; Riot control;
Riots; Social psychology**

x Mobs

xx **Riots; Social psychology**

Crucifixion of Christ. *See* **Jesus Christ—Crucifixion**

Cruelty

See also **Atrocities**

x Brutality

xx **Ethics**

Cruelty to animals. *See* **Animals—Treatment**

Cruelty to children

x Battered child syndrome; Child abuse;
Children, Cruelty to

xx **Child welfare; Children—Management;
Parent and child**

Crusades

See also **Chivalry**

xx **Chivalry; Church history—Middle
Ages; Middle Ages—History**

Crustacea

See also names of shellfish, e.g. **Crabs;
Crayfish; Lobsters;** etc.

x Shellfish

xx **Invertebrates**

✓ crop yields

148

Cryobiology

See also **Cold—Physiological effect**

x Freezing; Low temperature biology

xx **Biology; Cold; Low temperatures**

Cryogenic internment. *See* **Cryonics**

Cryogenic surgery. *See* **Cryosurgery**

Cryogenics. *See* **Low temperatures**

Cryonics

x Burial; Cryogenic internment; Freezing of human bodies; Human cold storage

Cryosurgery

x Cryogenic surgery

xx **Cold—Therapeutic use; Surgery**

Cryptography

See also **Ciphers**

x Secret writing

xx **Ciphers; Signs and symbols; Writing**

Crystal gazing. *See* **Divination**

Crystalline rocks. *See* **Rocks**

Crystallization. *See* **Crystallography**

Crystallography

See also **Mineralogy**

x Crystallization; Crystals

xx **Chemistry, Physical and theoretical; Petrology; Rocks; Science**

Crystals. *See* **Crystallography**

Cub Scouts. *See* **Boy Scouts**

Cuba

xx **Islands**

Cuba—History—1959-

Cuba—History—Invasion, 1961

x Bay of Pigs invasion; Operation Pluto; Pluto operation

Cubism

See also **Postimpressionism (Art)**

xx **Painting; Postimpressionism (Art)**

Cults and sects. *See* **Sects**

Cultural change. *See* **Social change**

Cultural relations

See also **Exchange of persons programs**

x Intercultural relations

xx **Intellectual cooperation; International cooperation; International relations**

Culturally handicapped. *See* **Socially handicapped**

Culturally handicapped children. *See* **Socially handicapped children**

Culture

Use for general discussions of refinement in manners, taste, etc. and the intellectual content of civilization. Works limited to the culture of individual nations are entered under names of countries with subdivisions *Civilization* or *Social life and customs*

See also **Acculturation; Biculturalism; Civilization; Education; Humanism; Learning and scholarship; Self-culture**

x Intellectual life

149

Culture—*Continued*

   xx Civilization; Education; Learning and scholarship

Cuneiform inscriptions

   x Assyro-Babylonian inscriptions; Babylonian inscriptions; Inscriptions, Assyrian; Inscriptions, Cuneiform

   xx **Writing**

Curates. *See* **Clergy**

Currency. *See* **Money**

Currency devaluation. *See* **Currency question**

Currency question (May subdiv. geog.)

   Use for works that discuss some or all of the following subjects: monetary policy and reform, stabilization, the commodity dollar, inflation, bimetallism, etc. General works on currency as a medium of exchange are entered under **Money**

   See also **Finance; Gold; Inflation (Finance); Money; Paper money; Precious metals; Silver**

   x Bimetallism; Currency devaluation; Devaluation of currency; Free coinage; Monetary question; Scrip

   xx **Coinage; Finance; Gold; Inflation (Finance); Money**

Currency question—U.S.

   x U.S.—Currency question

Current events

   Use for works on the study and teaching of current events. Periodicals and yearbooks devoted to the events themselves are entered under **History—Periodicals; History—Yearbooks**

   xx **History, Modern—Study and teaching**

Currents, Alternating. *See* **Electric currents, Alternating**

Currents, Electric. *See* **Electric currents**

Curricula (Courses of study). *See* **Education —Curricula**; also types of education and schools with the subdivision *Curricula,* e.g. **Library education—Curricula; Colleges and universities—Curricula;** etc.

Curriculum materials centers. *See* **Instructional materials centers**

Curtains. *See* **Drapery**

Customs (Tariff). *See* **Tariff**

Customs, Social. *See* **Manners and customs;** and names of ethnic groups, countries, cities, etc. with the subdivision *Social life and customs,* e.g. **Indians of North America—Social life and customs; U.S.—Social life and customs;** etc.

✓ Curling

✓ Custer Battlefield National monument

✓ customs administration

Cybernetics

> *See also* **Bionics; Computers; Systems engineering**
>
> *x* Automatic control; Mechanical brains
>
> *xx* **Calculating machines; Communication; Electronics**

Cycles, Motor. *See* **Motorcycles**

Cycling. *See* **Bicycles and bicycling; Motorcycles**

Cyclones

> Works on the cylonic storms of the West Indies are entered under **Hurricanes.** Storms of the China Seas and the Philippines are entered under **Typhoons**
>
> *See also* **Storms**
>
> *xx* **Hurricanes; Meteorology; Storms; Tornadoes; Winds**

Cyclopedias. *See* **Encyclopedias and dictionaries**

Cyclotron

> *x* Atom smashing; Magnetic resonance accelerator
>
> *xx* **Atoms; Nuclear physics; Transmutation (Chemistry)**

Cytology. *See* **Cells**

Czechoslovak Republic

Czechoslovak Republic—History—Intervention, 1968-

> *x* Russian intervention in the Czechoslovak Republic; Soviet invasion of the Czechoslovak Republic

Czechs

> *x* Bohemians

Czechs in the U.S.

> Use same form for Czechs in other countries, states, etc.

D Day. *See* **Normandy, Attack on, 1944**

DDT (Insecticide)

> *x* Dichloro-diphenyl-trichloroethane
>
> *xx* **Insecticides**

DNA

> *x* Deoxyribonucleic acid; Desoxyribonucleic acid
>
> *xx* **Cells; Heredity**

Dairies. *See* **Dairying**

Dairy cattle. *See* **Cows**

Dairy products

> *See also* **Dairying**; also names of dairy products, e.g. **Butter; Cheese; Milk;** etc.
>
> *x* Animal products; Products, Dairy
>
> *xx* **Dairying**

Dairying

> *See also* **Cattle; Cows; Dairy products; Milk**
>
> *x* Dairies
>
> *xx* **Agriculture; Cattle; Cows; Dairy products; Home economics; Livestock**

Dams

    See also names of dams, e.g. **Hoover Dam;** etc.

    xx **Civil engineering; Flood control; Hydraulic structures; Irrigation; Rivers; Water power; Water supply**

Dance music

    See also **Jazz music; Music, Popular (Songs, etc.)**

    xx **Dancing; Instrumental music; Music**

Dancers

    x Ballet dancers

    xx **Entertainers**

Dancing (May subdiv. geog.)

    See also **Ballet; Dance music; Folk dancing; Modern dance; Tap dancing**

    x Choreography

    xx **Amusements; Etiquette**

Dancing—U.S.

    x U.S.—Dancing

Dangerous occupations. *See* **Occupations, Dangerous**

Danish language

    May be subdivided like **English language**

    xx **Norwegian language; Scandinavian languages**

Danish literature

    May use same subdivisions and names of literary forms as for **English literature**

    xx **Scandinavian literature**

Dark Ages. *See* **Middle Ages**

Darwinism. *See* **Evolution**

Data processing. *See* **Electronic data processing; Information storage and retrieval systems**

Data storage and retrieval systems. *See* **Information storage and retrieval systems**

Date etiquette. *See* **Dating (Social customs)**

Dates. *See* **Chronology, Historical**

Dating, Radiocarbon. *See* **Radiocarbon dating**

Dating (Social customs)

    See also **Love; Marriage**

    x Courting; Courtship; Date etiquette

    xx **Etiquette; Love; Marriage**

Day care centers. *See* **Day nurseries**

Day nurseries

    See also **Nursery schools**

    x Day care centers; Nurseries, Day

    xx **Charities; Child welfare; Children—Institutional care; Nursery schools; Public welfare; Social settlements**

Days. *See* **Birthdays; Fasts and feasts; Festivals; Holidays;** and names of special days, e.g. **Christmas; Memorial Day;** etc.

The dead, Worship of. *See* **Ancestor worship**

Dead Sea scrolls

    x Qumran texts

Deaf
> *x* Dumb (Deafmutes)
> *xx* **Physically handicapped**

Deaf—Education
> *x* Education of the deaf
> *xx* **Education; Vocational education; Vocational guidance**

Deaf—Institutional care
> *x* Asylums; Charitable institutions; Homes (Institutions)

Deaf—Means of communication
> *x* Finger alphabet; Lip reading; Sign language

Deafness
> *See also* **Ear; Hearing; Hearing aids**
> *xx* **Hearing**

Death
> *See also* **Future life; Heaven; Hell; Mortality**
> *xx* **Biology; Eschatology; Life; Mortality**

Death masks. *See* **Masks (Sculpture)**

Death notices. *See* **Obituaries**

Death penalty. *See* **Capital punishment**

Death rate. *See* **Mortality; Vital statistics**

Deaths, Registers of. *See* **Registers of births, etc.**

Debates and debating
> *See also* **Discussion groups; Parliamentary practice; Radio addresses, debates, etc.**
> *x* Argumentation; Discussion; Speaking
> *xx* **Public speaking; Rhetoric**

Debtor and creditor
> Use for economic and statistical works about debt as well as for legal works involving debtor and creditor
> *See also* **Bankruptcy; Collecting of accounts; Credit**
> *xx* **Commercial law; Credit**

Debts, Public (May subdiv. geog.)
> *See also* **Bonds; European War, 1914-1918—Finance; World War, 1939-1945—Finance**
> *x* National debts; Public debts; State debts; War debts
> *xx* **Bonds; Credit; Economics; Finance; Loans**

Debts, Public—U.S.
> *x* U.S.—Debts, Public; U.S.—Public debts

Decalogue. *See* **Ten commandments**

Declaration of Independence. *See* **U.S. Declaration of Independence**

Decoration, Interior. *See* **Interior decoration**

Decoration and ornament (May subdiv. geog. adjective form, e.g. **Decoration and ornament, Mexican;** etc.)
> Use for books dealing with the forms and styles of decoration in various fields of fine arts or applied art; the history of such styles of ornament as Empire,

153

Decoration and ornament—*Continued*

Louis XV, etc.; and with manifestation in different countries or periods, as Chinese, Renaissance. Works limited to the decoration of houses are entered under **Interior decoration.** Works limited to the application of decoration to objects are entered under **Design, Decorative**

See also

Alphabets	Interior decoration
Art, Decorative	Ironwork
Bronzes	Jewelry
Carpets	Leatherwork
Design	Lettering
Design, Decorative	Metalwork
Enamel and enameling	Mosaics
	Painting
Flower arrangement	Plants in art
	Pottery
Furniture	Sculpture
Gems	Stencil work
Holiday decorations	Stucco
	Table setting and decoration
Illumination of books and manuscripts	Tapestry
	Terra cotta
Illustration of books	Wood carving

x Decorative arts; Ornament

xx **Art, Decorative; Arts and crafts; Design, Decorative**

Decoration and ornament, American

x American decoration and ornament; U.S.—Decoration and ornament

Decoration and ornament, Architectural

x Architectural decoration and ornament; Architecture—Decoration and ornament

xx **Architecture**

Decoration Day. *See* **Memorial Day**

Decorations, Holiday. *See* **Holiday decorations**

Decorations of honor

See also **Heraldry; Insignia; Medals**

x Badges of honor; Emblems

xx **Heraldry; Insignia; Medals**

Decorative art. *See* **Art, Decorative**

Decorative arts. *See* **Art, Decorative; Art industries and trade; Arts and crafts; Decoration and ornament; Design, Decorative; Interior decoration;** and the subjects referred to under these headings

Decorative metalwork. *See* **Art metalwork**

Decoupage

xx **Papercrafts**

Deduction (Logic). *See* **Logic**

Deep-sea diving. *See* **Skin diving**

Deep sea technology. *See* **Oceanography**

Deer

See also **Reindeer**

xx **Game and game birds**

Defective speech. *See* **Speech disorders**

Defectives. *See* **Handicapped**

Defectors, Military. *See* **Desertion, Military**

Defense, Civil. *See* **Civil defense**

Defenses, Air. *See* **Air defenses**

Defenses, National. *See* **Industrial mobilization**; and names of countries with the subdivision *Defenses,* e.g. **U.S.—Defenses**; etc.

Defenses, Radar. *See* **Radar defense network**

Degrees, Academic
> *x* Academic degrees; College degrees; Doctors' degrees; Honorary degrees; University degrees
>
> *xx* **Colleges and universities**

Degrees of latitude and longitude. *See* **Geodesy; Latitude; Longitude**

Dehydrated foods. *See* **Food, Dried**

Dehydrated milk. *See* **Milk, Dried**

Deism
> *See also* **Atheism; Christianity; Free thought; God; Positivism; Rationalism; Theism**
>
> *xx* **Atheism; Christianity; God; Pantheism; Rationalism; Religion; Theism; Theology**

Deities. *See* **Gods**

Delinquency, Juvenile. *See* **Juvenile delinquency**

Delinquents. *See* **Crime and criminals; Juvenile delinquency**

Delusions. *See* **Hallucinations and illusions; Superstition; Witchcraft**

Dementia. *See* **Insanity**

Democracy
> *See also*

Aristocracy	Referendum
Equality	Representative government and representation
Federal government	
Liberty	Republics
Middle classes	Socialism
Monarchy	Suffrage

> *x* Popular government; Self-government
>
> *xx* **Aristocracy; Constitutional history; Constitutional law; Equality; Federal government; Monarchy; Political science; Representative government and representation; Republics**

✓ **Democratic Party**
> *xx* **Political parties**

Demonology
> *See also* **Apparitions; Charms; Devil; Occult sciences; Superstition; Witchcraft**
>
> *x* Evil spirits; Spirits
>
> *xx* **Apparitions; Devil; Ghosts; Occult sciences; Superstition; Witchcraft**

Demonstrations (May subdiv. geog. country or state)

Use for works on large public gatherings, marches, etc. organized for non-violent protest even though incidental disturbances or incipient rioting may occur

See also **Riots; Youth movement;** also cities and institutions with the subdivision *Demonstrations,* e.g. **Chicago—Demonstrations;** etc.

x Marches (Demonstrations); Protest marches

xx **Crowds; Riots**

Demonstrations—U.S.

x U.S.—Demonstrations

Demonstrations for Negro civil rights. *See* **Negroes—Civil rights**

Demountable houses. *See* **Prefabricated houses**

Denatured alcohol. *See* **Alcohol, Denatured**

Denominational schools. *See* **Church schools**

Denominations, Religious. *See* **Sects;** and names of particular denominations and sects

Dentistry

See also **Teeth**

x Medicine, Dental

xx **Teeth**

Deoxyribonucleic acid. *See* **DNA**

Department stores

See also **Salesmen and salesmanship**

x Stores

xx **Business; Retail trade**

Dependencies. *See* **Colonies; Colonization**

Dependent children. *See* **Child welfare; Orphans and orphans' homes**

Depressions

x Business depressions; Economic depressions; Panics

xx **Business cycles; Economics**

Dermatology. *See* **Skin—Diseases**

Derricks. *See* **Cranes, derricks, etc.**

Dervishes

xx **Islam**

Descent. *See* **Genealogy; Heredity**

Description. *See* names of cities with the subdivision *Description* (e.g. **Chicago—Description;** etc.); names of modern countries, states and regions with the subdivision *Description and travel* (e.g. **U.S.—Description and travel;** etc.); and names of ancient countries with the subdivision *Description and geography,* e.g. **Greece—Description and geography;** etc.

Descriptive geometry. *See* **Geometry, Descriptive**

Desegregation. *See* **Segregation**

Desert animals

   See also **Camels**

   xx Animals; Deserts; Geographical distribution of animals and plants

Desert plants

   xx Botany—Ecology; Deserts; Geographical distribution of animals and plants; Plants

Desertion, Military (May subdiv. geog.)

   x Army desertion; Defectors, Military; Military desertion

   xx **Military offenses**

Desertion, Military—U.S.

   x U.S. Army—Desertions

Desertion and nonsupport

   x Nonsupport

   xx **Divorce**

Deserts

   See also **Desert animals; Desert plants**

Design

   Use for works on the theory of design

   See also **Costume design; Pattern making; Textile design**

   xx **Decoration and ornament; Pattern making**

Design, Architectural. *See* **Architecture—Details**

Design, Decorative

   Use for works dealing with purely ornamental features of design, e.g. design applied externally to objects. Works dealing with practical applications of the line, form or mass which objects may take are entered under **Design, Industrial**

   See also **Art, Decorative; Decoration and ornament; Drawing; Illumination of books and manuscripts; Lettering; Tapestry; Textile design**

   x Decorative arts; Designs, Floral; Floral design; Flowers in art; Nature in ornament; Ornamental design; Plant forms in design

   xx **Art; Art, Decorative; Arts and carfts; Decoration and ornament; Drawing**

Design, Industrial

   See also **Human engineering; Systems engineering**

   x Art, Applied; Industrial design

   xx **Art industries and trade**

Designs, Architectural. *See* **Architecture—Designs and plans**

Designs, Floral. *See* **Design, Decorative; Flower arrangement**

Desoxyribonucleic acid. *See* **DNA**

Desserts

   See also **Ice cream, ices, etc.**

   xx **Caterers and catering; Cookery; Dinners and dining**

Destiny. *See* **Fate and fatalism**

Destitution. *See* **Poverty**

Details, Architectural. *See* **Architecture—Details**

Detective stories. *See* **Mystery and detective stories**

Detectives

　See also **Criminal investigation; Police; Secret service; U.S. Federal Bureau of Investigation**

　xx **Crime and criminals; Criminal investigation; Police; Secret service**

Detergent pollution of rivers, lakes, etc.

　x Water—Detergent pollution

　xx **Detergents, Synthetic; Water—Pollution**

Detergents, Synthetic

　See also **Detergent pollution of rivers, lakes, etc.**

　x Synthetic detergents

　xx **Cleaning compounds; Soap**

Determinism and indeterminism. *See* **Free will and determinism**

Deuterium oxide

　x Heavy water; Water—Heavy water

Devaluation of currency. *See* **Currency question**

Developing countries. *See* **Underdeveloped areas**

Development. *See* **Embryology; Evolution; Growth**

Devices (Heraldry). *See* **Heraldry; Insignia; Symbolism**

Devil

　See also **Demonology**

　x Satan

　xx **Demonology; Folklore**

Devotion. *See* **Devotional exercises; Prayer; Worship**

Devotional exercises

　See also **Church music; Hymns; Liturgies; Lord's Prayer; Lord's Supper; Prayer**

　x Devotion; Family devotions; Family prayers; Theology, Devotional

　xx **Christian life; Prayer; Worship**

Devotional literature

　xx **Literature**

Dewey Decimal Classification. *See* **Classification, Dewey Decimal**

Diabetes

Diagnosis

　See also **Pain; Pathology**

　x Symptoms

　xx **Medicine—Practice; Pathology**

Diagrams, Statistical. *See* **Statistics—Graphic methods**

Dialectics. *See* **Logic**

Dialects. *See* names of languages with the subdivision *Dialects,* e.g. **English language—Dialects;** etc.

Diamonds

xx **Carbon; Precious stones**

Diaries. *See* **Autobiographies**

Dichloro-diphenyl-trichloroethane. *See* **DDT (Insecticide)**

Dictators

xx **Kings and rulers; Totalitarianism**

Dictionaries. *See* **Dictionaries, Polyglot; Encyclopedias and dictionaries;** and names of languages and subjects with the subdivision *Dictionaries,* e.g. **English language—Dictionaries; Chemistry—Dictionaries; English literature —Dictionaries; U.S.—Biography— Dictionaries;** etc.

Dictionaries, Classical. *See* **Classical dictionaries**

Dictionaries, Polyglot

x Dictionaries; Polyglot dictionaries

Dies (Metalworking)

xx **Metalwork**

Diesel engines

xx **Engines; Gas and oil engines**

Diet

See also **Beverages; Cookery; Digestion; Food; Indigestion; Menus; Nutrition; School children—Food; Vegetarianism; Weight control;** also names of diets, e.g. **Salt free diet;** etc.

x Dietetics

xx **Cookery; Digestion; Food; Hygiene; Nutrition; Weight control**

Diet in disease

See also **Cookery for the sick;** also names of diets, e.g., **Salt free diet;** etc.

xx **Therapeutics**

Dietetics. *See* **Diet**

Digestion

See also **Diet; Food; Indigestion; Nutrition**

xx **Diet; Nutrition; Physiological chemistry; Physiology; Stomach**

Diners. *See* **Restaurants, bars, etc.**

Dinners and dining

See also **Carving (Meat, etc.); Cookery; Desserts; Food; Menus**

x Banquets; Eating; Gastronomy

xx **Caterers and catering; Cookery; Entertaining; Etiquette; Food; Menus**

Dinosaurs

xx **Reptiles, Fossil**

Dioptrics. *See* **Refraction**

Diphtheria

xx **Children—Diseases; Diseases**

Diplomacy

See also **Diplomatic and consular service; Diplomats; Treaties;** also names of countries with the subdivision *Foreign relations,* e.g. **U.S.—Foreign relations;** etc.

159

Diplomacy—*Continued*

  xx **Diplomatic and consular service; International relations**

Diplomatic and consular service

  See also **Diplomacy; Diplomats;** also names of countries with the subdivision *Diplomatic and consular service,* e.g. **U.S.—Diplomatic and consular service;** etc.

  x Consulates; Embassies; Legations

  xx **Diplomacy; Diplomats; International relations**

Diplomats

  See also **Diplomatic and consular service**

  x Ambassadors; Consuls; Ministers (Diplomatic agents)

  xx **Diplomacy; Diplomatic and consular service; International relations; Statesmen**

Dipsomania. *See* **Alcoholism**

Diptera. *See* **Flies; Mosquitoes**

Direct current machinery. *See* **Electric machinery—Direct current**

Direct legislation. *See* **Referendum**

Direct primaries. *See* **Primaries**

Direct taxation. *See* **Income tax; Taxation**

Directories

  Use for works about directories and for bibliographies of directories

  See also names of countries, cities, etc. with the subdivision *Directories* (e.g. **U.S.—Directories;** etc.) ; classes of institutions with the subdivision *Directories* (e.g. **Junior colleges—Directories;** etc.) ; and classes of persons with the subdivision *Directories,* e.g. **Physicians —Directories;** etc.

Directory, French, 1795-1799. *See* **France—History—Revolution, 1789-1799**

Dirigible balloons. *See* **Airships**

Disability insurance. *See* **Insurance, Accident; Insurance, Health**

Disabled. *See* **Handicapped**

Disadvantaged. *See* **Socially handicapped**

Disadvantaged children. *See* **Socially handicapped children**

Disarmament

  See also **Arbitration, International; Peace; Sea power; Security, International**

  x Armaments; Arms control; Atomic weapons and disarmament; Limitation of armament; Military power; Nuclear test ban

  xx **Arbitration, International; Armies; International relations; Military art and science; Navies; Peace; Sea power; Security, International; War**

Disaster relief

    See also **Civil defense**

    x Emergency relief

    xx **Civil defense**

Disasters

    See also **Accidents; Earthquakes; Fires; Floods; Railroads—Accidents; Shipwrecks; Storms;** also names of particular disasters, e.g. **New England—Hurricane, 1938; San Francisco—Earthquake and fire, 1906;** etc.

    x Catastrophes; Natural disasters

    xx **Accidents**

Disciples, Twelve. *See* **Apostles**

Disciples of Christ

    x Campbellites; Christian Church (Disciples); Church of Christ (Disciples)

Discipline, Mental. *See* **Mental discipline**

Discipline of children. *See* **Children—Management; School discipline**

Discography. *See* **Phonograph records;** and subjects and names of persons with the subdivision *Discography,* e.g. **Music—Discography; Shakespeare, William—Discography;** etc.

Discoverers. *See* **Discoveries (in geography); Explorers**

Discoveries (in geography)

    See also **America—Discovery and exploration; Antarctic regions; Arctic regions; Explorers; Northeast Passage; Northwest Passage; Scientific expeditions; Voyages and travels;** also names of countries with the subdivision *Description and travel,* e.g. **U.S.—Description and travel;** etc.

    x Discoverers; Discoveries, Maritime; Explorations; Maritime discoveries; Navigators

    xx **Adventure and adventurers; Explorers; Geography; History; Voyages and travels**

Discoveries (in science). *See* **Inventions; Patents; Science**

Discoveries, Maritime. *See* **Discoveries (in geography)**

Discrimination

    Use for general works on discrimination by race, religion, sex, age, social status, or other factors

    See also **Civil rights; Minorities; Segregation; Sex discrimination; Toleration**

    xx **Human relations; Jews; Minorities; Negroes; Race problems; Segregation; Social problems; Toleration**

Discrimination in education

    See also **Segregation in education**

    x Education, Discrimination in

    xx **Segregation in education**

161

Discrimination in employment

    See also **Age and employment;** also names of social or racial groups with the subdivision *Employment,* e.g. **Woman—Employment; Negroes—Employment;** etc.

    x Employment discrimination; Fair employment practice; Job discrimination; Right to work

Discrimination in housing

    x Fair housing; Housing, Discrimination in; Open housing

Discrimination in public accommodations

    x Public accommodations, Discrimination in; Segregation in public accommodations

Discussion. *See* **Conversation; Debates and debating**

Discussion groups

    x Forums (Discussions); Great books program; Group discussion; Panel discussions

    xx **Debates and debating**

Disease (Pathology). *See* **Pathology**

Disease germs. *See* **Bacteriology; Germ theory of disease**

Diseases

    See also **Epidemics; Medicine—Practice;** also names of diseases and groups of diseases (e.g. **Diphtheria; Communicable diseases;** etc.); and subjects with the subdivision *Diseases,* e.g. **Children—Diseases; Skin—Diseases; Cattle—Diseases;** etc.

Diseases, Communicable. *See* **Communicable diseases**

Diseases, Contagious. *See* **Communicable diseases**

Diseases, Industrial. *See* **Occupational diseases**

Diseases, Infectious. *See* **Communicable diseases**

Diseases, Mental. *See* **Insanity; Mental illness; Psychology, Pathological**

Diseases, Occupational. *See* **Occupational diseases**

Diseases, Tropical. *See* **Tropics—Diseases and hygiene**

Diseases and pests. *See* **Agricultural pests; Bacteriology, Agricultural; Fungi; Household pests; Insects, Injurious and beneficial; Parasites; Plants—Diseases;** names of individual pests (e.g. **Locusts;** etc.); and names of crops, etc. with the subdivision *Diseases and pests,* e.g. **Fruit—Diseases and pests;** etc.

Diseases of animals. *See* **Veterinary medicine**

Diseases of children. *See* **Children—Diseases**

Diseases of occupation. *See* **Occupational diseases**

Diseases of plants. *See* **Plants—Diseases**
Diseases of the blood. *See* **Blood—Diseases**
Diseases of women. *See* **Woman—Diseases**
Dishes. *See* **Glassware; Porcelain; Pottery**
Dishonesty. *See* **Honesty**
Disinfection and disinfectants
    See also **Antiseptics; Fumigation**
    x Germicides
    xx **Antiseptics; Bacteriology; Chemistry,
        Medical and pharmaceutical; Com-
        municable diseases; Fumigation; Hy-
        giene; Public health; Sanitation**
Disneyland
    xx **Amusement parks**
Disobedience. *See* **Obedience**
Displaced persons. *See* **Refugees; Refugees,
    Political; World War, 1939-1945—
    Displaced persons**
Disposal of refuse. *See* **Refuse and refuse dis-
    posal**
Dissent
    x Noncomformity; Protest
    xx **Conformity**
Dissertations, Academic
    Use for works about theses and disserta-
        tions
    x Academic dissertations; Theses
    xx **Colleges and universities**
Distillation
    See also **Alcohol; Essences and essential
        oils; Liquors**
    x Stills
    xx **Alcohol; Liquors**
Distribution (Economics). *See* **Commerce;
    Marketing**
Distribution, Cooperative. *See* **Cooperation;
    Cooperative societies**
Distribution of animals and plants. *See* **Geo-
    graphical distribution of animals and
    plants**
Distribution of wealth. *See* **Economics; Wealth**
District libraries. *See* **Libraries, Regional**
District nurses. *See* **Nurses and nursing**
District schools. *See* **Rural schools**
Districting (in city planning). *See* **Zoning**
Dividends. *See* **Securities; Stocks**
Divination
    See also **Astrology; Clairvoyance;
        Dreams; Fortune telling; Occult sci-
        ences; Oracles; Palmistry; Proph-
        ecies; Superstition**
    x Crystal gazing; Necromancy; Soothsay-
        ing
    xx **Clairvoyance; Occult sciences; Ora-
        cles; Prophecies; Superstition**
Divine healing. *See* **Christian Science; Faith
    cure; Miracles**
Diving
    See also **Skin diving**
    xx **Swimming; Water sports**

[handwritten note: ✓Display workers]

Diving, Skin. *See* **Skin diving**

Diving, Submarine. *See* **Bathyscaphe; Skin diving**

Divinity of Christ. *See* **Jesus Christ—Divinity**

Divorce

    See also **Desertion and non-support; Marriage**

    x Annulment of marriage; Marriage—Annulment; Separation (Law)

    xx **Domestic relations; Family; Marriage; Social problems; Woman—Social conditions**

Docks

    See also **Harbors**

    xx **Harbors; Hydraulic structures**

Doctors. *See* **Physicians**

Doctors' degrees. *See* **Degrees, Academic**

Doctrinal theology. *See* **Theology**

Doctrines. *See* **Theology**

Documentary films. *See* **Moving pictures, Documentary**

Documentation

    See also **Archives; Bibliography; Cataloging; Classification—Books; Information storage and retrieval systems; Library science;** also subjects with the subdivision *Documentation,* e.g. **Agriculture—Documentation;** etc.

    xx **Information sciences**

Documents. *See* **Archives; Charters; Government publications**

Dog. *See* **Dogs**

Dog guides. *See* **Guide dogs**

Dogmatic theology. *See* **Theology**

Dogs

    See also classes of dogs, e.g. **Guide dogs;** etc.; also names of specific breeds, e.g. **Collies;** etc.

    x Dog

    xx **Animals; Domestic animals; Pets**

Dogs—Stories

    x Legends and stories of animals; Stories

    xx **Animals—Stories**

Dogs—Training

    xx **Animals—Training**

Dogs, War use of

    xx **Animals, War use of**

Dogs for the blind. *See* **Guide dogs**

Doll. *See* **Dolls**

Dollhouses

    x Miniature objects

    xx **Toys**

Dolls

    x Doll

    xx **Toys**

Domesday book

    x Doomsday book

Divining rod

Domestic animals

Use for general works on farm animals. Books limited to animals as pets are entered under **Pets.** Books on stock raising as an industry are entered under **Livestock.** Names of all animals are not included in this list but are to be added as needed

See also

Animals—Treatment	**Hogs**
Camels	**Horses**
Cats	**Livestock**
Cattle	**Pets**
Cows	**Poultry**
Dogs	**Reindeer**
Goats	**Sheep**

x Animal industry; Animals, Domestic; Farm animals

xx **Agriculture; Animals; Livestock; Pets; Zoology, Economic**

Domestic animals—Diseases. *See* **Veterinary medicine**

Domestic appliances. *See* **Household appliances, Electric; Household equipment and supplies**

Domestic architecture. *See* **Architecture, Domestic**

Domestic arts. *See* **Home economics**

Domestic finance. *See* **Budgets, Household**

Domestic relations

See also **Divorce; Family; Marriage; Parent and child**

x Family relations

xx **Family; Marriage**

Domestic service. *See* **Household employees**

Dominicans

x Black Friars; Friars, Blacks; Friars preachers; Jacobins (Dominicans); Mendicant orders; Preaching Friars; St. Dominic, Order of

xx **Monasticism and religious orders**

Dominion of the sea. *See* **Sea power**

Donations. *See* **Gifts**

Doomsday book. *See* **Domesday book**

Door to door selling. *See* **Peddlers and peddling**

Doors

xx **Architecture—Details; Building; Carpentry**

Double stars. *See* **Stars**

Doubt. *See* **Belief and doubt**

Draft, Military. *See* **Military service, Compulsory**

Drafting, Mechanical. *See* **Mechanical drawing**

Drainage

Use for works on land drainage. Works on house drainage are entered under **Drainage, House**

Drainage—*Continued*

  See also **Marshes; Sewerage**

  x Land drainage

  xx Agricultural engineering; Civil engineering; Hydraulic engineering; Municipal engineering; Reclamation of land; Sanitary engineering; Sewerage; Soils

Drainage, House

  See also **Plumbing; Sanitary engineering; Sewerage**

  x House drainage

  xx **Plumbing; Sanitation, Household**

Drama

  Use for general works on the drama. Works on the history and criticism of the drama as literature are entered under **Drama—History and criticism.** Works on criticism of the drama as presented on the stage are entered under **Dramatic criticism.** Works on the presentation of plays are entered under **Acting; Amateur theatricals; Theater—Production and direction.** Works on how to write plays are entered under **Drama—Technique.** Collections of plays are entered under **Drama—Collections; American drama—Collections; English drama—Collections;** etc.

  See also

Acting	One-act plays
Ballet	Opera
College and school drama	Pantomimes
	Passion plays
Comedy	Plots (Drama, fiction, etc.)
Dramatic criticism	
Dramatists	Puppets and puppet plays
Folk drama	
Masks (Plays)	Radio plays
Moralities	Religious drama
Moving picture plays	Television plays
	Theater
Mysteries and miracle plays	Tragedy

  also **American drama; English drama;** etc.; and names of special subjects, historical events and famous persons with the subdivision *Drama,* e.g. **Easter—Drama; U.S.—History—Civil War—Drama; Napoléon I, Emperor of the French—Drama;** etc.

  x Stage

  xx **Literature; Theater**

Drama—Collections

  Use for collections of plays by several authors

  See also **American drama—Collections; English drama—Collections;** etc.; also **Children's plays; Christmas**

166

Drama—Collections—*Continued*
    plays; College and school drama—
    Collections
    x Plays
Drama—History and criticism
    See also American drama—History and
    criticism; English drama—History
    and criticism; etc.
Drama—Plots. *See* Plots (Drama, fiction,
    etc.)
Drama, Religious. *See* Religious drama
Drama—Technique
    See also Radio plays—Technique; Tele-
    vision plays—Technique
    x Play writing; Playwriting
    xx Authorship; Characters and character-
    istics in literature
Drama in education
    See also Acting; Amateur theatricals;
    College and school drama; Religious
    drama; Theater
    xx Acting; Amateur theatricals; College
    and school drama; School assembly
    programs
Dramatic art. *See* Acting
Dramatic criticism
    Use for works on criticism of the drama
    as presented on the stage. Works on
    criticism of the drama as a literary
    form are entered under Drama—His-
    tory and criticism; American drama
    —History and criticism; etc.
    See also Moving picture plays—History
    and criticism
    x Theater criticism
    xx Criticism; Drama; Theater
Dramatic music. *See* Opera; Operetta
Dramatic plots. *See* Plots (Drama, fiction,
    etc.)
Dramatists (May subdiv. geog. adjective form,
    e.g. Dramatists, American; etc.)
    Use for works dealing largely with the per-
    sonal lives of several playwrights.
    Books treating of their literary work
    are entered under Drama—History
    and criticism; English drama—His-
    tory and criticism; etc.
    x Playwrights; Writers
    xx Authors; Drama; Poets
Dramatists, American
    x American dramatists; U.S.—Dramatists
Drapery
    x Curtains
    xx Interior decoration; Upholstery
Draughts. *See* Checkers
Drawing
    See also

Anatomy, Artistic	Commercial art
Architectural draw-ing	Crayon drawing
	Design, Decorative

167

Drawing—*Continued*

Drawings
Figure drawing
Geometrical draw-
ing
Graphic methods
Illustration of books
Landscape drawing
Mechanical drawing
Painting
Pastel drawing
Pen drawing
Pencil drawing
Perspective
Shades and
shadows
Topographical
drawing

   x Sketching
   xx Art; Design, Decorative; Graphic arts;
      Illustration of books; Perspective
Drawing materials. *See* **Artists' materials**
Drawings (May subdiv. geog. adjective form,
      e.g. **Drawings, American**; etc.)
   See also **Engravings; Etchings; Pastels**
   xx **Drawing**
Drawings, American
   x American drawings; U.S.—Drawings
Drawings, Architectural. *See* **Architectural**
      drawing
Dreams
   See also **Psychoanalysis; Sleep**
   xx **Brain; Divination; Fortune telling;**
      Mind and body; Psychical research;
      Psychoanalysis; Psychology, Phys-
      iological; Sleep; Subconsciousness;
      Superstition; Visions
Dredging
   xx **Civil engineering; Hydraulic engineer-**
      ing
Dress. *See* **Clothing and dress**
Dress accessories
   xx **Clothing and dress**
Dressing of ores. *See* **Ore dressing**
Dressmaking
   See also **Sewing; Tailoring**
   x Garment making; Patterns for dress-
      making
   xx **Clothing and dress; Costume; Fashion;**
      Needlework; Sewing; Tailoring
Dried flowers. *See* **Flowers, Drying**
Dried foods. *See* **Food, Dried**
Dried milk. *See* **Milk, Dried**
Drill (nonmilitary)
   x Marches (Exercise)
   xx **Physical education and training**
Drill and minor tactics
   See also **Military art and science**
   x Military drill; Minor tactics
   xx **Military art and science**
Drilling and boring
   Use for works relating to workshop op-
      erations in metal, wood, etc. Works re-
      lating to the operation of cutting holes
      in earth or rock are entered under
      Boring
   x Boring (Metal, wood, etc.)

Drilling and boring (Earth and rocks). *See*
Boring

Drink question. *See* **Liquor problem**

Drinks. *See* **Beverages; Liquors**

Driver education. See **Automobile drivers—
Education**

Drivers, Automobile. *See* **Automobile drivers**

Dromedaries. *See* **Camels**

Drop forging. *See* **Forging**

Dropouts
   x School dropouts; School withdrawals
   xx **Personnel service in education; School
     attendance; Youth**

Droughts
   See also **Dust storms; Rain and rainfall**
   xx **Meterology; Rain and rainfall**

Drug abuse
   Use for works on the misuse of drugs in a
   broad sense such as aspirin, alcohol,
   sedatives, LSD, marihuana and narcotics. Works limited to addiction to
   hard drugs such as opium, heroin, etc.
   are entered under **Narcotic habit**
   See also **Alcoholism; Drugs and youth;
   Narcotic habit**
   x Drug addiction; Drug habit; Drugs—
     Abuse; Drugs—Misuse

Drug abuse—Personal narratives
   x Personal narratives

Drug addiction. *See* **Drug abuse; Narcotic
habit**

Drug habit. *See* **Drug abuse; Narcotic habit**

Drugs
   See also **Materia medica; Pharmacology; Pharmacy; Poisons;** also names
   of individual drugs, and groups of
   drugs, e.g. **Narcotics;** etc.
   xx **Chemistry, Medical and pharmaceutical; Materia medica; Pharmacology;
   Pharmacy; Therapeutics**

Drugs—Abuse. *See* **Drug abuse**

Drugs—Adulteration and analysis
   xx **Consumer protection**

Drugs—Misuse. *See* **Drug abuse**

Drugs—Physiological effect

Drugs—Psychological aspects
   xx **Psychology, Applied**

Drugs and youth
   x Youth and drugs
   xx **Drug abuse; Juvenile delinquency;
   Narcotics and youth**

Druids and Druidism
   xx **Celts; Religions**

Drum
   xx **Musical instruments; Percussion instruments**

Drum majoring
   See also **Baton twirling**
   xx **Bands (Music); Baton twirling**

Drinking age

Drunkenness. *See* **Alcoholism; Liquor problem; Temperance**

Dry cleaning
    x Clothing and dress—Cleaning
    xx **Cleaning**

Dry farming
    x Farming, Dry
    xx **Agriculture; Irrigation**

Dry goods. *See* **Textile industry and fabrics**

Ducks
    xx **Poultry**

Ductless glands. *See* **Glands, Ductless**

Dual personality. *See* **Personality disorders**

Dueling
    See also **Fencing**
    x Fighting
    xx **Fencing; Manners and customs**

Dumb (Deaf-mutes). *See* **Deaf**

Dunes. *See* **Sand dunes**

Dungeons. *See* **Prisons**

Dunkards. *See* **Church of the Brethren**

Dunkers. *See* **Church of the Brethren**

Duplicate bridge. *See* **Bridge (Game)**

Duplicating processes. *See* **Copying processes and machines**

Dust, Radioactive. *See* **Radioactive fallout**

Dust storms
    xx **Droughts; Erosion; Storms**

Duties. *See* **Tariff; Taxation**

Duty
    See also **Conscience; Ethics**
    xx **Behavior; Ethics**

Dwarf trees
    x Bonsai
    xx **Trees**

Dwarfs
    See also **Pygmies**
    x Midgets
    xx **Monsters**

Dwellings. *See* **Architecture, Domestic; Houses; Prefabricated houses;** also classes of people with the subdivision *Dwellings;* e.g. **Aged—Dwellings;** etc.

Dyes and dyeing
    See also **Batik; Bleaching**
    xx **Bleaching; Chemistry, Technical; Cleaning; Color; Pigments; Textile chemistry; Textile industry and fabrics; Wool**

Dynamics
    See also

Aerodynamics	Motion
Astrodynamics	Physics
Force and energy	Quantum theory
Hydrodynamics	Statics
Kinematics	Thermodynamics
Matter	

    x Kinetics
    xx **Force and energy; Mathematics; Mechanics; Physics; Statics**

✓ *Dutch Elm Disease*

170

Dynamite

   xx **Explosives**

Dynamos. *See* **Electric generators**

Dyspepsia. *See* **Indigestion**

ESP. *See* **Extrasensory perception**

Eagles

   xx **Birds of prey**

Ear

   See also **Hearing**

   xx **Deafness; Head; Hearing**

Early Christian literature. *See* **Christian literature, Early**

Early warning system, Ballistic missile. *See* **Ballistic missile early warning system**

Earth

   Use for general works on the whole planet. Works limited to the structure and composition of the earth and the physical changes which it has undergone and is still undergoing are entered under **Geology**

   See also

Antarctic regions	**Glacial epoch**
Arctic regions	**Latitude**
Atmosphere	**Longitude**
Creation	**Meterology**
Earthquakes	**Ocean**
Geodesy	**Oceanography**
Geography	**Physical geography**
Geology	**Universe**
Geophysics	

   x World

   xx **Creation; Geology; Physical geography; Solar system; Universe**

Earth—Age

Earth—Chemical composition. *See* **Geochemistry**

Earth, Effect of man on. *See* **Man—Influence on nature**

Earth—Internal structure

Earth—Photographs from space

   xx **Space photography**

Earthenware. *See* **Pottery**

Earthquakes

   See also **Volcanoes**

   x Seismography; Seismology

   xx **Disasters; Earth; Geology; Physical geography**

Earthwork. *See* **Soils (Engineering)**

Earthworks (Archeology). *See* **Excavations (Archeology)**

East

   See also **Asia; Near East**

   x Orient

East (Far East)

   Use for works on the Far East including China, Japan, Korea, Formosa, Hongkong and Macao

   See also **Eastern question (Far East)**

   x Far East; Orient

East (Near East). *See* **Eastern question; Near East**

East Africa. *See* **Africa, East**

East and West
> Use for works on both acculturation and cultural conflict between Oriental and Occidental civilizations
>
> *See also* **Acculturation; Civilization, Occidental; Civilization, Oriental**
>
> *xx* **Acculturation; Eastern question; Eastern question (Far East)**

East Germany. *See* **Germany (Democratic Republic)**

East Indians
> *See also* **Hindus**
>
> *x* Indians (of India)
>
> *xx* **Hindus**

Easter
> *x* Ecclesiastical fasts and feasts; Religious festivals
>
> *xx* **Fasts and feasts; Holy Week; Lent**

Easter—Drama
> *xx* **Drama**

Eastern churches
> *See also* **Orthodox Eastern Church**

Eastern Empire. *See* **Byzantine Empire**

Eastern question
> Use for works dealing with problems of international policies in the countries of the Near East
>
> *See also* **East and West; World politics**
>
> *x* East (Near East); Near Eastern question
>
> *xx* **Near East; World poitics**

Eastern question (Far East)
> Use for works dealing with problems of international policies in the countries of the Far East
>
> *See also* **East and West**
>
> *x* Far Eastern question; Open door policy (Far East)
>
> *xx* **East (Far East)**

Eastern Seaboard. *See* **Atlantic States**

Eating. *See* **Dinners and dining**

Eavesdropping
> *See also* **Wire tapping**
>
> *x* Electronic eavesdropping; Listening devices
>
> *xx* **Criminal investigation; Privacy, Right of; Wire tapping**

Ecclesiastical antiquities. *See* **Christian antiquities**

Ecclesiastical architecture. *See* **Church architecture**

Ecclesiastical art. *See* **Christian art and symbolism**

Ecclesiastical biography. *See* **Christian biography**

Ecclesiastical fasts and feasts. *See* **Fasts and feasts;** and names of special fasts and feasts, e.g. **Easter; Lent;** etc.

Ecclesiastical furniture. *See* **Church furniture**

Ecclesiastical history. *See* **Church history**

Ecclesiastical law

    See also **Tithes**

    x Canon law; Church law; Law, Ecclesiastical

    xx **Church and state; Law**

Ecclesiastical rites and ceremonies. *See* **Liturgies; Rites and ceremonies; Sacraments;** and special rites and ceremonies, e.g. **Funeral rites and ceremonies; Lord's Supper;** etc.

Echo ranging. *See* **Sonar**

Eclipses, Lunar

    x Lunar eclipses; Moon—Eclipses

    xx **Astronomy**

Eclipses, Solar

    x Solar eclipses; Sun—Eclipses

    xx **Astronomy**

Ecology

    See also **Adaptation (Biology); Botany—Ecology; Geographical distribution of animals and plants;** and **Marine ecology;** and similar headings

    x Balance of nature; Biology—Ecology; Environment

Ecology, Human. *See* **Human ecology**

Ecology, Marine. *See* **Marine ecology**

Ecology, Social. *See* **Human ecology**

Economic assistance

    Use for general works on international economic aid given in the form of gifts, loans, relief grants, or technical assistance. Works limited to the latter are entered under **Technical assistance**

    See also **Reconstruction (1939-1951); Technical assistance; Underdeveloped areas; World War, 1939-1945—Civilian relief**

    x Aid to developing areas; Assistance to developing areas; Foreign aid program; Underdeveloped areas—Economic assistance

    xx **Economic policy: International cooperation; International economic relations; Reconstruction (1939-1951); Underdeveloped areas**

Economic assistance, Domestic

    See also **Poverty; Public works; Subsidies; Unemployed**

    x Anti-poverty programs; Poor relief

    xx **Economic policy; Unemployed**

Economic botany. *See* **Botany, Economic**

Economic conditions

    Use for general works on some or all of the following: natural resources, business, commerce, industry, labor, manu-

✓ *Economic development*

173

Economic conditions—*Continued*

    factures, financial conditions; and for the history of the economic development of several countries

    See also **Business cycles; Economic policy; Geography, Commercial; Labor supply; Natural resources; Statistics; Underdeveloped areas;** also classes of people and names of countries, cities, etc. with the subdivision *Economic conditions,* e.g., **Negroes—Economic conditions; U.S.—Economic conditions;** etc.

    x Business depressions; Economic development; Economic history; Stabilization in industry; World economics

    xx **Business; Economics; Geography, Commercial; Social conditions; Wealth**

Economic cycles. *See* **Business cycles**

Economic depressions. *See* **Depressions**

Economic development. *See* **Economic conditions**

Economic entomology. *See* **Insects, Injurious and beneficial**

Economic geography. *See* **Geography, Commercial**

Economic geology. *See* **Geology, Economic**

Economic history. *See* **Economic conditions**

Economic mobilization. *See* **Industrial mobilization**

Economic planning. *See* **Economic policy**

Economic policy

    Use for works on the policy of governments towards economic problems

    See also **Commercial policy; Economic assistance; Economic assistance, Domestic; Free trade and protection; Government ownership; Industrial mobilization; Industrialization; Industry and state; International economic relations; Manpower policy; Municipal ownership; Social policy; Subsidies; Tariff; Technical assistance;** also names of countries and states with the subdivision *Economic policy* (e.g. **U.S.—Economic policy; Ohio—Economic policy;** etc.); and names of countries with the subdivision *Commercial policy,* e.g. **U.S.—Commercial policy;** etc.

    x Economic planning; National planning; Planning, Economic; Planning, National; Welfare state; World economics

    xx **Economic conditions; Economics; Industry and state; Social policy**

Economic relations, Foreign. *See* **International economic relations**

Economic zoology. *See* **Zoology, Economic**

174

Economics

See also

Business
Capital
Capitalism
Christianity and
economics
Commerce
Consumption (Economics)
Cooperation
Cost and standard
of living
Credit
Debts (Public)
Depressions
Economic conditions
Economic policy
Finance
Free trade and protection
Government ownership
Income
Industry
Labor and laboring
classes
Land
Money
Monopolies
Population
Prices
Profit
Property
Saving and thrift
Socialism
Trusts, Industrial
Wages
Waste (Economics)
Wealth

also subjects with the subdivision *Economic
aspects,* e.g. **Agriculture—Economic
aspects;** etc.

x Distribution of wealth; Political economy; Production

xx **Social sciences**

Economics—History

Use for works describing the development
of economic theories. Works on the
economic conditions and development of
countries are entered under **Economic
conditions**

Economics, Medical. *See* **Medical economics**

Economics and Christianity. *See* **Christianity
and economics**

Economics of war. *See* **War—Economic aspects**

Economy. *See* **Saving and thrift**

Ecumenical councils. *See* **Councils and synods**

Ecumenical movement. *See* **Christian unity**

Eddas

xx **Icelandic and Old Norse** literature;
Poetry; Scandinavian literature

Eden

x Garden of Eden

Edible plants. *See* **Plants, Edible**

Editions. *See* **Bibliography—Editions**

Editors and editing. *See* **Journalism; Journalists; Publishers and publishing**

Education (May subdiv. geog.)

Subdivisions listed under this heading may
be used under other education headings
where applicable

See also

Adult education
Area studies
Audio-visual education
Books and reading
Business education
Character education
Child study

175

Education—*Continued*

Church and education
Classical education
Coeducation
Colleges and universities
Correspondence schools and courses
Culture
Education and state
Education of women
Educators
Evening and continuation schools
Illiteracy
International education
Learning and scholarship
Libraries
Library education
Military education
Naval education
Physical education and training
Professional education
Religious education
Scholarships, fellowships, etc.
Schools and references under that heading
Self-culture
Study, Method of
Teachers
Teaching
Technical education
Vocational education

also names of classes of people and social and ethnic groups with the subdivision *Education,* (e.g. **Automobile drivers—Education; Deaf—Education; Negroes—Education;** etc.) subjects with the subdivision *Study and teaching* (e.g. **Science—Study and teaching;** etc.) and headings beginning with the words **Education** and **Educational**

x Instruction; Pedagogy

xx **Civilization; Coeducation; Culture; Learning and scholarship; Schools; Teaching**

Education, Adult. *See* **Adult education**
Education—Aims and objectives
Education—Associations. *See* **Educational associations**
Education, Business. *See* **Business education**
Education, Character. *See* **Character education**
Education, Christian. *See* **Religious education**
Education, Classical. *See* **Classical education**
Education, Compulsory

See also **Child labor; Evening and continuation schools; School attendance**

x Compulsory education; Compulsory school attendance

xx **School attendance**

Education—Curricula

See also **Articulation (Education);** also types of education and schools with the subdivision *Curricula,* e.g. **Library education—Curricula; Colleges and universities—Curricula;** etc.

x Core curriculum; Courses of study; Curricula (Courses of study); Schools—Curricula; Study, Courses of

Education, Discrimination in. *See* **Discrimination in education**

Education, Elementary

    Use for general works on education of children below the secondary school level

    See also **Exceptional children; Kindergarten; Montessori method of education; Nursery schools**

    x Children—Education; Education, Primary; Education of children; Elementary education; Grammar schools; Primary education

    xx **Children**

Education, Ethical. *See* **Character education; Religious education**

Education—Experimental methods

    See also **Free schools; Mental tests; Nongraded schools**

    x Activity schools; Experimental methods in education; Progressive education; Teaching—Experimental methods

    xx **Mental tests**

Education—Federal aid. *See* **Federal aid to education**

Education—Finance

    See also **Federal aid to education; State aid to education**

    x School finance; School taxes; Tuition

    xx **Finance**

Education, Higher

    Use for general consideration of education above the secondary level, i.e. for works on college education, professional education, etc. Use for works not specific enough to be entered under **Colleges and universities**

    See also **Adult education; Classical education; College education, Value of; Colleges and universities; Junior colleges; Professional education; Technical education; University extension**

    x Higher education

    xx **Colleges and universities**

Education, Industrial. *See* **Industrial arts education; Technical education**

Education, Intercultural. *See* **Intercultural education**

Education, International. *See* **International education**

Education, Medical. *See* **Medicine—Study and teaching**

Education, Military. *See* **Military education**

Education, Moral. *See* **Character education**

Education, Musical. *See* **Music—Study and teaching**

Education, Naval. *See* **Naval education**

Education—Personnel service. *See* **Personnel service in education**

Education, Physical. *See* **Physical education and training**

Education, Preschool. *See* **Nursery schools**

177

Education, Primary. *See* **Education, Elementary**

Education, Professional. *See* **Professional education**

Education, Religious. *See* **Religious education**

Education, Scientific. *See* **Science—Study and teaching**

Education, Secondary

A more inclusive subject than **High schools**

See also **Adult education; Evening and continuation schools; High schools; Junior high schools; Private schools; Public schools**

x **High school education; Secondary education; Secondary schools**

xx **High schools**

Education, Segregation in. *See* **Segregation in education**

Education—State aid. *See* **State aid to education**

Education—Statistics

Education—Study and teaching

Use for works on the study and teaching of education as a science. Works limited to the methods of training teachers are entered under **Teachers—Training.** Works on the methods of teaching are entered under **Teaching**

See also **Teachers—Training; Teachers colleges**

x Pedagogy

Education, Technical. *See* **Technical education**

Education, Theological. *See* **Religious education; Theology—Study and teaching**

Education—U.S.

x U.S.—Education

Education, Vocational. *See* **Vocational education**

Education and church. *See* **Church and education**

Education and radio. *See* **Radio in education**

Education and religion. *See* **Church and education**

Education and state

See also **Federal aid to education; Scholarships, fellowships, etc.; State aid to education**

x State and education

xx **Education**

Education and television. *See* **Television in education**

Education associations. *See* **Educational associations**

Education for librarianship. *See* **Library education**

Education of adults. *See* **Adult education**

Education of children. *See* **Education, Elementary**

178

Education of criminals. *See* **Education of prisoners**

Education of girls. *See* **Education of women**

Education of prisoners
   x Education of criminals; Prison schools; Prisoners—Education
   xx **Adult education; Crime and criminals; Prisons**

Education of the blind. *See* **Blind—Education**

Education of the deaf. *See* **Deaf—Education**

Education of veterans. *See* **Veterans—Education**

Education of women
   See also **Coeducation**
   x Education of girls; Girls—Education; Woman—Education
   xx **Coeducation; Education; Girls; Young women**

Education of workers. *See* **Labor and laboring classes—Education**

Educational administration. *See* **School administration and organization**

Educational associations
   See also **Parents' and teachers' associations**
   x Education—Associations; Education associations
   xx **Societies; Teachers**

Educational films. *See* **Libraries and moving pictures; Moving pictures in education**

Educational guidance. *See* **Personnel service in education**

Educational measurements. *See* **Educational tests and measurements**

Educational psychology
   See also **Apperception; Attention; Child study; Imagination; Memory; Mental tests; Perception; Psychology, Applied; Thought and thinking**
   x Psychology, Educational
   xx **Child study; Psychology; Teaching**

Educational sociology
   x Social problems in education; Sociology, Educational
   xx **Sociology**

Educational surveys
   x School surveys; Surveys, Educational
   xx **Social surveys**

Educational television. *See* **Television in education**

Educational tests and measurements
   See also **Ability—Testing; Examinations; Grading and marking (Students); Mental tests**
   x Educational measurements; Tests
   xx **Mental tests**

✓ Educational exchanges

179

Educators

    See also **Teachers**

    x College teachers; Faculty (Education)

    xx **Education; Teachers**

Efficiency, Household. *See* **Home economics**

Efficiency, Industrial

    Use for works dealing with specific means of increasing efficiency and output in business and industries. Such books include time and motion studies, and the application of psychological principles

    See also **Executive ability; Factory management; Job analysis; Motion study; Office management; Personnel management; Time study**

    x Industrial efficiency

    xx **Business; Cost accounting; Engineering; Executive ability; Factory management; Industrial management; Industry; Management; Personnel management**

Eggs

    See also **Birds—Eggs and nests**

Egypt

Egypt—Antiquities

    x Egyptology

Egypt—History

    See also **Sinai Campaign, 1956**

Egyptology. *See* **Egypt—Antiquities**

Eight-hour day. *See* **Hours of labor**

Eighteenth century

    See note under **Nineteenth century**

Election (Theology). *See* **Predestination**

Electioneering. *See* **Politics, Practical**

Elections (May subdiv. geog.)

    See also **Campaign** funds; **Presidents—U.S.—Election; Primaries; Referendum; Representative government and representation; Suffrage**

    x Ballot; Franchise; Polls, Election; Voting

    xx **Politics, Practical; Primaries; Proportional representation; Representative government and representation**

Elections—U.S.

    x U.S.—Elections

Elections, Primary. *See* **Primaries**

Electoral college. *See* **Presidents—U.S.—Election**

Electric apparatus and appliances

    See also

Burglar alarms	Electric switchgear
Condensers (Electricity)	Electric toys
	Electric transformers
Electric batteries	
Electric generators	Electromagnets
Electric lamps	Household appliances, Electric
Electric machinery	
Electric meters	Induction coils
Electric motors	Storage batteries

Electric apparatus and appliances—*Continued*
> *x* Apparatus, Electric; Appliances, Electric; Electric appliances
>
> *xx* **Electric engineering; Scientific apparatus and instruments**

Electric apparatus and appliances, Domestic. *See* **Household appliances, Electric**

Electric appliances. *See* **Electric apparatus and appliances; Household appliances, Electric**

Electric automobiles. *See* **Automobiles, Electric**

Electric batteries
> *See also* **Solar batteries; Storage batteries**
>
> *x* Batteries, Electric; Cells, Electric
>
> *xx* **Electric apparatus and appliances; Electrochemistry; Storage batteries**

Electric circuits
> *See also* **Electronic circuits**
>
> *x* Circuits, Electric

Electric communication. *See* **Telecommunication**

Electric condensers. *See* **Condensers (Electricity)**

Electric conductors
> *See also* **Radio, Short wave**
>
> *x* Conductors, Electric

Electric controllers
> *x* Automatic control

Electric currents
> *See also* **Electric measurements; Electric transformers**
>
> *x* Currents, Electric

Electric currents, Alternating
> *x* Alternating currents; Currents, Alternating

Electric distribution. *See* **Electric lines; Electric power distribution**

Electric engineering
> *See also* **Electric apparatus and appliances; Electric lighting; Electric machinery; Electric power distribution; Electric railroads; Electricity in mining; Radio; Telegraph; Telephone**
>
> *xx* **Engineering; Mechanical engineering**

Electric engineering as a profession. *See* **Engineering as a profession**

Electric equipment of automobiles. *See* **Automobiles—Electric equipment**

Electric eye. *See* **Photoelectric cells**

Electric generators
> *x* Dynamos; Generators, Electric
>
> *xx* **Electric apparatus and appliances; Electric machinery**

Electric heating
> *x* Electricity in the home
>
> *xx* **Heating**

Electric household appliances. *See* **Household appliances, Electric**

Electric industries

    See also **Radio industry and trade**

    x Electric utilities; Industries, Electric

    xx **Public utilities**

Electric lamps

    See also **Electric lighting**

    x Incandescent lamps

    xx **Electric apparatus and appliances; Electric lighting; Lamps**

Electric light. *See* **Electric lighting; Photometry; Phototherapy**

Electric lighting

    See also **Electric lamps**

    x Arc light; Electric light; Electricity in the home; Light, Electric

    xx **Electric engineering; Electric lamps; Electric wiring; Lighting**

Electric lighting, Fluorescent. *See* **Fluorescent lighting**

Electric lines

    Use for works on general transmission systems

    See also **Electric wiring**

    x Electric distribution; Electric power transmission; Electric transmission; Electricity—Distribution; Power transmission, Electric; Transmission of power

    xx **Electric power distribution**

Electric machinery

    Use for discussions of more than one kind or class of machines. Works treating of the smaller machines and appliances are entered under **Electric apparatus and appliances**

    See also **Electric generators; Electric motors; Electric transformers; Electicity in mining**

    xx **Electric apparatus and appliances; Electric engineering; Machinery**

Electric machinery—Alternating current

    x Alternating current machinery

Electric machinery—Direct current

    x Direct current machinery

Electric measurements

    See also **Electric meters; Electric testing**

    x Measurements, Electric

    xx **Electric currents; Electric testing; Weights and measures**   .

Electric meters

    x Meters, Electric

    xx **Electric apparatus and appliances; Electric measurements**

Electric motors

    See also **Electric transformers; Electricity in mining**

    x Induction motors; Motors

    xx **Electric apparatus and appliances; Electric machinery**

Electric power
> *xx* **Power (Mechanics); Power resources**

Electric power—Interruptions. *See* **Electric power failures**

Electric power distribution
> *See also* **Electric lines; Electric wiring**
>
> *x* Electric distribution; Electric power transmission; Electric transmission; Electricity—Distribution; Power transmission, Electric; Rural electrification; Transmission of power
>
> *xx* **Electric engineering; Power transmission**

Electric power failures
> *x* Blackouts, Electric power; Brownouts; Electric power—Interruptions; Electric power interruptions; Power blackouts; Power failures

Electric power in mining. *See* **Electricity in mining**

Electric power interruptions. *See* **Electric power failures**

Electric power plants
> *x* Electric utilities; Power plants, Electric
>
> *xx* **Power plants**

Electric power transmission. *See* **Electric lines; Electric power distribution**

Electric railroads
> *See also* **Railroads—Electrification; Street railroads**
>
> *x* Interurban railroads; Railroads, Electric
>
> *xx* **Electric engineering; Public utilities; Railroads; Railroads — Electrification; Street railroads; Transportation**

Electric signs
> *See also* **Neon tubes**
>
> *x* Signs (Advertising); Signs, Electric
>
> *xx* **Advertising; Signs and signboards**

Electric smelting. *See* **Electrometallurgy**

Electric switches. *See* **Electric switchgear**

Electric switchgear
> *x* Electric switches; Switches, Electric
>
> *xx* **Electric apparatus and appliances**

Electric testing
> *See also* **Electric measurements**
>
> *xx* **Electric measurements**

Electric toys
> *xx* **Electric apparatus and appliances; Toys**

Electric transformers
> *x* Transformers, Electric
>
> *xx* **Electric apparatus and appliances; Electric currents; Electric machinery; Electric motors**

Electric transmissions. *See* **Electric lines; Electric power distribution**

Electric utilities. *See* **Electric industries; Electric power plants; Public utilities;** and names of specific utilities

Electric waves

See also **Electromagnetic waves; Microwaves; Radio, Short wave**

x Hertzian waves; Radio waves

xx **Waves**

Electric welding

x Arc welding; Resistance welding; Spot welding; Welding, Electric

xx **Welding**

Electric wiring

See also **Electric lighting; Telegraph; Telephone**

xx **Electric lines; Electric power distribution**

Electrical. See headings beginning with the word **Electric**

Electricity

See also **Electrons; Lightning; Magnetism; Radioactivity; Telegraph; Telephone; X rays;** also headings beginning with **Electric** and **Electro**

xx **Magnetism; Physics**

Electricity—Distribution. See **Electric lines; Electric power distribution**

Electricity, Medical. See **Electrotherapeutics**

Electricity in agriculture

Use same form for electricity in other endeavors, e.g. **Electricity in mining;** etc.

x Electricity on the farm; Rural electrification

xx **Agricultural engineering; Agricultural machinery**

Electricity in medicine. See **Electrotherapeutics**

Electricity in mining

See also **Mining engineering**

x Electric power in mining; Mining, Electric

xx **Electric engineering; Electric machinery; Electric motors; Mining engineering**

Electricity in the home. See **Electric heating; Electric lighting; Household appliances, Electric**

Electricity on the farm. See **Electricity in agriculture**

Electrification of railroads. See **Railroads—Electrification**

Electrochemistry

See also **Electric batteries; Electrometallurgy; Electroplating; Electrotyping**

xx **Chemistry, Physical and theoretical; Chemistry, Technical**

Electromagnetic waves

See also **Heat; Light; Microwaves; Ultraviolet rays; X-rays**

x Waves, Electromagnetic

xx **Electric waves; Radiation**

184

Electromagnetism

   See also **Masers**

   xx **Magnetism**

Electromagnets

   x Magnet winding

   xx **Electric apparatus and appliances; Magnetism; Magnets**

Electrometallurgy

   See also **Electroplating; Electrotyping**

   x Electric smelting

   xx **Electrochemistry; Electroplating; Electrotyping; Metallurgy; Smelting**

Electron microscope

   xx **Microscope and microscopy**

Electron tubes. *See* **Vacuum tubes**

Electronic apparatus and appliances

   See also **Computers; Intercommunication systems**

   x Apparatus, Electronic; Appliances, Electronic

   xx **Electronics; Scientific apparatus and appliances**

Electronic brains. *See* **Artificial intelligence; Computers**

Electronic calculating machines. *See* **Computers**

Electronic circuits

   xx **Electric circuits; Electronics**

Electronic computers. *See* **Computers**

Electronic data processing

   May be subdiv. by topic, e.g. **Electronic data processing—Library science;** etc.

   See also **Computers; On line data processing; Optical data processing; Programming (Electronic computers); Programming languages (Electronic computers)**

   x Automatic data processing; Data processing

   xx **Information sciences; Information storage and retrieval systems**

Electronic data processing—Library science

   x Library science—Electronic data processing

Electronic eavesdropping. *See* **Eavesdropping**

Electronic musical instruments. *See* **Musical instruments, Electronic**

Electronics

   See also **Cybernetics; Electronic apparatus and appliances; Electronic circuits; High-fidelity sound systems; Microelectronics; Semiconductors; Transistors**

   xx **Electrons; Photoelectric cells; Vacuum tubes**

Electrons
>   See also **Electronics**
>   *xx* **Atoms; Electricity; Neutrons; Nuclear physics; Physics; Protons; Radioactivity**

Electroplating
>   See also **Electrometallurgy**
>   *xx* **Electrochemistry; Electrometallurgy; Metalwork**

Electrotherapeutics
>   See also **Radiotherapy**
>   *x* Electricity, Medical; Electricity in medicine; Medical electricity
>   *xx* **Massage; Physical therapy; Therapeutics**

Electrotyping
>   See also **Electrometallurgy**
>   *xx* **Electrochemistry; Electrometallurgy; Printing**

Elementary education. See **Education, Elementary**

Elements, Chemical. See **Chemical elements**

Elephants
>   *xx* **Mammals**

Elevators
>   *x* Lifts
>   *xx* **Hoisting machinery**

Elizabeth II, Queen of Great Britain
>   *xx* **Kings and rulers; Queens**

Elk Mountain, Wyo.
>   *xx* **Mountains**

Elocution. See **Public speaking**

Elves. See **Fairies**

Emancipation of slaves. See **Slavery; Slavery in the U.S.**

Emancipation of women. See **Woman—Civil rights**

Embassies. See **Diplomatic and consular service**

Emblems. See **Decorations of honor; Heraldry; Insignia; Mottoes; Seals (Numismatics); Symbolism**

Embroidery
>   See also kinds of embroidery, e.g. **Beadwork; Crewelwork; etc.**
>   *xx* **Needlework; Sewing**

Embryology
>   See also **Cells; Protoplasm; Reproduction**
>   *x* Development
>   *xx* **Biology; Cells; Evolution; Protoplasm; Reproduction; Zoology**

Emergencies. See **Accidents; First aid**

Emergency relief. See **Disaster relief**

Emigration. See **Immigration and emigration**

Eminent domain
>   *x* Condemnation of land; Expropriation; Land, Condemnation of
>   *xx* **Constitutional law; Land; Property; Railroads; Real estate**

Emotionally disturbed children. *See* **Problem children**

Emotions
> *See also* **Attitude (Psychology)**; **Bashfulness**; **Belief and doubt**; **Fear**; **Joy and sorrow**; **Laughter**; **Love**; **Pain**; **Pleasure**; **Prejudices and antipathies**; **Sympathy**; and names of other emotions
> *x* Feelings; Frustration; Passions
> *xx* **Psychology**; **Psychology, Physiological**

Emperors. *See* **Kings and rulers**; **Roman emperors**; and names of emperors

Empiricism
> *See also* **Pragmatism**
> *x* Experience
> *xx* **Knowledge, Theory of**; **Philosophy**; **Pragmatism**; **Reality**

Employee absenteeism. *See* **Absenteeism (Labor)**

Employees, Clerical. *See* **Clerks**

Employees—Training
> *See also* **Apprentices**; **Occupational training**; **Retraining, Occupational**; **Technical education**
> *x* Factories—Training departments; Factory schools; In-service training; Training of employees
> *xx* **Apprentices**; **Personnel management**; **Technical education**; **Vocational education**

Employees and officials. *See* **Civil service**; and names of countries, cities, etc. and organizations with the subdivision *Officials and employees,* e.g. **Chicago—Officials and employees**; **United Nations—Officials and employees**; etc.

Employees' representation in management
> *See also* **Collective bargaining**
> *x* Company unions; Industrial councils; Labor representation in regulation of industry; Management, Employees' representation in; Shop committees; Workshop councils
> *xx* **Collective bargaining**; **Factory management**; **Industrial relations**; **Labor and laboring classes**; **Personnel management**

Employer-employee relations. *See* **Industrial relations**

Employers' liability. *See* **Workmen's compensation**

Employment. *See* **Labor and laboring classes**; **Vocational guidance**; also names of groups of people with the subdivision *Employment,* e.g. **Negroes—Employment**; **Veterans—Employment**; etc.

187

Employment agencies
>   *See also* **Labor supply**
>   *x* Jobs
>   *xx* **Labor and laboring classes; Labor sup-
>   ply; Labor turnover; Personnel man-
>   agement; Recruiting of employees;
>   Unemployed**

Employment and age. *See* **Age and employ-
    ment**

Employment discrimination. *See* **Discrimina-
    tion in employment**

Employment management. *See* **Personnel
    management**

Employment of children. *See* **Child labor**

Employment of veterans. *See* **Veterans—Em-
    ployment**

Employment of women. *See* **Woman—Em-
    ployment**

Employment references. *See* **Applications for
    positions**

Empresses. *See* **Queens**

Enamel and enameling
>   *x* Porcelain enamels
>   *xx* **Art, Decorative; Arts and crafts; Dec-
>   oration and ornament**

Enamel paints. *See* **Paint; Painting, Indus-
    trial; Varnish and varnishing**

Encyclicals, Papal
>   *x* Papal encyclicals
>   *xx* **Catholic Church—Doctrinal and con-
>   troversial works**

Encyclopedias and dictionaries
>   Use for collections of miscellaneous facts
>   *See also* names of languages and subjects
>   with the subdivision *Dictionaries,*
>   e.g. **English language—Dictionaries;
>   Chemistry—Dictionaries;** etc., for
>   works with meaning of words; and
>   subjects with the subdivision *Encyclo-
>   pedias,* e.g. **Sports—Encyclopedias;**
>   etc., for works with facts presented in
>   condensed form
>   *x* Cyclopedias; Dictionaries
>   *xx* **Reference books**

End of the world
>   *x* World, End of the
>   *xx* **Eschatology**

Endangered species. *See* **Rare animals**

Endocrinology. *See* **Glands, Ductless**

Endowed charities. *See* **Charities; Endowments**

Endowments
>   *See also* **Charities; Scholarships, fellow-
>   ships, etc.**
>   *x* Endowed charities; Foundations (En-
>   dowments); Hospital endowments;
>   Philanthropy; School endowments
>   *xx* **Charities**

Endurance, Physical. *See* **Physical fitness**

Enemy aliens. *See* **Aliens**

Energy. *See* **Force and energy**

188

Enforcement of law. *See* **Law enforcement**

Engineering

See also

Aeronautics
Agricultural engineering
Chemical engineering
Civil engineering
Efficiency, Industrial
Electric engineering
Engineers
Hydraulic engineering
Marine engineering
Mechanical drawing
Mechanical engineering
Mechanics
Military engineering
Mining engineering
Municipal engineering
Nuclear engineering
Railroad engineering
Reliability (Engineering)
Sanitary engineering
Steam engineering
Structural engineering
Systems engineering
Water supply engineering

x Construction
xx **Building; Mechanics; Technology**

Engineering—Periodicals
xx **Periodicals**

Engineering—Study and teaching
xx **Technical education**

Engineering, Structural. *See* **Structural engineering**

Engineering as a profession
x Civil engineering as a profession; Electric engineering as a profession
xx **Engineers**

Engineering drawing. *See* **Mechanical drawing**

Engineering instruments
x Instruments, Engineering
xx **Scientific apparatus and instruments**

Engineering materials. *See* **Materials**

Engineers
See also **Engineering as a profession; Inventors**
xx **Engineering**

Engines

See also

Airplanes—Engines
Automobiles—Engines
Diesel engines
Farm engines
Fire engines
Fuel
Gas and oil engines
Heat engines
Marine engines
Pumping machinery
Solar engines
Steam engines
Turbines

x Motors
xx **Machinery; Mechanical engineering**

England

Use with the subdivisions *Description and travel; Historic houses, etc.; Industries; Intellectual life; Social life and customs* for works limited to England

189

England—*Continued*
> *See also* **Great Britain**
> *xx* **Great Britain**

England, Church of. *See* **Church of England**

England—**History.** *See* **Gt. Brit.**—**History**

English authors. *See* **Authors, English**

English composition. *See* **English language**—
>   **Composition and exercises**

English drama
> *See also* **Moralities; Mysteries and mira-**
>   **cle plays**
> *xx* **Drama; English literature**

English drama—**Collections**
> *xx* **Drama**—**Collections**

English drama—**History and criticism**
> *xx* **Drama**—**History and criticism**

English essays
> Use for collections of literary essays by
>   several authors
> *xx* **English literature; Essays**

English fiction
> *x* Fiction, English
> *xx* **English literature; Fiction**

English fiction—**History and criticism**

English for foreigners. *See* **English language**
>   **—Textbooks for foreigners**

English grammar. *See* **English language**—
>   **Grammar**

English history. *See* **Gt. Brit.**—**History**

English in India. *See* **British in India**

English language
> Subdivisions used under this heading may
>   be used under other languages unless
>   otherwise specified
> *x* Language arts
> *xx* **Language and languages**

English language—**Acronyms.** *See* **Acronyms**

English language—**Americanisms.** *See* **Amer-**
>   **icanisms**

English language—**Antonyms.** *See* **English lan-**
>   **guage**—**Synonyms and antonyms**

English language—**Business English**
> *See also* **Business letters**
> *x* Business English
> *xx* **Business letters**

English language—**Composition and exercises**
> *See also* **Rhetoric**
> *x* Composition (Rhetoric); English com-
>   position
> *xx* **Rhetoric**

English language—Conversation and phrase
>   books. *See* **English language**—**Text-**
>   **books for foreigners**
> Use subdivision *Conversation and phrase*
>   *books* for languages other than English

English language—**Dialects**
> *See also* **Americanisms**
> *x* Dialects

English language—Dictionaries

> For dictionaries of English and another language use the name of the foreign language as a further subdivision under *Dictionaries,* e.g. **English language—Dictionaries—French**; etc.
>
> *See also* **English language—Terms and phrases**
>
> *x* Dictionaries; Glossaries
>
> *xx* **Encyclopedias and dictionaries; English language—Terms and phrases**

English language—Dictionaries—French

> Use for English-French dictionaries. For French-English dictionaries use **French language—Dictionaries—English.** Use both headings for an English-French and French-English dictionary

English language—Errors

English language—Etymology

> *x* Etymology

English language—Examinations, questions, etc.

> *xx* **Examinations**

English language—Foreign words and phrases

> *x* Foreign language phrases

English language—Grammar

> *x* English grammar
>
> *xx* **Grammar**

English language—History

> *xx* **History**

English language—Homonyms

> *x* Homonyms

English language—Idioms

> *See also* **English language—Provincialisms**
>
> *x* Idioms
>
> *xx* **English language—Provincialisms**

English language—Old English. *See* **Anglo-Saxon language**

English language—Orthography. *See* **English language—Spelling**

English language—Phonetics. *See* **English language—Pronunciation**

English language—Phrases and terms. *See* **English language — Terms and phrases**

English language—Pronunciation

> *x* English language—Phonetics; Phonology; Pronunciation
>
> *xx* **Phonetics**

English language—Provincialisms

> *See also* **English language—Idioms**
>
> *x* Localism; Provincialism
>
> *xx* **English language—Idioms**

English language—Punctuation. *See* **Punctuation**

191

English language—Readers. *See* **Readers**
> Use subdivision *Readers* for languages other than English, e.g. **French language—Readers;** etc.

English language—Rhetoric. *See* **Rhetoric**

English language—Rhyme
> *xx* **Rhyme**

English language—Slang
> *x* Slang

English language—Spelling
> *See also* **Spellers; Spelling reform**
> *x* English language—Orthography; Orthography; Spelling

English language—Spelling reform. *See* **Spelling reform**

English language—Study and teaching

English language—Synonyms and antonyms
> *x* Antonyms; English language—Antonyms; Synonyms

English language—Terms and phrases
> Use for general lists of words and phrases which are applicable to certain situations (curious expressions, public speaking phrases, etc.) rather than to a specific subject. If the list is limited to a special field use name of that subject with the subdivision *Dictionaries,* e.g. **Chemistry—Dictionaries;** etc.
>
> *See also* **English language—Dictionaries**
> *x* English language—Phrases and terms
> *xx* **English language—Dictionaries**

English language—Textbooks for foreigners
> Use under English language only. For other languages use the subdivision *Conversation and phrase books*
> *x* English for foreigners; English language—Conversation and phrase books
> *xx* **Textbooks**

English language—Versification. *See* **Versification**

English letters
> *xx* English literature; Letters

English literature
> Subdivisions used under this heading may be used under other literatures
>
> *See also* **Authors, English; English drama; English essays; English fiction; English letters; English newspapers; English orations; English periodicals; English poetry; English prose literature; English wit and humor; Parodies; Satire, English; Short stories**
> *xx* **Literature**

English literature—Bibliography

English literature—Bio-bibliography
> *x* Bio-bibliography
> *xx* **Authors, English**

English literature—Biography. *See* **Authors, English**

English literature—Collections
> Use for collections of poetry and prose by several authors. Collections of prose are entered under **English prose literature.** Collections of poetry are entered under **English poetry—Collections**
> *See also* **English poetry—Collections; English prose literature**
> *x* Collections of literature
> *xx* **Literature—Collections**

English literature—Criticism. *See* **English literature—History and criticism**

English literature—Dictionaries
> *See also* **English literature—Indexes**
> *x* Dictionaries
> *xx* **English literature—Indexes**

English literature—Examinations, questions, etc.
> *See also* **English literature—Study and teaching**

English literature—History and criticism
> *x* English literature—Criticism
> *xx* **Criticism; History**

English literature—Indexes
> *See also* **English literature—Dictionaries**
> *xx* **English literature—Dictionaries**

English literature—Old English. *See* **Anglo-Saxon literature**

English literature—Outlines, syllabi, etc.
> *See also* **English literature—Study and teaching**
> *x* Outlines, syllabi, etc.
> *xx* **English literature—Study and teaching; Literature—Outlines, syllabi, etc.**

English literature—Study and teaching
> *See also* **English literature—Examinations, questions, etc.; English literature—Outlines, syllabi, etc.**
> *xx* **English literature—Outlines, syllabi, etc.**

English metrical romances. *See* **Romances**

English newspapers
> *xx* **English literature; Newspapers**

English orations
> *xx* **English literature; Orations**

English parodies. *See* **Parodies**

English periodicals
> *xx* **English literature; Periodicals**

English poetry
> *xx* **English literature; Poetry**

English poetry—Collections
> *xx* **English literature—Collections; Poetry—Collections**

English poetry—History and criticism
> *xx* **Criticism; Poetry—History and criticism**

English prose literature

Use for collections of prose writings which may include several literary forms such as essays, fiction, orations, etc.

x Prose literature, English

xx **English literature; English literature —Collections**

English satire. *See* **Satire, English**

English short stories. *See* **Short stories**

English wit and humor

Use for collections of several authors. May be used also for works about **English wit and humor**

xx **English literature; Wit and humor**

Engravers

See also **Etchers; Lithographers**

xx **Artists**

Engraving (May subdiv. geog. adjective form, e.g. **Engraving, American;** etc.)

See also **Aquatint; Engravings; Etching; Gems; Linoleum block printing; Mezzotint engraving; Photoengraving; Wood engraving**

x Copper engraving; Line engraving; Steel engraving

xx **Art; Etching; Graphic arts; Illustration of books**

Engraving, American

x American engraving; U.S.—Engraving

Engravings (May subdiv. geog. adjective form, e.g. **Engravings, American;** etc.)

See also **Color prints; Etchings**

xx **Drawings; Engraving; Etchings; Pictures; Prints**

Engravings, American

x American engravings; U.S.—Engravings

Enlarging (Photography). *See* **Photography —Enlarging**

Enlistment. *See* **U.S. Army—Recruiting, enlistment, etc.; U.S. Navy—Recruiting, enlistment, etc.**

Ensembles (Mathematics). *See* **Set theory**

Ensigns. *See* **Flags**

Ensilage. *See* **Silage and silos**

Enteric fever. *See* **Typhoid fever**

Entertainers

See also **Actors and actresses; Clowns; Comedians; Dancers**

Entertaining

Use for works that treat of the art and skill of entertaining and hospitality

See also **Amusements; Dinners and dining; Etiquette; Games; Luncheons; Parties**

x Guests; Hospitality

xx **Amusements; Etiquette; Home economics**

Entertainments. *See* **Amusements; Christmas entertainments; Church entertainments; Skits**

Entomology. *See* **Insects**

Entomology, Economic. *See* **Insects, Injurious and beneficial**

Entozoa. *See* **Parasites**

Entrance requirements for colleges and universities. *See* **Colleges and universities—Entrance requirements**; and names of individual colleges and universities with the subdivision *Entrance requirements*

Environment. *See* **Adaptation (Biology)**; **Anthropogeography**; **Ecology**; **Human ecology**; **Man—Influence of environment**; **Man—Influence on nature**

Environment and pesticides. *See* **Pesticides and the environment**

Environment and state. *See* **Environmental policy**

Environment, Space. *See* **Space environment**

Environmental policy (May subdiv. geog.)

> *See also* **Conservation of natural resources**; **Human ecology**; **Man—Influence on nature**; **Natural resources**; **Pollution**
>
> *x* Environment and state; State and environment
>
> *xx* **Human ecology**; **Man—Influence on nature**

Environmental policy—U.S.

> *x* American environmental policy; U.S.—Environmental policy

Environmental pollution. *See* **Pollution**

Enzymes

> *See also* **Fermentation**

Eolithic period. *See* **Stone age**

Ephemerides. *See* **Nautical almanacs**

Epic poetry

> *See also* **Romances**
>
> *xx* **Poetry**

Epidemics

> *See also* **Communicable diseases**; also names of contagious diseases, e.g. **Smallpox**; etc.
>
> *x* Pestilences
>
> *xx* **Communicable diseases**; **Diseases**; **Public health**

Epigrams

> *See also* **Proverbs**; **Quotations**; **Toasts**
>
> *x* Sayings
>
> *xx* **Proverbs**; **Wit and humor**

Epigraphy. *See* **Inscriptions**

Epilepsy

> *xx* **Nervous system—Diseases**

Episcopal Church. *See* **Church of England**; **Protestant Episcopal Church in the U.S.A.**

Epistemology. *See* **Knowledge, Theory of**

Epitaphs

> *x* Burial; Graves
>
> *xx* **Biography**; **Cemeteries**; **Inscriptions**; **Tombs**

195

Epithets. *See* **Names; Nicknames**

Epizoa. *See* **Parasites**

Equality

> *See also* **Aristocracy; Democracy; Individualism; Social classes; Socialism**
>
> *x* Inequality; Social equality
>
> *xx* **Democracy; Liberty; Socialism; Sociology**

Equestrianism. *See* **Horsemanship**

Equipment and supplies. *See* appropriate subjects with the subdivision *Equipment and supplies,* e.g. **Sports—Equipment and supplies;** etc.

Ergomanics. *See* **Human engineering**

Erosion

> *See also* **Dust storms; Soil conservation**
>
> *x* Soil erosion
>
> *xx* **Soil conservation**

Errors

> Use for works on errors of judgment, errors of observation, scientific errors, popular misconceptions, etc. Errors in language are entered under names of languages with the subdivision *Errors,* e.g. **English language—Errors;** etc.
>
> *See also* **Superstition**
>
> *x* Fallacies; Mistakes
>
> *xx* **Superstition**

Eruptions. *See* **Geysers; Volcanoes**

Escape life style. *See* **Counter culture**

Escapes

> *x* Prison escapes
>
> *xx* **Adventure and adventurers; Prisons**

Eschatology

> *See also* **Death; End of the world; Future life; Heaven; Hell; Immortality; Millennium; Second Advent**
>
> *x* Intermediate state
>
> *xx* **Theology**

Eskimos

> *x* Esquimaux

Eskimos—Folklore. *See* **Folklore, Eskimo**

Esperanto

> *xx* **Language, Universal**

Espionage (May subdiv. geog. adj. form)

> *See also* **Spies**
>
> *xx* **Secret service; Subversive activities**

Espionage, American

> *x* American espionage

Esquimaux. *See* **Eskimos**

Essay

> Use for works on the appreciation of the essay and on writing the essay
>
> *xx* **Literature**

Essays

> Use for collections of literary essays by authors of different nationalities. Collections of literary essays by American authors are entered under **American essays;** by English authors, under **Eng-**

Essays—*Continued*

       lish essays; etc. Essays limited to a particular subject, by one or more authors, are entered under that subject. If it is not treated comprehensively, add the subdivision *Addresses and essays*

       See also **American essays; English essays**; etc.; also general subjects with the subdivision *Addresses and essays,* e.g. **Agriculture—Addresses and essays; U.S.—History—Addresses and essays**; etc.

    x Collections of literature

    xx **Literature—Collections**

Essences and essential oils

    See also **Flavoring essences; Perfumes**

    x Aromatic plant products; Oils, Essential; Vegetable oils; Volatile oils

    xx **Distillation; Oils and fats**

Estate planning

    See also **Inheritance and transfer tax; Insurance; Investments; Taxation**

    xx **Finance, Personal**

Estate tax. *See* **Inheritance and transfer tax**

Esthetics

    See also **Art appreciation; Color; Criticism; Painting; Poetry; Rhythm; Romanticism; Sculpture**

    x Aesthetics; Beauty; Taste (Esthetics)

    xx **Art**

Estimates. *See* technical subjects with the subdivision *Estimates,* e.g. **Building—Estimates**; etc.

Estrangement (Social psychology). *See* **Alienation (Social Psychology)**

Etchers

    xx **Artists; Engravers**

Etching

    See also **Aquatint; Engraving; Etchings**

    xx **Art; Engraving**

Etchings

    See also **Engravings**

    xx **Drawings; Engravings; Etching; Pictures; Prints**

Eternal life. *See* **Future life**

Eternal punishment. *See* **Hell**

Eternity

    Use for works on the philosophical concept of eternity. Works dealing with the character and form of a future life are entered under **Future life**

    See also **Future life**

    xx **Future life**

Ether (of space)

    xx **Physics; Waves**

Ethical education. *See* **Character education; Religious education**

Ethics (May subdiv. geog. adjective form, e.g.
  Ethics, Japanese; Ethics, Jewish;
  etc.)

  See also
  Behavior
  Business ethics   Joy and sorrow
  Character education   Justice
  Charity   Legal ethics
  Christian ethics   Medical ethics
  Conscience   Political ethics
  Cruelty   Professional ethics
  Duty   Sexual ethics
  Free will and de-   Sin
    terminism   Social ethics
  Friendship   Spiritual life
  Good and evil   Stoics
  Happiness   Utilitarianism
  Honesty
    x Moral philosophy; Morality; Morals;
      Natural law; Philosophy, Moral
    xx Behavior; Civilization; Duty; Life;
      Philosophy; Theology
Ethics, American
    x American ethics; U.S.—Ethics
Ethics, Christian. *See* **Christian ethics**
Ethics, Legal. *See* **Legal ethics**
Ethics, Medical. *See* **Medical ethics**
Ethics, Political. *See* **Political ethics**
Ethics, Professional. *See* **Professional ethics**
Ethics, Sexual. *See* **Sexual ethics**
Ethics, Social. *See* **Social ethics**
Ethiopian-Italian War, 1935-1936. *See* **Italo-Ethiopian War, 1935-1936**
Ethnic groups. *See* **Minorities**
Ethnic psychology. *See* **Race psychology**
Ethnography. *See* **Ethnology**
Ethnology (May subdiv. geog.)
  See also
  Acculturation   Man, Primitive
  Anthropogeography   Manners and cus-
  Anthropology   toms
  Anthropometry   Native races
  Archeology   Race
  Cannibalism   Race problems
  Civilization   Race psychology
  Color of man   Religion, Primitive
  Costume   Sacrifice
  Folklore   Society, Primitive
  Language and lan-   Somatology
    guages   Totems and totem-
  Man, Prehistoric   ism
    also names of races, tribes, and peoples
      (e.g. **Teutonic race; Negroes;** etc.),
      and names of countries with the sub-
      division *Social life and customs,* e.g.
      U.S—Social life and customs; etc.
    x Aborigines; Ethnography; Geographical
      distribution of man; Races of man
    xx **Anthropology; Archeology; Civiliza-**

Ethnology—*Continued*

tion; Geography; History; Man; Science

Ethnology—U.S.

x U.S.—Ethnology

Ethnopsychology. *See* **Race psychology**

Etiquette

See also **Courtesy; Dancing; Dating (Social customs); Dinners and dining; Entertaining; Letter writing; Manners and customs; Table etiquette;** also names of countries with the subdivision *Social life and customs*

x Ceremonies; Manners; Politeness; Salutations; Weddings

xx **Behavior; Courtesy; Entertaining; Manners and customs**

Etymology. *See* names of languages with the subdivision *Etymology,* e.g. **English language—Etymology;** etc.

Eucharist. *See* **Lord's Supper**

Eugenics

See also **Birth control; Heredity**

x Race improvement

xx **Anthropology; Family; Genetics; Heredity; Population; Social problems**

Europe, Central. *See* **Central Europe**

Europe—History

Europe—History—To 476

Europe—History—476-1492

See also **Holy Roman Empire; Hundred Years' War, 1339-1453; Middle Ages —History; Thirteenth century**

xx **Middle Ages—History**

Europe—History—1492-1789

See also names of wars, e.g. **Seven Years' War, 1756-1763; Spanish Succession, War of, 1701-1714; Thirty Years' War, 1618-1648;** etc.

xx **Reformation; Seven Years' War, 1756-1763**

Europe—History—1789-1900

x Europe—History—19th century; Napoleonic Wars

Europe—History—19th century. *See* **Europe—History—1789-1900**

Europe—History—20th century

Europe—History—1914-1945

See also **European War, 1914-1918; World War, 1939-1945**

Europe—History—1945-

Europe—Politics

May be subdivided by period using the same subdivisions as under **Europe—History,** e.g. **Europe—Politics—1789-1900**

See also **European federation**

European common market. *See* **European Economic Community**

199

European Economic Community

　　x Common market; European common
　　　market

European federation

　　x Federation of Europe; Paneuropean fed-
　　　eration; United States of Europe (pro-
　　　posed)

　　xx **Europe—Politics; Federal government;
　　　International organization**

European War, 1914-1918 (May subdiv. geog.)
　　May be subdivided like **World War, 1939-
　　1945**

　　x War of 1914; Wars; World War, 1914-
　　　1918

　　xx **Europe—History—1914-1945; History,
　　　Modern—20th century; World poli-
　　　tics**

European War, 1914-1918—Economic aspects

　　Use for works treating of the economic
　　causes of the war and the effect of the
　　war on commerce and industry

　　See also **European War, 1914-1918—Fi-
　　　nance**

　　xx **European War, 1914-1918—Finance;
　　　Reconstruction (1914-1939); War—
　　　Economic aspects**

European War, 1914-1918—Finance

　　Use for works on the cost and financing of
　　the war, including war debts, and the
　　effect of the war on financial systems,
　　including inflation

　　See also **European War, 1914-1918—Eco-
　　　nomic aspects**

　　x War debts

　　xx **Debts, Public; European War, 1914-
　　　1918—Economic aspects**

European, War, 1914-1918—Gas warfare. *See*
　　**Gases—Asphyxiating and poisonous
　　—War use**

European War, 1914-1918—German propa-
　　ganda. *See* **Propaganda, German**

European War, 1914-1918—Peace
　　See also **League of Nations**

European War, 1914-1918—Propaganda
　　See also **Propaganda, German**
　　xx **Propaganda**

European War, 1914-1918—Reconstruction. *See*
　　Reconstruction (1914-1939)

European War, 1914-1918—Reparations
　　x Reparations (European War)

**European War, 1914-1918—Territorial ques-
　　tions**
　　See also **Mandates**

European War, 1914-1918—U.S.
　　x U.S.—European War, 1914-1918; U.S.
　　　—History—European War, 1914-1918

European War, 1939-1945. *See* **World War,
　　1939-1945**

Evacuation of civilians. *See* names of wars with the subdivision *Evacuation of civilians,* e.g. **World War, 1939-1945—Evacuation of civilians;** etc.

Evaluation of literature. *See* **Book reviews; Books and reading; Books and reading—Best books; Criticism; Literature—History and criticism**

Evangelistic work
> *See also* **Conversion; Missions; Revivals; Salvation Army**
> *xx* **Church work; Missions; Revivals**

Evening and continuation schools
> *See also* **Adult education**
> *x* Continuation schools; Evening schools; Night schools
> *xx* **Adult education; Education; Education, Compulsory; Education, Secondary; Public schools; Schools; Technical education**

Evening schools. *See* **Evening and continuation schools**

Evergreens
> *xx* **Landscape gardening; Shrubs; Trees**

Evidences of Christianity. *See* **Apologetics**

Evidences of the Bible. *See* **Bible—Evidences, authority, etc.**

Evil. *See* **Good and evil**

Evil spirits. *See* **Demonology**

Evolution
> *See also*

Adaptation (Biology)	**Man—Influence of environment**
Anatomy, Comparative	**Man—Origin and antiquity**
Biology	**Mendel's law**
Color of animals	**Natural selection**
Color of man	**Religion and science**
Creation	
Embryology	**Social change**
Heredity	**Variation (Biology)**
Life—Origin	

> *x* Darwinism; Development; Mutation (Biology); Origin of species
> *xx* **Biology; Creation; Genetics; Heredity; Man—Origin and antiquity; Natural selection; Philosophy, Modern; Religion and science; Variation (Biology); Zoology**

Ex libris. *See* **Bookplates**

Examinations
> Use for general works about examinations, their value, etc. Works discussing the requirements for examinations in particular branches of study, or compilations of questions and answers for such examinations, are entered under the subject with the subdivision *Examinations, questions, etc.,* e.g. **English lan-**

Examinations—*Continued*

guage—**Examinations, questions, etc.;**
etc.

See also **Civil service—Examinations;
Colleges and universities—Entrance
requirements; Mental tests;** also particular branches of study with the subdivision *Examinations, questions, etc.,*
e.g. **English language—Examinations,
questions, etc.; Music—Examinations, questions, etc.;** etc.

x Achievement tests; Objective tests;
Tests

xx **Educational tests and measurements;
Teaching**

Ex-Catholic priests. *See* **Ex-priests**

Excavation

xx **Civil engineering; Tunnels**

Excavations (Archeology) (May subdiv.
geog.)

See also **Mounds and mound builders**

x Earthworks (Archeology) ; Ruins

xx **Archeology; Cities and towns; Ruined,
extinct, etc.; Mounds and mound
builders**

Excavations (Archeology)—U.S.

x U.S.—Excavations (Archeology)

Exceptional children

See also **Gifted children; Handicapped
children; Problem children; Slow
learning children**

x Abnormal children; Children, Abnormal;
Children, Exceptional

xx **Child study; Children; Education, Elementary**

Exchange

See also **Commerce; Foreign exchange;
Money; Stock exchange**

xx **Commerce**

Exchange, Bills of. *See* **Bills of exchange**

Exchange of persons programs

See also classes of persons participating
in an exchange; e.g. **Teachers, Interchange of;** etc.

x Interchange of visitors; Specialists exchange programs; Visitors' exchange
programs

xx **Cultural relations; International cooperation**

Exchange of prisoners of war. *See* **Prisoners
of war**

Exchange of teachers. *See* **Teachers, Interchange of**

Executions. *See* **Capital punishment**

Executive ability

See also **Efficiency, Industrial; Leadership**

x Administrative ability

xx **Ability; Efficiency, Industrial**

Executive departments. *See* names of countries, states, etc. with the subdivision *Executive departments,* e.g. **U.S.—Executive departments**; etc.

Executive investigations. *See* **Governmental investigations**

Executive power (May subdiv. geog.)

Use for works that discuss the duties and rights of the highest administrative authority of a country, often as compared or contrasted with the legislative power

See also **Monarchy; Presidents**

x Presidents—Powers and duties

xx **Constitutional law; Political science; Presidents**

Executive power—U.S.

x Presidents—U.S.—Power; U.S.—Executive power

Executors and administrators

See also **Wills**

x Administrators and executors

xx **Inheritance and succession; Wills**

Exegesis, Biblical. *See* **Bible—Criticism, interpretation, etc.**

Exercise

See also **Gymnastics; Physical education and training; Physical fitness;** also names of special kinds of exercises, e.g. **Rowing**; etc.

xx **Hygiene; Physical education and training; Weight control**

Exhaustion. *See* **Fatigue**

Exhibitions

See also **Fashion shows; Flower shows;** etc.; also subjects with the subdivision *Exhibitions,* e.g. **Art—Exhibitions; Printing—Exhibitions;** etc.; and names of exhibitions, e.g. **Expo '70**; etc.

x Expositions; Industrial exhibitions; International exhibitions; World's fairs

xx **Fairs**

Exiles. *See* **Refugees**

Existentialism

xx **Metaphysics; Ontology; Philosophy, Modern; Phenomenology**

Ex-nuns

xx **Monasticism and religious orders for women**

Exobiology. *See* **Space biology**

Exorcism. *See* **Witchcraft**

Expeditions, Antarctic and Arctic. *See* **Arctic regions; Antarctic regions;** and names of expeditions, e.g. **Byrd Antarctic Expedition, 1st, 1928-1930**; etc.

Expeditions, Scientific. *See* **Scientific expeditions**

Experience. *See* **Empiricism**

Experimental farms. *See* **Agricultural experiment stations**

Experimental films
    x Avant-garde films; Moving pictures, Experimental; Personal films; Underground films
    xx **Moving pictures**

Experimental methods in education. *See* **Education—Experimental methods**

Experimental psychology. *See* **Psychology, Physiological**

Experimental schools. *See* **Free schools**

Experimental theater
    x Avant-garde theater
    xx **Theater**

Experimental universities. *See* **Free universities**

Experiments, Scientific. *See* **Science—Experiments**; and particular branches of science with the subdivision *Experiments,* e.g. **Chemistry—Experiments**; etc.

Exploration, Submarine. *See* **Underwater exploration**

Exploration, Underwater. *See* **Underwater exploration**

Explorations. *See* **America—Discovery and exploration; Discoveries (in geography); Explorers;** and names of countries with the subdivision *Exploring expeditions,* e.g. **U.S.—Exploring expeditions**; etc.

Explorer (Artificial satellite)
    xx **Artificial satellites**

Explorers
    See also **America—Discovery and exploration; Discoveries (in geography); Travelers; Voyages and travels;** also names of countries with the subdivisions *Description and travel* and *Exploring expeditions,* e.g. **U.S.—Description and travel; U.S.—Exploring expeditions;** etc.; and names of individual explorers
    x Discoverers; Explorations; Navigators; Voyagers
    xx **Adventure and adventurers; America —Discovery and exploration; Discoveries (in geography); Heroes; Travelers; Voyages and travels**

Exploring expeditions. *See* names of countries with the subdivision *Exploring expeditions* (e.g. **U.S.—Exploring expeditions;** etc.); and names of expeditions, e.g. **Lewis and Clark Expedition;** etc.

Explosions
    xx **Accidents**

Explosives

> *See also* **Ammunition; Dynamite; Gunpowder; Torpedoes**
>
> *xx* **Chemistry**

Expo '70

> *x* Japan World's Exposition, Osaka, 1970; Osaka. World's Fair, 1970
>
> *xx* **Exhibitions; Fairs**

Exports. *See* **Commerce; Tariff**

Expositions. *See* **Exhibitions**

Express highways

> *x* Freeways; Limited access highways; Motorways; Parkways; Superhighways; Turnpikes (Modern); Toll roads
>
> *xx* **Roads; Traffic engineering**

Express service

> *See also* **Pony express**
>
> *xx* **Railroads; Transportation**

Expression. *See* **Nonverbal communication**

Expressionism (Art)

> *See also* **Postimpressionism (Art)**
>
> *xx* **Painting; Postimpressionism (Art)**

Ex-priests

> *x* Catholic ex-priests; Ex-Catholic priests
>
> *xx* **Catholic church—Clergy; Priests**

Expropriation. *See* **Eminent domain**

Ex-service men. *See* **Veterans**

Extension work, Agricultural. *See* **Agricultural extension work**

Extermination. *See* **Pest control**

Extinct animals

> *See also* **Rare animals;** also names of extinct animals, e.g. **Mastodon;** etc.
>
> *x* Animals, Extinct
>
> *xx* **Fossils; Rare animals**

Extinct cities. *See* **Cities and towns, Ruined, extinct, etc.**

Extinct plants. *See* **Plants, Fossil**

Extracurricular activities. *See* **Student activities**

Extragalactic nebulae. *See* **Galaxies**

Extrasensory perception

> *x* ESP
>
> *xx* **Clairvoyance; Psychical research; Thought transference**

Extraterrestrial environment. *See* **Space environment**

Extraterrestrial life. *See* **Life on other planets; Space biology**

Extravehicular activity (Manned space flight)

> *x* Space vehicles—Extravehicular activity; Walking in space
>
> *xx* **Manned space flight**

Extremism (Political science). *See* **Right and left (Political science)**

Eye

> *See also* **Optometry; Vision**
>
> *xx* **Head; Optometry; Vision**

Eyeglasses
    See also **Lenses**
    x Contact lenses; Spectacles; Sun glasses
FBI. *See* **U.S. Federal Bureau of Investigation**
FM Radio. *See* **Radio frequency modulation**
FORTRAN (Computer program language)
    x Formula translation (Computer program language); Fortran (Computer program language)
    xx **Programming languages (Electronic computers)**
Fables
    Use for books in which animals or inanimate objects speak and act like human beings. Also used for books about fables
    See also **Animals—Stories; Folklore; Parables**
    x Legends and stories of animals; Tales
    xx **Allegories; Animals—Stories; Fiction; Folklore; Legends; Literature; Parables**
Fabric pictures. *See* **Collage**
Fabrics. *See* **Textile industry and fabrics**
Fabrics, Synthetic. *See* **Synthetic fabrics**
Face
    See also **Nose; Physiognomy**
    xx **Head; Physiognomy**
Facetiae. *See* **Anecdotes; Wit and humor**
Factories
    See also **Mills and millwork; Workshops;** also headings beginning with the word **Factory**
    x Mill and factory buildings
    xx **Industrial buildings; Mills and millwork; Workshops**
Factories—Management. *See* **Factory management**
Factories—Training departments. *See* **Employees—Training**
Factory and trade waste
    See also **Pollution; Refuse and refuse disposal; Waste products; Water—Pollution**
    x Factory waste; Industrial wastes; Trade waste; Waste disposal
    xx **Refuse and refuse disposal; Waste products; Water—Pollution**
Factory management
    Use for works on the technical problems of manufacturing processes. Works on general principles of management of industries are entered under **Industrial management**
    See also **Efficiency, Industrial; Employees' representation in management; Foremen; Job analysis; Motion study; Office management; Personnel management; Time study**

Factory management—*Continued*

    x Factories—Management; Production engineering; Shop management

    xx **Efficiency, Industrial; Industrial management; Management; Personnel management**

Factory schools. *See* **Employees—Training**

Factory waste. *See* **Factory and trade waste**

Faculty (Education). *See* **Colleges and universities—Faculty; Educators; Teachers**

Faience. *See* **Pottery**

Failure (in business). *See* **Bankruptcy**

Fair employment practice. *See* **Discrimination in employment**

Fair housing. *See* **Discrimination in housing**

Fair trade. *See* **Competition, Unfair**

Fair trade (Tariff). *See* **Free trade and protection**

Fair use (Copyright)

    xx **Copyright**

Fairies

    See also **Fairy tales**

    x Elves; Gnomes; Goblins

    xx **Folklore; Superstition**

Fairs

    See also **Exhibitions; Markets;** also names of fairs; e.g. **Expo '70;** etc.

    x Bazaars; Trade fairs; World's fairs

    xx **Markets**

Fairy tales

    See also **Folklore**

    x Children's stories; Stories; Tales

    xx **Children's literature; Fairies; Fiction; Folklore; Legends; Literature**

Faith

    Use for works treating of religious faith and doubt. Works treating of doubt from the philosophical standpoint are entered under **Belief and doubt**

    See also **Agnosticism; Atheism; Salvation; Skepticism; Truth**

    x Religious belief; Trust in God

    xx **Christian life; Religion; Spiritual life; Theology**

Faith, Confessions of. *See* **Creeds**

Faith cure

    See also **Christian Science; Mental healing; Miracles; Therapeutics, Suggestive**

    x Divine healing; Mind cure; Spiritual healing

    xx **Christian Science; Medicine and religion; Mental healing; Mind and body; Subconsciousness; Therapeutics, Suggestive**

Faithfulness. *See* **Loyalty**

Falconry

    x Hawking

    xx **Game and game birds; Hunting**

Fall. *See* **Autumn**

Fallacies. *See* **Errors; Logic**
Falling stars. *See* **Meteors**
Fallout, Radioactive. *See* **Radioactive fallout**
Fallout shelters. *See* **Air raid shelters**
False advertising. *See* **Advertising, Fraudulent**
Falsehood. *See* **Truthfulness and falsehood**
Family

    See also

Clans and clan system	**Family life education**
Divorce	**Home**
Domestic relations	**Marriage**
Eugenics	**Parent and child**
	Woman

    also names of members of the family, e.g., **Children; Fathers; Mothers;** etc.

    x Family relations; Home life

    xx **Domestic relations; Home; Human relations; Marriage; Sociology**

Family—Religious life

    x Family devotions; Family prayers; Family worship

Family budget. *See* **Budgets, Household**
Family devotions. *See* **Devotional exercises; Family—Religious life**
Family life education

    See also **Counseling; Finance, Personal; Home economics; Human relations; Sex instruction**

    xx **Behavior; Family; Marriage**

Family histories. *See* **Genealogy**
Family names. *See* **Names, Personal**
Family planning. *See* **Birth control**
Family prayers. *See* **Devotional exercises; Family—Religious life**
Family relations. *See* **Domestic relations; Family**
Family social work. *See* **Social case work**
Family worship. *See* **Family—Religious life**
Famines

    xx **Food supply**

Fancy dress. *See* **Costume**
Fans

    xx **Costume**

Fantastic fiction

    See also **Ghost stories; Science fiction**

    xx **Fiction**

Far East. *See* **East (Far East)**
Far Eastern question. *See* **Eastern question (Far East)**
Farm animals. *See* **Domestic animals; Livestock**
Farm buildings

    x Architecture, Rural; Barns; Buildings, Farm; Farm houses; Farmhouses; Rural architecture; Stables

    xx **Architecture; Architecture, Domestic; Buildings**

Farm credit. *See* **Agricultural credit**
Farm crops. *See* **Farm produce**

Farm engines

>*See also* **Agricultural engineering; Tractors**

>*xx* **Agricultural machinery; Engines; Gas and oil engines; Steam engines**

Farm houses. *See* **Farm buildings**

Farm implements. *See* **Agricultural machinery**

Farm laborers. *See* **Agricultural laborers**

Farm life (May subdiv. geog.)

>*See also* **Country life; Ranch life; Sociology, Rural**

>*x* Rural life

>*xx* **Country life; Sociology, Rural**

Farm life—U.S.

>*x* U.S.—Farm life

Farm machinery. *See* **Agricultural machinery**

Farm management

>*See also* **Agriculture—Economic aspects**

>*xx* **Agriculture — Economic aspects; Farms; Management**

Farm mechanics. *See* **Agricultural engineering; Agricultural machinery**

Farm produce

>*See also* names of farm products, e.g. **Hay;** etc.

>*x* Agricultural products; Crops; Farm crops

>*xx* **Food; Raw materials**

Farm produce—Marketing

>*See also* **Agriculture—Economic aspects**

>*x* Food trade; Fruit—Marketing; Marketing of farm produce; Vegetables—Marketing

>*xx* **Agriculture—Economic aspects; Marketing; Prices**

Farm tenancy

>Use for works on the economic and social aspects of farm tenancy. Works that treat of the legal aspect are entered under **Landlord and tenant**

>*x* Agriculture—Tenant farming; Farming on shares; Sharecropping; Tenant farming

>*xx* **Farms; Land tenure; Landlord and tenant**

Farmers' cooperatives. *See* **Agriculture, Cooperative**

Farmhouses. *See* **Farm buildings**

Farming. *See* **Agriculture**

Farming, Dry. *See* **Dry farming**

Farming on shares. *See* **Farm tenancy**

Farms

>*See also* **Farm management; Farm tenancy**

>*xx* **Agriculture; Land; Real estate**

Farms, Experimental. *See* **Agricultural experiment stations**

Fascism (May subdiv. geog.)

>*See also* **National socialism**

>*x* Authoritarianism

Fascism—*Continued*

   xx **National socialism; Totalitarianism**

Fascism—Germany. *See* **National socialism**

Fascism—U.S.

   x U.S.—Fascism

Fashion

   Use for works describing the prevailing
      mode or style in dress. Historical works
      on styles of particular countries or
      periods are entered under **Costume**

   See also **Clothing and dress; Costume;
      Dressmaking; Tailoring**

   x Style in dress

   xx **Clothing and dress; Costume**

Fashion models. *See* **Models, Fashion**

Fashion shows

   xx **Exhibitions**

Fashionable society. *See* **Upper classes**

Faster reading. *See* **Rapid reading**

Fasting

   See also **Asceticism; Fasts and feasts**

   x Abstinence

Fasts and feasts

   Use for works on religious fasts and
      feasts in general and on Christian fes-
      tivals. Works limited to Jewish festi-
      vals are entered under **Fasts and
      feasts—Judaism.** Works on secular
      festivals are entered under **Festivals**

   See also **Christmas; Easter; Festivals;
      Good Friday; Holidays; Lent;
      Thanksgiving Day**

   x Bible—Festivals; Church festivals;
      Days; Ecclesiastical fasts and feasts;
      Feasts; Fiestas; Religious festivals

   xx **Christian antiquities; Fasting; Festi-
      vals; Holidays; Rites and ceremo-
      nies**

Fasts and feasts—Judaism

   See also names of individual fasts and
      feasts, e.g. **Yom Kippur;** etc.

   x Festivals—Jews; Jewish holidays; Jews
      —Festivals

Fat. *See* **Oils and fats; Weight control**

Fate and fatalism

   See also **Free will and determinism; Pre-
      destination**

   x Destiny; Fortune

   xx **Philosophy**

Fathers

   xx **Family; Parent and child**

Fathers of the church

   See also **Church history—Primitive and
      early church; Saints**

   x Church fathers

   xx **Christian biography; Christian litera-
      ture, Early; Church history; Church
      history—Primitive and early church;
      Saints**

Fatigue
> *See also* **Rest**
> *x* Exhaustion; Weariness
> *xx* **Physiology; Rest**

Fats. *See* **Oils and fats**

Fauna. *See* **Animals; Zoology**

Fayence. *See* **Pottery**

Fear
> *See also* **Courage**
> *x* Anxiety
> *xx* **Courage; Emotions; Nervous system—Diseases; Neuroses**

Feasts. *See* **Fasts and feasts**

Federal aid to education
> *x* Education—Federal aid
> *xx* **Colleges and universities—Finance; Education—Finance; Education and state**

Federal aid to libraries
> *x* Libraries—Federal aid
> *xx* **Libraries and state; Library finance**

Federal budget. *See* **Budget—U.S.**

Federal Bureau of Investigation. *See* **U.S. Federal Bureau of Investigation**

Federal courts. *See* **Courts—U.S.**

Federal government
> *See also* **Democracy; European federation; State governments**
> *x* Confederacies
> *xx* **Constitutional law; Democracy; Political science; Republics; State governments**

Federal libraries. *See* **Libraries, Governmental**

Federal Reserve banks
> *xx* **Banks and banking**

Federal revenue sharing. *See* **Intergovernmental tax relations**

Federal-state tax relations. *See* **Intergovernmental tax relations**

Federation, International. *See* **International organization**

Federation of Europe. *See* **European federation**

Feeble-minded. *See* **Mentally handicapped**

Feeding and feeds
> *See also* **Forage plants; Hay; Root crops; Silage and silos;** also names of feeds, e.g. **Oats;** etc.
> *x* Fodder
> *xx* **Grasses; Hay; Livestock; Root crops**

Feeling. *See* **Perception; Touch**

Feelings. *See* **Emotions**

Feet. *See* **Foot**

Fellowships. *See* **Scholarships, fellowships, etc.**

Felony. *See* **Crime and criminals**

Feminine psychology. *See* **Woman—Psychology**

Feminism. *See* **Woman—Social conditions**

Fencing

    See also **Dueling**

    x Fighting

    xx Dueling; Physical education and training

Fermentation

    See also **Bacteriology; Wine and wine making; Yeast**

    xx Bacteriology; Chemistry; Enzymes; Wine and wine making

Ferns

    xx **Plants**

Fertilization of plants

    x Plants—Fertilization; Pollination

    xx Flowers; Insects; Plant breeding; Plant physiology; Plants

Fertilizers and manures

    See also **Agricultural chemistry; Lime; Nitrates; Phosphates; Potash**

    x Compost; Manures

    xx **Agricultural chemistry; Soils**

Festivals (May subdiv. geog.)

    See note under **Fasts and feasts**

    See also **Fasts and feasts; Holidays; Music festivals; Pageants**

    x Carnivals; Days; Fiestas

    xx **Fasts and feasts; Manners and customs; Pageants**

Festivals—Jews. *See* **Fasts and feasts—Judaism**

Festivals—U.S.

    x U.S.—Festivals

Fetal death. *See* **Abortion**

Feudalism

    See also **Chivalry; Clans and clan system; Middle Ages; Peasantry**

    x Fiefs; Vassals

    xx Chivalry; Civilization, Medieval; Land; Land tenure; Middle Ages—History

Fever

    See also names of fevers, e.g. **Malaria**; etc.

    xx **Medicine—Practice; Therapeutics**

Fiat money. *See* **Paper money**

Fibers

    See also **Cotton; Flax; Hemp; Linen; Paper; Silk; Wool**

    x Textile fibers

    xx **Cotton; Hemp**

Fibers, Glass. *See* **Glass fibers**

Fiction

    Use for works dealing with fiction as a literary form

    See also

Allegories	Ghost stories
Animals—Stories	Historical fiction
College stories	Horror stories
Fables	Legends
Fairy tales	Mystery and detective stories
Fantastic fiction	
Folklore	Novelists

Fiction—*Continued*

Plots (Drama, fiction, etc.)
Romances
Romanticism
School stories
Science fiction
Sea stories
Short stories
Short story
Vocational stories

also **American fiction; English fiction;** etc.; and names of historical events and characters with the subdivision *Fiction,* e.g. **Slavery in the U.S.—Fiction; Napoléon I, Emperor of the French—Fiction;** etc.

x Novels; Stories

xx **Literature**

Fiction, American; Fiction, English; etc. *See* **American fiction; English fiction;** etc.

Fiction, Historical. *See* **Historical fiction**

Fiction—History and criticism

Fiction—Plots. *See* **Plots (Drama, fiction, etc.)**

Fiction—Technique

xx **Authorship**

Fictitious animals. *See* **Animals, Mythical**

Fictitious names. *See* **Pseudonyms**

Fiddle. *See* **Violin**

Fiefs. *See* **Feudalism; Land tenure**

Field athletics. *See* **Track athletics**

Field hockey

xx **Hockey**

Field hospitals. *See* **Hospitals, Military; Medicine, Military**

Field sports. *See* **Hunting; Sports**

Fiestas. *See* **Fasts and feasts; Festivals**

Fifth column. *See* **Subversive activities**

Fighting. *See* **Battles; Boxing; Bullfights; Dueling; Fencing; Gladiators; Military art and science; Naval art and science; Self-defense; War**

Figure drawing

See also **Figure painting**

x Human figure in art

xx **Anatomy, Artistic; Drawing; Figure painting**

Figure painting

See also **Figure drawing; Portrait painting**

x Human figure in art

xx **Anatomy, Artistic; Figure drawing; Painting; Portrait painting**

Figure skating. *See* **Skating**

Files and filing

See also **Indexing**

x Alphabeting; Filing systems

xx **Indexing**

Filing systems. *See* **Files and filing**

Filling stations. *See* **Automobiles—Service stations**

Filmstrips

See also **Slides (Photography)**

x Strip films

Filmstrips—*Continued*
>   *xx* Audio-visual materials; Photography;
>   Slides (Photography)

Finance (May subdiv. geog.)
>   *See also*
>
> | | |
> |---|---|
> | Bankruptcy | Interest and usury |
> | Banks and banking | Internal revenue |
> | Bonds | Investments |
> | Budget | Metropolitan |
> | Capital | finance |
> | Church finance | Money |
> | Commerce | Municipal finance |
> | Credit | Paper money |
> | Currency question | Prices |
> | Debts, Public | Securities |
> | Finance, Personal | Speculation |
> | Foreign exchange | Stock exchange |
> | Income | Tariff |
> | Income tax | Taxation |
> | Inflation (Finance) | Wealth |
> | Insurance | |
>
>   *also* subjects with the subdivision *Finance,*
>   e.g. **Education—Finance**; etc.
>   *x* Funds; Public finance
>   *xx* **Budget; Currency question; Economics**

Finance, Church. *See* **Church finance**
Finance, Municipal. *See* **Municipal finance**
Finance, Personal
>   *See also* **Budgets, Household; Consumer
>   credit; Estate planning; Insurance;
>   Investments; Saving and thrift**
>   *x* Budgets, Personal; Personal finance
>   *xx* **Family life education; Finance**

Finance—U.S.
>   *x* U.S.—Finance
>   ✓ *Financial disclosure law*

Financiers. *See* **Capitalists and financiers**
Fine arts. *See* **The arts**
Finger alphabet. *See* **Deaf—Means of com-
    munication**
Finger marks. *See* **Fingerprints**
Finger painting
>   *x* Painting, Finger
>   *xx* **Children as artists; Painting**

Fingerprints
>   *x* Finger marks
>   *xx* **Anthropometry; Crime and criminals
>   —Identification; Criminal investiga-
>   tion; Identification**

Finishes and finishing. *See* **Lacquer and lac-
    quering; Paint; Painting, Industrial;
    Varnish and varnishing; Wood fin-
    ishing**
Finno-Russian War, 1939-1940. *See* **Russo-Fin-
    nish War, 1939-1940**

Fire
>   *See also* **Combustion; Fires; Fuel; Heat;
>   Heating**
>   *xx* **Chemistry; Combustion; Heat**

Fire balls. See **Meteors**
Fire bombs. See **Incendiary bombs**

Fire departments

Fire engines

    xx **Engines; Fire extinction**

Fire extinction

    See also **Fire engines**

    xx **Fire prevention; Fires**

Fire insurance. *See* **Insurance, Fire**

Fire prevention

    See also **Fire extinction; Fireproofing;** also names of cities with the subdivision *Fires and fire prevention,* e.g. **Chicago—Fires and fire prevention;** etc.

    x Prevention of fire

    xx **Fires**

Firearms

    See also **Gunpowder; Ordnance; Pistols; Rifles; Shooting; Shotguns**

    x Guns; Small arms; Weapons

    xx **Arms and armor; Shooting**

Firearms industry and trade

    Use for works on the small arms industry. Works on heavy firearms are entered under **Ordnance**

Firemen

Fireplaces

    See also **Chimneys**

    xx **Architecture—Details; Heating**

Fireproofing

    xx **Fire prevention; Insurance, Fire**

Fires

    See also **Fire extinction; Fire prevention; Forest fires; Insurance, Fire;** also names of cities with the subdivision *Fires and fire prevention,* e.g. **Chicago—Fires and fire prevention;** etc.

    xx **Accidents; Disasters; Fire**

Fireworks

First aid

    See also **Accidents; Artificial respiration; Bandages and bandaging**

    x Emergencies; Injuries; Wounded, First aid to

    xx **Accidents; Hospitals, Military; Medicine, Military; Nurses and nursing; Rescue work; Sick**

First editions. *See* **Bibliography—First editions**

Fish. *See* **Fishes**

Fish as food. *See* **Sea food**

Fish culture

    x Fish hatcheries

    xx **Aquariums; Fishes**

Fish hatcheries. *See* **Fish culture**

Fisheries (May subdiv. geog.)

    Use for works on the fishing industry

    See also **Fishes; Pearlfisheries; Whaling**

    x Fishing industry; Sea fisheries

    xx **Fishes; Marine resources; Natural resources**

Fisheries—U.S.
    x U.S.—Fisheries
Fishes (May subdiv. geog.)
    Names of fishes are not included in this list but are to be added as needed, e.g. **Salmon**; etc.
    See also **Aquariums; Fish culture; Fisheries; Fishing; Sea food; Tropical fish**; also names of fishes, e.g. **Salmon**; etc.
    x Fish; Ichthyology
    xx **Fisheries; Marine animals; Vertebrates**
Fishes—Geographical distribution. *See* **Geographical distribution of animals and plants**
Fishes—Photography. *See* **Photography of fishes**
Fishes—U.S.
    x U.S.—Fishes
Fishing (May subdiv. geog.)
    Use for works on fishing as a sport. Works on fishing as an industry are entered under **Fisheries**
    See also **Flies, Artificial; Fly-casting; Spear fishing; Trout fishing**
    x Angling
    xx **Fishes; Water sports**
Fishing—Equipment and supplies
    x Fishing tackle
Fishing—U.S.
    x U.S.—Fishing
Fishing-flies. *See* **Flies, Artificial**
Fishing industry. *See* **Fisheries**
Fishing tackle. *See* **Fishing—Equipment and supplies**
Five-day work week. *See* **Hours of labor**
Flags (May subdiv. geog.)
    See also **Signals and signaling**
    x Banners; Ensigns
    xx **Heraldry; Signals and signaling**
Flags—U.S.
    x American flag; U.S.—Flags
Flats. *See* **Apartment houses**
Flatware, Silver. *See* **Silverware**
Flavoring essences
    xx **Cookery; Essences and essential oils; Food**
Flax
    See also **Linen**
    xx **Fibers; Linen; Yarn**
Flies
    See also names of flies; e.g., **Fruit flies**; etc.
    x Diptera; Fly; House flies; Pests
    xx **Household pests; Insects as carriers of disease**
Flies, Artificial
    See also **Fly-casting**
    x Artificial flies; Fishing-flies
    xx **Fishing**

Flight

> *See also* **Aeronautics**
>
> *x* Birds—Flight; Flying; Locomotion
>
> *xx* **Aeronautics; Birds**

Flight to the moon. *See* **Space flight to the moon**

Flight training. *See* **Aeronautics—Study and teaching; Airplanes—Piloting**

Flights around the world. *See* **Aeronautics—Flights**

Flint implements. *See* **Stone implements**

Floats (Parades). *See* **Parades**

Flood control

> *See also* **Dams; Forest influences; Rivers**
>
> *xx* **Forest influences; Hydraulic engineering**

Floods

> *See also* **Reclamation of land; Rivers;** also names of rivers, cities, etc. with the subdivision *Floods,* e.g. **Chicago—Floods;** etc.
>
> *xx* **Disasters; Meteorology; Rain and rainfall; Rivers; Water**

Floods and forests. *See* **Forest influences**

Floors

> *xx* **Architecture—Details; Building; Carpentry**

Flora. *See* **Botany; Plants**

Floral decoration. *See* **Flower arrangement**

Floral design. *See* **Design, Decorative**

Floriculture. *See* **Flower gardening**

Florists' designs. *See* **Flower arrangement**

Flour and flour mills

> *See also* **Grain; Wheat**
>
> *x* Breadstuffs; Grist mills; Milling (Flour)
>
> *xx* **Bread; Mills and millwork; Wheat**

Flower arrangement

> Use for works on the artistic arrangement of flowers, including decoration of houses, churches, etc. with flowers
>
> *x* Designs, Floral; Floral decoration; Florists' designs; Flowers—Arrangement
>
> *xx* **Decoration and ornament; Flowers; Table setting and arrangement**

Flower gardening

> Use for practical works on the cultivation of flowering plants for either commercial or private purposes
>
> *See also*

Annuals (Plants)	**Perennials**
Bulbs	**Plant breeding**
Flowers	**Plant propagation**
Greenhouses	**Plants, Ornamental**
House plants	**Window gardening**

> *also* names of flowers, e.g. **Roses;** etc.
>
> *x* Floriculture
>
> *xx* **Botany; Flowers; Gardening; Plants**

Flower painting and illustration
    x Flowers in art
    xx **Flowers; Painting; Plants in art**
Flower shows
    x Flowers—Exhibitions
    xx **Exhibitions**
Flowers (May subdiv. geog.)
    Use for general works on the botanical characteristics of flowers, guides for studying and classifying them or for study of flowers from the artistic point of view. Works limited to the cultivation of flowers are entered under **Flower gardening**
    Names of flowers are not included in this list but are to be added as needed, in the plural form; e.g. **Roses**; etc.
    See also

Annuals (Plants)	**Flower painting and**
Fertilization of	**illustration**
plants	**Perennials**
Flower arrange-	**Plants**
ment	**State flowers**
Flower gardening	**Wild flowers**
	Window gardening

    also names of flowers, e.g. **Roses**; etc.
    xx **Botany; Flower gardening; Plants**
Flowers—Arrangement. *See* **Flower arrangement**
Flowers, Artificial. *See* **Artificial flowers**
Flowers, Drying
    x Dried flowers
Flowers—Exhibitions. *See* **Flower shows**
Flowers, State. *See* **State flowers**
Flowers—Stories
    x Stories
Flowers—U.S.
    x U.S.—Flowers
Flowers, Wild. *See* **Wild flowers**
Flowers in art. *See* **Design, Decorative, Flower painting and illustration; Plants in art**
Fluorescent lighting
    x Electric lighting, Fluorescent; Light, Electric
    xx **Lighting**
Fluoridation of water. *See* **Water—Fluoridation**
Flute
    xx **Wind instruments**
Fly. *See* **Flies**
Fly-casting
    xx **Fishing; Flies, Artificial**
Flying. *See* **Flight**
Flying bombs. *See* **Guided missiles**
✓ **Flying saucers**
    x UFO; Unidentified flying objects
    xx **Aeronautics**
Fodder. *See* **Feeding and feeds**

✓ Flu. See Influenza

Fog

    xx **Meteorology; Water**

Fog signals. *See* **Signals and signaling**

Foliage. *See* **Leaves**

Folk art (May subdiv. geog. adjective form, e.g. **Folk art, Swedish;** etc.)

    Use for general and historical works on peasant and popular art in the fields of decorative arts, music, dancing, theater, etc.

    See also **Art, Primitive; Art industries and trade; Arts and crafts**

    x Peasant art

    xx **Art; Art, Primitive; Art and society; Art industries and trade; Arts and crafts**

Folk art, American

    x American folk art; U.S.—Folk art

Folk dancing (May subdiv. geog. adjective form, e.g. **Folk dancing, Swedish;** etc.)

    See also **Indians of North America— Dances; Square dancing**

    x Clog dances; National dances

    xx **Dancing**

Folk dancing, American

    x American folk dancing; U.S.—Folk dancing

Folk drama

    See also **Puppets and puppet plays**

    x Folk plays

    xx **Drama**

Folk lore. *See* **Folklore**

Folk music. *See* **Folk songs**

Folk plays. *See* **Folk drama**

Folk psychology. *See* **Race psychology**

Folk songs (May subdiv. geog. adjective form, except for the U.S. and states and regions of the U.S. where the noun form is used, e.g. **Folk songs, French;** etc.; but **Folk songs—U.S.; Folk songs— Ohio;** etc.)

    See note under **Ballads**

    See also **Ballads; Carols; Folklore; National songs**

    x Folk music

    xx **Ballads; Folklore; National songs; Songs; Vocal music**

Folk songs, African

    x Folk songs, Negro (African)

    xx **Negro songs**

Folk songs, American. *See* **Folk songs—U.S.**

Folk songs, Negro (African). *See* **Folk songs, African**

Folk songs, Negro (American). *See* **Negro songs**

Folk songs—U.S.

    x American folk songs; Folk songs, American; U.S.—Folk songs

    xx **Songs, American**

Folk tales. *See* **Folklore**

Folklore (May subdiv. geog. noun form (e.g.
      Folklore—Ireland; etc.) or, where
      country subdivision is not applicable,
      use ethnic subdivision, adjective form,
      e.g. **Folklore, Jewish**; etc.)

    Use for a discussion of folklore in general
      and also for a story or a collection of
      stories based on spoken rather than
      written traditions

    See also

Charms	Legends
Devil	Mythology
Fables	Nursery rhymes
Fairies	Plant lore
Fairy tales	Proverbs
Folk songs	Sagas
Ghosts	Superstition
Grail	Weather lore
Halloween	Witchcraft

    x Folk lore; Folk tales; Tales; Tall tales;
      Traditions

    xx **Ethnology; Fables; Fairy tales; Fic-
      tion; Folk songs; Legends; Mythol-
      ogy; Superstition**

Folklore, Eskimo
    x Eskimos—Folklore

Folklore, Indian
    Use for works on folklore of American In-
      dians. Collections of Indian legends,
      myths, tales, etc. are entered under
      Indians of North America—Legends

    See also **Indians of North America—
      Legends**

    x Indian folklore; Indians of North Amer-
      ica—Folklore; Indians of North Amer-
      ica—Mythology

    xx **Indians of North America—Legends**

Folklore, Jewish
    x Jews—Folklore

Folklore, Negro
    x Negro folklore

Folklore—U.S.
    x U.S.—Folklore

Folklore of plants. *See* **Plant lore**

Folkways. *See* **Manners and customs**

Food
    See also

Beverages	Meat
Cookery	Nutrition
Diet	Nuts
Dinners and dining	Poultry
Farm produce	Sea food
Flavoring essences	Vegetables
Fruit	Vegetarianism
Grain	Vitamins
Markets	

    also names of foods, e.g. **Bread**; etc.

    x Gastronomy

Food—*Continued*

    xx **Cookery; Diet; Digestion; Dinners and dining; Home economics; Hygiene; Nutrition**

Food—Analysis

    See also **Food additives**

    x Analysis (Chemistry) ; Analysis of food; Chemistry of food; Food chemistry

    xx **Chemistry, Technical**

Food, Canned. *See* **Canning and preserving**

Food—Contamination. *See* **Food contamination**

Food, Cost of. *See* **Cost and standard of living**

Food, Dehydrated. *See* **Food, Dried**

Food, Dried

    See also **Food, Freeze dried**

    x Dehydrated foods; Dried foods; Food, Dehydrated

    xx **Food—Preservation**

Food, Freeze dried

    x Freeze dried food

    xx **Food, Dried**

Food, Frozen

    See also **Ice cream, ices, etc.**

    x Frozen food

    xx **Food—Preservation**

Food—Laws and regulations

    See also **Food adulteration and inspection**

    x Food laws; Laws

    xx **Food adulteration and inspection; Law; Legislation**

Food—Preservation

    See also **Canning and preserving; Cold storage; Food, Dried; Food, Frozen; Food additives**

    x Food preservation; Preservation of food

    xx **Food supply**

Food additives

    x Additives, Food

    xx **Food—Analysis; Food—Preservation**

Food adulteration and inspection

    See also **Food—Laws and regulations; Meat inspection; Milk supply**

    x Analysis of food; Food inspection; Inspection of food; Pure food

    xx **Consumer protection; Food—Laws and regulations; Public health**

Food contamination

    x Contaminated food; Food—Contamination

Food chemistry. *See* **Food—Analysis**

Food control. *See* **Food supply**

Food for invalids. *See* **Cookery for the sick**

Food for school children. *See* **School children—Food**

Food inspection. *See* **Food adulteration and inspection**

Food laws. *See* **Food—Laws and regulations**

Food plants. *See* **Plants, Edible**

Food poisoning

    x Ptomaine poisoning

✓ Food consumption

✓ Food, Wild

221

Food preservation. *See* **Food—Preservation**

Food supply

    See also **Agriculture—Statistics; Famines; Food—Preservation; Meat industry and trade**

    x Food control

Food trade. *See* **Farm produce—Marketing**

Foot

    x Feet; Toes

Foot—Care and hygiene. *See* **Chiropody**

Football

    See also **Soccer**

    xx **College sports**

Football coaching

    xx **Coaching (Athletics)**

Forage plants

    See also **Grasses; Pastures; Silage and silos;** also names of specific forage plants, e.g., **Corn; Hay; Soybean;** etc.

    xx **Feeding and feeds; Grasses; Pastures; Plants**

Force and energy

    See also **Dynamics; Mechanics; Motion; Quantum theory**

    x Conservation of energy; Energy

    xx **Dynamics; Mechanics; Motion; Power (Mechanics); Quantum theory**

Force pumps. *See* **Pumping machinery**

Forced labor. *See* **Convict labor; Military service, Compulsory; Peonage; Slavery**

Ford automobile

    xx **Automobiles**

Forecasting, Business. *See* **Business forecasting**

Forecasting, Weather. *See* **Weather forecasting**

Foreign aid program. *See* **Economic assistance; Technical assistance**

Foreign area studies. *See* **Area studies**

Foreign automobiles. *See* **Automobiles, Foreign**

Foreign economic relations. *See* **International economic relations**

Foreign exchange

    See also **Bills of exchange**

    x Cambistry; International exchange

    xx **Banks and banking; Exchange; Finance; Money; Stock exchange**

Foreign language laboratories. *See* **Language laboratories**

Foreign language phrases. *See* **Languages, Modern—Conversation and phrase books;** and names of foreign languages with the subdivision *Conversation and phrase books,* e.g. **French language—Conversation and phrase books;** etc.

    For works on foreign words and phrases incorporated into languages see names of languages with the subdivision *For-*

Foreign language phrases—*Continued*
> *eign words and phrases,* e.g. **English language — Foreign words and phrases**; etc.

Foreign Legion (French Army). *See* **France. Army. Foreign Legion**

Foreign missions. *See* **Missions**

Foreign policy. *See* names of countries with the subdivision *Foreign relations,* e.g. **U.S.—Foreign relations**; etc.

Foreign population. *See* **Immigration and emigration**; names of countries with the subdivision *Immigration and emigration* (e.g. **U.S.—Immigration and emigration**; etc.) ; and names of countries, cities, etc. with the subdivision *Foreign population,* e.g. **Chicago—Foreign population**; etc.

Foreign relations. *See* **International relations**; and names of countries with the subdivision *Foreign relations,* e.g. **U.S.—Foreign relations**; etc.

Foreign students. *See* **Students, Foreign**

Foreign trade. *See* **Commerce**

Foreigners. *See* **Aliens; Citizenship; Naturalization**; names of countries, cities, etc. with the subdivision *Foreign population* (e.g. **U.S.—Foreign population**; etc.) ; **Italians in the U.S.**; and similar subjects

Foremen
> *xx* **Factory management; Personnel management**

Forenames. *See* **Names, Personal**

Forensic medicine. *See* **Medical jurisprudence**

Foreordination. *See* **Predestination**

Forest conservation. *See* **Forests and forestry**

✓ **Forest fires**
> *xx* **Fires**

Forest influences
> *See also* **Botany—Ecology; Flood control; Forests and forestry; Rain and rainfall**
> *x* Climate and forests; Floods and forests; Forests and climate; Forests and floods; Forests and rainfall; Forests and water supply; Rainfall and forests
> *xx* **Climate; Flood control; Rain and rainfall; Water supply**

Forest products
> *See also* **Gums and resins; Lumber and lumbering; Rubber; Wood; Wood pulp**
> *xx* **Botany, Economic; Commercial products; Raw materials**

Forest reserves
> *See also* **Forests and forestry; National parks and reserves; Wilderness areas**
> *x* National forests; Public lands
> *xx* **National parks and reserves**

Foresters

Forestry. *See* **Forests and forestry**

Forests and climate. *See* **Forest influences**

Forests and floods. *See* **Forest influences**

Forests and forestry (May subdiv. geog.)

    Use for general works on forests and on forest conservation

    See also **Lumber and lumbering; Pruning; Reforestation; Tree planting; Trees; Wood;** also headings beginning with the word **Forest**

    x Arboriculture; Conservation of forests; Forest conservation; Forestry; Jungles; Preservation of forests; Timber; Woods

    xx **Agriculture; Forest influences; Forest reserves; Natural resources; Trees; Wildlife—Conservation; Wood**

Forests and forestry—U.S.

    x U.S.—Forests and forestry

Forests and rainfall. *See* **Forest influences**

Forests and water supply. *See* **Forest influences**

Forgery

    See also **Counterfeits and counterfeiting**

    xx **Crime and criminals; Fraud; Impostors and imposture**

Forgery of works of art

    x Art—Forgeries; Art forgeries; Art objects, Forgery of

    xx **Art**

Forging

    See also **Blacksmithing; Ironwork; Welding**

    x Drop forging

    xx **Blacksmithing; Ironwork**

Form, Musical. *See* **Musical form**

Formal gardens. *See* **Gardens**

Formosa

    x Taiwan

Formosa—History—1949-

    x China—History—1949-

Formula translation (Computer program language). *See* **FORTRAN (Computer program language)**

Fortification

    See also **Military engineering;** also names of countries with the subdivision *Defenses,* e.g. **U.S.—Defenses;** etc.

    x Forts

    xx **Military art and science; Military engineering**

Fortran (Computer program language). *See* **FORTRAN (Computer program language)**

Forts. *See* **Fortification**

Fortune. *See* **Fate and fatalism; Probabilities; Success**

Fort Lincoln, Bank

Fortune telling
> *See also* **Astrology; Cards; Clairvoyance; Dreams; Palmistry**
> *xx* **Amusements; Card tricks; Cards; Clairvoyance; Divination; Occult sciences; Prophecies; Superstition**

Fortunes. *See* **Income; Wealth**

Forums (Discussions). *See* **Discussion groups**

Fossil mammals; Fossil plants; Fossil reptiles.
> *See* **Mammals, Fossil; Plants, Fossil; Reptiles, Fossil**

Fossils
> *See also* **Extinct animals; Mammals, Fossil; Plants, Fossil; Reptiles, Fossil**
> *x* Animals, Fossil; Animals, Prehistoric; Paleontology; Prehistoric animals
> *xx* **Geology, Stratigraphic; Natural history; Science; Zoology**

Foster home care
> *See also* **Adoption; Children—Institutional care**
> *x* Children—Placing out
> *xx* **Adoption; Child welfare; Children—Institutional care**

Foundations
> *See also* **Basements; Compressed air; Concrete; Masonry; Soils (Engineering); Walls**
> *xx* **Architecture—Details; Building; Civil engineering; Masonry; Structural engineering; Walls**

Foundations (Endowments). *See* **Endowments**

Founding
> Use for works on the melting and casting of metals
> *See also* **Brass; Metalwork; Pattern making; Type and type founding**
> *x* Casting; Foundry practice; Iron founding; Molding (Metal); Moulding (Metal)
> *xx* **Metalwork; Pattern making**

Foundlings. *See* **Orphans and orphans' homes**

Foundry practice. *See* **Founding**

4-H clubs
> *x* Boys' agricultural clubs; Girls' agricultural clubs
> *xx* **Agriculture—Societies; Boys' clubs; Girls' clubs**

Four-day work week. *See* **Hours of labor**

Fourth of July
> *x* Anniversaries; Independence Day (U.S.); July Fourth
> *xx* **Holidays; U.S.—History—Revolution**

Fractures
> *xx* **Bones**

Framing of pictures. *See* **Picture frames and framing**

225

France
>May be subdivided like U.S. except for
>>*History*

France. Army. Foreign Legion
>*x* Foreign Legion (French Army)

France—History

France—History—To 1328
>*See also* Celts

France—History—House of Valois, 1328-
1589
>*See also* Hundred Years' War, 1337-1453;
St. Bartholomew's Day, Massacre of,
1572

France—History—Bourbons, 1589-1789

France—History—Revolution, 1789-1799
>*x* Directory, French, 1795-1799; French
Revolution; Napoleonic Wars; Reign
of Terror; Revolution, French; Terror, Reign of
>*xx* Revolutions

France—History—1799-1914

France—History—War with Germany, 1870-
1871. *See* Franco-German War, 1870-
1871

France—History—1914-1940

France—History—German occupation, 1940-
1945
>*x* German occupation of France, 1940-1945

France—History—1945-1958

France—History—1958-

Franchise. *See* Citizenship; Elections; Suffrage

Franciscans
>*x* Friars, Gray; Friars, Minor; Gray
Friars; Grey Friars; Mendicant orders; Minorites; St. Francis, Order of
>*xx* Monasticism and religious orders

Franco-German War, 1870-1871
>*x* France—History—War with Germany,
1870-1871; Franco-Prussian War, 1870-
1871; Germany—History—War with
France, 1870-1871

Franco-Prussian War, 1870-1871. *See* Franco-
German War, 1870-1871

Fraternities and sororities
>*x* College fraternities; Greek letter soci-
eties; Sororities
>*xx* Colleges and universities; Secret so-
cieties; Students' societies

Fraud
>*See also* Forgery; Impostors and impos-
ture; Swindlers and swindling
>*xx* Impostors and imposture; Swindlers
and swindling

Fraudulent advertising. *See* Advertising, Fraudulent

Freaks. *See* Monsters

Free agency. *See* Free will and determinism

Free coinage. *See* Currency question

Free fall. *See* Weightlessness

Free love

 xx **Marriage; Sexual ethics**

Free material

 x Giveaways

Free press. *See* **Freedom of the press**

Free schools

 x Alternative schools; Experimental schools

 xx **Education—Experimental methods**

Free speech

 See also **Freedom of information; Libel and slander; Freedom of the press**

 x Freedom of speech; Liberty of speech; Speech, Liberty of

 xx **Censorship; Civil rights; Freedom of assembly; Freedom of information; Intellectual freedom; Libel and slander**

Free thought

 See also **Agnosticism; Bible—Evidences, authority, etc.; Rationalism; Religious liberty; Skepticism**

 xx **Deism; God; Freedom of conscience; Rationalism**

Free trade and protection

 See also **Tariff**

 x Fair trade (Tariff); Protection; Tariff question—Free trade and protection

 xx **Commerce; Commercial policy; Economic policy; Economics; Tariff**

Free universities

 x Alternative universities; Experimental universities

 xx **Colleges and universities**

Free verse

 x Vers libre

 xx **Poetry**

Free will and determinism

 x Choice, Freedom of; Determinism and indeterminism; Free agency; Freedom of choice; Freedom of the will; Indeterminism; Liberty of the will; Will

 xx **Ethics; Fate and fatalism; Philosophy; Predestination; Sin**

Freebooters. *See* **Pirates**

Freedom. *See* **Liberty; Slavery**

Freedom marches. *See* **Negroes—Civil rights**

Freedom of assembly

 See also **Free speech; Public meetings; Riots**

 x Assembly, Right of; Right of assembly

 xx **Civil rights**

Freedom of choice. *See* **Free will and determinism**

Freedom of conscience

 See also **Conscientious objectors; Free thought; Persecution; Public opinion; Religious liberty**

 x Intolerance

Freedom of conscience—*Continued*

    xx Church and state; Conscience; Persecution; Religious liberty; Toleration

Freedom of information

    See also Free speech; Freedom of the press; Government and the press; Moving pictures—Censorship; Radio —Censorship; Television—Censorship

    x Information, Freedom of

    xx Civil rights; Free speech; Freedom of the press; Intellectual freedom

Freedom of movement

    x Movement, Freedom of

    xx Civil rights

Freedom of religion. *See* Religious liberty

Freedom of speech. *See* Free speech

Freedom of teaching. *See* Academic freedom

Freedom of the press

    See also Books—Censorship; Freedom of information; Libel and slander

    x Free press; Liberty of the press; Press; Press censorship

    xx Censorship; Civil rights; Free speech; Freedom of information; Intellectual freedom; Journalism; Libel and slander; Newspapers; Periodicals

Freedom of the will. *See* Free will and determinism

Freedom of worship. *See* Religious liberty

Freemasons

    x Masons (Secret order)

    xx Secret societies

Freeways. *See* Express highways

Freeze dried food. *See* Food, Freeze dried

Freezers. *See* Refrigeration and refrigerating machinery

Freezing. *See* Cryobiology; Frost; Ice; Refrigeration and refrigerating machinery

Freezing of human bodies. *See* Cryonics

Freight and freightage

    See also Aeronautics, Commercial; Railroads—Rates

    x Railroads—Freight

    xx Maritime law; Materials handling; Railroads; Railroads—Rates; Transportation

French and Indian War. *See* U.S.—History—French and Indian War, 1755-1763

French Canadian literature

    May use same subdivisions and names of literary forms as for English literature

    x Canadian literature, French; French literature—Canada

    xx Canadian literature

French Canadians

    xx Canadians

French language
>   May be subdivided like **English language**
>   *xx* **Romance languages**
French language—**Conversation and phrase
     books**
>   *x* Conversation in foreign languages; For-
>   eign language phrases
French language—**Dictionaries—English**
>   See note under **English language—Dic-
>   tionaries—French**
French language—**Readers**
>   *xx* **Readers**
French literature
>   May use same subdivisions and names of
>   literary forms as for **English litera-
>   ture**
>   *xx* **Literature; Romance literature**
French literature—Canada. *See* **French Cana-
     dian literature**
French poetry
>   *See also* **Troubadours**
French Revolution. *See* **France—History—
     Revolution, 1789-1799**
Frequency modulation, Radio. *See* **Radio fre-
     quency modulation**
Fresco painting. *See* **Mural painting and dec-
     oration**
Fresh-water animals
>   *See also* **Aquariums; Marine animals;**
>   also names of individual fresh-water
>   animals, e.g. **Beavers;** etc.
>   *x* Animals, Aquatic; Animals, Fresh-
>   water; Aquatic animals; Water ani-
>   mals
>   *xx* **Animals; Fresh-water biology; Geo-
>   graphical distribution of animals and
>   plants; Marine animals**
Fresh-water biology
>   *See also* **Aquariums; Fresh-water ani-
>   mals; Fresh-water plants; Marine
>   biology**
>   *xx* **Biology; Marine biology; Natural his-
>   tory**
Fresh-water plants
>   *See also* **Aquariums; Marine plants**
>   *x* Aquatic plants; Water plants
>   *xx* **Fresh-water biology; Geographical dis-
>   tribution of animals and plants; Ma-
>   rine plants; Plants**
Friars, Black. *See* **Dominicans**
Friars, Gray. *See* **Franciscans**
Friars, Minor. *See* **Franciscans**
Friars preachers. *See* **Dominicans**
Friends, Society of
>   *x* Quakers; Society of Friends
>   *xx* **Congregationalism**
Friendship
>   *See also* **Love; Sympathy**
>   *x* Affection
>   *xx* **Behavior; Ethics; Love**

Frogmen. *See* **Skin diving**

Frogs

    x Tadpoles; Toads

    xx **Amphibians**

Frontier and pioneer life (May subdiv. geog. by state and region)

    See also **Cowboys; Indians of North America—Captivities; Overland journeys to the Pacific; Ranch life**

    x Border life; Pioneer life

    xx **Adventure and adventurers**

Frontiers. *See* **Boundaries;** and names of countries with the subdivision *Boundaries*

Frost

    See also **Ice; Refrigeration and refrigerating machinery**

    x Freezing

    xx **Meteorology; Water**

Frozen food. *See* **Food, Frozen; Ice cream, ices, etc.**

Fruit

    Names of fruits are not included in this list but are to be added as needed, usually in the singular form, e.g. **Apple;** etc.

    See also **Berries; Citrus fruit; Fruit culture;** also names of fruits, e.g. **Apple;** etc.

    xx **Botany; Food**

Fruit—Canning. *See* **Canning and preserving**

Fruit—Diseases and pests

    See also **Spraying** and dusting

    x Diseases and pests; Pests

    xx **Agricultural pests; Bacteriology, Agricultural; Insects, Injurious and beneficial; Plants—Diseases**

Fruit—Marketing. *See* **Farm produce—Marketing**

Fruit culture

    See also **Berries; Grafting; Nurseries (Horticulture); Plant propagation; Pruning;** also names of fruits

    x Arboriculture; Orchards

    xx **Agriculture; Fruit; Gardening; Trees**

Fruit flies

    xx **Flies**

Frustration. *See* **Attitude (Psychology); Emotions; Personality disorders**

Fuel

    See also **Charcoal; Coal; Gas; Heating; Petroleum as fuel; Wood**

    xx **Combustion; Engines; Fire; Heating; Home economics; Power resources; Smoke prevention**

Fuel, Liquid. *See* **Gasoline; Petroleum as fuel**

Fuel oil. *See* **Oil burners; Petroleum as fuel**

Fugue

    xx **Composition (Music); Counterpoint; Music—Theory; Musical form**

Fumigation

See also **Disinfection and disinfectants**

xx **Communicable diseases; Disinfection and disinfectants; Insecticides**

Fund raising

x Community chests; Money raising

Fundamental theology. *See* **Apologetics**

Fundamentalism

Use for works on the conservative interpretation of Christianity as opposed to Modernism

See also **Modernism**

xx **Modernism**

Funds. *See* **Finance**

Funeral directors. *See* **Undertakers and undertaking**

Funeral rites and ceremonies

See also **Ancestor worship; Cremation**

x Burial; Ecclesiastical rites and ceremonies; Graves; Mortuary customs; Mourning customs

xx **Archeology; Cremation; Manners and customs; Rites and ceremonies**

Fungi

See also **Bacteriology; Mushrooms; Plants—Diseases**

x Diseases and pests; Mycology; Pests

xx **Agricultural pests; Mushrooms**

Fungicides

See also **Spraying and dusting**

x Germicides

xx **Pesticides; Spraying and dusting**

Funnies. *See* **Comic books, strips, etc.**

Fur

See also **Hides and skins**

xx **Hides and skins**

Fur-bearing animals

See also names of fur-bearing animals, e.g. **Beavers**; etc.

xx **Animals; Zoology, Economic**

Fur seals. *See* **Seals (Animals)**

Fur trade

xx **Trapping**

Furnaces

See also **Blast furnaces; Smelting**

xx **Heating; Smoke prevention**

Furniture (May subdiv. geog. adjective form, e.g. **Furniture, American;** etc.)

See also **Built-in furniture; Cabinet work; Church furniture; Garden ornaments and furniture; Library equipment and supplies; Schools—Furniture, equipment, etc.; Upholstery; Veneers and veneering; Wood carving;** also names of articles of furniture, e.g. **Chairs; Mirrors;** etc.

xx **Art, Decorative; Art objects; Decoration and ornament; Home economics; Interior decoration; Manufactures; Upholstery; Woodwork**

Furniture, American

    x American furniture; Colonial furniture; Furniture, Colonial; U.S.—Furniture

Furniture, Built-in. *See* **Built-in furniture**

Furniture, Colonial. *See* **Furniture, American**

Furniture—Repairing

Future life

    Use for works dealing with the character and form of a future existence. Works dealing with the question of the endless existence of the soul are entered under **Immortality**. Works on the philosophical concept of eternity are entered under **Eternity**

    See also **Eternity; Immortality; Millennium; Soul; Spiritualism**

    x Eternal life; Future punishment; Hades; Intermediate state; Life, Future; Life after death; Resurrection; Retribution

    xx **Death; Eschatology; Eternity; Heaven; Immortality; Soul**

Future punishment. *See* **Future life**

Futurism (Art)

    See also **Kinetic sculpture; Postimpressionism (Art)**

    xx **Art; Painting; Postimpressionism (Art)**

G-men. *See* **U.S. Federal Bureau of Investigation**

G.I.s. *See* **Soldiers—U.S.; Veterans**

Galaxies

    x Extragalactic nebulae; Nebulae, Extragalactic

    xx **Stars**

Gaels. *See* **Celts**

Gales. *See* **Winds**

Galleries (Art). *See* **Art—Galleries and museums;** names of countries, cities, etc. with the subdivision *Galleries and museums* (e.g. **U.S.—Galleries and museums;** etc.) ; and names of galleries and museums

Gallup polls. *See* **Public opinion polls**

Gambling

    See also **Cards; Horse racing; Lotteries; Probabilities**

    x Betting; Gaming; Vice

Game and game birds

    See also **Falconry; Game protection; Hunting; Shooting; Trapping;** also names of animals and birds, e.g. **Deer; Pheasants;** etc.

    x Wild fowl

    xx **Animals; Birds; Hunting; Trapping**

Game preserves

    xx **Hunting; Wildlife—Conservation**

232

Game protection

    See also **Birds—Protection**

    x Game wardens; Protection of game

    xx **Birds—Protection; Game and game birds; Hunting; Wildlife—Conservation**

Game wardens. *See* **Game protection**

Games

    See also **Amusements; Cards; Indians of North America—Games; Indoor games; Kindergarten; Olympic games; Play; Singing games; Sports;** also names of games, e.g. **Chess; Tennis;** etc.

    x Indoor games; Pastimes

    xx **Amusements; Entertaining; Physical education and training; Play; Recreation; Sports**

Games, Olympic. *See* **Olympic games**

Gaming. *See* **Gambling**

Gangs. *See* **Crime and criminals; Juvenile delinquency**

Garages

Garbage. *See* **Refuse and refuse disposal**

Garden design. *See* **Landscape gardening**

Garden furniture. *See* **Garden ornaments and furniture**

Garden of Eden. *See* **Eden**

Garden ornaments and furniture

    See also **Sundials**

    x Garden furniture

    xx **Furniture; Gardens; Landscape architecture**

Garden pests. *See* **Agricultural pests; Insects, Injurious and beneficial; Plants—Diseases**

Gardening

    Use for practical works on the cultivation of flowers, fruits, lawns, vegetables, etc.

    See also

Bulbs
Climbing plants
Flower gardening
Fruit culture
Gardens
Grafting
Greenhouses
Grounds maintenance
Insects, Injurious and beneficial
Landscape gardening
Nurseries (Horticulture)
Organiculture
Plant propagation
Plants
Plants, Cultivated
Pruning
Vegetable gardening
Weeds
Window gardening

    x Horticulture; Planting

    xx **Agriculture; Plants**

Gardens

    Use for general works about the history of gardens, various types of gardens, and designs of gardens. Works limited to the cultivation of gardens are en-

233

Gardens—*Continued*

tered under **Gardening.** Works limited to garden design are entered under **Landscape gardening**

See also **Botanical gardens; Garden ornaments and furniture; Rock gardens**

x Formal gardens

xx **Gardening**

Gardens, Miniature

x Miniature gardens; Miniature objects; Tray gardens

xx **Terrariums**

Garment making. *See* **Dressmaking; Tailoring**

Garments, Leather. *See* **Leather garments**

Gas

See also **Coal-tar products; Gases; Petroleum**

x Coal gas; Illuminating gas

xx **Coal-tar products; Fuel; Public utilities**

Gas, Natural

See also **Boring**

x Gas wells; Natural gas

xx **Geology, Economic; Wells**

Gas, Poisonous. *See* **Gases, Asphyxiating and poisonous**

Gas and oil engines

See also **Airplanes—Engines; Automobiles—Engines; Carburetors; Diesel engines; Farm engines**

x Gas engines; Gasoline engines; Internal-combustion engines; Oil engines; Petroleum engines

xx **Engines**

Gas companies. *See* **Public utilities**

Gas engines. *See* **Gas and oil engines**

Gas stations. *See* **Automobiles—Service stations**

Gas turbines

xx **Turbines**

Gas warfare. *See* **Gases, Asphyxiating and poisonous—War use**

Gas wells. *See* **Gas, Natural**

Gases

See also **Pneumatics;** also names of gases, e.g. **Nitrogen;** etc.

xx **Gas; Hydrostatics; Mechanics; Physics; Pneumatics**

Gases, Asphyxiating and poisonous

x Asphyxiating gases; Gas, Poisonous; Poison gases

Gases, Asphyxiating and poisonous—War use

x European War, 1914-1918—Gas warfare; Gas warfare

xx **Chemical warfare**

Gasoline

x Fuel, Liquid; Liquid fuel

xx **Petroleum**

Gasoline engines. *See* **Gas and oil engines**

234

Gastronomy. *See* **Cookery; Dinners and din-**
   ing; Food; Menus
Gauchos. *See* **Cowboys**
Gay liberation. *See* **Homosexuality**
Gazetteers
   See also **Names, Geographical**; also names
      of countries, states, etc. with the sub-
      division—*Gazetteers*, e.g. **U.S.—Gazet-**
      teers; etc.
   xx **Names, Geographical**
Gearing
   See also **Automobiles—Transmission de-**
      vices; Mechanical movements
   x Bevel gearing; Cog wheels; Spiral gear-
      ing
   xx **Machinery; Mechanical movements;**
      Power transmission; Wheels
✓ **Geese**
   x Goose
   xx **Poultry**
Gemini project
   x Project Gemini
   xx **Manned space flight; Orbital rendez-**
      vous (Space environment)
Gems
   Use for works on cut and polished precious
      stones treated from the point of view
      of art or antiquity. Works on uncut
      stones treated from the mineralogical
      point of view are entered under **Pre-**
      cious stones. Works on gems in which
      the interest is in the setting are entered
      under **Jewelry**
   See also **Jewelry; Precious stones**
   x Jewels
   xx **Archeology; Art; Decoration and or-**
      nament; Engraving; Jewelry; Min-
      eralogy; Precious stones
Genealogy
   See also **Biography; Heraldry; Registers**
      of births, etc.; Wills; also names of
      families, e.g. **Lincoln family;** etc.
   x Ancestry; Descent; Family histories;
      Pedigrees
   xx **Biography; Heraldry; History**
Generals
   x Military biography
   xx **Soldiers**
Generation. *See* **Reproduction**
Generation gap. *See* **Conflict of generations**
Generative organs. *See* **Reproductive system**
Generators, Electric. *See* **Electric generators**
Genes. *See* **Heredity**
Genetics
   Use for comprehensive works dealing with
      reproduction, heredity, evolution and
      variation
   See also **Adaptation (Biology); Chromo-**
      somes; Eugenics; Evolution; Hered-
      ity; Life (Biology); Natural selec-

Genetics—*Continued*

tion; Reproduction; Variation (Biology)

xx Biology; Chromosomes; Life (Biology)

Genius

See also **Creation (Literary, artistic, etc.);
Gifted children**

x Talent

xx **Psychology**

Geochemistry

x Chemical geology; Earth—Chemical composition; Geological chemistry

xx **Chemistry; Petrology; Physical geography; Rocks**

Geodesy

See also **Latitude; Longitude; Surveying**

x Degrees of latitude and longitude

xx **Earth; Mensuration; Surveying**

Geographical atlases. *See* **Atlases**

Geographical distribution of animals and plants

See also **Alpine plants; Animals—Migration; Birds—Migration; Desert animals; Desert plants; Fresh-water animals; Fresh-water plants; Marine animals; Marine plants**

x Animals—Geographical distribution; Biogeography; Botany—Geographical distribution; Distribution of animals and plants; Fishes—Geographical distribution; Plants—Geographical distribution; Zoology—Geographical distribution

xx **Animals; Ecology; Natural history; Plants**

Geographical distribution of man. *See* **Anthropogeography; Ethnology**

Geographical names. *See* **Names, Geographical**

Geography

Use for general works, frequently textbooks, which describe the surface of the earth with its various peoples, animals, natural products and industries. For travel books limited to one country or region, use the name of the place with the subdivision *Description and travel.* Works that treat only of the physical features of the earth's surface and its atmosphere are entered under **Physical geography**

See also **Anthropogeography; Atlases; Boundaries; Discoveries (in geography); Ethnology; Maps; Physical geography; Surveying; Voyages and travels;** also names of countries, states, etc. with the subdivision *Description and travel,* and *Geography,* e.g. **U.S.—**

236

Geography—*Continued*

> Description and travel; U.S.—Geography; etc.
>
> *x* Social studies
>
> *xx* **Earth; Textbooks; World history**

Geography, Ancient

> Use for works on the geography of the ancient world in general
>
> *See also* names of countries of antiquity with the subdivision *Description and geography,* e.g. **Greece—Description and geography**; etc.
>
> *x* Ancient geography; Classical geography
>
> *xx* **Geography, Historical; History, Ancient**

Geography, Biblical. *See* **Bible—Geography**

Geography, Commercial

> *See also* **Economic conditions; Trade routes**
>
> *x* Commercial geography; Economic geography; Geography, Economic; World economics
>
> *xx* **Commerce; Commercial products; Economic conditions**

Geography—Dictionaries

> Use for dictionaries of geographic terms. Works listing names and descriptions of places are entered under **Gazetteers**

Geography, Economic. *See* **Geography, Commercial**

Geography, Historical

> Use for works that discuss the extent of territory held by states or nations at a given period of history. When limited to one country or region use the name of the place with the subdivision *Historical geography.* Under names of countries of antiquity use, instead, the subdivision *Description and geography*
>
> *See also* **Geography, Ancient**; also names of modern countries or regions with the subdivision *Historical geography* (e.g. **U.S.—Historical geography**; etc.); and names of ancient countries with the subdivision *Description and geography,* e.g. **Greece—Description and geography**; etc.
>
> *x* Historical geography
>
> *xx* **History**

Geography, Historical—Maps. *See* **Atlases, Historical**

Geography, Military. *See* **Military geography**

Geography, Physical. *See* **Physical geography**

Geography—Pictorial works. *See* **Views**

Geography, Political. *See* **Boundaries; Geopolitics**

Geography, Social. *See* **Anthropogeography**

Geological chemistry. *See* **Geochemistry**

Geological physics. *See* **Geophysics**

Geologists

    xx **Scientists**

Geology (May subdiv. geog.)

    See note under **Earth**

    See also

Coral reefs and is-	**Mountains**
lands	**Oceanography**
Creation	**Ore deposits**
Earth	**Petrology**
Earthquakes	**Physical geography**
Geysers	**Rocks**
Glaciers	**Submarine geology**
Mineralogy	**Volcanoes**

    x Geoscience

    xx **Creation; Earth; Natural history; Petrology; Rocks; Science**

Geology, Dynamic. *See* **Geophysics**

Geology, Economic

    See also **Coal; Gas, Natural; Mines and mineral resources; Ores; Petroleum —Geology; Quarries and quarrying; Soils; Stone;** also names of other geological products, e.g. **Asbestos; Gypsum;** etc.

    x Economic geology

Geology, Historical. *See* **Geology, Stratigraphic**

Geology, Lunar. *See* **Lunar geology**

Geology—Maps

    xx **Maps**

Geology, Moon. *See* **Lunar geology**

Geology, Stratigraphic

    See also **Fossils**

    x Geology, Historical; Historical geology; Rocks—Age; Stratigraphic geology

Geology, Submarine. *See* **Submarine geology**

Geology—U.S.

    x U.S.—Geology

Geometrical drawing

    See also **Geometry, Descriptive; Graphic methods; Mechanical drawing; Perspective**

    x Mathematical drawing; Plans

    xx **Drawing; Geometry; Mechanical drawing**

Geometry

    See also **Geometrical drawing; Trigonometry**

    x Geometry, Plane; Geometry, Solid; Plane geometry; Solid geometry

    xx **Mathematics**

Geometry, Analytic

    x Analytical geometry

Geometry, Descriptive

    See also **Perspective**

    x Descriptive geometry

    xx **Geometrical drawing**

Geometry, Plane. *See* **Geometry**

Geometry, Projective

    x Projective geometry

Geometry, Solid. *See* **Geometry**

Geophysics

   See also **Auroras; Meteorology; Oceanography**

   x Geological physics; Geology, Dynamic; Physics, Terrestrial; Terrestrial physics

   xx **Earth; Physical geography; Physics; Space sciences**

Geopolitics

   See also **Anthropogeography; Boundaries; World politics**

   x Geography, Political

   xx **Anthropogeography; Boundaries; International relations; Political science; World politics**

Geoscience. *See* **Geology**

Geriatrics. *See* **Aged—Diseases**

Germ theory. *See* **Life—Origin**

Germ theory of disease

   See also **Bacteriology**

   x Bacilli; Disease germs; Germs; Microbes

   xx **Bacteriology; Communicable diseases**

Germ warfare. *See* **Biological warfare**

German Baptist Brethren. *See* **Church of the Brethren**

German Hebrew. *See* **Yiddish language**

German language

   May be subdivided like **English language**

German literature

   May use same subdivisions and names of literary forms as for **English literature**

German occupation of France, [Netherlands, etc.] 1940-1945. *See* **France—History—German occupation, 1940-1945; Netherlands—History—German occupation, 1940-1945; etc.**

German propaganda. *See* **Propaganda, German**

Germans in Czechoslovak Republic

   Use same form for Germans in other countries, states, etc., except Pennsylvania

   xx **Minorities**

Germans in Pennsylvania. *See* **Pennsylvania Dutch**

Germany

   May be subdivided like U.S. except for *History*

Germany—History

Germany—History—To 1517

   See also **Holy Roman Empire**

Germany—History—1517-1740

   See also **Thirty Years' War, 1618-1648**

Germany—History—1740-1815

   See also **Seven Years' War, 1756-1763**

Germany—History—1815-1866

Germany—History—Revolution, 1848-1849

Germany—History—1866-1918

Germany—History—War with France, 1870-
1871. *See* **Franco-German War, 1870-
1871**

Germany—History—1918-1933

Germany—History—1933-1945

Germany—History—1945-

Germany (Democratic Republic)
    x East Germany

Germany (Federal Republic)
    x West Germany

Germicides. *See* **Disinfection and disinfectants;
Fungicides**

Germination
    x Seeds—Germination
    xx **Plant physiology**

Germs. *See* **Bacteriology; Germ theory of disease; Microorganisms**

Gerontology. *See* **Aged; Old age**

Gestalt psychology
    x Configuration (Psychology); Psychol-
ogy, Structural; Structural psychology
    xx **Consciousness; Knowledge, Theory
of; Perception; Psychology; Senses
and sensation**

Gesture. *See* **Nonverbal communication**

Gettysburg, Battle of, 1863
    xx **U.S.—History—Civil War—Campaigns
and battles; War**

Geysers
    x Eruptions; Hot springs
    xx **Geology; Physical geography; Water**

Ghost stories
    x Stories
    xx **Fantastic fiction; Fiction**

Ghost towns. See **Cities and towns, Ruined,
extinct, etc.**

Ghosts
    See also **Apparitions; Demonology; Hal-
lucinations and illusions; Psychical
research; Spiritualism; Superstition**
    x Haunted houses; Phantoms; Polter-
geists; Specters; Spirits
    xx **Apparitions; Folklore; Hallucinations
and illusions; Psychical research;
Spiritualism; Superstition**

Giants
    xx **Monsters**

Gift wrapping
    x Wrapping of gifts
    xx **Gifts; Packaging; Paper crafts**

Gifted children
    See also **Children as artists; Children as
authors**
    x Bright children; Children, Gifted; Pre-
cocious children; Superior children;
Talent
    xx **Exceptional children; Genius**

Gifts

See also **Gift wrapping**

x Bequests; Donations; Philanthropy; Presents

Gilds. *See* **Guilds**

Gipsies. *See* **Gypsies**

✓ **Girl Scouts**

xx **Girls' clubs; Scouts and scouting**

Girls

See also **Children; Education of women; Woman; Young women; Youth**

xx **Children; Woman; Young women; Youth**

Girls—Clubs. *See* **Girls' clubs**

Girls—Education. *See* **Coeducation; Education of women**

Girls—Employment. *See* **Child labor; Woman —Employment**

Girls—Societies and clubs. *See* **Girls' clubs**

Girls' agricultural clubs. *See* **Agriculture—Societies; Girls' clubs; 4-H clubs**

Girls' clubs

See also **Camp Fire Girls; 4-H clubs; Girl Scouts**

x Girls—Clubs; Girls—Societies and clubs; Girls' agricultural clubs

xx **Clubs; Social settlements; Societies; Women's clubs**

Giveaways. *See* **Free material**

Glacial epoch

x Ice age

xx **Earth**

Glaciers

xx **Geology; Ice; Physical geography; Water**

Gladiators

x Fighting

Gladness. *See* **Happiness**

Glands

Glands, Ductless

See also **Hormones**

x Ductless glands; Endocrinology

xx **Hormones**

Glass

xx **Ceramics; Windows**

Glass, Spun. *See* **Glass fibers**

Glass, Stained. *See* **Glass painting and staining**

Glass construction

xx **Building materials**

Glass fibers

x Fibers, Glass; Glass, Spun; Spun glass

Glass manufacture

xx **Ceramic industries**

Glass painting and staining

x Glass, Stained; Painted glass; Stained glass; Windows, Stained glass

xx **Art industries and trade; Arts and crafts; Painting**

✓ Girls state

241

Glassware

   See also **Vases**

   x Dishes

   xx **Tableware; Vases**

Glazes

   xx **Ceramics; Pottery**

Gliders (Aeronautics)

   x Aircraft

   xx **Aeronautics; Airplanes**

Gliding and soaring

   x Soaring flight

Global satellite communications systems. *See* **Artificial satellites in telecommunication**

Globes

Glossaries. *See* names of language or subject with the subdivision *Dictionaries,* e.g. **English language — Dictionaries; Chemistry—Dictionaries;** etc.

Gloves

Glue

   xx **Adhesives**

Gnomes. *See* **Fairies**

Gnosticism

   xx **Church history—Primitive and early church; Philosophy; Religions; Theosophy**

Go karts. *See* **Karts and karting**

Goats

   xx **Domestic animals; Livestock**

Goblins. *See* **Fairies**

God

   See also

Agnosticism	**Natural theology**
Atheism	**Ontology**
Christianity	**Pantheism**
Creation	**Providence and government of God**
Deism	
Free thought	**Rationalism**
Holy Spirit	**Religion**
Jesus Christ	**Theism**
Metaphysics	**Theology**
Mythology	**Trinity**

   xx **Christianity; Creation; Deism; Metaphysics; Philosophy; Religion; Theism; Theology; Trinity**

Gods

   See also **Mythology; Religions**

   x Deities

   xx **Mythology; Religions**

Gold

   See also **Coinage; Currency question; Gold mines and mining; Goldsmithing; Jewelry; Money**

   x Bimetallism; Bullion

   xx **Coinage; Currency question; Metals; Money; Precious metals**

Gold fish. *See* **Goldfish**

242

Gold mines and mining
>*See also* **Prospecting**
>*xx* **Gold**

Gold plate. *See* **Plate**

Gold rush. *See* **California—Gold discoveries;**
>>**Klondike gold fields**

Golden Gate Bridge
>*xx* **Bridges**

Goldfish
>*x* Gold fish
>*xx* **Aquariums**

Goldsmithing
>*See also* **Hallmarks; Jewelry; Metalwork;**
>>**Plate**
>*xx* **Gold; Hallmarks; Jewelry; Metalwork**

Golf

Golf links
>*xx* **Grounds maintenance**

Good and evil
>*See also* **Sin**
>*x* Evil
>*xx* **Ethics; Suffering; Theology**

Good Friday
>*xx* **Fasts and feasts; Holy Week; Lent**

Good grooming. *See* **Beauty, Personal; Groom-**
>>**ing for men**

Good Neighbor Policy. *See* **Pan-Americanism**

Goose. *See* **Geese**

Gorillas

Gothic architecture. *See* **Architecture, Gothic**

Goths. *See* **Teutonic race**

Gourds

Gout
>*See also* **Arthritis**

Government. *See* **Political science;** and names
>>of countries, cities, etc. with the sub-
>>division *Politics and government,* e.g.
>>**U.S.—Politics and government;** etc.

Government, Local. *See* **Local government**

Government, Mandatory. *See* **Mandates**

Government, Municipal. *See* **Municipal gov-**
>>**ernment**

Government, Resistance to
>*See also* **Revolutions**
>*x* Civil disobedience; Resistance to govern-
>>ment
>*xx* **Political crimes and offenses; Political**
>>**ethics; Political science; Revolutions**

Government and business. *See* **Industry and**
>>**state**

Government and the press
>*x* Press and government
>*xx* **Freedom of information; Journalism;**
>>**Reporters and reporting**

Government buildings. *See* **Public buildings**

Government by commission. *See* **Municipal**
>>**government by commission**

Government employees. *See* **Civil service;** and names of countries, cities, etc. with the subdivision *Officials and employees,* e.g. **U.S.—Officials and employees;** etc.

Government insurance. *See* **Insurance, Social**

Government investigations. *See* **Governmental investigations**

Government libraries. *See* **Libraries, Governmental**

Government ownership
> *See also* **Municipal ownership; Railroads and state**
> *x* Nationalization; Public ownership; Socialization of industry; State ownership
> *xx* **Corporations; Economic policy; Economics; Industry and state; Political science; Socialism**

Government ownership of railroads. *See* **Railroads and state**

Government publications
> *See also* names of countries, cities, etc. with the subdivision *Government publications,* e.g. **U.S.—Government publications;** etc.
> *x* Documents; Official publications; Public documents

Government records—Preservation. *See* **Archives**

Government regulation of commerce. *See* **Commercial policy; Interstate commerce;** and special methods of regulation, e.g. **Tariff;** etc.

Government regulation of industry. *See* **Industry and state**

Government regulation of railroads. *See* **Interstate commerce; Railroads and state**

Government service. *See* **Civil service**

Governmental investigations
> Use for works on investigations initiated by the legislative, executive or judicial branches of the government
> *x* Congressional investigations; Executive investigations; Government investigations; Investigations, Governmental; Judicial investigations; Legislative investigations
> *xx* **Justice, Administration of**

Governments in exile. *See* **World War, 1939-1945—Governments in exile**

Governors
> *xx* **State governments**

Graal. *See* **Grail**

Grace (Theology)
> *xx* **Conversion; Theology**

Grading and marking (Students)
> *See also* **Ability grouping in education; Mental tests; School reports**

Grading and marking (Students)—*Continued*

    x Marking (Students); Students—Grading and marking

    xx **Educational tests and measurements; School reports**

Graduation. *See* **Commencements**

Graft (in politics). *See* **Corruption (in politics)**

Grafting

    xx **Botany; Fruit culture; Gardening; Plant propagation; Trees**

Grail

    See also **Arthur, King**

    x Graal; Holy Grail

    xx **Arthur, King; Folklore; Legends**

Grain

    See also names of cereal plants, e.g. **Corn; Wheat;** etc.

    x Breadstuffs; Cereals

    xx **Botany, Economic; Flour and flour mills; Food**

                                        ✓ Grain - Export program

                                        ✓ Grain - Inspection

                                        ✓ Grain - Prices

Grammar

    See also **Language and languages; Philology, Comparative;** also names of languages with the subdivision *Grammar,* e.g. **English language—Grammar;** etc.

    xx **Language and languages**

Grammar schools. *See* **Education, Elementary; Public schools**

Gramophone. *See* **Phonograph**

Grand opera. *See* **Opera**

Grange

    xx **Agriculture—Societies**

                                        ✓ Grand jury

Granite

    xx **Petrology; Rocks**

Grants. *See* **Subsidies**

                                        ✓ Grants-in-aid - North Dakota

Grapes

    See also **Wine and wine making**

    x Vineyards

    xx **Wine and wine making**

Graphic arts (May subdiv. geog. adjective form, e.g. **Graphic arts, French;** etc.)

    See also **Drawing; Engraving; Painting; Printing; Prints**

    x Art, Graphic; Arts, Graphic

    xx **Art**

Graphic arts, American

    x American graphic arts; U.S.—Graphic arts

Graphic methods

    See also **Statistics—Graphic methods**

    x Graphs

    xx **Drawing; Geometrical drawing; Mechanical drawing**

Graphite

    x Black lead

    xx **Carbon**

Graphology
    See note under **Writing**
    x Handwriting
    xx **Penmanship; Writing**

Graphs. *See* **Graphic methods**

Grasses
    See also **Feeding and feeds; Forage plants; Hay; Pastures**
    x Herbage
    xx **Botany, Economic; Forage plants; Hay; Lawns; Pastures**

Grasshoppers. *See* **Locusts**

Graves. *See* **Cemeteries; Epitaphs; Funeral rites and ceremonies; Mounds and mound builders; Tombs**

Graveyards. *See* **Cemeteries**

Gravitation
    x Gravity
    xx **Physics**

Gravity. *See* **Gravitation**

Gravity free state. *See* **Weightlessness**

Gray Friars. *See* **Franciscans**

Grease. *See* **Lubrication and lubricants; Oils and fats**

Great books program. *See* **Discussion groups**

Great Britain
    May be subdivided like U.S. except for *History*. The abbreviation Gt. Brit. may be used when followed by a subdivision. For a list of subjects which may be used under either England or Great Britain, see **England**
    See also **Commonwealth of Nations; England**
    x United Kingdom
    xx **England**

Gt. Brit.—Colonies
    xx **Colonies; Commonwealth of Nations**

Gt. Brit.—History
    x England—History; English history

Gt. Brit.—History—To 1066
    See also **Anglo-Saxons; Celts**

Gt. Brit.—History—Norman period, 1066-1154
    See also **Hastings, Battle of, 1066; Normans**

Gt. Brit.—History—Plantagenets, 1154-1399

Gt. Brit.—History—Lancaster and York, 1399-1485
    See also **Hundred Years' War, 1339-1453**

Gt. Brit.—History—Wars of the Roses, 1455-1485
    x Wars of the Roses, 1455-1485

Gt. Brit.—History—Tudors, 1485-1603
    See also **Armada, 1588**

Gt. Brit.—History—Stuarts, 1603-1714
    See also **Spanish Succession, War of, 1701-1714**

Gt. Brit.—History—Civil War and Commonwealth, 1642-1660
  x Civil War—England; Commonwealth of England
Gt. Brit.—History—1714-1837
  See also **Seven Years' War, 1756-1763**
Gt. Brit.—History—19th century
  See also **South African War, 1899-1902**
  x Industrial revolution
Gt. Brit.—History—Crimean War, 1853-1856.
  See **Crimean War, 1853-1856**
Gt. Brit.—History—20th century
Gt. Brit.—History—1945-
Gt. Brit.—Kings and rulers
  xx **Kings and rulers; Queens**
Greece
  Use for works on ancient Greece from earliest times to 323 A.D. Works on medieval Greece, 323-1453, are entered under **Byzantine Empire.** Works on modern Greece from 1453-date are entered under **Greece, Modern**
Greece—Antiquities
  xx **Classical antiquities**
Greece—Biography
  x Classical biography
Greece—Civilization. *See* **Civilization, Greek**
Greece—Description and geography
  Use for descriptive and geographic works on ancient Greece instead of the subdivisions *Description and travel* and *Historical geography*
  x Description; Historical geography
  xx **Geography, Ancient; Geography, Historical**
Greece—History
  Use for works on ancient Greece from earliest times to 323 A.D.
Greece, Medieval, 323-1453. *See* **Byzantine Empire**
Greece, Modern
Greece, Modern—History
  Use for modern Greece from 1453-date
Greek antiquities. *See* **Classical antiquities**
Greek architecture. *See* **Architecture, Greek**
Greek art. *See* **Art, Greek**
Greek Church. *See* **Orthodox Eastern Church**
Greek civilization. *See* **Civilization, Greek; Hellenism**
Greek language
  May be subdivided like **English language**
  See also **Hellenism**
  x Classical languages
Greek language, Modern
  May be subdivided like **English language**
  x Romaic language
Greek letter societies. *See* **Fraternities and sororities; Secret societies**

Greek literature

May use same subdivisions and names of literary forms as for **English literature**

See also **Classical literature; Hellenism**

xx **Classical literature**

Greek literature, Modern

x Neo-Greek literature; Romaic literature

Greek mythology. *See* **Mythology, Classical**

Greek philosophy. *See* **Philosophy, Ancient**

Greek sculpture. *See* **Sculpture, Greek**

Greenbacks. *See* **Paper money**

Greenhouses

x Hothouses

xx **Flower gardening; Gardening**

Greeting cards

x Cards, Greeting; Christmas cards

Gregorian chant. *See* **Chants (Plain, Gregorian, etc.)**

Grey Friars. *See* **Franciscans**

Grief. *See* **Joy and sorrow**

Grinding and polishing

x Polishing

Grippe. *See* **Influenza**

Grist mills. *See* **Flour and flour mills**

Groceries

Grocery trade

See also **Supermarkets**

Grooming, Personal. *See* **Beauty, Personal; Grooming for men**

Grooming for men

See also **Men's clothing**

x Good grooming; Grooming, Personal; Male grooming; Personal appearance; Personal grooming

xx **Hygiene**

Grooming for women. *See* **Beauty, Personal**

Grottoes. *See* **Caves**

Ground cushion phenomena

See also **Ground effect machines**

x Air bearing lift

xx **Aerodynamics; Pneumatics**

Ground effect machines

See also **Helicopters; Vertically rising airplanes**

x Air bearing vehicles; Air cushion vehicles; Hovercraft; Ground proximity machines

xx **Ground cushion phenomena**

Ground proximity machines. *See* **Ground effect machines**

Grounds maintenance

Use for work on maintenance of public, industrial, and institutional grounds and large estates

See also **Golf links; Roadside improvement**

xx **Gardening**

Group discussion. *See* **Discussion groups**

248

Group health. *See* **Insurance, Health**

Group hospitalization. *See* **Insurance, Hospitalization**

Group insurance. *See* **Insurance, Group**

Group living. *See* **Collective settlements**

Group medical service. *See* **Insurance, Health**

Group work, Educational and social. *See* **Social group work**

Grouping by ability. *See* **Ability grouping in education**

Growth

Use for biological and psychological works on the growth and development of animal and human organisms

See also **Children—Growth; Growth (Plants)**

x Development; Stature

xx **Physiology**

Growth (Plants)

x Plants—Growth

xx **Growth; Plant physiology**

Guaranteed annual income

See also **Wages—Annual wage**

x Annual income guarantee; Guaranteed income

xx **Income**

Guaranteed income. *See* **Guaranteed annual income**

Guerrilla warfare

See also **World War, 1939-1945—Underground movements**

xx **Military art and science; Tactics; War**

Guests. *See* **Entertaining**

Guidance. *See* **Counseling; Personnel service in education; Vocational guidance**

Guide books. *See* names of countries, states, etc. with the subdivision *Description and travel—Guide books* (e.g. **U.S.—Description and travel—Guide books;** etc.) and names of cities with the subdivision *Description—Guide books,* e.g. **Chicago—Description—Guide books;** etc.

Guide dogs

x Blind, Dogs for the; Dog guides; Dogs for the blind; Seeing eye dogs

xx **Dogs**

Guide posts. *See* **Signs and signboards**

Guided missiles

✓ Guided missile bases

See also **Antimissile missiles; Ballistic missiles;** also names of specific missiles, e.g. **Nike rocket;** etc.

x Bombs, Flying; Flying bombs; Missiles, Guided

xx **Bombs; Projectiles; Rocketry; Rockets (Aeronautics)**

Guilds

See also **Labor and laboring classes; Labor unions**

x Gilds; Labor organizations

Guilds—*Continued*

   xx Corporations; Labor and laboring classes; Labor unions; Societies

Guitar

   xx Stringed instruments

Gulf States

   xx United States

Gums and resins

   x Resins; Rosin

   xx Chemistry, Technical; Forest products; Plastics

Gunning. *See* **Hunting**; **Shooting**

Gunpowder

   See also **Ammunition**

   x Powder, Smokeless; Smokeless powder

   xx Ammunition; Explosives; Firearms

Guns. *See* **Firearms**; **Ordnance**; **Rifles**; **Shotguns**

Gunsmithing

Gymnastics

   See also **Acrobats and acrobatics**; **Physical education and training**

   x Calisthenics

   xx Acrobats and acrobatics; Athletics; Exercise; Hygiene; Physical education and training; Sports

Gypsies

   x Gipsies

Gypsum

   x Plaster of paris

   xx Geology, Economic

Gyroscope

   xx Aeronautical instruments

H bomb. *See* **Hydrogen bomb**

Habit

   See also **Instinct**

   xx Behavior; Instinct; Psychology

Habitations, Human. *See* **Architecture, Domestic**; **Houses**; **Housing**

Habitations of animals. *See* **Animals—Habitations**

Habits of animals. *See* **Animals—Habits and behavior**

Hades. *See* **Future life**; **Hell**

Hair

   Includes works on hairdressing and haircutting

   See also **Wigs**

   xx Beauty, Personal; Head

Half-tone process. *See* **Photoengraving**

Hallmarks

   See also **Goldsmithing**; **Plate**; **Silversmithing**

   x Marks on plate

   xx Goldsmithing; Plate; Silversmithing

Halloween

   x All Hallows' Eve

   xx Folklore

Halfway houses

Hallucinations and illusions
>*See also* **Apparitions; Ghosts; Insanity;**
>>**Magic; Optical illusions; Personality**
>>**disorders**
>*x* Delusions; Illusions
>*xx* **Apparitions; Ghosts; Insanity; Per-**
>>**sonality disorders; Psychical re-**
>>**search; Psychology, Pathological;**
>>**Subconsciousness; Visions**

Hampton, Va. National Cemetery
>*xx* **Cemeteries**

Handbooks, manuals, etc. *See* general subjects
>with the subdivision *Handbooks, man-*
>*uals, etc.,* e.g. **Photography—Hand-**
>**books, manuals, etc.;** etc.

Handicapped
>*See also* **Mentally handicapped; Phys-**
>>**ically handicapped; Sick; Socially**
>>**handicapped**
>*x* Defectives; Disabled

Handicapped children
>*See also* **Mentally handicapped children;**
>>**Physically handicapped children; So-**
>>**cially handicapped children**
>*x* Abnormal children; Children, Abnormal
>*xx* **Child study; Exceptional children**

Handicraft
>*See also* **Hobbies; Industrial arts; Indus-**
>>**trial arts education; Occupational**
>>**therapy;** also names of crafts, e.g.,
>>**Leather work; Weaving;** etc.
>*x* Crafts
>*xx* **Arts and crafts; Hobbies; Industrial**
>>**arts education; Occupational therapy**

Handwriting. *See* **Autographs; Graphology;**
>**Penmanship; Writing**

Hanging. *See* **Capital punishment**

Happiness
>*See also* **Joy and sorrow; Pleasure**
>*x* Gladness
>*xx* **Ethics; Joy and sorrow; Pleasure**

Harbors
>*See also* **Docks; Pilots and pilotage;** also
>>names of cities with the subdivision
>>*Harbor,* e.g. **Chicago—Harbor;** etc.
>*x* Ports
>*xx* **Civil engineering; Docks; Hydraulic**
>>**structures; Merchant marine; Navi-**
>>**gation; Shipping; Transportation**

Hares. *See* **Rabbits**

Harmony
>*xx* **Composition (Music); Music; Music—**
>>**Study and teaching; Music—Theory**

Harry S. Truman Library, Independence, Mo.
>*xx* **Presidents—U.S.—Archives**

Harvesting machinery
>*x* Reapers
>*xx* **Agricultural machinery**

Handbell ringing

Hastings, Battle of, 1066
>*xx* Gt. Brit.—History—Norman period, 1066-1154
Hats
>*See also* Millinery
>*xx* Clothing and dress; Costume; Millinery
Haunted houses. *See* Ghosts
Hawking. *See* Falconry
Hay
>*See also* Feeding and feeds; Grasses; also names of hay crops, e.g. Alfalfa; etc.
>*xx* Farm produce; Feeding and feeds; Forage plants; Grasses
Head
>*See also* Brain; Ear; Eye; Face; Hair; Nose; Phrenology
>*x* Skull
>*xx* Brain
Healing, Mental. *See* Mental healing
Health. *See* Hygiene
Health, Mental. *See* Mental health
Health, Public. *See* Public health
Health boards
>*x* Boards of health; Public health boards
>*xx* Public health
Health care. *See* Medical care
Health education
>*See also* School hygiene
>*x* Hygiene—Study and teaching
>*xx* Children—Care and hygiene; Physical education and training
Health insurance. *See* Insurance, Health
Health of children. *See* Children—Care and hygiene
Health of infants. *See* Infants—Care and hygiene
Health of women. *See* Woman—Health and hygiene
Health resorts, spas, etc.
>*See also* Summer resorts; Winter resorts
>*x* Resorts; Sanatoriums; Spas
>*xx* Hydrotherapy; Medicine; Sick; Summer resorts; Travel; Winter resorts
Healths, Drinking of. *See* Toasts
Hearing
>*See also* Deafness; Ear
>*x* Acoustics
>*xx* Deafness; Ear; Senses and sensation; Sound
Hearing aids
>*xx* Deafness
Heart
>*See also* Blood—Circulation
>*xx* Anatomy; Physiology
Heart—Diseases
>*x* Angina pectoris; Cardiac diseases; Coronary heart diseases
Heart—Surgery
>*x* Open heart surgery
>*xx* Surgery

✓ Health facilities

252

Heart—Transplantation
 xx Transplantation of organs, tissues, etc.
Heat
 See also Combustion; Fire; Steam; Temperature; Thermodynamics; Thermometers and thermometry
 xx Combustion; Electromagnetic waves; Fire; Temperature; Thermodynamics
Heat—Conduction
Heat—Transmission
Heat engines
 See also Steam engines; Thermodynamics
 x Air engines; Hot air engines
 xx Engines; Thermodynamics
Heat pumps. *See* Pumping machinery
Heathenism. *See* Paganism
Heating
 See also Boilers; Chimneys; Electric heating; Fireplaces; Fuel; Furnaces; Hot air heating; Hot water heating; Insulation (Heat); Oil burners; Radiant heating; Steam heating; Stoves; Ventilation
 xx Fire; Fuel; Home economics; Ventilation
Heaven
 See also Future life
 xx Death; Eschatology
Heavy water. *See* Deuterium oxide
Hebrew language
 May be subdivided like English language
 See also Yiddish language
 x Jewish language; Jews—Language
Hebrew literature
 May use same subdivisions and names of literary forms as for English literature
 See also Bible; Jewish literature; Talmud
 x Jews—Literature
 xx Jewish literature
Hebrews. *See* Jews
Heirs. *See* Inheritance and succession
Helicopters
 x Aircraft
 xx Aeronautics; Ground effect machines
Heliports
 xx Airports
Helium
 xx Radioactivity
Hell
 x Eternal punishment; Hades; Retribution
 xx Death; Eschatology
Hellenism
 See also Neoplatonism
 x Greek civilization
 xx Civilization, Greek; Greek language; Greek literature; Humanism

Hemp
> *See also* Fibers; Rope
> *xx* Fibers; Linen; Rope

Heraldry
> *See also* Chivalry; Decorations of honor; Flags; Genealogy; Insignia; Knights and knighthood; Mottoes; Nobility; Seals (Numismatics)
> *x* Arms, Coats of; Coats of arms; Crests; Devices (Heraldry); Emblems; Pedigrees
> *xx* Archeology; Biography; Chivalry; Decorations of honor; Genealogy; Knights and knighthood; Nobility; Signs and symbols; Symbolism

Herbage. *See* **Grasses**

Herbals. *See* **Botany, Medical; Herbs; Materia medica**

Herbaria. *See* **Plants—Collection and preservation**

Herbs
> *x* Herbals

Herbs, Medical. *See* **Botany, Medical**

Hereditary succession. *See* **Inheritance and succession**

Heredity
> *See also* Blood groups; DNA; Eugenics; Evolution; Mendel's law; Natural selection; Variation (Biology)
> *x* Ancestry; Descent; Genes; Inheritance (Biology)
> *xx* Biology; Children; Eugenics; Evolution; Genetics; Man; Mendel's law; Natural selection; Sociology

Hermeneutics, Biblical. *See* **Bible—Criticism, interpretation, etc.**

Hermetic art and philosophy. *See* **Alchemy; Astrology; Occult sciences**

Hermits
> *x* Recluses
> *xx* Christian biography; Monasticism and religious orders; Saints

Heroes
> *See also* Courage; Explorers; Martyrs; Mythology; Saints
> *x* Heroines; Heroism
> *xx* Adventure and adventurers; Courage; Mythology

Heroines. *See* **Heroes; Woman—Biography; Women in literature and art; Women in the Bible**

Heroism. *See* **Courage; Heroes**

Hertzian waves. *See* **Electric waves**

Hibernation. See **Animals—Hibernation**

Hides and skins
> *See also* Fur; Leather; Tanning
> *x* Animal products; Pelts; Skins
> *xx* Fur; Leather; Tanning

✓ Herbicides

✓ Heritage Center

Hieroglyphics
> *See also* **Picture writing; Rosetta stone inscription**
>
> *xx* **Inscriptions; Picture writing; Writing**

Hi-fi systems. *See* **High-fidelity sound systems**

High-fidelity sound systems
> *See also* **Stereophonic sound systems**
>
> *x* Hi-fi systems
>
> *xx* **Electronics; Sound—Recording and reproducing**

High-frequency radio. *See* **Radio, Short wave**

High school education. *See* **Education, Secondary**

High school libraries. *See* **School libraries (High school)**

High schools
> *See also* **Commencements; Education, Secondary; Junior high schools;** also names of cities with the subdivision *Public schools,* e.g. **Chicago—Public schools;** etc.
>
> *x* Secondary schools
>
> *xx* **Education, Secondary; Public schools; Schools**

High schools, Junior. *See* **Junior high schools**

High schools, Rural. *See* **Rural schools**

High society. *See* **Upper classes**

High speed aerodynamics. *See* **Aerodynamics, Supersonic**

High speed aeronautics
> *See also* **Aerodynamics, Supersonic; Aerothermodynamics; Rocket planes; Rockets (Aeronautics)**
>
> *x* Aeronautics, High speed
>
> *xx* **Aeronautics**

High treason. *See* **Treason**

Higher criticism. *See* **Bible—Criticism, interpretation, etc.**

Higher education. *See* **Education, Higher**

Highjacking of airplanes. *See* **Hijacking of airplanes**

Highland clans. *See* **Clans and clan system**

Highland costume. *See* **Tartans**

Highway accidents. *See* **Traffic accidents**

Highway beautification. *See* **Roadside improvement**

Highway construction. *See* **Roads**

Highway engineering
> *See also* **Roads; Traffic engineering**
>
> *x* Road engineering
>
> *xx* **Civil engineering; Roads**

Highway transportation. *See* **Transportation, Highway**

Highwaymen. *See* **Robbers and outlaws**

Highways. *See* **Roads; Streets**

Hijacking of airplanes
> *x* Aeronautics, Commercial—Hijacking; Air lines—Hijacking; Air piracy; Air-

Hijacking of airplanes—*Continued*
planes—Hijacking; Highjacking of airplanes; Sky hijacking; Skyjacking
xx **Offenses against public safety**

Hiking
See also **Backpacking; Walking**
xx **Outdoor life; Walking**

Hindoos. *See* **Hindus**

Hinduism
See also **Brahmanism; Caste; Vedas; Yoga**
xx **Brahmanism; Religions**

Hindus
See also **East Indians**
x Hindoos
xx **East Indians**

Hippies (May subdiv. geog.)
x Yippies
xx **Bohemianism**

Hippies—Religious life
x Jesus people; Religious people

Hippies—U.S.
x U.S.—Hippies

Hire-purchase plan. *See* **Instalment plan**

Hispanic-American literature. *See* **Latin American literature**

Hispano-American War, 1898. *See* **U.S.—History—War of 1898**

Histochemistry. *See* **Physiological chemistry**

Histology. *See* **Anatomy; Anatomy, Comparative; Botany—Anatomy; Cells**

Historians (May subdiv. geog. adjective form, e.g. **Historians, English;** etc.)
See also **Archeologists**
x Writers
xx **Historiography; History**

Historians, American
x American historians; U.S.—Historians

✓ **Historic houses, etc.**
See also **Literary landmarks;** also names of countries, cities, etc. with the subdivision *Historic houses, etc.* e.g. **U.S. —Historic houses, etc.;** etc.
x Houses, Historic

Historical atlases. *See* **Atlases, Historical**

Historical chronology. *See* **Chronology, Historical**

Historical dictionaries. *See* **History—Dictionaries**

Historical fiction
Use for works about historical fiction. For historical novels see names of historical events and characters with the subdivision *Fiction,* e.g. **U.S.—History—Civil War—Fiction; Slavery in the U.S.—Fiction; Napoléon I, Emperor of the French—Fiction;** etc.
x Fiction, Historical
xx **Fiction; History**

[handwritten in right margin:] ✓ Historic sites   See also   ✓ Historic houses, etc.

Historical geography. *See* **Atlases, Historical; Geography, Historical;** names of modern countries or regions with the subdivision *Historical geography* (e.g. **U.S.—Historical geography;** etc.); and names of ancient countries with the subdivision *Description and geography,* e.g. **Greece—Description and geography;** etc.

Historical geology. *See* **Geology, Stratigraphic**

Historical records—Preservation. *See* **Archives**

Historical societies. *See* **History—Societies**

Historiography

See note under **History**

See also **Historians;** also subjects with the subdivision *History—Historiography,* e.g. **U.S.—History—Historiography;** etc.

x History—Criticism; History—Historiography

History

Use for general works on history as a science. This includes the principles of history, the influence of various factors on history and the relation of the science of history to other subjects. Works on the interpretation and meaning of history, the course of events and their resulting consequences, are entered under **History—Philosophy.** Works limited to the study and criticism of sources of history, methods of historical research and writing of history, are entered under **Historiography**

See also

Anthropogeography	Historical fiction
Archeology	Kings and rulers
Biography	Man
Church history	Middle Ages—History
Civilization	tory
Colonization	Military history
Constitutional history	Naval history
tory	Numismatics
Discoveries (in geography)	Oral history
ography)	Political science
Ethnology	Seals (Numismatics
Genealogy	ics
Geography, Historical	World history
cal	
Historians	

and headings beginning with the word **History;** also names of countries, states, etc. with the subdivisions *Antiquities; Foreign relations; History; Politics and government.* For the history of a subject see the name of the subject with the subdivision *History,* or, for literature and music headings, *History and criticism,* e.g. **Art—History; English language—History; English lit-**

History—*Continued*

erature—History and criticism; Music—History and criticism; etc.

x Social studies

History, Ancient

See also **Archeology; Bible; Civilization, Ancient; Classical dictionaries; Geography, Ancient; Inscriptions; Numismatics;** also names of ancient races and peoples (e.g. **Hittites;** etc.) ; and names of countries of antiquity

x Ancient history

xx **World history**

History—Atlases. *See* **Atlases, Historical**

History, Biblical. *See* **Bible—History of Biblical events**

History—Chronology. *See* **Chronology, Historical**

History, Church. *See* **Church history**

History, Constitutional. *See* **Constitutional history**

History—Criticism. *See* **Historiography**

History—Dictionaries

x Historical dictionaries

History—Historiography. *See* **Historiography;** also subjects with the subdivisions *History—Historiography,* e.g. **U.S.—History—Historiography;** etc.

History, Local. *See* names of countries, states, etc. with the subdivision *History, Local,* e.g. **U.S.—History, Local;** etc.

History, Medieval. *See* **Middle Ages—History**

History, Military. *See* **Military history;** and names of countries with the subdivision *History, Military,* e.g. **U.S.—History, Military;** etc.

History, Modern

Use for works covering the period after 1453

See also **Civilization, Modern; Reformation; Renaissance**

x Modern history

xx **Civilization, Modern; World history**

History, Modern—19th century

See also **Nineteenth century**

History, Modern—20th century

See also **European War, 1914-1918; Twentieth century; World War, 1939-1945**

History, Modern—Philosophy. *See* **History—Philosophy**

History, Modern—Study and teaching

See also **Current events**

History, Natural. *See* **Natural history**

History, Naval. *See* **Naval history;** and names of countries with the subdivision *History, Naval,* e.g. **U.S.—History, Naval;** etc.

History, Oral. *See* **Oral history**

History—Philosophy

See note under **History**

See also **Civilization**

x History, Modern—Philosophy; Philosophy of history

xx **Philosophy**

History—Societies

See also **U.S.—History—Societies**

x Historical societies

History—Sources

Use only for documents, records and other source materials upon which narrative history is based

See also **Archives; Charters;** also names of countries, states, etc. with the subdivision *History—Sources* (e.g. **U.S.—History—Sources;** etc.); and names of periods of history and names of wars with the subdivision *Sources,* e.g. **U.S.—History—Civil War—Sources; World War, 1939-1945—Sources;** etc.

History, Universal. *See* **World history**

Histrionics. *See* **Acting; Theater**

Hitchhiking. *See* **Walking**

Hittites

xx **History, Ancient**

Hoaxes. *See* **Impostors and Imposture**

Hobbies

See also **Collectors and collecting; Handicraft;** also names of hobbies

xx **Amusements; Handicraft; Leisure; Recreation**

Hockey

See also **Field hockey**

x Ice hockey

xx **Winter sports**

Hogs

See also **Pigs**

x Swine

xx **Domestic animals; Livestock**

Hoisting machinery

See also types of hoisting machinery; e.g. **Conveying machinery; Cranes, derricks, etc.; Elevators;** etc.

x Lifts

xx **Conveying machinery**

Holding companies

xx **Corporations; Public utilities; Trusts, Industrial**

Holiday decorations

x Decorations, Holiday

xx **Decoration and ornament**

Holidays

See also **Fasts and feasts; Vacations;** also names of holidays, e.g. **Fourth of July;** etc.

x Anniversaries; Days; Legal holidays; National holidays

xx **Fasts and feasts; Festivals; Manners and customs; Vacations**

259

Holland. *See* **Netherlands**

Holy Ghost. *See* **Holy Spirit**

Holy Grail. *See* **Grail**

Holy Roman Empire

 xx Austria—History; Europe—History—
  476-1492; Germany — History — To
  1517; Middle Ages—History

Holy Scriptures. *See* **Bible**

Holy See. *See* **Catholic Church; Papacy;
 Popes**

Holy Spirit

 See also **Trinity**

 x Holy Ghost; Spirit, Holy

 xx **God; Theology; Trinity**

Holy Week

 See also **Easter; Good Friday**

 xx **Lent**

Home

 See also **Family; Home economics; Marriage**

 xx **Family; Marriage**

Home and school

 See also **Parents' and teachers' associations**

 x Parents and teachers; School and home;
  Teachers and parents

 xx **Parents' and teachers' associations**

Home decoration. *See* **Interior decoration**

Home economics

 See also

Consumer education	House cleaning
Cookery	Household employees
Cost and standard	Household pests
of living	Interior decorations
Dairying	Laundry
Entertaining	Mobile home liv-
Food	ing
Fuel	Sewing
Furniture	Shopping
Heating	

 x Domestic arts; Efficiency, Household;
  Household management; Housekeeping

 xx **Family life education; Home**

Home economics—Accounting. *See* **Budgets,
 Household**

Home economics—Equipment and supplies. *See*
 Household equipment and supplies

Home economics as a profession

Home education. *See* **Correspondence schools
 and courses; Self-culture**

Home life. *See* **Family**

Home missions. *See* **Missions**

Home nursing

 See also **Sick**

 xx **Nurses and nursing; Sick**

Home repairing. *See* **Houses—Repairing**

Home study courses. *See* **Correspondence
 schools and courses; Self-culture**

Homeopathy

 xx **Medicine; Medicine—Practice**

260

Homes. *See* **Houses**

Homes (Institutions). *See* **Charities; Institutional care; Orphans and orphans' homes;** also classes of people with the subdivision *Institutional care*, e.g. **Blind—Institutional care; Children—Institutional care; Deaf—Institutional care;** etc.

Homes for the aged. *See* **Aged—Dwellings**

Homonyms. *See* names of languages with the subdivision *Homonyms*, e.g. **English language—Homonyms;** etc.

Homosexuality
>*See also* **Lesbianism**
>*x* Gay liberation

Honesty
>*See also* **Business ethics; Truthfulness and falsehood**
>*x* Dishonesty
>*xx* **Behavior; Business ethics; Ethics; Truthfulness and falsehood**

Honey
>*See also* **Bees**
>*xx* **Bees**

Honor system. *See* **Self-government (in education)**

Honorary degrees. *See* **Degrees, Academic**

Hooked rugs. *See* **Rugs, Hooked**

Hoover Dam
>*x* Boulder Dam; Colorado River—Hoover Dam
>*xx* **Dams**

Hormones
>*See also* **Glands, Ductless**
>*xx* **Glands, Ductless**

Hornbooks
>*xx* **Primers**

Horology. *See* **Clocks and watches; Sundials**

Horoscope. *See* **Astrology**

Horror stories
>*x* Stories
>*xx* **Fiction**

Horse. *See* **Horses**

Horse racing
>*x* Racing
>*xx* **Gambling**

Horsebreaking. *See* **Horses—Training**

Horsemanship
>*See also* **Rodeos**
>*x* Equestrianism; Riding

Horses
>*See also* **Ponies**
>*x* Horse
>*xx* **Domestic animals; Livestock**

Horses—Diseases

Horses—Training
>*x* Horsebreaking
>*xx* **Animals—Training**

Horseshoeing. *See* **Blacksmithing**

Horticulture. *See* **Gardening**

✓ *Horseshoe pitching*

Hosiery

    x Stockings

    xx **Clothing and dress; Textile industry and fabrics**

Hospital endowments. *See* **Endowments**

Hospital libraries

    x Libraries, Hospital

    xx **Libraries**

Hospitality. *See* **Entertaining**

Hospitalization insurance. *See* **Insurance, Hospitalization**

✓ **Hospitals** (May subdiv. geog. country or state)

    See also **Children—Hospitals; Medical centers; Nurses and nursing;** also names of cities with the subdivision *Hospitals,* e.g. **Chicago—Hospitals;** etc., and names of hospitals

    x Infirmaries; Institutions, Charitable and philanthropic; Sanatoriums

    xx **Charities, Medical; Institutional care; Medical centers; Medicine; Nurses and nursing; Public health; Public welfare; Sick**

Hospitals, Military

    See also **First aid;** also names of wars with the subdivision *Medical and sanitary affairs,* e.g. **World War, 1939-1945— Medical and sanitary affairs;** etc.

    x Field hospitals; Military hospitals; Veterans—Hospitals

    xx **Medicine, Military; Military art and science; Veterans**

Hospitals—U.S.

    x U.S.—Hospitals

Hostels, Youth. *See* **Youth hostels**

Hostesses, Air line. *See* **Air lines—Hostesses**

Hot air engines. *See* **Heat engines**

Hot air heating

    x Warm air heating

    xx **Heating**

Hot springs. *See* **Geysers**

Hot water heating

    xx **Heating**

✓ **Hotels, motels, etc.** (May subdiv. geog. country or state)

    See also names of cities with the subdivision *Hotels, motels, etc.,* e.g. **Chicago —Hotels, motels, etc.;** etc.

    x Auto courts; Boarding houses; Inns; Lodging houses; Motor courts; Rooming houses; Tourist accommodations

Hotels, motels, etc.—U.S.

    x U.S.—Hotels, motels, etc.

Hothouses. *See* **Greenhouses**

Hours of labor

    See also **Child labor; Woman—Employment**

    x Eight-hour day; Five-day work week; Four-day work week; Labor, Hours

Hospital chaplains
See chaplains, Hospital

✓ *Hot line*

Hours of labor—*Continued*
>   of; Overtime; Woman—Hours of
>   labor; Working day
>   *xx* **Child labor; Labor and laboring
>   classes; Woman—Employment**

House boats. *See* **Houseboats**

House cleaning
>   *xx* **Cleaning; Home economics; Sanita-
>   tion, Household**

House decoration. *See* **Interior decoration**

House drainage. *See* **Drainage, House**

House flies. *See* **Flies**

House furnishing. *See* **Interior decoration**

House painting
>   *xx* **Painting, Industrial**

House plans. *See* **Architecture, Domestic—
>   Designs and plans**

House plants
>   *xx* **Flower gardening; Plants; Plants, Cul-
>   tivated; Window gardening**

House repairing. *See* **Houses—Repairing**

House sanitation. *See* **Sanitation, Household**

House trailers. *See* **Travel trailers and camp-
>   ers**

Houseboats
>   *x* House boats
>   *xx* **Boats and boating**

Household appliances. *See* **Household equip-
>   ment and supplies**

Household appliances, Electric
>   *x* Appliances, Electric; Domestic appli-
>   ances; Electric apparatus and appli-
>   ances, Domestic; Electric appliances;
>   Electric household appliances; Elec-
>   tricity in the home; Labor saving de-
>   vices, Household
>   *xx* **Electric apparatus and appliances;
>   Household equipment and supplies**

Household budget. *See* **Budgets, Household**

Household equipment and supplies
>   *See also* **Household appliances, Electric**
>   *x* Cooking utensils; Domestic appliances;
>   Home economics—Equipment and sup-
>   plies; Household appliances; Imple-
>   ments, utensils, etc.; Kitchen utensils;
>   Labor saving devices, Household;
>   Utensils, Kitchen

Household employees
>   *x* Domestic service; Housemaids; Servants
>   *xx* **Home economics; Labor and laboring
>   classes**

Household expenses. *See* **Budgets, Household;
>   Cost and standard of living**

Household management. *See* **Home economics**

Household moving. *See* **Moving, Household**

Household pests
>   *See also* names of pests, e.g. **Flies**; etc.
>   *x* Diseases and pests; Pests; Vermin
>   *xx* **Home economics; Insects, Injurious
>   and beneficial; Sanitation, Household**

263

Household sanitation. *See* **Sanitation, Household**

Housekeeping. *See* **Home economics**

Housemaids. *See* **Household employees**

Houses

Use for general works on houses

See also **Apartment houses; Building; Building—Repair and reconstruction; Housing; Tenement houses**

x Cottages; Dwellings; Habitations, Human; Homes; Residences; Summer homes

xx **Architecture, Domestic**

Houses, Historic. *See* **Historic houses, etc.**

Houses, Prefabricated. *See* **Prefabricated houses**

Houses—Repairing

x Home repairing; House repairing

Houses of animals. *See* **Animals—Habitations**

Housing

Use for works on the social and economic aspects of the housing problem, including dwellings for the working classes, slum clearance, etc.

See also **Apartment houses; City planning; Tenement houses**

x Habitations, Human; Labor and laboring classes—Housing; Slums; Workingmen's dwellings

xx **Apartment houses; City planning; Houses; Landlord and tenant; Social problems; Tenement houses; Welfare work in industry**

Housing, Discrimination in. *See* **Discrimination in housing**

Housing, Negro. *See* **Negroes—Housing**

Housing for the aged. *See* **Aged—Dwellings**

Housing for the physically handicapped. *See* **Physically handicapped—Dwellings**

Houston, Tex. Baseball Club (National League). *See* **Houston Astros**

Houston Astros

x Astros; Houston, Tex. Baseball Club (National League)

Hovercraft. *See* **Ground effect machines**

Hudson River—Bridges

xx **Bridges**

Huguenots

xx **Christianity; Reformation; St. Bartholomew's Day, Massacre of, 1572**

Hull House, Chicago

xx **Social settlements**

Human body. *See* **Anatomy; Physiology**

Human cold storage. *See* **Cryonics**

Human ecology

See also **Anthropogeography; Environmental policy; Man—Influence of environment; Man—Influence on nature; Population**

264

Human ecology—*Continued*

    x Ecology, Human; Ecology, Social; Environment; Social ecology

  xx **Environmental policy; Sociology**

Human engineering

    Use for works on engineering design as related to man's anatomical, physiological and psychological capabilities and limitations

    See also **Life support systems (Space environment)**

    x Biomechanics; Ergomanics

  xx **Design, Industrial; Machinery—Design; Psychology, Applied**

Human figure in art. *See* **Anatomy, Artistic; Figure drawing; Figure painting**

Human race. *See* **Anthropology; Man**

Human relations

    Use for works that deal with the integration of people so that they can live and work together with psychological, social and economic satisfaction

    See also **Behavior; Conflict of generations; Discrimination; Family; Intercultural education; Personnel management; Prejudices and antipathies; Psychology, Applied; Social adjustment; Toleration;** also interpersonal relations between individuals or group of individuals, e.g. **Landlord and tenant; Parent and child;** etc.

    x Interpersonal relations

  xx **Behavior; Family life education; Psychology, Applied; Social psychology**

Human resource development. *See* **Manpower policy**

Human rights. *See* **Civil rights**

Humanism

    Use for works on culture founded on the study of the classics, sometimes narrowly for Greek and Roman scholarship

    See also **Classical education; Hellenism; Humanities; Learning and scholarship; Renaissance**

  xx **Classical education; Culture; Learning and scholarship; Literature; Philosophy; Renaissance**

Humanism—20th century

    Use for works on any intellectual, philosophical or religious movement or system which is centered in man rather than in nature, the supernatural, or the absolute

Humanities

    See also **Classical education;** and such subjects as **Art; Literature; Music; Philosophy;** etc.

  xx **Classical education; Humanism**

Humanities and science. *See* **Science and the humanities**

Humanity, Religion of. *See* **Positivism**

Humor. *See* **Wit and humor**

Humorists

  xx **Wit and humor**

Humorous pictures. *See* **Cartoons and caricatures; Comic books, strips, etc.**

Humorous poetry

  See also **Limericks; Nonsense verses**

Humorous stories. *See* **Wit and humor**

Hundred Years' War, 1339-1453

  xx **Europe—History—476-1492; France—History—House of Valois, 1328-1589; Gt. Brit.—History—Lancaster and York, 1399-1485**

Hungary—History

Hungary—History—Revolution, 1956

  xx **Revolutions**

Hunting (May subdiv. geog.)

  See also **Falconry; Game and game birds; Game preserves; Game protection; Shooting; Tracking and trailing; Trapping**

  x The chase; Field sports; Gunning

  xx **Game and game birds; Shooting; Trapping**

Hunting—U.S.

  x U.S.—Hunting

Hurricanes

  Use for storms originating in the region of the West Indies

  See also **Cyclones; Storms**; also names of particular hurricanes, e.g. **New England—Hurricane, 1938;** etc.

  xx **Meteorology; Storms; Winds**

Hybridization. *See* **Plant breeding**

Hydraulic cement. *See* **Cement**

Hydraulic engineering

  See also

Boring	Irrigation
Drainage	Pumping machinery
Dredging	Reclamation of land
Flood control	Rivers
Hydraulic structures	Turbines
	Water
Hydraulics	Water supply engineering
Hydrodynamics	
Hydrostatics	Wells

  xx **Civil engineering; Engineering; Hydraulics; Rivers; Water; Water power; Water supply engineering**

Hydraulic machinery

  See also **Turbines**

  xx **Machinery; Water power**

Hydraulic structures

  See also **Aqueducts; Canals; Dams; Docks; Harbors; Reservoirs**

  xx **Hydraulic engineering; Structural engineering**

Hydraulics

> Use for works on technical applications of the theory of hydrodynamics

> *See also* **Hydraulic engineering; Hydrodynamics; Hydrostatics; Water; Water power**

> *x* Water flow

> *xx* **Hydraulic engineering; Liquids; Mechanics; Physics**

Hydrodynamics

> Use for works on the theory of the motion and action of fluids. Works on the experimental investigation and technical application of this theory are entered under **Hydraulics**

> *See also* **Hydrostatics; Viscosity; Waves**

> *xx* **Dynamics; Hydraulic engineering; Hydraulics; Liquids; Mechanics**

Hydroelectric power. *See* **Water power**

Hydrofoil boats

Hydrogen

> *xx* **Chemical elements**

Hydrogen bomb

> *See also* **Atomic bomb; Radioactive fallout**

> *x* H bomb

> *xx* **Atomic bomb; Atomic warfare; Atomic weapons; Bombs**

Hydrogen nucleus. *See* **Protons**

Hydrology. *See* **Water**

Hydropathy. *See* **Hydrotherapy**

Hydrophobia. *See* **Rabies**

Hydroponics. *See* **Plants—Soilless culture**

Hydrostatics

> *See also* **Gases**

> *xx* **Hydraulic engineering; Hydraulics; Hydrodynamics; Liquids; Mechanics; Physics; Statics**

Hydrotherapy

> *See also* **Baths; Health resorts, spas, etc.**

> *x* Hydropathy; Water cure

> *xx* **Baths; Physical therapy; Therapeutics; Water**

Hygiene

> *See also*

Air	**Infants—Care and**
Baths	**hygiene**
Beauty, Personal	**Mental health**
Children—Care and	**Military hygiene**
hygiene	**Narcotics**
Clothing and dress	**Occupational dis-**
Diet	**eases**
Disinfection and	**Physical education**
disinfectants	**and training**
Exercise	**Physiology**
Food	**Rest**
Grooming	**Sanitation**
for men	**School hygiene**
Gymnastics	**Sleep**

Hygiene—*Continued*

 Stimulants

 Temperance

 Ventilation

 Water—Pollution

 Woman—Health
  and hygiene

    x Cleaniness; Health; Hygiene, Social; Medicine, Preventive; Preventive medicine; Social hygiene

    xx **Medicine; Sanitation**

Hygiene, Industrial. *See* **Occupational diseases**

Hygiene, Mental. *See* **Mental health**

Hygiene, Military. *See* **Military hygiene**

Hygiene, Public. *See* **Public health**

Hygiene, Rural

    x Rural hygiene

Hygiene, School. *See* **School hygiene**

Hygiene, Sexual. *See* **Sexual hygiene**

Hygiene, Social. *See* **Hygiene; Prostitution; Public health; Sexual hygiene; Venereal diseases**

Hygiene—Study and teaching. *See* **Health education**

Hygiene of employment. *See* **Occupational diseases**

Hymenoptera. *See* **Ants; Bees; Wasps**

Hymnology. *See* **Hymns**

Hymns

    See also **Carols; Church music; Religious poetry**

    x Hymnology; Psalmody

    xx **Church music; Devotional exercises; Poetry; Religious poetry; Songs; Vocal music**

Hypnotism

    See also **Mental suggestion; Mind and body; Personality disorders; Psychoanalysis; Subconsciousness; Therapeutics, Suggestive**

    x Animal magnetism; Autosuggestion; Mesmerism

    xx **Clairvoyance; Medicine; Mental healing; Mental suggestion; Mind and body; Mind reading; Personality disorders; Psychical research; Psychoanalysis; Psychology, Physiological; Subconsciousness; Therapeutics, Suggestive; Thought transference**

IBM 7090 (Computer)

    xx **Computers**

ICBM. *See* **Intercontinental ballistic missiles**

Ice

    See also **Glaciers; Icebergs**

    x Freezing

    xx **Cold; Frost; Physical geography; Water**

Ice age. *See* **Glacial epoch**

Ice boats. *See* **Iceboats**

Ice cream, ices, etc.

    See also **Confectionery**

    x Frozen food; Ices

    xx **Desserts; Food, Frozen**

Ice hockey. *See* **Hockey**

Ice manufacture. *See* **Refrigeration and refrigerating machinery**

Ice skating. *See* **Skating**

Ice sports. *See* **Winter sports**

Icebergs
 xx **Ice; Ocean; Physical geography**

Iceboats
 x Ice boats
 xx **Boats and boating; Winter sports**

Iceboxes. *See* **Refrigeration and refrigerating machinery**

Icelandic and Old Norse languages
 See also **Scandinavian languages**
 x Norse languages; Old Norse language
 xx **Scandinavian languages**

Icelandic and Old Norse literature
 See also **Eddas; Sagas; Scalds and scaldic poetry; Scandinavian literature**
 x Norse literature; Old Norse literature
 xx **Sagas; Scalds and scaldic poetry; Scandinavian literature**

Ices. *See* **Ice cream, ices, etc.**

Ichthyology. *See* **Fishes**

Icings, Cake. *See* **Cake decorating**

Iconography. *See* **Art; Christian art and symbolism; Portraits**

Ideal states. *See* **Utopias**

Idealism
 See also **Materialism; Realism; Transcendentalism**
 xx **Materialism; Philosophy; Positivism; Realism; Transcendentalism**

Identification
 See also **Fingerprints;** also subjects with the subdivision *Identification,* e.g. **Airplanes—Identification; Crime and criminals—Identification;** etc.

Identity, Personal. *See* **Personality**

Idiocy. *See* **Mentally handicapped**

Idioms. *See* names of languages with the subdivision *Idioms,* e.g. **English language —Idioms;** etc.

Illegitimacy
 x Bastardy; Children, Illegitimate; Legitimacy (Law)
 xx **Parent and child**

Illiteracy
 x Literacy
 xx **Education**

Illiterate societies. *See* **Society, Primitive**

Illuminated manuscripts. *See* **Illumination of books and manuscripts**

Illuminating gas. *See* **Gas**

Illumination. *See* **Lighting**

Illumination of books and manuscripts
 See also **Initials**
 x Illuminated manuscripts; Manuscripts, Illuminated; Miniatures (Illumination

269

Illumination of books and mansucripts
—*Continued*

of books and manuscripts) ; Ornamental alphabets

xx Alphabets; Art; Art, Medieval; Arts and crafts; Books; Christian art and symbolism; Decoration and ornament; Design, Decorative; Illustration of books; Initials; Manuscripts

Illusions. *See* Hallucinations and illusions; Optical illusions

Illustration of books

See also Caldecott Medal books; Drawing; Engraving; Illumination of books and manuscripts; Photomechanical processes

x Book illustration

xx Art; Art, Decorative; Books; Color printing; Decoration and ornament; Drawing

Illustrations. *See* subjects with the subdivision *Pictorial works;* e.g. Animals—Pictorial works; U.S.—History—Civil War—Pictorial works; etc.

Illustrations, Humorous. *See* Cartoons and caricatures

Illustrators (May subdiv. geog. adjective form, e.g. Illustrators, French; etc.)

xx Artists

Illustrators, American

x American illustrators; U.S.—Illustrators

Imaginary animals. *See* Animals, Mythical

Imagination

See also Creation (Literary, artistic, etc.)

xx Educational psychology; Intellect; Psychology

Imbecility. *See* Mentally handicapped

Immersion, Baptismal. *See* Baptism

Immigrants. *See* Immigration and emigration

Immigration and emigration

Use for works on migration from one country to another. Works on the movement of population within a country for permanent settlements are entered under Migration, Internal

See also Aliens; Anthropogeography; Colonization; Naturalization; Refugees; also names of countries with the subdivision *Immigration and emigration* (e.g. U.S.—Immigration and emigration; etc.) ; names of countries, cities, etc. with the subdivision *Foreign population* (e.g. U.S.—Foreign population; etc.) ; and names of nationalities, e.g. Italians in the U.S.; etc.

x Emigration; Foreign population; Immigrants; Migration; Population, Foreign

xx Colonies; Colonization; Race problems; Social problems; Sociology

Immoral art. *See* Pornography

Immoral literature. *See* **Pornography**

Immortality

Use for works dealing with the question of the endless existence of the soul. Works dealing with the character and form of a future existence are entered under **Future life**

See also **Future life**

x Life after death

xx **Eschatology; Future life; Soul; Theology**

Immunity

See also **Allergy; Communicable diseases; Vaccination**

x Medicine, Preventive; Preventive medicine

xx **Bacteriology; Communicable diseases; Pathology; Vaccination**

Impeachment. *See* **Recall**

Imperialism

See also names of countries with the subdivision *Foreign relations,* e.g. **U.S.— Foreign relations;** etc.

x Colonialism

xx **Political science**

Implements, utensils, etc. *See* **Agricultural machinery; Household equipment and supplies; Stone implements; Tools**

Imports. *See* **Commerce; Tariff**

Impostors and imposture

See also **Counterfeits and counterfeiting; Forgery; Fraud; Quacks and quackery; Swindlers and swindling**

x Hoaxes

xx **Fraud; Swindlers and swindling**

Impregnation, Artificial. *See* **Artificial insemination**

Impressionism (Art)

See also **Postimpressionism (Art)**

x Neo-impressionism (Art)

xx **Painting; Postimpressionism (Art)**

Imprisonment. *See* **Prisons**

In line data processing. *See* **On line data processing**

Inaudible sound. *See* **Ultrasonics**

Incandescent lamps. *See* **Electric lamps**

Incas

xx **Indians of South America**

Incendiary bombs

x Bombs, Incendiary; Fire bombs

xx **Bombs**

Incineration. *See* **Cremation; Refuse and refuse disposal**

Income

See also **Capital; Guaranteed annual income; Profit**

x Fortunes

xx **Economics; Finance; Profit; Property; Wealth**

271

Income tax

    x Direct taxation; Payroll taxes; Taxation of income

    xx **Finance; Internal revenue; Taxation; Wealth**

Independence Day (U.S.). *See* **Fourth of July**

Indeterminism. *See* **Free will and determinism**

Index librorum prohibitorum. *See* **Books—Censorship; Catholic literature**

Indexes

    See also **Subject headings**; also subjects with the subdivision *Indexes,* e.g. **Newspapers—Indexes; Periodicals—Indexes; Short stories—Indexes**; etc.

    xx **Bibliography**

Indexing

    See also **Cataloging; Files and filing**

    xx **Bibliography; Cataloging; Files and filing**

India rubber. *See* **Rubber**

Indian folklore. *See* **Folklore, Indian**

Indian languages (North American). *See* **Indians of North America—Languages**

Indian reservations. *See* **Indians of North America—Reservations**

Indians

    Use for works which treat of the Indians of both South and North America. Names of tribes and linguistic families are not included in this list but may be added as needed

    May be subdivided like **Indians of North America**

    See also **Indians of Central America; Indians of Mexico; Indians of North America; Indians of South America**

    x American Indians

Indians (of India). *See* **East Indians**

Indians of Canada. *See* **Indians of North America—Canada**

Indians of Central America

    May be subdivided like **Indians of North America**

    xx **Indians**

Indians of Mexico

    May be subdivided like **Indians of North America**

    See also **Aztecs; Mayas**

    xx **Indians**

Indians of North America (May subdiv. geog. state or region)

    Names of tribes and linguistic families are not included in this list but may be added as needed, e.g. **Cherokee Indians**; etc.

    See also **Cliff dwellers and cliff dwellings; Mounds and mound builders**; also **Indians of North America—Canada**; and names of tribes and linguistic families, e.g. **Cherokee Indians**; etc.

272

Indians of North America—*Continued*

    x Aborigines; American aborigines; American Indians; North American Indians

    xx **Indians**

Indians of North America—Amusements. *See* **Indians of North America—Games; Indians of North America—Social life and customs**

Indians of North America—Antiquities

    Antiquities of a special tribe are entered under name of tribe, e.g. **Cherokee Indians—Antiquities;** etc.

    See also **Mounds and mound builders**

    x Antiquities

    xx **Archeology; U.S.—Antiquities**

Indians of North America—Art

    x Art, Indian

    xx **Art, Primitive**

Indians of North America—Canada

    x Canadian Indians; Indians of Canada

    xx **Indians of North America**

Indians of North America—Captivities

    xx **Frontier and pioneer life**

Indians of North America—Children

    xx **Children**

Indians of North America—Claims

    x Indians of North America—Legal status, etc.

Indians of North America—Costume and adornment

    xx **Costume**

Indians of North America—Customs. *See* **Indians of North America—Social life and customs**

Indians of North America—Dances

    xx **Folk dancing; Indians of North America—Religion and mythology; Indians of North America—Social life and customs**

Indians of North America—Drama

Indians of North America—Economic conditions

Indians of North America—Education

    See also names of Indian schools

    x Indians of North America—Schools

Indians of North America—Fiction

Indians of North America—Folklore. *See* **Folklore, Indian**

Indians of North America—Games

    x Indians of North America—Amusements; Indians of North America—Recreations; Indians of North America—Sports

    xx **Games; Indians of North America—Social life and customs**

Indians of North America—Government relations

    x Indians of North America—Legal status, laws, etc.

    xx **Native races**

Indians of North America—History
   See also **Indians of North America—Wars**
Indians of North America—Industries
Indians of North America—Languages
   See also **Indians of North America—Sign language**
   x Indian languages (North American)
Indians of North America—Legal status, laws, etc. *See* **Indians of North America—Claims; Indians of North America—Government relations**
Indians of North America—Legends
   Use for collections of Indian legends, myths, tales, etc. Works about the folklore of American Indians are entered under **Folklore, Indian**
   See also **Folklore, Indian**
   x Indians of North America—Mythology; Legends, Indian
   xx **Folklore, Indian**
Indians of North America—Missions
   x Missions, Indian
Indians of North America—Music
   x Music, Indian
   xx **Music, Primitive**
Indians of North America—Mythology. *See* **Folklore, Indian; Indians of North America—Legends; Indians of North America—Religion and mythology**
Indians of North America—Names
Indians of North America—Origin
Indians of North America—Poetry
Indians of North America—Recreations. *See* **Indians of North America—Games**
Indians of North America—Religion and mythology
   See also **Indians of North America—Dances; Totems and totemism**
   x Indians of North America—Mythology; Mythology, Indian
   xx **Mythology; Religion; Religion, Primitive**
Indians of North America—Reservations
   x Indian reservations; Reservations, Indian
Indians of North America—Schools. *See* **Indians of North America—Education;** and names of Indian schools
Indians of North America—Sign language
   x Sign language
   xx **Indians of North America—Languages**
Indians of North America—Social conditions
   xx **Social conditions**
Indians of North America—Social life and customs
   See also **Indians of North America—Dances; Indians of North America—Games**
   x Customs, Social; Indians of North America—Amusements; Indians of North

Indians of North America—Social life and
customs—*Continued*
America—Customs; Social customs;
Social life and customs
xx **Manners and customs; Society, Primitive**
Indians of North America—Sports. *See* **Indians
of North America—Games**
Indians of North America—Treatment
Indians of North America—Wars
See also **Black Hawk War, 1832; King
Philip's War, 1675-1676; Pontiac's
Conspiracy, 1763-1765; U.S.—History—French and Indian War, 1755-1763; U.S.—History—King William's
War, 1689-1697;** etc.
xx **Indians of North America—History**
Indians of South America (May be subdiv.
by country, e.g. **Indians of South
America—Peru;** etc.)
May be subdivided like **Indians of North
America**
See also **Incas**
x American aborigines; American Indians
xx **Indians**
Indigestion
x Dyspepsia
xx **Diet; Digestion**
Individualism
See also **Communism; Socialism**
xx **Communism; Equality; Socialism; Sociology**
Individuality
See also **Conformity; Personality; Self**
xx **Conformity; Consciousness; Personality; Psychology**
Indochina. *See* **Asia, Southeastern**
Indoor games
See also **Amusements**
xx **Amusements; Games**
Induction (Logic). *See* **Logic**
Induction coils
See also **Condensers (Electricity)**
xx **Electric apparatus and appliances**
Induction motors. *See* **Electric motors**
Industrial alcohol. *See* **Alcohol, Denatured**
Industrial arbitration. *See* **Arbitration, Industrial**
Industrial arts
See also **Art industries and trade; Arts
and crafts; Technology;** also names
of specific industries, arts, trades (e.g.
Bookbinding; Printing; Shipbuilding;
etc.) ; and names of countries, cities,
etc. with the subdivision *Industries,*
e.g. **U.S.—Industries;** etc.
x Arts, Useful; Mechanic arts; Trades;
Useful arts
xx **Handicraft; Technology**

Industrial arts education

    See also **Arts and crafts; Basketmaking; Carpentry; Handicraft; Modeling; Technical education; Woodwork**

    x Education, Industrial; Industrial education; Industrial schools; Manual training

    xx **Arts and crafts; Handicraft; Technical education; Vocational education**

Industrial arts shops. *See* **School shops**

Industrial buildings

    See also **Factories; Office buildings; Skyscrapers**

    x Buildings, Industrial

    xx **Architecture**

Industrial chemistry. *See* **Chemical engineering; Chemical industries; Chemistry, Technical**

Industrial combinations. *See* **Trusts, Industrial**

Industrial conciliation. *See* **Arbitration, Industrial**

Industrial councils. *See* **Employees' representation in management**

Industrial design. *See* **Design, Industrial**

Industrial diseases. *See* **Occupational diseases**

Industrial drawing. *See* **Mechanical drawing**

Industrial education. *See* **Industrial arts education; Technical education**

Industrial efficiency. *See* **Efficiency, Industrial**

Industrial engineering. *See* **Industrial management**

Industrial exhibitions. *See* **Exhibitions**

Industrial hygiene. *See* **Occupational diseases**

Industrial insurance. *See* **Insurance, Industrial**

Industrial management

    Use for general works on the application of the principles of management to industries, including problems of production, marketing, financial control, office management, etc. Works limited to technical aspects of manufacturing processes are entered under **Factory management**

    See also

Business	**Marketing**
Buying	**Materials handling**
Efficiency, Industrial	**Office management**
Factory management	**Personnel management**
Industrial relations	**Sales management**
Job analysis	**Welfare work in industry**
Machinery	

    x Industrial engineering; Industrial organization; Industry—Organization, control, etc.; Management, Industrial

    xx **Business; Industry; Management**

Industrial materials. *See* **Materials**

Industrial mergers. *See* **Railroads—Consolidation; Trusts, Industrial**

Industrial mobilization

Use for material dealing with industrial and labor policies and programs for defense mobilization

See also **Munitions**

x Armaments; Defenses, National; Economic mobilization; Industry and war; Mobilization, Industrial; National defenses

xx **Economic policy; Military art and science; War—Economic aspects**

Industrial organization. *See* **Industrial management**

Industrial painting. *See* **Painting, Industrial**

Industrial psychology. *See* **Psychology, Applied**

Industrial relations

Use for general works on employer-employee relations. Works on problems of personnel and relations from the employer's point of view are entered under **Personnel management**

See also **Arbitration, Industrial; Collective bargaining; Employees' representation in management; Labor contract; Labor unions; Personnel management; Strikes and lockouts**

x Capital and labor; Employer-employee relations; Labor and capital; Labor-management relations; Labor relations

xx **Industrial management; Labor and laboring classes**

Industrial revolution. *See* **Gt. Brit.—History—19th century; Industry—History**

Industrial schools. *See* **Industrial arts education; Reformatories; Technical education**

Industrial trusts. *See* **Trusts, Industrial**

Industrial wastes. *See* **Factory and trade waste; Waste products**

Industrialization

Use for general works only. Works on the industrialization of individual countries, regions, etc. are entered under the name of the country, city, etc. with the subdivision *Industries*

See also **Technical assistance; Underdeveloped areas**

xx **Economic policy; Industry; Technical assistance**

Industries. *See* **Industry**; names of industries (e.g. **Steel industry and trade;** etc.) ; and names of countries, cities, etc. with the subdivision, *Industries*, e.g. **U.S.—Industries;** etc.

Industries, Chemical. *See* **Chemical industries**

Industries, Electric. *See* **Electric industries**

Industry, *N D.*

Use for general works on manufacturing and mechanical activities. Names of all

✓ *Industrial park - Mhd*

✓ *Industrial School. See N. D. Industrial School*

✓

277

Industry—*Continued*

individual industries are not included in this list but are to be added as needed, e.g. **Steel industry and trade;** etc.

See also **Efficiency, Industrial; Industrial management; Industrialization; Machinery in industry; Manufactures**

x Industries; Production

xx **Civilization; Economics**

Industry—History

x Industrial revolution

Industry—Organization, control, etc. *See* **Industrial management; Industry and state**

Industry and art. *See* **Art industries and trade**

Industry and state (May subdiv. geog.)

Use for works on the theory of state regulation of industry and for general works on the relations between government and business

See also

Agriculture and state	**Public service commissions**
Economic policy	**Railroads and state**
Government ownership	**Subsidies**

x Business and government; Government and business; Government regulation of industry; Industry—Organization, control, etc.; Laissez faire; Socialization of industry; State and industry; State regulation of industry

xx **Economic policy; Socialism**

Industry and state—U.S.

x U.S.—Industry and state

Industry and war. *See* **Industrial mobilization; War—Economic aspects**

Inebriates. *See* **Alcoholism; Liquor problem; Temperance**

Inequality. *See* **Equality**

Infallibility of the Pope. *See* **Popes—Infallibility**

Infantile paralysis. *See* **Poliomyelitis**

Infants

Use for works about children in the earliest period of life, usually the first two years only

See also **Children**

x Babies

xx **Children**

Infants—Care and hygiene

See also **Baby sitters**

x Health of infants

xx **Children—Care and hygiene; Hygiene; Nurses and nursing**

Infants—Clothing. *See* **Children's clothing**

Infants—Diseases. *See* **Children—Diseases**

Infants—Nutrition. *See* **Children—Nutrition**

Infection and infectious diseases. *See* **Communicable diseases**

Infirmaries. *See* **Hospitals**

Inflation (Finance)
> *See also* **Currency question; Paper money; Wage-price policy**
> *xx* **Currency question; Finance**

Influenza
> *x* Grippe
> *xx* **Cold (Disease)**

Information, Freedom of. *See* **Freedom of information**

Information sciences
> *See also* **Documentation; Electronic data processing; Information storage and retrieval systems; Library science**
> *xx* **Communication**

Information storage and retrieval systems
> *See also* **Electronic data processing; Libraries—Automation**
> *x* Automatic information retrieval; Data processing; Data storage and retrieval systems; Punched card systems
> *xx* **Bibliography; Computers; Documentation; Information sciences; Libraries—Automation**

Inheritance (Biology). *See* **Heredity**

Inheritance and succession
> *See also* **Executors and administrators; Inheritance and transfer tax; Land tenure; Wills**
> *x* Bequests; Heirs; Hereditary succession; Intestacy; Legacies; Succession, Intestate
> *xx* **Parent and child; Wealth; Wills**

Inheritance and transfer tax
> *x* Estate tax; Taxation of legacies; Transfer tax
> *xx* **Estate planning; Inheritance and succession; Internal revenue; Taxation**

Initialisms. *See* **Acronyms**

Initials
> *See also* **Alphabets; Illumination of books and manuscripts; Lettering; Monograms; Printing—Specimens; Type and type-founding**
> *xx* **Alphabets; Illumination of books and manuscripts; Lettering; Monograms; Type and type-founding**

Initiative and referendum. *See* **Referendum**

Injunctions
> *See also* **Strikes and lockouts**
> *xx* **Constitutional law; Labor unions; Strikes and lockouts**

Injuries. *See* **Accidents; First aid**

Injurious insects. *See* **Insects, Injurious and beneficial**

Injurious occupations. *See* **Occupations, Dangerous**

Ink drawing. *See* **Pen drawing**

Inland navigation

> *See also* Canals; Lakes; Rivers
>
> *x* Navigation, Inland
>
> *xx* Canals; Navigation; Rivers; Shipping; Transportation; Water resources development; Waterways

Inns. *See* Hotels, motels, etc.

Inoculation. *See* Vaccination

Inorganic chemistry. *See* Chemistry, Inorganic

Insane. *See* Insanity; Mental illness

Insane—Hospitals. *See* Mentally ill—Institutional care

Insane asylums. *See* Mentally ill—Institutional care

Insanity

> *See also* Hallucinations and illusions; Mental illness; Mentally handicapped; Personality disorders; Psychiatry; Psychology, Pathological; Suicide
>
> *x* Dementia; Diseases, Mental; Insane; Lunacy; Madness; Mental diseases; Psychoses
>
> *xx* Brain—Diseases; Hallucinations and illusions; Mental illness; Nervous system—Diseases; Personality disorders; Psychiatry; Psychology, Pathological

Inscriptions

> *See also* Brasses; Epitaphs; Hieroglyphics; Seals (Numismatics)
>
> *x* Epigraphy
>
> *xx* Archeology; History, Ancient

Inscriptions, Assyrian. *See* Cuneiform inscriptions

Inscriptions, Cuneiform. *See* Cuneiform inscriptions

Insecticides

> *See also* DDT (Insecticide); Fumigation; Insects, Injurious and beneficial; Spraying and dusting
>
> *xx* Insects, Injurious and beneficial; Pesticides; Spraying and dusting

Insects

> *See also* Fertilization of plants; also names of insects, e.g. Bees; Butterflies; Wasps; etc.
>
> *x* Bugs; Entomology
>
> *xx* Animals; Invertebrates

Insects, Destructive and useful. *See* Insects, Injurious and beneficial

Insects, Injurious and beneficial

> *See also* Aeronautics in agriculture; Agricultural pests; Household pests; Insecticides; Insects as carriers of disease; also names of injurious and beneficial insects (e.g. Locusts; Silkworms; etc.); and names of crops, trees, etc. with the subdivision *Diseases*

Insects, Injurious and beneficial—*Continued*
and pests, e.g. **Fruit—Diseases and pests;** etc.
  x Diseases and pests; Economic entomology; Entomology, Economic; Garden pests; Injurious insects; Insects, Destructive and useful; Pests
  xx **Agricultural pests; Gardening; Insecticides; Parasites; Zoology, Economic**

Insects as carriers of disease
  See also **Flies; Mosquitoes**
  xx **Communicable diseases; Insects, Injurious and beneficial**

Insemination, Artificial. *See* **Artificial insemination**

In-service training. *See* **Employees—Training**

Insignia
  See also **Decorations of honor; Medals; U.S. Army—Insignia; U.S. Army—Medals, badges, decorations, etc.; U.S. Navy—Insignia; U.S. Navy—Medals, badges, decorations, etc.**
  x Badges of honor; Devices (Heraldry); Emblems
  xx **Decorations of honor; Heraldry; Medals**

Insolvency. *See* **Bankruptcy**

Insomnia
  See also **Narcotics; Sleep**
  x Sleeplessness; Wakefulness
  xx **Sleep**

Inspection of food. *See* **Food adulteration and inspection**

Inspection of meat. *See* **Meat inspection**

Inspection of schools. *See* **School administration and organization; School supervision**

Inspiration. *See* **Creation (Literary, artistic, etc.)**

Inspiration, Biblical. *See* **Bible—Inspiration**

Instalment plan
  x Hire-purchase plan
  xx **Business; Buying; Consumer credit; Credit**

Instinct
  See also **Animal intelligence; Habit; Psychology, Comparative**
  x Animal instinct
  xx **Animal intelligence; Animals—Habits and behavior; Habit; Psychology; Psychology, Comparative**

Institutional care
  See also **Hospitals; Orphans and orphans' homes;** also classes of people with the subdivision *Institutional care,* e.g. **Blind—Institutional care; Children— Institutional care; Mentally ill—Institutional care;** etc.
  x Asylums; Benevolent institutions; Charitable institutions; Homes (Institutions)

281

Institutional care—*Continued*
    xx **Charities; Charities, Medical; Public welfare**
Institutions, Charitable and philanthropic. *See* **Charities; Children—Institutional care; Hospitals**
Instruction. *See* **Education; Teaching**
Instructional materials centers
    x Audio-visual materials centers; Curriculum materials centers; Learning centers; Media centers (Education); Multi-media centers
    xx **Libraries**
Instructional supervision. *See* **School supervision**
Instrumental music
    See also **Bands (Music); Chamber music; Dance music; Musical instruments; Orchestral music;** also **Piano music;** and similar headings
    x Music, Instrumental
    xx **Music; Musical instruments**
Instrumentation and orchestration
    See also **Musical instruments**
    x Orchestration
    xx **Bands (Music); Composition (Music); Music; Musical instruments; Orchestra**
Instruments, Aeronautical. *See* **Aeronautical instruments**
Instruments, Astronautical. *See* **Astronautical instruments**
Instruments, Astronomical. *See* **Astronomical instruments**
Instruments, Engineering. *See* **Engineering instruments**
Instruments, Measuring. *See* **Measuring instruments**
Instruments, Meteorological. *See* **Meteorological instruments**
Instruments, Musical. *See* **Musical instruments**
Instruments, Negotiable. *See* **Negotiable instruments**
Instruments, Scientific. *See* **Scientific apparatus and instruments**
Insulation (Heat)
    xx **Heating**
Insurance
    See also **Saving and thrift**
    x Underwriting
    xx **Estate planning; Finance; Finance, Personal**
Insurance, Accident
    See also **Workmen's compensation**
    x Accident insurance; Disability insurance; Insurance, Disability
    xx **Insurance, Casualty**
Insurance, Automobile
    x Automobile insurance

282

Insurance, Casualty
> *See also* **Insurance, Accident**
> *x* Casualty insurance

Insurance, Disability. *See* **Insurance, Accident;**
> **Insurance, Health**

Insurance, Fire
> *See also* **Fireproofing**
> *x* Fire insurance
> *xx* **Fires**

Insurance, Group
> Includes group life insurance. Works on group insurance in other fields are entered under the specific heading, **e.g. Insurance, Health;** etc.
> *x* Group insurance
> *xx* **Insurance, Life**

Insurance, Health
> *See also* **Insurance; Hospitalization; Workmen's compensation**
> *x* Disability insurance; Group health; Group medical service; Health insurance; Insurance, Disability; Insurance, Sickness; Medical care, Prepaid; Medical service, Prepaid; Prepaid medical care; Sickness insurance; Socialized medicine
> *xx* **Insurance, Social**

Insurance, Hospitalization
> *x* Group hospitalization; Hospitalization insurance; Socialized medicine
> *xx* **Insurance, Health**

Insurance, Industrial
> Use for works on insurance as carried on by companies whose agents collect the premiums from policy holders in small weekly payments
> *x* Industrial insurance
> *xx* **Insurance, Life; Labor and laboring classes; Saving and thrift**

Insurance, Life
> *See also* **Annuities; Insurance, Group; Insurance, Industrial; Probabilities**
> *x* Life insurance
> *xx* **Annuities**

Insurance, Marine
> *x* Marine insurance
> *xx* **Commerce; Maritime law; Merchant marine; Shipping**

Insurance, Old age. *See* **Old age pensions**

Insurance, Sickness. *See* **Insurance, Health**

Insurance, Social
> *See also* **Insurance, Health; Insurance, Unemployment; Mothers' pensions; Old age pensions; Workmen's compensation**
> *x* Government insurance; Insurance, State and compulsory; Insurance, Workingmen's; Labor and laboring classes—Insurance; Security, Social; Social in-

Insurance, Social—*Continued*

surance; Social security; State and insurance; Workingmen's insurance

xx **Pensions**

Insurance, State and compulsory. *See* **Insurance, Social**

Insurance, Unemployment

x Labor and laboring classes—Insurance; Payroll taxes; Security, Social; Social security; Unemployment insurance

xx **Insurance, Social**

Insurance, Workingmen's. *See* **Insurance, Social**

Insurance, Workmen's compensation. *See* **Workmen's compensation**

Integral calculus. *See* **Calculus**

Integrated churches. *See* **Church and race problems**

Integration, Racial. *See* **Negroes—Integration; Race problems**

Integration in education. *See* **Articulation (Education); Segregation in education**

Intellect

See also

Creation (Literary, artistic, etc.)	**Perception**
Imagination	**Reason**
Knowledge, Theory of	**Reasoning**
Logic	**Senses and sensation**
Memory	**Thought and thinking**
Mental tests	

x Intelligence; Mind; Understanding

xx **Knowledge, Theory of; Psychology; Reasoning; Thought and thinking**

Intellectual cooperation

See also **Congresses and conventions; Cultural relations; International education**

x Cooperation, Intellectual

xx **International cooperation; International education**

Intellectual freedom

See also **Academic freedom; Censorship; Free speech; Freedom of information; Freedom of the press**

xx **Liberty**

Intellectual life. *See* **Culture; Learning and scholarship;** and names of countries, cities, etc. with the subdivision *Intellectual life,* e.g. **U.S.—Intellectual life;** etc.

Intellectual property. *See* **Copyright; Inventions; Patents**

Intelligence. *See* **Intellect**

Intelligence, Artificial. *See* **Artificial intelligence**

Intelligence of animals. *See* **Animal intelligence**

Intelligence tests. *See* **Mental tests**

Intemperance. *See* **Alcoholism; Liquor problem; Temperance**

Inter-American relations. *See* **Pan-Americanism**

Interchange of teachers. *See* **Teachers, Interchange of**

Interchange of visitors. *See* **Exchange of persons programs**

Intercollegiate athletics. *See* **Athletics; College sports**

Intercommunication systems

See also **Closed circuit television; Microwave communication systems**

x Interoffice communication systems; Loud speakers

xx **Electronic apparatus and supplies; Sound—Recording and reproducing; Telecommunication**

Intercontinental ballistic missiles

See also names of specific ICBM missiles, e.g. **Atlas (Missile)**; etc.

x ICBM

xx **Atomic weapons; Ballistic missiles**

Intercultural education

Use for works dealing with the eradication of racial and religious prejudices by showing the nature and effects of race, creed and immigrant cultures

See also **International education**

x Education, Intercultural

xx **Acculturation; Human relations; International education; Race problems**

Intercultural marriage. *See* **Marriage, Mixed**

Intercultural relations. *See* **Cultural relations**

Interest and usury

x Usury

xx **Banks and banking; Business arithmetic; Capital; Finance; Loans**

Interest groups. *See* **Lobbying**

Interfaith marriage. *See* **Marriage, Mixed**

Interior decoration

See also

Carpets	**Paper hanging**
Coverlets	**Rugs**
Drapery	**Tapestry**
Furniture	**Upholstery**
Mural painting and decoration	**Wallpaper**

x Decoration, Interior; Decorative arts; Home decoration; House decoration; House furnishing

xx **Decoration and ornament; Home economics**

Intergovernmental tax relations

x Federal revenue sharing; Federal-state tax relations; Revenue sharing; State-local tax relations; Tax relations, Intergovernmental; Tax sharing

xx **Taxation**

285

Interlibrary loans. *See* **Libraries—Circulation, loans**

Interlocking signals. *See* **Railroads—Signaling**

Intermarriage. *See* **Marriage, Mixed**

Intermediate state. *See* **Eschatology; Future life**

Intermittent fever. *See* **Malaria**

Internal-combustion engines. *See* **Gas and oil engines**

Internal revenue
    See also **Income tax; Inheritance and transfer tax**
    x Revenue, Internal
    xx **Finance; Taxation**

Internal revenue law
    x Law, Internal revenue
    xx **Law**

Internal security
    See also **Subversive activities**
    x Loyalty oaths; National security; Security, Internal
    xx **Subversive activities**

International arbitration. *See* **Arbitration, International**

International conferences. *See* **Congresses and conventions**

International cooperation
    Use for general works on international cooperative activities, with or without the participation of governments
    See also **Arbitration, International; Congresses and conventions; Cultural relations; Economic assistance; Exchange of persons programs; Intellectual cooperation; International education; International organization; International police; League of Nations; Reconstruction; Reconstruction (1939-1951); Technical assistance; United Nations**
    x Cooperation, International
    xx **Cooperation; International education; International law; International organization; International relations; Reconstruction (1939-1951)**

International copyright. *See* **Copyright**

International economic relations
    See also **Balance of payments; Commercial policy; Economic assistance; Technical assistance**
    x Economic relations, Foreign; Foreign economic relations
    xx **Economic policy; International relations**

International education
    Use for works on education for international understanding, world citizenship, etc.
    See also **Comparative librarianship; Intellectual cooperation; Intercultural**

International education—*Continued*
education; International cooperation;
Teachers, Interchange of
x Education, International
xx Education; Intellectual cooperation;
Intercultural education; International
cooperation

International exchange. *See* **Foreign exchange**

International exhibitions. *See* **Exhibitions;** and
names of exhibitions

International federation. *See* **International organization**

International language. *See* **Language, Universal**

International law
See also

Aliens	Military law
Arbitration, International	Naturalization
	Neutrality
Boundaries	Pirates
International cooperation	Privateering
	Refugees, Political
International organizations	Salvage
	Slave trade
International relations	Space law
	Treaties
Mandates	War
Maritime law	

x Law, International; Law of nations;
Nations, Law of; Natural law
xx International organization; International relations; Law; War

International organization
Use for works on plans leading towards
political organizations of nations
See also **European federation;** International cooperation; International law;
International police; Mandates;
World politics; also names of specific
organizations, e.g. **United Nations;**
etc.
x Federation, International; International
federation; Organization, International;
World government; World organization
xx Congresses and conventions; International cooperation; International law;
International relations; Security, International; World politics

International police
x Interpol; Police, International
xx International cooperation; International organization; International relations; Security, International

International relations
Use for works on the theory of international
relations. Historical accounts are
entered under **World politics; Europe
—Politics;** etc. Works limited to rela-

✓ International music Camp, Peace Gardens

287

International relations—*Continued*
> tions between two countries are entered
> under the name of one or both countries
> with the subdivision *Foreign relations*
>
> *See also*

Arbitration, International
Boundaries
Catholic Church—Relations (Diplomatic)
Cultural relations
Diplomacy
Diplomatic and consular service
Diplomats
Disarmament
Geopolitics
International cooperation
International economic relations
International law
International organization
International police
Mandates
Monroe Doctrine
Munitions
Nationalism
Neutrality
Peace
Refugees, Political
Security, International
Treaties
World politics

> *also* names of countries with the subdivision *Foreign relations,* e.g. **U.S.—Foreign relations;** etc.
>
> *x* Foreign relations
> *xx* **International law; World politics**

International security. *See* **Security, International**

International space cooperation. *See* **Astronautics—International cooperation**

International trade. *See* **Commerce**

Internationalism. *See* **Nationalism**

Internment camps. *See* **Concentration camps**

Interoffice communication systems. *See* **Intercommunication systems**

Interpersonal relations. *See* **Human relations**

Interplanetary communication. *See* **Intersteller communication**

Interplanetary voyages
> See note under **Space flight**
> *See also* **Outer space—Exploration; Rockets (Aeronautics); Space flight**
> *x* Interstellar voyages; Space travel
> *xx* **Astronautics; Space flight**

Interpol. *See* **International police**

Interpreting and translating. *See* **Translating and interpreting**

Interpretive dancing. *See* Modern dance

Interracial marriage. *See* **Marriage, Mixed**

Interstate commerce
> *See also* **Railroads and state**
> *x* Commerce, Interstate; Government regulation of commerce; Government regulation of railroads
> *xx* **Commerce; Railroads—Rates; Railroads and state; Trusts, Industrial**

Interstellar communication

See also Astronautics—Communication systems; Radio astronomy

x Interplanetary communication; Outer space—Communication; Space communication; Space telecommunication

xx Life on other planets; Telecommunication

Interstellar voyages. See Interplanetary voyages

Interurban railroads. See Electric railroads; Street railroads

Interviewing

See also Counseling; Psychology, Applied

xx Applications for positions; Counseling; Psychology, Applied; Social psychology

Interviewing (Journalism). See Journalism; Reporters and reporting

Intestacy. See Inheritance and succession

Intolerance. See Freedom of conscience; Religious liberty; Toleration

Intoxicants. See Alcohol; Liquors; Stimulants

Intoxication. See Alcoholism; Liquor problem; Narcotic habit; Temperance

Intuition

See also Perception; Reality

xx Knowledge, Theory of; Perception; Philosophy; Psychology; Rationalism

Invalid cookery. See Cookery for the sick

Invalids. See Physically handicapped; Sick

Invasion of privacy. See Privacy, Right of

Inventions

See also Creation (Literary, artistic, etc.); Inventors; Patents

x Discoveries (in science); Intellectual property

xx Civilization; Inventors; Machinery; Patents; Technology

Inventors

See also Inventions

xx Engineers; Inventions

Invertebrates

See also Corals; Crustacea; Insects; Mollusks; Protozoa; Sponges; Worms

xx Zoology

Investigations, Governmental. See Governmental investigations

Investment trusts

x Mutual funds

xx Banks and banking; Trust companies

Investments

See also

Annuities	Saving and thrift
Bonds	Securities
Building and loan associations	Speculation
	Stock exchange
Mortgages	Stocks

Investments—*Continued*

    xx Banks and banking; Bonds; Capital; Estate planning; Finance; Finance, Personal; Loans; Saving and thrift; Securities; Speculation; Stock exchange; Stocks

Iran

    x Persia

Iron

    See also **Building, Iron and steel; Iron ores; Ironwork**

    xx **Steel**

Iron age

    See also **Archeology; Bronze age**

    x Prehistory

    xx **Archeology; Bronze age**

Iron and steel building. *See* **Building, Iron and steel**

Iron curtain countries. *See* **Communist countries**

Iron founding. *See* **Founding**

Iron industry and trade

    See also **Steel industry and trade**

    xx **Ironwork; Steel industry and trade**

Iron ores

    xx **Iron; Ore deposits; Ores**

Ironing. *See* **Laundry**

Ironwork

    See also **Blacksmithing; Forging; Iron industry and trade; Metalwork; Steel industry and trade; Welding**

    x Wrought iron work

    xx **Decoration and ornament; Forging; Iron; Metalwork**

Irrigation (May subdiv. geog.)

    See also **Dams; Dry farming; Reclamation of land; Water rights; Windmills**

    xx **Agricultural engineering; Civil engineering; Hydraulic engineering; Reclamation of land; Reservoirs; Soils; Water resources development; Water supply**

Irrigation—U.S.

    x U.S.—Irrigation

Islam

    Use for works on the religion. For books on the believers in this religion use **Muslims**

    See also **Bahaism; Dervishes; Koran; Mosques**

    x Islamism; Mohammedanism; Moslemism; Muhammadanism; Muslimism

    xx **Religions**

Islamism. *See* **Islam**

Islands

    See also **Coral reefs and islands;** also names of islands and groups of islands, e.g. **Cuba; Islands of the Pacific;** etc.

290

Islands of the Pacific

    x Oceania; Pacific Islands; South Sea Islands

    xx **Islands**

Isotopes

    See also **Radioisotopes**

Israel-Arab border conflicts. *See* **Jewish-Arab relations**

Israel-Arab War, 1956. *See* **Sinai Campaign, 1956**

Israel-Arab War, 1967-

    x Arab-Israel War, 1967-   ; Six Day War, 1967

Israelites. *See* **Jews**

Italian language

    May be subdivided like **English language**

Italian literature

    May use same subdivisions and names of literary forms as for **English literature**

Italians in the U.S.

    Use same form for Italians in other countries, states, etc., e.g. **Italians in Africa;** etc.

    x Foreigners

    xx **Aliens; Immigration and emigration; U.S.—Foreign population; U.S.—Immigration and emigration**

Italo-Ethiopian War, 1935-1936

    x Ethiopian-Italian War, 1935-1936

Italy

    May be subdivided like U.S. except for *History*

Italy—History

Italy—History—To 1559

Italy—History—1559-1789

Italy—History—1789-1815

Italy—History—1815-1915

Italy—History—1914-1946

Italy—History—1946-

Ivory

    x Animal products

Jacobins (Dominicans). *See* **Dominicans**

Jails. *See* **Prisons**

Japan

Japan—History

Japan—History—To 1868

Japan—History—1868-1945

Japan—History—Allied occupation, 1945-1952

    xx **Military occupation; World War, 1939-1945—Occupied territories**

Japan—History—1952-

Japan World's Exposition, Osaka, 1970. *See* **Expo '70**

Japanese color prints. *See* **Color prints, Japanese**

Japanese prints. *See* **Color prints, Japanese**

291

Jazz music
> *See also* **Blues (Songs, etc.)**
> *x* Soul music; Swing music
> *xx* **Dance music; Music**

Jeeps. *See* **Automobiles; Trucks**

Jesuits
> *x* Jesus, Society of; Society of Jesus
> *xx* **Monasticism and religious orders**

Jesus, Society of. *See* **Jesuits**

Jesus Christ
> *See also* **Atonement; Christianity; Lord's Supper; Millennium; Salvation; Second Advent; Trinity**
> *x* Christ; Christology
> *xx* **Christianity; God; Theology; Trinity**

Jesus Christ—Art
> *See also* **Bible—Pictorial works; Christian art and symbolism; Mary, Virgin—Art**
> *x* Jesus Christ—Iconography; Jesus Christ in art
> *xx* **Christian art and symbolism; Mary, Virgin—Art**

Jesus Christ—Atonement. *See* **Atonement**

Jesus Christ—Biography
> *See also* **Jesus Christ—Crucifixion; Jesus Christ—Nativity**

Jesus Christ—Birth. *See* **Jesus Christ—Nativity**

Jesus Christ—Crucifixion
> *x* Crucifixion of Christ
> *xx* **Jesus Christ—Biography**

Jesus Christ—Divinity
> *See also* **Trinity; Unitarianism**
> *x* Divinity of Christ
> *xx* **Unitarianism**

Jesus Christ—Drama
> *See also* **Passion plays**

Jesus Christ—Iconography. *See* **Jesus Christ—Art**

Jesus Christ—Last Supper. *See* **Lord's Supper**

Jesus Christ—Messiahship

Jesus Christ—Nativity
> *See also* **Christmas**
> *x* Jesus Christ—Birth; Nativity of Christ
> *xx* **Christmas; Jesus Christ—Biography**

Jesus Christ—Parables
> *x* Bible—Parables
> *xx* **Parables**

Jesus Christ—Prayers
> *See also* **Lord's Prayer**
> *xx* **Prayers**

Jesus Christ—Resurrection
> *x* Resurrection

Jesus Christ—Second Advent. *See* **Second Advent**

Jesus Christ—Sermon on the Mount. *See* **Sermon on the Mount**

Jesus Christ—Teachings
>   *x* Teachings of Jesus
Jesus Christ in art. *See* **Jesus Christ—Art**
Jesus people. *See* **Hippies—Religious life**
Jet planes
>   *See also* **Short take off and landing aircraft**
>   *x* Airplanes, Jet propelled
Jet propulsion
>   *See also* **Rockets (Aeronautics)**
>   *xx* **Airplanes—Engines; Rockets (Aeronautics)**
Jewelry
>   *See also* **Gems; Goldsmithing; Silversmithing**
>   *x* Jewels
>   *xx* **Art metalwork; Arts and crafts; Costume; Decoration and ornament; Gems; Gold; Goldsmithing; Metalwork; Silver; Silversmithing**
Jewelry—Repairing
Jewels. *See* **Gems; Jewelry; Precious stones**
Jewish-Arab relations
>   *x* Arab-Jewish relations; Israel-Arab border conflict
Jewish civilization. *See* **Jews—Civilization**
Jewish holidays. *See* **Fasts and feasts—Judaism**
Jewish language. *See* **Hebrew language; Yiddish language**
Jewish literature
>   *See also* **Bible; Hebrew literature; Talmud; Yiddish literature**
>   *x* Jews—Literature
>   *xx* **Hebrew literature**
Jewish question
>   Use for works on the relation of the Jews to non-Jews
>   *See also* **Zionism**
>   *x* Antisemitism
Jewish religion. *See* **Judaism**
Jews
>   *See also* **Discrimination**
>   *x* Hebrews; Israelites
>   *xx* **Church history; Judaism**
Jews—Antiquities
>   *x* Antiquities
Jews—Civilization
>   *x* Civilization, Jewish; Jewish civilization
Jews—Colonization
>   *xx* **Colonization**
Jews—Customs. *See* **Jews—Social life and customs**
Jews—Economic conditions
Jews—Festivals. *See* **Fasts and feasts—Judaism**
Jews—Folklore. *See* **Folklore, Jewish**
Jews—History
Jews—Language. *See* **Hebrew language; Yiddish language**

293

Jews—Literature. *See* **Hebrew literature; Jewish literature**

Jews—Persecutions
  xx Persecution
Jews—Political activity
Jews—Religion. *See* **Judaism**
Jews—Restoration
  Use for works dealing with the belief that the Jews, in fulfillment of Biblical prophecy, would some day return to Palestine
  See also **Zionism**
  xx Zionism
Jews—Rites and ceremonies
  xx Rites and ceremonies
Jews—Social conditions
  Use for works relating to social conditions of the Jews themselves. Works on the relation of the Jews to non-Jews are entered under **Jewish question**
  xx Social conditions
Jews—Social life and customs
  x Customs, Social; Jews—Customs; Social customs; Social life and customs
  xx Manners and customs
Jews in the U.S.
  Use same form for Jews in other countries, states, etc., e.g. **Jews in Russia**; etc.
Jiujitsu. *See* **Judo**
Job analysis
  See also **Motion study; Time study**
  x Personnel classification
  xx Efficiency, Industrial; Factory management; Industrial management; Occupations; Personnel management; Wages
Job discrimination. *See* **Discrimination in employment**
Job resumés. *See* **Applications for positions**
Job training. *See* **Occupational training**
Jobs. *See* **Employment** (agencies;) **Occupations; Professions** *omit*
Joint-stock companies. *See* **Stock companies**
Jokes. *See* **Wit and humor**
Journalism
  Use for works dealing with the composition of materials for the periodical press and with the editing of this material, or for works on journalism as an occupation. Books limited to the history, organization and management of newspapers are entered under **Newspapers**
  See also **College and school journalism; Libel and slander; Freedom of the press; Government and the press; Newspapers; Periodicals; Reporters and reporting**
  x Editors and editing; Interviewing (Journalism); Literature as a profession;

294

Journalism—*Continued*

Newspaper work; Press; Radio journalism; Writing (Authorship)

xx **Authorship; Literature; Newspapers; Reporters and reporting**

Journalistic photography. *See* **Photography, Journalistic**

Journalists

x Columnists; Editors and editing; Literature as a profession; Writers

Journals (Machinery). *See* **Bearings (Machinery)**

Journeys. *See* **Voyages and travels; Voyages around the world;** and names of countries with the subdivision *Description and travel,* e.g. **U.S.—Description and travel;** etc.

Joy and sorrow

See also **Happiness; Pleasure**

x Affliction; Grief; Sorrow

xx **Emotions; Ethics; Happiness; Suffering**

Judaeo-German. *See* **Yiddish language**

Judaism

See also **Jews; Sabbath; Synagogues; Talmud**

x Jewish religion; Jews—Religion

xx **Religions**

Judges

See also **Courts; Lawyers**

x Chief justices

xx **Courts; Law; Lawyers**

Judicial investigations. *See* **Governmental investigations**

Judo

See also **Karate**

x Jiujitsu

xx **Physical education and training; Self-defense; Wrestling**

July Fourth. *See* **Fourth of July**

Jungles. *See* **Forests and forestry; Tropics**

Junior colleges

x Community colleges

xx **Colleges and universities; Education, Higher; Schools**

Junior colleges—Directories

xx **Directories**

Junior high schools

x High schools, Junior; Secondary schools

xx **Education, Secondary; High schools; Public schools; Schools**

Junk. *See* **Waste products**

Jurisprudence. *See* **Law**

Jurisprudence, Medical. *See* **Medical jurisprudence**

Jurists. *See* **Lawyers**

Jury

x Trial by jury

xx **Courts; Criminal law; Law**

Justice
>   *xx* Behavior; Ethics; Law
Justice, Administration of
>   *See also* Courts; Crime and criminals; Governmental investigations
>   *x* Administration of justice
>   *xx* Courts; Crime and criminals
Juvenile courts
>   *See also* Probation
>   *x* Children's courts
>   *xx* Courts; Juvenile delinquency; Probation; Reformatories
Juvenile delinquency
>   *See also* Child welfare; Drugs and youth; Juvenile courts; Narcotics and youth; Reformatories
>   *x* Children, Delinquent; Delinquency, Juvenile; Delinquents; Gangs
>   *xx* Child welfare; Crime and criminals; Problem children; Reformatories; Social problems
Juvenile delinquency—Case studies
>   *x* Case studies
Juvenile literature. *See* Children's literature
K.K.K. *See* Ku Klux Klan
Karate
>   *xx* Judo; Self-defense
Karts and karting
>   *x* Go karts
>   *xx* Automobile racing
Kennedy, John Fitzgerald, Pres. U.S.
>   *xx* Presidents—U.S.
Keramics. *See* Ceramics
Kerosene. *See* Petroleum
Keys. *See* Locks and keys
Kibbutz. *See* Collective settlements
Kindergarten
>   *See also* Child study; Montessori method of education
>   *xx* Child study; Children; Education, Elementary; Games; Nursery schools; Schools; Teaching
Kindness to animals. *See* Animals—Treatment
Kinematics
>   *See also* Mechanical movements; Mechanics; Motion
>   *xx* Dynamics; Mechanics; Motion
Kinetic art
>   *See also* Kinetic sculpture
>   *x* Art, Kinetic; Art in motion
>   *xx* Art, Abstract; Art, Modern—20th century
Kinetic sculpture
>   *See also* Mobiles (Sculpture)
>   *x* Sculpture, Kinetic; Sculpture in motion
>   *xx* Futurism (Art); Kinetic art
Kinetics. *See* Dynamics; Motion

King Philip's War, 1675-1676

    x U.S.—History—King Philip's War, 1675-1676

    xx Indians of North America—Wars; U.S.—History—Colonial period

King William's War, 1689-1697. *See* **U.S.—History—King William's War, 1689-1697**

Kingdom of God

Kings and rulers

    See also **Courts and courtiers; Dictators; Presidents; Queens; Roman emperors;** also names of countries with the subdivision *Kings and rulers,* (e.g. **Gt. Brit.—Kings and rulers;** etc.) ; also names of individual kings and rulers, e.g. **Elizabeth II, Queen of Great Britain;** etc.

    x Emperors; Monarchs; Royalty; Rulers; Sovereigns

    xx **Courts and courtiers; History; Monarchy; Political science; Queens**

Kitchen gardens. *See* **Vegetable gardening**

Kitchen utensils. *See* **Household equipment and supplies**

Kitchens

Kites

    xx **Aeronautics**

Klondike gold fields

    x Gold rush

Knighthood. *See* **Knights and knighthood**

Knights and knighthood

    See also **Chivalry; Heraldry**

    x Knighthood

    xx **Chivalry; Heraldry; Middle Ages; Nobility**

Knights of the Round Table. *See* **Arthur, King**

Knitting

Knots and splices

    x Splicing

    xx **Navigation; Rope**

Knowledge, Theory of

    Use for works that treat of the origin, nature, methods and limits of human knowledge

    See also

Apperception	Pragmatism
Belief and doubt	Rationalism
Empiricism	Reality
Gestalt psychology	Senses and sensa-
Intellect	tion
Intuition	Truth
Perception	

    x Cognition; Epistemology; Understanding

    xx **Apperception; Consciousness; Intellect; Logic; Metaphysics; Philosophy; Reality; Truth**

Kodak camera
    x Cameras
Koran
    x Alkoran; Qur'an
    xx Islam; Sacred books
Korean War, 1950-1953
Ku Klux Klan (1865-1876)
    x K.K.K.
    xx Reconstruction
Ku Klux Klan (1915-   )
    x K.K.K.
LEM. *See* Lunar excursion module
Labor, Hours of. *See* Hours of labor
Labor, Migratory. *See* Migrant labor
Labor (Obstetrics). *See* Childbirth
Labor absenteeism. *See* Absenteeism (Labor)
Labor and capital. *See* Industrial relations
Labor and laboring classes (May subdiv. geog.)

   See also

Absenteeism (Labor)	Machinery in industry
Apprentices	Middle classes
Arbitration, Industrial	Migrant labor
Capitalism	Occupational diseases
Child labor	Occupations
Church and labor	Occupations, Dangerous
Collective bargaining	Old age pensions
Communism	Open and closed shop
Contract labor	Peasantry
Convict labor	Peonage
Cost and standard of living	Proletariat
Employees' representation in management	Slavery
Employment agencies	Socialism
Guilds	Strikes and lockouts
Hours of labor	Syndicalism
Household employees	Unemployed
Industrial relations	Wages
Insurance, Industrial	Welfare work in industry
Labor unions, and other headings beginning with the word **Labor**	Woman—Employment
	Workshops
	World War, 1939-1945—Manpower

   also names of classes of laborers (e.g. **Agricultural laborers; Miners;** etc.); and names of countries, cities, etc. with the subdivisions *Economic conditions* and *Social conditions,* e.g. **U.S.—Economic conditions; U.S.—Social conditions;** etc.
    x Employment; Laborers; Working classes
    xx **Capital; Economics; Guilds; Social**

Labor and laboring classes—*Continued*
>
> conditions; Socialism; Sociology; Work

Labor and laboring classes—Accidents

Labor and laboring classes—Education

> *x* Education of workers

Labor and laboring classes—Housing. *See* **Housing**

Labor and laboring classes—Insurance. *See* **Insurance, Social; Insurance, Unemployment; Old age pensions**

Labor and laboring classes—Library service. *See* **Libraries and labor**

Labor and laboring classes—U.S.

> *x* U.S.—Labor and laboring classes

Labor and the church. *See* **Church and labor**

Labor contract

> Use for books dealing with agreements between employer and employee in which the latter agrees to perform work in return for compensation from the former
>
> *See also* **Collective bargaining; Open and closed shop; Wages**
>
> *x* Collective labor agreements; Trade agreements (Labor)
>
> *xx* **Collective bargaining; Contracts; Industrial relations**

Labor disputes. *See* **Arbitration, Industrial; Collective bargaining; Strikes and lockouts**

Labor-management relations. *See* **Industrial relations**

Labor organizations. *See* **Guilds; Labor unions**

Labor relations. *See* **Industrial relations**

Labor representation in regulation of industry. *See* **Employees' representation in management**

Labor saving devices, Household. *See* **Household equipment and supplies; Household appliances, Electric**

Labor supply

> *See also* **Child labor; Employment agencies; Manpower policy; Retraining, Occupational; Unemployed; Woman —Employment; World War, 1939-1945—Manpower**
>
> *x* Man power; Manpower
>
> *xx* **Economic conditions; Employment agencies; Manpower policy; Unemployed**

Labor turnover

> *See also* **Employment agencies**
>
> *xx* **Personnel management**

Labor unions

> *See also* **Arbitration, Industrial; Collective bargaining; Guilds; Injunctions; Open and closed shop; Sabotage; Strikes and lockouts; Syndicalism;** also names of types of unions and

Labor unions—*Continued*

  names of individual labor unions, e.g.
  **Librarians' unions; United Steel-
  workers of America;** etc.

  x Labor organizations; Organized labor;
  Trade unions; Unions, Labor

  xx **Collective bargaining; Cooperation;
  Guilds; Industrial relations; Labor
  and laboring classes; Socialism; Societies; Strikes and lockouts**

Laboratories, Language. *See* **Language laboratories**

Laboratories, Space. *See* **Space stations**

Laboratory manuals. *See* scientific and technical
  subjects with the subdivision *Laboratory manuals,* e.g. **Chemistry—Laboratory manuals;** etc.

Laborers. *See* **Labor and laboring classes;** and
  names of classes of laborers, e.g. **Agricultural laborers; Miners;** etc.

Lace and lace making

  xx **Crocheting; Needlework; Weaving**

Lacquer and lacquering

  See also **Varnish and varnishing**

  x Finishes and finishing

  xx **Arts and crafts; Varnish and varnishing; Wood finishing**

Laissez faire. *See* **Industry and state**

Lakes

  xx **Inland navigation; Physical geography; Water; Waterways**

Lamps

  See also **Electric lamps**

  xx **Lighting**

Land

  Use for general works which cover such
  topics as types of land, the utilization,
  distribution and development of land
  and the economic factors which affect
  the value of land. Works which treat
  only of ownership of land are entered
  under **Real estate**

  See also

Agriculture	Feudalism
Agriculture—Eco-	Land tenure
nomic aspects	Real estate
Eminent domain	Reclamation of land
Farms	

  x Land use

  xx **Agriculture; Economics**

Land, Condemnation of. *See* **Eminent domain**

Land, Reclamation of. *See* **Reclamation of land**

Land drainage. *See* **Drainage**

Land question. *See* **Land tenure**

Land settlement. *See* **Colonization**

Land surveying. *See* **Surveying**

Land tenure

  Use for general and historical works on
  systems of holding land

Laboratory technicians

Land tenure—*Continued*

    See also Farm tenancy; Feudalism; Land-
        lord and tenant; Peasantry; Real es-
        tate

    x Agrarian question; Fiefs; Land ques-
        tion; Tenure of land

    xx Agriculture; Agriculture—Economic
        aspects; Inheritance and succession;
        Land; Peasantry; Real estate

Land use. *See* Land   ✓ *Landfills, Sanitary. See Sanitary landfills*

Landlord and tenant

    See note under **Farm tenancy**

    See also **Apartment houses; Farm ten-
        ancy; Housing; Tenement houses**

    x Tenants

    xx **Commercial law; Human relations;
        Land tenure; Real estate**

Landmarks, Literary. *See* **Literary landmarks**

Landmarks, Preservation of. *See* **Natural
    monuments**

Landscape architecture

    See also **Cemeteries; Garden ornaments
        and furniture; Landscape gardening;
        Landscape protection; Parks; Patios;
        Roadside improvement**

    x Landscape design

    xx **Landscape gardening; Landscape pro-
        tection**

Landscape design. *See* **Landscape architecture**

Landscape drawing

    See also **Landscape painting**

    xx **Drawing; Landscape painting**

Landscape gardening

    See also **Evergreens; Landscape architec-
        ture; Plants, Ornamental; Shrubs;
        Trees**

    x Garden design; Planting

    xx **Gardening; Landscape architecture;
        Parks; Shrubs; Trees**

Landscape painting

    See also **Landscape drawing**

    xx **Landscape drawing; Painting**

Landscape protection

    See also **Landscape architecture; Natural
        monuments; Regional planning**

    x Beautification of the landscape; Natural
        beauty conservation; Preservation of
        natural scenery; Protection of natural
        scenery; Scenery

    xx **Landscape architecture; Nature con-
        servation; Regional planning**

Language, International. *See* **Language, Uni-
    versal**

Language, Universal

    See also **Esperanto**

    x International language; Language, Inter-
        national; Universal language; World
        language

Language and languages

Use for general works on the history, philosophy, origin, etc. of language. Comparative studies of languages are entered under **Philology, Comparative**

See also

Bilingualism	**Rhetoric**
Conversation	**Semantics**
Grammar	**Speech**
Literature	**Translating and interpreting**
Philology, Comparative	**Voice**
Phonetics	**Writing**
Programming languages (Electronic computers)	

also names of languages or groups of cognate languages, e.g. **English language;** etc.; also classes of people with the subdivision *Language,* e.g. **Children—Language;** etc.

x Comparative linguistics; Linguistics; Philology

xx **Anthropology; Communication; Ethnology; Grammar; Philology, Comparative; Speech**

Language and languages—Comparative philology. *See* **Philology, Comparative**

Language arts. *See* **Communication; English language; Literature; Reading; Speech**

Language laboratories

See also **Languages, Modern—Study and teaching**

x Foreign language laboratories; Laboratories, Language

xx **Languages, Modern—Study and teaching**

Languages, Modern

May be subdivided like **English language.** Use for works on the living literary languages of Europe

x Languages, Western; Modern languages

Languages, Modern—Conversation and phrase books

x Conversation in foreign languages; Foreign language phrases

Languages, Modern—Study and teaching

See also **Language laboratories**

xx **Language laboratories**

Languages, Western. *See* **Languages, Modern**

Lantern projection. *See* **Projectors**

Lantern slides. *See* **Slides (Photography)**

Large print books

x Books—Large print; Books for sight saving; Large type books; Sight saving books

xx **Blind, Books for the**

Large type books. *See* **Large print books**

Lasers
    x Light amplification by stimulated emission of radiation; Masers, Optical; Optical masers
    xx **Light**

Last Supper. *See* **Lord's Supper**

Lathe work. *See* **Lathes; Turning**

Lathes
    See also **Turning**
    x Lathe work
    xx **Turning; Woodworking machinery**

Latin America
    See also **Pan-Americanism; South America;** and names of individual Latin American countries
    x Spanish America
    xx **America**

Latin America—Politics
    x Politics

Latin American literature
    Use for works on French, Portuguese, and/or Spanish literature of Latin American countries
    May use same subdivisions and names of literary forms as for **English literature**
    See also **Brazilian literature**
    x Hispanic-American literature; South American literature; Spanish American literature
    xx **American literature; Spanish literature**

Latin language
    May be subdivided like **English language**
    See also **Romance languages**
    x Classical languages

Latin literature
    May use same subdivisions and names of literary forms as for **English literature**
    See also **Christian literature, Early; Classical literature**
    x Roman literature
    xx **Classical literature**

Latitude
    x Degrees of latitude and longitude
    xx **Earth; Geodesy; Nautical astronomy**

Latter-Day Saints. *See* **Mormons and Mormonism**

Laughter
    See also **Wit and humor**
    xx **Emotions**

Launching of satellites. *See* **Artificial satellites—Launching**

Laundry
    x Ironing; Washing
    xx **Cleaning; Home economics; Sanitation, Household**

Law (May subdiv. geog.)

> *See also*

Courts	Legislation
Judges	Legislative bodies
Jury	Medical jurispru-
Justice	dence
Lawyers	Police

> Legal ethics

> > *also* special branches of law, e.g. **Administrative law; Commercial law; Constitutional law; Corporation law; Criminal law; Ecclesiastical law; Internal revenue law; International law; Maritime law; Military law; Space law;** etc. For laws on special subjects see names of subjects with the subdivision *Laws and regulations,* e.g. **Automobiles—Laws and regulations; Food—Laws and regulations;** etc.

> *x* Jurisprudence; Laws; Statutes

> *xx* **Legislation; Political science; Professions**

Law, Administrative. *See* **Administrative law**

Law, Business. *See* **Commercial law**

Law, Commercial. *See* **Commercial law**

Law, Constitutional. *See* **Constitutional law**

Law, Corporation. *See* **Corporation law**

Law, Criminal. *See* **Criminal law**

Law, Ecclesiastical. *See* **Ecclesiastical law**

Law, Internal revenue. *See* **Internal revenue law**

Law, International. *See* **International law**

Law, Maritime. *See* **Maritime law**

Law, Military. *See* **Military law**

Law, Space. *See* **Space law**

Law—U.S.

> *x* U.S.—Law

Law as a profession

> *xx* **Lawyers; Occupations; Professions; Vocational guidance**

Law enforcement

> *See also* **Police**

> *x* Enforcement of law

Law of nations. *See* **International law**

Law reform

> *x* Legal reform

Lawn tennis. *See* **Tennis**

Lawns

> *See also* **Grasses**

Laws. *See* **Law; Legislation;** and subjects with the subdivision *Laws and regulations,* e.g. **Automobiles—Laws and regulations; Food—Laws and regulations;** etc.

Lawyers

> *See also* **Judges; Law as a profession; Legal ethics**

> *x* Attorneys; Bar; Barristers; Jurists; Legal profession

> *xx* **Judges; Law**

Layout and typography. *See* **Printing**

Leadership

  xx Ability; Executive ability; Success

League of Nations

  xx Arbitration, International; European War, 1914-1918—Peace; International cooperation; Peace

League of Nations—Mandatory system. *See* **Mandates**

Learned societies. *See* **Societies**

Learning, Art of. *See* **Study, Method of**

Learning, Psychology of

  x Psychology of learning

  xx **Animal intelligence**

Learning and scholarship

  See also Culture; Education; Humanism; Professional education; Research

  x Intellectual life; Scholarship

  xx Civilization; Culture; Education; Humanism; Research

Learning centers. *See* **Instructional materials centers**

Lease and rental services

  x Lease services; Rental services

Lease services. *See* **Lease and rental services**

Leather

  See also Hides and skins; Tanning

  xx Hides and skins; Tanning

Leather garments

  x Clothing, Leather; Garments, Leather; Skin garments

  xx **Clothing and dress**

Leather industry and trade

  See also Bookbinding; Shoes and shoe industry

Leather work

  xx Art industries and trade; Arts and crafts; Decoration and ornament; Handicraft

Leaves

  x Foliage

  xx Botany; Trees

Lectures and lecturing

  Use for general works on the art of lecturing, effectiveness of the lecture method, announcements of lectures, etc. Collections of lectures on several subjects are entered under **Speeches, addresses, etc.** Lectures on one topic are entered under that subject. If it is not treated comprehensively add the subdivision *Addresses and essays*

  See also Radio addresses, debates, etc.; also general subjects with the subdivision *Addresses and essays,* e.g. **Agriculture—Addresses and essays; U.S.—History—Addresses and essays;** etc.

  x Addresses; Speaking

305

Lectures and lecturing—*Continued*
    xx Public speaking; Rhetoric; Speeches, addresses, etc.; Teaching

Left (Political science). *See* **Right and left (Political science)**

Legacies. *See* **Inheritance and succession; Wills**

Legal aid
    x Charities, Legal
    xx **Legal assistance to the poor**

Legal assistance to the poor
    See also **Legal aid**
    x Legal representative of the poor; Legal service for the poor
    xx **Public welfare**

Legal ethics
    x Ethics, Legal
    xx **Ethics; Law; Lawyers; Professional ethics**

Legal holidays. *See* **Holidays**

Legal medicine. *See* **Medical jurisprudence**

Legal profession. *See* **Lawyers**

Legal reform. *See* **Law reform**

Legal representative of the poor. *See* **Legal assistance to the poor**

Legal service for the poor. *See* **Legal assistance to the poor**

Legal tender. *See* **Paper money**

Legations. *See* **Diplomatic and consular service**

Legends (May subdiv. geog. noun form (e.g. **Legends—Ireland;** etc.) or, where country subdivision is not applicable, use ethnic subdivision, adjective form, e.g. **Legends, Jewish;** etc.
    Use for tales coming down from the past, especially those relating to actual events or persons. Collections of tales written between the eleventh and fourteenth centuries and dealing with the age of chivalry are entered under **Romances**
    See also **Fables; Fairy tales; Folklore; Grail; Mythology; Romances; Saints**
    x Stories; Tales; Tall tales; Traditions
    xx **Fiction; Folklore; Literature; Saints**

Legends, Celtic
    x Celtic legends

Legends, Indian. *See* **Indians of North America—Legends**

Legends, Norse
    x Norse legends

Legends—U.S.
    x U.S.—Legends

Legends and stories of animals. *See* **Animals —Stories; Fables;** and names of animals with the subdivision *Stories,* e.g. **Dogs—Stories;** etc.

Legerdemain. *See* **Magic**

Legislation
>Use for works on the theory of law-making and descriptions of the preparation and enactment of laws
>
>*See also* **Law; Legislative bodies; Parliamentary practice;** also subjects with the subdivision *Laws and regulations,* e.g. **Automobiles—Laws and regulations; Food—Laws and regulations;** etc.
>
>*x* Laws
>
>*xx* **Constitutional law; Law; Political science**

Legislation, Direct. *See* **Referendum**

Legislative bodies
>Use for descriptions and histories of law making bodies, discussions of one-house legislatures, etc.
>
>*See also* **Parliamentary practice;** also names of individual legislative bodies, e.g. **U.S. Congress;** etc.
>
>*x* Parliaments; Unicameral legislatures
>
>*xx* **Constitutional law; Law; Legislation; Representative government and representation**

Legislative investigations. *See* **Governmental investigations**

Legislative reapportionment. *See* **Apportionment (Election law)**

Legitimacy (Law). *See* **Illegitimacy**

Leisure
>*See also* **Hobbies; Recreation; Retirement**

Lem. *See* **Lunar excursion module**

Lending. *See* **Loans**

Lenses
>*xx* **Eyeglasses**

Lent
>*See also* **Easter; Good Friday; Holy Week**
>
>*x* Ecclesiastical fasts and feasts
>
>*xx* **Fasts and feasts**

Lepidoptera. *See* **Butterflies; Moths**

Lesbianism
>*xx* **Homosexuality**

Letter writing
>Use for works on the composition, forms, and etiquette of correspondence. Works limited to business correspondence are entered under **Business letters.** Collections of literary letters are entered under **Letters**
>
>*See also* **Business letters**
>
>*x* Correspondence; Salutations
>
>*x* **Etiquette; Rhetoric; Style, Literary**

Lettering
>*See also* **Alphabets; Initials; Monograms; Sign painting**
>
>*x* Ornamental alphabets
>
>*xx* **Alphabets; Decoration and ornament; Design, Decorative; Initials; Me-**

307

Lettering—*Continued*
  chanical drawing; Painting, Industrial; Sign painting
Letters
  Use for collections of literary letters
  See also **American letters; English letters; etc.**
  x Correspondence
  xx **Literature—Collections**
Letters of credit. *See* **Credit; Negotiable instruments**
Letters of marque. *See* **Privateering**
Letters of recommendation. *See* **Applications for positions**
Letters of the alphabet. *See* **Alphabet**
Leukemia
  xx **Blood—Diseases**
Levant. *See* **Near East**
Lewis and Clark Expedition
  x Exploring expeditions
  xx **U.S.—Exploring expeditions; U.S.—History—1783-1809**
Libel and slander
  See also **Free speech; Freedom of the press; Privacy, Right of**
  x Slander (Law)
  xx **Free speech; Freedom of the press; Journalism**
Liberalism
  See also **Right and Left (Political science)**
  xx **Right and left (Political science)**
Liberty
  See also **Anarchism and anarchists; Civil rights; Equality; Intellectual freedom; Religious liberty; Slavery**
  x Civil liberty; Freedom; Natural law; Personal liberty
  xx **Civil rights; Democracy; Political science**
Liberty of conscience. *See* **Freedom of conscience**
Liberty of speech. *See* **Free speech**
Liberty of the press. *See* **Freedom of the press**
Liberty of the will. *See* **Free will and determinism**
Librarians
  See also **Library technicians**
Librarians—Education. *See* **Library education**
Librarians—In-service training
  xx **Library education**
Librarians, Negro. *See* **Negro librarians**
Librarians—Recruiting
  xx **Recruiting of employees**
Librarians—Training. *See* **Library education**
Librarians' unions
  xx **Labor unions**
Librarianship. *See* **Library science**

Librarianship, Comparative. *See* **Comparative librarianship**

Libraries (May subdiv. geog. country or state)
See also special types of libraries, e.g. **Business libraries; Hospital libraries; Instructional materials centers; Music libraries; Public libraries; School libraries; School libraries (High school)**; names of cities with the subdivision *Libraries* (e.g. **Chicago —Libraries**; etc.) ; names of individual libraries (e.g. **U.S. Library of Congress**; etc.) ; and headings beginning with the words **Libraries** and **Library**
xx **Books; Books and reading; Education**

Libraries—Administration. *See* **Library administration**

Libraries—Advertising. *See* **Advertising—Libraries**

Libraries—Automation
See also **Information storage and retrieval systems; MARC project**
xx **Automation; Information storage and retrieval systems**

Libraries—Boards of trustees. *See* **Libraries—Trustees**

Libraries, Business. *See* **Business libraries**

Libraries—Catalogs. *See* **Library catalogs**

Libraries—Censorship

Libraries—Centralization
x Library systems

Libraries, Children's
See also **Children's literature; Libraries, Young adults'; Libraries and schools; School libraries**
x Children's libraries
xx **Children's literature; Libraries, Young adults'; Libraries and schools; School libraries**

Libraries, Church
x Church libraries ; Parish libraries

Libraries—Circulation, loans
x Book lending ; Interlibrary loans

Libraries—Classification. *See* **Classification—Books**

Libraries, College and university
x College libraries ; Libraries, University ; University libraries
xx **College and universities**

Libraries—Cooperation. *See* **Library cooperation**

Libraries, County
See also **Libraries, Regional**
x County libraries
xx **Libraries, Regional; Library extension**

Libraries—Federal aid. *See* **Federal aid to libraries**

Libraries—Finance. *See* **Library finance**

Libraries, Governmental
> *See also* **State libraries**
> *x* Federal libraries; Government libraries
> *xx* **State libraries**

Libraries, Hospital. *See* **Hospital libraries**

Libraries—Laws and regulations
> *x* Library laws; Library legislation

Libraries, Music. *See* **Music libraries**

Libraries—Order department. *See* **Acquisitions (Libraries)**

Libraries, Presidential. *See* **Presidents—U.S.—Archives**

Libraries, Public. *See* **Public libraries**

Libraries—Public relations. *See* **Public relations—Libraries**

Libraries—Reference service
> *xx* **Library service**

Libraries, Regional
> *See also* **Libraries, County**
> *x* District libraries; Regional libraries
> *xx* **Libraries, County; Library extension**

Libraries, School. *See* **School libraries; School libraries (High school)**

Libraries, Special
> *See also* types of special libraries, e.g. **Business libraries; Music libraries;** etc.
> *x* Special libraries

Libraries, State. *See* **State libraries**

Libraries—State aid. *See* **State aid to libraries**

Libraries—Statistics

Libraries—Technical services. *See* **Processing (Libraries)**

Libraries—Trustees
> *x* Libraries—Boards of trustees; Library boards; Library trustees
> *xx* **Library administration**

Libraries—U.S.
> *x* U.S.—Libraries

Libraries, University. *See* **Libraries, College and university**

Libraries, Young adults'
> *See also* **Libraries, Children's**
> *x* Young people's libraries
> *xx* **Libraries, Children's; School libraries; Youth**

Libraries and community
> *See also* **Public relations—Libraries**
> *x* Community and libraries

Libraries and labor
> *x* Labor and laboring classes—Library service

Libraries and moving pictures
> *x* Educational films; Moving pictures and libraries
> *xx* **Library service; Moving pictures in education**

Libraries and Negroes
 See also **Negro librarians**
 x Negroes—Libraries; Negroes and libraries
 xx **Negro librarians**
Libraries and pictures
 xx **Pictures**
Libraries and readers
 See note under **Library education**
 xx **Library service**
Libraries and schools
 See also **Children's literature; Libraries, Children's; Libraries and students; School libraries**
 x Schools and libraries
 xx **Children's literature; Libraries, Children's; School libraries; Schools**
Libraries and state
 See also **Federal aid to libraries; State aid to libraries; State libraries**
Libraries and students
 x Students and libraries
 xx **Libraries and schools**
Libraries and the aged
 x Aged—Library service
Library acquisitions. *See* **Acquisitions (Libraries)**
Library administration
 See also **Libraries—Trustees; Library finance**
 x Libraries—Administration; Library policies
Library advertising. *See* **Advertising—Libraries**
Library architecture
 x Buildings, Library; Library buildings
 xx **Architecture**
Library assistants. *See* **Library technicians**
Library boards. *See* **Libraries—Trustees**
Library buildings. *See* **Library architecture**
Library catalogs
 See also types of library catalogs, e.g., **Catalogs, Book; Catalogs, Card; Catalogs, Classified; Catalogs, Subject;** etc.
 x Catalogs; Catalogs, Library; Libraries—Catalogs
Library classification. *See* **Classification—Books**
Library cooperation
 x Cooperation, Library; Libraries—Cooperation
Library education
 Here are entered works on the education of librarians. Works dealing with the instruction of readers in library use are entered under the heading **Libraries and readers**
 See also **Librarians—In-service training; Library schools**

Library education—*Continued*

    x Education for librarianship; Librarians —Education; Librarians—Training; Library science—Study and teaching

    xx **Education; Professional education**

Library education—Audio-visual aids

    xx **Audio-visual education; Audio-visual materials**

Library education—Curricula

    x Core curriculum; Courses of study; Curriculum (Courses of study); Schools—Curriculum; Study, Courses of

    xx **Education—Curricula**

Library equipment and supplies

    x Library supplies

    xx **Furniture**

Library extension

    See also **Bookmobiles; Libraries, County; Libraries, Regional**

Library finance

    See also **Federal aid to libraries; State aid to libraries**

    x Libraries—Finance

    xx **Library administration**

Library laws. *See* **Libraries—Laws and regulations**

Library legislation. *See* **Libraries—Laws and regulations**

Library of Congress. *See* **U.S. Library of Congress**

Library policies. *See* **Library administration**

Library processing. *See* **Processing (Libraries)**

Library schools

    xx **Library education; Schools**

Library science

    Use for general works on the organization and administration of libraries. Works about services offered by libraries to patrons are entered under **Library service**

    See also **Bibliography; Cataloging; Classification—Books; Comparative librarianship; Library service; Library surveys; Processing (Libraries)**; also headings beginning with the words **Libraries** and **Library**

    x Librarianship

    xx **Bibliography; Documentation; Information sciences**

Library science—Electronic data processing. *See* **Electronic data processing—Library science**

Library science—Study and teaching. *See* **Library education**

Library service

    See note under **Library science**

    See also **Libraries—Reference service; Libraries and readers; Libraries and moving pictures**

    xx **Library science**

Library supplies. *See* **Library equipment and supplies**

Library surveys
   x Surveys, Library
   xx **Library science**

Library systems. *See* **Libraries—Centralization**

Library technicians
   x Library assistants; Nonprofessional library assistants; Subprofessional library assistants
   xx **Librarians**

Library trustees. *See* **Libraries—Trustees**

Librettos
   See also **Operas—Stories, plots, etc.;** also musical forms with the subdivision *Librettos,* e.g. **Operas—Librettos;** etc.

Life
   See also **Death; Ethics; Ontology**

Life, Christian. *See* **Christian life**

Life, Future. *See* **Future life**

Life—Origin
   x Germ theory; Origin of life
   xx **Evolution**

Life, Spiritual. *See* **Spiritual life**

Life (Biology)
   See also **Biology; Genetics; Middle age; Old age; Protoplasm; Reproduction**
   xx **Biology; Genetics**

Life after death. *See* **Future life; Immortality**

Life insurance. *See* **Insurance, Life**

Life on other planets
   See also **Interstellar communication**
   x Extraterrestrial life; Planets, Life on other
   xx **Astronomy; Planets; Space biology; Universe**

Life support systems (Space environment)
   See also **Astronauts—Clothing; Apollo project; Space ships**
   xx **Human engineering; Space medicine**

Lifts. *See* **Elevators; Hoisting machinery**

Light
   See also **Color; Lasers; Optics; Phosphorescence; Photometry; Radiation; Radioactivity; Refraction; Spectrum; X rays**
   xx **Electromagnetic waves; Optics; Photometry; Physics; Radiation; Spectrum; Vibration; Waves**

Light, Electric. *See* **Electric lighting; Fluorescent lighting; Photometry; Phototherapy**

Light amplification by stimulated emission of radiation. *See* **Lasers**

Light and shade. *See* **Shades and shadows**

Light ships. *See* **Lightships**

Lighthouses
   See also **Lightships**
   xx **Navigation**

313

Lighting

See also **Candles; Electric lighting; Fluorescent lighting; Lamps; Street lighting;** also subjects and names of cities with the subdivision *Lighting,* e.g. **Chicago—Lighting; Theaters—Lighting;** etc.

x Illumination

Lightning

xx **Electricity; Meteorology; Thunderstorms**

Lightships

x Light ships

xx **Lighthouses**

Lime

See also **Cement**

xx **Fertilizers and manures**

Limericks

See also **Nonsense verses**

x Rhymes

xx **Humorous poetry; Nonsense verses**

Limitation of armament. *See* **Disarmament**

Limited access highways. *See* **Express highways**

Lincoln Day. *See* **Lincoln's Birthday**

Lincoln family

xx **Genealogy**

Lincoln's Birthday

x Lincoln Day

Line engraving. *See* **Engraving**

Linen

See also **Flax; Hemp**

xx **Fibers; Flax; Textile industry and fabrics**

Linguistics. *See* **Language and languages**

Linoleum block printing

x Block printing

xx **Color prints; Engraving**

Linotype

xx **Printing; Type and type founding; Typesetting**

Lip reading. *See* **Deaf—Means of communication**

Liquid fuel. *See* **Gasoline; Petroleum as fuel**

Liquids

See also **Hydraulics; Hydrodynamics; Hydrostatics**

xx **Mechanics; Physics**

Liquor problem

Use for works of an administrative character including liquor control

See also **Alcoholism; Prohibition; Temperance**

x Drink question; Drunkenness; Inebriates; Intemperance; Intoxication

xx **Alcohol; Alcoholism; Prohibition; Social problems; Temperance**

314

Liquor traffic
>Use for works dealing with the liquor industry
>*x* Saloons
>*xx* **Alcohol; Temperance**

Liquors
>Use for technical works
>*See also* **Distillation**
>*x* Drinks; Intoxicants; Spirits, Alcoholic
>*xx* **Alcohol; Beverages; Distillation; Stimulants**

Listening
>*See also* **Attention**
>*xx* **Attention**

Listening devices. *See* **Eavesdropping**

Literacy. *See* **Illiteracy**

Literary awards. *See* **Literary prizes;** also names of awards, e.g. **Caldecott Medal books;** etc.

Literary characters. *See* **Characters and characteristics in literature**

Literary criticism. *See* **Criticism; Literature—History and criticism**

Literary landmarks (May subdiv. geog.)
>*x* Authors—Homes and haunts; Landmarks, Literary
>*xx* **Historic houses, etc.; Literature—History and criticism**

Literary landmarks—U.S.
>*x* U.S.—Literary landmarks

Literary prizes
>*See also* names of awards; e.g. **Caldecott Medal books;** etc.
>*x* Book awards; Book prizes; Literary awards; Literature—Prizes
>*xx* **Rewards (Prizes, etc.)**

Literary property. *See* **Copyright**

Literary style. *See* **Style, Literary**

Literature
>Use for works on literature in general, not limited to history, philosophy or any one aspect
>*See also*

Authorship	**Devotional literature**
Ballads	**ture**
Bible in literature	**Drama**
Biography (as a literary form)	**Essay**
	Fables
Books	**Fairy tales**
Catholic literature	**Fiction**
Characters and characteristics in literature	**Humanism**
	Journalism
	Legends
Children in literature and art	**Music and literature**
Children's literature	**Negro literature**
Christian literature, Early	**Parody**
	Plots (Drama, fiction, etc.)
Classical literature	
Criticism	**Poetry**

Literature—*Continued*

Realism in literature

Religious literature

Romanticism

Sagas

Satire

Short story

Style, Literary

Symbolism in literature

Wit and humor

Women in literature and art

also names of literatures, e.g. **English literature; French literature;** etc.

x Belles-lettres; Language arts

xx **Books; Books and reading; Humanities; Language and languages**

Literature—Bio-bibliography

See also **Authors**

xx **Authors**

Literature—Biography. *See* **Authors**

Literature, Classical. *See* **Classical literature**

Literature—Collections

See also **Essays; Letters; Orations, Parodies; Quotations; Romances; Short stories;** also names of literatures and names of literary forms with the subdivision *Collections,* e.g. **English literature — Collections; Poetry — Collections;** etc.

x Literature—Selections

Literature, Comparative

x Comparative literature

xx **Philology, Comparative**

Literature—Competitions

x Competitions

Literature—Criticism. *See* **Literature—History and criticism**

Literature—Dictionaries

See also **Literature—Indexes**

xx **Literature—Indexes**

Literature—Evaluation. *See* **Book reviews; Books and reading; Books and reading—Best books; Criticism; Literature—History and criticism**

Literature—History and criticism

See also **Authors; Criticism; Literary landmarks**

x Appraisal of books; Books—Appraisal; Evaluation of literature; Literary criticism; Literature—Criticism; Literature—Evaluation

xx **Authors; Style, Literary**

Literature, Immoral. *See* **Pornography**

Literature—Indexes

See also **Literature—Dictionaries**

xx **Literature—Dictionaries**

Literature, Medieval

May use same subdivisions as under **Literature**

See also **Christian literature, Early**

x Medieval literature

xx **Middle Ages; Renaissance**

316

Literature—Outlines, syllabi, etc.
> *See also* **English literature—Outlines, syllabi, etc.**

Literature—Prizes. *See* **Literary prizes,** also names of prizes, e.g. **Caldecott Medal books;** etc.

Literature—Selections. *See* **Literature—Collections**

Literature—Stories, plots, etc.
> Use for collections of stories, plots, etc. Works dealing with the construction and analysis of plots as a literary technique are entered under **Plots (Drama, fiction, etc.)**

Literature—Yearbooks
> *x* Annuals
> *xx* **Yearbooks**

Literature and communism. *See* **Communism and literature**

Literature as a profession. *See* **Authors; Authorship; Journalism; Journalists**

Lithographers
> *xx* **Engravers**

Lithography
> *See also* **Offset printing**
> *xx* **Color printing; Prints**

Lithoprinting. *See* **Offset printing**

Littering. *See* **Refuse and refuse disposal**

Little league baseball
> *xx* **Baseball**

Little theater. *See* **Theater—Little theater movement**

Liturgies
> *See also* **Mass**
> *x* Church service books; Ecclesiastical rites and ceremonies; Ritual; Service books
> *xx* **Church music; Devotional exercises; Theology**

Live poliovirus vaccine. *See* **Poliomyelitis vaccine**

Livestock
> Use for material on breeds of livestock and on stock raising as an industry. General descriptions of farm and other domestic animals are entered under **Domestic animals**
>
> *See also*

Cattle	Hogs
Cows	Horses
Dairying	Livestock judging
Domestic animals	Sheep
Feeding and feeds	Veterinary medicine
Goats	

> *x* Animal husbandry; Animal industry; Breeding; Farm animals; Stock and stock breeding; Stock raising
> *xx* **Agriculture; Cattle; Domestic animals**

Livestock judging
> *x* Stock judging
> *xx* **Livestock**

Living, Cost of. *See* **Cost and standard of living**

Living, Standard of. *See* **Cost and standard of living**

Lizards

   xx **Reptiles**

Loan associations. *See* **Building and loan associations**

Loan funds, Student. *See* **Student loan funds**

Loans

   Use for works on loans, particularly small loans, usually made by finance companies. Works on government loans are entered under **Debts, Public**

   See also **Building and loan associations; Debts, Public; Interest and usury; Investments**

   x Lending

   xx **Credit**

Lobbying

   See also **Corruption (in politics)**

   x Interest groups; Pressure groups

   xx **Corruption (in politics); Politics, Practical**

Lobsters

   xx **Crustacea**

Local government

   Use for works about local government of districts, counties, townships, etc. Works about county government only are entered under **County government**; works about city government are entered under **Municipal government**

   See also **Cities and towns; County government; Metropolitan government; Municipal government; Public administration; Villages**

   x Government, Local; Town officers

   xx **Administrative law; Political science; Villages**

Local history. *See* names of countries, states, etc. with the subdivision *History, Local,* e.g. **U.S.—History, Local;** etc.

Local transit

   See also **Buses; Street railroads; Subways;** also names of cities and metropolitan areas with the subdivision *Transit systems,* e.g. **Chicago—Transit systems; Chicago metropolitan area—Transit systems;** etc.

   x City transit; Municipal transit; Rapid transit; Transit systems

   xx **Traffic engineering; Transportation**

Localism. *See* **Sectionalism (U.S.);** and names of languages with the subdivision *Provincialisms,* e.g. **English language —Provincialisms;** etc.

Lockouts. *See* **Strikes and lockouts**

Locks and keys
    x Keys
    xx Burglary protection
Locomotion. *See* **Aeronautics; Animal loco-**
       motion; Automobiles; Boats and
       boating; Flight; Navigation; Trans-
       portation; Walking
Locomotives
    x Railroads—Rolling stock; Rolling stock
    xx **Machinery; Steam engines**
Locomotives—Models
    xx **Machinery—Models**
Locusts
    x Diseases and pests; Grasshoppers
    xx **Cicadas; Insects, Injurious and bene-**
       ficial
Locusts, Seventeen-year. *See* **Cicadas**
Lodging houses. *See* **Hotels, motels, etc.**
Log cabins
    x Cabins
Logarithms
    See also **Slide rule**
    xx **Algebra; Mathematics—Tables, etc.;**
       Trigonometry—Tables, etc.
Logging. *See* **Lumber and lumbering**
Logic
    See also **Knowledge, Theory of; Proba-**
       bilities; Reasoning; Thought and
       thinking
    x Argumentation; Deduction (Logic); Dia-
       lectics; Fallacies; Induction (Logic)
    xx **Intellect; Philosophy; Reasoning; Sci-**
       ence—Methodology; Thought and
       thinking
Logic, Symbolic and mathematical
    See also **Algebra, Boolean; Set theory**
    xx **Mathematics; Set theory**
Longevity. *See* **Old age**
Longitude
    See also **Time**
    x Degrees of latitude and longitude
    xx **Earth; Geodesy; Nautical astronomy**
Looking glasses. *See* **Mirrors**
Looms
    xx **Weaving**
Loran
    xx **Navigation**
Lord's Day. *See* **Sabbath**
Lord's Prayer
    xx **Devotional exercises; Jesus Christ—**
       Prayers
Lord's Supper
    See also **Mass**
    x Communion; Ecclesiastical rites and cere-
       monies; Eucharist; Jesus Christ—Last
       Supper; Last Supper
    xx **Devotional exercises; Jesus Christ;**
       Mass; Sacraments; Theology
Lotteries
    xx **Gambling**

319

Loud speakers. *See* **Amplifiers, Vacuum tube;**
    Intercommunication systems

Louisiana Purchase
    xx **U.S.—History—1783-1809**

Love
    See also **Dating (Social customs); Friend-
        ship; Marriage**
    x Affection
    xx **Behavior; Dating (Social customs);
        Emotions; Friendship**

Love (Theology)
    xx **Christian ethics**

Love poetry
    x Poetry of love
    xx **Poetry**

Low sodium diet. *See* **Salt free diet**

Low temperature biology. *See* **Cryobiology**

Low temperatures
    See also **Cold; Cryobiology**
    x Cryogenics; Temperatures, Low
    xx **Cold; Temperature**

Loyalists, American. *See* **American Loyalists**

Loyalty
    See also **Patriotism**
    x Faithfulness
    xx **Behavior; Patriotism**

Loyalty oaths. *See* **Internal security**

Lubrication and lubricants
    See also **Bearings (Machinery); Oils and
        fats**
    x Grease
    xx **Bearings (Machinery); Machinery;
        Oils and fats**

Lullabies
    x Cradle songs; Slumber songs
    xx **Children's poetry; Children's songs;
        Songs**

Lumber and lumbering
    Includes works on cut timber, its prepara-
        tion for construction and building pur-
        poses, and uses of various kinds of
        lumber
    x Logging; Timber
    xx **Forest products; Forests and forestry;
        Trees; Wood**

Luminescence. *See* **Phosphorescence**

Luminescence, Animal. *See* **Bioluminescence**

Lunacy. *See* **Insanity**

Lunar bases
    x Moon bases

Lunar cars. *See* **Moon cars**

Lunar eclipses. *See* **Eclipses, Lunar**

Lunar excursion module
    x LEM; Lem; Lunar module
    xx **Space vehicles**

Lunar expeditions. *See* **Space flight to the
    moon**

Lunar exploration. *See* **Moon—Exploration**

Lunar geology
> *See also* **Lunar petrology**
> *x* Geology, Lunar; Geology—Moon; Moon
> —Geology

Lunar module. *See* **Lunar excursion module**

Lunar petrology
> *x* Lunar rocks; Moon rocks; Rocks, Moon
> *xx* **Lunar geology; Petrology**

Lunar photography
> *See also* **Moon—Photographs**
> *x* Moon photography
> *xx* **Space photography**

Lunar probes
> *See also* names of space projects, e.g.
> **Mariner project;** etc.
> *x* Moon probes
> *xx* **Space probes**

Lunar rocks. *See* **Lunar petrology**

Lunar rover vehicles. *See* **Moon cars**

Lunar surface radio communication. *See* **Radio in astronautics**

Lunar surface vehicles. *See* **Moon cars**

Lunatic asylums. *See* **Mentally ill—Institutional care**

Lunch rooms. *See* **Restaurants, bars, etc.**

Luncheons
> *xx* **Caterers and catering; Cooking; Entertaining; Menus**

Lungs
> *See also* **Respiration**

Lungs—Diseases
> *See also* **Pneumonia; Tuberculosis**

Lutheran Church

Lying. *See* **Truthfulness and falsehood**

Lynching
> *See also* **Vigilance committees**
> *xx* **Crime and criminals**

MARC project
> *x* Machine readable catalog; Marc project; Project MARC
> *xx* **Libraries—Automation**

Machine design. *See* **Machinery—Design**

Machine intelligence. *See* **Artificial intelligence**

Machine language. *See* **Programming languages (Electronic computers)**

Machine readable catalog. *See* **MARC project**

Machine shop practice
> *x* Shop practice

Machine shops
> *x* Shops, Machine

Machine tools
> *See also* **Planing machines**
> *xx* **Machinery; Milling machines; Tools**

Machine translating. *See* **Translating and interpreting**

Machinery
> *See also*

| Agricultural machinery | Bearings (Machinery) |

Machinery—*Continued*

Belts and belting
Electric machinery
Engines
Gearing
Hydraulic machinery
Inventions
Locomotives
Lubrication and lubricants
Machine tools
Mechanical drawing
Mechanics
Metalworking machinery
Milling machines
Patents
Power transmission
Steam engines
Woodworking machinery

x Machines

xx Industrial management; Manufactures; Mechanical engineering; Mechanics; Mills and millwork; Power (Mechanics); Power transmission; Technology; Tools

Machinery, Automatic. *See* **Automation**

Machinery—Design

See also **Human engineering; Machinery —Models**

x Machine design

Machinery—Drawing. *See* **Mechanical drawing**

Machinery—Models

See also **Airplanes—Models; Automobiles — Models; Locomotives — Models; Motorboats — Models; Railroads — Models; Ships—Models**

x Mechanical models; Models, Mechanical

xx **Machinery—Design**

Machinery in industry

Use for works on the social and economic aspects of mechanization in the industrial world, the machine age, etc.

See also **Automation**

xx **Industry; Labor and laboring classes; Technology and civilization**

Machines. *See* **Machinery**

Madness. *See* **Insanity**

Madonna. *See* **Mary, Virgin**

Magazines. *See* **Periodicals**

Magic

Use for works dealing with modern ("parlor") magic, legerdemain, etc. Works on magic which seemingly requires the supernatural are entered under **Occult sciences**

See also **Card tricks; Occult sciences; Tricks**

x Conjuring; Legerdemain; Sleight of hand

xx **Amusements; Hallucinations and illusions; Occult sciences; Tricks**

Magna Carta

Magnet winding. *See* **Electromagnets**

Magnetic needle. *See* **Compass**

322

Magnetic resonance accelerator. *See* **Cyclotron**

Magnetic recorders and recording
  x Recorders, Tape; Tape recorders
  xx **Sound—Recordings and reproduction**

Magnetism
  See also **Compass; Electricity; Electro-magnetism; Electromagnets; Magnets**
  xx **Electricity; Physics**

Magneto
  xx **Gas and oil engines**

Magnets
  See also **Electromagnets**
  xx **Magnetism; Microwaves**

Mail-order business
  xx **Advertising; Business; Salesmen and salesmanship**

Mail service. *See* **Postal service**

Maize. *See* **Corn**

Make-up (Cosmetics). *See* **Cosmetics**

Make-up, Theatrical
  x Theatrical make-up
  xx **Amateur theatricals; Costume**

Maladjusted children. *See* **Problem children**

Maladjustment (Psychology). *See* **Adjustment (Psychology)**

Malaria
  x Ague; Chills and fever; Intermittent fever
  xx **Fever**

Malay race

Male grooming. *See* **Grooming for men**

Malnutrition. *See* **Nutrition**

Mammals
  See also **Primates;** also names of mammals, e.g. **Bats; Elephants;** etc.
  xx **Vertebrates; Zoology**

Mammals, Fossil
  See also names of extinct animals, e.g. **Mastodon;** etc.
  x Fossil mammals
  xx **Fossils**

Man
  See also **Anthropology; Anthropometry; Creation; Ethnology; Heredity**
  x Human race; Men
  xx **Anthropology; Creation; History; Primates; Woman**

Man—Antiquity. *See* **Man—Origin and antiquity**

Man—Color. *See* **Color of man**

Man—Influence of environment
  See also **Color of man; Weightlessness**
  x Acclimatization; Altitude, Influence of; Environment
  xx **Adaptation (Biology); Anthropogeography; Evolution; Human ecology**

Malls, Shopping
See Shopping malls

323

Man—Influence on nature
> *See also* **Environmental policy; Pollution**
>
> *x* Earth, Effect of man on; Environment; Nature, Effect of man on
>
> *xx* **Environmental policy; Human ecology**

Man—Origin and antiquity
> *See also* **Anatomy, Comparative; Evolution; Man, Prehistoric**
>
> *x* Antiquities; Man—Antiquity; Origin of man
>
> *xx* **Anatomy, Comparative; Evolution; Man, Prehistoric; Religion and science; Somatology**

Man, Prehistoric
> *See also* **Bronze age; Cave dwellers; Man —Origin and antiquity;** also names of countries, cities, etc. with the subdivision *Antiquities,* e.g. **U.S.—Antiquities;** etc.
>
> *x* Antiquities; Prehistoric man; Primitive man
>
> *xx* **Archeology; Civilization, Ancient; Ethnology; Man—Origin and antiquity; Society, Primitive; Stone age**

Man, Primitive
> *x* Primitive man
>
> *xx* **Ethnology**

Man (Theology)
> *See also* **Soul**
>
> *xx* **Theology**

Man in space. *See* **Manned space flight**

Man power. *See* **Labor supply; Military service, Compulsory;** and names of wars with the subdivision *Manpower,* e.g. **World War, 1939-1945—Manpower;** etc.

Management
> Use for general works on the principles of management in factories, industries, shops, etc. Works on the application of such principles are entered under the specific headings such as those listed below
>
> *See also* **Efficiency, Industrial; Factory management; Farm management; Industrial management; Office management; Personnel management; Sales management**
>
> *x* Administration; Management, Scientific; Organization and management; Scientific management

Management, Employees' representation in. *See* **Employees' representation in management**

Management, Industrial. *See* **Industrial management**

Management, Sales. *See* **Sales management**

Management, Scientific. *See* **Management**

Management of children. *See* **Children—Management; School discipline**

Mandates

    x Government, Mandatory; League of Nations—Mandatory system

    xx European War, 1914-1918—Territorial questions; International law; International organization; International relations

Manicuring

Manikins (Fashion models). *See* **Models, Fashion**

Manned space flight

    See also **Astronauts; Extravehicular activity (Manned space flight); Outer space—Exploration; Space medicine; Space ships;** also names of projects, e.g. **Gemini project;** etc.

    x Man in space; Space flight, Manned; Space travel

    xx **Astronautics; Space medicine**

Manned space flight—Rescue work. *See* **Space rescue operations**

Manned undersea research stations

    See also **Aquanauts;** and names of special research projects and stations, e.g. **Sealab project;** etc.

    x Sea laboratories; Submarine research stations, Manned; Undersea research stations, Manned; Underwater research stations, Manned

    xx **Oceanography—Research; Skin diving; Underwater exploration**

Manners. *See* **Courtesy; Etiquette**

Manners and customs

    See also

Bohemianism	Funeral rites and
Caste	ceremonies
Chivalry	Holidays
Clothing and dress	Marriage customs
Costume	and rites
Courts and cour-	Rites and ceremon-
tiers	ies
Dueling	Social classes
Etiquette	Travel
Festivals	

    also names of ethnic groups, countries, cities, etc. with the subdivision *Social life and customs,* e.g. **Indians of North America—Social life and customs; Jews—Social life and customs; U.S. —Social life and customs;** etc.

    x Ceremonies; Customs, Social; Folkways; Social customs; Social life and customs

    xx **Civilization; Ethnology; Etiquette; Rites and ceremonies**

Manpower. *See* **Labor supply; Military service, Compulsory;** and names of wars with the subdivision *Manpower,* e.g. **World War, 1939-1945—Manpower;** etc.

Manpower development and training. *See* **Occupational training**
Manpower policy
    See also **Labor supply; Retraining, Oc-
cupational; Vocational education**
    x Human resource development
    xx **Economic policy; Labor supply**
Manslaughter. *See* **Murder**
Manual training. *See* **Industrial arts education**
Manufactures
    See also **Machinery; Mills and millwork;
Patents; Prices; Trade-marks; Waste
products; Workshops;** also names of
articles manufactured (e.g. **Furniture;**
etc.) and names of industries (e.g.
Paper making and trade; etc.) ; also
names of countries, cities, etc. with the
subdivision *Industries,* e.g. **Chicago—
Industries;** etc.
    x Consumer goods
    xx **Business; Commercial products; In-
dustry; Technology**
Manures. *See* **Fertilizers and manures**
Manuscripts
    See also **Autographs; Charters; Illumina-
tion of books and manuscripts**
    x Papyrus manuscripts
    xx **Archives; Autographs; Bibliography;
Books; Charters**
Manuscripts, Illuminated. *See* **Illumination of
books and manuscripts**
Manuscripts—Prices. *See* **Books—Prices**
Map drawing
    See also **Topographical drawing**
    x Cartography; Chartography; Plans
    xx **Topographical drawing**
Maple sugar
    xx **Sugar**
Maps
    Use for general works about maps and their
history. Works on the methods of map
making and the mapping of areas are
entered under **Map drawing.** Collec-
tions of maps of several countries are
entered under **Atlases**
    See also **Atlases; Automobiles—Road
guides; Charts;** also subjects with the
subdivision *Maps* (e.g. **Geology—
Maps; Railroads—Maps;** etc.) and
names of countries, cities, etc. with the
subdivision *Maps,* e.g. **U.S.—Maps;
Chicago—Maps;** etc.
    x Cartography; Chartography; Plans
    xx **Charts; Geography**
Maps, Historical. *See* **Atlases, Historical**
Maps, Military. *See* **Military geography**
Maps, Road. *See* **Automobiles—Road guides**
Marble
    xx **Petrology; Stone**
Marc project. *See* **MARC project**

Marches. *See* **Military music**

Marches (Demonstrations). *See* **Demonstrations**

Marches (Exercises). *See* **Drill (nonmilitary)**

Marches for Negro civil rights. *See* **Negroes—Civil rights**

Margarine

    x Butter, Artificial; Oleomargarine

    xx **Butter**

Marine animals

    See also **Corals; Fishes; Fresh-water animals**

    x Animals, Aquatic; Animals, Marine; Animals, Sea; Aquatic animals; Marine fauna; Marine zoology; Sea animals: Water animals

    xx **Animals; Fresh-water animals; Geographical distribution of animals and plants; Marine biology**

Marine aquariums

    See also names of specific marine aquariums, e.g. **Marineland;** etc.

    x Aquariums, Saltwater; Oceanariums; Sea water aquariums

    xx **Aquariums**

Marine architecture. *See* **Naval architecture; Shipbuilding**

Marine biology

    See also **Fresh-water biology; Marine animals; Marine ecology; Marine plants; Marine resources; Photography, Submarine**

    x Biology, Marine; Ocean life

    xx **Biology; Fresh-water biology; Natural history; Oceanography; Underwater exploration**

Marine boilers. *See* **Boilers, Marine**

Marine ecology

    x Ecology, Marine

    xx **Ecology; Marine biology**

Marine engineering

    x Naval engineering

    xx **Civil engineering; Engineering; Mechanical engineering; Naval architecture; Naval art and science; Steam navigation**

Marine engines

    See also **Boilers, Marine**

    xx **Engines; Shipbuilding; Steam engines**

Marine fauna. *See* **Marine animals**

Marine flora. *See* **Marine plants**

Marine geology. *See* **Submarine geology**

Marine insurance. *See* **Insurance, Marine**

Marine law. *See* **Maritime law**

Marine mineral resources

    x Mineral resources, Marine; Ocean mineral resources

    xx **Marine resources; Mines and mineral resources**

Marine painting

x Sea in art; Seascapes; Ships in art

xx **Painting**

Marine plants

See also **Algae; Fresh-water plants**

x Aquatic plants; Marine flora; Water plants

xx **Fresh-water plants; Geographical distribution of animals and plants; Marine biology; Plants**

Marine pollution

x Ocean pollution; Offshore water pollution; Sea pollution

xx **Pollution**

Marine resources

See also **Fisheries; Marine mineral resources**

x Ocean—Economic aspects; Resources, Marine

xx **Commercial products; Marine biology; Natural resources; Oceanography**

Marine steam boilers. *See* **Boilers, Marine**

Marine zoology. *See* **Marine animals**

Marineland

xx **Marine aquariums**

Mariner project

x Project Mariner

xx **Lunar probes; Space probes**

Mariners. *See* **Seamen**

Mariner's compass. *See* **Compass**

Marionettes. *See* **Puppets and puppet plays**

Maritime discoveries. *See* **Discoveries (in geography)**

Maritime law

See also **Commercial law; Freight and freightage; Insurance, Marine; Merchant marine; Pirates; Salvage**

x Law, Maritime; Marine law; Merchant marine—Laws and legislation; Naval law; Navigation—Laws and legislation; Sea laws

xx **Commercial law; International law; Law; Shipping**

Market gardening. *See* **Vegetable gardening**

Market surveys

See also **Public opinion polls**

xx **Public opinion polls**

Marketing

Use for works on the principles and methods involved in the distribution of merchandise from producer to consumer

See also **Sales management;** and subjects with the subdivision *Marketing,* e.g. **Farm produce—Marketing;** etc.

x Distribution (Economics); Merchandising

xx **Advertising; Business; Industrial management; Salesmen and salesmanship**

Marketing (Home economics). *See* **Shopping**

Marketing of farm produce. *See* **Farm produce—Marketing**

Markets

See also **Fairs**

xx **Business; Cities and towns; Commerce; Fairs; Food**

Marking (Students). *See* **Grading and marking (Students)**

Marks, Potters'. *See* **Pottery—Marks**

Marks on plate. *See* **Hallmarks**

Marksmanship. *See* **Shooting**

Marriage

See also **Celibacy; Dating (Social customs); Divorce; Domestic relations; Family; Family life education; Free love; Home; Sex; Sexual ethics**

x Matrimony; Weddings

xx **Dating (Social customs); Divorce; Domestic relations; Family; Home; Love; Sacraments**

Marriage—Annulment. *See* **Divorce**

Marriage, Mixed

x Intercultural marriage; Interfaith marriage; Intermarriage; Interracial marriage; Mixed marriage

Marriage customs and rites

x Bridal customs; Weddings

xx **Manners and customs; Rites and ceremonies**

Marriage registers. *See* **Registers of births, etc.**

Marriage statistics. *See* **Vital statistics**

Mars (Planet)

See also **Mars probes**

Mars (Planet)—Exploration

Mars (Planet)—Photographs

Mars probes

x Martian probes

xx **Mars (Planet); Space probes**

Marshall Plan. *See* **Reconstruction (1939-1951)**

Marshes

x Bogs; Swamps

xx **Drainage; Reclamation of land**

Martian probes. *See* **Mars probes**

Martyrs

See also **Christian biography; Persecution; Saints**

xx **Christian biography; Church history; Heroes; Persecution; Saints**

Marxism. *See* **Communism; Socialism**

Mary, Virgin

x Madonna; Virgin Mary

Mary, Virgin—Art

See also **Jesus Christ—Art**

xx **Christian art and symbolism; Jesus Christ—Art**

Masers

x Microwave amplification by stimulated emission of radiation

Masers—*Continued*

   xx **Electromagnetism; Microwaves; Vacuum tubes**

Masers, Optical. *See* **Lasers**

Masks (for the face)

Masks (Plays)

   x Masques (Plays)

   xx **Drama; Pageants; Theater**

Masks (Sculpture)

   x Death masks

   xx **Sculpture**

Masonry

   See also **Bricklaying; Bridges; Cement; Concrete; Foundations; Plaster and plastering; Stonecutting; Walls**

   xx **Bricklaying; Building; Civil engineering; Foundations; Stone; Walls**

Masons (Secret order). *See* **Freemasons**

Masques (Plays). *See* **Masks (Plays)**

Mass

   See also **Lord's Supper**

   xx **Liturgies; Lord's Supper**

Mass communication. *See* **Communication; Mass media; Telecommunication**

Mass media

   See also **Moving pictures; Newspapers; Radio broadcasting; Television broadcasting**

   x Mass communication

   xx **Communication**

Mass psychology. *See* **Social psychology**

Massage

   See also **Electrotherapeutics; Osteopathy**

   xx **Medicine—Practice; Osteopathy; Physical therapy**

Mastodon

   xx **Extinct animals; Mammals, Fossil**

Materia medica

   See also **Anesthetics; Drugs; Pharmacology; Pharmacy; Poisons; Therapeutics;** also names of classes of drugs and and individual drugs, e.g. **Narcotics;** etc.

   x Herbals; Pharmacopoeias

   xx **Chemistry, Medical and pharmaceutical; Drugs; Medicine; Pharmacy; Therapeutics**

Materialism

   See also **Idealism; Realism**

   xx **Idealism; Monism; Philosophy; Positivism; Realism**

Materials

   Use for works on materials of engineering and industry

   See also **Building materials; Raw materials; Strength of materials**

   x Engineering materials; Industrial materials; Strategic materials

Materials, Strength of. *See* **Strength of materials**

Materials handling

    See also **Freight and freightage; Trucks**

    x Mechanical handling

    xx **Industrial management; Trucks**

Maternity. *See* **Mothers**

Mathematical drawing. *See* **Geometrical drawing; Mechanical drawing**

Mathematical recreations

    See also **Number games**

    x Recreations, Mathematical

    xx **Amusements; Puzzles; Scientific recreations**

Mathematical sets. *See* **Set theory**

Mathematicians

    xx **Scientists**

Mathematics

    See also

Algebra	**Logic, Symbolic**
Arithmetic	**and mathematical**
Binary system	**Mechanics**
(Mathematics)	**Mensuration**
Calculus	**Number theory**
Dynamics	**Set theory**
Geometry	**Trigonometry**

    xx **Science**

Mathematics—Tables, etc.

    See also **Logarithms; Trigonometry—Tables, etc.**

    x Ready reckoners

Matrimony. *See* **Marriage**

Matter

    xx **Dynamics; Physics**

Mausoleums. *See* **Tombs**

Maxims. *See* **Proverbs**

Mayas

    xx **Indians of Mexico**

Meal planning. *See* **Menus; Nutrition**

Meals for astronauts. *See* **Astronauts—Nutrition**

Meals for school children. *See* **School children—Food**

Measurements, Electric. *See* **Electric measurements**

Measures. *See* **Weights and measures**

Measuring. *See* **Mensuration**

Measuring instruments

    See also **Slide rule**

    x Instruments, Measuring

    xx **Mensuration; Weights and measures**

Meat

    See also **Beef; Carving (Meat, etc.)**

    xx **Food**

Meat industry and trade

    See also **Cold storage; Meat inspection**

    x Packing industry; Stockyards

    xx **Food supply**

Meat inspection

    x Inspection of meat

    xx **Food adulteration and inspection; Meat industry and trade; Public health**

Mechanic arts. *See* **Industrial arts**

Mechanical brains. *See* **Computers; Cybernetics**

Mechanical drawing

> *See also* **Architectural drawing; Geometrical drawing; Graphic methods; Lettering**
>
> *x* Drafting, Mechanical; Engineering drawing; Industrial drawing; Machinery—Drawing; Mathematical drawing; Plans; Structural drafting
>
> *xx* **Drawing; Engineering; Geometrical drawing; Machinery; Pattern making**

Mechanical engineering

> See note under **Mechanics, Applied**
>
> *See also* **Electric engineering; Engines; Machinery; Marine engineering; Mechanical movements; Power (Mechanics); Power transmission; Steam engineering**
>
> *xx* **Civil engineering; Engineering; Steam engineering**

Mechanical handling. *See* **Materials handling**

Mechanical models. *See* **Machinery—Models**

Mechanical movements

> *See also* **Automata; Gearing; Robots**
>
> *xx* **Gearing; Kinematics; Mechanical engineering; Mechanics; Motion**

Mechanical musical instruments. *See* **Musical instruments, Mechanical**

Mechanical painting. *See* **Painting, Industrial**

Mechanical stokers. *See* **Stokers, Mechanical**

Mechanical translating. *See* **Translating and interpreting**

Mechanics

> *See also*
>
> | | |
> |---|---|
> | **Dynamics** | **Motion** |
> | **Engineering** | **Power (Mechanics)** |
> | **Force and energy** | **Statics** |
> | **Gases** | **Steam engines** |
> | **Hydraulics** | **Strains and stresses** |
> | **Hydrodynamics** | **Strength of materials** |
> | **Hydrostatics** | |
> | **Kinematics** | **Vibration** |
> | **Liquids** | **Viscosity** |
> | **Machinery** | **Wave mechanics** |
> | **Mechanical movements** | |
>
> *xx* **Engineering; Force and energy; Kinematics; Machinery; Mathematics; Motion; Physics**

Mechanics, Applied

> Use for works on the application of the principles of mechanics to engineering structure other than machinery. Works on the application of the principles of mechanics to the design, construction and operation of machinery are entered under **Mechanical engineering**
>
> *x* Applied mechanics

332

Mechanics (Persons)

Medallions. *See* **Medals**

Medals

> *See also* **Decorations of honor; Insignia; Numismatics;** also **U.S. Army—Medals, badges, decorations, etc.; U.S. Navy—Medals, badges, decorations, etc.;** etc.
>
> *x* Badges of honor; Medallions
>
> *xx* **Decorations of honor; Insignia; Numismatics**

Media centers (Education). *See* **Instructional materials centers**

Mediation, Industrial. *See* **Arbitration, Industrial**

Medical botany. *See* **Botany, Medical**

Medical care

> *See also* **Charities, Medical;** also classes of people with the subdivision *Medical care,* e.g. **Aged—Medical care;** etc.
>
> *x* Health care; Medical service
>
> *xx* **Public health**

Medical care—Costs

> *x* Cost of medical care; Medical service, Cost of; Medicine—Cost of medical care
>
> *xx* **Medical economics**

Medical care, Prepaid. *See* **Insurance, Health**

Medical care for the aged. *See* **Aged—Medical care**

Medical centers

> *See also* **Hospitals; Medicine—Study and teaching**
>
> *xx* **Hospitals**

Medical charities. *See* **Charities, Medical**

Medical chemistry. *See* **Chemistry, Medical and pharmaceutical**

Medical colleges. *See* **Medicine—Study and teaching**

Medical economics

> Use for comprehensive works on the economic aspects of medical service from the point of view of both the practitioner and the public
>
> *See also* **Medical care—Costs; Medical care, Prepaid**
>
> *x* Economics, Medical

Medical education. *See* **Medicine—Study and teaching**

Medical electricity. *See* **Electrotherapeutics**

Medical ethics

> *x* Ethics, Medical
>
> *xx* **Ethics; Professional ethics**

Medical jurisprudence

> Use for works that treat of the relation and application of medical facts to legal medicine. Works that include laws, or discussion of those laws which affect medicine and the medical profession,

333

Medical jurisprudence—*Continued*
> are entered under **Medicine—Laws and regulations**
>
> *See also* **Medicine—Laws and regulations; Murder; Poisons; Suicide**
>
> *x* Forensic medicine; Jurisprudence, Medical; Legal medicine; Medicine, Legal
>
> *xx* **Criminal investigation; Criminal law; Law; Medicine—Laws and regulations; Medicine, State**

Medical laws and legislation. *See* **Medicine—Laws and regulations**

Medical missions. *See* **Missions, Medical**

Medical photography. *See* **Photography, Medical**

Medical profession. *See* **Medicine; Physicians; Surgeons**

Medical research. *See* **Medicine—Research**

Medical service. *See* **Medical care**

Medical service, Cost of. *See* **Medical care—Costs**

Medical service, Prepaid. *See* **Insurance, Health**

Medical technology
> *xx* **Medicine**

Medical transplantation. *See* **Transplantation of organs, tissues, etc.**

Medicare. *See* **Aged—Medical care**

Medicinal plants. *See* **Botany, Medical**

Medicine
> *See also*

Anatomy	**Medical technology**
Aviation medicine	**Mind and body**
Bacteriology	**Missions, Medical**
Botany, Medical	**Nurses and nursing**
Chemistry, Medical and pharmaceutical	**Osteopathy**
	Pathology
Health resorts, spas, etc.	**Pharmacology**
	Pharmacy
Homeopathy	**Physiology**
Hospitals	**Quacks and quackery**
Hygiene	**Submarine medicine**
Hypnotism	**Surgery**
Materia medica	

> *also* headings beginning with the word **Medical**
>
> *x* Medical profession
>
> *xx* **Pathology; Professions; Therapeutics**

Medicine, Atomic. *See* **Atomic medicine**

Medicine, Aviation. *See* **Aviation medicine**

Medicine—Biography
> Use for works on lives of workers in several branches of medicine. Collective biographies limited to physicians, surgeons, etc. are entered under **Physicians; Surgeons;** etc.
>
> *See also* **Nurses and nursing; Physicians; Radiologists; Surgeons**

Medicine—Cost of medical care. *See* **Medical care—Costs**

Medicine, Dental. *See* **Dentistry; Teeth**

Medicine—Laws and regulations

    See also **Medical jurisprudence**

    x Medical laws and legislation

    xx **Medical jurisprudence**

Medicine, Legal. *See* **Medical jurisprudence**

Medicine, Military

    See also **Armies—Medical and sanitary affairs; First aid; Hospitals, Military; Military hygiene;** also names of wars with the subdivision *Medical and sanitary affairs,* e.g. **World War, 1939-1945—Medical and sanitary affairs;** etc.

    x Field hospitals; Military medicine

    xx **Armies—Medical and sanitary affairs; Military hygiene**

Medicine, Pediatric. *See* **Children—Diseases**

Medicine—Physiological effect. *See* **Pharmacology**

Medicine, Popular

    Use for medical books for the layman

Medicine—Practice

    See also

Childbirth	**Massage**
Children—Diseases	**Nurses and nursing**
Communicable diseases	**Osteopathy**
Diagnosis	**Therapeutics**
Homeopathy	**Woman—Diseases**

    also names of diseases and groups of diseases, e.g. **Smallpox; Fever; Nervous system—Diseases;** etc.

    xx **Diseases**

Medicine, Preventive. *See* **Bacteriology; Hygiene; Immunity; Public health**

Medicine, Psychosomatic

    x Psychosomatic medicine

    xx **Mind and body; Neuroses; Psychoanalysis; Psychology, Pathological**

Medicine—Research

    x Medical research

    xx **Research**

Medicine, Socialized. *See* **Medicine, State**

Medicine, State

    Use for general works on the relations of the state to medicine, public health, medical legislation, examinations of physicians by state boards, etc.

    See also **Charities, Medical; Medical jurisprudence; Public health**

    x Medicine, Socialized; National health service; Socialized medicine; State medicine

Medicine—Study and teaching

    x Education, Medical; Medical colleges; Medical education

    xx **Medical centers; Professional education; Schools; Vocational education**

Medicine, Submarine. *See* **Submarine medicine**

Medicine, Tropical. *See* **Tropics—Diseases and hygiene**

Medicine, Veterinary. *See* **Veterinary medicine**

Medicine and religion
    See also **Christian Science; Faith cure; Mental healing**
    x Religion and medicine

Medicine as a profession
    See also **Women as physicians**
    xx **Physicians**

Medicine man
    xx **Occult sciences**

Medicines, Patent. *See* **Patent medicines**

Medieval architecture. *See* **Architecture, Medieval**

Medieval art. *See* **Art, Medieval**

Medieval civilization. *See* **Civilization, Medieval**

Medieval history. *See* **Middle Ages—History**

Medieval literature. *See* **Literature, Medieval**

Medieval philosophy. *See* **Philosophy, Medieval**

Meditations
    x Theology, Devotional
    xx **Spiritual life**

Meetings, Public. *See* **Public meetings**

Memoirs. *See* **Autobiographies; Biography**

Memorial Day
    x Days; Decoration Day; National holidays
    xx **School assembly programs**

Memory
    See also **Attention**
    x Mnemonics
    xx **Brain; Educational psychology; Intellect; Mental discipline; Psychology; Psychology, Physiological; Thought and thinking**

Men. *See* **Man; Young men**

Mendel's law
    See also **Heredity**
    xx **Evolution; Heredity; Variation (Biology)**

Mendicancy. *See* **Begging**

Mendicant orders. *See* **Dominicans; Franciscans**

Mending. *See* **Repairing;** and appropriate subjects with the subdivision *Repairing,* e.g. **Radio—Repairing;** etc.

Mennonites
    See also **Amish**
    xx **Baptists**

Menopause
    x Change of life in women
    xx **Woman—Health and hygiene**

✓ *melons*

Men's clothing

    x Clothing, Men's

    xx **Clothing and dress; Costume; Tailoring**

Mensuration

    See also **Geodesy; Measuring instruments; Surveying; Weights and measures**

    x Measuring; Metrology

    xx **Mathematics; Weights and measures**

Mental deficiency. *See* **Mentally handicapped**

Mental diseases. *See* **Insanity; Mental illness; Psychology, Pathological**

Mental healing

    See also **Christian Science; Faith cure; Hypnotism; Mental suggestion; Mind and body; New Thought; Psychotherapy; Subconsciousness; Therapeutics, Suggestive**

    x Healing, Mental; Mind cure

    xx **Christian Science; Faith cure; Medicine and religion; Mental suggestion; Mind and body; Psychotherapy; Subconsciousness; Therapeutics, Suggestive**

Mental health

    See also **Mental illness; Mind and body; Occupational therapy; Psychology, Pathological; Psychology, Physiological; Worry**

    x Health, Mental; Hygiene, Mental; Mental hygiene

    xx **Hygiene; Mental illness; Mind and body; Nervous system—Hygiene**

Mental hospitals. *See* **Mentally ill—Institutional care**

Mental hygiene. *See* **Mental health**

Mental illness

    See note under **Psychiatry**

    See also **Insanity; Mental health; Mentally handicapped**

    x Diseases, Mental; Insane; Mental diseases; Psychoses

    xx **Insanity; Mental health; Mentally handicapped; Psychiatry; Psychology, Pathological**

Mental institutions. *See* **Mentally ill—Institutional care**

Mental philosophy. *See* **Philosophy; Psychology**

Mental suggestion

    See also **Brainwashing; Hypnotism; Mental healing; Therapeutics, Suggestive**

    x Autosuggestion; Suggestion, Mental

    xx **Hypnotism; Mental healing; Mind and body; Psychical research; Subconsciousness; Therapeutics, Suggestive; Thought transference**

Mental telepathy. *See* **Thought transference**

Mental tests
> *See also* **Ability testing; Education—Ex-**
> **perimental methods; Educational**
> **tests and measurements**
>
> *x* Intelligence tests; Objective tests; Psy-
> chological tests; Tests
>
> *xx* **Child study; Education—Experimen-**
> **tal methods; Educational psychology;**
> **Educational tests and measurements;**
> **Examinations; Grading and marking**
> **(Students); Intellect; Psychology,**
> **Physiological**

✓ **Mentally handicapped**
> *See also* **Mental illness**
>
> *x* Feeble-minded; Handicapped; Idiocy;
> Imbecility; Mental deficiency; Men-
> tally retarded; Morons
>
> *xx* **Handicapped; Insanity; Mental illness**

Mentally handicapped children
> *See also* **Slow learning children**
>
> *x* Backward children; Children, Backward;
> Children, Retarded; Mentally retarded
> children; Retarded children
>
> *xx* **Child psychiatry; Handicapped chil-**
> **dren**

Mentally ill—Institutional care
> *x* Asylums; Charitable institutions; Insane
> —Hospitals; Insane asylums; Lunatic
> asylums; Mental hospitals; Mental in-
> stitutions; Psychiatric hospitals
>
> *xx* **Institutional care**

Mentally retarded. *See* **Mentally handicapped**

Mentally retarded children. *See* **Mentally hand-**
> **icapped children**

Menus
> *See also* **Caterers and catering; Dinners**
> **and dining; Luncheons**
>
> *x* Bills of fare; Gastronomy; Meal plan-
> ning
>
> *xx* **Caterers and catering; Cookery; Diet;**
> **Dinners and dining**

Menus for space flight. *See* **Astronauts—Nu-**
> **trition**

Mercantile law. *See* **Commercial law**

Mercantile marine. *See* **Merchant marine**

Merchandise. *See* **Commercial products**

Merchandising. *See* **Marketing; Retail trade**

Merchant marine (May subdiv. geog.)
> *See also* **Harbors; Insurance, Marine;**
> **Shipping**
>
> *x* Mercantile marine
>
> *xx* **Maritime law; Seamen; Shipping;**
> **Ships; Transportation**

Merchant marine—Laws and legislation. *See*
> **Maritime law**

Merchant marine—U.S.
> *x* U.S.—Merchant marine

Merchants
> *xx* **Business; Commerce**

Mercury

    x Quicksilver

Mergers, Conglomerate. *See* **Conglomerate corporations**

Mergers, Industrial. *See* **Railroads—Consolidation; Trusts, Industrial**

Mesmerism. *See* **Hypnotism**

Messages to Congress. *See* **Presidents—U.S.—Messages**

Metabolism

    See also **Nutrition**

    xx **Biochemistry; Nutrition; Physiological chemistry**

Metal work. *See* **Metalwork**

Metallography

    Use for works on the science of metal structures and alloys, especially the study of such structures visually, with the microscope. Works dealing with the science and art of extracting metals from their ores, refining and preparing them for use, are entered under **Metallurgy**

    x Analysis, Microscopic; Micrographic analysis; Microscopic analysis

    xx **Metals; Microscope and microscopy**

Metallurgy

    See note under **Metallography**

    See also **Alloys; Chemical engineering; Chemistry, Technical; Electrometallurgy; Metals; Smelting**

    xx **Alloys; Chemical engineering; Ores; Smelting**

Metals

    See also **Alloys; Metallography; Mineralogy; Precious metals; Solder and soldering;** also names of metals, e.g. **Gold;** etc.

    xx **Chemistry, Inorganic; Metallurgy; Ores**

Metals, Transmutation of. *See* **Transmutation (Chemistry);** and for early works on transmutation of metals, see **Alchemy**

Metalwork

    See also

Architectural metalwork	Ironwork
Art metalwork	Jewelry
Bronzes	Plate-metal work
Coppersmithing	Sheet-metal work
Dies (Metalworking)	Silversmithing
Electroplating	Solder and soldering
Founding	Steel
Goldsmithing	Tinsmithing
	Welding

    x Metal work

    xx **Arts and crafts; Decoration and ornament; Founding; Goldsmithing; Ironwork; Silversmithing**

339

Metalwork, Architectural. *See* **Architectural metalwork**

Metalwork, Art. *See* **Art metalwork**

Metalworking machinery
   xx **Machinery**

Metamorphic rocks. *See* **Rocks**

Metaphysics
   See also **Existentialism; God; Knowledge, Theory of; Ontology; Universe**
   xx **God; Ontology; Philosophy**

Meteorites
   xx **Astronomy; Meteors**

Meteorological instruments
   See also **Barometer; Thermometers and thermometry**
   x Instruments, Meteorological
   xx **Scientific apparatus and instruments**

Meteorological observatories. *See* **Meteorology —Observatories**

Meteorological satellites
   See also names of satellites, e.g. **Tiros (Meteorological satellite)**; etc.
   x Weather satellites
   xx **Artificial satellites**

Meteorology
   See note under **Climate**
   See also

Air	**Rain and rainfall**
Atmosphere	**Seasons**
Auroras	**Snow**
Climate	**Solar radiation**
Clouds	**Storms**
Cyclones	**Sunspots**
Droughts	**Thunderstorms**
Floods	**Tornadoes**
Fog	**Weather**
Frost	**Weather forecasting**
Hurricanes	**Weather lore**
Lightning	**Winds**

   xx **Atmosphere; Climate; Earth; Geophysics; Physical geography; Rain and rainfall; Science; Storms; Weather**

Meteorology—Observatories
   x Meteorological observatories; Observatories, Meteorological

Meteorology—Tables, etc.

Meteorology in aeronautics
   x Aeronautics, Meteorology in
   xx **Aeronautics; Weather forecasting**

Meteors
   See also **Meteorites**
   x Falling stars; Fire balls; Shooting stars; Stars, Falling
   xx **Astronomy; Solar system; Stars**

Meter. *See* **Musical meter and rhythm; Versification**

Meters, Electric. *See* **Electric meters**

Method of study. *See* **Study, Method of**

Methodism

Methodist Church
  xx Protestant churches; Sects
Methodist Church in California
    Use same form for Methodist Church, and
        for other churches, in other states,
        countries, etc., **e.g. Methodist Church
        in Europe; Catholic Church in the
        U.S.;** etc.
Methodology. *See* special subjects with the sub-
        division *Methodology,* e.g. **Science—
        Methodology;** etc.
✓ Metric system
  xx Weights and measures
Metrology. *See* **Mensuration; Weights and
        measures**
Metropolitan areas
    See also **Cities and towns; Urban renewal;**
        also names of metropolitan areas, e.g.
        Chicago metropolitan area; etc.
  x Suburban areas; Urban areas
Metropolitan finance
  xx **Finance; Municipal finance**
Metropolitan government
    See also **Municipal government;** also
        names of metropolitan areas with the
        subdivision *Politics and government,*
        e.g. **Chicago metropolitan area—
        Politics and government;** etc.
  xx **Local government; Municipal govern-
        ment**
Mexican literature
    May use same subdivisions and names of
        literary forms as for **English litera-
        ture**
Mexican War, 1845-1848. *See* **U.S.—History
        —War with Mexico, 1845-1848**
Mexico—Presidents
  xx **Presidents**
Mezzotint engraving
  xx **Engraving**
Mice
  x Mouse
Microbes. *See* **Bacteriology; Germ theory of
        disease; Microorganisms; Viruses**
Microbiology
    See also **Bacteriology; Microorganisms;
        Microscope and microscopy;** also
        subjects with the subdivision *Micro-
        biology,* e.g. **Air—Microbiology;** etc.
  xx **Biology; Microorganisms; Microscope
        and microscopy**
Microchemistry
  xx **Chemistry; Microscope and microscopy**
Microelectronics
  x Microminiature electronic equipment;
        Microminiaturization (Electronics)
  xx **Electronics; Semiconductors**
Microfilming. *See* **Microphotography**
Microfilms
  xx **Microforms**

✓ Metropolitan Council of governments

Microforms
> *See also* types of microforms, e.g. **Micro-films**; etc.
> *xx* **Microphotography**

Micrographic analysis. *See* **Metallography;
Microscope and microscopy**

Microminiature electronic equipment. *See* **Mi-croelectronics**

Microminiaturization (Electronics). *See* **Micro-electronics**

Microorganisms
> *See also* **Bacteriology; Microbiology; Mi-croscope and microscopy; Protozoa; Viruses**
> *x* Germs; Microbes; Microscopic organ-isms
> *xx* **Bacteriology; Microbiology**

Microphotography
> Use for works dealing with the photograph-ing of objects of any size upon a micro-scopic or very small scale
> *See also* **Microforms**
> *x* Microfilming
> *xx* **Photography**

Microscope and microscopy
> *See also* **Electron microscope; Metallog-raphy; Microbiology; Microchemis-try**
> *x* Analysis, Microscopic; Micrographic analysis; Microscopic analysis
> *xx* **Microbiology; Microorganisms**

Microscopic analysis. *See* **Metallography; Mi-croscope and microscopy**

Microscopic organisms. *See* **Microorganisms**

Microwave amplification by stimulated emission of radiation. *See* **Masers**

Microwave communication systems
> *See also* **Citizens radio service (Class D); Closed-circuit television**
> *xx* **Intercommunication** systems; **Radio, Short wave; Telecommunication; Television**

Microwave cookery
> *x* Cookery, Microwave

Microwaves
> *See also* **Magnets; Masers**
> *xx* **Electric** waves; **Electromagnetic** waves; **Radio, Short wave**

Middle age
> *See also* **Old age**
> *x* Age
> *xx* **Life (Biology)**

Middle Ages
> *See also* **Renaissance; Thirteenth century;** also **Architecture, Medieval; Art, Medieval; Chivalry; Church history —Middle Ages; Civilization, Medi-eval; Knights and knighthood; Liter-ature, Medieval; Philosophy, Medi-eval**

Middle Ages—*Continued*

    x Dark Ages

    xx **Civilization, Medieval; Feudalism; Renaissance**

Middle Ages—History

    See also **Civilization, Medieval; Crusades; Europe—History—476-1492; Feudalism; Holy Roman Empire; Monasticism and religious orders**

    x History, Medieval; Medieval history

    xx **Europe—History—476-1492; History; World history**

Middle Atlantic States. *See* **Atlantic States**

Middle classes

    x Bourgeoisie; Middle-income class

    xx **Democracy; Labor and laboring classes; Social classes**

Middle East. *See* **Asia; Near East**

Middle-income class. *See* **Middle classes**

Middle West

    x Central States; Midwest; North Central States

    xx **Mississippi Valley; Northwest, Old; United States**

Midgets. *See* **Dwarfs**

Midshipmen

    xx **Naval education; Seamen**

Midwest. *See* **Middle West**

Midwifery. *See* **Childbirth**

Migrant labor

    Use for works dealing with casual or seasonal workers who move from place to place in search of employment. Works on the movement of population within a country for permanent settlements are entered under **Migration, Internal**

    x Labor, Migratory; Migratory workers

    xx **Agricultural laborers; Labor and laboring classes; Social problems; Unemployed**

Migration. *See* **Immigration and emigration**

Migration, Internal

    See note under **Migrant labor**

    x **Colonization; Population**

Migration of animals. *See* **Animals—Migration**

Migration of birds. *See* **Birds—Migration**

Migratory workers. *See* **Migrant labor**

Military aeronautics. *See* **Aeronautics, Military**

Military aid. *See* **Military assistance**

Military air bases. *See* **Air bases**

Military airplanes. *See* **Airplanes, Military**

Military art and science

    See also

Aeronautics, Military	**Battles**
Armies	**Biological warfare**
Arms and armor	**Camouflage**
	Camps (Military)

343

Military art and sciences—*Continued*

Chemical warfare	Ordnance
Civil defense	Psychological war-
Disarmament	fare
Drill and minor	Signals and signal-
tactics	ing
Fortification	Soldiers
Guerrilla warfare	Spies
Hospitals, Military	Strategy
Industrial mobiliza-	Tactics
tion	Transportation, Mil-
Naval art and sci-	itary
ence	War

also headings beginning with the word **Military**

x Army; Fighting; Military power; Military science

xx **Armies; Drill and minor tactics; Naval art and science; Soldiers; Strategy; War**

Military art and science—Study and teaching. *See* **Military education**

Military assistance (May subdiv. geog. adjective form)

x Military aid; Mutual defense assistance program

Military assistance, American

x American military assistance

Military atrocities. *See* names of wars with the subdivision *Atrocities,* e.g. **World War, 1939-1945—Atrocities;** and names of individual acts of atrocities

Military biography. *See* **Generals;** and names of armies and navies with the subdivision *Biography,* e.g. **U.S. Army—Biography; U.S. Navy—Biography;** etc.

Military camps. *See* **Camps (Military)**

Military career. *See* **Military service as a profession**

Military costume. *See* **Uniforms, Military**

Military crimes. *See* **Military offenses**

Military desertion. *See* **Desertion, Military**

Military draft. *See* **Military service, Compulsory**

Military drill. *See* **Drill and minor tactics**

Military education

See also **Military training camps;** also names of military schools, e.g. **U.S. Military Academy, West Point;** etc.

x Army schools; Education, Military; Military art and science—Study and teaching; Military schools; Military training; Schools, Military

xx **Education**

Military engineering

See also **Fortification**

xx **Civil engineering; Engineering; Fortification**

Military forces. *See* **Armies; Navies;** and
names of countries with the subdivision
Armed Forces, e.g. **U.S.—Armed
Forces;** etc.

Military geography
   x Geography, Military; Maps, Military

Military history
   See also **Battles; Military policy; Naval
history;** also names of countries with
the subhead *Army* or the subdivision
History, Military (e.g. **U.S. Army;
U.S.—History, Military;** etc.); and
names of wars, battles, sieges, etc.
   x History, Military; Wars
   xx **History; Naval history**

Military hospitals. *See* **Hospitals, Military**

Military hygiene
   See also **Armies—Medical and sanitary
affairs; Medicine, Military;** also
names of wars with the subdivision
Medical and sanitary affairs, e.g. **World
War, 1939-1945—Medical and sani-
tary affairs;** etc.
   x Hygiene, Military; Soldiers—Hygiene
   xx **Armies—Medical and sanitary affairs;
Hygiene; Medicine, Military; Sanitation**

Military law
   See also **Courts martial and courts of inquiry; Military offenses; Military
service, Compulsory; Veterans—
Laws and regulations**
   x Articles of war; Law, Military; War,
Articles of
   xx **Courts martial and courts of inquiry;
International law; Law; War**

Military life. *See* **Soldiers;** and names of countries with the subdivision *Army—Mili-
tary life,* e.g. **U.S. Army—Military
life;** etc.

Military medicine. *See* **Medicine, Military**

Military motorization. *See* **Transportation,
Military**

Military music
   See also **Bands (Music);** also names of
wars with the subdivision *Songs and
music,* e.g. **World War, 1939-1945—
Songs and music;** etc.
   x Marches; Music, Military
   xx **Bands (Music); Music**

Military occupation
   See also **World War, 1939-1945—Occupied territories;** also names of occupied countries with the subdivision
*History—German occupation, 1940-
1945; History—Allied occupation,
1945-* , e.g. **Netherlands—History
—German occupation, 1940-1945;
Japan—History—Allied occupation,
1945-1952;** etc.

Military occupation—*Continued*

    x Occupation, Military; Occupied territory

Military offenses (May subdiv. geog.)

    See also names of military crimes, e.g. **Desertion, Military;** etc.

    x Crimes, Military; Military crimes; Offenses, Military

    xx **Criminal law; Military law**

Military offenses—U.S.

    x U.S. Army—Crimes and misdemeanors; U.S.—Military offenses

Military pensions. *See* **Pensions, Military**

Military policy

    See also names of countries with the subdivision *Military policy,* e.g. **U.S.—Military policy;** etc.

    xx **Military history**

Military posts

    x Army posts

Military power. *See* **Armies; Disarmament; Military art and science; Navies; Sea power**

Military schools. *See* **Military education**

Military science. *See* **Military art and science**

Military service, Compulsory

    See also **Conscientious objectors**

    x Compulsory military service; Conscription, Military; Draft, Military; Forced labor; Man power; Manpower; Military draft; Military training, Universal; Selective service; Service, Compulsory military

    xx **Armies; Military law**

Military service as a profession

    x Military career

    xx **Soldiers**

Military signaling. *See* **Signals and signaling**

Military strategy. *See* **Strategy**

Military tactics. *See* **Tactics**

Military training. *See* **Military education**

Military training, Universal. *See* **Military service, Compulsory**

Military training camps

    x Students' military training camps; Training camp, Military

    xx **Military education**

Military transportation. *See* **Transportation, Military**

Military uniforms. *See* **Uniforms, Military**

Military vehicles. *See* **Vehicles, Military**

Militia. *See* names of countries and states with the subdivision *Militia,* e.g. **U.S.—Militia;** etc.

Milk

    See also **Butter; Cheese**

    xx **Cows; Dairy products; Dairying**

Milk—Analysis

Milk, Dried

    x Dehydrated milk; Dried milk; Powdered milk

Milk supply

　　xx Food adulteration and inspection; Public health

Mill and factory buildings. *See* **Factories**

Millennium

　　See also Second Advent

　　xx Eschatology; Future life; Jesus Christ; Second Advent

Millikan rays. *See* **Cosmic rays**

Millinery

　　See also Hats

　　xx Costume; Hats

Milling (Flour). *See* **Flour and flour mills**

Milling machines

　　See also Machine tools

　　xx Machinery

Millionaires

　　See also Wealth

　　xx Capitalists and financiers; Wealth

Mills and millwork

　　See also Factories; Flour and flour mills; Machinery

　　xx Factories; Manufactures; Technology

Mind. *See* Intellect; Psychology

Mind and body

　　See also

Consciousness	Phrenology
Dreams	Psychoanalysis
Faith cure	Psychology, Patho-
Hypnotism	logical
Medicine, Psycho-	Psychology, Physi-
somatic	ological
Mental healing	Sleep
Mental health	Subconsciousness.
Mental suggestion	Temperament
Nervous system	
Personality dis-	
orders	

　　x Body and mind; Mind cure

　　xx Brain; Hypnotism; Medicine; Mental healing; Mental health; Philosophy; Phrenology; Psychical research; Psychoanalysis; Psychology, Physiological; Subconsciousness

Mind cure. *See* Christian Science; Faith cure; Mental healing; Mind and body

Mind reading

　　See also Clairvoyance; Hypnotism; Thought transference

　　xx Clairvoyance; Psychical research; Thought transference

Mine surveying

　　xx Mining engineering; Prospecting; Surveying

Mineral industries. *See* **Mines and mineral resources**

Mineral lands. *See* **Mines and mineral resources**

Mineral oil. *See* **Petroleum**

Mineral resources. *See* **Mines and mineral resources**

Mineral resources, Marine. *See* **Marine mineral resources**

Mineralogy

    See also **Gems; Petrology; Phosphorescence; Precious stones;** also names of minerals, e.g. **Quartz;** etc.

    x Minerals

    xx **Crystallography; Geology; Metals; Mines and mineral resources; Natural history; Ores; Petrology; Rocks; Science**

Minerals. *See* **Mineralogy; Mines and mineral resources;** and names of minerals, e.g. **Quartz;** etc.

Miners

    x Coal miners; Laborers

    xx **Labor and laboring classes**

Mines and mineral resources (May subdiv. geog.)

    Use for general descriptive works and for technical and economic works on mining, metallurgy and minerals of economic value

    See also **Marine mineral resources; Mineralogy; Mining engineering; Precious metals; Prospecting;** also specific types of mines and mining, e.g. **Coal mines and mining;** etc.

    x Mineral industries; Mineral lands; Mineral resources; Minerals; Mining

    xx **Geology, Economic; Natural resources; Ores; Raw materials**

Mines and mineral resources—U.S.

    x U.S.—Mines and mineral resources

Miniature cameras. *See* **Cameras**

Miniature gardens. *See* **Gardens, Miniature**

Miniature objects. *See* **Dollhouses; Gardens, Miniature; Models and model making; Toys;** and names of objects with the subdivision *Models,* e.g. **Airplanes—Models;** etc.

Miniature painting

    See also **Portrait painting**

    x Miniatures (Portraits)

    xx **Painting; Portrait painting**

Miniatures (Illumination of books and manuscripts). *See* **Illumination of books and manuscripts**

Miniatures (Portraits). *See* **Miniature painting**

Minimum wage. *See* **Wages—Minimum wage**

Mining. *See* **Mines and mineral resources; Mining engineering**

Mining, Electric. *See* **Electricity in mining**

Mining engineering

    See also **Boring; Electricity in mining; Mine surveying**

    x Mining

    xx **Civil engineering; Coal mines and min-**

Mining engineering—*Continued*

    ing; Electricity in mining; Engineer-
    ing; Mines and mineral resources

Ministers (Diplomatic agents). *See* **Diplomats**

Ministers of state. *See* **Cabinet officers**

Ministers of the gospel. *See* **Clergy**

Minor tactics. *See* **Drill and minor tactics**

Minorites. *See* **Franciscans**

Minorities

    See also **Discrimination; Nationalism;
    Race problems; Segregation;** also
    names of races or peoples living within
    a country, state, or city dominated by
    another nationality (e.g. **Germans in
    Czechoslovak Republic; Puerto
    Ricans in New York (City);** etc.);
    and names of countries with the sub-
    divisions *Foreign population* and *Race
    relations,* e.g. **U.S.—Foreign popula-
    tion; U.S.—Race relations;** etc.

    x Ethnic groups

    xx **Discrimination; Nationalism; Segrega-
    tion**

Minstrels

    See also **Troubadours**

    xx **Poets**

Minstrels, Negro. *See* **Negro minstrels**

Mints

    See also **Coinage**

    xx **Coinage; Money**

Miracle plays. *See* **Mysteries and miracle plays**

Miracles

    See also **Supernatural**

    x Bible—Miracles; Divine healing

    xx **Apparitions; Bible—Evidences, author-
    ity, etc; Christianity; Church history;
    Faith cure; Shrines; Supernatural**

Mirrors

    x Looking glasses

    xx **Furniture**

Miscarriage. *See* **Abortion**

Misdemeanors (Law). *See* **Criminal law**

Missiles, Ballistic. *See* **Ballistic missiles**

Missiles, Guided. *See* **Guided missiles**

Missionaries

    xx **Christian biography; Missions**

Missions (May subdiv. geog. except U.S.)

    See also **Evangelistic work; Missionaries;
    Salvation Army;** also names of
    churches, denominations, religious
    orders, etc. with the subdivision *Mis-
    sions,* e.g. **Catholic Church—Missions;**
    etc.

    x Foreign missions; Home missions

    xx **Christianity; Church history; Church
    work; Evangelistic work**

Missions, Indian. *See* **Indians of North Amer-
    ica—Missions**

Missions, Medical
> *x* Medical missions
> *xx* **Medicine**

Mississippi Valley
> *See also* **Middle West**
> *xx* **United States**

Mississippi Valley—History
> *x* New France—History

Mistakes. *See* **Errors**

Mixed marriages. *See* **Marriage, Mixed**

Mnemonics. *See* **Memory**

Mobile home living
> *xx* **Home economics**

Mobile homes. *See* **Travel trailers and campers**

Mobiles (Sculpture)
> *xx* **Kinetic sculpture; Sculpture**

Mobilization, Industrial. *See* **Industrial mobilization**

Mobs. *See* **Crowds; Riots**

Model airplanes; Model cars; etc. *See* **Airplanes —Models; Automobiles—Models**; etc.

Modeling
> *See also* **Sculpture—Technique; Soap sculpture**
> *x* Clay modeling
> *xx* **Arts and crafts; Clay; Industrial arts education; Sculpture; Sculpture— Technique**

Models. *See* **Models and model making;** and names of objects with the subdivision *Models,* e.g. **Airplanes—Models**; etc.

Models, Fashion
> *x* Fashion models; Manikins (Fashion models); Style manikins

Models, Mechanical. *See* **Machinery—Models**

Models and model making
> *See also* names of objects with the subdivision *Models,* e.g. **Airplanes— Models**; etc.
> *x* Miniature objects; Models

Modern architecture. *See* **Architecture, Modern—20th century**

Modern art. *See* **Art, Modern**

Modern civilization. *See* **Civilization, Modern**

Modern dance
> *x* Interpretive dancing
> *xx* **Dancing**

Modern history. *See* **History, Modern**

Modern languages. *See* **Languages, Modern**

Modern painting. *See* **Painting, Modern**

Modern paintings. *See* **Paintings, Modern**

Modern philosophy. *See* **Philosophy, Modern**

Modern sculpture. *See* **Sculpture, Modern**

Modernism
> Use for works on the movement in the Protestant churches which applies modern critical methods to Biblical study and the history of dogma and emphasizes the spiritual and ethical side of

Modernism—*Continued*
>> Christianity rather than historic dogmas
>> and creeds
> *See also* **Fundamentalism**
> *xx* **Fundamentalism**

Mohammedan art. *See* **Art, Islamic**

Mohammedanism. *See* **Islam**

Mohammedans. *See* **Muslims**

Molding (Metal). *See* **Founding**

Molecular biochemistry. *See* **Molecular biology**

Molecular biology
> *x* Biology, Molecular; Molecular bio-
>> chemistry; Molecular biophysics
> *xx* **Biochemistry; Biophysics**

Molecular biophysics. *See* **Molecular biology**

Molecular physiology. *See* **Biophysics**

Molecules
> *xx* **Chemistry, Physical and theoretical**

Mollusks
> *See also* **Shells**
> *x* Conchology; Shellfish
> *xx* **Invertebrates; Shells**

Monarchs. *See* **Kings and rulers; Queens**

Monarchy
> *See also* **Democracy; Kings and rulers;**
>> **Queens**
> *x* Sovereigns
> *xx* **Constitutional history; Constitutional**
>> **law; Democracy; Executive power;**
>> **Political science**

Monasteries
> *See also* **Abbeys; Convents; Monasticism**
>> **and religious orders**
> *x* Cloisters
> *xx* **Abbeys; Convents; Monasticism and**
>> **religious orders**

Monastic orders. *See* **Monasticism and re-**
>> **ligious orders**

✓ **Monasticism and religious orders**
> *See also*

Asceticism	**Hermits**
Celibacy	**Jesuits**
Dominicans	**Monasteries**
Franciscans	**Religious life**

> *x* Monastic orders; Monks; Orders, Monas-
>> tic; Religious orders
> *xx* **Asceticism; Christian biography;**
>> **Church history; Civilization, Medie-**
>> **val; Clergy; Middle Ages—History;**
>> **Monasteries**

Monasticism and religious orders for women
> *See also* **Convents; Ex-nuns**
> *x* Nuns; Sisterhoods
> *xx* **Convents**

Monetary question. *See* **Currency question;**
>> **Money**

Money
> Use for works on currency as a medium
>> of exchange or measure of value

Money—*Continued*
> *See also*

Banks and banking	Currency question
Bills of exchange	Foreign exchange
Capital	Gold
Coinage	Mints
Coins	Paper money
Counterfeits and	Silver
counterfeiting	Wealth

Credit
> *x* Bullion; Currency; Monetary question; Specie; Standard of value
>
> *xx* Banks and banking; Coinage; Currency question; Economics; Exchange; Finance; Gold; Silver; Wealth

Money, Paper. *See* Paper money

Money raising. *See* Fund raising

Monkeys
> *xx* Primates

Monks. *See* Monasticism and religious orders

Monograms
> *See also* Initials
>
> *x* Ciphers (Lettering)
>
> *xx* Alphabets; Initials; Lettering

Monoplanes. *See* Airplanes

Monopolies
> *See also* Capitalism; Competition; Corporation law; Railroads—Consolidation; Trusts, Industrial
>
> *xx* Capital; Commerce; Competition; Economics; Trusts, Industrial

Monorails
> *x* Railroads, Single rail; Single rail railroads

Monroe Doctrine
> *xx* International relations; Pan-Americanism; U.S.—Foreign relations

Monsters
> *See also* Dwarfs; Giants
>
> *x* Freaks; Monstrosities

Monstrosities. *See* Monsters

Montessori method of education
> *xx* Education, Elementary; Kindergarten; Teaching

Months

Monumental brasses. *See* Brasses

Monuments
> *See also* Obelisks; Pyramids; Tombs
>
> *x* Statues
>
> *xx* Architecture; Sculpture

Monuments, Natural. *See* Natural monuments

Moon
> *See also* Tides
>
> *xx* Astronomy; Solar system

Moon—Eclipses. *See* Eclipses, Lunar

Moon—Exploration
> *x* Lunar exploration
>
> *xx* Space flight to the moon

Moon—Geology. *See* Lunar geology

Moon—Maps

Moon—Photographs
  xx Lunar photography
Moon—Photographs from space
  xx Space photography
Moon—Surface
Moon, Voyages to. *See* **Space flight to the moon**
Moon bases. *See* **Lunar bases**
Moon cars
  x Lunar cars; Lunar rover vehicles; Lunar surface vehicles
Moon photography. *See* **Lunar photography**
Moon probes. *See* **Lunar probes**
Moon rocks. *See* **Lunar petrology**
Moorish art. *See* **Art, Islamic**
Moors
  xx Arabs
Moral conditions
  See also names of countries, cities, etc. with the subdivision *Moral conditions,* e.g. **U.S.—Moral conditions**; etc.
  x Morals
  xx Social conditions
Moral education. *See* **Character education**
Moral philosophy. *See* **Ethics**
Morale
  See also **Psychological warfare**
  xx Courage
Moralities
  See also **Mysteries and miracle plays**
  x Morality plays
  xx Drama; English drama; Mysteries and miracle plays; Religious drama; Theater
Morality. *See* **Ethics**
Morality plays. *See* **Moralities**
Morals. *See* **Behavior; Ethics; Moral conditions**
Moravians
  x United Brethren
Mormons and Mormonism
  x Church of Christ of Latter-Day Saints; Latter-Day Saints
Morons. *See* **Mentally handicapped**
Morphology. *See* **Anatomy; Anatomy, Comparative; Biology; Botany—Anatomy**
Morse code. *See* **Cipher and telegraph codes**
Mortality
  See also **Death**
  x Burial statistics; Death rate; Mortuary statistics
  xx Death; Population; Vital statistics
Mortar
  xx Adhesives; Plaster and plastering
Mortgages
  See also **Agricultural credit**
  x Chattel mortgages
  xx Commercial law; Contracts; Investments; Real estate; Securities
Morticians. *See* **Undertakers and undertaking**

Mortuary customs. *See* **Cremation; Funeral rites and ceremonies**

Mortuary statistics. *See* **Mortality; Vital statistics**

Mosaics
    See also **Mural painting and decoration**
    xx **Art, Decorative; Arts and crafts; Decoration and ornament; Mural painting and decoration**

Moslem art. *See* **Art, Islamic**

Moslemism. *See* **Islam**

Moslems. *See* **Muslims**

Mosques
    xx **Architecture; Architecture, Oriental; Church architecture; Islam; Temples**

✓ **Mosquitoes** – *control*
    x Diptera
    xx **Insects as carriers of disease**

Mosquitoes—Control
    xx **Pest control**

Mosses
    xx **Plants**

Motels. *See* **Hotels, motels, etc.**

Mothers
    x Maternity
    xx **Family; Parent and child; Woman**

Mothers' pensions
    See also **Child welfare**
    xx **Child welfare; Insurance, Social; Pensions**

Moths
    See also **Butterflies; Caterpillars; Silkworms**
    x Cocoons; Lepidoptera
    xx **Butterflies; Caterpillars**

Motion
    See also **Force and energy; Kinematics; Mechanical movements; Mechanics; Speed**
    x Kinetics
    xx **Dynamics; Force and energy; Kinematics; Mechanics**

Motion pictures. *See* **Moving pictures**

Motion study
    See also **Time study**
    xx **Efficiency, Industrial; Factory management; Job analysis; Personnel management; Time study**

Motivation (Psychology)
    xx **Psychology**

Motor boats. *See* **Motorboats**

Motor buses. *See* **Buses**

Motor cars. *See* **Automobiles**

Motor courts. *See* **Hotels, motels, etc.**

Motor cycles. *See* **Motorcycles**

Motor trucks. *See* **Trucks**

Motorboat racing. *See* **Boat racing**

Motorboats

    x Motor boats; Outboard motorboats; Power boats

    xx Boats and boating

Motorboats—Models

    xx Machinery—Models

Motorcycles

    x Cycles, Motor; Cycling; Motor cycles

    xx Bicycles and bicycling

Motoring. *See* **Automobiles—Touring**

Motorization, Military. *See* **Transportation, Military**

Motors. *See* **Electric motors; Engines**

Motorways. *See* **Express highways**

Mottoes

    x Emblems

    xx Heraldry

Moulding (Metal). *See* **Founding**

Mounds and mound builders

    See also **Excavations (Archeology)**

    x Barrows; Burial; Graves

    xx Archeology; Cliff dwellers and cliff dwellings; Excavations (Archeology); Indians of North America; Indians of North America—Antiquities; Tombs

Mountain climbing. *See* **Mountaineering**

Mountain life—Southern States

    x Mountaineers of the South

Mountain plants. *See* **Alpine plants**

Mountaineering

    x Mountain climbing; Rock climbing

    xx Mountains; Outdoor life

Mountaineers of the South. *See* **Mountain life —Southern States**

Mountains

    Names of mountain ranges and mountains are not included in this list but are to be added as needed, e.g. **Rocky Mountains; Elk Mountain, Wyo.;** etc.

    See also **Mountaineering; Volcanoes;** also names of mountain ranges (e.g. **Rocky Mountains;** etc.) ; and names of mountains, e.g. **Elk Mountain, Wyo.;** etc.

    xx Geology; Physical geography

Mourning customs. *See* **Funeral rites and ceremonies**

Mouse. *See* **Mice**

Movement, Freedom of. *See* **Freedom of movement**

Movements of animals. *See* **Animal locomotion**

Movies. *See* **Moving pictures**

Moving, Household

    x Household moving

Moving picture cameras. *See* **Cameras; Moving picture photography**

Moving picture cartoons

    x Animated cartoons

    xx Cartoons and caricatures

Moving picture industry

355

Moving picture photography

　　x Moving picture cameras; Photography—
　　　　Moving pictures

　　xx **Photography**

Moving picture plays

　　Use for individual scenarios, for collections
　　　　of plays, and for works on writing and
　　　　producing scenarios

　　x Moving pictures—Play writing; Photo-
　　　　plays; Play production; Play writing;
　　　　Playwriting; Scenarios

　　xx **Drama; Theater—Production and di-
　　　　rection**

Moving picture plays—History and criticism

　　xx **Dramatic criticism**

Moving picture projectors. *See* **Projectors**

Moving pictures

　　See also **Experimental films; Sound—Re-
　　　　cording and reproducing**

　　x Cinema; Motion pictures; Movies; Talk-
　　　　ing pictures

　　xx **Amusements; Audio-visual materials;
　　　　Mass media; Theater**

Moving pictures—Biography

　　xx **Actors and actresses**

Moving pictures—Catalogs

　　x Catalogs

Moving pictures—Censorship

　　xx **Censorship; Freedom of information**

Moving pictures, Documentary

　　x Documentary films

Moving pictures, Experimental. *See* **Experi-
　　mental films**

Moving pictures—Moral and religious aspects

Moving pictures—Play writing. *See* **Moving
　　picture plays**

Moving pictures and children

　　Use for works dealing with the effect of
　　　　moving pictures on children and youth

　　See also **Television and children**

　　x Children and moving pictures

　　xx **Children; Television and children**

Moving pictures and libraries. *See* **Libraries and
　　moving pictures**

Moving pictures as a profession

　　See also **Acting as a profession**

Moving pictures in education

　　See also **Libraries and moving pictures**

　　x Educational films

　　xx **Audio-visual education; Teaching—
　　　　Aids and devices**

Muhammedanism. *See* **Islam**

Muhammedans. *See* **Muslims**

Multi-age grouping. *See* **Nongraded schools**

Multiple consciousness. *See* **Personality dis-
　　orders**

Multi-media centers. *See* **Instructional ma-
　　terials center**

Mummies

    x Burial

    xx Archeology

Municipal administration. *See* **Municipal government**

Municipal art. *See* **Art, Municipal**

Municipal corporations

    Use for formal legal treatises and collections of statutes concerning municipal corporations. Works on public service corporations in cities are entered under **Public utilities**

    See also **Cities and towns; Municipal finance; Municipal government**

    xx **Administrative law; Charters; Corporations; Municipal government**

Municipal employees. *See* **Civil service; Municipal government;** and names of cities with the subdivision *Officials and employees,* e.g. **Chicago—Officials and employees;** etc.

Municipal engineering

    See also **Drainage; Refuse and refuse disposal; Sanitary engineering; Sewerage; Street cleaning; Water supply**

    xx **Engineering; Public works; Sanitary engineering**

Municipal finance

    See also **Metropolitan finance**

    x Finance, Municipal

    xx **Finance; Municipal corporations; Municipal government**

Municipal government (May subdiv. geog.)

    Use for works on the government of cities in general and, when subdivided by country, for general consideration of municipal government of countries, or regions. Collections of statutes are entered under **Municipal corporations.** Works on the government of individual cities, towns, or areas are entered under the name of city, town, or area with the subdivision *Politics and government*

    See also **Cities and towns; Metropolitan government; Municipal corporations; Municipal finance; Public administration;** also names of cities with the subdivision *Politics and government,* e.g. **Chicago—Politics and government;** etc.

    x City government; Government, Municipal; Municipal administration; Municipal employees; Municipalities

    xx **Local government; Metropolitan government; Municipal corporations; Political science**

Municipal government—U.S.

    x U.S.—Municipal government

Municipal government by city manager

    x City manager; Commission government with city manager

Municipal government by commission

    x Commission government; Government by commission

Municipal improvements. *See* **Art, Municipal; Cities and towns—Civic improvement;** and names of cities with the subdivision *Public works,* e.g. **Chicago—Public works;** etc.

Municipal ownership

    x Public ownership

    xx Corporations; Economic policy; Government ownership

Municipal transit. *See* **Local transit**

Municipalities. *See* **Cities and towns; Municipal government**

Munitions

    x Armaments

    xx Industrial mobilization; International relations; War; War—Economic aspects

Mural painting and decoration

    See also **Cave drawings; Mosaics**

    x Fresco painting; Wall decoration; Wall painting

    xx Art, Decorative; Arts and crafts; Interior decoration; Mosaics; Painting; Walls

Murder

    See also **Assassination; Capital punishment**

    x Manslaughter

    xx Assassination; Crime and criminals; Criminal law; Medical jurisprudence; Offenses against the person

Muscles

    xx Physiology

Museums

    See also **Art—Galleries and museums;** also names of countries, cities, etc. with the subdivision *Galleries and museums* (e.g. **U.S.—Galleries and museums;** etc.); and names of galleries and museums, e.g. **Boston Museum of Fine Arts;** etc.

Museums and schools

    x Schools and museums

    xx Schools

Mushrooms

    See also **Fungi**

    x Toadstools

    xx **Fungi**

✓ Music (May subdiv. geog. adjective form, e.g. **Music, American;** etc.)

    ✓*See also*

Chamber music	**Composition (Music)**
Church music	

✓Country & western music

Music—*Continued*

Concerts
Dance music
Harmony
Instrumental music
Instrumentation
  and orchestration
Jazz music
Military music
Musicians
Radio and music
Romanticism
Sound
Vocal music

    also **Orchestral music; Organ music; Piano music**; etc. and headings beginning with the words **Music** and **Musical**

  xx **Humanities**

Music—Acoustics and physics
  See also **Sound**
  x Acoustics
  xx **Music—Theory; Physics; Sound**

Music, American
  See also **Negro songs; Negro spirituals**
  x American music; U.S.—Music

Music—Analysis, appreciation
  x Appreciation of music; Music—Appreciation; Music appreciation; Musical appreciation

Music—Anecdotes, facetiae, satire, etc.
  xx **Anecdotes; Wit and humor**

Music—Appreciation. *See* **Music—Analysis, appreciation**

Music—Biography. *See* **Musicians**

Music—Cataloging. *See* **Cataloging—Music**

Music, Choral. *See* **Choral music**

Music, Community. *See* **Community music**

Music—Composition. *See* **Composition (Music)**

Music—Discography
  x Discography

Music, Dramatic. *See* **Opera; Operetta**

Music—Examinations, questions, etc.
  xx **Examinations; Questions and answers**

Music—History and criticism
  x Musical criticism
  xx **Criticism; History**

Music, Indian. *See* **Indians of North America —Music**

Music, Influence of. *See* **Music—Psychology**

Music—Instruction and study. *See* **Music— Study and teaching**

Music, Instrumental. *See* **Instrumental music**

Music, Military. *See* **Military music**

Music, Negro. *See* **Negro music**

Music—Notation. *See* **Musical notation**

Music, Popular (Songs, etc.)
  See also names of types of popular music, e.g. **Blues (Songs, etc.); Rock music**; etc.
  x Popular music; Songs, Popular; Soul music
  xx **Dance music; Songs**

Music, Popular (Songs, etc.)—Writing and publishing
  x Song writing
  xx **Composition (Music)**
Music, Primitive
  See also **Indians of North America—Music**
  xx **Society, Primitive**
Music—Psychology
  x Music, Influence of; Psychology of music
  xx **Psychology**
Music, Rock. *See* **Rock music**
Music, Sacred. *See* **Church music**
Music—Study and teaching
  See also **Composition (Music); Conducting; Harmony; Musical form**
  x Education, Musical; Music—Instruction and study; Musical education; Musical instruction; School music
Music—Theory
  See also **Composition (Music); Counterpoint; Fugue; Harmony; Music—Acoustics and physics; Musical form; Musical meter and rhythm**
Music, Vocal. *See* **Vocal music**
Music and literature
  x Music and poetry; Poetry and music
  xx **Literature**
Music and poetry. *See* **Music and literature**
Music and radio. *See* **Radio and music**
Music appreciation. *See* **Music—Analysis, appreciation**
Music as a profession
  xx **Musicians; Occupations; Professions; Vocational guidance**
Music box
  xx **Musical instruments, Mechanical**
Music conductors. *See* **Conductors (Music)**
Music festivals
  x Music festivals
  xx **Concerts; Festivals**
Music libraries
  x Libraries, Music
  xx **Libraries; Libraries, Special**
Musical ability
  x Musical talent; Talent
  xx **Ability**
Musical accompaniment
  x Accompaniment, Musical
  xx **Composition (Music)**
Musical appreciation. *See* **Music—Analysis, appreciation**
Musical comedies. *See* **Musical revues, comedies, etc.**
Musical composition. *See* **Composition (Music)**
Musical criticism. *See* **Music—History and criticism**
Musical education. *See* **Music—Study and teaching**
Musical festivals. *See* **Music festivals**

Musical form

    See also Concerto; Fugue; Opera; Op-
        eretta; Oratorio; Sonata; Symphony

    x Form, Musical

    xx Music—Study and teaching; Music—
        Theory

Musical instruction. *See* Music—Study and
    teaching

Musical instruments

    See also Instrumental music; Instrumen-
        tation and orchestration; Orchestra;
        Tuning; also groups of instruments,
        e.g. Percussion instruments; Stringed
        instruments; Wind instruments; etc.;
        also names of musical instruments,
        e.g. Drum; Organ; etc.

    x Instruments, Musical

    xx Instrumental music; Instrumentation
        and orchestration

Musical instruments, Electronic

    x Electronic musical instruments

Musical instruments, Mechanical

    See also names of instruments, e.g. Music
        box; etc.

    x Mechanical musical instruments

Musical meter and rhythm

    x Meter

    xx Music—Theory; Rhythm

Musical notation

    x Music—Notation; Notation, Musical

Musical revues, comedies, etc.

    x Musical comedies

    xx Operas; Operetta

Musical talent. *See* Musical ability

Musicians (May subdiv. geog. adjective form,
        e.g. Musicians, American; etc.)

    Use for works about several musicians

    See also Composers; Conductors (Mu-
        sic); Music as a profession; Organ-
        ists; Pianists; Singers; Violinists,
        violoncellists, etc.; also names of mu-
        sicians

    x Music—Biography

    xx Biography; Music

Musicians, American

    x American musicians; U.S.—Musicians

Musicians, Negro. *See* Negro musicians

Musicians—Portraits

    xx Portraits

Muslimism. *See* Islam

Muslims

    x Mohammedans; Moslems; Muhamme-
        dans; Mussulmans

Muslims, Black. *See* Black Muslims

Mussulmans. *See* Muslims

Mutation (Biology). *See* Evolution; Variation
    (Biology)

Mutual defense assistance program. *See* Mili-
    tary assistance

Mutual funds. *See* Investment trusts

Mycology. *See* **Fungi**

Mysteries and miracle plays

See also **Moralities**

x Bible—Drama; Bible plays; Miracle plays

xx **Drama; English drama; Moralities; Pageants; Passion plays; Religious drama; Theater**

Mystery and detective stories

May be used for single novels as well as for collections of stories

x Detective stories; Stories

xx **Fiction**

Mysticism

See also **Christian art and symbolism; Spiritual life**

xx **Philosophy; Religion; Theology**

Mythical animals. *See* **Animals, Mythical**

Mythology (May use ethnic or geog. subdiv. adjective form, e.g. **Mythology, Celtic;** etc.)

See also

Ancestor worship	Indians of North
Animals, Mythical	America—Reli-
Art and mythology	gion and mythol-
Folklore	ogy
Gods	Religion, Primitive
Heroes	Symbolism
	Totems and totem-
	ism

x Myths

xx **Creation; Folklore; God; Gods; Heroes; Legends; Religion; Religions**

Mythology, Classical

x Classical mythology; Greek mythology; Roman mythology

xx **Classical antiquities**

Mythology, Indian. *See* **Indians of North America—Religion and mythology**

Mythology in art. *See* **Art and mythology**

Myths. *See* **Mythology**

NATO. *See* **North Atlantic Treaty Organization**

Names

x Epithets; Nomenclature; Proper names; Terminology

Names, Fictitious. *See* **Pseudonyms**

Names, Geographical

See also **Gazetteers**

x Geographical names; Place names

xx **Gazetteers**

Names, Personal

May be subdivided by nationality or by country, e.g. **Names, Personal—Scottish; Names, Personal—U.S.;** etc.

See also **Nicknames; Pseudonyms**

x Christian names; Family names; Forenames; Personal names; Surnames

Names, Personal—U.S.
x American names; U.S.—Names, Personal; U.S.—Personal names

Names—Pronunciation
x Pronunciation

Napoléon I, Emperor of the French—Drama
xx Drama

Napoléon I, Emperor of the French—Fiction
xx Fiction; Historical fiction

Napoleonic Wars. *See* **Europe—History, 1789-1900; France—History—Revolution, 1789-1799**

Narcotic habit
See note under **Drug abuse**
See also **Narcotics and youth**
x Drug addiction; Drug habit; Intoxication
xx Drug abuse; Temperance

Narcotics
See also **Stimulants;** and names of specific narcotics, e.g. **Opium;** etc.
x Opiates; Soporifics
xx Drugs; Hygiene; Insomnia; Materia medica; Stimulants; Therapeutics

Narcotics and youth
See also **Drugs and youth**
x Youth and narcotics
xx Juvenile delinquency; Narcotic habit

Nation of Islam. *See* **Black Muslims**

National anthems. *See* **National songs**

National characteristics (May subdiv. geog. adjective form, e.g. **National characteristics, French;** etc.)
See also **Race psychology**
x Characteristics, National; National psychology; Psychology, National
xx Anthropology; Nationalism; Race psychology; Social psychology

National characteristics, American
x American characteristics; American national characteristics; U.S.—National characteristics

National consciousness. *See* **Nationalism**

National dances. *See* **Folk dancing**

National debts. *See* **Debts, Public**

National defenses. *See* **Industrial mobilization;** and names of countries with the subdivision *Defenses,* e.g. **U.S.—Defenses;** etc.

National forests. *See* **Forest reserves**

National Guard (U.S.). *See* **U.S.—National Guard**

National health service. *See* **Medicine, State**

National holidays. *See* **Holidays;** and names of national holidays, e.g. **Memorial Day;** etc.

National hymns. *See* **National songs**

National monuments. *See* **National parks and reserves; Natural monuments**

National parks and reserves (May subdiv. geog.)

    See also **Forest reserves; Natural monuments; Wilderness areas;** also names of national parks, e.g. **Yellowstone National Park;** etc.

    x National monuments; Public lands

    xx **Forest reserves; Parks; Wildlife—Conservation**

National parks and reserves—U.S.

    x U.S.—National parks and reserves

National planning. *See* **Economic policy; Social policy;** and names of countries with the subdivision *Economic policy; Social policy;* e.g. **U.S.—Economic policy; U.S.—Social policy;** etc.

National psychology. *See* **National characteristics; Race psychology**

National resources. *See* **Natural resources;** and names of countries with the subdivision *Economic conditions,* e.g. **U.S.—Economic conditions;** etc.

National security. *See* **Internal security; U.S.—Defenses**

National socialism

    See also **Fascism; Socialism**

    x Fascism—Germany; Nazi movement

    xx **Fascism; Socialism; Totalitarianism**

National songs (May subdiv. geog. adjective form, e.g. **National Songs, German;** etc.)

    See also **Folk songs; Patriotic poetry; War songs**

    x National anthems; National hymns; Patriotic songs; Songs, National

    xx **Folk songs; Songs**

National songs, American

    x American national songs; U.S.—National songs

    xx **Songs, American**

Nationalism

    See also **Minorities; National characteristics; Patriotism**

    x Internationalism; National consciousness; Regionalism

    xx **International relations; Minorities; Patriotism; Political science**

Nationalism, Black. *See* **Black nationalism**

Nationalism, Negro. *See* **Black nationalism**

Nationality (Citizenship). *See* **Citizenship**

Nationalization. *See* **Government ownership**

Nationalization of railroads. *See* **Railroads and state**

Nations, Law of. *See* **International law**

Native races

    Use for works on the relations between the governing authorities and the aboriginal inhabitants of colonial or other areas

    See also **Race problems;** also **Africa—**

Native races—*Continued*
> Native races; Indians of North America—Government relations

  x Aborigines

  xx **Ethnology**

Nativity of Christ. *See* **Jesus Christ—Nativity**

Natural beauty conservation. *See* **Landscape protection**

Natural Bridge, Va.

  xx **Natural monuments**

Natural disasters. *See* **Disasters**

Natural gas. *See* **Gas, Natural**

Natural history (May subdiv. geog.)
> Use for popular works describing animals, plants, minerals and nature in general. Handbooks on the detailed study of birds, flowers, etc. are entered under **Nature study**

  See also

Aquariums	Geology
Biology	Marine biology
Botany	Mineralogy
Fossils	Plant lore
Fresh-water biology	Zoology
Geographical distribution of animals and plants	

  x Animal lore; History, Natural

  xx **Animals; Biology; Science; Zoology**

Natural history, Biblical. *See* **Bible—Natural history**

Natural history—Outdoor books. See **Nature study**

Natural history—U.S.

  x U.S.—Natural history

Natural law. *See* **Civil rights; Ethics; International law; Liberty**

Natural monuments (May subdiv. geog.)
> Use for general works on natural objects of historic or scientific interest such as caves, cliffs, natural bridges, and for those created as national monuments by presidential proclamation

  See also **Wilderness areas;** also names of natural monuments, e.g. **Natural Bridge, Va.;** etc.

  x Landmarks, Preservation of; Monuments, Natural; National monuments; Preservation of natural scenery; Protection of natural scenery

  xx **Landscape protection; National parks and reserves; Nature conservation**

Natural monuments—U.S.

  x U.S.—Natural monuments

Natural religion. *See* **Natural theology**

Natural resources (May subdiv. geog.)
> *See also* **Conservation of natural resources; Fisheries; Forests and forestry; Marine resources; Mines and mineral resources; Power resources;**

Natural resources—*Continued*

> Reclamation of land; Soil conservation; Water power; Water resources development; Water supply

> *x* National resources; Resources, Natural

> *xx* **Economic conditions; Environmental policy; Wildlife—Conservation**

Natural resources—U.S.

> *See also* **U.S.—Economic conditions**

> *x* U.S.—Natural resources

Natural selection

> *See also* **Evolution; Heredity**

> *x* Selection, Natural; Survival of the fittest

> *xx* **Evolution; Genetics; Heredity; Variation (Biology)**

Natural theology

> Use for works that treat of the knowledge of God's existence obtained by observing the visible processes of nature

> *See also* **Creation; Religion and science**

> *x* Natural religion; Theology, Natural

> *xx* **Apologetics; God; Religion; Religion and science; Theology**

Naturalism in literature. *See* **Realism in literature**

Naturalists

> *See also* names of classes of naturalists, e.g. **Biologists; Botanists;** etc.

> *xx* **Scientists**

Naturalization

> *See also* **Aliens; Citizenship**

> *x* Foreigners

> *xx* **Aliens; Americanization; Citizenship; Immigration and emigration; International law; Suffrage**

Nature

Nature, Effect of man on. *See* **Man—Influence on nature**

Nature conservation

> *See also* **Landscape protection; Natural monuments; Wildlife—Conservation**

> *x* Conservation of nature; Nature protection; Preservation of natural scenery; Protection of natural scenery

> *xx* **Conservation of natural resources**

Nature in literature

> *See also* **Animals in literature; Birds in literature; Nature in poetry**

Nature in ornament. *See* **Design, Decorative**

Nature in poetry

> *x* Nature poetry; Poetry of nature

> *xx* **Nature in literature; Poetry**

Nature photography

> *See also* **Photography of animals; Photography of birds; Photography of fishes; Photography of plants;** and similar headings

> *x* Photography of nature

> *xx* **Nature study; Photography**

Nature poetry. *See* **Nature in poetry**

Nature protection. *See* **Nature conservation**

Nature study (May subdiv. geog.)

> See note under **Natural history**
>
> *See also* **Animals—Habits and behavior; Botany; Nature photography; Zoology**
>
> *x* Natural history—Outdoor books
>
> *xx* **Animals—Habits and behavior; Outdoor life; Science—Study and teaching**

Nature study—U.S.

> *x* U.S.—Nature study

Nautical almanacs

> *x* Ephemerides
>
> *xx* **Almanacs; Navigation**

Nautical astronomy

> *See also* **Latitude; Longitude; Navigation**
>
> *x* Astronomy, Nautical
>
> *xx* **Astronomy; Navigation**

Naval Academy, Annapolis. *See* **U.S. Naval Academy, Annapolis**

Naval administration. *See* **Naval art and science**; and names of countries with the subhead *Navy*, e.g. **U.S. Navy**; etc.

Naval aeronautics. *See* **Aeronautics, Military**

Naval air bases. *See* **Air bases**

Naval airplanes. *See* **Airplanes, Military**

Naval architecture

> *See also* **Boatbuilding; Marine engineering; Shipbuilding; Ships; Steamboats; Warships**
>
> *x* Architecture, Naval; Marine architecture
>
> *xx* **Architecture; Shipbuilding**

Naval art and science

> *See also*

Camouflage	Seamen
Marine engineering	Shipbuilding
Military art and science	Signals and signaling
Navies	Strategy
Navigation	Submarine warfare
Navy yards and naval stations	Submarines
Privateering	Torpedoes
Sea power	Warships

> *x* Fighting; Naval administration; Naval science; Naval warfare; Navy
>
> *xx* **Military art and science; Navies; Navigation; Strategy; War**

Naval art and science—Study and teaching. *See* **Naval education**

Naval bases. *See* **Navy yards and naval stations**

Naval battles

> *See also* **Battles; Naval history**; also names of countries with the subdivision *History, Naval*, e.g. **U.S.—History, Naval**; etc.; and names of battles
>
> *x* Naval warfare

Naval battles—*Continued*

    xx Battles; Sea power

Naval biography

    See also **Admirals; Seamen;** also names of navies with the subdivision *Biography,* e.g. **U.S. Navy—Biography;** etc.

    xx **Biography; Naval history; Seamen**

Naval boilers. *See* **Boilers, Marine**

Naval education

    See also **Midshipmen; U.S. Naval Academy, Annapolis**

    x Education, Naval; Naval art and science—Study and teaching; Naval schools

    xx **Education**

Naval engineering. *See* **Marine engineering**

Naval history

    See also **Military history; Naval biography; Pirates; Privateering; Sea power;** also names of countries with the subhead *Navy* or the subdivision *History, Naval,* e.g. **U.S. Navy; U.S. —History, Naval;** etc.

    x History, Naval; Wars

    xx **History; Military history; Naval battles; Sea power**

Naval law. *See* **Maritime law**

Naval pensions. *See* **Pensions, Military**

Naval schools. *See* **Naval education**

Naval science. *See* **Naval art and science**

Naval signaling. *See* **Signals and signaling**

Naval strategy. *See* **Strategy**

Naval uniforms. *See* **Uniforms, Military**

Naval warfare. *See* **Naval art and science; Naval battles; Submarine warfare**

Navies

    See also **Armies; Disarmament; Naval art and science; Sea power; Warships;** also names of countries with the subhead *Navy,* e.g. **U.S. Navy;** etc.

    x Armaments; Armed forces; Military forces; Military power; Navy

    xx **Armies; Naval art and science; Sea power; Ships; War; Warships**

Navigation

    See also

Compass	**Pilot guides**
Harbors	**Pilots and pilotage**
Inland navigation	**Radar**
Knots and splices	**Sailing**
Lighthouses	**Shipwrecks**
Loran	**Signals and signaling**
Nautical almanacs	
Nautical astronomy	**Steam navigation**
Naval art and science	**Tides**
	Winds

    x Locomotion; Seamanship

    xx **Nautical astronomy; Naval art and science; Oceanography; Pilots and pilotage; Sailing; Ships; Steam navigation**

Navigation (Aeronautics)

    See also **Airplanes—Piloting; Radio in aeronautics**

    x Aerial navigation; Aeronautics— Navigation; Air navigation; Navigation, Aerial

    xx **Aeronautics**

Navigation (Astronautics)

    See also **Astronautical instruments; Space flight; Space ships—Piloting**

    x Astronavigation

    xx **Astrodynamics; Astronautics; Space flight**

Navigation, Aerial. *See* **Navigation (Aeronautics)**

Navigation, Inland. *See* **Inland navigation**

Navigation—Laws and legislation. *See* **Maritime law**

Navigation, Steam. *See* **Steam navigation**

Navigators. *See* **Discoveries (in geography); Explorers; Seamen**

Navy. *See* **Naval art and science; Navies; Sea power;** and names of countries with the subhead *Navy,* e.g. **U.S. Navy;** etc.

Navy Sealab project. *See* **Sealab project**

Navy yards and naval stations

    x Naval bases

    xx **Naval art and science**

Nazi movement. *See* **National socialism**

Near East

    See also **Eastern question**

    x East (Near East) ; Levant; Middle East

    xx **East**

Near Eastern question. *See* **Eastern question**

Nebulae, Extragalactic. *See* **Galaxies**

Necrologies. *See* **Obituaries**

Necromancy. *See* **Divination; Witchcraft**

Needlework

    See also names of needlework; e.g. **Dressmaking; Embroidery; Lace and lace making; Sewing; Tapestry;** etc.

    xx **Art, Decorative; Arts and crafts; Dressmaking; Sewing**

Negotiable instruments

    See also **Bills of exchange; Bonds**

    x Bills and notes; Bills of credit; Commercial paper; Instruments, Negotiable; Letters of credit

    xx **Banks and banking; Bills of exchange; Commercial law; Contracts; Credit**

Negritude. *See* **Negroes—Race identity**

Negro actors

    xx **Actors and actresses**

Negro art

    See also **Negro artists**

    x Art, Negro ; Negroes—Art

    xx **Negro artists**

Negro artists

 See also **Negro art**

 x Artists, Negro

 xx **Artists; Negro art**

Negro athletes

 x Athletes, Negro

Negro authors

 Use for works dealing with the lives of several Negro writers. Criticism of their literary productions is entered under **Negro literature—History and criticism; Negro poetry—History and criticism;** etc.

 x Authors, Negro

 xx **Authors**

Negro businessmen

 x Negroes as businessmen

Negro folklore. *See* **Folklore, Negro**

Negro librarians

 See also **Libraries and Negroes**

 x Librarians, Negro

 xx **Libraries and Negroes**

Negro literature

 May use same subdivisions and names of literary forms as for **English literature**

 x Black literature

 xx **American literature; Literature**

Negro minstrels

 x Minstrels, Negro

Negro music

 See also **Negro songs; Negro spirituals**

 x Music, Negro

Negro musicians

 x Musicians, Negro

Negro nationalism. *See* **Black Muslims; Black nationalism**

Negro poetry

 xx **American poetry; Poetry—Collections**

Negro race. *See* **Negroes**

Negro songs

 See also **Blues (Songs, etc.); Folk songs, African; Negro spirituals**

 x Folk songs, Negro (American)

 xx **Music, American; Negro music; Songs**

Negro spirituals

 See also **Blues (Songs, etc.)**

 x Spirituals, Negro

 xx **Music, American; Negro music; Negro songs**

Negro suffrage. *See* **Negroes—Suffrage**

Negroes

 Use for general works on the Negro race and for Negroes in the U.S. If limited to a particular area in the U.S. may use geog. subdiv., e.g. **Negroes—Arkansas; Negroes—Chicago; Negroes—Southern States;** etc. Works dealing with Negroes in other countries

Negroes—*Continued*
>are entered under **Negroes in Africa; Negroes in France;** etc.
>*See also* **Discrimination; Slavery in the U.S.; U.S.—Race relations;** and headings beginning with the word **Negro**
>*x* African Americans; Afro-Americans; Black Americans; Blacks (U.S.); Colored people (U.S.); Negro race
>*xx* **Ethnology; Reconstruction; Slavery in the U.S.**

Negroes—Art. *See* **Negro art**

Negroes—Biography
>*xx* **Biography**

Negroes—Civil rights
>*See also* **Black power**
>*x* Civil rights demonstrations; Demonstrations for Negro civil rights; Freedom marches; Marches for Negro civil rights
>*xx* **Civil rights**

Negroes—Economic conditions
>*See also* **Black power**
>*xx* **Economic conditions**

Negroes—Education
>*See also* **Afro-American studies; Segregation in education**
>*xx* **Education**

Negroes—Employment
>*x* Employment; Negroes in business
>*xx* **Discrimination in employment**

Negroes—Housing
>*x* Housing, Negro

Negroes—Integration
>*See also* **Negroes—Segregation**
>*x* Integration, Racial
>*xx* **Negroes—Segregation**

Negroes—Libraries. *See* **Libraries and Negroes**

Negroes—Political activity
>*See also* **Black nationalism; Black power**

Negroes—Race identity
>*See also* **Afro-American studies; Black nationalism**
>*x* Negritude; Race identity; Racial identity
>*xx* **Race awareness; Race psychology**

Negroes—Religion
>*See also* **Black Muslims**
>*xx* **Religion**

Negroes—Segregation
>*See also* **Negroes—Integration; Segregation in education**
>*xx* **Negroes—Integration; Segregation**

Negroes—Social conditions

Negroes—Social life and customs

Negroes—Suffrage
>*x* Negro suffrage
>*xx* **Suffrage**

Negroes and libraries. *See* **Libraries and Negroes**

Negroes as businessmen. *See* **Negro business-men**

Negroes in Africa
Use same form for Negroes in other countries except the U.S. See note under **Negroes**
xx **Africa—Native races**

Negroes in art. *See* **Negroes in literature and art**

Negroes in business. *See* **Negroes—Employment**

Negroes in literature and art
Use for works treating of Negro characters in literature and Negroes depicted in works of art. For works of Negro authors or artists see **Negro literature; Negro art.** For works about Negro authors or artists see **Negro authors; Negro artists**
x Negroes in art
xx **Art; Characters and characteristics in literature**

Neighborhood. See **Community life;** and other headings beginning with the word **Community**

Neighborhood centers. *See* **Social settlements**

Neighborhood schools. *See* **Schools**

Neo-Greek literature. *See* **Greek literature, Modern**

Neo-impressionism (Art). *See* **Impressionism (Art)**

Neo-Latin languages. *See* **Romance languages**

Neolithic period. *See* **Stone age**

Neon tubes
xx **Electric signs**

Neoplatonism
xx **Church history—Primitive and early church; Hellenism; Philosophy; Philosophy, Ancient; Theosophy**

Nero, Emperor of Rome
xx **Roman emperors**

Nerves
See also **Nervous system**
xx **Nervous system**

Nerves—Diseases. *See* **Nervous system—Diseases**

Nervous exhaustion. *See* **Neurasthenia**

Nervous prostration. *See* **Neurasthenia**

Nervous system
See also **Brain; Nerves; Psychology, Pathological; Psychology, Physiological**
x Neurology
xx **Anatomy; Brain; Mind and body; Nerves; Physiology**

Nervous system—Diseases
See also **Epilepsy; Fear; Insanity; Neurasthenia; Worry**
x Nerves—Diseases; Neuropathology
xx **Medicine—Practice; Therapeutics**

Nervous system—Hygiene
  See also Mental health
Nests. *See* Birds—Eggs and nests
Netherlands
  x Holland
Netherlands—History
Netherlands—History—German occupation,
    1940-1945
    x German occupation of Netherlands, 1940-
      1945
    xx Military occupation; World War, 1939-
      1945—Occupied territories
Neurasthenia
    x Nervous exhaustion; Nervous prostra-
      tion
    xx Nervous system—Diseases
Neurology. *See* Nervous system
Neuropathology. *See* Nervous system—Dis-
    eases
Neuroses
    See also Fear; Medicine, Psychosomatic
    xx Psychology, Pathological
Neutrality
    See also names of countries with the sub-
      division *Neutrality,* e.g. U.S.—Neu-
      trality; etc.
    xx International law; International rela-
      tions; Privateering; Security, Inter-
      national
Neutrons
    See also Atoms; Electrons; Protons
    xx Nuclear physics; Quantum theory
New Church. *See* New Jerusalem Church
New England
    xx United States
New England—Hurricane, 1938
    xx Disasters; Hurricanes
New France—History. *See* Canada—History
      —To 1763 (New France); Missis-
      sippi Valley—History
New Jerusalem Church
    x Church of the New Jerusalem; New
      Church; Swedenborgianism
New nations. *See* States, New
New Testament. *See* Bible. New Testament
New Thought
    xx Mental healing; Psychology; Thera-
      peutics, Suggestive
New words. *See* Words, New
News agencies
    x Press
News broadcasts. *See* Radio broadcasting;
      Television broadcasting
News photography. *See* Photography, Jour-
      nalistic
Newsboys
    xx Boys; Child labor
Newspaper clippings. *See* Clippings (Books,
      newspapers, etc.)

373

Newspaper work. *See* **Journalism; Reporters and reporting**

✓ **Newspapers**
    See note under **Journalism**
    See also **Clippings (Books, newspapers, etc.) Freedom of the press; Journalism; Periodicals; Reporters and reporting; also American newspapers; English newspapers; etc.**
    x Press
    xx **Communication; Journalism; Mass media; Periodicals**

Newspapers—Indexes
    xx **Indexes**

Nicene Creed
    xx **Creeds**

Nicknames
    x Epithets; Sobriquets; Soubriquets
    xx **Names, Personal**

Night schools. *See* **Evening and continuation schools**

Nike rocket
    xx **Guided missiles**

Nineteenth century
    Use for general works covering progress and development during this period in one or in several countries
    xx **History, Modern—19th century**

Nitrates
    xx **Fertilizers and manures**

Nitrogen
    xx **Gases**

Nobel prizes
    xx **Rewards (Prizes, etc.)**

Nobility
    See also **Aristocracy; Heraldry; Knights and knighthood**
    x Baronage; Peerage
    xx **Aristocracy; Heraldry; Social classes**

Noise
    See also subjects with the subdivision *Noise*, e.g. **Airplanes—Noise;** etc.
    xx **Public health; Sound**

Noise pollution
    See also subjects with the subdivision *Noise*, e.g. **Airplanes—Noise;** etc.
    xx **Pollution**

Nomenclature. *See* **Names;** and scientific and technical subjects with the subdivision *Terminology,* e.g. **Botany—Terminology;** etc.

Nomination of presidents. *See* **Presidents—U.S.—Nomination**

Nonbook materials. See **Audio-visual materials**

Nonconformity. *See* **Conformity; Dissent**

Nongraded schools
    x Multi-age grouping; Schools, Nongraded; Schools, Ungraded; Ungraded schools

Nongraded schools—*Continued*
    xx Ability grouping in education; Education—Experimental methods
Noninstitutional churches
    x Avant-garde churches; Churches—Avant-garde; Churches, Noninstitutional
Nonobjective art. *See* Art, Abstract
Nonprint materials. *See* Audio-visual materials
Nonprofessional library assistants. *See* Library technicians
Nonpublic schools. *See* Church schools; Private schools
Nonsense verses
    See also Limericks
    x Rhymes
    xx Humorous poetry; Limericks; Poetry—Collections; Wit and humor
Nonsupport. *See* Desertion and nonsupport
Nonverbal communication
    x Expression; Gesture
    xx Communication
Nonviolence
    See also Pacifism; Passive resistance
    xx Pacifism; Passive resistance; War and religion
Nonviolent noncooperation. *See* Passive resistance
Nordic race. *See* Teutonic race
Normal schools. *See* Teachers colleges
Normandy, Attack on, 1944
    x D Day
Normans
    See also Northmen
    xx Gt. Brit.—History—Norman period, 1066-1154; Northmen
Norse languages. *See* Icelandic and Old Norse languages; Scandinavian languages
Norse legends. *See* Legends, Norse
Norse literature. *See* Icelandic and Old Norse literature; Scandinavian literature
Norsemen. *See* Northmen
North Africa. *See* Africa, North
North America
    xx America
North America—Discovery and exploration. *See* America—Discovery and exploration
North American Indians. *See* Indians of North America
North Atlantic Treaty, 1949
    xx Treaties
North Atlantic Treaty Organization
    x NATO
North Central States. *See* Middle West
North Pole
    See also Arctic regions
    x Polar expeditions
    xx Arctic regions; Polar regions

North Dakota Republican Convention
    See also Republican Party.

Northeast Passage

    xx **Arctic regions; Discoveries (in geography); Voyages and travels**

Northern lights. *See* **Auroras**

Northmen

    Use for works on the early Scandinavian people. Works on the people since the 10th century are entered under **Scandinavians**

    See also **Normans**

    x Norsemen; Vikings

    xx **Normans; Scandinavians**

Northwest, Canadian

    x Canada, Northwest; Canadian Northwest

    xx **Canada**

Northwest, Old

    Use for works on the region between the Ohio and Mississippi Rivers and the Great Lakes

    See also **Middle West**

    xx **United States**

Northwest, Pacific

    Use for works on the old Oregon country, comprising the present states of Oregon, Washington and Idaho, parts of Montana and Wyoming and the province of British Columbia

    x Pacific Northwest

    xx **United States; The West**

Northwest Passage

    xx **America—Discovery and exploration; Arctic regions; Discoveries (in geography); Voyages and travels**

Norwegian language

    May be subdivided like **English language**

    See also **Danish language**

    xx **Scandinavian languages**

Norwegian literature

    May use same subdivisions and names of literary forms as for **English literature**

    xx **Scandinavian literature**

Nose

    xx **Face; Head; Smell**

Notation, Musical. *See* **Musical notation**

Novelists (May subdiv. geog. adjective form, e.g. **Novelists, French;** etc.)

    Use for works, mainly biographical, treating of several novelists. Works on their literary output are entered under **Fiction—History and criticism; English fiction—History and criticism;** etc.

    xx **Authors; Fiction**

Novelists, American

    x American novelists; U.S.—Novelists

Novels. *See* **Fiction**

Novels—Plots. *See* **Plots (Drama, fiction, etc.)**

Nuclear energy. *See* **Atomic energy**

Nuclear engineering

    See also **Nuclear reactors; Radioisotopes**

    xx **Atomic energy; Engineering; Nuclear physics**

Nuclear physics

    See also **Atomic energy; Chemistry, Physical and theoretical; Cosmic rays; Cyclotron; Electrons; Neutrons; Nuclear engineering; Nuclear reactors; Protons; Radioactivity; Radiobiology; Transmutation (Chemistry)**

    x Atomic nuclei; Physics, Nuclear

    xx **Atoms; Chemistry, Physical and theoretical; Physics; Radioactivity**

Nuclear propulsion

    See also **Nuclear reactors;** also specific applications; e.g. **Atomic submarines;** etc.

    x Atomic powered vehicles

    xx **Atomic energy**

Nuclear reactors

    x Atomic piles; Reactors (Nuclear physics)

    xx **Atomic energy; Nuclear engineering; Nuclear physics; Nuclear propulsion**

Nuclear submarines. *See* **Atomic submarines**

Nuclear test ban. *See* **Disarmament**

Nuclear warfare. *See* **Atomic warfare**

Nuclear weapons. *See* **Atomic weapons**

Nudity in the performing arts

    xx **Performing arts**

Number games

    xx **Arithmetic—Study and teaching; Counting books; Mathematical recreations**

Numbers theory

    x Theory of numbers

    xx **Algebra; Mathematics; Set theory**

Numismatics

    Use for works on coins, medals and tokens considered as works of art, as historical specimens, or as aids to the study of history, archeology, etc.

    See also **Coins; Medals; Seals (Numismatics)**

    xx **Archeology; Coins; History; History, Ancient; Medals**

Nunneries. *See* **Convents**

Nuns. *See* **Monasticism and religious orders for women**

Nurseries (Horticulture)

    See also **Plant propagation**

    xx **Fruit culture; Gardening; Trees**

Nurseries, Day. *See* **Day nurseries**

Nursery rhymes

    x Poetry for children; Rhymes

    xx **Children's poetry; Children's songs; Folklore**

377

Nursery schools

  See also **Day nurseries; Kindergarten**

  x Education, Preschool; Preschool education

  xx **Day nurseries; Education, Elementary**

Nurses and nursing

  See also **Children—Care and hygiene; Cookery for the sick; First aid; Home nursing; Hospitals; Infants—Care and hygiene; Practical nurses and nursing; Red Cross; School nurses; Sick**

  x District nurses; Nursing; Trained nurses

  xx **Children—Care and hygiene; Hospitals; Medicine; Medicine—Biography; Medicine—Practice; Sick; Therapeutics; Woman—Employment**

Nursing. *See* **Nurses and nursing**

Nutrition

  See also **Diet; Digestion; Food; Metabolism; Vitamins**

  x Malnutrition; Meal planning

  xx **Diet; Digestion; Food; Metabolism; Physiology; Therapeutics**

Nutrition of astronauts. *See* **Astronauts—Nutrition**

Nutrition of children. *See* **Children—Nutrition**

Nutrition of plants. *See* **Plants—Nutrition**

Nuts

  Names of nuts are not included in this list but are to be added as needed, in the singular form, e.g. **Pecan**; etc.

  See also names of nuts, e.g. **Pecan**; etc.

  xx **Food; Trees**

Nylon

  xx **Synthetic fabrics; Texile industry and fabrics**

Oak

  xx **Trees; Wood**

Oats

  xx **Feeding and feeds**

Obedience

  x Disobedience

  xx **Behavior**

Obelisks

  xx **Archeology; Architecture; Monuments; Pyramids**

Obesity. *See* **Weight control**

Obituaries

  x Death notices; Necrologies

  xx **Biography**

Objective tests. *See* **Examinations; Mental tests**

Obscene literature. *See* **Pornography**

Obscenity (Law)

  See also **Pornography**

Observatories, Astronomical. *See* **Astronomical observatories**

Observatories, Meteorological. *See* **Meteorology—Observatories**

Obstetrics. *See* **Childbirth**

Occidental civilization. *See* **Civilization, Occidental**

Occult sciences

    See also

Alchemy	**Medicine man**
Astrology	**Oracles**
Clairvoyance	**Palmistry**
Demonology	**Prophecies**
Divination	**Spiritualism**
Fortune telling	**Superstition**
Magic	**Witchcraft**

    x Hermetic art and philosophy; Sorcery

    xx **Astrology; Demonology; Divination; Magic; Supernatural; Superstition; Witchcraft**

Occupation, Choice of. *See* **Vocational guidance**

Occupation, Military. *See* **Military occupation**

Occupational diseases

    See also **Occupations, Dangerous; Workmen's compensation**

    x Diseases, Industrial; Diseases, Occupational; Diseases of occupation; Hygiene, Industrial; Hygiene of employment; Industrial diseases; Industrial hygiene; Occupations—Diseases and hygiene

    xx **Hygiene; Labor and laboring classes; Occupations, Dangerous; Public health**

Occupational therapy

    See also Handicraft

    xx **Handicraft; Mental health; Physical therapy; Physically handicapped—Rehabilitation; Therapeutics**

Occupational retraining. *See* **Retraining, Occupational**

Occupational training

    Use for works on teaching people a skill after formal education. For teaching a skill during the educational process use **Vocational education.** For on the job training use **Employees—Training.** For retraining use **Retraining, Occupational**

    See also **Employees—Training; Retraining, Occupational**

    x Job training; Manpower development and training; Training, Occupational; Training, Vocational; Vocational training

    xx **Technical education; Vocational education**

Occupations

    Use for descriptions and lists of occupations

    See also **Job analysis; Professions; Voca-**

Occupations—*Continued*

    tional guidance; also names of countries, cities, etc. with the subdivision *Occupations* (e.g. **U.S.—Occupations; Chicago—Occupations**; etc.) also such headings as **Law as a profession; Music as a profession**; etc.

    x Careers; Jobs; Trades; Vocations

    xx **Business; Labor and laboring classes; Professions; Vocational guidance; Woman—Employment**

Occupations, Dangerous

    See also **Occupational diseases**

    x Dangerous occupations; Injurious occupations

    xx **Accidents; Labor and laboring classes; Occupational diseases**

Occupations—Diseases and hygiene. *See* **Occupational diseases**

Occupied territory. *See* **Military occupation**

Ocean

    See also **Icebergs; Oceanography; Seashore; Storms; Tides**; also names of oceans and seas, e.g. **Atlantic Ocean**; etc.

    x Sea

    xx **Earth; Physical geography; Water**

Ocean—Economic aspects. *See* **Marine resources; Shipping**

Ocean cables. *See* **Cables, Submarine**

Ocean life. *See* **Marine biology**

Ocean mineral resources. *See* **Marine mineral resources**

Ocean pollution. *See* **Marine pollution**

Ocean routes. *See* **Trade routes**

Ocean travel

    See also **Steamboats; Yachts and yachting**

    x Sea travel

    xx **Transportation; Travel; Voyages and travels**

Ocean waves

    x Sea waves; Surf; Tidal waves

    xx **Oceanography; Waves**

Oceanariums. *See* **Marine aquariums**

Oceania. *See* **Islands of the Pacific**

Oceanographic research. *See* **Oceanography—Research**

Oceanography (May subdiv. geog. area e.g. **Oceanography—Atlantic Ocean**; etc.)

    See also **Marine biology; Marine resources; Navigation; Ocean waves; Submarine geology**

    x Deep sea technology; Oceanology; Undersea technology

    xx **Earth; Geology; Geophysics; Ocean**

Oceanography—Computer programs

    xx **Computer programs**

Oceanography—Research
> *See also* Bathyscaphe; Manned undersea research stations; Skin diving; Underwater exploration
> *x* Oceanographic research

Oceanology. *See* **Oceanography**

Offenses, Military. *See* **Military offenses**

Offenses against public safety
> *See also* names of specific offenses, e.g. **Hijacking of airplanes; Riots; Sabotage; etc.**
> *x* Crimes against public safety; Public safety, Crimes against
> *xx* **Criminal law**

Offenses against the person
> *See also* names of specific offenses, e.g. **Assassination; Murder; etc.**
> *x* Crimes against the person; Persons, Crimes against
> *xx* **Criminal law**

Office, Tenure of. *See* **Civil service**

Office buildings
> *See also* **Skyscrapers;** also names of cities with the subdivision *Office buildings,* e.g. **Chicago—Office buildings; etc.**
> *x* Buildings, Office
> *xx* **Industrial buildings**

Office employees. *See* **Clerks**

Office equipment and supplies
> *See also* **Calculating machines; Typewriters**
> *x* Business machines; Office machines
> *xx* **Bookkeeping; Office management**

Office machines. *See* **Office equipment and supplies**

Office management
> *See also* **Office equipment and supplies; Personnel management; Secretaries**
> *x* Office procedures
> *xx* **Business; Efficiency, Industrial; Factory management; Industrial management; Management; Personnel management**

Office procedures. *See* **Office management**

Office supplies. *See* **Office equipment and supplies**

Office work—Training. *See* **Business education**

Official publications. *See* **Government publications;** and names of countries, cities, etc. with the subdivision *Government publications,* e.g. **U.S.—Government publications; etc.**

Officials. *See* **Civil service;** and names of countries, cities, etc. and organizations with the subdivision *Officials and employees,* e.g. **U.S.—Officials and employees; Chicago—Officials and employees; United Nations—Officials and employees; etc.**

Offset printing

    x Lithoprinting; Printing, Offset

    xx **Lithography; Printing**

Offshore water pollution. *See* **Marine pollution**

Ohio

    Subdivisions have been given under this subject to serve as a guide to the subdivisions that may be used under the name of any state or province. They are examples of the application of directions given in the general references under various headings throughout the list. References are given only for those headings that are cited specifically under the general references. The subdivisions under **United States** may be consulted as a guide for formulating other references that may be needed

Ohio—Antiquities

Ohio—Bibliography

Ohio—Bio-bibliography

Ohio—Biography

Ohio—Biography—Dictionaries

Ohio—Biography—Portraits

Ohio—Boundaries

Ohio—Census

Ohio—Church history

Ohio—Civilization

Ohio—Climate

Ohio—Commerce

Ohio. Constitution

    xx **Constitutions, State**

Ohio—Constitutional history

Ohio—Description and travel

Ohio—Description and travel—Guide books

Ohio—Description and travel—Views

Ohio—Directories

    Use for lists of names and addresses. Lists of names without addresses are entered under **Ohio—Registers**

    See also **Ohio—Registers**

    xx **Ohio—Registers**

Ohio—Economic conditions

Ohio—Economic policy

    x State planning

    xx **Economic policy**

Ohio—Executive departments

Ohio—Foreign population

Ohio—Galleries and museums

Ohio—Gazetteers

Ohio—Government publications

Ohio—Historic houses, etc.

Ohio—History

Ohio—History, Local

Ohio—History—Societies

Ohio—History—Sources

Ohio—Industries

    x Ohio—Manufactures

Ohio—Intellectual life

Ohio—Manufactures. *See* **Ohio—Industries**

Ohio—Maps
Ohio—Militia
Ohio—Moral conditions
Ohio—Occupations
Ohio—Officials and employees
Ohio—Politics and government
> *xx* State governments

Ohio—Population
Ohio—Public buildings
Ohio—Public lands
Ohio—Public works
Ohio—Race relations
Ohio—Registers
> Use for lists of names without addresses. List of names that include addresses are entered under **Ohio—Directories**
> *See also* **Ohio—Directories**
> *xx* **Ohio—Directories**

Ohio—Religion
Ohio—Social conditions
Ohio—Social life and customs
Ohio—Social policy
> *x* State planning

Ohio—Statistics
Oil. *See* **Oils and fats; Petroleum**
Oil burners
> *x* Fuel oil
> *xx* **Heating; Petroleum as fuel**

Oil engines. *See* **Gas and oil engines**
Oil fuel. *See* **Petroleum as fuel**
Oil painting. *See* **Painting**
Oil wells. *See* **Petroleum**
Oils, Essential. *See* **Essences and essential oils**
Oils and fats
> *See also* **Essences and essential oils; Lubrication and lubricants; Petroleum**
> *x* Animal oils; Fat; Fats; Grease; Oil; Vegetable oils
> *xx* **Coal-tar products; Lubrication and lubricants**

Old age
> *See also* **Age and employment; Aged; Old age pensions; Retirement**
> *x* Age; Gerontology; Longevity
> *xx* **Life (Biology); Middle age; Physiology**

Old age homes. *See* **Aged—Dwellings**
Old age pensions
> *x* Insurance, Old age; Labor and laboring classes—Insurance; Payroll taxes; Retirement income; Security, Social; Social security
> *xx* **Insurance, Social; Labor and laboring classes; Old age; Pensions; Saving and thrift; Social problems; Socialism**

Old English language. *See* **Anglo-Saxon language**
Old English literature. *See* **Anglo-Saxon literature**

Old Norse language. *See* **Icelandic and Old Norse languages**

Old Norse literature. *See* **Icelandic and Old Norse literature**

Old Testament. *See* **Bible. Old Testament**

Oleomargarine. *See* **Margarine**

Olympic games
> *x* Games, Olympic
> *xx* **Athletics; Games; Sports**

Ombudsman
> *x* Citizen's defender

On line data processing
> *x* In line data processing
> *xx* **Electronic data processing**

One-act plays
> *x* Plays
> *xx* **Amateur theatricals; Drama**

Ontology
> *See also* **Existentialism; Metaphysics; Philosophy**
> *x* Being
> *xx* **God; Life; Metaphysics**

Opaque projectors. *See* **Projectors**

Open and closed shop
> *x* Closed shop; Right to work
> *xx* **Labor and laboring classes; Labor contract; Labor unions**

Open door policy (Far East). *See* **Eastern question (Far East)**

Open heart surgery. *See* **Heart—Surgery**

Open housing. *See* **Discrimination in housing**

Opera
> *See also* **Ballet; Operetta**
> *x* Comic opera; Dramatic music; Grand opera; Music, Dramatic
> *xx* **Drama; Musical form; Theater**

Opera houses. *See* **Theaters**

Operas
> *See also* **Musical revues, comedies, etc.**
> *xx* **Vocal music**

Operas—Librettos
> *xx* **Librettos**

Operas—Stories, plots, etc.
> *x* Stories
> *xx* **Librettos; Plots (Drama, fiction, etc.)**

Operation Pluto. *See* **Cuba—History—Invasion, 1961**

Operations, Surgical. *See* **Surgery**

Operations research
> *See also* **Queuing theory; Systems engineering**
> *xx* **Research; Systems engineering**

Operetta
> *See also* **Musical revues, comedies, etc.**
> *x* Comic opera; Dramatic music; Music, Dramatic
> *xx* **Musical form; Opera; Vocal music**

Opiates. *See* **Narcotics**

Opinion, Public. *See* **Public opinion**

Opium
xx Narcotics

Opium—Physiological effect
x Physiological effect
xx Pharmacology

Optical data processing
x Visual data processing
xx Bionics; Electronic data processing

Optical illusions
x Illusions
xx Hallucinations and illusions; Psychology, Physiological; Vision

Optical masers. *See* **Lasers**

Optics
See also Color; Light; Perspective; Phosphorescence; Photometry; Radiation; Refraction; Spectrum; Vision
xx Light; Photometry; Physics

Options. *See* **Contracts; Stock exchange**

Optometry
See also **Eye**
xx Eye

Oracles
See also **Divination**
xx Divination; Occult sciences; Prophecies

Oral history
Use for works on recording the recollections of events by persons. Use appropriate subject headings for the content of the recollections
x History, oral
xx History

Orange
xx Citrus fruit

Orations
Use for collections of orations by several authors, especially those delivered on formal occasions and in a more formal manner than those entered under **Speeches, addresses, etc.**
See also **After-dinner speeches;** also **American orations; English orations;** etc.
x Addresses
xx Literature—Collections; Public speaking; Speeches, addresses, etc.

Oratorio
xx Church music; Musical form; Vocal music

Oratory. *See* **Public speaking**

Orbital laboratories. *See* **Space stations**

Orbital rendezvous (Space flight)
See also names of projects, e.g. **Apollo project; Gemini project;** etc.; also names of space ships
x Rendezvous in space; Space orbital rendezvous
xx Space flight; Space ships; Space stations

Orbiting vehicles. *See* **Artificial satellites**

Orchards. *See* **Fruit culture**

Orchestra

> *See also* **Bands (Music); Conducting; Conductors (Music); Instrumentation and orchestration; Orchestral music**
>
> *xx* **Bands (Music); Conducting; Musical instruments**

Orchestral music

> *See also* **Chamber music; Symphonies**
>
> *xx* **Instrumental music; Music; Orchestra**

Orchestration. *See* **Instrumentation and orchestration**

Orders, Architectural. *See* **Architecture—Orders**

Orders, Monastic. *See* **Monasticism and religious orders**

Ordnance

> *See also* names of general and specific military ordnance, e.g. **Atomic weapons; Bombs; Projectiles;** etc.; also names of armies with the subdivision *Ordnance and ordnance stores,* e.g. **U.S. Army—Ordnance and ordnance stores;** etc.
>
> *x* Cannon; Guns
>
> *xx* **Arms and armor; Artillery; Firearms; Military art and science; Projectiles**

Ore deposits

> *See also* **Ores;** also names of ores, e.g. **Iron ores;** etc.
>
> *xx* **Geology; Ores**

Ore dressing

> *x* Dressing of ores
>
> *xx* Smelting

Oregon Trail

> *xx* **Overland journeys to the Pacific; United States**

Ores

> *See also* **Metallurgy; Metals; Minerology; Mines and mineral resources; Ore deposits;** also names of ores, e.g. **Iron ores;** etc.
>
> *xx* **Geology, Economic; Ore deposits**

Organ

> *x* Pipe organ
>
> *xx* **Musical instruments**

Organ music

> *xx* **Church music; Music**

Organ preservation. *See* **Preservation of organs, tissues, etc.**

Organ transplantation. *See* **Transplantation of organs, tissues, etc.**

Organic chemistry. *See* **Chemistry, Organic**

Organic farming. *See* **Organiculture**

Organic gardening. *See* **Organiculture**

Organiculture

> *x* Organic farming; Organic gardening
>
> *xx* **Agriculture; Gardening**

Organists

    xx **Musicians**

Organization, International. *See* **International organization**

Organization and management. *See* **Management**

Organizations. *See* **Associations**

Organized crime. *See* **Racketeering**

Organized labor. *See* **Labor unions**

Organs, Artificial. *See* **Artificial organs**

Organs, Preservation. *See* **Preservation of organs, tissues, etc.**

Orient. *See* **East; East (Far East)**

Oriental architecture. *See* **Architecture, Oriental**

Oriental art. *See* **Art, Oriental**

Oriental civilization. *See* **Civilization, Oriental**

Oriental rugs. *See* **Rugs, Oriental**

Origami

    xx **Paper crafts**

Origin of life. *See* **Life—Origin**

Origin of man. *See* **Man—Origin and antiquity**

Origin of species. *See* **Evolution**

Ornament. *See* **Decoration and ornament**

Ornamental alphabets. *See* **Illumination of books and manuscripts; Lettering**

Ornamental design. *See* **Design, Decorative**

Ornamental plants. *See* **Plants, Ornamental**

Ornithology. *See* **Birds**

Orphans and orphans' homes

    See also **Child welfare**

    x Charitable institutions; Dependent children; Foundlings; Homes (Institutions)

    xx **Charities; Child welfare; Children—Institutional care; Institutional care; Public welfare**

Orthodox Eastern Church

    x Greek Church

    xx **Eastern churches**

Orthodox Eastern Church, Russian

    x Russian Church

Orthography. *See* **Spelling reform**; and names of languages with the subdivision *Spelling,* e.g. **English language—Spelling**; etc.

Orthopedia

    See also **Physically handicapped**

    x Orthopedic surgery; Surgery, Orthopedic

    xx **Physically handicapped; Surgery**

Orthopedic surgery. *See* **Orthopedia**

Osaka. World's Fair, 1970. *See* **Expo '70**

Osteology. *See* **Bones**

Osteopathy

    See also **Massage**

    xx **Massage; Medicine; Medicine—Practice**

Ostrogoths. *See* **Teutonic race**

Outboard motorboats. *See* **Motorboats**

Outdoor cookery
  x Barbecue cooking; Camp cooking; Cooking, Outdoor
  xx Camping; Cookery
Outdoor life
  See also Camping; Country life; Hiking; Mountaineering; Nature study; Sports; Wilderness survival
  x Rural life
  xx Camping; Country life; Sports
Outdoor recreation
  See also Camping; Parks
  xx Recreation
Outdoor survival. *See* Wilderness survival
Outer space
  See also Space environment
  x Space, Outer
  xx Astronautics; Astronomy; Space sciences
Outer space—Communication. *See* Intersteller communication
Outer space—Exploration
  See also Space probes
  x Space exploration (Astronautics); Space research
  xx Interplanetary voyages; Manned space flights; Space flight
Outer space and civilization. *See* Astronautics and civilization
Outlaws. *See* Robbers and outlaws
Outlines, syllabi, etc. *See* general subjects with the subdivision *Outlines, syllabi, etc.* e.g. English literature—Outlines, syllabi, etc.; etc.
Overland journeys to the Pacific
  Use for works on the pioneers' crossing of the continent toward the Pacific by foot, horseback, wagon, etc.
  See also Oregon Trail
  x Transcontinental journeys; Travels
  xx Frontier and pioneer life; Voyages and travels
Overtime. *See* Hours of labor; Wages
Overweight. *See* Weight control
Ownership. *See* Property
Oxyacetylene welding. *See* Welding
Oxygen
  See also Ozone
Oysters, Pearl. *See* Pearlfisheries
Ozone
  xx Oxygen
POW. *See* Prisoners of war
PTA. *See* Parents' and teachers' associations
Pacific cable. *See* Cables, Submarine
Pacific Islands. *See* Islands of the Pacific
Pacific Northwest. *See* Northwest, Pacific
Pacific States
  xx The West

Pacifism

See also **Conscientious objectors; Non-violence**

xx **Conscientious objectors; Nonviolence; Peace; War and religion**

Pack transportation. *See* **Backpacking**

Packaged houses. *See* **Prefabricated houses**

Packaging

See also **Gift wrapping**

xx **Advertising; Retail trade**

Packing industry. *See* **Meat industry and trade**

Paganism

x Heathenism

xx **Christianity and other religions; Religions**

Pageants

See also **Festivals; Masks (Plays); Mysteries and miracle plays**

xx **Acting; Festivals**

Pain

See also **Anesthetics; Pleasure; Suffering**

xx **Diagnosis; Emotions; Pleasure; Psychology, Physiological; Senses and sensation; Suffering**

Paint

See also **Corrosion and anticorrosives; Pigments**

x Enamel paints; Finishes and finishing

xx **Corrosion and anticorrosives; Painting, Industrial; Pigments**

Painted glass. *See* **Glass painting and staining**

Painters (May subdiv. geog. adjective form, e.g. **Painters, French;** etc.)

See also **Artists;** also names of individual painters

xx **Artists**

Painters, American

x American painters; U.S.—Painters

Painters' materials. *See* **Artists' materials**

Painting (May subdiv. geog. adjective form, e.g. **Painting, Dutch;** etc.)

See also

Animal painting and illustration

China painting

Color

Composition (Art)

Cubism

Expressionism (Art)

Figure painting

Finger painting

Flower painting and illustration

Futurism (Art)

Glass painting and staining

Impressionism (Art)

Landscape painting

Marine painting

Miniature painting

Mural painting and decoration

Paintings

Perspective

Portrait painting

Postimpressionism (Art)

Pre-Raphaelitism

Scene painting

Stencil work

Textile painting

Water color painting

x Oil painting

Painting—*Continued*

    xx Art; Composition (Art); Decoration and ornament; Drawing; Esthetics; Graphic arts

Painting, American

    x American painting; U.S.—Painting

Painting, Finger. *See* **Finger painting**

Painting, Industrial

    See also House painting; Lettering; Paint; Sign painting; Varnish and varnishing; Wood finishing

    x Enamel paints; Finishes and finishing; Industrial painting; Mechanical painting; Painting, Mechanical

Painting, Mechanical. *See* **Painting, Industrial**

Painting, Modern

    x Modern painting

Painting, Modern—19th century

Painting, Modern—20th century

Painting, Religious. *See* **Christian art and symbolism**

Painting, Romanesque

    x Romanesque painting

    xx **Art, Romanesque**

Painting—Technique

Paintings (May subdiv. geog. adjective form, e.g. **Paintings, French**; etc.)

    Use for collections of reproductions of paintings in which the reproductions are more important than the text

    See also Portraits; Water colors

    xx **Painting; Pictures**

Paintings, Abstract. *See* **Art, Abstract**

Paintings, American

    x American paintings; U.S.—Paintings

Paintings—Color reproduction. *See* **Color prints**

Paintings—Conservation and restoration

    x Conservation of works of art; Preservation of works of art; Restoration of works of art

Paintings, Modern

    Divide like **Painting, Modern**

    x Modern paintings

Pair system. *See* **Binary system (Mathematics)**

Palaces

    xx **Architecture**

Paleobotany. *See* **Plants, Fossil**

Paleolithic period. *See* **Stone age**

Paleontology. *See* **Fossils**

Palmistry

    xx **Divination; Fortune telling; Occult sciences**

Palsy, Cerebral. *See* **Cerebral palsy**

Pamphlets

Pan-Africanism

    x African relations

    xx **Africa**

Pan-Americanism
  Use for works on the relations between the United States and the republics of Latin America
  See also America—Politics; Monroe Doctrine
  x Good Neighbor Policy; Inter-American relations
  xx America—Politics; Latin America
Panama Canal
  xx Canals
Panel discussions. *See* Discussion groups
Panel heating. *See* Radiant heating
Paneuropean federation. *See* European federation
Pangermanism
  See also Propaganda, German
Panics. See Depressions
Pantheism
  See also Deism; Theism
  xx God; Philosophy; Religion; Theism; Theology
Pantomimes
  See also Shadow pantomimes and plays
  xx Acting; Amateur theatricals; Ballet; Drama; Theater
Papacy
  See also Popes
  x Holy See
  xx Catholic Church; Church history; Church history—Middle Ages; Popes
Papal encyclicals. *See* Encyclicals, Papal
Paper
  xx Fibers
Paper bound books. *See* Paperback books
Paper crafts
  See also Gift wrapping; also names of paper crafts, e.g. Decoupage; Origami; etc.
  x Paper folding; Paper sculpture; Paper work; Papier-mâché
Paper folding. *See* Paper crafts
Paper hanging
  See also Wallpaper
  xx Interior decoration; Wallpaper
Paper making and trade
  See also Book industries and trade; Wood pulp
  xx Book industries and trade; Chemical industries; Manufactures
Paper money
  x Bills of credit; Fiat money; Greenbacks; Legal tender; Money, Paper
  xx Currency question; Finance; Inflation (Finance); Money
Paper sculpture. *See* Paper crafts
Paper work. *See* Paper crafts
Paperback books
  x Bibliography—Paperback editions; Books, Paperback; Paper bound books

Paperback books—*Continued*
>   *xx* Bibliography—Editions; Books; Publishers and publishing

Papier-mâché. *See* **Paper crafts**

Papyrus manuscripts. *See* **Manuscripts**

Parables
>   *See also* **Allegories; Fables; Jesus Christ —Parables**
>   *xx* **Allegories; Fables**

Parachute troops
>   *See also* names of armies with the subdivision *Parachute troops,* e.g. **U.S. Army—Parachute troops;** etc.
>   *x* Paratroops
>   *xx* **Aeronautics, Military; Parachutes**

Parachutes
>   *See also* **Parachute troops**
>   *xx* **Aeronautics**

Parades
>   *x* Floats (Parades) ; Processions

Paralysis, Anterior spinal. *See* **Poliomyelitis**

Paralysis, Cerebral. *See* **Cerebral palsy**

Paralysis, Infantile. *See* **Poliomyelitis**

Paralysis, Spastic. *See* **Cerebral palsy**

Parapsychology. *See* **Psychical research**

Parasites
>   *See also* **Bacteriology; Insects, Injurious and beneficial**
>   *x* Animal parasites ; Diseases and pests ; Entozoa ; Epizoa ; Pests

Parasols. *See* **Umbrellas and parasols**

Paratroops. *See* **Parachute troops**

Parcel post. *See* **Postal service**

Parent and child
>   *See also* **Children—Management; Conflict of generations; Cruelty to children; Fathers; Illegitimacy; Inheritance and succession; Mothers**
>   *x* Child and parent
>   *xx* **Child study; Conflict of generations; Domestic relations; Family; Human relations**

Parents and teachers. *See* **Home and school**

Parents' and teachers' associations
>   *See also* **Home and school**
>   *x* PTA ; Teachers and parents
>   *xx* **Child study; Community and school; Educational associations; Home and school; Societies**

Parish libraries. *See* **Libraries, Church**

Parish registers. *See* **Registers of births, etc.**

✓ **Parks** (May subdiv. geog. country or state)
>   *See also* **Amusement parks; Botanical gardens; National parks and reserves; Playgrounds; Zoological gardens;** also names of cities with the subdivision *Parks,* e.g. **Chicago—Parks;** etc.
>   *xx* **Cities and towns; Landscape architec-**

Parks—*Continued*

ture; Landscape gardening; **Outdoor recreation; Playgrounds**

Parks—U.S.

x U.S.—Parks

Parkways. *See* **Express highways**

Parliamentary government. *See* **Representative government and representation**

Parliamentary practice

x Rules of order

xx **Debates and debating; Legislation; Legislative bodies; Public meetings**

Parliaments. *See* **Legislative bodies**

Parochial schools. *See* **Church schools**

Parodies

May be used for collections by one author as well as for collections by several authors

See also names of prominent authors with the subdivision *Parodies, travesties, etc.* e.g. **Shakespeare, William—Parodies, travesties, etc.**; etc.

x English parodies; Travesties

xx **English literature; Literature—Collections; Poetry—Collections**

Parody

Use for works about parody. Collections of parodies are entered under **Parodies**

x Comic literature

xx **Literature; Poetry; Satire; Wit and humor**

Parole

See also **Probation**

xx **Crime and criminals; Probations; Social case work**

Parties

See also names of parties, e.g. **Shower (Parties)**; etc.

xx **Entertaining**

Parties, Political. *See* **Political parties**

Passion plays

See also **Mysteries and miracle plays**

xx **Drama; Jesus Christ—Drama; Religious drama; Theater**

Passions. *See* **Emotions**

Passive resistance

See also **Nonviolence**

x Boycott; Civil disobedience; Nonviolent noncooperation

xx **Nonviolence**

Pastel drawing

See also **Crayon drawing**

xx **Crayon drawing; Drawing; Portrait painting**

Pastels

xx **Drawings**

Pastimes. *See* **Amusements; Games; Recreation; Sports**

Pastoral psychiatry. *See* **Psychology, Pastoral**

Pastoral psychology. *See* **Psychology, Pastoral**

✓ *Pastoral counseling*

393

Pastoral theology. *See* **Pastoral work**
Pastoral work
> *See also* **Church work; Clergy; Preaching; Psychology, Pastoral**
> *x* Pastoral theology; Theology, Pastoral

Pastors. *See* **Clergy; Priests**
Pastors' wives. *See* **Clergymen's wives**
Pastry
> *xx* **Baking; Cookery**

Pastures
> *See also* **Forage plants; Grasses**
> *xx* **Agriculture; Cattle; Forage plants; Grasses**

Patent medicines
> *x* Medicines, Patent
> *xx* **Quacks and quackery**

Patents
> *See also* **Inventions; Trade-marks**
> *x* Discoveries (in science); Intellectual property
> *xx* **Inventions; Machinery; Manufactures; Trade-marks**

Pathological botany. *See* **Plants—Diseases**
Pathological chemistry. *See* **Chemistry, Medical and pharmaceutical; Physiological chemistry**
Pathological psychology. *See* **Psychology, Pathological**
Pathology
> *See also* **Bacteriology; Diagnosis; Immunity; Medicine; Physiological chemistry; Therapeutics**
> *x* Disease (Pathology)
> *xx* **Diagnosis; Medicine**

Pathology, Vegetable. *See* **Plants—Diseases**
Patience (Game). *See* **Solitaire (Game)**
Patients. *See* **Sick**
Patios
> *xx* Landscape architecture

Patriotic poetry
> *xx* National songs; Poetry—Collections

Patriotic songs. *See* **National songs**
Patriotism
> *See also* **Loyalty; Nationalism**
> *xx* **Behavior; Citizenship; Loyalty; Nationalism**

Pattern making
> *See also* **Design; Founding; Mechanical drawing**
> *xx* **Design; Founding**

Patterns for dressmaking. *See* **Dressmaking**
Pauperism. *See* **Poverty**
Pavements
> *See also* **Asphalt; Roads; Streets**
> *xx* **Cement; Concrete; Roads; Streets**

Pay television. *See* **Subscription television**
Payroll taxes. *See* **Income tax; Insurance, Unemployment; Old age pensions**

394

Peace

See also **Arbitration, International; Disarmament; League of Nations; Pacifism; Security, International; War;** also names of wars with the subdivision *Peace,* e.g. **World War, 1939-1945—Peace;** etc.

xx **Arbitration, International; Disarmament; International relations; Reconstruction (1914-1939); Reconstruction (1939-1951); Security, International; War**

Pearl diving and divers

x Ama

Pearl Harbor, Attack on, 1941

xx **World War, 1939-1945; World War, 1939-1945—Campaigns and battles**

Pearlfisheries

x Oysters, Pearl

xx **Fisheries**

Pearls

Peasant art. *See* **Art industries and trade; Folk art**

Peasantry

See also **Agricultural laborers; Land tenure; Sociology, Rural**

x Rural life

xx **Agricultural laborers; Feudalism; Labor and laboring classes; Land tenure; Sociology, Rural**

Pebbles. *See* **Rocks**

Pecan

xx **Nuts**

Pedagogy. *See* **Education; Education—Study and teaching; Teaching**

Peddlers and peddling

x Door to door selling

xx **Salesmen and salesmanship**

Pediatric psychiatry. *See* **Child psychiatry**

Pediatrics. *See* **Children—Care and hygiene; Children—Diseases**

Pedigrees. *See* **Genealogy; Heraldry**

Peerage. *See* **Nobility**

Pelts. *See* **Hides and skins**

Pen drawing

x Ink drawing

xx **Drawing**

Pen names. *See* **Pseudonyms**

Penal codes. *See* **Criminal law**

Penal colonies

x Convicts

xx **Colonies; Colonization; Crime and criminals; Prisons; Punishment**

Penal institutions. *See* **Prisons; Reformatories**

Penal law. *See* **Criminal law**

Pencil drawing

xx **Drawing**

Penguins

xx **Water birds**

✓ Peace Corps. See United States – action corps

Penicillin

    xx **Antibiotics**

Penitentiaries. *See* **Prisons**

Penmanship

    Use for practical manuals. Works on the history and art of writing are entered under **Writing**. Works on handwriting as an expression of the writer's character are entered under **Graphology**

    See also **Graphology; Writing**

    x Copybooks; Handwriting

    xx **Business education; Writing**

Pennsylvania Dutch

    x Germans in Pennsylvania; Pennsylvania Germans

Pennsylvania Germans. *See* **Pennsylvania Dutch**

Penology. *See* **Prisons; Punishment; Reformatories**

Pensions

    See also **Insurance, Social; Mothers' pensions; Old age pensions**

    x Compensation; Retirement income

    xx **Annuities**

Pensions, Military

    See also **Veterans**

    x Bonus, Soldiers'; Military pensions; Naval pensions; Pensions, Naval; Soldiers' bonus; War pensions

    xx **Veterans**

Pensions, Naval. *See* **Pensions, Military**

Peonage

    See also **Contract labor; Convict labor**

    x Compulsory labor; Forced labor

    xx **Contract labor; Convict labor; Labor and laboring classes; Slavery**

People's banks. *See* **Banks and banking, Cooperative**

People's democracies. *See* **Communist countries**

People's Republic of China. *See* **China (People's Republic of China, 1949-   )**

Perception

    See also **Apperception; Consciousness; Gestalt psychology; Intuition**

    x Feeling

    xx **Appreciation; Educational psychology; Intellect; Intuition; Knowledge, Theory of; Psychology; Thought and thinking**

Percussion instruments

    See also names of percussion instruments, e.g. **Drums;** etc.

    xx **Musical instruments**

Perennials

    xx **Flower gardening; Flowers**

Performing arts

    See also **Centers for the performing arts; Nudity in the performing arts; Theater;** also art forms performed on stage or screen, e.g. **Ballet;** etc.

[handwritten annotation: ✓ Penitentiary. See North Dakota State Penitentiary]

Perfumes

    xx Cosmetics; Essences and essential oils

Periodic law

    xx Chemical elements; Chemistry, Physical and theoretical

Periodicals

    Use for general works about and lists of journals issued at stated intervals, i.e. weekly, monthly, etc. Works limited to dailies are entered under **Newspapers**

    See also **Freedom of the press**; **Newspapers**; also **American periodicals**; **English periodicals**; etc.; and general subjects with the subdivision *Periodicals,* e.g. **Engineering—Periodicals**; etc.

    x Magazines; Press; Serials

    xx Journalism; Newspapers

Periodicals—Indexes

    xx Indexes

Periodicity

    See also **Rhythm**; **Time**

    xx Rhythm; Time

Persecution

    See also **Freedom of conscience**; **Jews—Persecutions**; **Martyrs**; **Religious liberty**

    xx Atrocities; Church history; Church history—Primitive and early church; Freedom of conscience; Martyrs; Religious liberty

Persia. *See* **Iran**

Persian rugs. *See* **Rugs, Oriental**

Personal appearance. *See* **Beauty, Personal**; **Grooming for men**

Personal development. *See* **Personality**; **Success**

Personal films. *See* **Experimental films**

Personal finance. *See* **Finance, Personal**

Personal grooming. *See* **Beauty, Personal**; **Grooming for men**

Personal liberty. *See* **Liberty**

Personal names. *See* **Names, Personal**

Personal narratives. *See* subjects with the subdivision *Personal narratives,* e.g. **Opium—Personal narratives**; etc.

Personal radiotelephone. *See* **Citizens radio service (Class D)**

Personality

    See also **Character**; **Individuality**; **Self**; **Soul**

    x Identity, Personal; Personal development

    xx Consciousness; Individuality; Psychology; Soul

Personality disorders

    See also **Hallucinations and illusions**; **Hypnotism**; **Insanity**

    x Consciousness, Multiple; Dual person-

Personality disorders—*Continued*

ality; Frustration; Multiple consciousness

xx Hallucinations and illusions; Hypnotism; Insanity; Mind and body; Psychical research; Psychology, Pathological; Subconsciousness

Personnel classification. *See* **Job analysis**

Personnel management

Use for works dealing with problems of personnel in factories, business, etc., hiring and dismissing employees, and general questions of relationship between officials and employees

See also

Absenteeism (Labor)	**Employment agencies**
Applications for positions	**Factory management**
Counseling	**Foremen**
Efficiency, Industrial	**Job analysis**
	Labor turnover
Employees—Training	**Motion study**
	Office management
Employees' representation in management	**Recruiting of employees**
	Time study

x Employment management; Supervision of employees

xx Efficiency, Industrial; Factory management; Human relations; Industrial management; Industrial relations; Management; Office management

Personnel service in education

See also **Counseling; Dropouts; School psychologists; Vocational guidance**

x Education—Personnel service; Educational guidance; Guidance; Student guidance; Students—Personnel work

xx **Counseling; Vocational guidance**

Persons, Crimes against. *See* **Offenses against the person**

Perspective

See also **Drawing**

x Architectural perspective

xx **Drawing; Geometrical drawing; Geometry, Descriptive; Optics; Painting**

Persuasion (Rhetoric). *See* **Public speaking; Rhetoric**

Pest control

See also **Pesticides;** also names of specific pests with the subdivision *Control,* e.g. **Mosquitoes—Control;** etc.

x Control of pests; Extermination; Pests—Control; Pests—Extermination

xx **Agricultural pests; Zoology, Economic**

Pest control—Biological control

    x Agricultural pests—Biological control;
        Biological control of pests

Pesticide pollution. *See* **Pesticides and the environment**

Pesticides

    See also **Fungicides; Insecticides**

    xx **Agricultural chemistry; Pest control;
        Poisons**

Pesticides and the environment

    x Environment and pesticides; Pesticide
        pollution

    xx **Pollution**

Pesticides and wildlife

    x Wildlife and pesticides

    xx **Wildlife—Conservation**

Pestilences. *See* **Epidemics**

Pests. *See* **Agricultural pests; Fungi; House-
        hold pests; Insects, Injurious and
        beneficial; Parasites; Zoology, Eco-
        nomic;** and names of crops, trees, etc.
        with the subdivision *Diseases and pests*
        (e.g. **Fruit—Diseases and pests;**
        etc.) ; and names of pests, e.g. **Flies;**
        etc.

Pests—Control. *See* **Pest control**

Pests—Extermination. *See* **Pest control**

Petroleum

    See also **Boring; Coal-tar products; Gas-
        oline**

    x Coal oil; Kerosene; Mineral Oil; Oil
        wells

    xx **Gas; Oils and fats; Wells**

Petroleum—Geology

    xx **Geology, Economic; Prospecting**

Petroleum as fuel

    See also **Oil burners**

    x Fuel, Liquid; Fuel oil; Liquid fuel; Oil
        fuel

    xx **Fuel**

Petroleum engines. *See* **Gas and oil engines**

Petroleum industry and trade

Petroleum pollution of water

    x Water—Petroleum pollution

    xx **Water—Pollution**

Petrology

    See also **Crystallography; Geochemistry;
        Geology; Lunar petrology; Mineral-
        ogy; Rocks; Stone;** also varieties of
        rocks, e.g. **Granite; Marble;** etc.

    xx **Geology; Mineralogy; Rocks; Science;
        Stone**

Pets

    See also **Domestic animals;** also names of
        animals, e.g. **Cats; Dogs;** etc.

    xx **Animals; Domestic animals**

Pewter

    xx **Alloys; Plate; Tin**

Phantoms. *See* **Apparitions; Ghosts**

Pharmaceutical chemistry. *See* **Chemistry, Medical and pharmaceutical**

Pharmacodynamics. *See* **Pharmacology**

Pharmacology

Use for works on the action of drugs in general. For action of specific drugs see name of drug with the subdivision *Physiological effect*, e.g. **Opium—Physiological effect**; etc.

See also **Drugs; Pharmacy**

x Medicine—Physiological effect; Pharmacodynamics

xx **Drugs; Materia medica; Medicine; Pharmacy; Physiological chemistry**

Pharmacopoeias. *See* **Materia medica**

Pharmacy

See also **Botany, Medical; Chemistry, Medical and pharmaceutical; Drugs; Materia medica; Pharmacology**

xx **Chemistry; Chemistry, Medical and pharmaceutical; Drugs; Materia medica; Medicine; Pharmacology**

Pharmacy – Laws and legislation

Pheasants

xx **Game and game birds**

Phenomenology

See also **Existentialism**

xx **Philosophy, Modern**

Philanthropists

Philanthropy. *See* **Charities; Charity organization; Endowments; Gifts; Social work**

Philately. *See* **Postage stamps—Collectors and collecting**

Philology. *See* **Language and languages; Philology, Comparative**

Philology, Comparative

Use for comparative studies of languages. General works on the history, philosophy, origin, etc. of languages are entered under **Language and languages**

See also **Language and languages; Literature, Comparative**

x Comparative philology; Language and languages — Comparative philology; Philology

xx **Grammar; Language and languages**

Philosophers (May subdiv. geog. adjective form, e.g. **Philosophers, German**; etc.)

Philosophers, American

x American philosophers; U.S.—Philosophers

Philosophers' stone. *See* **Alchemy**

Philosophy (May subdiv. geog. adjective form, e.g. **Philosophy, French**; etc.)

See also

Belief and doubt	**Free will and determinism**
Empiricism	
Ethics	**Gnosticism**
Fate and fatalism	**God**

Philosophy—*Continued*

Humanism	Positivism
Idealism	Pragmatism
Intuition	Psychology
Knowledge, Theory	Rationalism
of	Realism
Logic	Reality
Materialism	Skepticism
Metaphysics	Soul
Mind and body	Theism
Mysticism	Transcendentalism
Neoplatonism	Truth
Pantheism	Universe

    also general subjects with the subdivision *Philosophy,* e.g. **History—Philosophy;** etc.

    x Mental philosophy

    xx **Humanities; Ontology**

Philosophy, American

    x American philosophy; U.S.—Philosophy

Philosophy, Ancient

    See also **Neoplatonism; Stoics**

    x Ancient philosophy; Greek philosophy, Philosophy, Greek; Philosophy, Roman; Roman philosophy

Philosophy, Greek. *See* **Philosophy, Ancient**

Philosophy, Hindu

    See also **Yoga**

Philosophy, Medieval

    x Medieval philosophy

    xx **Middle Ages**

Philosophy, Modern

    See also **Evolution; Existentialism; Phenomenology**

    x Modern philosophy

Philosophy, Moral. *See* **Ethics**

Philosophy, Roman. *See* **Philosophy, Ancient**

Philosophy and religion

    See also **Religion—Philosophy**

    x Religion and philosophy

    xx **Religion—Philosophy**

Philosophy of history. *See* **History—Philosophy**

Philosophy of religion. *See* **Religion—Philosophy**

Phonetic spelling. *See* **Spelling reform**

Phonetics

    See also **Speech; Voice;** also names of languages with the subdivision *Pronunciation,* e.g. **English language—Pronunciation;** etc.

    x Phonics; Phonology

    xx **Language and languages; Sound; Speech; Voice**

Phonics. *See* **Phonetics**

Phonograph

    See also **Sound—Recording and reproducing**

    x Gramophone; Record players

Phonograph records
> *See also* **Talking books**
> *x* Discography; Records, Phonograph
> *xx* **Audio-visual education; Audio-visual materials**

Phonology. *See* **Phonetics**; and names of languages with the subdivision *Pronunciation,* e.g. **English language—Pronunciation**; etc.

Phosphates
> *xx* **Fertilizers and manures**

Phosphorescence
> *See also* **Bioluminescence**
> *x* Luminescence
> *xx* **Light; Mineralogy; Optics; Radiation; Radioactivity**

Photocopying machines. *See* **Copying processes and machines**

Photoelectric cells
> *See also* **Electronics**
> *x* Electric eye

Photoengraving
> *See also* **Photomechanical processes**
> *x* Half-tone process
> *xx* **Engraving; Photomechanical processes**

Photographic chemistry
> Use for works on the chemical processes employed in photography
> *x* Chemistry, Photographic
> *xx* **Chemistry**

Photographic supplies. *See* **Photography—Equipment and supplies**

Photography
> *See also*

Astronomical photography	Nature photography
Cameras	Photomechanical processes
Color photography	Slides (Photography)
Filmstrips	
Microphotography	Space photography
Moving picture photography	Telephotography

Photography, Aerial
> Includes photography from airplanes, balloons, high buildings, etc.
> *x* Aerial photography

Photography—Equipment and supplies
> *See also* **Cameras**
> *x* Photographic supplies

Photography, Artistic
> *x* Artistic photography; Photography—Esthetics
> *xx* **Art**

Photography, Astronomical. *See* **Astronomical photography**

Photography, Color. *See* **Color photography**

Photography, Commercial
> *x* Commercial photography

Photography—Enlarging
> *x* Enlarging (Photography)

Photography—Esthetics. *See* **Photography, Artistic**

Photography—Handbooks, manuals, etc.
x Handbooks, manuals, etc.

Photography, Immoral. *See* **Pornography**

Photography, Journalistic
x Journalistic photography; News photography

Photography—Lighting

Photography, Medical
x Medical photography
xx **Photography—Scientific applications**

Photography—Moving pictures. *See* **Moving picture photography**

Photography—Portraits
xx Portraits

Photography—Printing processes

Photography—Retouching
x Retouching (Photography)

Photography—Scientific applications
See also specific applications, e.g. **Photography, Medical;** etc.

Photography, Space. *See* **Space photography**

Photography, Stereoscopic
x Stereophotography

Photography, Submarine
x Submarine photography; Underwater photography
xx **Marine biology**

Photography in astronautics. *See* **Space photography**

Photography of animals
Use for works on the technique and accounts of photographing animals. Works consisting of photographs and pictures of animals are entered under **Animals—Pictorial works**
See also **Animal painting and illustration; Animals—Pictorial works**
x Animal photography; Animals—Photography
xx **Animal painting and illustration; Animals—Pictorial works; Nature photography**

Photography of birds
x Bird photography; Birds—Photography
xx **Nature photography**

Photography of fishes
x Fishes—Photography
xx **Nature photography**

Photography of nature. *See* **Nature photography**

Photography of plants
x Plants—Photography
xx **Nature photography**

Photomechanical processes
See also **Photoengraving**
xx **Illustration of books; Photoengraving; Photography**

Photometry
>See also< **Color; Light; Optics**
x Electric light; Light, Electric
xx **Light; Optics**
Photoplays. *See* **Moving picture plays**
Photosynthesis
Phototherapy
>See also< **Radiotherapy; Ultraviolet rays**
x Electric light; Light, Electric
xx **Physical therapy; Radiotherapy; Therapeutics**
Phrenology
See also **Mind and body; Physiognomy**
x Skull
xx **Brain; Head; Mind and body; Physiognomy; Psychology**
Physical anthropology. *See* **Somatology**
Physical chemistry. *See* **Chemistry, Physical and theoretical**
Physical culture. *See* **Physical education and training**
Physical education and training
See also

Athletics	**Gymnastics**
Coaching (Athletics)	**Health education**
Drill (nonmilitary)	**Physical fitness**
Exercise	**Posture**
Games	**Sports**

also names of kinds of exercises, e.g.
Fencing; Judo; etc.
x Calisthenics; Education, Physical; Physical culture; Physical training
xx **Athletics; Education; Exercise; Gymnastics; Hygiene; Sports; Woman—Health and hygiene**
Physical fitness
x Endurance, Physical; Physical stamina; Stamina, Physical
xx **Exercise; Physical education and training**
Physical geography (May subdiv. geog.)
See note under Geography
See also

Climate	**Lakes**
Earth	**Meteorology**
Earthquakes	**Mountains**
Geochemistry	**Ocean**
Geophysics	**Rivers**
Geysers	**Tides**
Glaciers	**Volcanoes**
Ice	**Winds**
Icebergs	

x Geography, Physical; Physiography
xx **Earth; Geography; Geology**
Physical geography—U.S.
x U.S.—Physical geography
Physical stamina. *See* **Physical fitness**

Physical therapy

 See also **Baths; Electrotherapeutics; Hydrotherapy; Massage; Occupational therapy; Phototherapy; Radiotherapy**

 x Physiotherapy

 xx **Therapeutics**

Physical training. *See* **Physical education and training**

Physically handicapped

 See also **Blind; Deaf; Orthopedia**

 x Cripples; Disabled; Handicapped; Invalids; Soldiers, Disabled; War cripples

 xx **Handicapped; Orthopedia**

Physically handicapped—Dwellings

 x Housing for the physically handicapped

Physically handicapped—Rehabilitation

 See also **Occupational therapy**

 x Rehabilitation

Physically handicapped children

 x Children, Crippled; Crippled children

 xx **Handicapped children**

Physicians

 Use for works about several physicians

 See also **Medicine as a profession; Women as physicians;** also names of specialists, e.g. **Radiologists; Surgeons;** etc.

 x Doctors; Medical profession

 xx **Medicine—Biography**

Physicians—Directories

 xx **Directories**

Physicists

 xx **Scientists**

Physics

 See also

Astrophysics	Magnetism
Biophysics	Matter
Chemistry, Physical and theoretical	Mechanics
	Music—Acoustics and physics
Dynamics	
Electricity	Nuclear physics
Electronics	Optics
Ether (of space)	Pneumatics
Gases	Quantum theory
Geophysics	Radiation
Gravitation	Radioactivity
Hydraulics	Relativity (Physics)
Hydrostatics	Sound
Light	Statics
Liquids	Thermodynamics

 xx **Dynamics; Science**

Physics, Astronomical. *See* **Astrophysics**

Physics, Biological. *See* **Biophysics**

Physics, Nuclear. *See* **Nuclear physics**

Physics, Terrestrial. *See* **Geophysics**

Physiognomy

 See also **Face; Phrenology**

 xx **Face; Phrenology; Psychology**

Physiography. *See* **Physical geography**

Physiological chemistry

    See also Biochemistry; Cells; Chemistry, Medical and pharmaceutical; Chemistry, Organic; Digestion; Metabolism; Pharmacology; Poisons; Proteins; Vitamins

    x Animal chemistry; Chemistry, Animal; Chemistry, Pathological; Chemistry, Physiological; Histochemistry; Pathological chemistry

    xx Biochemistry; Chemistry; Pathology; Physiology

Physiological effect. *See* appropriate subjects with the subdivision *Physiological effect,* e.g., **Alcohol—Physiological effect; Opium—Physiological effect;** etc.

Physiological psychology. *See* **Psychology, Physiological**

Physiology

    See also

Anatomy	Old age
Blood	Physiological chem-
Bones	istry
Cells	Psychology, Physio-
Digestion	logical
Fatigue	Reproduction
Growth	Respiration
Muscles	Senses and sensa-
Nervous system	tion
Nutrition	

    also names of organs, e.g. **Heart;** etc.

    x Body, Human; Human body

    xx **Anatomy; Biology; Hygiene; Medicine; Science**

Physiology, Comparative

    x Comparative physiology

    xx **Zoology**

Physiology, Molecular. *See* **Biophysics**

Physiology of plants. *See* **Plant physiology**

Physiotherapy. *See* **Physical therapy**

Pianists

    xx **Musicians**

Piano

Piano—Tuning. *See* **Tuning**

Piano music

    xx **Instrumental music; Music**

Pickling. *See* **Canning and preserving**

Pickup campers. *See* **Travel trailers and campers**

Pictographs. *See* **Picture writing**

Pictorial works. *See* **Pictures;** and subjects with the subdivision *Pictorial works,* e.g. **Animals—Pictorial works;** etc.

Picture frames and framing

    x Framing of pictures

Picture galleries. *See* **Art—Galleries and museums**

Picture posters. *See* **Posters**

Picture writing

    See also **Cave drawings; Hieroglyphics**

    x Pictographs

    xx **Hieroglyphics; Writing**

Pictures

    Use for general works on the study and use of pictures; also for miscellaneous collections of pictures

    See also **Cartoons and caricatures; Engravings; Etchings; Libraries and pictures; Paintings; Portraits;** also subjects with the subdivision *Pictorial works,* e.g. **Animals—Pictorial works; U.S.—History—Civil War—Pictorial works;** etc.; also names of countries, states, etc. with the subdivision *Description and travel—Views,* e.g. **U.S. —Description and travel—Views;** etc.; and names of cities with the subdivision *Description—Views,* e.g. **Chicago—Description—Views;** etc.

    x Pictorial works

    xx **Art**

Pictures, Humorous. *See* **Cartoons and caricatures**

Pigmentation. *See* **Color of animals; Color of man**

Pigments

    See also **Dyes and dyeing; Paint**

    xx **Paint**

Pigmies. *See* **Pygmies**

Pigs

    xx **Hogs**

Pilgrim Fathers

    xx **Christian biography; Puritans; U.S.— History—Colonial period**

Pilgrims and pilgrimages

    See also **Saints; Shrines**

    xx **Shrines; Voyages and travels**

Pilot guides

    x Coast pilot guides

    xx **Navigation; Pilots and pilotage**

Piloting (Aeronautics). *See* **Airplanes—Piloting**

Piloting (Astronautics). *See* **Space vehicles— Piloting**

Pilots, Airplane. *See* **Air pilots**

Pilots and pilotage

    See also **Navigation; Pilot guides**

    xx **Harbors; Navigation; Seamen**

Ping-pong

    x Table tennis

Pioneer life. *See* **Frontier and pioneer life**

Pipe fitting

    See also **Plumbing**

    x Steam fitting

    xx **Plumbing**

Pipe organ. *See* **Organ**

Pipes, Tobacco
    x Tobacco pipes
    xx **Smoking**
Pirates
    See also **Privateering; U.S.—History—Tripolitan War, 1801-1805**
    x Barbary corsairs; Buccaneers; Corsairs; Freebooters
    xx **Crime and criminals; International law; Maritime law; Naval history**
Pistols
    xx **Firearms**
Pity. *See* **Sympathy**
Place names. *See* **Names, Geographical**
Plague
    x Black death; Bubonic plague
Plain chant. *See* **Chants (Plain, Gregorian, etc.)**
Plainsong. *See* **Chants (Plain, Gregorian, etc.)**
Plane geometry. *See* **Geometry**
Plane trigonometry. *See* **Trigonometry**
Planets
    See also **Life on other planets; Solar system; Stars;** also names of planets, e.g. **Venus (Planet);** etc.
    xx **Astronomy; Solar system; Stars**
Planets, Life on other. *See* **Life on other planets**
Planing machines
    xx **Machine tools**
Planned parenthood. *See* **Birth control**
Planning, City. *Cee* **City planning**
Planning, Economic. *See* **Economic policy;** and names of countries, states, etc. with the subdivision *Economic policy,* e.g. **U.S.—Economic policy;** etc.
Planning, National. *See* **Economic policy; Social policy;** and names of countries with the subdivision *Economic policy, Social policy;* e.g. **U.S.—Economic policy; U.S.—Social policy;** etc.
Planning, Regional. *See* **Regional planning**
Plans. *See* **Architectural drawing; Geometrical drawing; Map drawing; Maps; Mechanical drawing**
Plant anatomy. *See* **Botany—Anatomy**
Plant breeding
    Use for works on that form of plant propagation which aims to improve plants, as by selection after controlled mating, etc.
    See also **Fertilization of plants; Plant propagation**
    x Breeding; Hybridization
    xx **Agriculture; Flower gardening; Plant propagation**
Plant chemistry. *See* **Botanical chemistry; Plants—Chemical analysis**
Plant diseases. *See* **Plants—Diseases**
Plant forms in design. *See* **Design, Decorative**

Plant introduction

    x Acclimatization

    xx Botany, Economic

Plant lore

    x Folklore of plants; Plants—Folklore

    xx **Folklore; Natural history; Plant names, Popular; Trees**

Plant names, Popular

    See also **Botany—Terminology; Plant lore**

    x Botany—Nomenclature

    xx **Botany—Terminology**

Plant names, Scientific. *See* **Botany—Terminology**

Plant nutrition. *See* **Plants—Nutrition**

Plant pathology. *See* **Plants—Diseases**

Plant physiology

    See also **Fertilization of plants; Germination; Growth (Plants); Plants—Nutrition**

    x Botany—Physiology; Physiology of plants

    xx **Botany**

Plant propagation

    Use for works on the continuance or multiplication of plants by successive production. Works dealing with methods adopted to secure new and improved varieties are entered under **Plant breeding**

    See also **Grafting; Plant breeding; Seeds**

    x Plants—Propagation; Propagation of plants

    xx **Flower gardening; Fruit culture; Gardening; Nurseries (Horticulture); Plant breeding**

Plantation life

Planting. *See* **Agriculture; Gardening; Landscape gardening; Tree planting**

Plants

    See also

Alpine plants	Gardening
Climbing plants	Geographical distribution of animals
Desert plants	and plants
Fertilization of	House plants
plants	Marine plants
Flower gardening	Poisonous plants
Flowers	Shrubs
Forage plants	Weeds
Fresh-water plants	

    also names of plants (e.g. **Ferns; Mosses;** etc.) ; and headings beginning with the words **Plant** and **Plants**

    x Flora; Vegetable kingdom

    xx **Botany; Flowers; Gardening; Trees**

Plants—Anatomy. *See* **Botany—Anatomy**

Plants—Chemical analysis

    See also **Botanical chemistry**

    x Plant chemistry

    xx **Botanical chemistry**

Plants—Collection and preservation
> *x* Botanical specimens—Collection and preservation; Herbaria; Preservation of botanical specimens; Specimens, Preservation of

Plants, Cultivated (May subdiv. geog.)
> *See also* **Annuals (Plants); House plants; Plants, Edible; Plants, Ornamental**
> *xx* **Gardening**

Plants, Cultivated—U.S.
> *x* U.S.—Plants, Cultivated

Plants—Diseases
> *See also* names of crops, etc. with the subdivision *Diseases and pests,* e.g. **Fruit—Diseases and pests;** etc.
> *x* Botany—Pathology; Diseases and pests; Diseases of plants; Garden pests; Pathological botany; Pathology, Vegetable; Plant diseases; Plant pathology; Vegetable pathology
> *xx* **Agricultural pests; Fungi**

Plants—Ecology. *See* **Botany—Ecology**

Plants, Edible
> *x* Edible plants; Food plants; Plants, Useful
> *xx* **Botany, Economic; Plants, Cultivated**

Plants, Extinct. *See* **Plants, Fossil**

Plants—Fertilization. *See* **Fertilization of plants**

Plants—Folklore. *See* **Plant lore**

Plants, Fossil
> *x* Botany, Fossil; Extinct plants; Fossil plants; Paleobotany; Plants, Extinct
> *xx* **Botany; Fossils**

Plants—Geographical distribution. *See* **Geographical distribution of animals and plants**

Plants—Growth. *See* **Growth (Plants)**

Plants, Medicinal. *See* **Botany, Medical**

Plants—Nutrition
> *x* Nutrition of plants; Plant nutrition
> *xx* **Plant physiology**

Plants, Ornamental
> *x* Ornamental plants
> *xx* **Flower gardening; Landscape gardening; Plants, Cultivated; Shrubs**

Plants—Photography. *See* **Photography of plants**

Plants—Propagation. *See* **Plant propagation**

Plants—Soilless culture
> *x* Agriculture, Soilless; Chemiculture; Hydroponics; Soilless agriculture; Water farming

Plants, Useful. *See* **Botany, Economic; Plants, Edible**

Plants in art
> *See also* **Flower painting and illustration**
> *x* Flowers in art; Trees in art
> *xx* **Art; Decoration and ornament**

Plaster and plastering
>See also Cement; Concrete; Mortar;
>>Stucco
>x Plastering
>xx Masonry

Plaster casts
>x Casting; Casts, Plaster
>xx Sculpture

Plaster of paris. See Gypsum
Plastering. See Plaster and plastering
Plastic materials. See Plastics
Plastic surgery. See Surgery, Plastic

Plastics
>See also Chemistry, Organic—Synthesis;
>>Gums and resins; Rubber, Artificial;
>>Synthetic products; also names of
>>plastics
>x Plastic materials
>xx Chemistry, Organic—Synthesis; Poly-
>>mers and polymerization; Synthetic
>>products

Plate
>See also Hallmarks; Pewter; Sheffield
>>plate
>x Gold plate
>xx Goldsmithing;   Hallmarks;   Silver-
>>smithing

Plate-metal work
>xx Metalwork; Sheet-metal work

Play
>See also Amusements; Games; Recrea-
>>tion; Sports
>xx Amusements; Child study; Children;
>>Games; Recreation

Play centers. See Community centers; Play-
>grounds

Play direction (Theater). See Theater—Pro-
>duction and direction

Play production. See Amateur theatricals;
>Moving picture plays; Theater—Pro-
>duction and direction

Play writing. See Drama—Technique; Mov-
>ing picture plays; Radio plays—
>Technique; Television plays—Tech-
>nique

Playgrounds
>See also Community centers; Parks; Va-
>>cation schools
>x Play   centers;   Public   playgrounds;
>>School playgrounds
>xx Child welfare; Children; Community
>>centers; Parks; Recreation; Social
>>settlements

Playhouses. See Theaters
Playing cards. See Cards
Plays. See Drama—Collections; One-act plays
Plays, Bible. See Religious drama
Plays, Christmas. See Christmas plays
Plays, College. See College and school drama
>—Collections

Plays, Community. *See* **Community plays**

Plays for children. *See* **Children's plays**

Playwrights. *See* **Dramatists**

Playwriting. *See* **Drama—Technique; Moving picture plays; Radio plays—Technique; Television plays—Technique**

Pleasure

> *See also* **Happiness; Pain**
>
> *xx* **Emotions; Happiness; Joy and sorrow; Pain; Senses and sensation**

Plots (Drama, fiction, etc.)

> Use for works dealing with the construction and analysis of plots as a literary technique. Collections of plots are entered under **Literature—Stories, plots, etc.**
>
> *See also* literary or musical forms with the subdivision *Stories, plots, etc.* e.g. **Ballets—Stories, plots, etc.; Operas —Stories, plots, etc.**; etc.
>
> *x* Drama—Plot; Dramatic plots; Fiction— Plots; Novels—Plots; Scenarios
>
> *xx* **Authorship; Characters and characteristics in literature; Drama; Fiction; Literature**

Plows

> *xx* **Agricultural machinery**

Plumbing

> *See also* **Drainage, House; Gas fitting; Pipe fitting; Sanitary engineering; Sanitation, Household; Sewerage; Solder and soldering**
>
> *xx* **Drainage, House; Gas fitting; Pipe fitting; Sanitation, Household**

Pluto operation. *See* **Cuba—History—Invasion, 1961**

Plywood

> *xx* **Wood**

Pneumatic transmission. *See* **Compressed air**

Pneumatics

> *See also* **Aerodynamics; Compressed air; Gases; Ground cushion** phenomena; **Sound**
>
> *xx* **Gases; Physics**

Pneumonia

> *xx* **Lungs—Diseases**

Poetics

> Use for works on the art and technique of poetry. Works on the appreciation and philosophy of poetry are entered under **Poetry**
>
> *See also* **Rhyme; Rhythm; Versification**
>
> *x* Poetry—Technique

Poetry

> See note under **Poetics**
>
> Names of all types of poetry are not included in this list but are to be added as needed

Poetry—*Continued*

  See also

Ballads	Hymns
Children in	Love poetry
poetry	Nature in poetry
Eddas	Parody
Epic poetry	Scalds and scal-
Free verse	dic poetry

    also **American poetry; English poetry;** etc.; and general subjects, names of historical events, places and famous persons with the subdivision *Poetry,* e.g. **Animals—Poetry; Bunker Hill, Battle of, 1775—Poetry; Chicago— Poetry; Shakespeare, William—Po- etry;** etc.

  x Poetry—Philosophy

  xx **Esthetics; Literature; Versification**

Poetry—Collections

  See also **American poetry—Collections; English poetry—Collections;** etc.; also **Children's poetry; Christmas poetry; Negro poetry; Nonsense verses; Parodies; Patriotic poetry; Religious poetry; School verse; Sea poetry; Songs; War poetry**

  x Collections of literature; Poetry—Selec- tions; Rhymes

  xx **Literature—Collections**

Poetry—History and criticism

  See also **American poetry—History and criticism; English poetry—History and criticism;** etc.

Poetry—Philosophy. *See* **Poetry**

Poetry—Selections. *See* **Poetry—Collections**

Poetry—Technique. *See* **Poetics**

Poetry and music. *See* **Music and literature**

Poetry for children. *See* **Children's poetry; Nursery rhymes**

Poetry of love. *See* **Love poetry**

Poetry of nature. *See* **Nature in poetry**

Poets (May subdiv. geog. adjective form, e.g. **Poets, German;** etc.)

  Use for works dealing with the personal lives of several poets. Works about their literary productions are entered under **Poetry—History and criticism; English poetry—History and criti- cism;** etc.

  See also **Dramatists; Minstrels; Scalds and scaldic poetry; Troubadours**

  xx **Authors**

Poets, American

  x American poets; U.S.—Poets

Point Four program. *See* **Reconstruction (1939-1951)**

Poison gases. *See* **Gases, Asphyxiating and poisonous**

Poisonous plants

> *xx* **Botany, Economic; Chemistry, Medical and pharmaceutical; Plants; Poisons**

Poisons

> *See also* **Pesticides; Poisonous plants**
>
> *x* Antidotes; Toxicology; Venom
>
> *xx* **Accidents; Chemistry; Chemistry, Medical and pharmaceutical; Drugs; Materia medica; Medical jurisprudence; Physiological chemistry**

Polar expeditions. *See* **Antarctic regions; Arctic regions; North Pole; Polar regions; Scientific expeditions; South Pole**; and names of exploring expeditions, and names of explorers

Polar lights. *See* **Auroras**

Polar regions

> Use for works dealing with both the Antarctic and Arctic regions
>
> *See also* **Antarctic regions; Arctic regions; North Pole; South Pole**
>
> *x* Polar expeditions

Police (May subdiv. geog. country or state)

> *See also* **Crime and criminals; Criminal investigation; Detectives; Secret service**; also names of cities with the subdivision *Police,* e.g. **Chicago—Police;** etc.
>
> *xx* **Crime and criminals; Criminal investigation; Detectives; Law; Law enforcement**

Police, International. *See* **International police**

Police, State

> *x* State police

Police—U.S.

> *x* U.S.—Police

Policewomen

> *x* Women as police

Polio. *See* **Poliomyelitis**

Poliomyelitis

> *x* Infantile paralysis; Paralysis, Anterior spinal; Paralysis, Infantile; Polio; Spinal paralysis, Anterior

Poliomyelitis vaccine

> *x* Live poliovirus vaccine; Sabine vaccine; Salk vaccine

Polishing. *See* **Grinding and polishing**

Politeness. *See* **Courtesy; Etiquette**

Political assessments. *See* **Campaign funds**

Political behavior. *See* **Political psychology**

Political conventions

> *See also* **Political parties; Primaries**
>
> *x* Conventions, Political
>
> *xx* **Political parties; Political science**

Political corruption. *See* **Corruption (in politics)**

Political crimes and offenses

> *See also* **Anarchism and anarchists; Assassination; Concentration camps;**

414

Political crimes and offenses—*Continued*
>
> Corruption (in politics); Government, Resistance to; Political prisoners; Treason

x Crimes, Political; Sedition

xx Political ethics; Subversive activities

Political economy. *See* Economics

Political ethics
>
> *See also* Citizenship; Corruption (in politics); Government, Resistance to; Political crimes and offenses

x Ethics, Political

xx Ethics; Political science; Social ethics

Political geography. *See* Boundaries

Political parties
>
> *See also* Political conventions; Politics, Practical; Right and left (Political science) also names of parties, e.g. Democratic Party; Republican Party; etc.

x Parties, Political

xx Political conventions; Political science

Political parties—Finance. *See* Campaign funds

Political prisoners

x Prisoners, Political

xx Political crimes and offenses; Prisons

Political psychology
>
> *See also* Propaganda; Public opinion

x Political behavior; Politics, Practical—Psychology; Psychology, Political

xx Political science; Psychology; Social psychology

Political refugees. *See* Refugees, Political

Political science
>
> *See also*

Anarchism and anarchists	Liberty
Aristocracy	Local government
Church and state	Monarchy
Citizenship	Municipal government
Civil rights	Nationalism
Civil service	Political conventions
Communism	Political ethics
Constitutional history	Political parties
Constitutional law	Political psychology
Constitutions	Politics, Practical
Constitutions, State	Power (Social sciences)
Democracy	
Executive power	Public administration
Federal government	
Geopolitics	Representative government and representation
Government, Resistance to	
Government ownership	Republics
	Revolutions
Imperialism	Right and left (Political science)
Kings and rulers	
Law	Socialism
Legislation	The State

415

Political science—*Continued*

State governments	Taxation
State rights	Utopias
Suffrage	World politics

also names of countries and states with the subhead *Constitution* (e.g. **U.S. Constitution;** etc.) ; also names of countries, cities, etc. with the subdivision *Politics and government,* e.g. **U.S.—Politics and government;** etc.

x Administration; Civics; Civil government; The Commonwealth; Government

xx **Constitutional history; Constitutional law; History; Social sciences; The State**

Politics. *See* names of continents, or groups of countries that have common political problems, with the subdivision *Politics,* e.g. **Asia—Politics; Latin America—Politics;** etc.; and names of countries, states, counties, cities with the subdivision *Politics and government,* e.g. **U.S—Politics and government; Chicago—Politics and government;** etc.

Politics, Corruption in. *See* **Corruption (in politics)**

Politics, Practical

Use for works dealing with practical politics in general, such as electioneering, political machines, etc. Works on the science of politics are entered under **Political science**

See also **Campaign funds; Campaign literature; Corruption (in politics); Elections; Lobbying; Primaries; Television in politics;** also names of countries, cities, etc. with the subdivision *Politics and government* (e.g. **U.S.—Politics and government;** etc.) ; also classes of people with the subdivision *Political activity,* e.g. **College students—Political activity; Students—Political activity;** etc. and headings beginning with the word **Political**

x Campaigns, Political; Electioneering; Practical politics

xx **Political parties; Political science**

Politics, Practical—Psychology. *See* **Political psychology**

Politics and Christianity. *See* **Christianity and politics**

Politics and students. *See* **Students—Political activity**

Poll tax. *See* **Taxation**

Pollination. *See* **Fertilization of plants**

Polls, Election. *See* **Elections**

Polls, Public opinion. *See* **Public opinion polls**

Pollution

> *See also* **Air—Pollution; Marine pollution; Noise pollution; Pesticides and the environment; Radioactive fallout; Water—Pollution** and similar headings

> *x* Contamination of the environment; Environmental pollution

> *xx* **Environmental policy; Factory and trade wastes; Man—Influence on nature; Public health; Sanitary engineering; Sanitation**

Pollution control devices. (Motor vehicles). *See* **Automobiles—Pollution control devices**

Pollution of air. *See* **Air—Pollution**

Pollution of water. *See* **Water—Pollution**

Poltergeists. *See* **Ghosts**

Polyglot dictionaries. *See* **Dictionaries, Polyglot**

Polymers and polymerization

> *See also* **Plastics**

> *xx* **Chemistry, Organic—Synthesis; Chemistry, Physical and theoretical**

Ponies

> *xx* **Horses**

Pontiac's Conspiracy, 1763-1765

> *xx* **Indians of North America—Wars; U.S.—History—Colonial period; U.S.—History—French and Indian War, 1755-1763**

Pony express

> *xx* **Express service; Postal service**

Poor. *See* **Poverty;** and names of cities with the subdivision *Poor,* e.g. **Chicago—Poor;** etc.

Poor relief. *See* **Charities; Economic assistance, Domestic; Public welfare**

Popes

> *See also* **Papacy**

> *x* Holy See

> *xx* **Christian biography; Church history; Papacy**

Popes—Infallibility

> *x* Infallibility of the Pope

Popes—Temporal power

> *See also* **Church and state**

> *x* Temporal power of the Pope

> *xx* **Church and state; Church history—Middle Ages**

Popular government. *See* **Democracy**

Popular music. *See* **Music, Popular (Songs, etc.)**

Popularity

> *xx* **Sociometry**

Population

> *See also* **Birth control; Birth rate; Census; Eugenics; Migration, Internal; Mortality;** also names of countries, cities, etc. with the subdivision *Pop-*

417

Population—*Continued*

 ulation, e.g. **U.S.—Population; Chicago—Population;** etc.

 xx **Birth rate; Economics; Human ecology; Sociology; Vital statistics**

Population, Foreign. *See* **Immigration and emigration;** names of countries with the subdivision *Immigration and emigration* (e.g. **U.S.—Immigration and emigration;** etc.) ; and names of countries, cities, etc. with the subdivision *Foreign population,* e.g. **U.S.—Foreign population; Chicago—Foreign population;** etc.

Porcelain

 See also **China painting**

 x China (Porcelain) ; Chinaware ; Dishes

 xx **Pottery**

Porcelain enamels. *See* **Enamel and enameling**

Porcelain painting. *See* **China painting**

Pornography

 x Art, Immoral ; Immoral art ; Immoral literature ; Literature, Immoral ; Obscene literature ; Photography, Immoral

 xx **Obscenity (Law)**

Portland cement. *See* **Cement**

Portrait painting

 See also **Crayon drawing; Figure painting; Miniature painting; Pastel drawing**

 xx **Figure painting; Miniature painting; Painting**

Portraits

 See also **Cartoons and caricatures; Photography—Portraits;** also headings for collective and individual biography with the subdivision *Portraits,* e.g. **U.S.—Biography—Portraits; Musicians—Portraits; Shakespeare, William—Portraits;** etc.

 x Iconography

 xx **Art; Biography; Paintings; Pictures**

Ports. *See* **Harbors**

Portuguese language

Portuguese literature

 See also **Brazilian literature**

 xx **Brazilian literature**

Positivism

 See also **Agnosticism; Idealism; Materialism; Pragmatism; Realism**

 x Humanity, Religion of ; Religion of humanity

 xx **Agnosticism; Deism; Philosophy; Rationalism; Realism**

Post-impressionism. *See* **Postimpressionism (Art)**

Post office. *See* **Postal service**

Postage stamps

 x Stamps, Postage

Postage stamps—Collectors and collecting

    x Collection of objects; Philately

    xx **Collectors and collecting**

Postal service (May subdiv. geog.)   *n. D.*

    See also **Air mail service; Pony express; Postal savings banks; Railway mail service**

    x Mail service; Parcel post; Post office; U.S.—Mail

    xx **Communication; Transportation**

Postal service—U.S.

    x U.S.—Mail; U.S.—Postal service

Posters

    See also **Signs and signboards**

    x Advertising, Pictorial; Picture posters

    xx **Advertising; Commercial art; Signs signboards**

Postimpressionism (Art)

    See also **Cubism; Expressionism (Art); Futurism (Art); Impressionism (Art); Surrealism**

    x Post-impressionism

    xx **Art, Modern—19th century; Cubism; Expressionism (Art); Futurism (Art); Impressionism (Art); Painting**

Posture

    xx **Physical education and training**

Potash

    xx **Fertilizers and manures**

Potatoes

    xx **Vegetables**

Potters

    xx **Artists**

Pottery (May subdiv. geog. adjective form, e.g. **Pottery, Chinese;** etc.)

    See also **Glazes; Porcelain; Terra cotta; Tiles; Vases**

    x Crockery; Dishes; Earthenware; Faience; Fayence; Stoneware

    xx **Archeology; Art, Decorative; Art objects; Arts and crafts; Ceramics; Clay industries; Decoration and ornament; Tableware; Vases**

Pottery, American

    x American pottery; U.S.—Pottery

Pottery—Marks

    x Marks, Potters'

Poultry

    See also names of domesticated birds, **e.g. Ducks; Geese; Turkeys;** etc.

    xx **Domestic animals; Food**

Poverty

    See also **Charities; Public welfare;** also names of countries with the subdivisions *Economic conditions* and *Social conditions* (e.g. **U.S.—Economic conditions; U.S.—Social conditions;** etc.); also names of cities with the

Poverty—*Continued*

    subdivision *Poor,* e.g. **Chicago—Poor;** etc.

    x Destitution; Pauperism; Poor

    xx **Economic assistance, Domestic; Wealth**

Powder, Smokeless. *See* **Gunpowder**

Powdered milk. *See* **Milk, Dried**

Power (Mechanics)

    See note under **Power resources**

    See also **Compressed air; Electric power; Force and energy; Machinery; Power resources; Power transmission; Steam; Water power**

    xx **Mechanical engineering; Mechanics; Steam engineering**

Power (Social sciences)

    xx **Political science**

Power boats. *See* **Motorboats**

Power blackouts. *See* **Electric power failures**

Power failures. *See* **Electric power failures**

Power plants

    See also **Atomic power plants; Electric power plants; Steam power plants**

    x Power stations

Power plants, Atomic. *See* **Atomic power plants**

Power plants, Electric. *See* **Electric power plants**

Power plants, Steam. *See* **Steam power plants**

Power politics. *See* **Balance of power; World politics—1945-1965; World politics, 1965-**

Power resources

    Use for works on the available sources of mechanical power in general. Works on the physics and engineering aspects of power are entered under **Power (Mechanics)**

    See also **Electric power; Fuel; Solar energy; Water power**

    x Power supply

    xx **Natural resources; Power (Mechanics)**

Power stations. *See* **Power plants**

Power supply. *See* **Power resources**

Power tools

    xx **Tools**

Power transmission

    See also **Belts and belting; Cables; Electric power distribution; Gearing; Machinery**

    x Transmission of power

    xx **Belts and belting; Machinery; Mechanical engineering; Power (Mechanics)**

Power transmission, Electric. *See* **Electric lines; Electric power distribution**

Practical nurses and nursing

    xx **Nurses nd nursing**

Practical politics. *See* **Politics, Practical**

Practice teaching. *See* **Student teaching**

Pragmatism

    See also **Empiricism; Reality; Truth; Utilitarianism**

    xx **Empiricism; Knowledge, Theory of; Philosophy; Positivism; Realism; Reality; Truth; Utilitarianism**

Prairies

Prayer

    See also **Devotional exercises; Prayers**

    x Devotion

    xx **Christian life; Devotional exercises; Prayers; Worship**

Prayer meetings

Prayers

    See also **Jesus Christ—Prayers; Prayer**

    x Collects; Theology, Devotional

    xx **Prayer**

Prayers in the public schools. *See* **Religion in the public schools**

Preachers. *See* **Clergy**

Preachers' wives. *See* **Clergymen's wives**

Preaching

    See also **Sermons**

    x Speaking

    xx **Public speaking; Rhetoric; Sermons; Pastoral work**

Preaching friars. *See* **Dominicans**

Precious metals

    See also **Gold; Silver**

    xx **Currency question; Metals; Mines and mineral resources**

Precious stones

    Use for mineralogical and technological works on the subject. Works treating of stones and jewels from the point of view of art are entered under **Gems**

    See also **Gems**; also names of precious stones, e.g. **Diamonds**; etc.

    x Jewels; Stones, Precious

    xx **Gems; Mineralogy**

Precocious children. *See* **Gifted children**

Predestination

    See also **Free will and determinism**

    x Election (Theology); Foreordination

    xx **Calvinism; Fate and fatalism; Theology**

Predictions. *See* **Prophecies**

Prefabricated houses

    x Demountable houses; Dwellings; Houses, Prefabricated; Packaged houses

    xx **Architecture, Domestic; Buildings, Prefabricated**

Pregnancy

    See also **Childbirth**

    xx **Childbirth; Reproduction**

Prehistoric animals. *See* **Fossils**

Prehistoric art. *See* **Art, Primitive**

Prehistoric man. *See* **Man, Prehistoric**

Prehistory. *See* **Archeology; Bronze age; Iron age; Stone age;** and names of countries, cities, etc. with the subdivision *Antiquities,* e.g. **U.S.—Antiquities;** etc.

Prejudices and antipathies
    x Antipathies
    xx **Emotions; Human relations; Race awareness**

Prepaid medical care. *See* **Insurance, Health**

Pre-Raphaelitism
    xx **Painting**

Presbyterian Church
    x Religious denominations

Preschool education. *See* **Nursery schools**

Presents. *See* **Gifts**

Preservation of botanical specimens. *See* **Plants—Collection and preservation**

Preservation of buildings. *See* **Architecture—Conservation and restoration**

Preservation of food. *See* **Food—Preservation**

Preservation of forests. *See* **Forests and forestry**

Preservation of historical records. *See* **Archives**

Preservation of natural resources. *See* **Conservation of natural resources**

Preservation of natural scenery. *See* **Landscape protection; Natural monuments; Nature conservation; Wilderness areas**

Preservation of organs, tissues, etc.
    See also **Transplantation of organs, tissues, etc.**
    x Organ preservation; Organs, Preservation

Preservation of wildlife. *See* **Wildlife—Conservation**

Preservation of wood. *See* **Wood—Preservation**

Preservation of works of art. *See* subjects with the subdivision *Conservation and restoration,* e.g. **Paintings—Conservation and restoration;** etc.

Preservation of zoological specimens. *See* **Zoological specimens—Collection and preservation**

Preserving. *See* **Canning and preserving**

Presidential libraries. *See* **Presidents—U.S.—Archives;** and names of libraries

Presidents
    See also **Executive power; Presidents—U.S.;** also names of other countries with the subdivision *Presidents* (e.g. **Mexico—Presidents;** etc.) ; and names of presidents
    xx **Executive power; Kings and rulers**

Presidents—Powers and duties. *See* **Executive power**

Presidents—U.S.

When applicable, the following subdivisions may be used under names of presidents

For works on presidents of other countries, use names of countries with the subdivision *Presidents,* e.g. **Mexico—Presidents**; etc.

See also names of presidents, e.g. **Kennedy, John Fitzgerald, Pres. U.S.;** etc.

x U.S.—Presidents

xx **Presidents**

Presidents—U.S.—Addresses and essays

See also **Presidents—U.S.—Inaugural addresses**

Presidents—U.S.—Archives

See also names of libraries, e.g. **Harry S. Truman Library, Independence, Mo.;** etc.

x Libraries, Presidential; Presidential libraries

Presidents—U.S.—Assassination

xx **Assassination**

Presidents—U.S.—Children

Presidents—U.S.—Election

x Campaigns, Presidential; Electoral college

xx **Elections**

Presidents—U.S.—Family

Presidents—U.S.—Funeral and memorial services

x Presidents—U.S.—Memorial services

Presidents—U.S.—Health

x Presidents—U.S.—Illness

Presidents—U.S.—Illness. *See* **Presidents—U.S.—Health**

Presidents—U.S.—Inability. *See* **Presidents—U.S.—Succession**

Presidents—U.S.—Inaugural addresses

xx Presidents—U.S.—Addresses and essays; Presidents—U.S.—Inauguration

Presidents—U.S.—Inauguration

See also **Presidents—U.S.—Inaugural addresses**

Presidents—U.S.—Medals

Presidents—U.S.—Memorial services. *See* **Presidents—U.S.—Funeral and memorial services**

Presidents—U.S.—Messages

x Messages to Congress; Presidents—U.S.—State of the Union messages; State of the Union messages

Presidents—U.S.—Nomination

x Nomination of presidents

Presidents—U.S.—Portraits

Presidents—U.S.—Power

See **Executive power—U.S.**

Presidents—U.S.—Protection

Presidents—U.S.—Quotations

xx **Quotations**

Presidents—U.S.—Religion
Presidents—U.S.—Sports
Presidents—U.S.—Staff
   xx **U.S.—Executive departments**
Presidents—U.S.—State of the Union messages.
   See **Presidents—U.S.—Messages**
Presidents—U.S.—Succession
   x Presidents—U.S.—Inability
Presidents—U.S.—Tomb
Presidents—U.S.—Travel
Presidents—U.S.—Wives
   x Presidents' wives; Wives of presidents
   xx **Women in the U.S.**
Presidents' wives. *See* **Presidents—U.S.—
   Wives**
Press. *See* **Freedom of the press; Journalism;
   News agencies; Newspapers; Period-
   icals; Underground press**
Press, Underground. *See* **Underground press**
Press and government. *See* **Government and
   the press**
Press censorship. *See* **Freedom of the press**
Press clippings. *See* **Clippings (Books, news-
   papers, etc.)**
Press working of metal. *See* **Sheet-metal work**
Pressure groups. *See* **Lobbying**
Pressure suits. *See* **Astronauts—Clothing**
Prevention of accidents. *See* **Accidents—Pre-
   vention**
Prevention of crime. *See* **Crime prevention**
Prevention of cruelty to animals. *See* **Animals
   —Treatment**
Prevention of fire. *See* **Fire prevention**
Prevention of smoke. *See* **Smoke prevention**
Preventive medicine. *See* **Bacteriology; Hy-
   giene; Immunity; Public health**
Price controls. *See* **Wage-price policy**
Price-wage policy. *See* **Wage-price policy**
Prices
   See also **Cost and standard of living;
   Farm produce—Marketing; Wage-
   price policy; Wages;** also subjects
   with the subdivision *Prices,* e.g. Art—
   Prices; Books—Prices; etc.
   xx **Commerce; Consumption (Econom-
   ics); Cost and standard of living;
   Economics; Finance; Manufactures;
   Wages**
Priests
   See also **Ex-priests**
   x Pastors
   xx **Clergy; Catholic Church—Clergy**
Primaries
   See also **Elections**
   x Direct primaries; Elections, Primary
   xx **Elections; Political conventions; Politics, Practical; Representative government and representation**
Primary education. *See* **Education, Elementary**

Primates
>   *See also* **Man; Monkeys**
>   *xx* **Mammals**

Primers
>   *See also* **Alphabet books; Hornbooks**
>   *xx* **Readers**

Primitive art. *See* **Art, Primitive**

Primitive Christianity. *See* **Church history—Primitive and early church**

Primitive man. *See* **Man, Primitive**

Primitive religion. *See* **Religion, Primitive**

Primitive society. *See* **Society, Primitive**

Princes and princesses
>   *x* Royalty

Printing
>   *See also* **Advertising layout and typography; Books; Color printing; Electrotyping; Linotype; Offset printing; Proofreading; Type and type founding; Typesetting**
>   *x* Layout and typography; Typography
>   *xx* **Bibliography; Book industries and trade; Books; Graphic arts; Industrial arts; Publishers and publishing; Typesetting**

Printing—Exhibitions
>   *See also* **Book industries and trade—Exhibitions**
>   *x* Books—Exhibitions
>   *xx* **Book industries and trade—Exhibitions; Exhibitions**

Printing, Offset. *See* **Offset printing**

Printing—Specimens
>   *See also* **Type and type founding**
>   *x* Type specimens
>   *xx* **Advertising; Initials; Type and type founding**

Printing—Style manuals
>   *See also* **Authorship—Handbooks, manuals, etc.**
>   *x* Style manuals
>   *xx* **Authorship—Handbooks, manuals, etc.**

Printing, Textile. *See* **Textile printing**

Printing as a trade

Prints (May subdiv. geog. adjective form)
>   *See also* **Engravings; Etchings; Lithography**
>   *xx* **Graphic arts**

Prints, American
>   *x* American prints; U.S.—Prints

Prison escapes. *See* **Escapes**

Prison labor. *See* **Convict labor**

Prison schools. *See* **Education of prisoners**

Prisoners—Education. *See* **Education of prisoners**

Prisoners, Political. *See* **Political prisoners**

Prisoners of war (May subdiv. geog. adjective form)
>   *See also* **Concentration camps;** also names of wars with the subdivision *Prisons*

Prisoners of war—*Continued*

 and prisoners, e.g. **World War, 1939-1945—Prisons and prisoners;** etc.

 x Exchange of prisoners of war; **POW;** War prisoners

✓**Prisons** (May subdiv. geog.)

 See also **Convict labor; Crime and criminals; Criminal law; Education of prisoners; Escapes; Penal colonies; Political prisoners; Probation; Reformatories;** also names of prisons

 x Convicts; Correctional institutions; Dungeons; Imprisonment; Jails; Penal institutions; Penitentiaries; Penology

 xx **Convict labor; Crime and criminals; Punishment**

Prisons—U.S.

 x U.S.—Prisons

Privacy, Right of

 See also **Eavesdropping**

 x Invasion of privacy; Right of privacy

 xx **Libel and slander**

Private schools

 See also **Church schools**

 x Boarding schools; Nonpublic schools; Secondary schools

 xx **Education, Secondary; Schools**

Private theatricals. *See* **Amateur theatricals**

Privateering

 See also **Neutrality**

 x Letters of marque

 xx **International law; Naval art and science; Naval history; Pirates**

Prize fighting. *See* **Boxing**

Prizes (Rewards). *See* **Rewards (Prizes, etc.);** and names of prizes

Probabilities

 See also **Sampling (Statistics)**

 x Certainty; Fortune

 xx **Algebra; Gambling; Insurance, Life; Logic; Statistics**

Probation

 See also **Juvenile courts; Parole**

 x Reform of criminals; Suspended sentence

 xx **Criminal law; Juvenile courts; Parole; Prisons; Punishment; Reformatories; Social case work**

Probes, Space. *See* **Space probes**

Problem children

 Use for works on children with behavior difficulties caused by emotional instability or social environment

 See also **Juvenile delinquency**

 x Behavior problems (Children); Children, Emotionally disturbed; Emotionally disturbed children; Maladjusted children

 xx **Child study; Children—Management; Exceptional children**

Processing (Libraries)

> See also **Acquisitions (Libraries)**; **Cataloging**; **Classifications—Books**
>
> x Centralized processing (Libraries); Libraries—Technical services; Library processing; Technical services (Libraries)
>
> xx **Library science**

Processions. See **Parades**

Production. See **Economics**; **Industry**

Production engineering. See **Factory management**

Products, Commercial. See **Commercial products**

Products, Dairy. See **Dairy products**

Products, Waste. See **Waste products**

Profession, Choice of. See **Vocational guidance**

Professional associations. See **Trade and professional associations**

Professional education

> See also **Colleges and universities**; **Library education**; **Technical education**; **Vocational education**; also names of professions with the subdivision *Study and teaching,* e.g. **Medicine—Study and teaching**; etc.
>
> x Education, Professional
>
> xx **Education**; **Education, Higher**; **Learning and scholarship**; **Technical education**; **Vocational education**

Professional ethics

> See also **Business ethics**; **Legal ethics**; **Medical ethics**
>
> x Ethics, Professional
>
> xx **Ethics**

Professions

> See also **Occupations**; **Vocational guidance**; also names of professions (e.g. **Law**; **Medicine**; etc.); also **Law as a profession**; **Music as a profession**, and similar headings
>
> x Careers; Jobs; Vocations
>
> xx **Occupations**; **Vocational guidance**

Professors. See **Teachers**

Profit

> See also **Capitalism**; **Income**
>
> xx **Business**; **Capital**; **Economics**; **Income**; **Wealth**

Profit sharing

> See also **Cooperation**
>
> xx **Commerce**; **Cooperation**; **Wages**

Programmed instruction

> See also **Teaching machines**; also subjects with the subdivision *Programmed instruction,* e.g. **Trigonometry—Programmed instruction**; etc.
>
> x Programmed textbooks
>
> xx **Teaching—Aids and devices**

Programmed textbooks. See **Programmed instruction**

Programming (Electronic computers)

> *See also* Computer programs; Programming languages (Electronic computers); also subjects with the subdivision *Computer programs*, e.g. **Oceanography—Computer programs**; etc.
>
> *x* Computer programming; Computer software; Computers—Programming; Software, Computer
>
> *xx* **Electronic data processing**

Programming languages (Electronic computers)

> *See also* specific languages, e.g. **FORTRAN (Computer program language)**; etc.
>
> *x* Autocodes; Automatic programming languages; Computer program languages; Computer software; Machine language; Software, Computer
>
> *xx* **Electronic data processing; Language and languages; Programming (Electronic computers)**

Programs, Computer. *See* **Computer programs**

Programs, School assembly. *See* **School assembly programs**

Progress

> *See also* **Civilization; Science and civilization; Social change; War and civilization**
>
> *xx* **Civilization**

Progressive education. *See* **Education—Experimental methods**

Prohibited books. *See* **Books—Censorship**

Prohibition

> Use for works dealing with the legal prohibition of liquor traffic and liquor manufacture
>
> *See also* **Liquor problem; Temperance**
>
> *xx* **Liquor problem; Temperance**

Project method in teaching

> *xx* **Teaching**

Project Apollo. *See* **Apollo project**

Project Gemini. *See* **Gemini project**

Project MARC. *See* **MARC project**

Project Mariner. *See* **Mariner proect**

Project Sealab. *See* **Sealab project**

Project Telstar. *See* **Telstar project**

Projectiles

> *See also* **Ammunition; Bombs; Guided missiles; Ordnance; Rockets (Aeronautics)**
>
> *x* Bullets; Shells (Projectiles)
>
> *xx* **Ordnance**

Projective geometry. *See* **Geometry, Projective**

Projectors

> *x* Lantern projection; Moving picture projectors; Opaque projectors; Slide projectors

Proletariat
   xx Labor and laboring classes; Socialism

Pronunciation. *See* **Names—Pronunciation;**
      and names of languages with the sub-
      division *Pronunciation,* e.g. **English
      language—Pronunciation**; etc.

Proofreading
   xx Printing

Propaganda (May subdiv. geog. adjective
      form, e.g. **Propaganda, German**; etc.)
   See also **Advertising; European War,
      1914-1918 — Propaganda; Political
      psychology; Psychological warfare;
      World War, 1939-1945—Propaganda**
   xx **Advertising; Public opinion; Publicity**

Propaganda, American
   x American propaganda; U.S. — Propa-
      ganda

Propaganda, German
   x European War, 1914-1918—German prop-
      aganda; German propaganda
   xx **European War, 1914-1918 — Propa-
      ganda; Pangermanism; World War,
      1939-1945—Propaganda**

Propagation of plants. *See* **Plant propagation**

Propellers, Aerial
   x Airplanes—Propellers
   xx **Airplanes**

Proper names. *See* **Names**

Property
   See also **Eminent domain; Income; Real
      estate; Wealth**
   x Ownership
   xx **Economics; Wealth**

Property, Literary. *See* **Copyright**

Property, Real. *See* **Real estate**

Prophecies
   See also **Astrology; Bible—Prophecies;
      Divination; Fortune telling; Oracles**
   x Predictions
   xx **Divination; Occult sciences; Super-
      natural**

Prophets
   xx **Bible—Biography**

Proportion (Architecture). *See* **Architecture—
      Composition, proportion,** etc.

Proportional representation
   See also **Elections**
   x Representation, Proportional; Voting,
      Cumulative
   xx **Constitutional law; Representative gov-
      ernment and representation**

Prose literature, American; Prose literature,
      English; etc. *See* **American prose lit-
      erature; English prose literature**; etc.

Prosody. *See* **Versification**

Prospecting

    See also **Mine surveying; Petroleum—Geology**

    xx **Gold mines and mining; Mines and mineral resources; Silver mines and mining**

Prosthesis. *See* **Artificial organs; Transplantation of organs, tissues, etc.**

Prostitution

    See also **Sexual ethics; Sexual hygiene; Venereal diseases**

    x Hygiene, Social; Social hygiene; Vice; White slave traffic

    xx **Crime and criminals; Sexual ethics; Sexual hygiene; Social problems; Woman—Social conditions**

Protection. *See* **Free trade and protection**

Protection against burglary. *See* **Burglary protection**

Protection of animals. *See* **Animals—Treatment**

Protection of birds. *See* **Birds—Protection**

Protection of children. *See* **Child welfare**

Protection of game. *See* **Game protection**

Protection of natural scenery. *See* **Landscape protection; Natural monuments; Nature conservation; Wilderness areas**

Protection of wildlife. *See* **Wildlife—Conservation**

Protest. *See* **Dissent**

Protest marches. *See* **Demonstrations**

Proteins

    xx **Physiological chemistry**

Protestant churches

    See also **Protestantism**; also names of churches, e.g. **Methodist Church**; etc.

    xx **Church history; Protestantism**

Protestant Episcopal Church in the U.S.A.

    x Episcopal Church

Protestant Reformation. *See* **Reformation**

Protestantism

    See also **Protestant churches; Reformation**

    xx **Christianity; Church history; Protestant churches; Reformation**

Protons

    See also **Atoms; Electrons**

    x Hydrogen nucleus

    xx **Neutrons; Nuclear physics**

Protoplasm

    See also **Cells; Embryology**

    xx **Biology; Cells; Embryology; Life (Biology)**

Protozoa

    xx **Cells; Invertebrates; Microorganisms**

Proverbs

    See also **Epigrams**

    x Adages; Maxims; Sayings

    xx **Epigrams; Folklore; Quotations**

Providence and government of God
    xx God; Theology
Provincialism. *See* **Sectionalism (U.S.)**; and
    names of languages with the subdivi-
    sion *Provincialisms,* e.g. **English lan-
    guage—Provincialisms;** etc.
Pruning
    xx **Forests and forestry; Fruit culture;
    Gardening; Trees**
Psalmody. *See* **Church music; Hymns**
Pseudonyms
    x Anonyms; Fictitious names; Names,
    Fictitious; Pen names
Psychiatric hospitals. *See* **Mentally ill—Insti-
    tutional care**
Psychiatrists
    x Psychopathologists
    xx **Psychologists**
Psychiatry
    Use for works on clinical aspects of mental
    disorders, including therapy. Popular
    works and works on regional or social
    aspects of mental disorders are entered
    under **Mental illness.** Systematic de-
    scriptions of mental disorders are
    entered under **Psychology, Pathologi-
    cal**
    See also **Adolescent psychiatry; Child
    psychiatry; Insanity; Mental illness;
    Psychology, Pathological; Psycho-
    therapy**
    xx **Insanity; Psychology, Pathological**
Psychiatry, Adolescent. *See* **Adolescent psy-
    chiatry**
Psychiatry, Child. *See* **Child psychiatry**
Psychical research
    Use for works on investigations of phe-
    nomena that appear to be contrary to
    physical laws and beyond the normal
    sense perceptions
    See also

Apparitions	Mental suggestion
Clairvoyance	Mind and body
Dreams	Mind reading
Extrasensory per-	Personality dis-
ception	orders
Ghosts	Spiritualism
Hallucinations and	Subconsciousness
illusions	Thought transfer-
Hypnotism	ence

    x Parapsychology
    xx **Ghosts; Psychology; Research; Spirit-
    ualism; Supernatural**
Psychoanalysis
    See also **Dreams; Hypnotism; Medicine,
    Psychosomatic; Mind and body;
    Psychology; Psychology, Pathologi-
    cal; Psychology, Physiological; Sub-
    consciousness**
    xx **Dreams; Hypnotism; Mind and body;**

Psychoanalysis—*Continued*

> Psychology; Psychology, Pathological; Psychology, Physiological; Subconsciousness

Psychological tests. *See* **Mental tests**

Psychological warfare

> Use for works dealing with the methods used to undermine the morale of the civilian population and the military forces of an enemy country
>
> *x* Cold war; War of nerves
>
> *xx* **Military art and science; Morale; Propaganda; Psychology, Applied; War**

Psychologists

> *See also* **Psychiatrists**

Psychologists, School. *See* **School psychologists**

Psychology

> *See also*

Adjustment (Psychology)	**Motivation (Psychology)**
Apperception	**New Thought**
Attention	**Perception**
Attitude (Psychology)	**Personality**
Behaviorism (Psychology)	**Phrenology**
Consciousness	**Physiognomy**
Educational psychology	**Political psychology**
Emotions	**Psychical research**
Genius	**Psychoanalysis**
Gestalt psychology	**Race psychology**
Habit	**Reasoning**
Imagination	**Senses and sensation**
Individuality	**Social psychology**
Instinct	**Subconsciousness**
Intellect	**Temperament**
Intuition	**Thought and thinking**
Memory	

> *also* subjects with the subdivision *Psychology;* e.g. **Color—Psychology; Music —Psychology;** etc.
>
> *x* Mental philosophy; Mind
>
> *xx* **Brain; Philosophy; Psychoanalysis; Soul**

Psychology, Abnormal. *See* **Psychology, Pathological**

Psychology, Applied

> *See also* **Counseling; Human engineering; Human relations; Interviewing; Psychological warfare; Psychology, Pastoral;** also subjects with the subdivision *Psychological aspects.* e.g. **Drugs— Psychological aspects;** etc.
>
> *x* Applied psychology; Industrial psychology; Psychology, Industrial; Psychology, Practical
>
> *xx* **Educational psychology; Human rela-**

Psychology, Applied—*Continued*
    tions; Interviewing; Public relations;
    Social psychology
Psychology, Biblical. *See* Bible—Psychology
Psychology, Child. *See* Child study
Psychology, Comparative
    See also Animal intelligence; Instinct
    x Animal psychology; Comparative psychology
    xx Animal intelligence; Instinct; Zoology
Psychology, Criminal. *See* Criminal psychology
Psychology, Educational. *See* Educational psychology
Psychology, Experimental. *See* Psychology, Physiological
Psychology, Industrial. *See* Psychology, Applied
Psychology, Medical. *See* Psychology, Pathological
Psychology, National. *See* National characteristics; Race psychology
Psychology, Pastoral
    Use for works on the application of psychology and psychiatry by clergymen to the spiritual problems of individuals
    See also Counseling
    x Pastoral psychiatry; Pastoral psychology
    xx Christian ethics; Church work; Counseling; Psychology, Applied; Pastoral work; Therapeutics, Suggestive
Psychology, Pathological
    See note under Psychiatry
    See also Criminal psychology; Hallucinations and illusions; Insanity; Medicine, Psychosomatic; Mental illness; Neuroses; Personality disorders; Psychiatry; Psychoanalysis; Subconsciousness
    x Abnormal psychology; Diseases, Mental; Mental diseases; Pathological psychology; Psychology, Abnormal; Psychology, Medical; Psychopathology; Psychopathy
    xx Criminal psychology; Insanity; Mental health; Mind and body; Nervous system; Psychiatry; Psychoanalysis
Psychology, Physiological
    See also

Color sense	Optical illusions
Dreams	Pain
Emotions	Psychoanalysis
Hypnotism	Senses and sensation
Memory	tion
Mental tests	Sleep
Mind and body	Temperament

    x Experimental psychology; Physiological psychology; Psychology, Experimental; Psychophysics
    xx Mental health; Mind and body; Ner-

Psychology, Physiological—*Continued*
　　vous system; Physiology; Psycho-
　　analysis
Psychology, Political. *See* Political psychology
Psychology, Practical. *See* Psychology, Ap-
　　plied
Psychology, Racial. *See* Race psychology
Psychology, Social. *See* Social psychology
Psychology, Structural. *See* Gestalt psychology
Psychology of color. *See* Color—Psychology
Psychology of learning. *See* Learning, Psy-
　　chology of
Psychology of music. *See* Music—Psychology
Psychopathologists. *See* Psychiatrists
Psychopathology. *See* Psychology, Pathologi-
　　cal
Psychopathy. *See* Psychology, Pathological
Psychophysics. *See* Psychology, Physiological
Psychoses. *See* Insanity; Mental illness
Psychosomatic medicine. *See* Medicine, Psy-
　　chosomatic
Psychotherapy
　　See also Mental healing; Therapeutics,
　　　Suggestive
　　xx Mental healing; Psychiatry; Therapeu-
　　　tics, Suggestive
Ptomaine poisoning. *See* Food poisoning
Public accommodations, Discrimination in. *See*
　　Discrimination in public accommo-
　　dations
Public administration
　　Use for general works on the principles and
　　　techniques involved in the conduct of
　　　public business. Works limited to the
　　　governmental processes of a particular
　　　country, state, etc. are entered under
　　　the name of the area with the sub-
　　　division *Politics and government*
　　See also Administrative law; Civil service;
　　　also names of countries, cities, etc. with
　　　the subdivision *Politics and government,*
　　　e.g. U.S.—Politics and government;
　　　etc.
　　x Administration
　　xx Administrative law; Local government;
　　　Municipal government; Political sci-
　　　ence
Public assistance. *See* Public welfare
Public buildings
　　See also names of countries, cities, etc. with
　　　the subdivision *Public buildings,* e.g.
　　　U.S.—Public buildings; Chicago—
　　　Public buildings; etc.
　　x Buildings, Public; Government buildings
　　xx Architecture; Art, Municipal; Public
　　　works
Public charities. *See* Public welfare
Public debts. *See* Debts, Public
Public documents. *See* Government publica-
　　tions

Public finance. *See* **Finance**

Public health (May subdiv. geog.)

 See also

Cemeteries	Noise
Charities, Medical	Occupational dis-
Communicable	eases
diseases	Pollution
Cremation	Refuse and refuse
Disinfection and	disposal
disinfectants	Sanitary engineering
Epidemics	Sanitation
Food adulteration	School hygiene
and inspection	Sewage disposal
Health boards	Street cleaning
Hospitals	Vaccination
Meat inspection	Water—Pollution
Medical care	Water supply
Milk supply	

 x Health, Public; Hygiene, Public; Hygiene, Social; Medicine, Preventive; Preventive medicine; Social hygiene

 xx **Medicine, State; Sanitation; Social problems**

Public health—U.S.

 x U.S.—Public health

Public health boards. *See* **Health boards**

Public lands. *See* **Forest reserves; National parks and reserves;** and names of countries, states, etc. with the subdivision *Public lands,* e.g. **U.S.—Public lands;** etc.

Public libraries

 x Libraries, Public

 xx **Libraries**

Public meetings

 See also **Parliamentary practice**

 x Meetings, Public

 xx **Freedom of assembly**

Public opinion

 See also **Attitude (Psychology); Political psychology; Propaganda; Public relations; Publicity;** also subjects with the subdivision *Public opinion,* e.g. **World War, 1939-1945—Public opinion;** etc.; and names of countries with the subdivision *Foreign opinion,* **U.S. —Foreign opinion;** etc.

 x Opinion, Public

 xx **Attitude (Psychology); Freedom of conscience; Public relations**

Public opinion polls

 See also **Market surveys**

 x Gallup polls; Polls, Public opinion; Straw votes

 xx **Market surveys**

Public ownership. *See* **Government ownership; Municipal ownership**

Public playgrounds. *See* **Playgrounds**

Public records—Preservation. *See* **Archives**

Public relations
> Use for general works on public relations including works on training in public relation policies and procedures. May be subdivided by topic, e.g. **Public relations—Libraries**; etc.
>
> *See also* **Advertising; Psychology, Applied; Public opinion; Publicity**
>
> *xx* **Advertising; Public opinion; Publicity**

Public relations—Libraries
> *x* Libraries—Public relations
>
> *xx* **Libraries and community**

Public safety, Crimes against. *See* **Offenses against public safety**

Public schools (May subdiv. geog. country or state)
> *See also* **Evening and continuation schools; High schools; Junior high schools; Rural schools; Schools; Vacation schools**; also names of cities with the subdivision *Public schools* (e.g. **Chicago—Public schools**; etc.) ; and headings beginning with the word **School**
>
> *x* Common schools; Grammar schools; Secondary schools
>
> *xx* **Education, Secondary; Schools**

Public schools—U.S.
> *x* U.S.—Public schools

Public schools and religion. *See* **Religion in the public schools**

Public service commissions
> Use for works on bodies appointed to regulate or control public utilities
>
> *x* Public utility commissions
>
> *xx* **Corporation law; Corporations; Industry and state**

Public service corporations. See **Public utilities**

Public speaking
> *See also* **Acting; Debates and debating; Lectures and lecturing; Orations; Preaching; Voice**
>
> *x* Elocution; Oratory; Persuasion (Rhetoric) ; Speaking
>
> *xx* **Voice**

Public utilities
> *See also* **Corporation law; Corporations; Electric industries; Electric railroads; Gas; Holding companies; Railroads; Railroads and state; Street railroads; Telegraph; Telephone; Water supply**
>
> *x* Electric utilities; Gas companies; Public service corporations; Utilities, Public
>
> *xx* **Corporation law; Corporations**

Public utility commissions. *See* **Public service commissions**

Public welfare

Use for works on tax-supported welfare activities. Works on privately supported welfare activities are entered under **Charities.** Works on the methods employed in welfare work, public or private, are entered under **Social work**

See also

Charities
Child welfare
Children—Hospitals
Day nurseries
Hospitals
Institutional care

Legal assistance
 to the poor
Orphans and orphans' homes
Unemployed

 x Charities, Public; Poor relief; Public assistance; Public charities; Relief, Public; Social security; Social welfare; Welfare state; Welfare work

 xx **Charities; Poverty; Social work**

Public works

See also **Municipal engineering; Public buildings;** also names of countries, cities, etc. with the subdivision *Public works,* e.g. **U.S.—Public works; Chicago—Public works;** etc.

 xx **Civil engineering; Economic assistance, Domestic**

Public worship

 x Church attendance

 xx **Worship**

Publicity

See also **Advertising; Propaganda; Public relations**

 xx **Advertising; Public opinion; Public relations**

Publishers and authors. *See* **Authors and publishers**

Publishers and publishing

See also **Authors and publishers; Book industries and trade; Books; Booksellers and bookselling; Catalogs, Publishers'; Copyright; Paperback books; Printing; Publishers' standard book numbers**

 x Book trade; Editors and editing; Publishing

 xx **Book industries and trade; Books; Booksellers and bookselling; Copyright**

Publishers' catalogs. *See* **Catalogs, Publishers'**

Publishers' standard book numbers

 x Book numbers, Publishers' standard; Standard book numbers

 xx **Publishers and publishing**

Publishing. *See* **Publishers and publishing**

Puerto Ricans in New York (City)

Use same form for Puerto Ricans in other cities, countries, etc.

 xx **Minorities**

Pugilism. *See* **Boxing**

437

Pulpwood. *See* **Wood pulp**

Pumping machinery

 x Force pumps; Heat pumps; Pumps; Steam pumps

 xx **Engines; Hydraulic engineering**

Pumps. *See* **Pumping machinery**

Punch and Judy. *See* **Puppets and puppet plays**

Punched card systems. *See* **Information storage and retrieval systems**

Punctuation

 x English language—Punctuation

 xx **Rhetoric**

Punishment

 See also **Capital punishment; Crime and criminals; Criminal law; Penal colonies; Prisons; Probation; Reformatories**

 x Penology

 xx **Crime and criminals; Criminal law**

Punishment in schools. *See* **School discipline**

Puppets and puppet plays

 See also **Shadow pantomimes and plays**

 x Marionettes; Punch and Judy

 xx **Drama; Folk drama; Theater**

Purchasing. *See* **Buying; Shopping**

Pure food. *See* **Food adulteration and inspection**

Puritans

 See also **Calvinism; Church of England; Congregationalism; Pilgrim Fathers**

 xx **Calvinism; Christian biography; Church of England; Congregationalism; U.S.—History—Colonial period**

Puzzles

 See also **Crossword puzzles; Mathematical recreations; Riddles**

 xx **Amusements; Riddles**

Pygmies

 x Pigmies

 xx **Dwarfs**

Pyramids

 See also **Obelisks**

 xx **Archeology; Architecture, Ancient; Monuments**

Quacks and quackery

 See also **Patent medicines**

 xx **Imposters and imposture; Medicine; Swindlers and swindling**

Quakers. *See* **Friends, Society of**

Qualitative analysis. *See* **Chemistry, Analytic**

Quality control

 See also specific industries with the subdivision *Quality control,* e.g. **Steel industry and trade—Quality control;** etc.

 xx **Reliability (Engineering); Sampling (Statistics)**

Quantitative analysis. *See* **Chemistry, Analytic**

Quantity cookery. *See* **Cookery for institutions, etc.**

Quantum mechanics. *See* **Quantum theory**

Quantum theory

    See also Atomic theory; Chemistry, Physical and theoretical; Force and energy; Neutrons; Radiation; Relativity (Physics); Thermodynamics; Wave mechanics

    x Quantum mechanics

    xx Atomic theory; Chemistry, Physical and theoretical; Dynamics; Force and energy; Physics; Radiation; Relativity (Physics); Thermodynamics

Quarantine. *See* **Communicable diseases**

Quarries and quarrying

    See also Stone

    x Stone quarries

    xx Geology, Economic; Stone

Quartz

    x Minerals; Rock crystal

    xx Mineralogy

Quasars

    x Quasi-stellar radio sources

    xx Astronomy; Radio astronomy

Quasi-stellar radio sources. *See* **Quasars**

Queens

    See also Courts and courtiers; Kings and rulers; also names of countries with the subdivision *Kings and rulers* (e.g. Gt. Brit.—Kings and rulers; etc.); and names of queens, e.g. Elizabeth II, Queen of Great Britain; etc.

    x Empresses; Monarchs; Royalty; Rulers; Sovereigns

    xx Courts and courtiers; Kings and rulers; Monarchy

Queries. *See* **Questions and answers**

Quebec (Province)

Quebec (Province)—History

Quebec (Province) — History — Autonomy and independence movements

    x Quebec (Province)—Separatist movement; Separatist movement in Quebec (Province)

    xx Canada—English-French relations

Quebec (Province)—Separatist movement. *See* **Quebec (Province) — History — Autonomy and independence movement**

Questions and answers

    Use for informal quiz books of miscellany. Questions on a particular subject are entered under the subject with the subdivision *Examinations, questions, etc.* e.g. **Music—Examinations, questions, etc.;** etc.

    See also subjects with the subdivision *Examinations, questions, etc.,* e.g. **Music —Examinations, questions, etc.;** etc.

    x Answers to questions; Queries; Quiz books

Queuing theory
>   *x* Waiting line theory
>   *xx* **Operations research**

Quicksilver. *See* **Mercury**

Quilts. *See* **Coverlets**

Quiz books. *See* **Questions and answers**

Qumran texts. *See* **Dead Sea scrolls**

Quotations
>   *See also* **Proverbs;** also subjects and names
>   of people with the subdivision *Quota-*
>   *tions,* e.g. **Presidents—U.S.—Quota-**
>   **tions;** etc.
>   *x* Sayings
>   *xx* **Epigrams; Literature—Collections**

Qur'an. *See* **Koran**

Rabbits
>   *x* Hares

Rabies
>   *x* Hydrophobia

Race
>   *xx* **Ethnology**

Race awareness
>   *See also* **Prejudices and antipathies; Race**
>   **problems; Negroes—Race identity**

Race discrimination. *See* **Race problems**

Race improvement. *See* **Eugenics**

Race identity. *See* names of races with the sub-
>   division *Race identity,* e.g. **Negroes—**
>   **Race identity;** etc.

Race problems
>   *See also* **Acculturation; Discrimination;**
>   **Immigration and emigration; Inter-**
>   **cultural education; Race awareness;**
>   also names of countries, cities, etc. with
>   the subdivision *Race relations,* e.g. **U.S.**
>   **—Race relations; Chicago—Race re-**
>   **lations;** etc.
>   *x* Integration, Racial; Race discrimination;
>   Racial discrimination
>   *xx* **Ethnology; Minorities; Native races;**
>   **Social problems; Sociology**

Race problems and the church. *See* **Church and**
>   **race problems**

Race psychology
>   *See also* **National characteristics; Negroes**
>   **—Race identity; Social psychology**
>   *x* Ethnic psychology; Ethnopsychology;
>   Folk psychology; National psychology;
>   Psychology, National; Psychology, Ra-
>   cial
>   *xx* **Anthropology; Ethnology; National**
>   **characteristics; Psychology; Social**
>   **psychology; Sociology**

Races of man. *See* **Ethnology**

Racial balance in schools. *See* **Busing (School**
>   **integration); Segregation in educa-**
>   **tion**

Racial discrimination. *See* **Race problems**

440

Racial identity. *See* names of races with the subdivision *Race identity,* e.g. **Negroes —Race identity;** etc.

Racing. *See* names of type of racing, e.g. **Automobile racing; Bicycle racing; Boat racing; Horse racing; Soap box derbies;** etc.

Racketeering
  x Organized crime
  xx **Crime and criminals**

Radar
  xx **Navigation; Radio**

Radar defense networks
  See also **Ballistic missile early warning system**
  x Defenses, Radar
  xx **Air defenses**

Radiant heating
  x Panel heating
  xx **Heating**

Radiation
  See also

Cosmic rays	**Radioactivity**
Electromagnetic	**Radium**
waves	**Sound**
Light	**Spectrum**
Phosphorescence	**Ultraviolet rays**
Quantum theory	**X rays**

  xx **Light; Optics; Physics; Quantum theory; Waves**

Radiation—Physiological effect
  See also **Atomic bomb—Physiological effect; Atomic medicine**
  xx **Atomic bomb—Physiological effect**

Radiation—Safety measures

Radiation, Solar. *See* **Solar radiation**

Radiation biology. *See* **Radiobiology**

Radiation chemistry. *See* **Radiochemistry**

Radicals and radicalism. *See* **Reformers; Revolutions; Right and left (Political science)**

Radio
  See also **Radar; Sound—Recording and reproducing**
  xx **Electric engineering; Signals and signaling; Telecommunication; Wireless**

Radio—Apparatus and supplies
  See also **Amplifiers, Vacuum tube; Radio —Receivers and reception**
  xx **Radio industry and trade**

Radio—Broadcasting. *See* **Radio broadcasting**

Radio—Censorship
  xx **Freedom of information**

Radio—Operators. *See* **Radio operators**

Radio—Receivers and reception
  x Radio receivers; Radio reception
  xx **Radio—Apparatus and supplies**

Radio—Repairing
  x Radio repairing; Radio servicing
  xx **Repairing**

Radio, Short wave
> *See also* Amateur radio stations; Micro-
> wave communication systems; Micro-
> waves
>
> *x* High-frequency radio; Short wave re-
> ceivers; UHF radio; Ultrahigh fre-
> quency radio
>
> *xx* Electric conductors; Electric waves;
> Radio frequency modulation

Radio—Stations. *See* Radio stations

Radio addresses, debates, etc.
> *x* Radio lectures
>
> *xx* Debates and debating; Lectures and
> lecturing; Radio broadcasting; Radio
> scripts

Radio advertising
> *x* Advertising, Radio; Commercials, Radio;
> Radio commercials
>
> *xx* Advertising; Radio broadcasting;
> Radio industry and trade

Radio and music
> *x* Music and radio
>
> *xx* Music

Radio apparatus industry. *See* Radio industry
> and trade

Radio as a profession

Radio astronomy
> *See also* names of celestial radio sources,
> e.g. Quasars; etc.
>
> *xx* Astronomy; Interstellar communica-
> tion

Radio authorship
> *See also* Radio plays—Technique; Radio
> scripts
>
> *x* Radio script writing; Radio writing
>
> *xx* Authorship; Radio broadcasting; Radio
> scripts

Radio broadcasting
> *See also* Radio addresses, debates, etc.;
> Radio advertising; Radio authorship;
> Radio plays; Television broadcasting
>
> *x* Broadcasting; News broadcasts; Radio—
> Broadcasting; Radio journalism
>
> *xx* Mass media

Radio chemistry. *See* Radiochemistry

Radio commercials. *See* Radio advertising

Radio frequency modulation
> *See also* Radio, Short wave
>
> *x* FM Radio; Frequency modulation, Radio

Radio in aeronautics
> *x* Aeronautics, Radio in
>
> *xx* Aeronautics; Navigation (Aeronautics)

Radio in astronautics
> *x* Lunar surface radio communication
>
> *xx* Astronautics—Communication systems

Radio in education
> *x* Education and radio
>
> *xx* Audio-visual education; Teaching—
> Aids and devices

442

Radio industry and trade
    See also **Radio—Apparatus and supplies;
        Radio advertising**
    x Radio apparatus industry
    xx **Electric industries**
Radio journalism. *See* **Journalism; Radio
        broadcasting**
Radio lectures. *See* **Radio addresses, debates,
        etc.**
Radio operators
    x Radio—Operators
Radio plays
    Use for individual radio plays, for collec-
        tions of plays, and for works about
        them. Works on how to write radio
        plays are entered under **Radio plays—
        Technique**
    x Scenarios
    xx **Drama; Radio broadcasting; Radio
        scripts**
Radio plays—Technique
    See also **Television plays—Technique**
    x Play writing; Playwriting
    xx **Drama—Technique; Radio authorship;
        Television plays—Technique**
Radio receivers. *See* **Radio—Receivers and re-
        ception**
Radio reception. *See* **Radio—Receivers and
        reception**
Radio repairing. *See* **Radio—Repairing**
Radio script writing. *See* **Radio authorship**
Radio scripts
    See also **Radio addresses, debates, etc.;
        Radio authorship; Radio plays; Tele-
        vision scripts**
    xx **Radio authorship; Television scripts**
Radio servicing. *See* **Radio—Repairing**
Radio stations
    x Radio—Stations
Radio stations, Amateur. *See* **Amateur radio
        stations**
Radio waves. *See* **Electric waves**
Radio writing. *See* **Radio authorship**
Radioactive fallout
    x Dust, Radioactive; Fallout, Radioactive
    xx **Atomic bomb; Hydrogen bomb; Pol-
        lution**
Radioactive isotopes. *See* **Radioisotopes**
Radioactive substances. *See* **Radioactivity**
Radioactivity
    See also

Cosmic rays	**Radiotherapy**
Electrons	**Radium**
Helium	**Transmutation**
Nuclear physics	**(Chemistry)**
Phosphorescence	**Uranium**
Radiobiology	**X-rays**
Radiochemistry	

    x Radioactive substances
    xx **Electricity; Light; Nuclear physics;**

Radioactivity—*Continued*
>Physics; Radiation; Radiotherapy; Radium

Radiobiology
>*x* Radiation biology
>
>*xx* **Biology; Biophysics; Nuclear physics; Radioactivity**

Radiocarbon dating
>*x* Carbon 14 dating; Dating, Radiocarbon
>
>*xx* **Archeology**

Radiochemistry
>*x* Radiation chemistry; Radio chemistry
>
>*xx* **Chemistry, Physical and theoretical; Radioactivity**

Radiography. *See* **X rays**

Radioisotopes
>*x* Radioactive isotopes
>
>*xx* **Isotopes; Nuclear engineering**

Radiologists
>*x* Roentgenologists
>
>*xx* **Medicine—Biography; Physicians; Radiotherapy; X rays**

Radiotelephone, Private. *See* **Citizens radio service (Class D)**

Radiotherapy
>*See also* **Photography; Radioactivity; Radiologists; Radium; Ultraviolet rays; X rays**
>
>*xx* **Electrotherapeutics; Phototherapy; Physical therapy; Radioactivity; Radium; Therapeutics; X rays**

Radium
>*See also* **Radioactivity; Radiotherapy**
>
>*xx* **Radiation; Radioactivity; Radiotherapy**

Railroad accidents. *See* **Railroads—Accidents**

Railroad construction. *See* **Railroad engineering**

Railroad engineering
>*x* Railroad construction
>
>*xx* **Civil engineering; Engineering; Railroads**

Railroad fares. *See* **Railroads—Rates**

Railroad mergers. *See* **Railroads—Consolidation**

Railroad rates. *See* **Railroads—Rates**

Railroad workers. *See* **Railroads—Employees**

Railroads (May subdivide geog. except U.S.)
>*See also*

Electric railroads	**Railroads and state**
Eminent domain	**Railway mail ser-**
Express service	**vice**
Freight and freight-	**Street railroads**
age	**Subways**
Railroad engineer-	
ing	

>*also* names of individual railroads
>
>*x* Railways; Trains, Railroad
>
>*xx* **Public utilities; Transportation**

Railroads—Accidents

  See also **Railroads—Safety appliances;
    Railroads—Signaling**

  x Collisions, Railroad; Railroad accidents;
    Wrecks

  xx **Accidents; Disasters**

Railroads—Consolidation

  x Business combinations; Industrial mer-
    gers; Mergers, Industrial; Railroad
    mergers

  xx **Monopolies; Trusts, Industrial**

Railroads, Electric. *See* **Electric railroads**

Railroads—Electrification

  See also **Electric railroads**

  x Electrification of railroads

  xx **Electric railroads**

Railroads—Employees

  x Railroad workers

Railroads—Fares. *See* **Railroads—Rates**

Railroads—Finance

  See also **Railroads—Rates; Railroads—
    Statistics**

  x Capitalization (Finance)

Railroads—Freight. *See* **Freight and freightage**

Railroads—Government ownership. *See* **Railroads and state**

Railroads—Maps

  xx **Maps**

Railroads—Models

  xx **Machinery—Models**

Railroads, Nationalization of. *See* **Railroads
  and state**

Railroads—Rates

  See also **Freight and freightage; Inter-
    state commerce**

  x Railroad fares; Railroad rates; Rail-
    roads—Fares; Rebates (Railroads)

  xx **Freight and freightage; Railroads—
    Finance; Railroads and state**

Railroads—Rolling stock. *See* **Locomotives**

Railroads—Safety appliances

  See also **Brakes; Railroads—Signaling**

  xx **Accidents—Prevention; Brakes; Rail-
    roads—Accidents; Safety appliances**

Railroads—Signaling

  x Block signal systems; Interlocking sig-
    nals

  xx **Railroads — Accidents;   Railroads—
    Safety appliances; Signals and sig-
    naling**

Railroads, Single rail. *See* **Monorails**

Railroads—Statistics

  xx **Railroads—Finance**

Railroads, Street. *See* **Street railroads**

Railroads, Underground. *See* **Subways**

Railroads and state

  See also **Interstate commerce; Railroads
    —Rates; Railway mail service**

  x Government ownership of railroads;

445

Railroads and state—*Continued*

Government regulation of railroads; Nationalization of railroads; Railroads —Government ownership; Railroads, Nationalization of; State and railroads; State ownership of railroads

xx **Government ownership; Industry and state; Interstate commerce; Public utilities; Railroads**

Railway mail service

xx **Postal service; Railroads; Railroads and state**

Railways. *See* **Railroads**

Rain and rainfall

See also **Droughts; Floods; Forest influences; Meteorology; Snow; Storms**

x Rainfall

xx **Climate; Droughts; Forest influences; Meteorology; Storms; Water; Weather**

Rainfall. *See* **Rain and rainfall**

Rainfall and forests. *See* **Forest influences**

Rain making. *See* **Weather control**

Ranch life

See also **Cowboys**

xx **Farm life; Frontier and pioneer life**

Rank. *See* **Social classes**

Rapid reading

x Accelerated reading; Faster reading; Speed reading

xx **Reading—Remedial teaching**

Rapid transit. *See* **Local transit**

Rare animals

See also **Extinct animals**

x Animals, Rare; Endangered species; Vanishing animals

xx **Extinct animals; Wildlife—Conservation**

Rare birds

x Birds, Rare

Rare books

x Bibliography—Rare books; Book rarities; Books, Rare

Rationalism

See also

Agnosticism	**Positivism**
Atheism	**Realism**
Belief and doubt	**Reason**
Deism	**Skepticism**
Free thought	**Theism**
Intuition	

xx **Agnosticism; Atheism; Belief and doubt; Deism; Free thought; God; Knowledge, Theory of; Philosophy; Realism; Religion**

Raw materials

See also **Farm produce; Forest products; Mines and mineral resources**

xx **Commercial products; Materials**

Rayon

    x Acetate silk; Artificial silk; Silk, Artificial

    xx **Synthetic fabrics; Synthetic products**

Rays, Roentgen. *See* **X rays**

Rays, Ultra-violet. *See* **Ultraviolet rays**

Reactors (Nuclear physics). *See* **Nuclear reactors**

Readability (Literary style)

    xx **Books and reading; Reading; Style, Literary**

Readers

    Use for school readers in English. For readers in other languages, use the name of the language with the subdivision *Readers,* e.g. **French language—Readers;** etc.

    See also **Primers; Reading and recitations**

    x English language—Readers

    xx **Children's literature; Textbooks**

Reading

    Use for books on methods of teaching reading, and general books on the art of reading. Works on teaching retarded readers are entered under **Reading—Remedial teaching.** Books on the cultural aspects of reading and general discussions of books to read are entered under **Books and reading**

    See also **Books and reading; Readability (Literary style)**

    x Children's reading; Language arts; Reading—Study and teaching

Reading—Remedial teaching

    See also **Rapid reading**

    x Reading clinics; Remedial reading

Reading—Study and teaching. *See* **Reading**

Reading clinics. *See* **Reading—Remedial teaching**

Reading interests. *See* **Books and reading**

Readings and recitations

    x Recitations and readings; Speakers (Recitation books)

    xx **Readers; School assembly programs**

Ready reckoners. *See* **Mathematics—Tables, etc.**

Real estate

    Use for general works on real property in the legal sense, i.e., ownership of land and buildings (immovable property) as opposed to personal property. Works limited to the buying and selling of real property are entered under **Real estate business.** General works on land without the ownership aspect are entered under **Land.** Works on the assessment of property are entered under **Taxation**

    See also **Eminent domain; Farms; Land**

Real estate—*Continued*

> tenure; Landlord and tenant; Mortgages; Real estate business

>> *x* Property, Real; Real property; Realty

>> *xx* Land; Land tenure; Property

Real estate business

> *xx* Business; Real estate

Real property. *See* **Real estate**

Realism

> *See also* **Idealism; Materialism; Positivism; Pragmatism; Rationalism**

> *xx* **Idealism; Materialism; Philosophy; Positivism; Rationalism**

Realism in literature

> Use same form for realism in other forms of the arts

> *See also* **Romanticism**

> *x* Naturalism in literature

> *xx* **Literature; Romanticism**

Reality

> *See also* **Empiricism; Knowledge, Theory of; Pragmatism**

> *xx* **Intuition; Knowledge, Theory of; Philosophy; Pragmatism; Truth**

Realty. *See* **Real estate**

Reapers. *See* **Harvesting machinery**

Reapportionment (Election law). *See* **Apportionment (Election law)**

Reason

> *See also* **Reasoning**

> *xx* **Intellect; Rationalism**

Reasoning

> *See also* **Intellect; Logic**

> *xx* **Intellect; Logic; Psychology; Reason; Thought and thinking**

Rebates (Railroads). *See* **Railroads—Rates**

Rebuses. *See* **Riddles**

Recall

> *x* Impeachment

> *xx* **Representative government and representation**

Recipes. *See* **Cookery**

Reciprocity. *See* **Commercial policy**

Recitations and readings. *See* **Readings and recitations**

Reclamation of land

> Use for general works on reclamation, including drainage and irrigation

> *See also* **Drainage; Irrigation; Marshes; Sand dunes**

> *x* Clearing of land; Land, Reclamation of

> *xx* **Agriculture; Civil engineering; Floods; Hydraulic engineering; Irrigation; Land; Natural resources; Soils**

Recluses. *See* **Hermits**

Recommendations for positions. *See* **Applications for positions**

Reconstruction

> Use for works dealing with reconstruction in the U.S. following the Civil War

Reconstruction—*Continued*

> *See also* **Ku Klux Klan (1865-1876)**; **Ne-groes**
>
> *x* Carpetbag rule
>
> *xx* **U.S.—History—1865-1898**

Reconstruction (1914-1939)

> *See also* **European War, 1914-1918—Eco-nomic aspects**; **Peace**; **Veterans—Education**; **Veterans—Employment**
>
> *x* European War, 1914-1918—Reconstruc-tion

Reconstruction (1939-1951) (May subdiv. geog. except U.S.)

> *See also* **Economic assistance**; **Interna-tional cooperation**; **Peace**; **Veterans—Education**; **Veterans—Employment**; **World War, 1939-1945—Civilian re-lief**; **World War, 1939-1945—Eco-nomic aspects**; **World War, 1939-1945—Reparations**
>
> *x* Marshall Plan; Point Four program; World War, 1939-1945—Reconstruc-tion
>
> *xx* **Economic assistance**; **International co-operation**; **World War, 1939-1945—Economic aspects**

Record players. *See* **Phonograph**

Recorders, Tape. *See* **Magnetic recorders and recording**

Records, Phonograph. *See* **Phonograph rec-ords**

Records—Preservation. *See* **Archives**

Records of births, etc. *See* **Registers of births, etc.**; **Vital statistics**

Recreation

> Use for works on the psychological and social aspects of recreation and for works on organized recreational proj-ects
>
> *See also* **Amusements**; **Community cen-ters**; **Games**; **Hobbies**; **Outdoor rec-reation**; **Play**; **Playgrounds**; **Sports**; **Vacations**; also classes of people with the subdivision *Recreation,* e.g. **Aged—Recreation**; etc.
>
> *x* Pastimes; Relaxation
>
> *xx* **Amusements**; **Leisure**; **Play**

Recreation centers. *See* **Community centers**

Recreational vehicles. *See* **Automobiles—Trail-ers**; **Travel trailers and campers**

Recreations, Mathematical. *See* **Mathematical recreations**

Recreations, Scientific. *See* **Scientific recrea-tions**

Recruiting and enlistment. *See* **U.S. Army—Recruiting, enlistment, etc.**; **U.S. Navy—Recruiting, enlistment, etc.**

449

Recruiting of employees

    See also **Employment agencies;** also names of professions with the subdivision *Recruiting,* e.g., **Librarians— Recruiting;** etc.

    xx **Personnel management**

Rectors. *See* **Clergy**

Recycling of waste. *See* **Salvage (Waste, etc.)**

Red

    xx **Color**

Red China. *See* **China (People's Republic of China)**

Red Cross

    xx **Charities; Nurses and nursing**

Redemption. *See* **Atonement; Salvation**

Reducing (Body weight control). *See* **Weight control**

Reference books

    See also **Books and reading—Best books; Encyclopedias and dictionaries**

    x Bibliography—Reference books

    xx **Books and reading**

Referendum

    x Direct legislation; Initiative and referendum; Legislation, Direct

    xx **Constitutional law; Democracy; Elections; Representative government and representation**

Reforestation

    See also **Tree planting**

    xx **Forests and forestry; Tree planting**

Reform, Social. *See* **Social problems**

Reform of criminals. *See* **Crime and criminals; Probation; Reformatories**

Reform schools. *See* **Reformatories**

Reformation

    See also **Calvinism; Europe—History— 1492-1789; Protestantism; Sixteenth century;** also names of religious sects, e.g. **Huguenots;** etc.

    x Anti-Reformation; Church history—Reformation; Counter-Reformation; Protestant Reformation

    xx **Christianity; Church history; History, Modern; Protestantism; Sixteenth century**

Reformatories

    See also **Juvenile courts; Juvenile delinquency; Probation**

    x Correctional institutions; Industrial schools; Penal institutions; Penology; Reform of criminals; Reform schools

    xx **Children—Institutional care; Crime and criminals; Juvenile delinquency; Prisons; Punishment**

Reformers

    Includes works about political, social, religious, etc. reformers

    x Radicals and radicalism

Refraction
    x Dioptrics
    xx **Light; Optics**
Refrigeration and refrigerating machinery
    See also **Air conditioning; Cold storage**
    x Cooling appliances; Freezers; Freezing;
        Ice manufacture; Iceboxes
    xx **Air conditioning; Cold storage; Frost**
Refugees (May subdiv. geog. or by ethnic
        groups, adjective form, e.g. **Refugees,
        Arabic; Refugees, Jewish;** etc.)
    x Displaced persons; Exiles
    xx **Aliens; Immigration and emigration**
Refugees, American
    x American refugees; U.S.—Refugees
Refugees, Political ·
    See also names of wars with the subdivision
        Refugees, e.g. **World War, 1939-1945
        —Refugees;** etc.
    x Displaced persons; Political refugees
    xx **International law; International rela-
        tions**
Refuse and refuse disposal
    See also **Factory and trade waste; Sal-
        vage (Waste, etc.); Sewage disposal;
        Street cleaning; Waste products;
        Water—Pollution**
    x Disposal of refuse; Garbage; Incinera-
        tion; Littering; Waste disposal
    xx **Factory and trade waste; Municipal
        engineering; Public health; Salvage
        (Waste, etc.); Sanitary engineering;
        Sanitation; Sewage disposal; Street
        cleaning; Waste products; Water—
        Pollution**
Regattas. *See* **Rowing; Yachts and yachting**
Regional libraries. *See* **Libraries, Regional**
Regional planning *See* *Metropolitan Council of Governments*
    See also **City planning; Landscape pro-
        tection; Social surveys**
    x County planning; Planning, Regional;
        State planning
    xx **Landscape protection**
Regionalism. *See* **Nationalism; Sectionalism
        (U.S.)**
Registers of births, etc.
    See also **Vital statistics; Wills**
    x Birth records; Births, Registers of;
        Burial statistics; Deaths, Registers of;
        Marriage registers; Parish registers;
        Records of births, etc.; Vital records
    xx **Genealogy; Vital statistics**
Registers of persons. *See* names of countries,
        cities, etc. and names of colleges, uni-
        versities, etc. with the subdivision *Reg-
        isters,* e.g. **U.S.—Registers; U.S. Mil-
        itary Academy, West Point—Regis-
        ters;** etc.
Rehabilitation. *See* classes of people with the
        subdivision *Rehabilitation,* e.g. **Physi-**

✓ Rehabilitation

451

Rehabilitation—*Continued*
>   cally   handicapped — **Rehabilitation;**
>   etc.

Reign of Terror. *See* **France—History—Rev-**
>   **olution, 1789-1799**

Reindeer
>   *xx* **Deer; Domestic animals**

Reinforced concrete. *See* **Concrete, Reinforced**

Relativity (Physics)
>   *See also* **Quantum theory**
>   *x* Space and time
>   *xx* **Physics; Quantum theory**

Relaxation. *See* **Recreation; Rest**

Reliability (Engineering)
>   *See also* **Quality control**
>   *xx* **Engineering**

Relief, Public. *See* **Public welfare**

Religion
>   *See also*

Agnosticism	Religions
Atheism	Revelation
Belief and doubt	Sacrifice
Deism	Skepticism
Faith	Spiritual life
God	Supernatural
Mysticism	Superstition
Mythology	Theism
Natural theology	Theology
Pantheism	Theosophy
Rationalism	Worship

>   *also* **Indians of North America—Religion**
>   **and mythology; Negroes—Religion;**
>   and names of countries, states, etc. with
>   the subdivision *Religion* (e.g. **U.S.—**
>   **Religion;** etc.) ; and headings begin-
>   ning with the words **Religion** and **Re-**
>   **ligious**
>   *xx* **God; Religions; Theology**

Religion—Philosophy
>   *See also* **Philosophy and religion**
>   *x* Philosophy of religion
>   *xx* **Philosophy and religion**

Religion, Primitive
>   *See also* **Ancestor worship; Indians of**
>   **North America—Religion and myth-**
>   **ology; Sacrifice; Superstition; To-**
>   **tems and totemism**
>   *x* Primitive religion
>   *xx* **Ethnology; Mythology; Society, Prim-**
>   **itive**

Religion—Study and teaching. *See* **Religious**
>   **education;   Theology—Study   and**
>   **teaching**

Religion and art. *See* **Art and religion**

Religion and astronautics
>   *x* Astronautics and religion
>   *xx* **Astronautics and civilization; Religion**
>   **and science**

Religion and communism. *See* **Communism and**
>   **religion**

452

Religion and education. *See* **Church and education**

Religion and literature. *See* **Religion in literature**

Religion and medicine. *See* **Medicine and religion**

Religion and philosophy. *See* **Philosophy and religion**

Religion and science

> *See also* **Bible and science; Creation; Evolution; Man—Origin and antiquity; Natural theology; Religion and astronautics**
>
> *x* Christianity and science; Science and religion
>
> *xx* **Apologetics; Evolution; Natural theology; Theology**

Religion and social problems. *See* **Church and social problems**

Religion and state. *See* **Church and state**

Religion and war. *See* **War and religion**

Religion in literature

> *See also* **Bible in literature**
>
> *x* Religion and literature
>
> *xx* **Bible in literature**

Religion in the public schools

> *x* Bible in the schools; Prayers in the public schools; Public schools and religion; Schools—Prayers
>
> *xx* **Church and education; Church and state; Religious education**

Religion of humanity. *See* **Positivism**

Religions

> *See also*

Bahaism	Hinduism
Brahmanism	Islam
Buddha and Buddhism	Judaism
	Mythology
Christianity	Paganism
Confucius and Confucianism	Religion
	Sects
Druids and Druidism	Shinto
	Taoism
Gnosticism	Theosophy
Gods	Zoroastrianism

> *x* Comparative religion
>
> *xx* **Civilization; Gods; Religion**

Religions—Biography

> Use for collections of biographies of religious leaders not limited to the Christian religion
>
> *See also* **Christian biography**
>
> *x* Religious biography
>
> *xx* **Biography**

Religious art. *See* **Art, Medieval; Christian art and symbolism; Church architecture**

Religious belief. *See* **Belief and doubt; Faith**

Religious biography. *See* **Christian biography; Religions—Biography**

Religious ceremonies. *See* **Rites and ceremonies**

Religious denominations. *See* **Sects**; and names of churches and sects, e.g. **Presbyterian Church**; etc.

Religious drama

    See also **Christmas plays; Moralities; Mysteries and miracle plays; Passion plays**

    x Bible—Drama; Bible plays; Drama, Religious; Plays, Bible

    xx **Drama; Drama in education; Religious literature**

Religious education

    See note under **Church and education**

    See also **Bible—Study; Catechisms; Character education; Church and education; Religion in the public schools; Sunday schools; Theology —Study and teaching**

    x Christian education; Education, Christian; Education, Ethical; Education, Religious; Education, Theological; Ethical education; Religion—Study and teaching

    xx **Christian life; Education; Theology— Study and teaching**

Religious festivals. *See* **Fasts and feasts**; and names of festivals, e.g. **Christmas; Easter**; etc.

Religious freedom. *See* **Religious liberty**

Religious hippies. *See* **Hippies—Religious life**

Religious history. *See* **Church history**

Religious liberty

    See also **Church and state; Freedom of conscience; Persecution**

    x Freedom of religion; Freedom of worship; Intolerance; Religious freedom

    xx **Church and state; Civil rights; Free thought; Freedom of conscience; Liberty; Persecution; Toleration**

Religious life

    See also **Christian life**; also classes of people with the subdivision *Religious life,* e.g. **Children—Religious life**; etc.

    xx **Christian life; Monasticism and religious orders**

Religious literature

    See also **Bible as literature; Catholic literature; Christian literature, Early; Religious drama; Religious poetry; Sacred books**

    xx **Bible as literature; Literature**

Religious music. *See* **Church music**

Religious orders. *See* **Monasticism and religious orders**

Religious painting. *See* **Christian art and symbolism**

Religious poetry

    See also **Carols; Hymns**

Religious poetry—*Continued*

    xx Hymns; Poetry—Collections; Religious literature

Religious symbolism. *See* **Christian art and symbolism**

Remedial reading. *See* **Reading—Remedial teaching**

Remodeling of buildings. *See* **Building—Repair and reconstruction**

Renaissance

    See also **Architecture, Renaissance; Art, Renaissance; Civilization, Medieval; Humanism; Literature, Medieval; Middle Ages; Sixteenth century**

    x Revival of letters

    xx **Civilization, Modern; History, Modern; Humanism; Middle Ages**

Rendezvous in space. *See* **Orbital rendezvous (Space flight)**

Rental services. *See* **Lease and rental services**

Repairing

    See also **Building—Repair and reconstruction**; also names of appropriate subjects with the subdivision *Repairing,* e.g. **Radio—Repairing**; etc.

    x Mending

Reparations (European War). *See* **European War, 1914-1918—Reparations**

Reparations (World War, 1939-1945). *See* **World War, 1939-1945—Reparations**

Report writing

    x Reports—Preparation

    xx **Authorship**

Reporters and reporting

    See also **Government and the press; Journalism**

    x Interviewing (Journalism); Newspaper work

    xx **Journalism; Newspapers**

Reports—Preparation. *See* **Report writing**

Representation. *See* **Representative government and representation**

Representation, Proportional. *See* **Proportional representation**

Representative government and representation

    See also

Apportionment (Election law)	Proportional representation
Constitutions	Recall
Democracy	Referendum
Elections	Republics
Legislative bodies	Suffrage
Primaries	

    x Parliamentary government; Representation; Self-government

    xx **Constitutional history; Constitutional law; Constitutions; Democracy; Elections; Political science; Republics; Suffrage**

Representatives—U.S. *See* **U.S. Congress. House**

Reprints. *See* **Bibliography—Editions**

Reproduction
> *See also* **Cells; Embryology; Pregnancy; Sex**
> *x* Generation
> *xx* **Biology; Embryology; Genetics; Life (Biology); Physiology; Sex**

Reproduction processes. *See* **Copying processes and machines**

Reproductive system
> *x* Generative organs

Reprography. *See* **Copying processes and machines**

Reptiles
> *See also* **Crocodiles; Lizards; Snakes; Turtles**
> *xx* **Vertebrates**

Reptiles, Fossil
> *See also* **Dinosaurs**
> *x* Fossil reptiles
> *xx* **Fossils**

Republican Party
> *xx* **Political parties**

Republics
> *See also* **Democracy; Federal government; Representative government and representation**
> *x* The Commonwealth
> *xx* **Constitutional history; Constitutional law; Democracy; Political science; Representative government and representation**

Rescue operations, Space. *See* **Space rescue operations**

Rescue work
> *See also* **First aid; Space rescue operations**
> *x* Search and rescue operations
> *xx* **Civil defense**

Research
> *See also* **Learning and scholarship; Operations research; Psychical research;** also subjects with the subdivision *Research,* e.g. **Agriculture—Research; Medicine—Research;** etc.
> *xx* **Learning and scholarship**

Reservations, Indian. *See* **Indians of North America—Reservations**

Reservoirs
> *See also* **Irrigation; Water supply**
> *xx* **Hydraulic structures; Water supply**

Residences. *See* **Architecture, Domestic; Houses**

Resins. *See* **Gums and resins**

Resistance of materials. *See* **Strength of materials**

Resistance to government. *See* **Government, Resistance to**

456

Resistance welding. *See* **Electric welding**

Resorts. *See* **Health resorts, spas, etc.; Summer resorts; Winter resorts**

Resources, Marine. *See* **Marine resources**

Resources, Natural. *See* **Natural resources**

Respiration
    x Breathing
    xx **Lungs; Physiology; Singing; Voice**

Respiration, Artificial. *See* **Artificial respiration**

Rest
    See also **Fatigue; Sleep**
    x Relaxation
    xx **Fatigue; Hygiene**

Restaurants, bars, etc.
    See also **Coffee houses**
    x Bars and restaurants; Cafeterias; Diners; Lunch rooms; Saloons; Taverns; Tea rooms; Tearooms

Restoration of buildings. *See* **Architecture—Conservation and restoration**

Restoration of works of art. *See* subjects with the subdivision *Conservation and restoration,* e.g. **Paintings—Conservation and restoration**; etc.

Resumés (Employment). *See* **Applications for positions**

Resurrection. *See* **Future life; Jesus Christ—Resurrection**

Retail trade
    See also **Advertising; Chain stores; Department stores; Packaging; Salesmen and salesmanship; Shopping centers; Supermarkets**
    x Merchandising
    xx **Commerce**

Retaining wall. *See* **Walls**

Retarded children. *See* **Mentally handicapped children; Slow learning children**

Retirement
    xx **Leisure; Old age**

Retirement income. *See* **Annuities; Old age pensions; Pensions**

Retouching (Photography). *See* **Photography—Retouching**

Retraining, Occupational
    See note under **Occupational training**
    x Occupational retraining
    xx **Employees—Training; Labor supply; Manpower policy; Occupational training; Technical education; Unemployed; Vocational education**

Retribution. *See* **Future life; Hell**

Reuse of waste. *See* **Salvage (Waste, etc.)**

Revelation
    xx **Bible—Inspiration; Religion; Supernatural; Theology**

Revenue. *See* **Tariff; Taxation**

Revenue, Internal. *See* **Internal revenue**

Revenue sharing. *See* ~~Intergovernmental tax relations~~

Reviews. *See* **Book reviews**

Revival of letters. *See* **Renaissance**

Revivals

    See also **Evangelistic work**

    xx **Christian life; Church history; Church work; Evangelistic work**

Revolution, American. *See* **U.S.—History—Revolution**

Revolution, French. *See* **France—History—Revolution, 1789-1799**

Revolution, Russian. *See* **Russia—History—Revolution, 1917-1921**

Revolutions

    See also **Class struggle; France—History—Revolution, 1789-1799; Government, Resistance to; Hungary—History—Revolution, 1956; Russia—History—Revolution, 1917-1921; U.S.—History—Revolution**

    x Coups d'état; Radicals and radicalism; Sedition

    xx **Government, Resistance to; Political science**

Rewards (Prizes, etc.)

    See also **Literary prizes;** also names of prizes, e.g. **Nobel prizes;** etc.

    x Awards; Competitions; Prizes (Rewards)

Rh factor. *See* **Blood groups**

Rhetoric

    See also

Criticism	**Letter writing**
Debates and debating	**Preaching**
	Punctuation
Lectures and lecturing	**Satire**
	Style, Literary

    also names of languages with the subdivision *Composition and exercises,* e.g. **English language—Composition and exercises;** etc.

    x Composition (Rhetoric); English language—Rhetoric; Persuasion (Rhetoric); Speaking

    xx **English language—Composition and exercises; Language and languages; Style, Literary**

Rheumatism

    See also **Arthritis**

Rhyme

    See also **Rhythm; Stories in rhyme;** also names of languages with the subdivision *Rhyme,* e.g. **English language—Rhyme;** etc.

    x Rime

    xx **Poetics; Versification**

Rhymes. *See* **Limericks; Nonsense verses; Nursery rhymes; Poetry—Collections**

Rhythm

See also **Musical meter and rhythm; Periodicity; Versification**

xx **Esthetics; Periodicity; Poetics; Rhyme**

Riches. See **Wealth**

Riddles

See also **Charades; Puzzles**

x Conundrums; Rebuses

xx **Amusements; Puzzles**

Riding. See **Horsemanship**

Rifles

x Carbines; Guns

xx **Arms and armor; Firearms**

Right (Political science). See **Right and left (Political science)**

Right and left (Political science)

See also **Conservatism; Liberalism**

x Extremism (Political science); Left (Political science); Radicals and radicalism; Right (Political science)

xx **Conservatism; Liberalism; Political parties; Political science**

Right of assembly. See **Freedom of assembly**

Right of privacy. See **Privacy, Right of**

Right to work. See **Discrimination in employment; Open and closed shop**

Rights, Civil. See **Civil rights**

Rights of women. See **Woman—Civil rights**

Rime. See **Rhyme**

Riot control

x Riots—Control

xx **Crowds; Riots**

Riots

See also **Crowds; Demonstrations; Riot control;** also names of cities, and institutions with the subdivision *Riots,* e.g. **Chicago—Riots;** etc.; also names of specific riots

x Civil disorders; Mobs

xx **Crime and criminals; Crowds; Demonstrations; Freedom of assembly; Offenses against public safety**

Riots—Control. See **Riot control**

Rites and ceremonies

See also **Baptism; Fasts and feasts; Funeral rites and ceremonies; Manners and customs; Marriage customs and rites; Sacraments; Secret societies;** also classes of people and ethnic groups with the subdivision *Rites and ceremonies,* e.g. **Jews—Rites and ceremonies;** etc.

x Ceremonies; Ecclesiastical rites and ceremonies; Religious ceremonies; Ritual

xx **Manners and customs**

Ritual. See **Liturgies; Rites and ceremonies**

Rivers

See also **Dams; Floods; Hydraulic engineering; Inland navigation; Water—**

459

Rivers—*Continued*

Pollution; Water power; Water rights; also names of rivers

xx Civil engineering; Flood control; Floods; Hydraulic engineering; Inland navigation; Physical geography; Water; Waterways

Rivers—Pollution. *See* **Water—Pollution**

Road construction. *See* **Roads**

Road engineering. *See* **Highway engineering**

Road maps. *See* **Automobiles—Road guides**

Road signs. *See* **Signs and signboards**

Roads

See also **Express highways; Highway engineering; Pavements; Roadside improvements; Soils (Engineering); Street cleaning; Streets**

x Construction of roads; Highway construction; Highways; Road construction; Thoroughfares

xx Civil engineering; Highway engineering; Pavements; Streets; Transportation

Roads—Maps. *See* **Automobiles—Road guides**

Roadside improvement

x Highway beautification

xx Grounds maintenance; Landscape architecture; Roads

Robbers and outlaws

See also **Rogues and vagabonds**

x Bandits; Brigands; Burglars; Highwaymen; Outlaws; Thieves

xx Crime and criminals; Rogues and vagabonds

Robots

See note under **Automata**

See also **Automata**

xx Automata; Mechanical movements

Rochdale system. *See* **Cooperation**

Rock and roll music. *See* **Rock music**

Rock climbing. *See* **Mountaineering**

Rock crystal. *See* **Quartz**

Rock gardens

xx **Gardens**

Rock music

x Music, Rock; Rock and roll music

xx **Music, Popular (Songs, etc.)**

Rock tombs. *See* **Tombs**

Rocket flight. *See* **Space flight**

Rocket planes

See also names of rocket planes, e.g. **X-15 (Rocket aircraft)**; etc.

x Airplanes, Rocket propelled

xx High speed aeronautics; Space ships

Rocketry

See also **Ballistic missiles; Guided missiles; Rockets (Aeronautics); Space ships; Space vehicles**

xx Aeronautics; Astronautics

Rockets (Aeronautics)

    See also Artificial satellites—Launching;
        Ballistic missiles; Guided missiles;
        Jet propulsion

    x Aerial rockets

    xx Aeronautics; High speed aeronautics;
        Interplanetary voyages; Jet propul-
        sion; Projectiles; Rocketry

Rocks

    See also Crystallography; Geochemistry;
        Geology; Mineralogy; Petrology;
        Stone; also varieties of rock, e.g.
        Granite; etc.

    x Crystalline rocks; Metamorphic rocks;
        Pebbles

    xx Geology; Petrology; Stone

Rocks—Age. *See* Geology, Stratigraphic

Rocks, Moon. *See* Lunar petrology

Rocky Mountains

    xx Mountains

Rodeos

    xx Cowboys; Horsemanship; Sports

Roentgen rays. *See* X rays

Roentgenologists. *See* Radiologists

Rogues and vagabonds

    See also Robbers and outlaws; Tramps

    x Vagabonds

    xx Crime and criminals; Robbers and out-
        laws; Tramps

Roller skating

    xx Skating

Rolling stock. *See* Locomotives

Romaic language. *See* Greek language, Mod-
    ern

Romaic literature. *See* Greek literature, Mod-
    ern

Roman antiquities. *See* Classical antiquities;
    Rome—Antiquities; Rome (City)—
    Antiquities

Roman architecture. *See* Architecture, Roman

Roman art. *See* Art, Roman

Roman Catholic Church. *See* Catholic Church

Roman emperors

    See also names of Roman emperors, e.g.
        Nero, Emperor of Rome; etc.

    x Emperors; Sovereigns

    xx Kings and rulers

Roman literature. *See* Latin literature

Roman mythology. *See* Mythology, Classical

Roman philosophy. *See* Philosophy, Ancient

Romance languages

    See also names of languages belonging to
        the Romance group, e.g. French lan-
        guage; etc.

    x Neo-Latin languages

    xx Latin language

Romance literature

    See also names of literatures belonging to
        the Romance group, e.g. French litera-
        ture; etc.

Romances

Use for collections of medieval tales dealing with the age of chivalry; they may be either metrical or prose versions and may or may not have a factual basis

x English metrical romances; Stories

xx **Chivalry; Epic poetry; Fiction; Legends; Literature—Collections**

Romanesque architecture. *See* **Architecture, Romanesque**

Romanesque art. *See* **Art, Romanesque**

Romanesque painting. *See* **Painting, Romanesque**

Romanticism

See also **Realism in literature**

xx **Esthetics; Fiction; Literature; Music; Realism in literature**

Rome

Use for works about the Roman Empire. Works treating only of the modern city of Rome are entered under **Rome (City)**

Rome—Antiquities

x Roman antiquities

Rome—Biography

x Classical biography

Rome—Description and geography

Use for descriptive and geographic works on ancient Rome instead of the subdivisions *Description and travel* and *Historical geography*

Rome—History

Rome—History—Kings, 753-510 B.C.

Rome—History—Republic, 510-30 B.C.

Rome—History—Empire, 30 B.C.-476 A.D.

Rome (City)

See note under **Rome**

Rome (City)—Antiquities

x Roman antiquities; Ruins

Rome (City)—Description

Rome (City)—History

Roofs

xx **Architecture—Details; Building; Building, Iron and steel; Carpentry**

Rooming houses. *See* **Hotels, motels, etc.**

Root crops

See also **Feeding and feeds**

xx **Feeding and feeds; Vegetables**

Rope

See also **Cables; Hemp; Knots and splices**

xx **Hemp**

Roses

xx **Flower gardening; Flowers**

Rosetta stone inscription

xx **Hieroglyphics**

Rosin. *See* **Gums and resins**

Rotation of crops

x Crops, Rotation of

xx **Agriculture**

Round stage. *See* **Arena theater**

Round Table. *See* **Arthur, King**
Routes of trade. *See* **Trade routes**
Rowing
> *x* Regattas; Sculling
> *xx* Athletics; Boats and boating; College
> sports; Exercise; Water sports
Royalty. *See* **Kings and rulers; Princes and**
> **princesses; Queens**
Rubber
> *x* India rubber
> *xx* **Forest products**
Rubber, Artificial
> *x* Artificial rubber; Synthetic rubber
> *xx* **Plastics; Synthetic products**
Rubber tires. *See* **Tires**
Rugs
> *See also* **Carpets**
> *xx* **Arts and crafts; Carpets; Interior deco-**
> ration
Rugs, Hooked
> *x* Hooked rugs
Rugs, Oriental
> *x* Oriental rugs; Persian rugs
Ruins. *See* **Archeology; Cities and towns,**
> **Ruined, extinct, etc.; Excavations**
> **(Archeology);** and names of countries,
> cities, etc. with the subdivision *Antiqui-*
> *ties,* e.g. **Rome (City)—Antiquities;**
> etc.
Rulers. *See* **Kings and rulers; Queens;** and
> names of individual rulers
Rules of order. *See* **Parliamentary practice**
Runaways
> *x* Children, Runaway; Youth, Runaway
> *xx* **Children; Youth**
Running. *See* **Track athletics**
Rural architecture. *See* **Architecture, Domes-**
> **tic; Farm buildings**
Rural churches
> *x* Church work, Rural; Churches, Country;
> Churches, Rural; Country churches
> *xx* **Church work**
Rural credit. *See* **Agricultural credit**
Rural electrification. *See* **Electric power dis-**
> **tribution; Electricity in agriculture**
Rural high schools. *See* **Rural schools**
Rural hygiene. *See* **Hygiene, Rural**
Rural life. *See* **Country life; Farm life; Out-**
> **door life; Peasantry**
Rural schools
> *x* Country schools; District schools; High
> schools, Rural; Rural high schools
> *xx* **Public schools; Schools**
Rural sociology. *See* **Sociology, Rural**
Russia
> *x* Soviet Union; USSR
Russia—Communism. *See* **Communism—Rus-**
> **sia**
Russia—History
Russia—History—Revolution of 1905

Russia—History—1917-

Russia—History—Revolution, 1917-1921
> *x* Revolution, Russian; Russian revolution
> *xx* **Revolutions**

Russia—History—1925-1953

Russia—History—War with Finland, 1939-1940.
> *See* **Russio-Finnish War, 1939-1940**

Russia—History—1953-

Russian artificial satellites. *See* **Artificial satellites, Russian**

Russian Church. *See* **Orthodox Eastern Church, Russian**

Russian communism. *See* **Communism—Russia**

Russian intervention in the Czechoslovak Republic. *See* **Czechoslovak Republic—History—Intervention, 1968-**

Russian revolution. *See* **Russia—History—Revolution, 1917-1921**

Russian satellite countries. *See* **Communist countries**

Russo-Finnish War, 1939-1940
> *x* Finno-Russian War, 1939-1940; Russia—History—War with Finland, 1939-1940

Russo-Turkish War, 1853-1856. *See* **Crimean War, 1853-1856**

Rust. *See* **Corrosion and anticorrosives**

Rustless coatings. *See* **Corrosion and anticorrosives**

SST. *See* **Supersonic transport planes**

STOL aircraft. *See* **Short take off and landing aircraft**

Sabbath
> *x* Lord's Day; Sunday
> *xx* **Judaism**

Sabine vaccine. *See* **Poliomyelitis vaccine**

Sabotage
> *xx* **Labor unions; Offenses against public safety; Strikes and lockouts; Subversive activities**

Sacraments
> *See also* **Baptism; Lord's Supper; Marriage**
> *x* Ecclesiastical rites and ceremonies
> *xx* **Rites and ceremonies; Theology**

Sacred art. *See* **Christian art and symbolism**

Sacred books
> *See also* names of sacred books, e.g. **Avesta; Bible; Koran; Vedas;** etc.
> *x* Books, Sacred
> *xx* **Religious literature**

Sacred music. *See* **Church music**

Sacrifice
> *See also* **Atonement**
> *xx* **Ethnology; Religion; Religion, Primitive; Theology; Worship**

Safety appliances
> *See also* Accidents—Prevention; also subjects with the subdivision *Safety appliances,* e.g. Railroads—Safety appliances; etc.
> *x* Safety devices
> *xx* Accidents—Prevention

Safety devices. *See* Safety appliances

Safety education
> *See also* Accidents—Prevention
> *xx* Accidents—Prevention

Safety measures. *See* Accidents—Prevention; and subjects with the subdivision *Safety measures,* e.g. Aeronautics—Safety measures; etc.

Sagas
> *See also* Icelandic and Old Norse literature
> *xx* Folklore; Icelandic and Old Norse literature; Literature; Scandinavian literature

Sailing
> *See also* Boats and boating; Navigation; Yachts and yachting
> *xx* Boats and boating; Navigation; Ships; Water sports; Yachts and yachting

Sailors. *See* Seamen

Sailors' life. *See* Seafaring life

Sailors' songs. *See* Sea songs

St. Bartholomew's Day, Massacre of, 1572
> *See also* Huguenots
> *xx* France—History—House of Valois, 1328-1589

St. Dominic, Order of. *See* Dominicans

St. Francis, Order of. *See* Franciscans

St. Valentine's Day. *See* Valentine's Day

Saints
> *See also* Apostles; Fathers of the church; Hermits; Legends; Martyrs; Shrines; also names of saints
> *xx* Christian biography; Fathers of the church; Heroes; Legends; Martyrs; Pilgrims and pilgrimages; Shrines

Salads
> *xx* Cookery

Salamanders
> *xx* Amphibians

Sales, Auction. *See* Auctions

Sales management
> *x* Management, Sales
> *xx* Industrial management; Management; Marketing; Salesmen and salesmanship

Sales tax
> *x* Taxation of sales
> *xx* Taxation

Salesmen and salesmanship
> *See also* Advertising; Booksellers and bookselling; Business; Clerks; Mail-

465

Salesmen and salesmanship—*Continued*
    order business; Marketing; Peddlers
    and peddling; Sales management
  x Agents; Clerks (Salesmen); Commercial
    travelers; Selling
  xx Advertising; Business; Department
    stores; Retail trade
Salk vaccine. *See* Poliomyelitis vaccine
Salmon
  xx Fishes
Saloons. *See* Restaurants, bars, etc.; Liquor
    traffic
Salt free diet
  x Low sodium diet
  xx Diet; Diet in disease; Cookery for the
    sick
Salt water. *See* Sea water
Salutations. *See* Etiquette; Letter writing
Salvage
  See also Skin diving; Shipwrecks
  xx International law; Maritime law; Ship-
    wrecks
Salvage (Waste, etc.)
  See also Refuse and refuse disposal;
    Waste products
  x Recycling of waste; Reuse of waste;
    Utilization of waste; Waste products—
    Recycling; Waste reclamation
  xx Refuse and refuse disposal; Waste
    products
Salvation
  See also Atonement; Sanctification; Sin
  x Redemption
  xx Conversion; Faith; Jesus Christ; The-
    ology
Salvation Army
  xx Evangelistic work; Missions
Sampling (Statistics)
  See also Quality control
  xx Probabilities; Statistics
San Francisco—Earthquake and fire, 1906
  xx Disasters
Sanatoriums. *See* Health resorts, spas, etc.;
    Hospitals
Sanctification
  xx Christian life; Salvation; Spiritual life;
    Theology
Sand dunes
  x Dunes
  xx Reclamation of land; Seashore
Sandwiches
  xx Cookery
Sanitary affairs. *See* Sanitary engineering;
    Sanitation
Sanitary engineering
  See also Drainage; Municipal engineer-
    ing; Pollution; Refuse and refuse dis-
    posal; Sanitation; Sewerage; Soil
    bacteriology; Street cleaning; Water
    supply

Sanitary engineering—*Continued*
>   *x* Sanitary affairs
>   *xx* Building; Civil engineering; Drainage, House; Engineering; Municipal engineering; Plumbing; Public health; Sanitation

Sanitation
>   *See also*
>
>   Cemeteries
>   Cremation
>   Disinfection and disinfectants
>   Hygiene
>   Military hygiene
>   Pollution
>   Public health
>   Refuse and refuse disposal
>
>   Sanitary engineering
>   School hygiene
>   Ventilation
>   Water—Purification
>   Water supply
>   World War, 1939-1945—Medical and sanitary affairs
>
>   *x* Cleanliness; Sanitary affairs
>   *xx* Hygiene; Public health; Sanitary engineering

Sanitation, Household
>   *See also* Drainage, House; House cleaning; Household pests; Laundry; Plumbing; Ventilation
>   *x* House sanitation; Household sanitation
>   *xx* Plumbing

Santa Claus
>   *xx* Christmas

Satan. *See* Devil

Satellites, Artificial. *See* Artificial satellites

Satire (May subdiv. geog. adjective form, e.g. Satire, English; etc.)
>   *See also* Parody
>   *x* Comic literature
>   *xx* Literature; Rhetoric; Wit and humor

Satire, American
>   *x* American satire

Satire, English
>   *x* English satire
>   *xx* English literature

Saving and thrift
>   *See also* Building and loan associations; Cost and standard of living; Insurance, Industrial; Investments; Old age pensions; Savings banks
>   *x* Economy; Thrift
>   *xx* Cost and standard of living; Economics; Finance, Personal; Insurance; Investments; Success

Savings and loan associations. *See* Building and loan associations

Savings banks
>   *See also* Building and loan associations
>   *xx* Banks and banking; Cooperation; Saving and thrift

Saws
>   *xx* Carpentry—Tools; Tools

Saxons. *See* Anglo-Saxons; Teutonic race

Sayings. *See* Epigrams; Proverbs; Quotations

Scalds and scaldic poetry
> *See also* Icelandic and Old Norse literature; Troubadours
>
> *xx* Icelandic and Old Norse literature; Poetry; Poets

Scandinavian civilization. *See* **Civilization, Scandinavian**

Scandinavian languages
> *See also* Danish language; Icelandic and Old Norse languages; Norwegian language; Swedish language
>
> *x* Norse languages
>
> *xx* Icelandic and Old Norse languages

Scandinavian literature
> *See also* Danish literature; Eddas; Icelandic and Old Norse literature; Norwegian literature; Sagas; Swedish literature
>
> *x* Norse literature
>
> *xx* Icelandic and Old Norse literature

Scandinavians
> Use for works on the people since the 10th century. Works on the early Scandinavians are entered under Northmen
>
> *See also* **Northmen**

Scenarios. *See* Moving picture plays; Plots (Drama, fiction, etc.); Radio plays; Television plays

Scene painting
> *xx* Painting; Theaters—Stage setting and scenery

Scenery. *See* Landscape protection; Views; and names of countries, states, etc. with the subdivision *Description and travel—Views* (e.g. **U.S.—Description and travel—Views**; etc.) ; and names of cities with the subdivision *Description—Views,* e.g. **Chicago—Description—Views**; etc.

Scenery (Stage). *See* Theaters—Stage setting and scenery

Scepticism. *See* Skepticism

Scholarship. *See* Learning and scholarship

Scholarships, fellowships, etc.
> *See also* Student loan funds
>
> *x* Fellowships; Student aid
>
> *xx* Colleges and universities; Education; Education and state; Endowments; Student loan funds

School administration and organization
> See note under School supervision
>
> *See also* Articulation (Education); School boards; School discipline; School superintendents and principals; School supervision; Self-government (in education); Teaching
>
> *x* Educational administration; Inspection of schools; School inspection; School management; School organization; Schools

School administration and organization
—Continued
—Administration; Schools—Management and organization
School and community. *See* **Community and school**
School and home. *See* **Home and school**
School architecture. *See* **School buildings**
School assembly programs
Use for general works on school entertainments, literary and otherwise, assembly programs, etc. Collections of prose and poetry for public speaking are entered under **Readings and recitations**

See also **Commencements; Drama in education; Readings and recitations;** also names of days observed, e.g. **Memorial Day;** etc.

x Assembly programs, School; Programs, School assembly; School entertainments; Schools—Exercises and recreations; Schools—Opening exercises

xx **Student activities**
School attendance
See also **Child labor; Dropouts; Education, Compulsory**
x Absence from school; Attendance, School; Compulsory school attendance; School enrollment; Truancy (Schools)
xx **Education, Compulsory**
School boards
x Boards of education
xx **School administration and organization**
School books. *See* **Textbooks**
School buildings
x Buildings, School; School architecture; School houses; Schoolhouses
xx **Architecture; Buildings; Schools**
School buildings as recreation centers. *See* **Community centers**
School busing. *See* **Busing (School integration)**
School children—Food
x Food for school children; Meals for school children; School lunches
xx **Children—Care and hygiene; Children—Nutrition; Diet**
School children—Transportation
School clubs. *See* **Students' societies**
School discipline
See also **Classroom management; Self-government (in education)**
x Discipline of children; Management of children; Punishment in schools
xx **Children—Management; School administration and organization; Teaching**
School drama. *See* **College and school drama**
School dropouts. *See* **Dropouts**
School endowments. *See* **Endowments**
School enrollment. *See* **School attendance**

School entertainments. *See* **School assembly programs**

School finance. *See* **Education—Finance**

School furniture. *See* **Schools—Furniture, equipment, etc.**

School houses. *See* **School buildings**

School hygiene
>*x* Children—Health; Hygiene, School
>
>*xx* **Children—Care and hygiene; Health education; Hygiene; Public health; Sanitation**

School inspection. *See* **School administration and organization; School supervision**

School integration. *See* **Busing (School integration); Segregation in education**

School journalism. *See* **College and school journalism**

School libraries
>*See also* **Children's literature; Libraries, Children's; Libraries, Young adults'; Libraries and schools**
>
>*x* Children's libraries; Libraries, School
>
>*xx* **Libraries; Libraries, Children's; Libraries and schools**

School libraries (High school)
>*x* High school libraries; Libraries, School
>
>*xx* **Libraries**

School life. *See* **Students**

School lunches. *See* **School children—Food**

School management. *See* **School administration and organization**

School music. *See* **Music—Study and teaching; School songbooks; Singing**

School newspapers. *See* **College and school journalism**

School nurses
>*xx* **Children—Care and hygiene; Nurses and nursing**

School organization. *See* **School administration and organization**

School playgrounds. *See* **Playgrounds**

School plays. *See* **Children's plays; College and school drama—Collections**

School principals. *See* **School superintendents and principals**

School psychologists
>*x* Psychologists, School
>
>*xx* **Personnel service in education**

School reports
>*See also* **Grading and marking (Students)**
>
>*xx* **Grading and marking (Students)**

School savings banks
>*xx* **Banks and banking**

School shops
>*x* Industrial arts shops
>
>*xx* **Technical education**

School songbooks
>*See also* **Children's songs**
>
>*x* School music; Songbooks, School
>
>*xx* **Singing; Songbooks; Songs**

School sports
> *See also* **Coaching (Athletics); College sports**
>
> *xx* **Sports; Student activities**

School stories
> *See also* **College stories**
>
> *x* Stories
>
> *xx* **College stories; Fiction**

School superintendents and principals
> *See also* **School supervision**
>
> *x* School principals; Superintendents of schools
>
> *xx* **School administration and organization; School supervision; Teachers; Teaching**

School supervision
> Use for works on the supervision of instruction. Works on the administrative duties of an educator are entered under **School administration and organization**
>
> *See also* **School superintendents and principals**
>
> *x* Inspection of schools; Instructional supervision; School inspection; Supervision of schools
>
> *xx* **School administration and organization; School superintendents and principals; Teaching**

School surveys. *See* **Educational surveys**

School taxes. *See* **Education—Finance**

School teaching. *See* **Teaching**

School verse
> *xx* **Poetry—Collections**

School withdrawals. *See* **Dropouts**

Schoolhouses. *See* **School buildings**

Schools (May subdiv. geog. country or states)
> *See also*

Church schools	Kindergarten
Colleges and universities	Libraries and schools
Correspondence schools and courses	Library schools
	Museums and schools
Education	Private schools
Evening and continuation schools	Public schools
	Rural schools
High schools	School buildings
Junior colleges	Sunday schools
Junior high schools	Vacation schools

> *also* subjects with the subdivision *Study and teaching* (e.g. **Medicine—Study and teaching**; etc.); names of cities with the subdivision *Public schools* (e.g. **Chicago—Public schools**; etc.); headings beginning with the word **School**; and names of individual schools
>
> *x* Community schools; Neighborhood schools
>
> *xx* **Education; Public schools**

471

Schools—Administration. *See* **School administration and organization**
Schools—Centralization
x Consolidation of schools
Schools, Commercial. *See* **Business education**
Schools—Curricula. *See* **Education—Curricula;**
also types of education and schools
with the subdivision *Curricula,* e.g.
**Library education—Curricula; Col-
leges and universities—Curricula;** etc.
Schools—Exercises and recreation. *See* **School
assembly programs**
Schools—Furniture, equipment, etc.
x School furniture
xx **Furniture**
Schools—Management and organization. *See*
**School administration and organiza-
tion**
Schools, Military. *See* **Military education**
Schools, Nongraded. *See* **Nongraded schools**
Schools—Opening exercises. *See* **School as-
sembly programs**
Schools, Parochial. *See* **Church schools**
Schools—Prayers. *See* **Religion in the public
schools**
Schools, Ungraded. *See* **Nongraded schools**
Schools—U.S.
x U.S.—Schools
Schools and libraries. *See* **Libraries and
schools**
Schools and museums. *See* **Museums and
schools**
Schools as social centers. *See* **Community cen-
ters**
Science (May subdiv. geog.)
See also

Astonomy	Mathematics
Bacteriology	Meteorology
Biology	Mineralogy
Botany	Natural history
Chemistry	Petrology
Crystallography	Physics
Ethnology	Physiology
Fossils	Space sciences
Geology	Zoology

also headings beginning with the word
Scientific
x Discoveries (in science)
Science—Exhibitions
x Science fairs
Science—Experiments
See also particular branches of science with
the subdivision *Experiments,* e.g.
Chemistry—Experiments; etc.
x Experiments, Scientific; Scientific experi-
ments
Science—Fiction. *See* **Science fiction**
Science—Methodology
See also **Logic**
x Methodology; Scientific method

472

Science—Social aspects. *See* **Science and civilization**

Science—Societies

    x Scientific societies

Science—Study and teaching

    See also **Nature study**

    x Education, Scientific; Scientific education

    xx **Education; Teaching**

Science—U.S.

    x American science; U.S.—Science

Science and civilization

    x Civilization and science; Science—Social aspects

    xx **Civilization; Progress**

Science and religion. *See* **Religion and science**

Science and space. *See* **Space sciences**

Science and state

    x State and science

Science and the Bible. *See* **Bible and science**

Science and the humanities

    x Humanities and science

Science as a profession

    xx **Scientists**

Science fairs. *See* **Science—Exhibitions**

Science fiction

    May be used for single novels as well as for collections of stories

    x Science—Fiction

    xx **Fantastic fiction; Fiction**

Scientific apparatus and instruments

    See also names of groups of instruments, e.g. **Aeronautical instruments; Astronomical instruments; Chemical apparatus; Electric apparatus and appliances; Electronic apparatus and appliances; Engineering instruments; Meteorological instruments;** etc.; also names of particular instruments

    x Apparatus, Scientific; Instruments, Scientific; Scientific instruments

Scientific education. *See* **Science—Study and teaching**

Scientific expeditions

    See also names of regions explored, e.g. **Antarctic regions; Arctic regions;** and names of expeditions

    x Expeditions, Scientific; Polar expeditions; Travels

    xx **Antarctic regions; Arctic regions; Discoveries (in geography); Voyages and travels**

Scientific experiments. *See* **Science—Experiments;** and particular branches of science with the subdivision *Experiments,* e.g. **Chemistry—Experiments;** etc.

Scientific instruments. *See* **Scientific apparatus and instruments**

Scientific management. *See* **Management**

Scientific method. *See* special subjects with the
subdivision *Methodology,* e.g. **Science—
Methodology;** etc.
Scientific recreations
See also **Mathematical recreations**
x Recreations, Scientific
xx **Amusements**
Scientific societies. *See* **Science—Societies**
Scientific writing. *See* **Technical writing**
Scientists
See also **Science as a profession;** also
classes of scientists, e.g. **Astrono-
mers; Chemists; Geologists; Mathe-
maticians; Naturalists; Physicists;**
etc. and names of scientists
Scottish clans. *See* **Clans and clan system**
Scottish tartans. *See* **Tartans**
Scouts and scouting
See also **Boy Scouts; Girl Scouts**
xx **Soldiers**
Screen printing. *See* **Silk screen printing**
Scrip. *See* **Currency question**
Scriptures, Holy. *See* **Bible**
Scuba diving. *See* **Skin diving**
Sculling. *See* **Rowing**
Sculptors (May subdiv. geog. adjective form,
e.g. **Sculptors, French;** etc.)
xx **Artists**
Sculptors, American
x American sculptors; U.S.—Sculptors
Sculpture (May subdiv. geog. adjective form,
e.g. **Sculpture, African;** etc.)
See also **Brasses; Bronzes; Masks (Sculp-
ture); Mobiles (Sculpture); Model-
ing; Monuments; Plaster casts; Soap
sculpture; Wood carving**
x Statues
xx **Art; Decoration and ornament; Es-
thetics**
Sculpture, American
x American sculpture; U.S.—Sculpture
Sculpture, Kinetic. *See* **Kinetic sculpture**
Sculpture, Modern
x Modern sculpture
Sculpture, Modern—20th century
Sculpture, Religious. *See* **Christian art and
symbolism**
Sculpture—Technique
See also **Modeling**
xx **Modeling**
Sculpture in motion. *See* **Kinetic sculpture**
Sea. *See* **Ocean**
Sea animals. *See* **Marine animals**
Sea fisheries. *See* **Fisheries**
Sea food
See also names of fish used for food
x Fish as food
xx **Fishes; Food**
Sea in art. *See* **Marine painting**

Sea laboratories. *See* **Manned undersea research stations; Oceanography—Research**

Sea laws. *See* **Maritime law**

Sea life. *See* **Seafaring life; Seamen;** and names of countries with the subhead *Navy,* e.g. **U.S. Navy;** etc.

Sea lions. *See* **Seals (Animals)**

Sea mosses. *See* **Algae**

Sea poetry

    See also **Sea songs**

    xx **Poetry—Collections**

Sea pollution. *See* **Marine pollution**

Sea power

    See also **Disarmament; Naval battles; Naval history; Navies; Warships;** also names of countries with the subhead *Navy* or the subdivision *History, Naval,* e.g. **U.S. Navy; U.S.—History, Naval;** etc.

    x Dominion of the sea; Military power; Navy

    xx **Disarmament; Naval art and science; Naval history; Navies**

Sea routes. *See* **Trade routes**

Sea shells. *See* **Shells**

Sea-shore. *See* **Seashore**

Sea songs

    x Chanties; Sailors' songs

    xx **Sea poetry; Songs**

Sea stories

    x Stories

    xx **Adventure and adventurers; Fiction**

Sea travel. *See* **Ocean travel**

Sea water

    x Salt water

    xx **Water**

Sea water aquariums. *See* **Marine aquariums**

Sea waves. *See* **Ocean waves**

Seafaring life

    See also **Seamen**

    x Sailors' life; Sea life

    xx **Adventure and adventurers; Seamen; Voyages and travels**

Sealab project

    x Navy Sealab project; Project Sealab; U.S. Navy—Sealab project

    xx **Manned undersea research stations**

Seals (Animals)

    x Fur seals; Sea lions

Seals (Numismatics)

    x Emblems; Signets

    xx **Heraldry; History; Inscriptions; Numismatics**

Seamanship. *See* **Navigation**

Seamen

    See also **Merchant marine; Midshipmen; Naval biography; Pilots and pilotage; Seafaring life; Veterans;** also names

Seamen—*Continued*

    of countries with the subhead *Navy,*
e.g. **U.S. Navy;** etc.

    x Armed forces; Mariners; Navigators;
Sailors; Sea life

    xx **Naval art and science; Naval biography; Seafaring life; Veterans; Voyages and travels**

Search and rescue operations. *See* **Rescue work**

Seascapes. *See* **Marine painting**

Seashore

    See also **Sand dunes**

    x Beaches; Sea-shore

    xx **Ocean**

Seasons

    See also names of the seasons, e.g. **Autumn;** etc.

    xx **Astronomy; Climate; Meteorology**

Seaweeds. *See* **Algae**

Secession. *See* **State rights; U.S.—History—Civil War—Causes**

Second Advent

    See also **Millennium**

    x Jesus Christ—Second Advent

    xx **Eschatology; Jesus Christ; Millennium**

Secondary education. *See* **Education, Secondary**

Secondary schools. *See* **Education, Secondary; High schools; Junior high schools; Private schools; Public schools**

Secret service

    See also **Detectives; Espionage; Spies;** also names of wars with the subdivision *Secret service,* e.g. **World War, 1939-1945—Secret service;** etc.

    xx **Detectives; Police; Spies**

Secret societies

    See also **Fraternities and sororities;** also names of secret societies, e.g. **Freemasons;** etc.

    x Greek letter societies

    xx **Rites and ceremonies; Societies**

Secret writing. *See* **Cryptography**

Secretaries

    xx **Business education; Office management**

Secretaries of state. *See* **Cabinet officers**

Sectionalism (U.S.)

    x Localism; Provincialism; Regionalism

Sects

    See also names of churches and sects, e.g. **Methodist Church;** etc.

    x Church denominations; Cults and sects; Denominations, Religious; Religious denominations

    xx **Church history; Religions**

Securities

    See also **Bonds; Investments; Mortgages; Stocks**

    x Capitalization (Finance); Dividends

Securities—*Continued*

> *xx* Bonds; Finance; Investments; Speculation; Stock exchange; Stocks

Securities exchange. *See* Stock exchange

Security, Internal. *See* Internal security

Security, International

> *See also* Arbitration, International; Disarmament; International organization; International police; Neutrality; Peace

> *x* International security

> *xx* Disarmament; International relations; Peace

Security, Social. *See* Insurance, Social; Insurance, Unemployment; Old age pensions

Sedition. *See* Political crimes and offenses; Revolutions

Seeds

> *xx* Botany; Plant propagation

Seeds—Germination. *See* Germination

Seeing eye dogs. *See* Guide dogs

Segregation

> *See also* Discrimination; Minorities; also names of groups of people with the subdivision *Segregation,* e.g. **Negroes—Segregation;** etc.

> *x* Apartheid; Desegregation

> *xx* Discrimination; Minorities

Segregation in education

> *See also* Busing (School integration); Discrimination in education

> *x* Education, Segregation in; Integration in education; Racial balance in schools; School integration

> *xx* Discrimination in education; Negroes—Education; Negroes—Segregation

Segregation in public accommodations. *See* Discrimination in public accommodations

Seismography. *See* Earthquakes

Seismology. *See* Earthquakes

Selection, Natural. *See* Natural selection

Selective service. *See* Military service, Compulsory

Self

> *xx* Consciousness; Individuality; Personality

Self-consciousness

Self-control

> *xx* Behavior

Self-culture

> *See also* Books and reading

> *x* Home education; Home study courses; Self-instruction

> *xx* Behavior; Culture; Education; Study, Method of

Self-defense

> *See also* Boxing; Judo; Karate

> *x* Fighting

Self-government. *See* **Democracy; Representative government and representation**

Self-government (in education)
- *x* Honor system; Student self-government
- *xx* School administration and organization; School discipline

Self-instruction. *See* **Correspondence schools and courses; Self-culture;** also names of subjects with subdivision *Programmed instruction,* e.g. **Trigonometry—Programmed instruction;** etc.

Selling. *See* **Salesmen and salesmanship**

Semantics
- *See also* **Words, New**
- *xx* **Language and languages**

Semiconductors
- *See also* **Microelectronics; Transistors**
- *xx* **Electronics**

Semitic race
- *xx* **Anthropology**

Senators—U.S. *See* **U.S. Congress. Senate**

Senior citizens. *See* **Aged**

Senses and sensation
- *See also* **Color sense; Gestalt psychology; Hearing; Pain; Pleasure; Smell; Taste; Touch; Vision**
- *xx* **Intellect; Knowledge, Theory of; Physiology; Psychology; Psychology, Physiological**

Separation (Law). *See* **Divorce**

Separatism, Black. *See* **Black nationalism**

Separatist movement in Quebec (Province). *See* **Quebec (Province)—History — Autonomy and independence movements**

Sepulchers. *See* **Tombs**

Sepulchral brasses. *See* **Brasses**

Serials. *See* **Periodicals**

Serigraphy. *See* **Silk screen printing**

Sermon on the Mount
- *x* Jesus Christ—Sermon on the Mount

Sermons
- *See also* **Preaching**
- *xx* **Preaching**

Serpents. *See* **Snakes**

Servants. *See* **Household employees**

Service, Compulsory military. *See* **Military service, Compulsory**

Service books. *See* **Liturgies**

Service stations, Automobile. *See* **Automobiles —Service stations**

Servomechanisms
- *x* Automatic control
- *xx* **Automation**

Set theory
- *See also* **Algebra, Boolean; Arithmetic; Logic, Symbolic and mathematical; Number theory**
- *x* Aggregates; Classes (Mathematics); Ensembles (Mathematics); Mathemat-

478

Set theory—*Continued*
ical sets; Sets (Mathematics); Theory of sets

xx **Logic, Symbolic and mathematical; Mathematics**

Sets (Mathematics). *See* **Set theory**

Settlements, Social. *See* **Social settlements**

Seven Years' War, 1756-1763
See also Europe—History—1492-1789; U.S.—History—French and Indian War, 1755-1763

x Silesian War, 3d, 1756-1763

xx **Austria—History; Europe—History—1492-1789; Germany—History—1740-1815; Gt. Brit.—History—1714-1837**

Seventeen-year locusts. *See* **Cicadas**

Seventeenth century
See note under **Nineteenth century**

Sewage disposal
See also **Refuse and refuse disposal; Water—Pollution**

x Waste disposal

xx **Public health; Refuse and refuse disposal; Water—Pollution**

Sewerage
See also **Drainage**

x Sewers

xx **Drainage; Drainage, House; Municipal engineering; Plumbing; Sanitary engineering**

Sewers. *See* **Sewerage**

Sewing
See also **Dressmaking; Embroidery; Needlework**

xx **Dressmaking; Home economics; Needlework**

Sex
See also **Reproduction;** also classes of people with the subdivision *Sexual behavior,* e.g. **College students—Sexual behavior;** etc. also headings beginning with the word **Sexual**

xx **Biology; Marriage; Reproduction**

Sex discrimination
See also **Woman—Civil rights**

xx **Discrimination**

Sex instruction
See also **Sexual hygiene**

x Sexual education

xx **Family life education; Sexual hygiene**

Sexual education. *See* **Sex instruction**

Sexual ethics
See also **Birth control; Free love; Prostitution; Sexual hygiene**

x Ethics, Sexual

xx **Ethics; Marriage; Prostitution; Sexual hygiene; Social ethics**

Sexual hygiene

    See also **Birth control; Prostitution; Sex instruction; Sexual ethics; Venereal diseases; Woman—Health and hygiene**

    x Hygiene, Sexual; Hygiene, Social; Social hygiene

    xx **Prostitution; Sex instruction; Sexual ethics; Venereal diseases**

Shades and shadows

    x Light and shade

    xx **Drawing**

Shadow pantomimes and plays

    xx **Amateur theatricals; Pantomimes; Puppets and puppet plays; Theater**

Shaft sinking. *See* **Boring**

Shakers

Shakespeare, William

    When applicable, the following subdivisions may be used for other voluminous authors, e.g. **Dante; Goethe;** etc. The following subjects are to be used for works about Shakespeare and about his writings. The texts of his plays, etc. are not given subject headings

Shakespeare, William—Adaptations

    x Shakespeare, William—Paraphrases

Shakespeare, William—Anniversaries

Shakespeare, William—Authorship

    x Bacon-Shakespeare controversy

Shakespeare, William—Bibliography

    xx **Bibliography**

Shakespeare, William—Biography

Shakespeare, William—Characters

    xx **Characters and characteristics in literature**

Shakespeare, William—Comedies

    Use for criticism, etc. of the comedies, not for the texts of the plays

Shakespeare, William—Concordances

    x Concordances; Shakespeare, William—Indexes

    xx **Shakespeare, William—Dictionaries**

Shakespeare, William—Contemporary England

Shakespeare, William—Criticism, interpretation, etc.

    Use for criticism of the plays in general; criticism of the comedies is entered under **Shakespeare, William—Comedies;** criticism of the tragedies under **Shakespeare, William — Tragedies;** criticism of an individual play is entered under **Shakespeare, William,** followed by the title of the play

    xx **Criticism**

Shakespeare, William—Dictionaries

    See also **Shakespeare, William—Concordances**

    x Shakespeare, William—Indexes

Shakespeare, William—Discography
 x Discography
Shakespeare, William—Drama
 x Shakespeare in fiction, drama, poetry, etc.
Shakespeare, William—Fiction
 x Shakespeare in fiction, drama, poetry, etc.
Shakespeare, William—Histories
Shakespeare, William—Indexes. *See* **Shakespeare, William — Concordances; Shakespeare, William—Dictionaries**
Shakespeare, William—Music. *See* **Shakespeare, William—Songs and music**
Shakespeare, William — Paraphrases. *See* **Shakespeare, William—Adaptations**
Shakespeare, William—Parodies, travesties, etc.
 xx Parodies
Shakespeare, William—Poetry
 x Shakespeare in fiction, drama, poetry, etc.
 xx Poetry
Shakespeare, William—Portraits
 xx Portraits
Shakespeare, William—Quotations
Shakespeare, William—Religion and ethics
Shakespeare, William—Songs and music
 x Shakespeare, William—Music
Shakespeare, William—Sonnets
Shakespeare, William—Stage history
 xx Theater
Shakespeare, William—Stage setting and scenery
Shakespeare, William—Style. *See* **Shakespeare, William—Technique**
Shakespeare, William—Technique
 x Shakespeare, William—Style
Shakespeare, William—Tragedies
 Use for criticism, etc. of the tragedies, not for the texts of the plays
Shakespeare in fiction, drama, poetry, etc. *See* **Shakespeare, William — Drama; Shakespeare, William — Fiction; Shakespeare, William—Poetry**
Shape. *See* **Size and shape**
Sharecropping. *See* **Farm tenancy**
Shares of stock. *See* **Stocks**
Sheep
 xx **Domestic animals; Livestock**
Sheet-metal work
 See also **Plate-metal work**
 x Press working of metal
 xx **Metalwork**
Sheffield plate
 xx **Plate**
Shellfish. *See* **Crustacea; Mollusks**
Shells
 See also **Mollusks**
 x Conchology; Sea shells
 xx **Mollusks**

481

Shells (Projectiles). *See* **Projectiles**

Shelterbelts. *See* **Windbreaks** *and shelterbreaks*

Shelters, Air raid. *See* **Air raid shelters**

Shinto
> *See also* **Ancestor worship**
> *xx* **Religions**

Ship building. *See* **Shipbuilding**

Ship models. *See* **Ships—Models**

Shipbuilding
> *See also* **Boatbuilding; Marine engines; Naval architecture; Ships; Ships—Models; Steamboats**
> *x* Architecture, Naval; Marine architecture; Ship building
> *xx* **Boatbuilding; Industrial arts; Naval architecture; Naval art and science**

Shipping (May subdiv. geog.)
> *See also* **Harbors; Inland navigation; Insurance, Marine; Maritime law; Merchant marine**
> *x* Ocean—Economic aspects
> *xx* **Merchant marine; Transportation**

Shipping—U.S.
> *x* U.S.—Shipping

Ships
> *See also*
>
> | | |
> |---|---|
> | Boats and boating | Steamboats |
> | Clipper ships | Submarines |
> | Merchant marine | Warships |
> | Navies | Yachts and yacht- |
> | Navigation | ing |
> | Sailing | |
>
> *also* names of ships, e.g. **Bounty (Ship);** etc.
> *x* Vessels (Ships)
> *xx* **Boats and boating; Naval architecture; Shipbuilding**

Ships—Models
> *x* Ship models
> *xx* **Machinery—Models; Shipbuilding**

Ships in art. *See* **Marine painting**

Shipwrecks
> *See also* **Salvage; Survival (after airplane accidents, shipwrecks, etc.);** also names of wrecked ships
> *x* Wrecks
> *xx* **Accidents; Adventure and adventurers; Disasters; Navigation; Salvage; Voyages and travels**

Shoes and shoe industry

Shoemakers

> *x* Boots
> *xx* **Clothing and dress; Leather industry and trade**

Shooting
> Use for works on the use of firearms. Works on shooting game are entered under **Hunting**
> *See also* **Archery; Firearms; Hunting**
> *x* Gunning; Marksmanship

Shooting—*Continued*
    xx Firearms; Game and game birds; Hunting

Shooting stars. *See* **Meteors**

Shop committees. *See* **Employees' representation in management**

Shop management. *See* **Factory management**

Shop practice. *See* **Machine shop practice**

Shop windows. *See* **Show windows**

Shoppers' guides. *See* **Consumer education; Shopping**

Shopping
    Use for works on buying by the consumer. Works on buying by government agencies and commercial and industrial enterprises are entered under **Buying**
    See also **Buying; Consumer education; Consumers**
    x Buyers' guides; Marketing (Home economics); Purchasing; Shoppers' guides
    xx **Buying; Consumer education; Home economics**

Shopping centers - *See* Shopping malls
    xx **Retail trade**

Shops, Machine. *See* **Machine shops**

Short stories
    May be used for collections of short stories by one author as well as for collections by several authors. Works on the technique of writing short stories are entered under **Short story**
    x Collections of literature; English short stories; Stories
    xx **English literature; Fiction; Literature —Collections**

Short stories—Indexes
    xx **Indexes**

Short story
    Use for works on the technique of short story writing. Collections of stories are entered under **Short stories**
    See also **Storytelling**
    xx **Authorship; Fiction; Literature; Storytelling**

Short take off and landing aircraft
    x STOL aircraft
    xx **Jet planes**

Short wave receivers. *See* **Radio, Short wave**

Shorthand
    See also **Abbreviations**
    x Stenography
    xx **Abbreviations; Business education; Writing**

Shotguns
    x Guns
    xx **Firearms**

Show windows
    x Shop windows; Window dressing
    xx **Advertising; Windows**

Showers (Parties)

    xx Parties

Shrines

    See also Miracles; Pilgrims and pilgrimages; Saints; Tombs

    xx Pilgrims and pilgrimages; Saints

Shrubs

    See also Evergreens; Landscape gardening; Plants, Ornamental

    xx Botany; Landscape gardening; Plants; Trees

Shyness. *See* Bashfulness

Sick

    See also Cookery for the sick; First aid; Health resorts, spas, etc.; Home nursing; Hospitals; Nurses and nursing

    x Invalids; Patients

    xx Handicapped; Home nursing; Nurses and nursing

Sickness insurance. *See* Insurance, Health

Sidereal sysem. *See* Stars

Sieges. *See* Battles

Sight. *See* Vision

Sight saving books. *See* Large print books

Sign boards. *See* Signs and signboards

Sign language. *See* Deaf—Means of communication; Indians of North America—Sign language

Sign painting

    See also Alphabets; Lettering; Signs and signboards

    xx Advertising; Lettering; Painting, Industrial; Signs and signboards

Signals and signaling

    See also Flags; Radio; Railroads—Signaling; Sonar

    x Coastal signals; Fog signals; Military signaling; Naval signaling

    xx Flags; Military art and science; Naval art and science; Navigation; Signs and symbols

Signers of the Declaration of Independence. *See* U.S. Declaration of Independence

Signets. *See* Seals (Numismatics)

Signs (Advertising). *See* Electric signs; Signs and signboards

Signs, Electric. *See* Electric signs

Signs and signboards

    See also Electric signs; Posters; Sign painting

    x Billboards; Guide posts; Road signs; Sign boards; Signs (Advertising)

    xx Advertising; Posters; Sign painting

Signs and symbols

    See also Abbreviations; Ciphers; Cryptography; Heraldry; Signals and signaling; Symbolism; Weather lore

Siamese Twins

Signs and symbols—*Continued*

    x Symbols

    xx **Abbreviations; Symbolism**

Silage and silos

    x Ensilages; Silos

    xx **Feeding and feeds; Forage plants**

Silesian War, 3d, 1756-1763. *See* **Seven Years' War, 1756-1763**

Silk

    See also **Silkworms**

    xx **Fibers; Textile industry and fabrics**

Silk, Artificial. *See* **Rayon**

Silk screen printing

    x Screen printing; Serigraphy

    xx **Color printing; Stencil work**

Silkworms

    x Cocoons

    xx **Insects, Injurious and beneficial; Moths; Silk**

Silos. *See* **Silage and silos**

Silver

    See also **Coinage; Jewelry; Money; Silversmithing; Silverware**

    x Bimetallism; Bullion

    xx **Coinage; Currency question; Money; Precious metals**

Silver mines and mining

    See also **Prospecting**

Silversmithing

    See also **Hallmarks; Jewelry; Metalwork; Plate; Silverware**

    xx **Hallmarks; Jewelry; Metalwork; Silver**

Silverware

    x Flatware, Silver

    xx **Silver; Silversmithing; Tableware**

Sin

    See also **Atonement; Free will and determinism**

    xx **Christian ethics; Ethics; Good and evil; Salvation; Theology**

Sinai Campaign, 1956

    x Anglo-French intervention in Egypt, 1956; Israel-Arab War, 1956

    xx **Egypt—History**

Singers

    xx **Musicians**

Singing

    See also **Choirs (Music); Respiration; School songbooks; Vocal music; Voice**

    x School music; Vocal culture; Voice culture

    xx **Choirs (Music); Vocal music; Voice**

Singing games

    xx **Games**

Singing societies. *See* **Choral societies**

Single rail railroads. *See* **Monorails**

Single women

    See also **Widows**

Single women—*Continued*

    x Spinsters; Unmarried women

    xx **Woman**

Sisterhoods. *See* **Monasticism and religious orders for women**

Sit-down strikes. *See* **Strikes and lockouts**

Six day war. *See* **Israel-Arab War, 1967**

Sixteenth century

    See note under **Nineteenth century**

    See also **Reformation**

    xx **Reformation; Renaissance**

Size and shape

    x Shape

Skating

    See also **Roller skating**

    x Figure skating; Ice skating

    xx **Winter sports**

Skepticism

    See also **Agnosticism; Belief and doubt; Truth**

    x Scepticism

    xx **Agnosticism; Atheism; Belief and doubt; Faith; Free thought; Philosophy; Rationalism; Religion; Truth**

Sketching. *See* **Drawing**

Skiing. *See* **Skis and skiing**

Skiing, Water. *See* **Water skiing**

Skin

Skin, Color of. *See* **Color of man**

Skin—Diseases

    See also names of skin diseases, e.g. **Acne;** etc.

    x Dermatology

    xx **Diseases**

Skin diving

    See also **Manned undersea research stations; Underwater exploration**

    x Deep-sea diving; Diving, Skin; Diving, Submarine; Frogmen; Snorkeling; Scuba diving; Submarine diving; Underwater swimming

    xx **Diving; Oceanography—Research; Salvage; Underwater exploration; Water sports**

Skin garments. *See* **Leather garments**

Skins. *See* **Hides and skins**

Skis and skiing

    See also **Water skiing**

    x Skiing

    xx **Winter sports**

Skits

    x Entertainments

Skull. *See* **Brain; Head; Phrenology**

Sky diving. *See* **Skydiving**

Sky hijacking. *See* **Hijacking of airplanes**

Sky laboratories. *See* **Space stations**

Skydiving

    x Sky diving

    xx **Aeronautical sports**

Skyjacking. *See* **Hijacking of airplanes**

486

Skyscrapers
  xx Architecture; Building, Iron and steel;
    Industrial buildings; Office buildings
Slander (Law). *See* Libel and slander
Slang. *See* English language—Slang
Slave trade
  xx International law; Slavery; Slavery in
    the U.S.
Slavery
  See also Peonage; Slave trade
  x Abolition of slavery; Antislavery; Com-
    pulsory labor; Emancipation of slaves;
    Forced labor; Freedom
  xx Contract labor; Labor and laboring
    classes; Liberty; Sociology
Slavery in the U.S.
  Use same form for slavery in other coun-
    tries
  See also

Abolitionists	State rights
Negroes	Underground
Slave trade	railroad

  Southern States—
    History
  x Emancipation of slaves
  xx Negroes; Underground railroad; U.S.
    —History—Civil War
Slavery in the U.S.—Fiction
  xx Fiction; Historical fiction
Slavic race. *See* Slavs
Slavs
  See also names of peoples belonging to the
    Slavic race
  x Slavic race
Sleep
  See also Dreams; Insomnia
  xx Brain; Dreams; Hygiene; Insomnia;
    Mind and body; Psychology, Phys-
    iological; Rest; Subconsciousness
Sleeping sickness
  xx Tropics—Diseases and hygiene
Sleeplessness. *See* Insomnia
Sleight of hand. *See* Magic
Slide projectors. *See* Projectors
Slide rule
  xx Calculating machines; Logarithms;
    Measuring instruments
Slides (Photography)
  See also Filmstrips
  x Color slides; Lantern slides
  xx Filmstrips; Photography
Slow learning children
  x Backward children; Children, Backward;
    Children, Retarded; Retarded children
  xx Exceptional children; Mentally handi-
    capped children
Slumber songs. *See* Lullabies
Slums. *See* Housing; Tenement houses
Small arms. *See* Firearms

Small business
  Use for works on small independent enterprises as contrasted with "big business"
  x Business, Small
  xx **Business**
Smallpox
  See also **Vaccination**
  xx Epidemics; Communicable diseases; Medicine—Practice; Therapeutics; Vaccination
Smell
  See also **Nose**
  xx Senses and sensations
Smelting
  See also Blast furnaces; Electrometallurgy; Metallurgy; Ore dressing
  xx Furnaces; Metallurgy
Smoke prevention
  See also Fuel; Furnaces
  x Prevention of smoke
Smoke stacks. *See* **Chimneys**
Smokeless powder. *See* **Gunpowder**
Smoking
  See also Cigarettes; Cigars; Pipes, Tobacco; Tobacco; Tobacco habit
  xx Tobacco
Smuggling
  xx Crime and criminals; Tariff
Snakes
  x Serpents; Vipers
  xx **Reptiles**
Snorkeling. *See* **Skin diving**
Snow
  xx Meteorology; Rain and rainfall; Storms; Water; Weather

✓ Snowmobiles

Soap
  See also Detergents, Synthetic
  xx Cleaning; Cleaning compounds
Soap box derbies
  x Racing
Soap carving. *See* **Soap sculpture**
Soap sculpture
  x Soap carving
  xx Modeling; Sculpture
Soaring flight. *See* **Gliding and soaring**
Sobriquets. *See* **Nicknames**
Soccer
  x Ball games
  xx College sports; Football
Social adjustment
  See also Socially handicapped
  x Adjustment, Social
  xx Behavior; Human relations; Social psychology
Social alienation. *See* **Alienation (Social psychology)**
Social case work
  See also Counseling; Parole; Probation
  x Case work, Social; Family social work
  xx Counseling; Social work

Social centers. *See* **Community centers**

Social change

    x Change, Social; Cultural change; Social evolution

    xx **Anthropology; Evolution; Progress; Social sciences; Sociology**

Social classes

    See also **Aristocracy; Caste; Middle classes; Nobility; Upper classes**

    x Class distinction; Rank; Social distinctions

    xx **Equality; Manners and customs; Social conflict; Sociology**

Social conditions

    Use for general works relating to several or all of the following topics: labor, poverty, education, health, housing, recreation, moral conditions

    See also **Cost and standard of living; Counter culture; Economic conditions; Labor and laboring classes; Moral conditions; Social problems; Social surveys;** also **Indians of North America—Social conditions; Jews—Social conditions; Negroes—Social conditions;** and names of countries, cities, etc. with the subdivision *Social conditions,* e.g. **U.S.—Social conditions; Chicago—Social conditions;** etc.

    x Social history

    xx **Social ethics; Sociology**

Social conflict

    See also **Conflict of generations; Social classes**

    x Class conflict; Class struggle; Conflict. Social

    xx **Communism; Revolutions; Socialism**

Social conformity. *See* **Conformity**

Social customs. *See* **Manners and customs;** and names of ethnic groups, countries, cities, etc. with the subdivision *Social life and customs,* e.g. **Indians of North America—Social life and customs; Jews—Social life and customs; U.S. —Social life and customs;** etc.

Social democracy. *See* **Socialism**

Social distinctions. *See* **Social classes**

Social ecology. *See* **Human ecology**

Social equality. *See* **Equality**

Social ethics

    See also **Christian ethics; Citizenship; Crime and criminals; Political ethics; Sexual ethics; Social conditions; Social problems; Sociology, Christian**

    x Ethics, Social

    xx **Christian ethics; Ethics; Social problems; Sociology, Christian**

Social evolution. *See* **Social change**

489

Social group work
> x Group work, Educational and social
> xx **Adult education; Clubs; Social work**

Social history. *See* **Social conditions**

Social hygiene. *See* **Hygiene; Prostitution; Public health; Sexual hygiene; Venereal diseases**

Social insurance. *See* **Insurance, Social**

Social life and customs. *See* **Manners and customs;** and names of ethnic groups, countries, cities, etc. with the subdivision *Social life and customs,* e.g. **Indians of North America—Social life and customs; Jews—Social life and customs; U.S.—Social life and customs;** etc.

Social policy
> *See also* **Economic policy;** also names of countries, cities, etc. with the subdivision *Social policy,* e.g. **U.S.—Social policy;** etc.
> x National planning; Planning, National; State planning
> xx **Economic policy**

Social problems
> *See also*

Charities	Migrant labor
Child labor	Old age pensions
Community centers	Prostitution
Cost and standard of living	Public health
Crime and criminals	Race problems
Discrimination	Social ethics
Divorce	Social surveys
Eugenics	Suicide
Housing	Tenement houses
Immigration and emigration	Unemployed
	Woman—Employment
Juvenile delinquency	Woman—Social conditions
Liquor problem	

> x Reform, Social; Social reform; Social welfare
> xx **Civilization; Social conditions; Social ethics; Sociology**

Social problems and the church. *See* **Church and social problems**

Social problems in education. *See* **Educational sociology**

Social psychology
> *See also* **Alienation (Social psychology); Attitude (Psychology); Crowds; Human relations; Interviewing; National characteristics; Political psychology; Psychology, Applied; Race psychology; Social adjustment; Sociometry; Violence**
> x Mass psychology; Psychology, Social
> xx **Crowds; Psychology; Race psychology; Sociology**

490

Social reform. *See* **Social problems**

Social sciences

Use for general and comprehensive works dealing with sociology, political science and economics

See also **Economics; Political science; Social change; Sociology**

x Social studies

Social security. *See* **Insurance, Social; Insurance, Unemployment; Old age pensions; Public welfare**

Social service. ~~*See* **Social work**~~

Social settlements

See also **Boys' clubs; Community centers; Day nurseries; Girls' clubs; Playgrounds;** also names of settlements, e.g. **Hull House, Chicago;** etc.

x Church settlements; Neighborhood centers; Settlements, Social

xx **Charities; Social work; Welfare work in industry**

Social studies. *See* **Geography; History; Social sciences**

Social surveys (May subdiv. geog.)

Use for works on the methods employed in conducting surveys of social and economic conditions of communities and also for surveys of individual regions or cities. In the latter case a second heading may be used for name of region or city followed by the subdivision *Social conditions*

See also **Educational surveys**

x Community surveys; Surveys, Social

xx **City planning; Regional planning; Social conditions; Social problems; Sociology**

Social surveys—U.S.

x U.S.—Social surveys

Social welfare. *See* **Charities; Public welfare; Social problems; Social work**

Social work

Use for works on the methods employed in welfare work, public or private

See also **Charities; Public welfare; Social case work; Social group work; Social settlements; Welfare work in industry**

x Philanthropy; Social service; Social welfare; Welfare work

Socialism (May subdiv. geog.)

See also

Capitalism	Labor and laboring
Class struggle	classes
Communism	Labor unions
Equality	National socialism
Government owner-	Old age pensions
ship	Proletariat
Individualism	Syndicalism
Industry and state	Utopias

491

Socialism—*Continued*

    x Collectivism; Marxism; Social democracy

    xx Capitalism; Communism; Cooperation; Democracy; Economics; Equality; Individualism; Labor and laboring classes; National socialism; Political science; Sociology; Syndicalism

Socialism, Christian

    See also **Christianity and economics; Church and social problems**

    x Christian socialism

    xx **Christianity; Church and social problems**

Socialism—U.S.

    x U.S.—Socialism

Socialization of industry. *See* **Government ownership; Industry and state**

Socialized medicine. *See* **Charities, Medical; Insurance, Health; Insurance, Hospitalization; Medicine, State**

Socially handicapped

    x Culturally handicapped; Disadvantaged; Underprivileged

    xx **Handicapped; Social adjustment**

Socially handicapped children

    x Culturally handicapped children; Disadvantaged children; Underprivileged children

    xx **Handicapped children**

Socials. *See* **Church entertainments**

Societies

    Use for general works about societies, etc. The headings enumerated below represent various types of societies and associations. Works about, and publications of, societies devoted to specific subjects are entered under the subject with the subdivision *Societies,* e.g. **Agriculture—Societies;** etc.

    See also

Associations	Girls' clubs
Boys' clubs	Guilds
Choral societies	Labor unions
Clubs	Parents' and teach-
Cooperative soci-	ers' associations
eties	Secret societies
Educational associa-	Students' societies
tions	Women's clubs

    also general subjects with the subdivision *Societies* (e.g. **Agriculture—Societies;** etc.) ; and names of individual societies

    x Learned societies

    xx **Associations; Clubs**

Societies, Cooperative. *See* **Cooperative societies**

Society, Primitive

    See also **Art, Primitive; Cannibalism; Clans and clan system; Indians of North America—Social life and cus-**

Society, Primitive—*Continued*
    toms; Man, Prehistoric; Music,
    Primitive; Religion, Primitive
  x Illiterate societies; Primitive society
  xx **Civilization; Ethnology; Sociology**
Society, Upper. *See* **Upper classes**
Society and art. *See* **Art and society**
Society of Friends. *See* **Friends, Society of**
Society of Jesus. *See* **Jesuits**
Sociology
    Use for systematic studies on the structure
    of society. General works dealing with
    sociology, political science and eco-
    nomics are entered under **Social sci-
    ences**

  See also

Aristocracy	Population
Cities and towns	Race problems
Civilization	Race psychology
Communism	Slavery
Educational sociol-	Social classes
ogy	Social change
Equality	Social conditions
Family	Social problems
Heredity	Social psychology
Human ecology	Social surveys
Immigration and	Socialism
emigration	Society, Primitive
Individualism	Unemployed
Labor and laboring	
classes	

  xx **Social sciences**
Sociology, Christian
    See note under **Church and social prob-
    lems**
  See also **Christianity and economics; So-
    cial ethics**
  x Christian sociology
  xx **Social ethics**
Sociology, Educational. *See* **Educational so-
    ciology**
Sociology, Rural
    Use for works which treat of social organi-
    zation and conditions in rural com-
    munities. Descriptive, popular and
    literary works on living in the country
    are entered under **Country life**
  See also **Country life; Farm life; Peas-
    antry**
  x Rural sociology
  xx **Country life; Farm life; Peasantry**
Sociology, Urban
  See also **Cities and towns; Urban renewal**
  x Urban sociology
  xx **Cities and towns**
Sociometry
  See also **Popularity**
  xx **Social psychology**
Softball
  xx **Baseball**

493

Software, Computer. *See* **Computer programs;**
        Programming (Electronic com-
        puters); Programming languages
        (Electronic computers)

Soil bacteriology. *See* **Soils—Bacteriology**

Soil conservation
    See also **Erosion**
    x Conservation of the soil
    xx **Erosion; Natural resources**

Soil erosion. *See* **Erosion**

Soil fertility. *See* **Soils**

Soil mechanics. *See* **Soils (Engineering)**

Soiling crops. *See* **Feeding and feeds**

Soilless agriculture. *See* **Plants—Soilless cul-**
        ture

Soils
    See also **Agricultural chemistry; Clay;**
        Drainage; Fertilizers and manures;
        Irrigation; Reclamation of land;
        Soils (Engineering); also headings
        beginning with the word **Soil**
    x Soil fertility
    xx **Agricultural chemistry; Agriculture;**
        Geology, Economic

Soils—Bacteriology
    See also **Bacteriology, Agricultural**
    xx **Bacteriology, Agricultural; Sanitary**
        engineering

Soils (Engineering)
    x Earthwork; Soil mechanics
    xx **Foundations; Roads; Soils; Structural**
        engineering

Solar batteries
    x Sun powered batteries
    xx **Electric batteries; Solar radiation**

Solar eclipses. *See* **Eclipses, Solar**

Solar energy
    See also **Solar engines**
    x Solar heat; Solar power
    xx **Power resources; Solar radiation; Sun**

Solar engines
    xx **Engines; Solar energy**

Solar heat. *See* **Solar energy; Sun**

Solar physics. *See* **Sun**

Solar power. *See* **Solar energy**

Solar radiation
    See also **Solar batteries; Solar energy;**
        Sunspots
    x Radiation, Solar; Sun—Radiation
    xx **Meteorology; Space environment**

Solar system
    See also **Comets; Earth; Meteors; Moon;**
        Planets; Sun; also names of planets,
        e.g. **Venus (Planet);** etc.
    xx **Astronomy; Planets; Stars; Sun**

Solder and soldering
    See also **Alloys; Welding**
    x Brazing
    xx **Metals; Metalwork; Plumbing; Weld-**
        ing

✓ Solar heating

Soldiers (May subdiv. geog.)

Use for works dealing with members of the armed forces in general, including the Navy, Marine Corps, etc. as well as the Army

See also **Armies; Generals; Military art and science; Military service as a profession; Scouts and scouting; Veterans;** also names of countries with the subdivision *Army—Military life,* e.g. **U.S. Army—Military life;** etc.

x Armed forces; Army life; Military life; Soldiers' life

xx **Armies; Military art and science; Veterans; War**

Soldiers, Disabled. *See* **Physically handicapped**

Soldiers—Hygiene. *See* **Military hygiene**

Soldiers—U.S.

x G.I.s; U.S.—Soldiers

Soldiers' bonus. *See* **Pensions, Military**

Soldiers' handbooks. *See* **U.S. Army—Handbooks, manuals, etc.**

Soldiers' life. *See* **Soldiers;** and names of countries with the subdivision *Army—Military life,* e.g. **U.S. Army—Military life;** etc.

Soldiers' songs. *See* **War songs**

Solid geometry. *See* **Geometry**

Solitaire (Game)

x Patience (Game)

Somatology

See also **Color of man; Man—Origin and antiquity**

x Anthropology, Physical; Physical anthropology

xx **Anthropology; Ethnology**

Sonar

x Echo ranging; Sound navigation

xx **Signals and signaling**

Sonata

xx **Musical form**

Song books. *See* **Songbooks**

Song writing. *See* **Composition (Music); Music, Popular (Songs, etc.)—Writing and publishing**

Songbooks

See also **School songbooks**

x Community songbooks; Song books

xx **Songs**

Songbooks, School. *See* **School songbooks**

Songs (May subdiv. geog. adjective form, e.g. **Songs, American;** etc.)

Use for collections of songs which include both words and music, and for works about songs. Collections of songs which contain the words but not the music are entered under **Poetry**

See also

Ballads	**Childrens' songs**
Carols	**Folk songs**

[handwritten: ✓ Solid waste management. See Refuse and refuse disposal]

495

Songs—*Continued*

Hymns	School songbooks
Lullabies	Sea songs
Music, Popular	Songbooks
(Songs, etc.)	State songs
National songs	Students' songs
Negro songs	War songs

    also general subjects, names of classes of
      persons and of schools, colleges, etc.
      with the subdivision *Songs and music,*
      e.g. **Aeronautics—Songs and music;**
      Cowboys—Songs and music; U.S.
      Military Academy, West Point—
      Songs and music; etc.; and names of
      individual songs

    xx **Poetry—Collections; Vocal music**

Songs, American

    See also **Folk songs—U.S.; National**
      songs, American

    x American songs; U.S.—Songs

Songs, National. *See* **National songs**

Songs, Popular. *See* **Music, Popular (Songs,**
    etc.)

Soothsaying. *See* **Divination**

Soporifics. *See* **Narcotics**

Sorcery. *See* **Occult sciences; Witchcraft**

Sororities. *See* **Fraternities and sororities**

Sorrow. *See* **Joy and sorrow**

Soubriquets. *See* **Nicknames**

Soul

    See also **Future life; Immortality; Per-**
      sonality; Psychology; Spiritual life

    x Spirit

    xx **Future life; Man (Theology); Person-**
      ality; Philosophy

Soul music. *See* **Blues (Songs, etc.); Jazz**
    music; Music, Popular (Songs, etc.);
    Negro music

Sound

    See also **Architectural acoustics; Hear-**
      ing; Music—Acoustics and physics;
      Noise; Phonetics; Soundproofing;
      Sounds; Ultrasonics; Vibration

    x Acoustics

    xx **Music; Music—Acoustics and physics;**
      Physics; Pneumatics; Radiation

Sound—Recording and reproducing

    See also **High-fidelity sound systems;**
      Intercommunication systems; Stereo-
      phonic sound systems; also methods
      of recording, e.g. **Magnetic recorders**
      and recording; etc.

    xx **Moving pictures; Phonograph; Radio**

Sound effects. *See* **Sounds**

Sound navigation. *See* **Sonar**

Sound waves

    See also **Ultrasonic waves**

    xx **Vibration; Waves**

Soundproofing

    xx **Architectural acoustics; Sound**

Sounds
> *x* Sound effects
> *xx* **Sound**

Soups
> *xx* **Cookery**

The South. *See* **Southern States**

South Africa. *See* **Africa, South**

South African War, 1899-1902
> *x* Boer War, 1899-1902; Transvaal War, 1899-1902
> *xx* **Africa, South—History; Gt. Brit.—History—19th century**

South America
> *xx* **America; Latin America**

South America—Discovery and exploration. *See* **America—Discovery and exploration**

South American literature. *See* **Latin American literature**

South Atlantic States. *See* **Atlantic States**

South Pole
> *See also* **Antarctic regions**
> *x* Polar expeditions
> *xx* **Antarctic regions; Polar regions**

South Sea Islands. *See* **Islands of the Pacific**

Southeast Asia. *See* **Asia, Southeastern**

Southern Africa. *See* **Africa, Southern**

Southern States
> *x* The South
> *xx* **United States**

Southern States—History
> *xx* **Slavery in the U.S.**

Southwest, New
> Use for works on that part of the United States which corresponds roughly with the old Spanish province of New Mexico, including the present Arizona, New Mexico, southern Colorado, Utah, Nevada and California
> *xx* **United States**

Southwest, Old
> Use for works on the section which comprised the southwestern part of the United States before the cessions of land from Mexico following the Mexican War. It included Louisiana, Texas, Arkansas, Tennessee, Kentucky and Missouri
> *xx* **United States**

Sovereigns. *See* **Kings and rulers; Monarchy; Queens; Roman emperors**

Soviet bloc. *See* **Communist countries**

Soviet invasion of the Czechoslovak Republic. *See* **Czechoslovak Republic—History Intervention, 1968-**

Soviet Union. *See* **Russia**

Soybean
> *xx* **Forage plants**

Space, Outer. *See* **Outer space**

Space and time. *See* **Relativity (Physics)**

497

Space biology

See also **Life on other planets**

x Astrobiology; Bioastronautics; Cosmobiology; Exobiology; Extraterrestrial life

xx **Biology; Space sciences**

Space communication. *See* **Astronautics—Communication systems; Interstellar communication**

Space craft. *See* **Space ships**

Space environment

See also **Cosmic rays; Solar radiation**

x Environment, Space; Extraterrestrial environment; Space weather

xx **Astronomy; Outer space**

Space exploration (Astronautics). *See* **Outer space—Exploration**

Space flight

Use for works on the physics and technique of flying in outer space. The early, imaginary, and descriptive accounts of travel beyond the earth's atmosphere are entered under **Interplanetary voyages**

See also **Astrodynamics; Interplanetary voyages; Navigation (Astronautics); Orbital rendezvous (Space flight); Outer space—Exploration**

x Rocket flight; Space travel

xx **Aeronautics—Flights; Astrodynamics; Astronautics; Interplanetary voyages; Navigation (Astronautics)**

Space flight—Laws and regulations. *See* **Space law**

Space flight, Manned. *See* **Manned space flight**

Space flight to the moon

Use same form for space flight to other planets

See also **Apollo project; Moon—Exploration**

x Flight to the moon; Lunar expeditions; Moon, Voyages to; Voyages to the moon

xx **Astronautics**

Space laboratories. *See* **Space stations**

Space law

x Aerospace (Law); Air space law; Airspace (Law); Artificial satellites—Laws and regulations; Astronautics—Laws and regulations; Law, Space; Space flight—Laws and regulations; Space stations—Laws and regulations

xx **Astronautics and civilization; International law; Law**

Space medicine

See also **Aviation medicine; Life support systems (Space environment); Manned space flight; Weightlessness**

x Aerospace medicine; Bioastronautics

498

Space medicine—*Continued*
>   *xx* Aviation medicine; Manned space
>   flight; Space sciences

Space nutrition. *See* Astronauts—Nutrition

Space orbital rendezvous. *See* Orbital rendez-
>   vous (Space flight)

Space photography
>   *See also* Lunar photography; also objects
>   with the subdivision *Photographs from
>   space,* e.g. Earth—Photographs from
>   space; Moon—Photographs from
>   space; etc.
>   *x* Astronautics, Photography in; Photog-
>   raphy, Space; Photography in astro-
>   nautics
>   *xx* Photography

Space platforms. *See* Space stations

Space power. *See* Astronautics and civilization

Space probes
>   *See also* names of types of probes, e.g.
>   Lunar probes; Mars probes; etc.;
>   also names of space vehicles and space
>   projects, e.g. Mariner project; etc.
>   *x* Probes, Space
>   *xx* Outer space—Exploration; Space ve-
>   hicles

Space rescue operations
>   *x* Manned space flight—Rescue work;
>   Rescue operations, Space; Space ships—
>   Rescue work
>   *xx* Rescue work

Space research. *See* Outer space—Explora-
>   tion; Space sciences

Space sciences
>   Use for general works, for scientific results
>   of space exploration and scientific ap-
>   plications of space flight
>   *See also* Astronautics; Astronomy; Geo-
>   physics; Outer space; Space biology;
>   Space medicine
>   *x* Science and space; Space research
>   *xx* Astronautics; Astronomy; Science

Space science—International cooperation

Space ships
>   Use for works on manned space vehicles.
>   For works on both manned and un-
>   manned craft use Space vehicles
>   *See also* Orbital rendezvous (Space
>   flight); Rocket planes
>   *x* Space craft
>   *xx* Astronautics; Manned space flight;
>   Life support systems (Space environ-
>   ment); Rocketry; Space vehicles

Space ships—Accidents. *See* Astronautics—
>   Accidents

Space ships—Pilots. *See* Astronauts

Space ships—Rescue work. *See* Space rescue
>   operations

499

Space stations
>   *See also* **Orbital rendezvous (Space flight)**
>   *x* Laboratories, Space; Orbital laboratories; Sky laboratories; Space laboratories; Space platforms
>   *xx* **Astronautics; Artificial satellites; Space vehicles**

Space stations—Laws and regulations. *See* **Space law**

Space suits. *See* **Astronauts—Clothing**

Space telecommunication. *See* **Interstellar communication**

Space television. *See* **Television in astronautics**

Space travel. *See* **Interplanetary voyages; Manned space flight; Space flight**

Space vehicles
>   Use for works on both manned and unmanned vehicles
>   *See also* **Artificial satellites; Astronautics; Lunar excursion module; Space probes; Space ships; Space stations**
>   *x* Space rockets
>   *xx* **Artificial satellites; Astronautics; Rocketry**

Space vehicles—Accidents. *See* **Astronautics—Accidents**

Space vehicles—Extravehicular activity. *See* **Extravehicular activity (Manned space flight)**

Space vehicles—Guidance systems

Space vehicles—Instruments. *See* **Astronautical instruments**

Space vehicles—Piloting
>   *x* Piloting (Astronautics)
>   *xx* **Astronauts; Navigation (Astronautics)**

Space vehicles—Propulsion systems

Space vehicles—Thermodynamics
>   *xx* **Thermodynamics**

Space vehicles—Tracking
>   *x* Tracking of satellites

Space weather. *See* **Space environment**

Spain
>   May be subdivided like U.S. except for *History*

Spain—History

Spain—History—War of 1898. *See* **U.S.—History—War of 1898**

Spain—History—Civil War, 1936-1939

Spain—History—1939-

Spaniards in the U.S.
>   Use same form for Spaniards in other countries, states, etc.
>   *x* Spanish in the U.S.

Spanish America. *See* **Latin America**

Spanish-American literature. *See* **Latin American literature**

Spanish-American War, 1898. *See* **U.S.—History—War of 1898**

Spanish Armada. *See* **Armada, 1588**

Spanish in the U.S. *See* **Spaniards in the U.S.**

Spanish language

    May be subdivided like **English language**

Spanish literature

    May use same subdivisions and names of literary forms as for **English literature**

    See also **Latin American literature**

Spanish Succession, War of, 1701-1714

    x War of the Spanish Succession, 1701-1714

    xx **Europe—History—1492-1789; Gt. Brit. —History—Stuarts, 1603-1714**

Sparring. *See* **Boxing**

Spas. *See* **Health resorts, spas, etc.**

Spastic paralysis. *See* **Cerebral palsy**

Speakers (Recitation books). *See* **Readings and recitations**

Speaking. *See* **Debates and debating; Lectures and lecturing; Preaching; Public speaking; Rhetoric; Voice**

Spear fishing

    xx **Fishing**

Special libraries. *See* **Libraries, Special**

Specialists exchange programs. *See* **Exchange of persons programs**

Specie. *See* **Money**

Specimens, Preservation of. *See* **Taxidermy; Zoological specimens — Collection and preservation**; and names of natural specimens with the subdivision *Collection and preservation,* e.g. **Birds—Collection and preservation; Plants —Collection and preservation;** etc.

Spectacles. *See* **Eyeglasses**

Specters. *See* **Apparitions; Ghosts**

Spectra. *See* **Spectrum**

Spectroscopy. *See* **Spectrum**

Spectrum

    See also **Light; Ultraviolet rays**

    x Analysis, Spectrum; Astronomical spectroscopy; Spectra; Spectroscopy

    xx **Astronomy; Chemistry; Light; Optics; Radiation**

Speculation

    See also **Investments; Securities; Stock exchange**

    xx **Finance; Investments; Stock exchange**

Speech

    See also **Language and languages; Phonetics; Voice**

    x Language arts; Talking

    xx **Language and languages; Phonetics; Voice**

Speech, Liberty of. *See* **Free speech**

Speech disorders

    x Defective speech; Speech pathology; Stammering; Stuttering

Speech pathology. *See* **Speech disorders**

Speeches, addresses, etc.

    Use for collections of speeches of a general nature which are less formal than those entered under **Orations** and gen-

Special education. See Exceptional children

Special weapons and tactics teams

Speeches, addresses, etc.—*Continued*

erally treat of less important subjects

See also **After-dinner speeches; Lectures and lecturing; Orations; Toasts;** also general subjects with the subdivision *Addresses and essays,* e.g. **Agriculture —Addresses and essays; U.S.—History—Addresses and essay;** etc.

x Addresses

xx **After-dinner speeches**

Speed

x Velocity

xx **Motion**

Speed, Supersonic. *See* **Aerodynamics, Supersonic**

Speed reading. *See* **Rapid reading**

Speleology. *See* **Caves**

Spellers

xx **English language—Spelling**

Spelling. *See* names of languages with the subdivision *Spelling,* e.g. **English language —Spelling;** etc.

Spelling reform

x English language—Spelling reform; Orthography; Phonetic spelling

xx **English language—Spelling**

Spells. *See* **Charms**

Spherical trigonometry. *See* **Trigonometry**

Spiders

x Arachnida

Spies

See also **Secret service; World War, 1939-1945—Underground movements**

xx **Espionage; Military art and science; Secret service; Subversive activities**

Spinal paralysis, Anterior. *See* **Poliomyelitis**

Spinning

xx **Textile industry and fabrics**

Spinsters. *See* **Single women**

Spiral gearing. *See* **Gearing**

Spires

x Steeples

xx **Architecture; Church architecture**

Spirit. *See* **Soul**

Spirit, Holy. *See* **Holy Spirit**

Spiritism. *See* **Spiritualism**

Spirits. *See* **Apparitions; Demonology; Ghosts; Spiritualism; Witchcraft**

Spirits, Alcoholic. *See* **Liquors**

Spiritual healing. *See* **Faith cure**

Spiritual life

See also **Christian life; Faith; Meditations; Sanctification**

x Life, Spiritual

xx **Behavior; Christian life; Ethics; Mysticism; Religion; Soul; Theology**

Spiritualism

    See also **Apparitions; Clairvoyance; Ghosts; Psychical research**

    x Spiritism; Spirits

    xx **Apparitions; Future life; Ghosts; Occult sciences; Psychical research; Supernatural**

Spirituals, Negro. *See* **Negro spirituals**

Splicing. *See* **Knots and splices**

Spoils system. *See* **Corruption (in politics)**

Sponges

    xx **Invertebrates**

Spontaneous combustion. *See* **Combustion**

Sports

    See also

Aeronautical sports	**Outdoor life**
Amusements	**Physical education**
Athletics	**and training**
Coaching (Athletics)	**Rodeos**
College sports	**School sports**
Games	**Water sports**
Gymnastics	**Winter sports**
Olympic games	

    also names of sports, e.g. **Baseball**; etc.

    x Field sports; Pastimes

    xx **Amusements; Athletics; Games; Outdoor life; Physical education and training; Play; Recreation**

Sports—Encyclopedias

    xx **Encyclopedias and dictionaries**

Sports—Equipment and supplies

    x Equipment and supplies

Sports cars

    See also names of specific sports cars

    xx **Automobiles**

Spot welding. *See* **Electric welding**

Spraying and dusting

    See also **Aeronautics in agriculture; Fungicides; Insecticides**

    xx **Agricultural pests; Fruit—Diseases and pests; Fungicides; Insecticides**

Spun glass. *See* **Glass fibers**

Sputniks. *See* **Artificial satellites, Russian**

Square dancing

    xx **Folk dancing**

Squirrels

    See also **Chipmunks**

Stabilization in industry. *See* **Business cycles; Economic conditions; Unemployed**

Stables. *See* **Farm buildings**

Stage. *See* **Acting; Actors and actresses; Drama; Theater**

Stage lighting. *See* **Theaters—Lighting**

Stage scenery. *See* **Theaters—Stage setting and scenery**

Stage setting. *See* **Theaters—Stage setting and scenery**

Stained glass. *See* **Glass painting and staining**

Stamina, Physical. *See* **Physical fitness**

Stammering. *See* **Speech disorders**

Stamps, Postage. *See* **Postage stamps**

Standard book numbers. *See* **Publishers' standard book numbers**

Standard of living. *See* **Cost and standard of living**

Standard of value. *See* **Money**

Standard time. *See* **Time**

Stars

> *See also* **Astrology; Astronomy; Astrophysics; Galaxies; Meteors; Planets; Solar system;** also names of stars and groups of stars

> *x* Constellations; Double stars; Sidereal system

> *xx* **Astronomy; Planets**

Stars—Atlases

> *x* Astronomy—Atlases; Atlases, Astronomical

Stars, Falling. *See* **Meteors**

The State

> *See also* **Political science**

> *x* Administration; The Commonwealth; Welfare state

> *xx* **Political science**

State aid to education

> *x* Education—State aid

> *xx* **Education—Finance; Education and state**

State aid to libraries

> *x* Libraries—State aid

> *xx* **Libraries and state; Library finance**

State and agriculture. *See* **Agriculture and state**

State and church. *See* **Church and state**

State and education. *See* **Education and state**

State and environment. *See* **Environmental policy**

State and industry. *See* **Industry and state**

State and insurance. *See* **Insurance, Social**

State and railroads. *See* **Railroads and state**

State and science. *See* **Science and state**

State and the arts. *See* **Art and state**

State birds

> *xx* **Birds**

State church. See **Church and state**

State constitutions. *See* **Constitutions, State**

State debts. *See* **Debts, Public**

State encouragement of the arts. *See* **Art and state**

State flowers

> *x* Flowers, State

> *xx* **Flowers**

State governments

> Use for general works on state government. Works on the government of a particular state are entered under the name of the state with the subdivision *Politics and government*

> *See also* **Constitutions, State; Federal government; Governors;** and names

State governments—*Continued*
>of states with the subdivision *Politics and government,* e.g. **Ohio—Politics and government;** etc.

>*x* U.S.—State governments

>*xx* **Constitutions, State; Federal government; Political science**

State libraries
>*See also* **Libraries, Governmental**

>*x* Libraries, State

>*xx* **Libraries, Governmental; Libraries and state**

State-local tax relations. *See* **Intergovernmental tax relations**

State medicine. *See* **Medicine, State**

State of the Union messages. *See* **Presidents—U.S.—Messages**

State ownership. *See* **Government ownership**

State ownership of railroads. *See* **Railroads and state**

State planning. *See* **Regional planning; Social policy;** and names of states with the subdivision *Economic policy; Social policy,* e.g. **Ohio—Economic policy; Ohio—Social policy;** etc.

State police. *See* **Police, State**

State regulation of industry. *See* **Industry and state**

State rights
>*x* Secession; States' rights

>*xx* **Political science; Slavery in the U.S.**

State songs
>*xx* **Songs**

States, New
>*x* New nations

>*xx* **Underdeveloped areas**

States' rights. *See* **State rights**

Statesmen (May subdiv. geog. adjective form, e.g. **Statesmen, British;** etc.)
>*See also* **Diplomats**

Statesmen, American
>*x* American statesmen; U.S.—Statesmen

Statics
>*See also* **Dynamics; Hydrostatics; Strains and stresses**

>*xx* **Dynamics; Mechanics; Physics**

Statistics
>Use for works on the theory and methods of statistics

>*See also* **Census; Probabilities; Sampling (Statistics); Vital statistics;** also general subjects and names of countries, cities, etc. with the subdivision *Statistics,* e.g. **Agriculture—Statistics; U.S.—Statistics; Chicago—Statistics;** etc.

>*xx* **Census; Commerce; Economic conditions**

Statistics—Graphic methods
  x Diagrams, Statistical
  xx **Graphic methods**
Statues. *See* **Monuments; Sculpture**
Stature. *See* **Growth**
Statutes. *See* **Law**
Steam
  xx **Heat; Power (Mechanics); Water**
Steam engineering
  See also **Mechanical engineering; Power
    (Mechanics); Steam engines; Steam
    navigation; Steam power plants**
  xx **Engineering; Mechanical engineering**
Steam engines
  See also **Boilers; Condensers (Steam);
    Farm engines; Locomotives; Marine
    engines; Steam turbines**
  xx **Engines; Heat engines; Machinery;
    Mechanics; Steam engineering**
Steam fitting. *See* **Pipe fitting**
Steam heating
  xx **Heating**
Steam navigation
  See also **Boilers, Marine; Marine engi-
    neering; Navigation; Steam turbines;
    Steamboats**
  x Navigation, Steam
  xx **Navigation; Steam engineering; Steam-
    boats; Transportation**
Steam power plants
  x Power plants, Steam
  xx **Power plants; Steam engineering**
Steam pumps. *See* **Pumping machinery**
Steam turbines
  xx **Steam engines; Steam navigation; Tur-
    bines**
Steamboats
  See also **Steam navigation**
  x Steamships
  xx **Boats and boating; Naval architecture;
    Ocean travel; Shipbuilding; Ships;
    Steam navigation; Transportation**
Steamboilers. *See* **Boilers**
Steamships. *See* **Steamboats**
Steel
  See also **Building, Iron and steel; Iron;**
    also headings beginning with the word
    Steel
  xx **Metalwork**
Steel, Structural
  See also **Building, Iron and steel**
  x Steel construction; Structural steel
  xx **Building, Iron and steel; Building ma-
    terials; Civil engineering**
Steel construction. *See* **Building, Iron and
    steel; Steel, Structural**
Steel engraving. *See* **Engraving**

Steel industry and trade

    See also Iron industry and trade

    x Industries

    xx Industry; Iron industry and trade; Ironwork

Steel industry and trade—Quality control

    xx Quality control

Steeples. *See* Spires

Stencil work

    See also Silk screen printing

    xx Arts and crafts; Decoration and ornament; Painting

Stenography. *See* Shorthand

Stereophonic sound systems

    xx High fidelity sound systems; Sound—Recording and reproducing

Stereophotography. *See* Photography, Stereoscopic

Sterilization (Birth control)

    x Vasectomy

    xx Birth control

Stewardesses, Air line. *See* Air lines—Hostesses

Stills. *See* Distillation

Stimulants

    See also Alcohol; Liquors; Narcotics

    x Intoxicants

    xx Hygiene; Narcotics; Temperance; Therapeutics

Stock and stock breeding. *See* Livestock

Stock companies

    See also Corporations

    x Companies, Stock; Joint-stock companies

    xx Corporations; Stocks

Stock exchange

    See also Bonds; Foreign exchange; Investments; Securities; Speculation; Stocks; Wall Street

    x Options; Securities exchange; Stock market

    xx Commerce; Exchange; Finance; Investments; Speculation; Stocks

Stock judging. *See* Livestock judging

Stock market. *See* Stock exchange

Stock raising. *See* Livestock

Stockings. *See* Hosiery

Stocks

    See also Bonds; Corporations; Investments; Securities; Stock companies; Stock exchange

    x Dividends; Shares of stock

    xx Bonds; Commerce; Investments; Securities; Stock exchange

Stockyards. *See* Meat industry and trade

Stoics

    xx Ethics; Philosophy, Ancient

Stokers, Mechanical

    x Mechanical stokers

Stomach

> *See also* Digestion

Stone

> *See also* Masonry; Petrology; Quarries
> and quarrying; Rocks; Stonecutting;
> also names of stones, e.g. Marble; etc.
>
> *xx* Building materials; Geology, Eco-
> nomic; Petrology; Quarries and
> quarrying; Rocks

Stone age

> *See also* Man, Prehistoric; Stone imple-
> ments
>
> *x* Eolithic period; Neolithic period; Paleo-
> lithic period; Prehistory
>
> *xx* Archeology

Stone-cutting. *See* Stonecutting

Stone implements

> *x* Flint implements; Implements, utensils,
> etc.
>
> *xx* Archeology; Stone age

Stone quarries. *See* Quarries and quarrying

Stonecutting

> *x* Stone-cutting
>
> *xx* Masonry; Stone

Stones, Precious. *See* Precious stones

Stoneware. *See* Pottery

Storage batteries

> *See also* Electric batteries
>
> *x* Batteries, Electric
>
> *xx* Electric apparatus and appliances;
> Electric batteries

Stores. *See* Chain stores; Cooperative societies; Department stores; Supermarkets

Stories. *See* Anecdotes; Animals—Stories;
Ballets—Stories, plots, etc.; Bible—
Stories; Birds—Stories; Christmas
stories; College stories; Fairy tales;
Fiction; Flowers—Stories; Ghost
stories; Horror stories; Legends;
Mystery and detective stories; Operas—Stories, plots, etc.; Romances;
School stories; Sea stories; Short
stories; Stories in rhyme; Storytelling; Trees—Stories; Vocational stories; and names of individual animals,
birds, flowers, fruits, trees, vegetables,
and holidays with the subdivision *Stories,* e.g. Dogs—Stories; Thanksgiving Day—Stories; etc.

Stories in rhyme

> *x* Stories
>
> *xx* Rhyme

Storms

> *See also* Blizzards; Cyclones; Dust
> storms; Hurricanes; Meteorology;
> Rain and rainfall; Snow; Thunder-
> storms; Tornadoes; Typhoons;
> Winds; and other kinds of storms
>
> *xx* Cyclones; Disasters; Hurricanes; Me-

Storms—*Continued*
> teorology; Ocean; Rain and rainfall; Tornadoes; Weather; Winds

Storytelling
> *See also* **Short story**
> *x* Stories
> *xx* **Children's literature; Short story**

Stoves
> *xx* **Heating**

Strains and stresses
> *See also* **Strength of materials**
> *x* Architectural engineering; Stresses
> *xx* **Architecture; Mechanics; Statics; Strength of materials; Structures, Theory of**

Strategic materials. *See* **Materials**

Strategy
> *See also* **Armies; Military art and science; Naval art and science; Tactics**
> *x* Military strategy; Naval strategy
> *xx* **Military art and science; Naval art and science; War**

Stratigraphic geology. *See* **Geology, Stratigraphic**

Stratosphere
> *xx* **Atmosphere, Upper**

Straw votes. *See* **Public opinion polls**

Strawberries
> *xx* **Berries**

Streamlining. *See* **Aerodynamics**

Street cars. *See* **Street railroads**

Street cleaning
> *See also* **Refuse and refuse disposal**
> *xx* **Cleaning; Municipal engineering; Public health; Refuse and refuse disposal; Roads; Sanitary engineering; Streets**

Street lighting
> *See also* cities with the subdivision *Lighting,* e.g. **Chicago—Lighting**; etc.
> *x* Cities and towns—Lighting; Streets—Lighting
> *xx* **Lighting; Streets**

Street railroads
> *See also* **Electric railroads; Subways**
> *x* Interurban railroads; Railroads, Street; Street cars; Trams; Trolley cars
> *xx* **Electric railroads; Local transit; Public utilities; Railroads; Transportation**

Street traffic. *See* **City traffic; Traffic engineering; Traffic regulations**

Streets
> *See also* **City traffic; Pavements; Roads; Street cleaning; Street lighting**; also names of cities with the subdivision *Streets,* e.g. **Chicago—Streets**; etc.
> *x* Alleys; Highways; Thoroughfares
> *xx* **Cities and towns; Civil engineering; Pavements; Roads; Transportation**

Streets—Lighting. *See* **Street lighting**

Strength of materials

 See also **Building materials; Strains and stresses;** also special materials and forms with the subdivision *Testing,* e.g. **Concrete—Testing;** etc.

 x Architectural engineering; Materials, Strength of; Resistance of materials

 xx **Architecture; Building; Building, Iron and steel; Building materials; Civil engineering; Materials; Mechanics; Strains and stresses; Structures, Theory of**

Stress (Physiology)

 x Tension

Stresses. *See* **Strains and stresses**

Strikes and lockouts

 See also **Arbitration, Industrial; Collective bargaining; Injunctions; Labor unions; Sabotage; Syndicalism**

 x Boycott; Labor disputes; Lockouts; Sit-down strikes; Work stoppage

 xx **Arbitration, Industrial; Collective bargaining; Industrial relations; Injunctions; Labor and laboring classes; Labor unions**

Stringed instruments

 See also names of stringed instruments, e.g. **Guitar; Violin;** etc.

 x Bowed instruments

 xx **Musical instruments**

Strip films. *See* **Filmstrips**

Structural botany. *See* **Botany—Anatomy**

Structural drafting. *See* **Mechanical drawing**

Structural engineering

 See also **Building; Foundations; Hydraulic structures; Soils (Engineering); Structures, Theory of**

 x Engineering, Structural

 xx **Architecture; Building materials; Civil engineering; Engineering; Structures, Theory of**

Structural materials. *See* **Building materials**

Structural psychology. *See* **Gestalt psychology**

Structural steel. *See* **Steel, Structural**

Structures, Theory of

 See also **Building; Strains and stresses; Strength of materials; Structural engineering**

 x Architectural engineering; Theory of structures

 xx **Building, Iron and steel; Structural engineering**

Stucco

 xx **Building materials; Decoration and ornament; Plaster and plastering**

Student activities

 See also **College and school drama; College and school journalism; School assembly programs; School sports**

 x Extracurricular activities

Student aid. *See* **Scholarships, fellowships, etc.; Student loan funds**
Student clubs. *See* **Students' societies**
Student evaluation of teachers
 x Student rating of teachers; Teachers, Rating of (by students)
Student guidance. *See* **Personnel service in education; Vocational guidance**
Student life and customs. *See* **Students**
Student loan funds
 See also **Scholarships, fellowships, etc.**
 x Loan funds, Student; Student aid
 xx **Scholarships, fellowships, etc.**
Student movement. *See* **Youth movement**
Student protests. *See* **Students—Political activity; Youth movement**
Student rating of teachers. *See* **Student evaluation of teachers**
Student revolt. *See* **Students—Political activity; Youth movement**
Student self-government. *See* **Self-government (in education)**
Student societies. *See* **Students' societies**
Student teaching
 x Practice teaching; Teachers—Practice teaching
 xx **Teachers—Training; Teaching**
Students (May subdiv. geog.)
 See also types of students, e.g. **College students;** etc. also headings beginning with the words **College** and **School**
 x School life; Student life and customs
 xx **Colleges and universities**
Students, Foreign
 x Foreign students
Students—Grading and marking. *See* **Grading and marking (Students)**
Students—Personnel work. *See* **Personnel service in education**
Students—Political activity
 x Politics and students; Student protests; Student revolt
 xx **Politics, Practical; Youth movement**
Students—Societies. *See* **Students' societies**
Students—U.S.
 x U.S.—Students
Students and libraries. *See* **Libraries and students**
Students' military training camps. *See* **Military training camps**
Students' societies
 See also **Fraternities and sororities**
 x College fraternities; School clubs; Student clubs; Student societies; Students—Societies
 xx **Societies**
Students' songs
 x College songs
 xx **Songs**

[handwritten:] ✓ Student housing

[handwritten:] ✓ Students, Interchange of

Study, Courses of. *See* **Education—Curricula;** also types of education and schools with the subdivision *Curricula,* e.g. **Library education—Curricula; Colleges and universities—Curricula;** etc.

Study, Method of

See also **Self-culture;** also subjects with the subdivision *Study and teaching,* e.g. **Art—Study and teaching;** etc.

x Learning, Art of; Method of study

xx **Education; Teaching**

Stuttering. *See* **Speech disorders**

Style, Literary

See also **Criticism; Letter writing; Literature—History and criticism; Readability (Literary style); Rhetoric**

x Literary style

xx **Criticism; Literature; Rhetoric**

Style in dress. *See* **Costume; Fashion**

Style manikins. *See* **Models, Fashion**

Style manuals. *See* **Printing—Style manuals**

Subconscious

See also

Consciousness	**Mind and body**
Dreams	**Personality disorders**
Faith cure	
Hallucinations and illusions	**Psychoanalysis**
	Sleep
Hypnotism	**Thought transference**
Mental healing	
Mental suggestion	

xx **Consciousness; Hypnotism; Mental healing; Mind and body; Psychical research; Psychoanalysis; Psychology; Psychology, Pathological; Therapeutics, Suggestive**

Subgravity state. *See* **Weightlessness**

Subject headings

See also **Classification—Books**

xx **Cataloging; Catalogs, Subject; Indexes**

Submarine boats

See note under **Submarines**

See also **Submarines**

x Boats, Submarine

xx **Submarines**

Submarine cables. *See* **Cables, Submarine**

Submarine diving. *See* **Skin diving**

Submarine exploration. *See* **Underwater exploration**

Submarine geology

x Geology, Submarine; Marine geology; Underwater geology

xx **Geology; Oceanography**

Submarine medicine

x Medicine, Submarine; Underwater physiology; Underwater medicine

xx **Medicine**

Submarine photography. *See* **Photography, Submarine**

Submarine research stations, Manned. *See* **Manned undersea research stations**

Submarine telegraph. *See* **Cables, Submarine**

Submarine warfare

> *See also* **Submarines; Torpedoes**
>
> *x* Naval warfare; Warfare, Submarine
>
> *xx* **Naval art and science; War**

Submarines

> Use for works on submarines only. Works on other underwater craft are entered under **Submarine boats**
>
> *See also* **Submarine boats**
>
> *x* Boats, Submarine; U boats
>
> *xx* **Boats and boating; Naval art and science; Ships; Submarine boats; Submarine warfare; Warships**

Submarines, Atomic. *See* **Atomic submarines**

Subprofessional library assistants. *See* **Library technicians**

Subscription television

> *x* Pay television; Television, Subscription
>
> *xx* **Television**

Subsidies

> *x* Bounties; Grants; Subventions
>
> *xx* **Commercial policy; Economic assistance, Domestic; Economic policy; Industry and state**

Suburban areas. *See* **Metropolitan areas**

Suburban homes. *See* **Architecture, Domestic**

Suburban life

> *See also* names of cities with the subdivision *Suburbs and environs,* e.g. **Chicago—Suburbs and environs;** etc.

Subventions. *See* **Subsidies**

Subversive activities

> *See also* **Espionage; Internal security; Political crimes and offenses; Sabotage; Spies**
>
> *x* Fifth column
>
> *xx* **Internal security**

Subways

> *x* Railroads, Underground; Underground railroads
>
> *xx* **Civil engineering; Local transit; Railroads; Street railroads; Transportation; Tunnels**

Success

> *See also* **Ability; Business; Leadership; Saving and thrift**
>
> *x* Fortune; Personal development
>
> *xx* **Business ethics; Wealth**

Succession, Intestate. *See* **Inheritance and succession**

Suffering

> *See also* **Good and evil; Joy and sorrow; Pain**
>
> *xx* **Pain**

513

Suffrage

 See also **Naturalization; Representative government and representation;** also classes of people with the subdivision *Suffrage,* e.g. **Negroes—Suffrage; Woman—Suffrage;** etc.

 x Franchise; Voting

 xx **Citizenship; Constitutional law; Democracy; Elections; Political science; Representative government and representation**

Suffragettes. *See* **Woman—Suffrage**

Sugar

 See also **Beets and beet sugar; Maple sugar; Syrups**

Sugar beets. *See* Beets and beet sugar ✓ *Sugar beets*

Sugar cane

Suggestion, Mental. *See* **Mental suggestion**

Suggestive therapeutics. *See* **Therapeutics, Suggestive**

Suicide

 xx **Insanity; Medical jurisprudence; Social problems**

Sulfa drugs. *See* **Sulfonamides**

Sulfonamides

 x Sulfa drugs

Sulfur. *See* **Sulphur**

Sulphur

 x Sulfur

Summer camps. *See* **Camps**

Summer homes. *See* **Architecture, Domestic; Houses**

Summer resorts

 See also **Health resorts, spas, etc.**

 x Resorts

 xx **Health resorts, spas, etc.**

Summer schools. *See* **Vacation schools**

Sun

 See also **Solar energy; Solar system; Sunspots**

 x Solar physics

 xx **Astronomy; Solar system**

Sun—Eclipses. *See* **Eclipses, Solar**

Sun—Radiation. *See* **Solar radiation**

Sun-dials. *See* **Sundials**

Sun glasses. *See* **Eyeglasses**

Sun-powered batteries. *See* **Solar batteries**

Sun-spots. *See* **Sunspots**

Sunday. *See* **Sabbath**

Sunday schools

 See also **Bible—Study**

 x Bible classes

 xx **Church work; Religious education; Schools**

Sundials

 x Horology; Sun-dials

 xx **Clocks and watches; Garden ornaments and furniture; Time**

Sunken cities. *See* **Cities and towns, Ruined, extinct, etc.**

514

Sunken treasure. *See* **Buried treasure**

Sunspots

    x Sun-spots

    xx **Meteorology; Solar radiation; Sun**

Super markets. *See* **Supermarkets**

Superhighways. *See* **Express highways**

Superintendents of schools. *See* **School superintendents and principals**

Superior children. *See* **Gifted children**

Supermarkets

    x Stores; Super markets

    xx **Grocery trade; Retail trade**

Supernatural

    See also **Divination; Miracles; Occult sciences; Prophecies; Psychical research; Revelation; Spiritualism; Superstition**

    xx **Miracles; Religion**

Supersonic aerodynamics. *See* **Aerodynamics, Supersonic**

Supersonic airliners. *See* **Supersonic transport planes**

Supersonic transport planes

    x SST; Supersonic airliners

Supersonic waves. *See* **Ultrasonic waves**

Supersonics. *See* **Ultrasonics**

Superstition

    See also

Alchemy	Errors
Apparitions	Fairies
Astrology	Folklore
Charms	Fortune telling
Demonology	Ghosts
Divination	Occult sciences
Dreams	Witchcraft

    x Delusions; Traditions

    xx **Demonology; Divination; Errors; Folklore; Ghosts; Occult sciences; Religion; Religion, Primitive; Supernatural**

Supervision of employees. *See* **Personnel management**

Supervision of schools. *See* **School supervision**

Supreme Court—U.S. *See* **U.S. Supreme Court**

Surf. *See* **Ocean waves**

Surf riding. *See* **Surfing**

Surfing

    x Surf riding

    xx **Water sports**

Surgeons

    See also **Physicians**

    x Medical profession

    xx **Medicine—Biography; Physicians**

Surgery

    See also **Anesthetics; Antiseptics; Cryosurgery; Orthopedia; Transplantation of organs, tissues, etc.; Vivisec-**

Surgery—*Continued*

tion; also names of organs and regions of the body with the subdivision *Surgery,* e.g. **Heart—Surgery;** etc.

   x Operations, Surgical

  xx **Medicine**

Surgery, Orthopedic. *See* **Orthopedia**

Surgery, Plastic

   x Plastic surgery

  xx **Transplantation of organs, tissues, etc.**

Surgical transplantation. *See* **Transplantation of organs, tissues, etc.**

Surnames. *See* **Names, Personal**

Surrealism

  xx **Art; Postimpressionism (Art)**

Surveying

  See also **Geodesy; Mine surveying; Topographical drawing**

   x Land surveying

  xx **Civil engineering; Geodesy; Geography; Mensuration**

Surveys, Educational. *See* **Educational surveys**

Surveys, Library. *See* **Library surveys**

Surveys, Social. *See* **Social surveys**

Survival (after airplane accidents, shipwrecks, etc.)

  See also **Wilderness survival**

   x Castaways

  xx **Aeronautics—Accidents; Shipwrecks**

Survival of the fittest. *See* **Natural selection**

Suspended sentence. *See* **Probation**

Suspension bridges. *See* **Bridges**

Swamps. *See* **Marshes**

Swedenborgianism. *See* **New Jerusalem Church**

Swedish language

  May be subdivided like **English language**

  xx **Scandinavian languages**

Swedish literature

  May use same subdivisions and names of literary forms as for **English literature**

  xx **Scandinavian literature**

Swimming

  See also **Diving; Synchronized swimming**

  xx **Water sports**

Swimming pools

Swindlers and swindling

  See also **Counterfeits and counterfeiting; Fraud; Impostors and imposture; Quacks and quackery**

  xx **Crime and criminals; Fraud; Impostors and imposture**

Swine. *See* **Hogs**

Swing music. *See* **Jazz music**

Switches, Electric. *See* **Electric switchgear**

Symbiosis. *See* **Botany—Ecology**

Symbolism
> *See also* **Christian art and symbolism;**
> **Heraldry; Signs and symbols**
> *x* Devices (Heraldry) ; Emblems
> *xx* **Art; Mythology; Signs and symbols**

Symbolism in literature
> *See also* **Allegories**
> *xx* **Literature**

Symbols. *See* **Abbreviations; Signs and symbols**

Sympathy
> *x* Compassion; Consolation; Pity
> *xx* **Behavior; Emotions; Friendship**

Symphonies
> Use for musical scores
> *xx* **Orchestral music**

Symphony
> Use for works on the symphony as a musical form
> *xx* **Musical form**

Symptoms. *See* **Diagnosis**

Synagogues
> *See also* names of cities with the subdivision *Synagogues,* e.g. **Chicago—Synagogues;** etc.
> *xx* **Architecture; Judaism**

Synchronized swimming
> *x* Ballet, Water; Water ballet
> *xx* **Swimming**

Syndicalism
> *See also* **Anarchism and anarchists; Communism; Socialism**
> *xx* **Labor and laboring classes; Labor unions; Socialism; Strikes and lockouts**

Synods. *See* **Councils and synods**

Synonyms. *See* names of languages with the subdivision *Synonyms and antonyms,* e.g. **English language—Synonyms and antonyms;** etc.

Synthetic chemistry. *See* **Chemistry, Organic —Synthesis**

Synthetic detergents. *See* **Detergents, Synthetic**

Synthetic fabrics
> *See also* **Nylon; Rayon**
> *x* Fabrics, Synthetic
> *xx* **Textile industry and fabrics**

Synthetic products
> *See also* **Chemurgy; Plastics;** also names of synthetic products, e.g. **Rubber, Artificial; Rayon;** etc.
> *xx* **Chemistry, Organic—Synthesis; Chemistry, Technical; Chemurgy; Plastics**

Synthetic rubber. *See* **Rubber, Artificial**

Syphilis
> *xx* **Venereal diseases**

Syrups
> *xx* **Sugar**

517

Systems engineering
> *See also* Bionics; Operations research
> *xx* Automation; Cybernetics; Design, Industrial; Engineering; Operations research

TIROS (Meteorological satellite). *See* Tiros (Meteorological satellite)

TV. *See* Television

Table decoration. *See* Table setting and decoration

Table etiquette
> *xx* Etiquette

Table setting and decoration
> *See also* Flower arrangement; Tableware
> *x* Table decoration
> *xx* Decoration and ornament

Table talk. *See* Conversation

Table tennis. *See* Ping-pong

Tables (Systematic lists). *See* scientific and economic subjects with the subdivision *Tables, etc.,* e.g. Trigonometry—Tables, etc.; etc.

Tableware
> *See also* Glassware; Pottery; Silverware
> *xx* Table setting and decoration

Tactics
> *See also* Biological warfare; Guerrilla warfare
> *x* Military tactics
> *xx* Military art and science; Strategy

Tadpoles. *See* Frogs

Tailoring
> Use for works on the cutting and making of men's, or men's and women's clothing. Works limited to the cutting and making of women's clothes are entered under Dressmaking
> *See also* Dressmaking; Men's clothing; Uniforms, Military
> *x* Garment making
> *xx* Clothing and dress; Clothing trade; Dressmaking; Fashion

Taiwan. *See* Formosa

Talent. *See* Genius; Gifted children; Musical ability

Tales. *See* Fables; Fairy tales; Folklore; Legends

Talismans. *See* Charms

Talking. *See* Conversation; Speech

Talking books
> *x* Books, Talking
> *xx* Blind, Books for the; Phonograph records

Talking pictures. *See* Moving pictures

Tall tales. *See* American wit and humor; Folklore; Legends

Talmud
> *xx* Hebrew literature; Jewish literature; Judaism

Tanks (Military science)
    x Armored cars (Tanks); Cars, Armored
        (Tanks)
Tanning
    See also **Hides and skins; Leather**
    xx **Chemistry, Technical; Hides and skins;**
        Leather
Taoism
    xx **Religions**
Tap dancing
    x Clog dancing
    xx **Dancing**
Tape recorders. *See* **Magnetic recorders and**
    recordings
Tapestry
    xx **Decoration and ornament; Design,**
        Decorative; Interior decoration;
        Needlework; Textile industry and
        fabrics
Tariff (May subdiv. geog.)
    See also **Free trade and protection;**
        Smuggling
    x Customs (Tariff); Duties; Exports;
        Government regulation of commerce;
        Imports; Revenue
    xx **Commerce; Commercial policy; Eco-**
        nomic policy; Finance; Free trade
        and protection; Taxation; Trusts, In-
        dustrial
Tariff—U.S.
    x U.S.—Tariff
Tariff question—Free trade and protection. *See*
    Free trade and protection
Tartans
    x Highland costume; Scottish tartans
    xx **Clans and clan system**
Taste
    xx **Senses and sensation**
Taste (Esthetics). *See* **Esthetics**
Tax relations, Intergovernmental. *See* **Inter-**
    governmental tax relations
Tax sharing. *See* **Intergovernmental tax rela-**
    tions
Taverns. *See* **Restaurants, bars, etc.**
Taxation (May subdiv. geog.)
    See also **Assessment; Income tax; Inher-**
        itance and transfer tax; Intergovern-
        mental tax relations; Internal rev-
        enue; Sales tax; Tariff; Tithes
    x Direct taxation; Duties; Poll tax; Rev-
        enus; Taxes
    xx **Assessment; Estate planning; Finance;**
        Political science
Taxation—U.S.
    x U.S.—Taxation
Taxation of income. *See* **Income tax**
Taxation of legacies. *See* **Inheritance and**
    transfer tax
Taxation of sales. *See* **Sales tax**
Taxes. *See* **Taxation**

Taxidermy

> *See also* **Zoological specimens—Collection and preservation;** also names of specimens with the subdivision *Collection and preservation,* e.g. **Birds—Collection and preservation;** etc.
>
> *x* Specimens, Preservation of
>
> *xx* **Zoological specimens—Collection and preservation**

Tea rooms. *See* **Restaurants, bars, etc.**

Teacher training. *See* **Teachers—Training; Teachers colleges**

✓ **Teachers**

> *See also* **Educational associations; Educators; School superintendents and principals; Teaching**
>
> *x* College teachers; Faculty (Education); Professors
>
> *xx* **Education; Educators**

Teachers, Exchange of. *See* **Teachers, Interchange of**

Teachers, Interchange of

> *x* Exchange of teachers; Interchange of teachers; Teachers, Exchange of
>
> *xx* **Exchange of persons programs; International education**

Teachers—Practice teaching. *See* **Student teaching**

Teachers, Rating of (by students). *See* **Student evaluation of teachers**

Teachers—Training

> Use for works dealing with the history and methods of training teachers, including the educational functions of teachers colleges. Works on the study of education as a science are entered under **Education—Study and teaching.** See note under **Teachers colleges**
>
> *See also* **Student teaching; Teachers colleges; Teachers' workshops**
>
> *x* Teacher training
>
> *xx* **Education — Study and teaching; Teachers colleges; Teaching**

Teachers and parents. *See* **Home and school; Parents' and teachers' associations**

Teachers colleges

> Use for general and historical works about teachers colleges. Works dealing with their educational functions are entered under **Teachers—Training**
>
> *See also* **Teachers—Training;** also names of teachers colleges
>
> *x* Normal schools; Teacher training; Training colleges for teachers
>
> *xx* **Colleges and universities; Education—Study and teaching; Teachers—Training**

Teachers' institutes. *See* **Teachers' workshops**

520

Teachers' workshops

　　x Teachers' institutes; Workshops, Teachers'

　xx **Teachers—Training**

Teaching

　　Use for works on the art and method of teaching

　　See also

Child study

Classroom management

Education

Educational psychology

Examinations

Kindergarten

Lectures and lecturing

Montessori method of education

Project method in teaching

School discipline

School superintendents and principals

School supervision

Student teaching

Study, Method of

Teachers—Training

Teaching teams

　　also subjects with the subdivision *Study and teaching,* e.g. **Science—Study and teaching**; etc.

　　x Instruction; Pedagogy; School teaching

　　xx **Education; School administration and organization; Teachers; Vocational guidance**

Teaching—Aids and devices

　　See also **Audio-visual materials; Moving pictures in education; Programmed instruction; Radio in education; Teaching machines; Television in education**

Teaching—Experimental methods. *See* **Education—Experimental methods**

Teaching, Freedom of. *See* **Academic freedom**

Teaching machines

　　x Automatic teaching; Tutorial machines

　　xx **Programmed instruction; Teaching—Aids and devices**

Teaching teams

　　x Team teaching

　　xx **Teaching**

Teachings of Jesus. *See* **Jesus Christ—Teachings**

Team teaching. *See* **Teaching teams**

Tearooms. *See* **Restaurants, bars, etc.**

Technical assistance

　　See note under **Economic assistance**

　　See also **Industrialization; Underdeveloped areas**

　　x Aid to developing areas; Assistance to developing areas; Foreign aid program

　　xx **Economic assistance; Economic policy; Industrialization; International cooperation; International economic relations; Underdeveloped areas**

Technical chemistry. *See* **Chemistry, Technical**

Technical education

See also **Apprentices; Correspondence schools and courses; Employees— Training; Evening and continuation schools; Industrial arts education; Occupational training; Professional education; Retraining, Occupational; School shops; Vocational education;** also technical subjects with the subdivision *Study and teaching,* e.g. **Engineering—Study and teaching;** etc.

x Education, Industrial; Education, Technical; Industrial education; Industrial schools; Technical schools; Trade schools

xx **Education; Education, Higher; Employees—Training; Industrial arts education; Professional education; Technology; Vocational education**

Technical services (Libraries). *See* **Processing (Libraries)**

Technical schools. *See* **Technical education**

Technical terms. *See* **Technology—Dictionaries**

Technical writing

  x Scientific writing

  xx **Authorship; Technology—Language**

Technology

  See also

Building	Inventions
Chemistry, Technical	Machinery
	Manufactures
Engineering	Mills and millwork
Industrial arts	Technical education

  x Applied science; Arts, Useful; Useful arts

  xx **Industrial arts**

Technology—Dictionaries

  x Technical terms

Technology—Language

  See also **Technical writing**

Technology and civilization

  See also **Machinery in industry**

  x Civilization and technology

  xx **Civilization**

Teen age. *See* **Adolescence; Youth**

Teen age consumers. *See* **Youth as consumers**

Teeth

  See also **Dentistry**

  x Anatomy, Dental; Medicine, Dental

  xx **Dentistry**

Teeth—Diseases

  See also **Water—Fluoridation**

Telecommunication

  See also **Artificial satellites in telecommunication; Cables, Submarine; Intercommunication systems; Interstellar communication; Microwave communication systems; Radio; Telegraph; Telephone; Television;** also

Telecommunication—*Continued*

subjects with the subdivision *Communication systems,* e.g. **Astronautics —Communication systems;** etc.

x Electric communication; Mass communication

xx **Communication**

Telegraph

See also **Cables, Submarine; Cipher and telegraph codes**

xx **Electric engineering; Electric wiring; Electricity; Public utilities; Telecommunication**

Telegraph, Submarine. *See* **Cables, Submarine**

Telegraph codes. *See* **Cipher and telegraph codes**

Telepathy. *See* **Thought transference**

Telephone

xx **Electric engineering; Electric wiring; Electricity; Public utilities; Telecommunication**

Telephotography

xx **Photography**

Telescope

xx **Astronomical instruments**

Television

See also **Closed-circuit television; Color television; Microwave communication systems; Subscription television**

x TV

xx **Telecommunication**

Television—Apparatus and supplies

Television — Broadcasting. *See* **Television broadcasting**

Television, Cable. *See* **Community antenna television**

Television—Censorship

xx **Freedom of information**

Television, Closed-circuit. *See* **Closed-circuit television**

Television, Color. *See* **Color television**

Television—Production and direction

Television—Receivers and reception

Television—Repairing

x Television repairing

Television, Space. *See* **Television in astronautics**

Television—Stations. *See* **Television stations**

Television, Subscription. *See* **Subscription television**

Television advertising

x Advertising, Television; Commercials, Television; Television commercials

xx **Advertising**

Television and children

Use for works dealing with the effect of television on children

See also **Moving pictures and children**

x Children and television

xx **Children; Moving pictures and children**

Television and youth
> *x* Youth and television
> *xx* **Youth**

Television and infrared observation satellite.
> *See* **Tiros (Meteorological satellite)**

Television authorship
> *See also* **Television plays—Technique**
> *x* Television writing
> *xx* **Authorship**

Television broadcasting
> *See also* **Community antenna television; Television in education; Television in politics; Television scripts; Video tape recorders and recording**
> *x* Broadcasting; News broadcasts; Television—Broadcasting
> *xx* **Mass media; Radio broadcasting**

Television broadcasting—Vocational guidance
> *xx* **Vocational guidance**

Television in astronautics
> *x* Space television; Television, Space
> *xx* **Astronautics—Communication systems**

Television commercials. *See* **Television advertising**

Television in education
> *See also* **Closed-circuit television**
> *x* Education and television; Educational television
> *xx* **Audio-visual education; Closed-circuit television; Teaching—Aids and devices; Television broadcasting**

Television in politics
> *xx* **Politics, Practical; Television broadcasting**

Television plays
> Use for individual television plays, for collections of plays, and for works about them. Works on how to write television plays are entered under **Television plays—Technique**
> *x* Scenarios
> *xx* **Drama; Television scripts**

Television plays—Technique
> *See also* **Radio plays—Technique**
> *x* Play writing
> *xx* **Drama — Technique; Radio plays — Technique; Television authorship**

Television repairing. *See* **Television—Repairing**

Television scripts
> *See also* **Radio scripts; Television plays**
> *xx* **Radio scripts; Television broadcasting**

Television stations
> *x* Television—Stations

Television writing. *See* **Television authorship**

Telstar project
> *x* Bell System Telstar; Project Telstar
> *xx* **Artificial satellites in telecommunication**

Temperament

    See also **Character**

    xx **Character; Mind and body; Psychology; Psychology, Physiological**

Temperance

    Use for general works on the temperance question and the temperance movement

    See also

Alcohol—Physiological effect	**Narcotic habit**
	Prohibition
Alcoholism	**Restaurants, bars,**
Liquor problem	**etc.**
Liquor traffic	**Stimulants**

    x Abstinence; Drunkenness; Inebriates; Intemperance; Intoxication; Total abstinence

    xx **Alcohol; Alcoholism; Behavior; Hygiene; Liquor problem; Prohibition**

Temperature

    See also **Heat; Low temperature; Thermometers and thermometry**

    xx **Heat; Thermometers and thermometry**

Temperatures, Low. *See* **Low temperatures**

Temples

    See also **Mosques**

    xx **Archeology; Architecture; Architecture, Ancient; Church architecture**

Temporal power of the Pope. *See* **Popes—Temporal power**

Ten commandments

    x Commandments, Ten; Decalogue

Tenant farming. *See* **Farm tenancy**

Tenants. *See* **Landlord and tenant**

Tenement houses

    See also **City planning; Housing**

    x Slums

    xx **Cities and towns; Houses; Housing; Landlord and tenant; Social problems**

Tennis

    x Lawn tennis

    xx **Games**

Tenpins. *See* **Bowling**

Tension. *See* **Stress (Physiology)**

Tents

    xx **Camping**

Tenure of land. *See* **Land tenure**

Tenure of office. *See* **Civil service**

Terminology. *See* **Names;** and subjects with the subdivision *Terminology,* e.g. **Botany—Terminology;** etc.

Terra cotta

    xx **Building materials; Decoration and ornament; Pottery**

Terrariums

    See also **Gardens, Miniature**

    x Vivariums

Terrestrial physics. *See* **Geophysics**

Terror, Reign of. *See* **France—History—Revolution, 1789-1799**

Test pilots. *See* **Air pilots; Airplanes—Testing**

Tests. *See* **Educational tests and measurements; Examinations; Mental tests**

Teutonic race

　See also **Anglo-Saxons**

　　x Goths; Nordic race; Ostrogoths; Saxons; Visigoths

　xx **Ethnology**

Textbooks

　Use for books about textbooks not for textbooks of a subject. The latter are entered under the name of subject only

　See also **English language—Textbooks for foreigners**; and names of branches of study, e.g. **Arithmetic; Geography;** etc.

　　x School books

Textile chemistry

　See also **Dyes and dyeing**

　　x Chemistry, Textile; Textile industry and fabrics—Chemistry

　xx **Chemistry, Technical; Textile industry and fabrics**

Textile design

　See also **Textile painting**

　xx **Commercial art; Design; Design, Decorative**

Textile fabrics. *See* **Textile industry and fabrics**

Textile fibers. *See* **Fibers**

Textile industry and fabrics

　See also **Bleaching; Cotton manufacture and trade; Dyes and dyeing; Spinning; Synthetic fabrics; Tapestry; Textile chemistry; Textile printing; Weaving; Yarn**; also names of special textile fabrics, (e.g. **Linen; Nylon; Silk;** etc.) ; and names of articles manufactured, e.g. **Carpets; Hosiery;** etc.

　　x Cloth; Dry goods; Fabrics; Textile fabrics

　xx **Weaving**

Textile industry and fabrics—Chemistry. *See* **Textile chemistry**

Textile painting

　xx **Painting; Textile design**

Textile printing

　　x Block printing; Printing, Textile

　xx **Textile industry and fabrics**

Thanksgiving Day

　xx **Fasts and feasts**

Thanksgiving Day—Stories

　　x Stories

Theater (May subdiv. geog.)

　Use for works dealing with the drama as acted on the stage, and with the historical, moral, and religious aspects of the theater. Works treating of the drama from a literary point of view are

526

Theater—*Continued*

entered under **Drama; American** drama; English drama; etc.

See also

Acting	Opera
Actors and actresses	Pantomimes
Arena theater	Passion plays
Ballet	Puppets and puppet
Children's plays	plays
Drama	Shadow panto-
Dramatic criticism	mimes and plays
Experimental the-	Shakespeare, Wil-
ater	liam—Stage his-
Masks (Plays)	tory
Moralities	Theaters
Moving pictures	Vaudeville
Mysteries and mir-	
acle plays	

x Histrionics; Stage

xx Acting; Actors and actresses; Amusements; Drama; Drama in education; Performing arts

Theater—Little theater movement

x Little theater

Theater—Production and direction

See also **Amateur theatricals; Moving picture plays**

x Play direction (Theater); Play production

xx **Amateur theatricals**

Theater—U.S.

x U.S.—Theater

Theater criticism. *See* **Dramatic criticism**

Theater-in-the-round. *See* **Arena theater**

Theaters

Use for works dealing only with theater buildings, their architecture, construction, decoration, sanitation, etc.

x Opera houses; Playhouses

xx **Architecture; Centers for the performing arts; Theater**

Theaters—Lighting

x Stage lighting

xx **Lighting**

Theaters—Stage setting and scenery

See also **Scene painting**

x Scenery (Stage); Stage scenery; Stage setting; Theatrical scenery

Theatrical costume. *See* **Costume**

Theatrical make-up. *See* **Make-up, Theatrical**

Theatrical scenery. *See* **Theaters—Stage setting and scenery**

Theatricals, Amateur. *See* **Amateur theatricals**

Theatricals, College. *See* **College and school drama**

Theism

See also **Atheism; Christianity; Deism; God; Pantheism**

xx **Atheism; Christianity; Deism; God;**

527

Theism—*Continued*
>> Pantheism; Philosophy; Rationalism; Religion; Theology

Theology
See also

Atheism	Mysticism
Atonement	Natural theology
Baptism	Pantheism
Christianity	Predestination
Church	Providence and
Conversion	government of
Creeds	God
Deism	Religion
Eschatology	Religion and sci-
Ethics	ence
Faith	Revelation
God	Sacraments
Good and evil	Sacrifice
Grace (Theology)	Salvation
Holy Spirit	Sanctification
Immortality	Sin
Jesus Christ	Spiritual life
Liturgies	Theism
Lord's Supper	Trinity
Man (Theology)	Worship

>> *x* Bible—Theology; Christian doctrine; Doctrinal theology; Doctrines; Dogmatic theology
>> *xx* Christianity; Creation; God; Religion

Theology, Devotional. *See* **Devotional exercises; Meditations; Prayers**

Theology, Natural. *See* **Natural theology**

Theology, Pastoral. *See* **Pastoral work**

Theology — Philosophy. *See* **Christianity — Philosophy**

Theology—Study and teaching
>> *See also* **Catechisms; Church and education; Religious education**
>> *x* Education, Theological; Religion—Study and teaching
>> *xx* **Church and education; Religious education**

Theoretical chemistry. *See* **Chemistry, Physical and theoretical**

Theory of numbers. *See* **Number theory**

Theory of sets. *See* **Set theory**

Theory of structures. *See* **Structures, Theory of**

Theosophy
>> *See also* **Buddha and Buddhism; Gnosticism; Neoplatonism; Yoga**
>> *xx* **Buddha and Buddhism; Religion; Religions**

Therapeutics
See also

Antiseptics	Drugs
Chemistry, Medical	Electrotherapeutics
and pharmaceuti-	Hydrotherapy
cal	Materia medica
Diet in disease	Medicine

Therapeutics—*Continued*

Narcotics
Nurses and nursing
Nutrition
Occupational
  therapy

Phototherapy
Physical therapy
Radiotherapy
Stimulants
X rays

also names of diseases and groups of diseases, e.g. **Smallpox; Fever; Nervous system—Diseases;** etc.

xx **Materia medica; Medicine—Practice; Pathology**

Therapeutics, Suggestive

See also **Faith cure; Hypnotism; Mental healing; Mental suggestion; New Thought; Psychology, Pastoral; Psychotherapy; Subconsciousness**

x Suggestive therapeutics

xx **Faith cure; Hypnotism; Mental healing; Mental suggestion; Psychotherapy**

Thermoaerodynamics. *See* **Aerothermodynamics**

Thermodynamics

See also **Aerothermodynamics; Heat; Heat engines; Quantum theory;** also subjects with the subdivision *Thermodynamics,* e.g. **Space vehicles—Thermodynamics;** etc.

xx **Chemistry, Physical and theoretical; Dynamics; Heat; Heat engines; Physics; Quantum theory**

Thermometers and thermometry

See also **Temperature**

xx **Heat; Meteorological instruments; Temperature**

Theses. *See* **Dissertations, Academic**

Thieves. *See* **Robbers and outlaws**

Thinking. *See* **Thought and thinking**

Third world. *See* **Underdeveloped areas**

Thirteenth century

See note under **Nineteenth century**

xx **Europe — History — 476-1492; Middle Ages**

Thirty Years' War, 1618-1648

xx **Europe—History—1492-1789; Germany —History, 1517-1740**

Thoroughfares. *See* **Roads; Streets**

Thought and thinking

See also **Attention; Intellect; Logic; Memory; Perception; Reasoning**

x Thinking

xx **Educational psychology; Intellect; Logic; Psychology**

Thought transference

See also **Clairvoyance; Extrasensory perception; Hypnotism; Mental suggestion; Mind reading**

x Mental telepathy; Telepathy

xx **Clairvoyance; Mind reading; Psychical research; Subconsciousness**

Thermal pollution of rivers, lakes, etc. See Water Pollution

Thrift. *See* **Saving and thrift**

Throat
    See also **Voice**
    xx **Anatomy**

Thunderstorms
    See also **Lightning**
    xx **Meteorology; Storms**

Tidal waves. *See* **Ocean waves**

Tides
    xx **Astronomy; Moon; Navigation; Ocean-
        ography; Physical geography**

Tiles
    xx **Bricks; Building materials; Ceramics;
        Clay industries; Pottery**

Timber. *See* **Forests and forestry; Lumber
        and lumbering; Trees; Wood**

Time
    See also **Calendars; Clocks and watches;
        Periodicity; Sundials**
    x Chronology; Standard time
    xx **Longitude; Periodicity**

Time study
    See also **Motion study**
    xx **Efficiency, Industrial; Factory manage-
        ment; Job analysis; Motion study;
        Personnel management**

Tin
    See also **Pewter**

Tinsmithing
    xx **Metalwork**

Tires
    x Rubber tires
    xx **Wheels**

Tiros (Meteorological satellite)
    x TIROS (Meteorological satellite); Tele-
        vision and infrared observation satellite
    xx **Meteorological satellites**

Tithes
    xx **Church finance; Ecclesiastical law;
        Taxation**

Toads. *See* **Frogs**

Toadstools. *See* **Mushrooms**

Toasts
    See also **After-dinner speeches**
    x Healths, Drinking of
    xx **After-dinner speeches; Epigrams;
        Speeches, addresses, etc.**

Tobacco
    See also **Smoking**
    xx **Smoking**

Tobacco habit
    xx **Smoking**

Tobacco pipes. *See* **Pipes, Tobacco**

Toes. *See* **Foot**

Toilet. *See* **Beauty, Personal**

Toilet preparations. *See* **Cosmetics**

Toleration
> *See also* **Academic freedom; Discrimination; Freedom of conscience; Religious liberty**
>
> *x* Bigotry; Intolerance
>
> *xx* **Discrimination; Human relations**

Toll roads. *See* **Express highways**

Tombs
> *See also* **Brasses; Catacombs; Cemeteries; Epitaphs; Mound and mound builders**
>
> *x* Burial; Graves; Mausoleums; Rock tombs; Sepulchers; Vaults (Sepulchral)
>
> *xx* **Archeology; Architecture; Cemeteries; Monuments; Shrines**

Tools
> *See also* **Agricultural machinery; Carpentry—Tools; Machine tools; Machinery; Power tools;** also names of specific tools, e.g. **Saws;** etc.
>
> *x* Implements, utensils, etc.

Topographical drawing
> *See also* **Map drawing**
>
> *xx* **Drawing; Map drawing; Surveying**

Tories, American. *See* **American Loyalists**

Tornadoes
> *See also* **Cyclones; Storms**
>
> *xx* **Meteorology; Storms; Winds**

Torpedoes
> *xx* **Explosives; Naval art and science; Submarine warfare**

Tortoises. *See* **Turtles**

Total abstinence. *See* **Temperance**

Totalitarianism
> *See also* **Communism; Dictators; Fascism; National socialism**
>
> *x* Authoritarianism

Totems and totemism
> *xx* **Ethnology; Indians of North America—Religion and mythology; Mythology; Religion, Primitive**

Touch
> *x* Feeling
>
> *xx* **Senses and sensation**

Tourist accommodations. *See* **Hotels, motels, etc.; Youth hostels**

Tourist trade
> *See also* **Travel**
>
> *xx* **Travel**

Town officers. *See* **Local government**

Town planning. *See* **City planning**

Towns. *See* **Cities and towns**

Toxicology. *See* **Poisons**

Toys
> *See also* **Dollhouses; Dolls; Electric toys**
>
> *x* Miniature objects
>
> *xx* **Amusements**

Track athletics

See also **Walking**

x Cross-country running; Field athletics; Running

xx **Athletics; College sports**

Tracking and trailing

x Trailing

xx **Animals—Habits and behavior; Hunting**

Tracking of satellites. *See* **Artificial satellites —Tracking; Space vehicles—Tracking**

Traction engines. *See* **Tractors**

Tractors

x Traction engines

xx **Agricultural machinery; Farm engines**

Trade. *See* **Business; Commerce**

Trade, Boards of. *See* **Chambers of commerce**

Trade agreements (Labor). *See* **Arbitration, Industrial; Labor contract**

Trade and professional associations

Use for works on business or professional organizations whose aim is the protection or advancement of their common interests without regard to the relations of employer and employee

x Professional associations

xx **Associations**

Trade barriers. *See* **Commercial policy**

Trade fairs. *See* **Fairs**

Trade-marks

See also **Patents**

x Brand names

xx **Commerce; Manufactures; Patents**

Trade routes

x Ocean routes; Routes of trade; Sea routes

xx **Commerce; Geography, Commercial; Transportation**

Trade schools. *See* **Technical education**

Trade unions. *See* **Labor unions**

Trade waste. *See* **Factory and trade waste; Waste products**

Trades. *See* **Industrial arts; Occupations**

Traditions. *See* **Folklore; Legends; Superstition**

Traffic, City. *See* **City traffic**

Traffic accidents

x Automobile accidents; Automobiles—Accidents; Highway accidents

xx **Accidents; Traffic regulations**

Traffic engineering

Use for works on the planning of the flow of traffic and related topics, largely as they concern street transportation in cities and metropolitan areas

See also **City traffic; Express highways; Local transit**

x Street traffic

xx **Highway engineering; Transportation**

Traffic regulations

    See also **Automobiles—Laws and regulations; Traffic accidents**

    x Street traffic

    xx **Automobiles—Laws and regulations; Transportation**

Tragedy

    xx **Drama**

Trailer parks

    x Mobile home parks

    xx **Campgrounds**

Trailers. *See* **Automobiles—Trailers; Travel trailers and campers**

Trailing. *See* **Tracking and trailing**

Trained nurses. *See* **Nurses and nursing**

Training, Occupational. *See* **Occupational training**

Training, Vocational. *See* **Occupational training**

Training camps, Military. *See* **Military training camps**

Training colleges for teachers. *See* **Teachers colleges**

Training of animals. *See* **Animals—Training**

Training of children. *See* **Children—Management**

Training of employees. *See* **Employees—Training**

Trains, Railroad. *See* **Railroads**

Tramps

    See also **Begging; Rogues and vagabonds; Unemployed**

    x Vagabonds; Vagrancy

    xx **Begging; Rogues and vagabonds; Unemployed**

Trams. *See* **Street railroads**

Transatlantic flights. *See* **Aeronautics—Flights**

Transcendentalism

    See also **Idealism**

    xx **Idealism; Philosophy**

Transcontinental journeys. *See* **Overland journeys to the Pacific**

Transfer tax. *See* **Inheritance and transfer tax**

Transformers, Electric. *See* **Electric transformers**

Transistors

    xx **Electronics; Semiconductors**

Transit systems. *See* **Local transit;** and names of cities and metropolitan areas with the subdivision *Transit systems,* e.g. **Chicago—Transit systems; Chicago metropolitan area—Transit systems;** etc.

Translating and interpreting

    x Interpreting and translating; Machine translating; Mechanical translating

    xx **Language and languages**

Transmission of power. *See* **Electric lines; Electric power distribution; Power transmission**

Transmissions, Automobile. *See* **Automobiles—
Transmission devices**

Transmutation (Chemistry)

Use for modern works on the transmutation
of metals. Works that treat of the
medieval attempts to transmute baser
metals into gold are entered under
Alchemy

See also **Cyclotron**

x Metals, Transmutation of; Transmutation of metals

xx **Alchemy; Atoms; Nuclear physics;
Radioactivity**

Transmutation of metals. *See* **Transmutation
(Chemistry)**; for early works on transmutation of metals see **Alchemy**

Transplantation of organs, tissues, etc.

See also **Surgery, Plastic**; also names of
organs of the body with the subdivision
Transplantation, e.g. **Heart—Transplantation;** etc.

x Medical transplantation; Organ transplantation; Prosthesis; Surgical transplantation

xx **Preservation of organs, tissues, etc.;
Surgery**

Transportation

Use for general works on the transportation of persons or goods

See also

Aeronautics, Com- mercial	**Postal service**
Automobiles	**Railroads**
Bridges	**Roads**
Buses	**Shipping**
Canals	**Steam navigation**
Carriages and carts	**Steamboats**
Commerce	**Street railroads**
Electric railroads	**Streets**
Express service	**Subways**
Freight and freight- age	**Trade routes**
Harbors	**Traffic engineering**
	Traffic regulations
Inland navigation	**Trucks**
Local transit	**Waterways**
Merchant marine	**World War, 1939-**
Ocean travel	**1945—Transporta- tion**

x Locomotion

xx **Commerce**

Transportation, Highway

See also **Automobiles; Buses; Trucks**

x Highway transportation

Transportation, Military

See also **Vehicles, Military**

x Military motorization; Military transportation; Motorization, Military

xx **Military art and science**

Transvaal War, 1899-1902. *See* **South African
War, 1899-1902**

Trapping

See also **Fur trade; Game and game birds; Hunting**

xx **Game and game birds; Hunting**

Travel

Use for general works on the enjoyment of travel, advice to travelers, etc. Descriptions of actual voyages are entered under **Voyages and travels** or under names of places with the subdivision *Description and travel*

See also **Automobiles—Touring; Health resorts, spas, etc.; Ocean travel; Tourist trade; Voyages and travels; Voyages around the world;** also names of countries, states, etc. with the subdivision *Description and travel,* e.g. **U.S.—Description and travel;** etc.

xx **Manners and customs; Tourist trade; Voyages and travels**

Travel trailers and campers

x Campers and trailers; House trailers; Mobile homes; Pickup campers; Recreational vehicles; Trailers

xx **Automobiles—Trailers; Camping**

Travelers (May subdiv. geog. adjectice form, e.g. **Travelers, German;** etc.)

See also **Explorers**

x Voyagers

xx **Explorers; Voyages and travels**

Travelers, American

x American travelers; U.S.—Travelers

Travels. *See* **Overland journeys to the Pacific; Scientific expeditions; Voyages and travels; Voyages around the world;** and names of countries, states, etc. with the subdivision *Description and travel,* e.g. **U.S.—Description and travel;** etc.

Travesties. *See* **Parodies**

Tray gardens. *See* **Gardens, Miniature**

Treason

x Collaborationists; High treason

xx **Crime and criminals; Political crimes and offenses**

Treasure-trove. *See* **Buried treasure**

Treaties

Names of treaties are not included in this list but are to be added as needed, e.g. **Versailles, Treaty of, 1919;** etc.

See also **Arbitration, International;** also names of treaties (e.g. **North Atlantic Treaty, 1949; Versailles, Treaty of, 1919;** etc.) ; and names of countries with the subdivision *Foreign relations—Treaties,* e.g. **U.S.—Foreign relations—Treaties;** etc.

xx **Congresses and conventions; Diplomacy; International law; International relations**

Tree planting

 See also Reforestation; Trees; Windbreaks

 x Planting

 xx Forests and forestry; Reforestation; Trees

Trees (May subdiv. geog.)

 Use for works on the structure, care, characteristics and use of trees

 Names of trees are not included in this list but are to be added as needed, in the singular form, e.g. **Oak**; etc.

 See also

Dwarf trees	Nurseries (Horticulture)
Evergreens	
Forests and forestry	Nuts
Fruit culture	Plant lore
Grafting	Plants
Landscape gardening	Pruning
	Shrubs
Leaves	Tree planting
Lumber and lumbering	Wood

 also names of trees, e.g. **Oak**; etc.

 x Arboriculture; Timber

 xx Botany; Forests and forestry; Landscape gardening; Tree planting

Trees—Stories

 x Stories

Trees—U.S.

 x U.S.—Trees

Trees in art. *See* Plants in art

Trent Affair, 1861

 xx U.S.—History—Civil War

Trial by jury. *See* Jury

Trials

 See also Courts martial and courts of inquiry; Crime and criminals

 xx Crime and criminals; Criminal law

Tricks

 See also Card tricks; Magic

 xx Magic

Tricycles. *See* Bicycles and bicycling

Trigonometry

 x Plane trigonometry; Spherical trigonometry

 xx Geometry; Mathematics

Trigonometry—Programmed instruction

 x Self-instruction

 xx Programmed instruction

Trigonometry—Tables, etc.

 See also Logarithms

 x Tables (Systematic lists)

 xx Mathematics—Tables, etc.

Trinity

 See also God; Holy Spirit; Jesus Christ

 xx God; Holy Spirit; Jesus Christ; Jesus Christ—Divinity; Theology; Unitarianism

Tripoline War. *See* **U.S.—History—Tripolitan War, 1801-1805**

Trolley cars. *See* **Street railroads**

Tropical diseases. *See* **Tropics—Diseases and hygiene**

Tropical fish
    xx **Fishes**

Tropics
    See also subjects with the subdivision *Tropics,* e.g. **Agriculture—Tropics;** etc.
    x Jungles

Tropics—Diseases and hygiene
    See also names of tropical diseases, e.g. **Sleeping sickness; Yellow fever;** etc.
    x Diseases, Tropical; Medicine, Tropical; Tropical diseases

Troubadours
    xx **French poetry; Minstrels; Poets; Scalds and scaldic poetry**

Trout fishing
    xx **Fishing**

Truancy (Schools). *See* **School attendance**

Truck farming. *See* **Vegetable gardening**

Trucks
    See also **Materials handling**
    x Automobile trucks; Jeeps; Motor trucks
    xx **Automobiles; Materials handling; Transportation; Transportation, Highway**

Trust companies
    See also **Banks and banking; Investment trusts**
    x Companies, Trust
    xx **Banks and banking; Business; Clearing house; Corporations**

Trust in God. *See* **Faith**

Trusts, Industrial
    See also **Capitalism; Competition; Corporations; Holding companies; Interstate commerce; Monopolies; Railroads—Consolidation; Tariff**
    x Business combinations; Cartels; Combinations, Industrial; Industrial combinations; Industrial mergers; Industrial trusts; Mergers, Industrial
    xx **Capital; Commerce; Competition; Corporation law; Corporations; Economics; Monopolies**

Truth
    See also **Agnosticism; Knowledge, Theory of; Pragmatism; Reality; Skepticism; Truthfulness and falsehood**
    x Certainty
    xx **Belief and doubt; Faith; Knowledge, Theory of; Philosophy; Pragmatism; Skepticism**

Truth in advertising. *See* **Advertising, Fraudulent**

Truthfulness and falsehood
> *See also* **Honesty**
> *x* Credibility; Falsehood; Lying
> *xx* **Behavior; Honesty; Truth**

Tuberculosis
> *xx* **Lungs—Diseases**

Tugboats

Tuition. *See* **College costs; Colleges and universities—Finance; Education—Finance**

Tumbling
> *xx* **Acrobats and acrobatics**

Tumors
> *See also* **Cancer**

Tuning
> *x* Piano—Tuning
> *xx* **Musical instruments**

Tunnels
> *See also* **Boring; Excavation; Subways**
> *xx* **Civil engineering**

Turbines
> *See also* **Gas turbines; Steam turbines**
> *xx* **Engines; Hydraulic engineering; Hydraulic machinery; Wheels**

Turkeys
> *xx* **Poultry**

Turning
> *See also* **Lathes; Woodwork**
> *x* Lathe work; Wood turning
> *xx* **Carpentry; Lathes; Woodwork**

Turnpikes (Modern). *See* **Express highways**

Turtles
> *x* Tortoises
> *xx* **Reptiles**

Tutorial machines. *See* **Teaching machines**

Twentieth century
> See note under **Nineteenth century**
> *xx* **History, Modern—20th century**

Twenty-first century

Type and type founding
> *See also* **Advertising layout and typography; Initials; Linotype; Printing—Specimens; Typesetting**
> *xx* **Founding; Initials; Printing; Printing—Specimens; Typesetting**

Type specimens. *See* **Printing—Specimens**

Typesetting
> *See also* **Linotype; Printing; Type and type founding**
> *x* Composition (Printing)
> *xx* **Printing; Type and type founding**

Typewriters
> *xx* **Office equipment and supplies**

Typewriting
> *xx* Business education; Writing

Typhoid fever
> *x* Enteric fever

Typhoons

See note under **Cyclones**

xx **Storms; Winds**

Typography. *See* **Printing**

U boats. *See* **Submarines**

UFO. *See* **Flying saucers**

U.H.F. radio. *See* **Radio, Short wave**

U.N. *See* **United Nations**

U.S.S.R. *See* **Russia**

Ultrahigh frequency radio. *See* **Radio, Short wave**

Ultrasonic waves

x Supersonic waves; Waves, Ultrasonic

xx **Sound waves; Ultrasonics**

Ultrasonics

See also **Ultrasonic waves**

x Inaudible sound; Supersonics

xx **Sound**

Ultraviolet rays

x Rays, Ultra-violet

xx **Electromagnetic waves; Phototherapy; Radiation; Radiotherapy; Spectrum**

Umbrellas and parasols

x Parasols

Undenominational churches. *See* **Community churches**

Under water exploration. *See* **Underwater exploration**

Underdeveloped areas

See also **Economic assistance; States, New; Technical assistance**

x Backward areas; Developing countries; Third world

xx **Economic assistance; Economic conditions; Industrialization; Technical assistance**

Underdeveloped areas—Economic assistance. *See* **Economic assistance**

Undergraduates. *See* **College students**

Underground, Anti-Communist. *See* **Anti-Communist movements**

Underground films. *See* **Experimental films**

Underground literature

See also **Underground press**

Underground movements (World War, 1939-1945). *See* **World War, 1939-1945— Underground movements**

Underground press

x Alternative press; Press, Underground

xx **Underground literature**

Underground railroad

See also **Slavery in the U.S.**

xx **Slavery in the U.S.**

Underground railroads. *See* **Subways**

Underprivileged. *See* **Socially handicapped**

Underprivileged children. *See* **Socially handicapped children**

Undersea exploration. *See* **Underwater exploration**

Undersea research stations, Manned. *See* **Manned undersea research stations**

Undersea technology. *See* **Oceanography**

Understanding. *See* **Intellect; Knowledge, Theory of**

Undertakers and undertaking
   x Funeral directors; Morticians

Underwater exploration
   See also **Aquanauts; Manned undersea research stations; Marine biology; Skin diving**
   x Exploration, Submarine; Exploration, Underwater; Submarine exploration; Under water exploration; Undersea exploration
   xx **Adventure and adventurers; Oceanography—Research; Skin diving**

Underwater geology. *See* **Submarine geology**

Underwater medicine. *See* **Submarine medicine**

Underwater photography. *See* **Photography, Submarine**

Underwater physiology. *See* **Submarine medicine**

Underwater research stations, Manned. *See* **Manned undersea research stations**

Underwater swimming. *See* **Skin diving**

Underwriting. *See* **Insurance**

Unemployed
   See also **Economic assistance, Domestic; Employment agencies; Insurance, Unemployment; Labor supply; Migrant labor; Retraining, Occupational; Tramps**
   x Stabilization in industry
   xx **Charities; Economic assistance, Domestic; Labor and laboring classes; Labor supply; Public welfare; Social problems; Sociology; Tramps**

Unemployment insurance. *See* **Insurance, Unemployment**

Unfair competition. *See* **Competition, Unfair**

Ungraded schools. *See* **Nongraded schools**

Unicameral legislatures. *See* **Legislative bodies**

Unicorns
   xx **Animals, Mythical**

Unidentified flying objects. *See* **Flying saucers**

Uniforms, Military
   x Costume, Military; Military costume; Military uniforms; Naval uniforms; Uniforms, Naval
   xx **Costume; Tailoring**

Uniforms, Naval. *See* **Uniforms, Military**

Union churches. *See* **Community churches**

Union of South Africa. *See* **Africa, South**

Unions, Labor. *See* **Labor unions**

Unison speaking. *See* **Choral speaking**

Unitarianism

    See also **Jesus Christ—Divinity; Trinity**

    xx **Congregationalism; Jesus Christ—Divinity**

United Brethren. *See* **Moravians**

United Brethren in Christ

United Kingdom. *See* **Great Britain**

United Nations

    x U.N.

    xx **Arbitration, International; International cooperation; International organization**

United Nations—Armed Forces

United Nations—Finance

United Nations—Officials and employees

    x Employees and officials; Officials

United Nations—Yearbooks

    x Annuals

    xx **Yearbooks**

United States

    The abbreviation U.S. may be used when followed by a subdivision

    The subject subdivisions under this heading may be used under the name of any country or region, with the exception of the period divisions of history. For subdivisions that may be used under names of states, see **Ohio;** under names of cities, see **Chicago**

    Most of these subdivisions are examples of the directions given in the general references under various headings throughout the list. *See* references are supplied more liberally than any library may need but they were included here in order to show what subjects are given geographic treatment, not only as a subdivision under the name of a country, but also as a heading subdivided by name of country or by national adjective

    Corporate entries, that is those official bodies which may be used also as author entries, are included only when they have been used as examples or as references or when they are subdivided by subject. Corporate entries are distinguished by using a period between parts instead of the dash, e.g. **U.S. Army**

    See also names of regions of the U.S. and groups of states, e.g. **Atlantic States; Gulf States; Middle West; Mississippi Valley; New England; Northwest, Old; Northwest, Pacific; Oregon Trail; Southern States; Southwest, New; Southwest, Old; The West;** etc. and headings beginning with the word **American**

U.S.—Actors and actresses. *See* **Actors and actresses, American**

U.S.—Aged. *See* **Aged—U.S.**

U.S.—Agriculture. *See* **Agriculture—U.S.**

U.S.—Air—Pollution. *See* **Air—Pollution—U.S.**

U.S.—Animals. *See* **Animals—U.S.**

U.S.—Antiquities
> *See also* **Indians of North America—Antiquities**
> *x* Antiquities; Prehistory
> *xx* **Archeology; Art, Primitive; Man, Prehistoric**

U.S.—Appropriations and expenditures
> *xx* **Budget—U.S.**

U.S.—Architecture. *See* **Architecture, American**

U.S.—Archives. *See* **Archives—U.S.**

U.S.—Armed Forces
> *See also* official names of branches of the Armed Forces, e.g. **U.S. Army; U.S. Navy;** etc.
> *x* Armed forces; Military forces

U.S. Army
> Subdivisions used under this heading may be used under armies of other countries
> *x* Army
> *xx* **Armies; Military history; U.S.—Armed Forces**

U.S. Army—Appointments and retirements
> *x* U.S. Army—Retirements

U.S. Army—Biography
> *x* Military biography

U.S. Army—Chaplains
> *xx* **Chaplains; Clergy**

U.S. Army—Crimes and misdemeanors. *See* **Military offenses—U.S.**

U.S. Army—Demobilization

U.S. Army—Desertions. *See* **Desertion, Military—U.S.**

U.S. Army—Enlistment. *See* **U.S. Army—Recruiting, enlistment, etc.**

U.S. Army—Examinations
> *x* Army tests

U.S. Army—Handbooks, manuals, etc.
> *x* Soldiers' handbooks; U.S. Army—Officers' handbooks; U.S. Army—Soldiers' handbooks

U.S. Army—Insignia
> *xx* **Insignia**

U.S. Army—Medals, badges, decorations, etc.
> *xx* **Insignia; Medals**

U.S. Army—Military life
> *x* Army life; Military life; Soldiers' life
> *xx* **Soldiers**

U.S. Army—Music. *See* **U.S. Army—Songs and music**

U.S. Army—Officers

U.S. Army—Officers' handbooks. *See* **U.S. Army—Handbooks, manuals, etc.**

U.S. Army—Ordnance and ordnance stores
> *xx* **Ordnance**

U.S. Army—Parachute troops
  x U.S.—Parachute troops
  xx **Parachute troops**
U.S. Army—Recruiting, enlistment, etc.
  x Enlistment; Recruiting and enlistment;
    U.S. Army—Enlistment
U.S. Army—Retirements. *See* **U.S. Army—**
    Appointments and retirements
U.S. Army—Soldiers' handbooks. *See* **U.S.**
    Army—Handbooks, manuals, etc.
U.S. Army—Songs and music
  x U.S. Army—Music
U.S.—Art. *See* **Art, American**
U.S.—Art industries and trade. *See* **Art indus-**
    tries and trade—U.S.
U.S.—Artificial satellites. *See* **Artificial satel-**
    lites, American
U.S.—Artists. *See* **Artists, American**
U.S.—Astronautics. *See* **Astronautics—U.S.**
U.S.—Atlases. *See* **U.S.—Maps**
U.S.—Authors. *See* **Authors, American**
U.S.—Ballads. *See* **Ballads, American**
U.S.—Banks and banking. *See* **Banks and**
    banking—U.S.
U.S.—Bibliography
  xx **Bibliography**
U.S.—Bicentennial celebrations. *See* **U.S.—**
    Centennial celebrations, etc.
U.S.—Bio-bibliography
  x Bio-bibliography
U.S.—Biography
  xx **Biography**
U.S.—Biography—Dictionaries
  x Dictionaries
U.S.—Biography—Portraits
  x U.S.—History—Portraits
  xx **Portraits**
U.S.—Birds. *See* **Birds—U.S.**
U.S.—Botany. *See* **Botany—U.S.**
U.S.—Boundaries
  xx **Boundaries**
U.S.—Budget. *See* **Budget—U.S.**
U.S.—Cathedrals. *See* **Cathedrals—U.S.**
U.S.—Census
  xx **Census**
U.S.—Centennial celebrations, etc.
  x U.S.—Bicentennial celebrations
U.S.—Child labor. *See* **Child labor—U.S.**
U.S.—Christmas. *See* **Christmas—U.S.**
U.S.—Church history
  See also **U.S.—Religion**
  x U.S.—Religious history
  xx **Church history; U.S.—Religion**
U.S.—Churches. *See* **Churches—U.S.**
U.S.—Cities and towns. *See* **Cities and towns**
    —U.S.
U.S.—City planning. *See* **City planning—U.S.**
U.S.—Civil service. *See* **Civil service—U.S.**

U.S.—Civilization
  x American civilization
  xx **Civilization**
U.S.—Civilization—Foreign influences
U.S.—Civilization, 1960-1970
U.S.—Civilization, 1970-
U.S.—Climate
  xx **Climate; Weather**
U.S.—Collective settlements. *See* **Collective settlements—U.S.**
U.S.—Colleges. *See* **Colleges and universities —U.S.**
U.S.—Colonies. *See* **U.S.—Territories and possessions.** For other countries use *Colonies* as a subdivision
U.S.—Commerce
  xx **Commerce**
U.S.—Commercial policy
  xx **Commercial policy; Economic** policy
U.S.—Communism. *See* **Communism—U.S.**
U.S.—Composers. *See* **Composers, American**
U.S. Congress
  x Congress—U.S.
  xx **Legislative bodies**
U.S. Congress. House
  x Representatives—U.S.
U.S. Congress. Senate
  x Senators—U.S.
U.S. Constitution
  x Constitution
  xx **Constitutions; Political science**
U.S. Constitution—Amendments
  x Bill of rights; Constitutional amendments—U.S.
U.S.—Constitutional history
  xx **Constitutional history; U.S.—History; U.S.—History—1783-1809**
U.S.—Constitutional law
  xx **Constitutional law**
U.S.—Consular service. *See* **U.S.—Diplomatic and consular service**
U.S.—Country life. *See* **Country life—U.S.**
U.S.—Courts. *See* **Courts—U.S.**
U.S.—Crime and criminals. *See* **Crime and criminals—U.S.**
U.S.—Currency question. *See* **Currency question—U.S.**
U.S.—Dancing. *See* **Dancing—U.S.**
U.S.—Debts, Public. *See* **Debts, Public—U.S.**
U.S. Declaration of Independence
  x Declaration of Independence; Signers of the Declaration of Independence
  xx **U.S.—History—Revolution**
U.S.—Decoration and ornament. *See* **Decoration and ornament, American**
U.S.—Defenses
  x Defenses, National; National defenses; National security
  xx **Fortification**

U.S.—Description and travel
    x Description; Journeys; Travels
    xx **Discoveries (in geography); Explorers; Geography; Travel; Voyages and travels**
U.S.—Description and travel—Guide books
    x Guide books; U.S.—Guide books
U.S.—Description and travel—Maps. *See* **U.S.—Maps**
U.S.—Description and travel—Views
    x Scenery
    xx **Pictures; Views**
U.S.—Diplomatic and consular service
    x U.S.—Consular service
    xx **Diplomatic and consular service**
U.S.—Directories
    Use for lists of names and addresses. Lists of names without addresses are entered under **U.S.—Registers**
    See also **U.S.—Registers**
    xx **Directories; U.S.—Registers**
U.S.—Discovery and exploration. *See* **America—Discovery and exploration; U.S.—Exploring expeditions; The West—Discovery and exploration**
U.S.—Dramatists. *See* **Dramatists, American**
U.S.—Drawings. *See* **Drawings, American**
U.S.—Economic conditions
    May be subdivided by period using the subdivisions under **U.S—History**, e.g. **U.S.—Economic conditions—Colonial period**; etc.
    x National resources; U.S.—History, Economic; U.S.—Natural resources
    xx **Economic conditions; Labor and laboring classes; Natural resources—U.S.; Poverty**
U.S.—Economic policy
    x National planning; Planning, Economic; Planning, National
    xx **Economic policy**
U.S.—Education. *See* **Education—U.S.**
U.S.—Elections. *See* **Elections—U.S.**
U.S.—Emigration. *See* **U.S.—Immigration and emigration**
U.S.—Employees. *See* **U.S.—Officials and employees**
U.S.—Engraving. *See* **Engraving, American**
U.S.—Engravings. *See* **Engravings, American**
U.S.—Environmental policy. *See* **Environmental policy—U.S.**
U.S.—Ethics. *See* **Ethics, American**
U.S.—Ethnology. *See* **Ethnology—U.S.**
U.S.—European War, 1914-1918. *See* **European War, 1914-1918—U.S.**
U.S.—Excavations (Archeology). *See* **Excavations (Archeology)—U.S.**
U.S.—Executive departments
    See also **Presidents—U.S.—Staff**
    x Executive departments

U.S.—Executive power. *See* **Executive power —U.S.**

U.S.—Exploring expeditions

Use for works on exploration within the U.S. and for explorations in other countries which are sponsored by the U.S. Works on early exploration in territory which became a part of the U.S. are entered under **America—Discovery and exploration**

See also names of expeditions (e.g. **Lewis and Clark Expedition;** etc.) ; and names of explorers

x Explorations; Exploring expeditions; U.S.—Discovery and exploration

xx **America—Discovery and exploration; Explorers**

U.S.—Farm life. *See* **Farm life—U.S.**

U.S.—Fascism. *See* **Fascism—U.S.**

U.S. Federal Bureau of Investigation

x FBI; Federal Bureau of Investigation; G-men

xx **Crime and criminals; Detectives**

U.S.—Festivals. *See* **Festivals—U.S.**

U.S.—Finance. *See* **Finance—U.S.**

U.S.—Fisheries. *See* **Fisheries—U.S.**

U.S.—Fishes. *See* **Fishes—U.S.**

U.S.—Fishing. *See* **Fishing—U.S.**

U.S.—Flags. *See* **Flags—U.S.**

U.S.—Flowers. *See* **Flowers—U.S.**

U.S.—Folk art. *See* **Folk art, American**

U.S.—Folk dancing. *See* **Folk dancing, American**

U.S.—Folk songs. *See* **Folk songs—U.S.**

U.S.—Folklore. *See* **Folklore—U.S.**

U.S.—Foreign opinion

x Anti-Americanism

xx **Public opinion**

U.S.—Foreign policy. *See* **U.S.—Foreign relations**

U.S.—Foreign population

See also **U.S.—Immigration and emigration;** also **Italians in the U.S.;** and similar headings

x Foreigners; Population, Foreign

xx **Americanization; Immigration and emigration; Minorities; U.S.—Immigration and emigration**

U.S.—Foreign relations (May subdiv. geog.)

See also **Monroe Doctrine; U.S.—Neutrality**

x Foreign policy; Foreign relations; U.S. —Foreign policy

xx **Diplomacy; Imperialism; International relations; U.S.—Neutrality; World politics**

U.S.—Foreign relations—Treaties

x U.S.—Treaties

xx **Treaties**

546

U.S.—Forests and forestry. *See* **Forests and forestry—U.S.**

U.S.—Furniture. *See* **Furniture, American**

U.S.—Galleries and museums
 x Galleries (Art) ; U.S.—Museums
 xx **Art—Galleries and museums; Museums**

U.S.—Gazetteers
 xx **Gazetteers**

U.S.—Geography
 xx **Geography**

U.S.—Geology. *See* **Geology—U.S.**

U.S.—Government. *See* **U.S.—Politics and government**

U.S.—Government buildings. *See* **U.S.—Public buildings**

U.S.—Government employees. *See* **U.S.—Officials and employees**

U.S.—Government publications
 x Official publications; U.S.—Public documents
 xx **Government publications**

U.S.—Graphic arts. *See* **Graphic arts, American**

U.S.—Guide books. *See* **U.S.—Description and travel—Guide books**

U.S.—Hippies. *See* **Hippies—U.S.**

U.S.—Historians. *See* **Historians, American**

U.S.—Historic houses, etc.
 xx **Historic houses, etc.**

U.S.—Historical geography
 x Historical geography
 xx **Geography, Historical**

U.S.—Historical geography—Maps
 xx **U.S.—Maps**

U.S.—History
 The subdivisions by period have been listed after the subject subdivisions of **U.S. —History**, i.e. following **U.S.—History—Study and teaching**
 See also **U.S.—Constitutional history**
 x American history

U.S.—History—Addresses and essays
 x Addresses
 xx **Essays; Lectures and lecturing; Speeches, addresses, etc.**

U.S.—History—Bibliography

U.S.—History—Chronology. *See* **Chronology, Historical**

U.S.—History—Dictionaries

U.S.—History—Drama

U.S.—History, Economic. *See* **U.S.—Economic conditions**

U.S.—History—Examinations, questions, etc.
 See also **U.S.—History—Study and teaching**
 xx **U.S.—History—Study and teaching**

U.S.—History—Fiction

U.S.—History—Historiography

   x History—Historiography

  xx **Historiography**

U.S.—History, Local

   x History, Local; Local history

U.S.—History, Military

   x History, Military; U.S.—Military history

  xx **Military history**

U.S.—History, Naval

   x History, Naval; U.S.—Naval history

  xx **Naval battles; Naval history; Sea power**

U.S.—History—Outlines, syllabi, etc.

  xx **U.S.—History—Study and teaching**

U.S.—History—Periodicals

U.S.—History—Poetry

U.S.—History, Political. *See* **U.S.—Politics and government**

U.S.—History—Portraits. *See* **U.S.—Biography—Portraits**

U.S.—History—Societies

  xx **History—Societies**

U.S.—History—Sources

  xx **History—Sources**

U.S.—History—Study and teaching

   See also **U.S.—History—Examinations, questions, etc.; U.S.—History—Outlines, syllabi, etc.**

  xx **U.S.—History—Examinations, questions, etc.**

U.S.—History—Colonial period

   Use for the period from the earliest permanent English settlements on the Atlantic coast to the American Revolution, i.e. 1607-1775. Works dealing with the period of discovery are entered under **America—Discovery and exploration**

   See also **Bacon's Rebellion, 1676; King Philip's War, 1675-1676; Pilgrim Fathers; Pontiac's Conspiracy, 1763-1765; Puritans; U.S.—History—King William's War, 1689-1697; U.S.—History—French and Indian War, 1755-1763**

   x American colonies; Colonial history (U.S.); Colonial life and customs (U.S.)

U.S.—History—King Philip's War, 1675-1676. *See* **King Philip's War, 1675-1676**

U.S.—History—King William's War, 1689-1697

   x King William's War, 1689-1697

  xx **Indians of North America—Wars; U.S.—History—Colonial period**

U.S.—History—French and Indian War, 1755-1763

   See also **Pontiac's Conspiracy, 1763-1765**

   x French and Indian War

U.S.—History—French and Indian War, 1755-1763—*Continued*
  xx Indians of North America—Wars; Seven Years' War, 1756-1763; U.S. —History—Colonial period
U.S.—History—Revolution
  May be subdivided like **U.S.—History— Civil War**
  See also **American Loyalists; Canadian Invasion, 1775-1776; Fourth of July; U.S. Declaration of Independence**
  x American Revolution; Revolution, American; War of the American Revolution
  xx **Revolutions**
U.S.—History—1783-1809
  See also **Lewis and Clark Expedition; Louisiana Purchase; U.S.—Constitutional history**
  x Confederation of American colonies
U.S.—History—1783-1865
U.S.—History—Tripolitan War, 1801-1805
  x Tripoline War
  xx **Pirates**
U.S.—History—War of 1812
  x War of 1812
U.S.—History—1815-1861
  See also **Black Hawk War, 1832**
U.S.—History—War with Mexico, 1845-1848
  x Mexican War, 1845-1848
U.S.—History—Civil War
  See also **Confederate States of America; Slavery in the U.S.; Trent Affair, 1861**
  x American Civil War; Civil War—U.S.; War of Secession (U.S.)
  xx **War**
U.S.—History—Civil War—Biography
U.S.—History—Civil War—Campaigns and battles
  See also names of battles, e.g. **Gettysburg, Battle of, 1863;** etc.
  xx **Battles**
U.S.—History—Civil War—Causes
  x Secession
U.S.—History—Civil War—Centennial celebrations, etc.
U.S.—History—Civil War—Drama
  xx **Drama**
U.S.—History—Civil War—Fiction
  xx **Historical fiction**
U.S.—History—Civil War—Medical and sanitary affairs
U.S.—History—Civil War—Naval operations
U.S.—History—Civil War—Personal narratives
  Use for miscellaneous accounts and reports written by soldiers, officers, journalists and other observers. Accounts limited to a special topic are entered under the specific subject

549

U.S.—History—Civil War—Pictorial works
 x Illustrations
xx **Pictures**
U.S.—History—Civil War—Prisoners and prisons
U.S.—History—Civil War—Sources
 xx **History—Sources**
U.S.—History—1865-1898
 See also **Reconstruction**
U.S.—History—War of 1898
 x American-Spanish War, 1898; Hispano-American War, 1898; Spain—History—War of 1898; Spanish-American War, 1898
U.S.—History—20th century
U.S.—History—1898-1919
U.S.—History—European War, 1914-1918. *See* **European War, 1914-1918—U.S.**
U.S.—History—1919-1933
U.S.—History—1933-1945
U.S.—History—World War, 1939-1945. *See* **World War, 1939-1945—U.S.**
U.S.—History—1945-1953
U.S.—History—1953-1961
U.S.—History—1961-
U.S.—Hospitals. *See* **Hospitals—U.S.**
U.S.—Hotels, motels, etc. *See* **Hotels, motels, etc.—U.S.**
U.S.—Hunting. *See* **Hunting—U.S.**
U.S.—Illustrators. *See* **Illustrators, American**
U.S.—Immigration and emigration
 See also **U.S.—Foreign population;** also **Italians in the U.S.;** and similar headings
 x Foreign population; Population, Foreign; U.S.—Emigration
 xx **Americanization; Colonization; Immigration and emigration; U.S.—Foreign population**
U.S.—Industries
 x Industries; U.S.—Manufactures
 xx **Industrial arts**
U.S.—Industry and state. *See* **Industry and state—U.S.**
U.S.—Insular possessions. *See* **U.S.—Territories and possessions**
U.S.—Intellectual life
 x Intellectual life
U.S.—Irrigation. *See* **Irrigation—U.S.**
U.S.—Labor and laboring classes. *See* **Labor and laboring classes—U.S.**
U.S.—Law. *See* **Law—U.S.**
U.S.—Legends. *See* **Legends—U.S.**
U.S.—Libraries. *See* **Libraries—U.S.**
U.S. Library of Congress
 x Library of Congress
 xx **Libraries**
U.S.—Literary landmarks. *See* **Literary landmarks—U.S.**
U.S.—Literature. *See* **American literature**

U.S.—Mail. *See* **Postal service—U.S.**

U.S.—Manners and customs. *See* **U.S.—Social life and customs**

U.S.—Manufactures. *See* **U.S.—Industries**

U.S.—Maps

    See also **U.S.—Historical geography— Maps**

    x U.S.—Atlases; U.S.—Description and travel—Maps

    xx **Atlases; Maps**

U.S.—Merchant marine. *See* **Merchant marine —U.S.**

U.S. Military Academy, West Point

    x West Point Military Academy

    xx **Military education**

U.S. Military Academy, West Point—Registers

    Use for lists of graduates, etc.

    x Registers of persons

U.S. Military Academy, West Point—Songs and music

    xx **Songs**

U.S.—Military history. *See* **U.S.—History, Military**

U.S.—Military offenses. *See* **Military offenses —U.S.**

U.S.—Military policy

    xx **Military policy**

U.S.—Militia

    See also **U.S.—National Guard**

    x Militia

U.S.—Mines and mineral resources. *See* **Mines and mineral resources—U.S.**

U.S.—Moral conditions

    xx **Moral conditions**

U.S.—Municipal government. *See* **Municipal government—U.S.**

U.S.—Museums. *See* **U.S.—Galleries and museums**

U.S.—Music. *See* **Music, American**

U.S.—Musicians. *See* **Musicians, American**

U.S.—Names, Personal. *See* **Names, Personal —U.S.**

U.S.—National characteristics. *See* **National characteristics, American**

U.S.—National Guard

    x National Guard (U.S.)

    xx **U.S.—Militia**

U.S.—National parks and reserves. *See* **National parks and reserves—U.S.**

U.S.—National songs. *See* **National songs, American**

U.S.—Natural history. *See* **Natural history— U.S.**

U.S.—Natural monuments. *See* **Natural monuments—U.S.**

U.S.—Natural resources. *See* **Natural resources —U.S.; U.S.—Economic conditions**

U.S.—Nature study. *See* **Nature study—U.S.**

551

U.S. Naval Academy, Annapolis
    x Annapolis Naval Academy; Naval Academy, Annapolis
    xx **Naval education**
U.S.—Naval history. *See* **U.S.—History—Naval**
U.S. Navy
    x Naval administration; Navy; Sea life
    xx **Naval history; Navies; Sea power; Seamen; U.S.—Armed Forces; Warships**
U.S. Navy—Biography
    x Military biography
    xx **Naval biography**
U.S. Navy—Enlistment. *See* **U.S. Navy—Recruiting, enlistment, etc.**
U.S. Navy—Handbooks, manuals, etc.
    x U.S. Navy—Officers' handbooks
U.S. Navy—Insignia
    xx **Insignia**
U.S. Navy—Medals, badges, decorations, etc.
    xx **Insignia; Medals**
U.S. Navy—Officers
U.S. Navy—Officers' handbooks. *See* **U.S. Navy—Handbooks, manuals, etc.**
U.S. Navy—Recruiting, enlistment, etc.
    x Enlistment; Recruiting and enlistment; U.S. Navy—Enlistment
U.S. Navy—Sealab project. *See* **Sealab project**
U.S.—Neutrality
    See also **U.S.—Foreign relations**
    xx **Neutrality; U.S.—Foreign relations**
U.S.—Novelists. *See* **Novelists, American**
U.S.—Occupations
    xx **Occupations**
U.S.—Officials and employees
    See also **Civil service—U.S.**
    x Government employees; Officials; U.S.—Employees; U.S.—Government employees
    xx **Civil service—U.S.**
U.S.—Painters. *See* **Painters, American**
U.S.—Painting. *See* **Painting, American**
U.S.—Paintings. *See* **Paintings, American**
U.S.—Parachute troops. *See* **U.S. Army—Parachute troops**
U.S.—Parks. *See* **Parks—U.S.**
U.S.—Personal names. *See* **Names, Personal—U.S.**
U.S. Philosophers. *See* **Philosophers, American**
U.S.—Philosophy. *See* **Philosophy, American**
U.S.—Physical geography. *See* **Physical geography—U.S.**
U.S.—Plants, Cultivated. *See* **Plants, Cultivated—U.S.**
U.S.—Poets. *See* **Poets, American**
U.S.—Police. *See* **Police—U.S.**

U.S.—Politics and government

   May be subdivided by period using the sub-
      divisions under **U.S.—History,** e.g.
      U.S.—Politics and government—
      Colonial period; etc.

   x Administration; Civics; Civil govern-
      ment; Government; Politics; U.S.—
      Government; U.S.—History, Political

   xx **Political science; Politics, Practical;**
      Public administration; World politics

U.S.—Population

   xx **Population**

U.S.—Postal service. *See* **Postal service—U.S.**

U.S.—Pottery. *See* **Pottery, American**

U.S.—Presidents. *See* **Presidents—U.S.** For
      works on presidents of other countries
      see names of countries with the sub-
      division *Presidents,* e.g. **Mexico—**
      Presidents; etc.

U.S.—Prints. *See* **Prints, American**

U.S.—Prisons. *See* **Prisons—U.S.**

U.S.—Propaganda. *See* **Propaganda, American**

U.S.—Public buildings

   x U.S.—Government buildings

   xx **Public buildings**

U.S.—Public debts. *See* **Debts, Public—U.S.**

U.S.—Public documents. *See* **U.S.—Govern-**
      ment publications

U.S.—Public health. *See* **Public health—U.S.**

U.S.—Public lands

   x Public lands

U.S.—Public schools. *See* **Public schools—U.S.**

U.S.—Public works

   xx **Public works**

U.S.—Race relations

   See also **Black Muslims**

   xx **Anthropology; Minorities; Negroes;**
      Race problems

U.S.—Refugees. *See* **Refugees, American**

U.S.—Registers

   Use for lists of names without addresses.
      Lists of names that include addresses
      are entered under **U.S.—Directories**

   See also **U.S.—Directories**

   x Registers of persons

   xx **U.S.—Directories**

U.S.—Religion

   See also **U.S.—Church history**

   xx **Religion; U.S.—Church history**

U.S.—Religious history. *See* **U.S.—Church**
      history

U.S.—Schools. *See* **Schools—U.S.**

U.S.—Science. *See* **Science—U.S.**

U.S.—Sculptors. *See* **Sculptors, American**

U.S.—Sculpture. *See* **Sculpture, American**

U.S.—Shipping. *See* **Shipping—U.S.**

U.S.—Social conditions

   xx **Labor and laboring classes; Poverty;**
      Social conditions

U.S.—Social life and customs
> *x* Customs, Social; Social customs; Social
> life and customs; U.S.—Manners and
> customs
> *xx* **Ethnology; Manners and customs**

**U.S.—Social life and customs—Colonial
period**
> *x* Colonial life and customs (U.S.)

U.S.—Social policy
> *x* National planning; Planning, National
> *xx* **Social policy**

U.S.—Social surveys. *See* **Social surveys—U.S.**

U.S.—Socialism. *See* **Socialism—U.S.**

U.S.—Soldiers. *See* **Soldiers—U.S.**

U.S.—Songs. *See* **Songs, American**

U.S.—State governments. *See* **State governments**

U.S.—Statesmen. *See* **Statesmen, American**

U.S.—Statistics
> *x* Burial statistics
> *xx* **Statistics**

U.S.—Students. *See* **Students—U.S.**

U.S. Supreme Court
> *x* Supreme Court—U.S.

U.S. Supreme Court—Biography

U.S.—Tariff. *See* **Tariff—U.S.**

U.S.—Taxation. *See* **Taxation—U.S.**

U.S.—Territorial expansion

U.S.—Territories and possessions
> Use this subdivision under U.S. only. For
> other countries use the subdivision
> *Colonies*
> *x* U.S.—Colonies; U.S.—Insular posses-
> sions
> *xx* **Colonies**

U.S.—Theater. *See* **Theater—U.S.**

U.S.—Travelers. *See* **Travelers, American**

U.S.—Treaties. *See* **U.S.—Foreign relations—
Treaties**

U.S.—Trees. *See* **Trees—U.S.**

U.S.—Universities. *See* **Colleges and universities—U.S.**

U.S.—Urban renewal. *See* **Urban renewal—
U.S.**

U.S.—Vice-Presidents. *See* **Vice-Presidents—
U.S.**

U.S.—Women. *See* **Women in the U.S.**

U.S.—World War, 1939-1945. *See* **World War,
1939-1945—U.S.**

U.S.—Youth. *See* **Youth—U.S.**

U.S.—Zoology. *See* **Zoology—U.S.**

United States of Europe (Proposed). *See*
European federation

United Steelworkers of America
> *xx* **Labor Unions**

Universal history. *See* **World history**

Universal language. *See* **Language, Universal**

√ United Tribes of N. Dak
√ United Way of America

554

Universe
> See also **Astronomy; Creation; Earth; Life on other planets**
> x Cosmogony; Cosmography; Cosmology
> xx **Creation; Earth; Metaphysics; Philosophy**

Universities. See **Colleges and universities**
University degrees. See **Degrees, Academic**
University extension
> See also **Adult education; Correspondence schools and courses**
> xx **Colleges and universities; Education, Higher**

University libraries. See **Libraries, College and university**
University students. See **College students**
Unmarried women. See **Single women**
Upholstery
> See also **Drapery; Furniture**
> xx **Furniture; Interior decoration**

Upper atmosphere. See **Atmosphere, Upper**
Upper classes
> x Fashionable society; High society; Society, Upper
> xx **Aristocracy; Social classes**

Uranium
> xx **Radioactivity**

Urban areas. See **Metropolitan areas**
Urban renewal (May subdiv. geog.)
> Use for works on urban redevelopment and the economic, sociological and political factors involved. For architectural and engineering aspects use **City planning**
> See also **City planning**
> xx **City planning; Metropolitan areas; Sociology, Urban**

Urban renewal—Chicago
> x Chicago—Urban renewal

Urban renewal—U.S.
> x U.S.—Urban renewal

Urban sociology. See **Sociology, Urban**
Urban traffic. See **City traffic**
Useful arts. See **Industrial arts; Technology**
Usury. See **Interest and usury**
Utensils, Kitchen. See **Household equipment and supplies**
Utilitarianism
> See also **Pragmatism**
> xx **Ethics; Pragmatism**

Utilities, Public. See **Public utilities**
Utilization of waste. See **Salvage (Waste, etc.)**
Utopias
> x Ideal states
> xx **Political science; Socialism**

VTOL. See **Vertically rising airplanes**
Vacation church schools. See **Vacation schools, Religious**
Vacation schools
> x Summer schools
> xx **Playgrounds; Public schools; Schools**

University of N. Dak.—Art

555

Vacation schools, Religious
 x Bible classes; Vacation church schools
Vacations
 See also **Holidays**
 xx **Holidays; Recreation**
Vaccination
 See also **Immunity; Smallpox**
 x Inoculation
 xx **Communicable diseases; Immunity; Public health; Smallpox**
Vacuum tubes
 See also **Amplifiers, Vacuum tube; Cathode ray tubes; Electronics; Masers**
 x Electron tubes
 xx **X rays**
Vagabonds. *See* **Rogues and vagabonds; Tramps**
Vagrancy. *See* **Begging; Tramps**
Valentine's Day
 x St. Valentine's Day
Valuation
 Use for general works only. Works on valuation of special classes of property are entered under the class (e.g. **Real estate;** etc.). Works on valuation for taxing purposes are entered under **Assessment**
 x Appraisal; Capitalization (Finance)
 xx **Assessment**
Vanishing animals. *See* **Rare animals**
Variation (Biology)
 See also **Adaptation (Biology); Color of animals; Evolution; Mendel's law; Natural selection**
 x Mutation (Biology)
 xx **Biology; Botany; Evolution; Genetics; Heredity; Zoology**
Varnish and varnishing
 See also **Lacquer and lacquering**
 x Enamel paints; Finishes and finishing
 xx **Lacquer and lacquering; Painting, Industrial; Wood finishing**
Vasectomy. *See* **Sterilization (Birth control)**
Vases
 See also **Glassware; Pottery**
 xx **Glassware; Pottery**
Vassals. *See* **Feudalism**
Vatican Council, 2d, 1962-1965
 xx **Councils and synods**
Vaudeville
 xx **Amusements; Theater**
Vaults (Sepulchral). *See* **Tombs**
Vedas
 xx **Hinduism; Sacred books**
Vegetable anatomy. *See* **Botany—Anatomy**
Vegetable gardening
 See also **Vegetables**
 x Kitchen gardens; Market gardening; Truck farming
 xx **Gardening; Vegetables**

✓ Vandalism

Vegetable kingdom. *See* **Botany; Plants**

Vegetable oils. *See* **Essences and essential oils; Oils and fats**

Vegetable pathology. *See* **Plants—Diseases**

Vegetables

Names of vegetables are not included in this list but are to be added as needed, e.g. **Celery; Potatoes;** etc.

See also **Cookery—Vegetables; Root crops; Vegetable gardening; Vegetarianism;** also names of vegetables, e.g. **Celery; Potatoes;** etc.

xx **Botany; Food; Vegetable gardening**

Vegetables—Canning. *See* **Canning and preserving**

Vegetables—Marketing. *See* **Farm produce—Marketing**

Vegetarian cooking. *See* **Cookery—Vegetables**

Vegetarianism

xx **Diet; Food; Vegetables**

Vehicles, Military

x Army vehicles; Military vehicles

xx **Transportation, Military**

Velocity. *See* **Speed**

Veneers and veneering

xx **Cabinet work; Furniture**

Venereal diseases

See also **Sexual hygiene;** also names of venereal diseases, e.g. **Syphilis;** etc.

x Hygiene, Social; Social hygiene

xx **Prostitution; Sexual hygiene**

Venom. *See* **Poisons**

Ventilation

See also **Air conditioning; Chimneys; Heating**

xx **Air; Air conditioning; Heating; Home economics; Hygiene; Sanitation; Sanitation, Household**

Ventriloquism

xx **Amusements; Voice**

Venus (Planet)

xx **Planets; Solar system**

Vermin. *See* **Household pests**

Vers libre. *See* **Free verse**

Versailles, Treaty of, 1919

xx **Treaties**

Versification

See also **Poetry; Rhyme**

x English language—Versification; Meter; Prosody

xx **Authorship; Poetics; Rhythm**

Vertebrates

See also **Amphibians; Birds; Fishes; Mammals; Reptiles**

xx **Zoology**

Vertically rising airplanes

x Airplanes, Vertically rising; VTOL

xx **Airplanes; Ground effect machines**

Vessels (Ships). *See* **Ships**

557

Veterans
> *See also* **Hospitals, Military; Pensions, Military; Seamen; Soldiers**
> *x* Ex-service men; G.I.s; War veterans
> *xx* **Pensions, Military; Seamen; Soldiers**

Veterans—Education
> *x* Education of veterans
> *xx* **Reconstruction (1914-1939); Reconstruction (1939-1951)**

Veterans—Employment
> *x* Employment; Employment of veterans
> *xx* **Reconstruction (1914-1939); Reconstruction (1939-1951)**

Veterans—Hospitals. *See* **Hospitals, Military**

Veterans—Laws and regulations
> *xx* **Military law**

Veterans Day
> *x* Armistice Day

Veterinarians

Veterinary medicine
> *See also* names of animals with the subdivision *Diseases,* e.g. **Cattle—Diseases;** etc.
> *x* Animals—Diseases; Diseases of animals; Domestic animals—Diseases; Medicine, Veterinary
> *xx* **Cattle; Livestock**

Viaducts. *See* **Bridges**

Vibration
> *See also* **Light; Sound waves; Waves**
> *xx* **Mechanics; Sound**

Vice. *See* **Crime and criminals;** and names of specific vices, e.g. **Gambling; Prostitution;** etc.

Vice-Presidents—U.S.
> *x* U.S.—Vice-Presidents

Video tape recorders and recording
> *xx* **Television broadcasting**

Vietnam War, 1961- . *See* **Vietnamese Conflict, 1961-**

Vietnamese Conflict, 1961-
> May use appropriate subdivisions under **World War, 1939-1945**

Views
> Use for collections of pictures of many lands
> *See also* names of countries, states, etc. with the subdivision *Description and travel—Views* (e.g. **U.S.—Description and travel—Views;** etc.); and names of cities with the subdivision *Description—Views,* e.g. **Chicago—Description—Views;** etc.
> *x* Geography—Pictorial works; Scenery

Vigilance committees
> *xx* **Crime and criminals; Criminal law; Lynching**

Vikings. *See* **Northmen**

✓ *Vietnamese*

Villages
> *See also* **Local government**
> *xx* **Cities and towns; Local government**

Villas. *See* **Architecture, Domestic**

Vines. *See* **Climbing plants**

Vineyards. *See* **Grapes**

Violence
> *xx* **Aggressiveness (Psychology); Social psychology**

Violin
> *x* Fiddle
> *xx* **Stringed instruments**

Violin music

Violinists, violoncellists, etc.
> *x* Violoncellists
> *xx* **Musicians**

Violoncellists. *See* **Violinists, violoncellists, etc.**

Violoncello
> *x* Cello

Vipers. *See* **Snakes**

Virgin Mary. *See* **Mary, Virgin**

Viruses
> *x* Microbes
> *xx* **Microorganisms**

Viscosity
> *xx* **Hydrodynamics; Mechanics**

Visigoths. *See* **Teutonic race**

Vision
> *See also* **Blind; Color blindness; Color sense; Eye; Optical illusions**
> *x* Sight
> *xx* **Eye; Optics; Senses and sensation**

Visions
> *See also* **Apparitions; Dreams; Hallucinations and illusions**
> *xx* **Apparitions**

Visitors' exchange programs. *See* **Exchange of persons programs**

Visual data processing. *See* **Optical data processing**

Visual instruction. *See* **Audio-visual education**

Vital records. *See* **Registers of birth, etc.**

Vital statistics
> *See also* **Census; Mortality; Population; Registers of births, etc.**
> *x* Burial statistics; Death rate; Marriage statistics; Mortuary statistics; Records of births, etc.
> *xx* **Registers of births, etc.; Statistics**

Vitamins
> *xx* **Food; Nutrition; Physiological chemistry**

Vivariums. *See* **Terrariums**

Vivisection
> *See also* **Animals—Treatment**
> *x* Antivivisection
> *xx* **Animals—Treatment; Surgery**

Vocabulary
> *See also* **Words, New**
> *x* Words

Vocal culture. *See* **Singing; Voice**
Vocal music

    See also **Carols; Choral music; Folk songs; Hymns; Operas; Operetta; Oratorio; Singing; Songs**

    x Music, Vocal

    xx **Music; Singing**

Vocation, Choice of. *See* **Vocational guidance**

Vocational education

    See note under **Occupational training**

    See also **Blind—Education; Deaf—Education; Employees—Training; Industrial arts education; Occupational training; Professional education; Retraining, Occupational; Technical education; Vocational guidance;** also names of industries, professions, etc. with the subdivision *Study and teaching,* e.g. **Agriculture—Study and teaching; Medicine — Study and ing;** etc.

    x Education, Vocational

    xx **Education; Manpower policy; Professional education; Technical education**

Vocational guidance

    . Use for general works only. Works on guidance in a specific vocation are entered under such headings as **Law as a profession; Music as a profession;** etc.

    See also **Blind—Education; Counseling; Deaf—Education; Occupations; Personnel service in education; Professions;** also fields of knowledge and industries and trades with the subdivision *Vocational guidance,* e.g. **Television broadcasting—Vocational guidance;** etc.; also names of occupations (e.g. **Teaching;** etc.) ; and such headings as **Law as a profession; Music as a profession;** etc.

    x Business, Choice of; Careers; Choice of profession; Employment; Guidance; Occupation, Choice of; Profession, Choice of; Student guidance; Vocation, Choice of

    xx **Counseling; Occupations; Personnel service in education; Professions; Vocational education**

Vocational stories

    x Career stories; Stories

    xx **Fiction**

Vocational training. *See* **Occupational training**

Vocations. *See* **Occupations; Professions**

Voice

    See also **Phonetics; Public speaking; Respiration; Singing; Speech; Ventriloquism**

    x Speaking; Vocal culture; Voice culture

    xx **Language and languages; Phonetics;**

Voice—*Continued*
>> Public speaking; Singing; Speech;
>> Throat

Voice culture. *See* **Singing; Voice**

Volatile oils. *See* **Essences and essential oils**

Volcanoes
>> *x* Eruptions
>> *xx* Earthquakes; Geology; Mountains;
>> Physical geography

Volleyball

Voluntary associations. *See* **Associations**

Voluntary work. *See* **Volunteer workers**

Volunteer workers
>> *x* Voluntary work

Voting. *See* **Elections; Suffrage**

Voting, Cumulative. *See* **Proportional representation**

Voyagers. *See* **Explorers; Travelers**

Voyages and travels
>> *See also*

Adventure and ad-venturers	Scientific expedi-tions
Aeronautics—Flights	Seafaring life
	Seamen
Discoveries (in ge-ography)	Shipwrecks
	Travel
Explorers	Travelers
Northeast Passage	Voyages around the world
Northwest Passage	
Ocean travel	Whaling
Overland journeys to the Pacific	Yachts and yacht-ing
Pilgrims and pil-grimages	

>> *also* names of countries, continents, etc. with
>> the subdivision *Description and travel*
>> (e.g. **U.S.—Description and travel;**
>> etc.) ; also names of regions (e.g.
>> **Antarctic regions;** etc.) ; and names
>> of ships, e.g. **Bounty (Ship);** etc.
>> *x* Journeys; Travels
>> *xx* **Adventure and adventurers; Discover-
>> ies (in geography); Explorers; Geog-
>> raphy; Travel**

Voyages around the world
>> *x* Circumnavigation; Journeys; Travels
>> *xx* **Travel; Voyages and travels**

Voyages to the moon. *See* **Space flight to the
moon**

Wage-price controls. *See* **Wage-price policy**

Wage-price policy
>> *x* Price controls; Price-wage policy;
>> Wage-price controls
>> *xx* **Inflation (Finance); Prices; Wages**

✓ **Wages** *See Salaries*
>> *See also* **Cost and standard of living; Job
>> analysis; Prices; Profit sharing;
>> Wage-price policy**
>> *x* Compensation; Overtime
>> *xx* **Cost and standard of living; Eco-**

Wages—*Continued*
> nomics; Labor and laboring classes; Labor contract; Prices

Wages—Annual wage
> *x* Annual wage plans
> *xx* Guaranteed annual income

Wages—Minimum wage
> *x* Minimum wage

Wagons. *See* **Carriages and carts**

Waiting line theory. *See* **Queuing theory**

Wakefulness. *See* **Insomnia**

Walking
> *See also* **Hiking**
> *x* Hitchhiking; Locomotion
> *xx* **Hiking; Track athletics**

Walking in space. *See* **Extravehicular activity (Manned space flight)**

Wall decoration. *See* **Mural painting and decoration**

Wall painting. *See* **Mural painting and decoration**

Wall Street
> Use for works on the activities of Wall Street as a financial district. Historical and descriptive works on Wall Street as a street are entered under **New York (City)—Streets**
> *xx* **Stock exchange**

Wallpaper
> *See also* **Paper hanging**
> *xx* **Interior decoration; Paper hanging**

Walls
> *See also* **Foundations; Masonry; Mural painting and decoration**
> *x* Retaining walls
> *xx* **Building; Carpentry; Civil engineering; Foundations; Masonry**

War
> *See also*

Aeronautics, Military	**Military law**
Armies	**Munitions**
Battles	**Naval art and science**
Chemical warfare	**Navies**
Disarmament	**Peace**
Guerrilla warfare	**Psychological warfare**
International law	
Military art and science	**Soldiers**
	Strategy
	Submarine warfare

> *also* names of wars, battles, etc., e.g. **U.S.—History—Civil War; Gettysburg, Battle of, 1863;** etc.
> *x* Fighting; Wars
> *xx* **Armies; International law; Militarism; Military art and science; Peace**

War, Articles of. *See* **Military law**

War—Economic aspects

Use for works discussing the economic causes of war and the effect of war on industry and trade

See also **Industrial mobilization; Munitions; World War, 1939-1945—Manpower;** also names of wars with the subdivision *Economic aspects,* e.g. **European War, 1914-1918—Economic aspects; World War, 1939-1945—Economic aspects;** etc.

x Economics of war; Industry and war, War and industry

War and civilization

x Civilization and war

xx **Civilization; Progress**

War and industry. *See* **War—Economic aspects**

War and religion

See also **Conscientious objectors; Nonviolence; Pacifism; World War, 1939-1945—Religious aspects**

x Christianity and war; Church and war; Religion and war

War crime trials

xx **World War, 1939-1945—Atrocities**

War cripples. *See* **Physically handicapped**

War debts. *See* **Debts, Public; European War, 1914-1918 — Finance; World War, 1939-1945—Finance**

War of 1812. *See* **U.S.—History—War of 1812**

War of nerves. *See* **Psychological warfare**

War of 1914. *See* **European War, 1914-1918**

War of 1939-1945. *See* **World War, 1939-1945**

War of Secession (U.S.). *See* **U.S.—History—Civil War**

War of the American Revolution. *See* **U.S.—History—Revolution**

War of the Spanish Succession, 1701-1714. *See* **Spanish Succession, War of, 1701-1714**

War pensions. *See* **Pensions, Military**

War poetry

See also **War songs**

xx **Poetry—Collections; War songs**

War prisoners. *See* **Prisoners of war**

War ships. *See* **Warships**

War songs

See also **War poetry; World War, 1939-1945—Songs and music**

x Battle songs; Soldiers' songs

xx **National songs; Songs; War poetry**

War veterans. *See* **Veterans**

War work. *See* names of wars with the subdivision *War work,* e.g. **World War, 1939-1945—War work;** etc.

Warfare, Submarine. *See* **Submarine warfare**

Warm air heating. *See* **Hot air heating**

Wars. *See* **Military history; Naval history; War;** and names of wars, e.g. **World War, 1939-1945;** etc.

Wars of the Roses, 1455-1485. *See.* **Gt. Brit.— History—Wars of the Roses, 1455-1485**

Warships
> *See also* **Aircraft carriers; Navies; Submarines;** also names of countries with the subhead *Navy* (e.g. **U.S. Navy;** etc.) ; and names of warships
> *x* Battle ships; Battleships; War ships
> *xx* **Naval architecture; Naval art and science; Navies; Sea power; Ships**

Washing. *See* **Laundry**

Wasps
> *x* Hymenoptera
> *xx* **Insects**

Waste (Economics)
> *xx* **Economics**

Waste disposal. *See* **Factory and trade waste; Refuse and refuse disposal; Sewage disposal; Waste products**

Waste products
> *See also* **Factory and trade waste; Refuse and refuse disposal; Salvage (Waste, etc.)**
> *x* By-products; Industrial wastes; Junk: Products, Waste; Trade waste; Waste disposal
> *xx* **Chemistry, Technical; Factory and trade waste; Manufactures; Refuse and refuse disposal; Salvage (Waste, etc.)**

Waste products—Recycling. *See* **Salvage (Waste, etc.)**

Waste reclamation. *See* **Salvage (Waste, etc.)**

Watches. *See* **Clocks and watches**

Water
> *See also*

Floods	Ice
Fog	Lakes
Frost	Ocean
Geysers	Rain and rainfall
Glaciers	Rivers
Hydraulic engineering	Sea water
Hydrotherapy	Snow
	Steam

> *x* Hydrology
> *xx* **Hydraulic engineering; Hydraulics**

Water—Analysis
> *x* Chemical analysis; Water analysis
> *xx* **Chemistry, Analytic; Water—Pollution**

Water—Conservation. *See* **Water conservation**

Water—Detergent pollution. *See* **Detergent pollution of rivers, lakes, etc.**

Water—Fluoridation
> *x* Fluoridation of water; Water fluoridation
> *xx* **Teeth—Diseases**

Water—Heavy water. *See* **Deuterium oxide**

[handwritten note:] Waste water reclamation. See Water reuse.

Water—Petroleum pollution. *See* **Petroleum pollution of water**

Water—Pollution

> *See also* **Factory and trade waste; Refuse and refuse disposal; Sewage disposal; Water—Analysis; Water supply**; also **Detergent pollution of rivers, lakes, etc.; Petroleum pollution of water** and similar headings
>
> *x* Pollution of water; Rivers—Pollution; Water pollution
>
> *xx* **Factory and trade waste; Hygiene; Pollution; Public health; Refuse and refuse disposal; Rivers; Sewage disposal; Water supply**

Water—Purification

> *x* Water purification
>
> *xx* **Sanitation; Water supply**

Water analysis. *See* **Water—Analysis**

Water animals. *See* **Fresh-water animals; Marine animals**

Water ballet. *See* **Synchronized swimming**

Water birds

> *See also* names of water birds, e.g. **Penguins**; etc.
>
> *x* Aquatic birds; Birds, Aquatic; Water fowl; Wild fowl
>
> *xx* **Birds**

Water color painting

> *xx* **Painting**

Water colors

> *xx* **Paintings**

Water conduits. *See* **Aqueducts**

Water conservation

> *See also* **Water supply**
>
> *x* Conservation of water; Water—Conservation
>
> *xx* **Water supply**

Water cure. *See* **Hydrotherapy**

Water farming. *See* **Plants—Soilless culture**

Water flow. *See* **Hydraulics**

Water fluoridation. *See* **Water—Fluoridation**

Water fowl. *See* **Water birds**

Water plants. *See* **Fresh-water plants; Marine plants**

Water pollution. *See* **Water—Pollution**

Water power

> *See also* **Dams; Hydraulic engineering; Hydraulic machinery**
>
> *x* Hydroelectric power
>
> *xx* **Hydraulics; Natural resources; Power (Mechanics); Power resources; Rivers; Water resources development**

Water purification. *See* **Water—Purification**

Water resources development

> *See also* **Inland navigation; Irrigation; Water power; Water supply**
>
> *xx* **Natural resources**

Water rights

> *xx* **Irrigation; Rivers**

See Waterfoul
Water pollution

Water reuse

565

Water skiing
   x Skiing, Water
  xx **Skiis and skiing**
Water sports
   See also **Boats and boating; Canoes and canoeing; Diving; Fishing; Rowing; Sailing; Skin diving; Surfing; Swimming; Yachts and Yachting;** and names of other water sports
   x Aquatic sports
  xx **Sports**
Water supply
   See also **Aqueducts; Dams; Forest influences; Irrigation; Reservoirs; Water — Pollution; Water — Purification; Water conservation; Wells;** also names of cities with the subdivision *Water supply,* e.g. **Chicago—Water supply;** etc.
   x Waterworks
  xx **Civil engineering; Municipal engineering; Natural resources; Public health; Public utilities; Reservoirs; Sanitary engineering; Sanitation; Water—Pollution; Water conservation; Water resources development; Wells**
Water supply engineering
   See also **Boring; Hydraulic engineering**
  xx **Engineering; Hydraulic engineering**
Watering places. *See* **Health resorts, spas, etc.**
Waterways
   Use for general works on rivers, lakes, canals as highways for transportation or commerce
   See also **Canals; Inland navigation; Lakes; Rivers**
  xx **Transportation**
Waterworks. *See* **Water supply**
Wave mechanics
  xx **Mechanics; Quantum theory; Waves**
Waves
   See also **Electric waves; Ether (of space); Light; Ocean waves; Radiation; Sound waves; Wave mechanics**
  xx **Hydrodynamics; Vibration**
Waves, Electromagnetic. *See* **Electromagnetic waves**
Wealth
   See also

Capital	Inheritance and succession
Capitalists and financiers	Millionaires
Cost and standard of living	Money
Economic conditions	Poverty
Income	Profit
Income tax	Property
	Success

   x Distribution of wealth; Fortune, Riches

[handwritten annotations, right margin:] ✓ Water witching. See Divining rod ✓ Watersheds ✓ Waterfowl

Wealth—*Continued*

    xx Capital; Economics; Finance; Millionaires; Money; Property

Weapons. *See* **Arms and armor; Firearms**

Weapons, Atomic. *See* **Atomic weapons**

Weariness. *See* **Fatigue**

Weather

    See note under **Climate**

    See also **Climate; Meteorology; Rain and rainfall; Snow; Storms; Weather control; Weather forecasting; Winds;** also names of countries, cities, etc. with the subdivision *Climate,* e.g. **U.S.— Climate;** etc.

    xx **Climate; Meteorology**

Weather control

    x Artificial weather control; Cloud seeding; Rain making

    xx **Weather**

Weather forecasting

    See also **Meteorology in aeronautics; Weather lore**

    x Forecasting, Weather

    xx **Meteorology; Weather**

Weather lore

    xx **Folklore; Meteorology; Signs and symbols; Weather forecasting**

Weather satellites. *See* **Meteorological satellites**

Weaving

    See also **Basket making; Beadwork; Lace and lace making; Looms; Textile industry and fabrics;** also names of woven articles, e.g. **Carpets;** etc.

    xx **Arts and crafts; Carpets; Handicraft; Textile industry and fabrics**

Weddings. *See* **Etiquette; Marriage; Marriage customs and rites**

Weeds

    xx **Agricultural pests; Botany; Botany, Economic; Gardening; Plants**

Weight control

    See also **Diet; Exercise**

    x Body weight control; Corpulence; Fat; Obesity; Overweight; Reducing (Body weight control)

    xx **Diet**

Weightlessness

    x Free fall; Gravity free state; Subgravity state; Zero gravity

    xx **Man—Influence of environment; Space medicine**

Weights and measures

    See also **Electric measurements; Measuring instruments; Mensuration; Metric system**

    x Cambistry; Measures; Metrology

    xx **Mensuration**

Welding

> *See also* **Electric welding; Solder and soldering**
>
> *x* Oxyacetylene welding
>
> *xx* **Blacksmithing; Forging; Ironwork; Metalwork; Solder and soldering**

Welding, Electric. *See* **Electric welding**

Welfare agencies. *See* **Charities**

Welfare state. *See* **Economic policy; Public welfare; The State**

Welfare ~~work~~. *See* **~~Charities~~; Public welfare; Social work**

Welfare work in industry

> *See also* **Counseling; Housing; Social settlements**
>
> *xx* **Industrial management; Labor and laboring classes; Social work**

Well boring. *See* **Boring**

Wells

> *See also* **Boring; Gas, Natural; Petroleum; Water supply**
>
> *x* Artesian wells
>
> *xx* **Boring; Hydraulic engineering; Water supply**

The West

> Use for the region west of the Mississippi River
>
> *See also* **Northwest, Pacific; Pacific States;** also names of individual states in this region
>
> *xx* **United States**

The West—Discovery and exploration

> *x* U.S.—Discovery and exploration

West Africa. *See* **Africa, West**

West Germany. *See* **Germany (Federal Republic)**

West Point Military Academy. *See* **U.S. Military Academy, West Point**

Western civilization. *See* **Civilization, Occidental**

Westminster Abbey

> *xx* **Abbeys**

Whales

Whaling

> *xx* **Fisheries; Voyages and travels**

Wheat

> *See also* **Flour and flour mills**
>
> *x* Breadstuffs
>
> *xx* **Flour and flour mills; Grain**

Wheels

> *See also* **Gearing; Tires; Turbines**
>
> *x* Car wheels

White slave traffic. *See* **Prostitution**

Whittling. *See* **Wood carving**

Widows

> *xx* **Single women; Woman**

Wigs

> *xx* **Costume; Hair**

Wild animals. *See* **Animals**

✓ Wetlands

Wild flowers

    x Flowers, Wild

    xx **Flowers**

Wild fowl. *See* **Game and game birds; Water birds**

Wild life—Conservation. *See* **Wildlife—Conservation**

Wilderness areas

    x Preservation of natural scenery; Protection of natural scenery

    xx **Forest reserves; National parks and reserves; Natural monuments**

Wilderness survival

    x Bush survival; Outdoor survival

    xx **Camping; Outdoor life; Survival (after airplane accidents, shipwrecks, etc.)**

Wildlife—Conservation

    See also **Birds—Protection; Forests and forestry; Game preserves; Game protection; National parks and reserves; Natural resources; Pesticides and wildlife; Rare animals;** also names of specific wildlife refuges

    x Conservation of wildlife; Preservation of wildlife; Protection of wildlife; Wild life—Conservation

    xx **Nature conservation**

Wildlife and pesticides. *See* **Pesticides and wildlife**

Will. *See* **Brainwashing; Free will and determinism**

Wills

    See also **Executors and administrators; Inheritance and succession**

    x Bequests; Legacies

    xx **Executors and administrators; Genealogy; Inheritance and succession; Registers of birth, etc.**

Wind. *See* **Winds**

Wind instruments

    See also **Bands (Music);** also names of wind instruments, e.g. **Flute;** etc.

    x Brass instruments; Woodwind instruments

    xx **Bands (Music); Musical instruments**

Windbreaks

    x Shelterbelts

    xx **Tree planting**

Windmills

    xx **Irrigation**

Window dressing. *See* **Show windows**

Window gardening

    See also **House plants**

    xx **Flower gardening; Flowers; Gardening**

Windows

    See also **Glass; Show windows**

    xx **Architecture—Details; Building**

Windows, Stained glass. *See* **Glass painting and staining**

569

Winds

See also **Cyclones; Hurricanes; Storms; Tornadoes; Typhoons**

x Gales; Wind

xx **Meteorology; Navigation; Physical geography; Storms; Weather**

Wine and wine making

See also **Fermentation; Grapes**

xx **Fermentation; Grapes**

Winter resorts

See also **Health resorts, spas, etc.**

x Resorts

xx **Health resorts, spas, etc.**

Winter sports

See also **Hockey; Iceboats; Skating; Skis and skiing;** and names of other winter sports

x Ice sports

xx **Sports**

Wire tapping

See also **Eavesdropping**

xx **Criminal investigation; Eavesdropping**

Wireless. *See* **Radio**

Wit and humor

See also **Anecdotes; Comedy; Epigrams; Humorists; Nonsense verses; Parody; Satire;** also **American wit and humor; English wit and humor;** etc.; and subjects with the subdivision *Anecdotes, facetiae, satire, etc.,* e.g. **Music—Anecdotes, facetiae, satire, etc.;** etc.

x Facetiae; Humor; Humorous stories; Jokes

xx **Laughter; Literature**

Witchcraft

See also **Charms; Demonology; Occult sciences; Witches**

x Black magic; Delusions; Exorcism; Necromancy; Sorcery; Spirits

xx **Demonology; Folklore; Occult sciences; Superstition**

Witches

xx **Witchcraft**

Witnesses

x Cross-examination

Wives of clergymen. *See* **Clergymen's wives**

Wives of presidents. *See* **Presidents—U.S.— Wives**

Woman

See also **Girls; Man; Mothers; Single women; Widows; Young women;** also **Women as artists; Women as authors; Women as physicians;** and similar headings; also **Women in aeronautics; Women in literature and art; Women in the U.S.;** and similar subjects

x Women

Woman—*Continued*

   xx Anthropology; Family; Girls; Young women

Woman—Biography

   x Heroines

   xx Biography

Woman—Civil rights

   See also **Woman—Suffrage; Women's Liberation Movement**

   x Emancipation of women; Rights of women; Woman — Emancipation; Woman—Equal rights; Woman—Rights of women; Women's rights

   xx Civil rights; Sex discrimination; **Woman—Suffrage**

Woman—Clothing. *See* **Clothing and dress**

Woman—Clubs. *See* **Women's clubs**

Woman—Diseases

   See also **Woman—Health and hygiene**

   x Diseases of women

   xx Medicine—Practice; **Woman—Health and hygiene**

Woman—Dress. *See* **Clothing and dress; Costume**

Woman—Education. *See* **Education of women**

Woman—Emancipation. *See* **Woman—Civil rights**

Woman—Employment

   See also **Discrimination in employment; Hours of labor; Occupations;** and names of occupations, e.g. **Dressmaking; Nurses and nursing;** etc.

   x Employment of women; Girls—Employment; Woman—Occupations; Women in industry; Working girls; Working women

   xx Hours of labor; Labor and laboring classes; Labor supply; Social problems; **Woman—Health and hygiene**

Woman—Enfranchisement. *See* **Woman—Suffrage**

Woman—Equal rights. *See* **Woman—Civil rights**

Woman—Health and hygiene

   See also **Clothing and dress; Menopause; Physical education and training; Woman—Diseases; Woman—Employment**

   x Health of women

   xx Hygiene; Sexual hygiene; **Woman—Diseases**

Woman—History and condition of women. *See* **Woman—Social conditions**

Woman—Hours of labor. *See* **Hours of labor**

Woman—Occupations. *See* **Woman—Employment**

Woman—Psychology

   x Feminine psychology

Woman—Rights of women. *See* **Woman—Civil rights**

Woman—Social conditions

　　See also **Divorce; Prostitution; Women in public life; Women's clubs; Women's Liberation Movement**

　　x Feminism; Woman—History and condition of women

　　xx **Social problems**

Woman—Societies and clubs. *See* **Women's clubs**

Woman—Suffrage

　　See also **Woman—Civil rights**

　　x Suffragettes; Woman—Enfranchisement

　　xx **Suffrage; Woman—Civil rights**

Women. *See* **Woman**; and headings beginning with the word **Women**

Women as air pilots. *See* **Women in aeronautics**

Women as artists

　　Use same form for the attainments of women in other professions and capacities, e.g. **Women as scientists**; etc.

　　xx **Artists; Woman**

Women as authors

　　xx **Authors; Woman**

Women as physicians

　　xx **Medicine as a profession; Physicians; Woman**

Women as police. *See* **Policewomen**

Women in aeronautics

　　Use same form for women working in other professions or trades

　　See also **Air lines—Hostesses**

　　x Women as air pilots

　　xx **Aeronautics—Biography; Aeronautics as a profession; Air pilots; Woman**

Women in art. *See* **Women in literature and art**

Women in industry. *See* **Woman—Employment**

Women in literature and art

　　Use for works treating of women in literature, and women depicted in works of art. Works on the attainments of women in literature and art are entered under **Women as authors; Women as artists**

　　x Heroines; Women in art

　　xx **Art; Characters and characteristics in literature; Literature; Woman**

Women in public life

　　xx **Woman—Social conditions**

Women in the Bible

　　x Bible—Women; Heroines

　　xx **Bible—Biogaphy**

Women in the U.S.

　　Use same form for women in other countries, e.g. **Women in France**; etc.

　　See also **Presidents—U.S.—Wives**

　　x U.S.—Women

　　xx **Woman**

Women's clothing. *See* **Clothing and dress**

Women's clubs

> *See also* **Girls' clubs**
>
> *x* Woman—Clubs; Woman—Societies and clubs
>
> *xx* **Clubs; Societies; Woman—Social conditions**

Women's lib. *See* **Women's Liberation Movement**

Women's Liberation Movement

> *x* Women's lib
>
> *xx* **Woman—Civil rights; Woman—Social conditions**

Women's rights. *See* **Woman—Civil rights**

Wood

> Use for works on the chemical and physical properties of different kinds of wood and how they are used
>
> *See also* **Forests and forestry; Lumber and lumbering; Plywood; Woodwork;** also kinds of wood, e.g. **Oak,** etc.
>
> *x* Timber
>
> *xx* **Building materials; Forest products; Forests and forestry; Fuel; Trees**

Wood—Preservation

> *x* Preservation of wood

Wood block printing. *See* **Wood engraving**

Wood carving

> *x* Carving, Wood; Whittling
>
> *xx* **Arts and crafts; Decoration and ornament; Furniture; Sculpture; Woodwork**

Wood engraving

> *x* Block printing; Wood block printing; Woodcuts
>
> *xx* **Engraving**

Wood finishing

> *See also* **Lacquer and lacquering; Varnish and varnishing**
>
> *x* Finishes and finishing
>
> *xx* **Painting, Industrial**

Wood pulp

> *x* Pulpwood
>
> *xx* **Forest products; Paper making and trade**

Wood turning. *See* **Turning**

Wood wind instruments. *See* **Wind instruments**

Woodcuts. *See* **Wood engraving**

Woods. *See* **Forests and forestry**

Woodwork

> *See also* **Cabinet work; Carpentry; Furniture; Turning; Wood carving**
>
> *xx* **Architecture—Details; Cabinet work; Carpentry; Industrial arts education; Turning; Wood**

Woodworking machinery

> *See also* special kinds of machines, e.g. **Lathes;** etc.
>
> *xx* **Machinery**

Wool

　　See also **Dyes and dyeing; Yarn**

　　xx **Fibers; Yarn**

Word games

　　See also names of specific word games; e.g., **Crossword puzzles**; etc.

Words. *See* **Vocabulary**

Words, New

　　x Coinage of words; New words

　　xx **Semantics; Vocabulary**

Work

　　See also **Labor and laboring classes**

Work stoppages. *See* **Strikes and lockouts**

Working classes. *See* **Labor and laboring classes**

Working day. *See* **Hours of labor**

Working girls. *See* **Child labor; Woman—Employment**

Working women. *See* **Woman—Employment**

Workingmen's dwellings. *See* **Housing**

Workingmen's insurance. *See* **Insurance, Social**

Workmen's compensation

　　x Compensation; Employers' liability; Insurance, Workmen's compensation

　　xx **Insurance, Accident; Insurance, Health; Insurance, Social; Occupational diseases**

Workshop councils. *See* **Employees' representation in management**

Workshops

　　See also **Factories**

　　xx **Factories; Labor and laboring classes; Manufactures**

Workshops, Teachers'. *See* **Teachers' workshops**

World. *See* **Earth**

World, End of the. *See* **End of the world**

World economics. *See* **Commercial policy; Economic conditions; Economic policy; Geography, Commercial**

World government. *See* **International organization**

World history

　　See also **Geography; History, Ancient; History, Modern; Middle Ages—History**

　　x History, Universal; Universal history

　　xx **History**

World language. *See* **Language, Universal**

World organization. *See* **International organization**

World politics

　　See note under **International relations**

　　See also **Eastern question; European War, 1914-1918; Geopolitics; International organization; International relations; World War, 1939-1945**; also names of countries with the subdivisions *Foreign relations* and *Politics and government,*

World politics—*Continued*
  e.g. **U.S.—Foreign relations; U.S.—Politics and government; etc.**
  xx **Eastern question; Geopolitics; International organization; International relations; Political science**
World politics—1945-1965
  x Cold war; Power politics
World politics, 1965-
  x Cold war; Power politics
World War, 1914-1918. *See* **European War, 1914-1918**
World War, 1939-1945 (May subdiv. geog.)
  Subdivisions used under this heading may be used under other wars
  See also names of battles, sieges, etc. e.g. **Ardennes, Battle of the, 1944-1945; Pearl Harbor, Attack on, 1941; etc.**
  x European War, 1939-1945; War of 1939-1945
  xx **Europe—History—1914-1945; History, Modern—20th century; World politics**
World War, 1939-1945—Aerial operations
  x Air warfare
  xx **Aeronautics, Military**
World War, 1939-1945—Amphibious operations
  xx **World War, 1939-1945—Naval operations**
World War, 1939-1945—Art and war
World War, 1939-1945—Atrocities
  See also **War crime trials**
  x Military atrocities
  xx **Atrocities**
World War, 1939-1945—Battles. *See* **World War, 1939-1945—Campaigns and battles**
World War, 1939-1945—Biography
World War, 1939-1945—Blockades
World War, 1939-1945—Campaigns and battles (May subdiv. geog.)
  See also names of battles, campaigns, sieges, etc. e.g. **Ardennes, Battle of the, 1944-1945; Pearl Harbor, Attack on, 1941; etc.**
  x World War, 1939-1945—Battles
  xx **Battles**
World War, 1939-1945—Cartoons. *See* **World War, 1939-1945—Humor, caricatures, etc.**
World War, 1939-1945—Causes
World War, 1939-1945—Censorship
World War, 1939-1945—Charities. *See* **World War, 1939-1945—Civilian relief; World War, 1939-1945—War work**
World War, 1939-1945—Children
  xx **Children**
World War, 1939-1945—Civilian defense. *See* **Civil defense**

World War, 1939-1945—Civilian evacuation.
See **World War, 1939-1945—Evacuation of civilians**

World War, 1939-1945—Civilian relief
 See also **World War, 1939-1945—Refugees**
 x World War, 1939-1945—Charities
 xx **Charities; Reconstruction (1939-1951); Economic assistance; World War, 1939-1945—Food question; World War, 1939-1945—Medical and sanitary affairs, World War, 1939-1945—Refugees; World War, 1939-1945—War work**

World War, 1939-1945—Congresses, conferences, etc.

World War, 1939-1945—Conscientious objectors
 xx **Conscientious objectors**

World War, 1939-1945—Correspondents. *See* **World War, 1939-1945—Journalists**

World War, 1939-1945—Damage to property. *See* **World War, 1939-1945—Destruction and pillage**

World War, 1939-1945—Destruction and pillage
 x World War, 1939-1945—Damage to property

World War, 1939-1945—Diplomatic history
 See also **World War, 1939-1945—Governments in exile**

World War, 1939-1945—Displaced persons
 x Displaced persons
 xx **World War, 1939-1945—Refugees**

World War, 1939-1945—Economic aspects
 Use for works treating of the economic causes of the war and the effect of the war on commerce and industry
 See also **Reconstruction (1939-1951); World War, 1939-1945—Finance; World War, 1939-1945—Manpower; World War, 1939-1945—Reparations**
 xx **Reconstruction (1939-1951); War—Economic aspects**

World War, 1939-1945—Engineering and construction

World War, 1939-1945—Evacuation of civilians
 x Civilian evacuation; Evacuation of civilians; World War, 1939-1945—Civilian evacuation
 xx **Civil defense; World War, 1939-1945—Refugees**

World War, 1939-1945—Finance
 Use for works on the cost and financing of the war, including war debts, and the effect of the war on financial systems, including inflation
 x War debts

576

World War, 1939-1945—Finance—*Continued*
    xx Debts, Public; World War, 1939-1945
       —Economic aspects
World War, 1939-1945—Food question
    See also World War, 1939-1945—Civilian
       relief
World War, 1939-1945—Governments in
       exile
    x Governments in exile
    xx World War, 1939-1945—Diplomatic
       history
World War, 1939-1945—Guerrillas. *See* World
       War, 1939-1945—Underground move-
       ments
World War, 1939-1945—Hospitals. *See* World
       War, 1939-1945—Medical and sani-
       tary affairs
World War, 1939-1945—Humor, caricatures,
       etc.
    x World War, 1939-1945—Cartoons
    xx Cartoons and caricatures
World War, 1939-1945—Influence and re-
       sults
World War, 1939-1945—Jews
World War, 1939-1945—Journalists
    x World War, 1939-1945—Correspondents;
       World War, 1939-1945—War corre-
       spondents
World War, 1939-1945—Manpower
    x Man power; Manpower
    xx Armies; Labor and laboring classes;
       Labor supply; War—Economic as-
       pects; World War, 1939-1945—Eco-
       nomic aspects
World War, 1939-1945—Maps
World War, 1939-1945—Medical and sanitary
       affairs
    See also World War, 1939-1945—Civilian
       relief
    x World War, 1939-1945—Hospitals;
       World War, 1939-1945—Sanitary af-
       fairs
    xx Armies—Medical and sanitary affairs;
       Hospitals, Military; Medicine, Mili-
       tary; Military hygiene; Sanitation
World War, 1939-1945—Moral aspects
World War, 1939-1945—Naval operations
    See also World War, 1939-1945—Amphib-
       ious operation; also names of naval
       battles
World War, 1939-1945—Naval operations—
       Submarine
    x World War, 1939-1945—Submarine op-
       erations
World War, 1939-1945—Negroes
World War, 1939-1945—Occupied territories
    Use for general treatment of the subject.
       For occupation of specific countries,
       use the name of the country with the
       subdivision *History—German occupa-*

World War, 1939-1945—Occupied territories
—*Continued*

> tion, 1940-1945 or *History—Allied occupation, 1945-* , e.g. Netherlands History—German occupation, 1940-1945; Japan—History—Allied occupation, 1945-1952; etc.

> *See also* World War, 1939-1945—Underground movements; also names of countries with the subdivision *History—German occupation, 1940-1945,* e.g. Netherlands—History—German occupation, 1940-1945; etc.

xx Military occupation; World War, 1939-1945—Territorial questions

World War, 1939-1945—Peace
xx Peace

World War, 1939-1945—Personal narratives
> Use for miscellaneous accounts and reports written by soldiers, officers, journalists and other observers. Accounts limited to a special topic are entered under the specific subject

World War, 1939-1945—Pictorial works

World War, 1939-1945—Prisoners and prisons
> *See also* Concentration camps; Prisoners of war

World War, 1939-1945—Propaganda
> *See also* Propaganda, German
xx Propaganda

World War, 1939-1945—Public opinion
xx Public opinion

World War, 1939-1945—Railroads. *See* World War, 1939-1945—Transportation

World War, 1939-1945—Reconstruction. *See* Reconstruction (1939-1951)

World War, 1939-1945—Refugees
> *See also* World War, 1939-1945—Civilian relief; World War, 1939-1945—Evacuation of civilians; World War, 1939-1945—Displaced persons
xx Refugees, Political; World War, 1939-1945—Civilian relief

World War, 1939-1945—Regimental histories

World War, 1939-1945—Religious aspects
xx War and religion

World War, 1939-1945—Reparations
x Reparations (World War, 1939-1945)
xx Reconstruction (1939-1951); World War, 1939-1945—Economic aspects

World War, 1939-1945—Secret service
xx Secret service

World War, 1939-1945—Sanitary affairs. *See* World War, 1939-1945—Medical and Sanitary affairs

World War, 1939-1945—Social work. *See* World War, 1939-1945—War work

World War, 1939-1945—Songs and music
xx Military music; War songs

World War, 1939-1945—Sources
>> *xx* History—Sources
World War, 1939-1945—Submarine operations.
>> *See* **World War, 1939-1945—Naval operations—Submarine**
World War, 1939-1945—Supplies
World War, 1939-1945—Territorial questions
>> *See also* **World War, 1939-1945—Occupied territories**
>> *xx* **Boundaries**
World War, 1939-1945—Transportation
>> *x* World War, 1939-1945—Railroads
>> *xx* **Transportation**
World War, 1939-1945—Underground movements
>> *x* World War, 1939-1945 — Guerrillas; Underground movements (World War, 1939-1945)
>> *xx* **Guerrilla warfare; Spies; World War, 1939-1945—Occupied territories**
World War, 1939-1945—U.S.
>> *x* U.S.—History—World War, 1939-1945; U.S.—World War, 1939-1945
World War, 1939-1945—War correspondents.
>> *See* **World War, 1939-1945—Journalists**
World War, 1939-1945—War work
>> *See also* **World War, 1939-1945—Civilian relief**
>> *x* War work; World War, 1939-1945—Charities; World War, 1939-1945—Social work
World War, 1939-1945—Women
World's fairs. *See* **Exhibitions; Fairs**
Worms
>> *xx* **Invertebrates**
Worry
>> *x* Anxiety
>> *xx* **Mental health; Nervous system—Diseases**
Worship
>> *See also* **Ancestor worship; Devotional exercises; Prayer; Public worship; Sacrifice**
>> *x* Devotion
>> *xx* **Religion; Theology**
Wounded, First aid to. *See* **First aid**
Wrapping of gifts. *See* **Gift wrapping**
Wrecks. *See* **Railroads—Accidents; Shipwrecks**
Wrestling
>> *See also* **Judo**
Writers. *See* **Authors**; and special classes of writers, e.g. **Dramatists; Historians; Journalists**; etc.
Writing
>> Use for general works on the history and art of writing and on elegant handwriting. Practical manuals are entered under **Penmanship.** Works on hand-

Writing—*Continued*

writing as an expression of the writer's character are entered under **Graphology**

See also

Abbreviations	**Graphology**
Alphabet	**Hieroglyphics**
Autographs	**Penmanship**
Ciphers	**Picture writing**
Cryptography	**Shorthand**
Cuneiform inscrip-	**Typewriting**
tions	

x Calligraphy; Handwriting

xx **Alphabet; Ciphers; Communication; Language and languages; Penmanship**

Writing (Authorship). *See* **Authorship; Journalism**

Wrought iron work. *See* **Ironwork**

X-15 (Rocket aircraft)

xx **Rocket planes**

X rays

See also **Radiologists; Radiotherapy; Vacuum tubes**

x Radiography; Rays, Roentgen; Roentgen rays

xx **Electricity; Electromagnetic waves; Light; Radiation; Radioactivity; Radiotherapy; Therapeutics**

Xerography

xx **Copying processes and machines**

Yacht racing. *See* **Boat racing**

Yachts and yachting

See also **Sailing**

x Regattas

xx **Boatbuilding; Boats and boating; Ocean travel; Sailing; Ships; Voyages and travels; Water sports**

Yarn

See also **Cotton; Flax; Wool**

xx **Textile industry and fabrics; Wool**

Yearbooks

See also **Almanacs; Calendars;** and general subjects and names of organizations with the subdivision *Yearbooks,* e.g. **Literature—Yearbooks; United Nations—Yearbooks;** etc.

x Annuals

xx **Almanacs**

Yeast

xx **Fermentation**

Yellow fever

xx **Tropics—Diseases and hygiene**

Yellowstone National Park

xx **National parks and reserves**

Yiddish language

May be subdivided like **English language**

x German Hebrew; Jewish language; Jews —Language; Judaeo-German

xx **Hebrew language**

Yiddish literature
   May use same subdivisions and names of
      literary forms as for **English literature**
   xx Jewish literature
Yippies. *See* **Hippies**
Yoga
   xx Hinduism; Philosophy, Hindu; Theos-
      ophy
Yom Kippur
   xx Fasts and feasts—Judaism
Young adults. *See* **Youth**
Young men
   See also **Boys; Youth**
   x Men
   xx Boys; Youth
Young Men's Christian Associations
Young people's libraries. *See* **Libraries, Young
   adults'**
Young women
   See also **Education of women; Girls;
      Woman; Youth**
   xx Girls; Woman; Youth
Young Women's Christian Associations
Youth (May subdiv. geog.)
   See also **Adolescence; Boys; Children;
      Church work with youth; Dropouts;
      Girls; Libraries, Young adults'; Run-
      aways; Young men; Young women;
      Youth and television**
   x Age; Campus disorders; Teen age;
      Young adults
   xx Boys; Children; Girls; Young men;
      Young women
Youth—Attitudes
   xx Attitude (Psychology)
Youth—Religious life
Youth, Runaway. *See* **Runaways**
Youth—U.S.
   x American youth; U.S.—Youth
Youth and drugs. *See* **Drugs and youth**
Youth and narcotics. *See* **Narcotics and youth**
Youth and television. *See* **Television and youth**
Youth as consumers
   x Children as consumers; Teenage con-
      sumers; Youth market
   xx **Consumers**
Youth hostels
   x Hostels, Youth; Tourist accommodations
Youth market. *See* **Youth as consumers**
Youth movement
   See also **Demonstrations; Students—
      Political activity**
   x Student movement; Student protests;
      Student revolt
Zen Buddhism
   xx Buddha and Buddhism
Zend-Avesta. *See* **Avesta**
Zeppelins. *See* **Airships**
Zero gravity. *See* **Weightlessness**

*Youth conservation Corps
(YCC)*

581

Zinc

    See also **Brass**

Zionism

    See also **Jews—Restoration**

    xx **Jewish question; Jews—Restoration**

Zodiac

    xx **Astronomy**

Zoning

    x City planning—Zone system; Districting
        (in city planning)

    xx **City planning**

Zoological gardens

    See also names of zoological gardens

    x Zoos

    xx **Animals; Parks**

Zoological specimens—Collection and preservation

    See also **Taxidermy**; also names of specimens with the subdivision *Collection and preservation*, e.g. **Birds—Collection and preservation**; etc.

    x Collections of natural specimens; Preservation of zoological specimens; Specimens, Preservation of

    xx **Collectors and collecting; Taxidermy**

Zoology (May subdiv. geog.)

    See also

Anatomy, Comparative	**Natural history**
Animals	**Physiology, Comparative**
Embryology	**Psychology, Comparative**
Evolution	
Fossils	**Variation (Biology)**

    also names of divisions, classes, etc. of the animal kingdom (e.g. **Invertebrates; Vertebrates; Birds; Mammals;** etc.); and names of animals

    x Animal kingdom; Animal physiology; Fauna

    xx **Animals; Biology; Natural history; Nature study; Science**

Zoology—Anatomy. *See* **Anatomy, Comparative**

Zoology, Economic

    Use for general works on animals injurious and beneficial to man and to agriculture, and for works on the extermination of wild animals, venomous snakes, etc.

    See also **Agricultural pests; Domestic animals; Fur-bearing animals; Insects, Injurious and beneficial; Pest control**

    x Animals, Useful and harmful; Biology, Economic; Economic zoology; Pests

Zoology—Geographic distribution. *See* **Geographical distribution of animals and plants**

Zoology—U.S.

    x U.S.—Zoology

✓ *Zoo animals*

Zoology of the Bible. *See* Bible—Natural history
Zoos. *See* Zoological gardens
Zoroastrianism
 See also Avesta
 xx Avesta; Religions

APPENDIX
Black Subject Headings

This suggested list of Black subject headings is the rewording of the subject headings that exist in the Sears List under the words Negro and Negroes. Under very general subjects (e.g. **Ethnology**; **Literature**; etc.) only those references are listed here that apply to the headings in the Appendix. The cataloger must consult the general headings in their alphabetic places in the List to find the complete list of applicable references and to write in the Black headings.

Actors and actresses
　See also **Black actors**
Africa—Native races
　See also **Blacks in Africa**
African Americans. *See* **Blacks**
Afro-American studies. *See* **Black studies**
Afro-Americans. *See* **Blacks**
American literature
　See also **Black literature**
American poetry
　See also **Black poetry**
Area studies
　xx **Black studies**
Art
　See also **Blacks in literature and art**
Arts, Black. *See* **Black art**
Art, Negro. *See* **Black art**
Artists
　See also **Black artists**
Artists, Black. *See* **Black artists**
Artists, Negro. *See* **Black artists**
Arts, Black. *See* **Black art**
Arts, Negro. *See* **Black art**
Athletes, Black. *See* **Black athletes**
Athletes, Negro. *See* **Black athletes**
Authors
　See also **Black authors**
Authors, Black. *See* **Black authors**
Authors, Negro. *See* **Black authors**
Biography
　See also **Blacks—Biography**
Black actors
　xx **Actors and actresses**
Black Americans. *See* **Blacks**
Black art
　See also **Black artists**
　x Art, Black; Art, Negro; Arts, Black;
　　Arts, Negro; Blacks—Art; Negroes—
　　Art
　xx **Black artists**
Black art (Magic). *See* **Witchcraft**

Black artists
    See also **Black art**
    x Artists, Black; Artists, Negro; Negro artists
    xx **Artists; Black art**
Black athletes
    x Athletes, Black; Athletes, Negro; Negro athletes
Black authors
    Use for works dealing with the lives of several Black writers. Criticism of their literary production is entered under **Black literature—History and criticism; Black poetry—History and criticism;** etc.
    x Authors, Black; Authors, Negro; Negro authors
    xx **Authors**
Black businessmen
    x Blacks as businessmen; Businessmen, Black; Negroes as businessmen
Black folklore
    x Folklore, Black; Folklore, Negro; Negro folklore
Black librarians
    See also **Libraries and Blacks**
    x Librarians, Black; Librarians, Negro; Negro librarians
    xx **Libraries and Blacks**
Black literature
    May use same divisions and names of literary forms as for **English language**
    x Negro literature
    xx **American literature; Literature**
Black minstrels
    x Minstrels, Black; Minstrels, Negro; Negro minstrels
Black music
    See also **Black songs; Spirituals**
    x Music, Black; Music, Negro; Negro music
Black musicians
    x Musicians, Black; Musicians, Negro; Negro musicians
Black Muslims
    xx **Black nationalism; Blacks—Religion**
Black nationalism
    See also **Black Muslims**
    x Black separatism; Nationalism, Black; Nationalism, Negro; Negro nationalism; Separatism, Black
    xx **Blacks—Political activity; Blacks—Race identity**
Black poetry
    x Negro poetry
    xx **American poetry; Poetry—Collections**
Black power
    xx **Blacks—Civil rights; Blacks—Economic conditions; Blacks—Political activity**

586

Black race. *See* **Negro race**

Black separatism. *See* **Black natonalism**

Black songs

    See also **Blues (Songs, etc.); Folk songs, African; Spirituals**

    x Folk songs, Black (American); Folk songs, Negro (American); Negro folk songs

    xx **Black music; Music, American; Songs**

Black spirituals. *See* **Spirituals**

Black studies

    x Afro-American studies

    xx **Area studies; Blacks—Education; Blacks—Race identity**

Black suffrage. *See* **Blacks—Suffrage**

Blacks

    Use for general works on the Blacks in the U.S. If limited to a particular area in the U.S. may use geog. subdiv., e.g., **Blacks—Arkansas; Blacks—Chicago; Blacks—Southern States;** etc. Works dealing with Blacks in other countries are entered under **Blacks in Africa; Blacks in France,** etc.

    See also **Slavery in the U.S.**

    x African Americans; Afro-Americans; Black Americans; Colored people (U.S.); Negroes

    xx **Ethnology**

Blacks—Art. *See* **Black art**

Blacks—Biography

    xx **Biography**

Blacks—Civil rights

    See also **Black power**

    x Civil rights demonstrations; Demonstrations for Black civil rights; Freedom marches; Marches for Black civil rights

    xx **Civil rights**

Blacks—Economic conditions

    See also **Black power**

Blacks—Education

    See also **Black studies; Segregation in education**

    xx **Education**

Blacks—Employment

    x Blacks in business; Employment

    xx **Discrimination in employment**

Blacks—Housing

    x Housing, Black; Housing, Negro

Blacks—Integration

    x Integration, Racial

Blacks—Libraries. *See* **Libraries and Blacks**

Blacks—Political activity

    See also **Black nationalism; Black power**

Blacks—Race identity

    See also **Black studies; Black nationalism**

    x Negritude; Race identity; Racial identity

    xx **Race awareness; Race psychology**

Blacks—Religion

    See also **Black Muslims**

    xx **Religion**

Blacks—Segregation
  See also Segregation in education
Blacks—Social conditions
Blacks—Social life and customs
Blacks—Suffrage
  x Black suffrage; Negro suffrage
  xx Suffrage
Blacks and libraries. *See* Libraries and Blacks
Blacks as businessmen. *See* Black businessmen
Blacks in Africa
  Use same form for Blacks in other countries except U.S. See note under Blacks
  xx Africa—Native races
Blacks in art. *See* Blacks in literature and art
Blacks in business. *See* Blacks—Employment
Blacks in literature and art
  Use for works treating of Blacks in literature and Blacks depicted in works of art. For works of Black authors or artists see Black literature, Black art. For works about Black authors or artists see Black authors; Black artists
  x Blacks in art; Negroes in art
  xx Art; Characters and characteristics in literature
Blues (Songs, etc.)
  xx Black songs; Spirituals
Businessmen, Black. *See* Black businessmen
Characters and characteristics in literature
  See also Blacks in literature and art
Civil rights
  See also Blacks—Civil rights
Civil rights demonstrations. *See* Blacks—Civil rights
Color of man
  xx Negro race
Colored people (U.S.). *See* Blacks
Demonstrations for Black civil rights. *See* Blacks—Civil rights
Discrimination in employment
  See also Blacks—Employment
Education
  See also Blacks—Education
Employment. *See* Blacks—Employment
Ethnology
  See also Blacks
  xx Negro race
Folk songs, African
  xx Black songs
Folk songs, Black (American). *See* Black songs
Folk songs, Negro (American). *See* Black songs
Folklore, Black. *See* Black folklore
Folklore, Negro. *See* Black folklore
Freedom marches. *See* Blacks—Civil rights
Housing, Black. *See* Blacks—Housing
Housing, Negro. *See* Blacks—Housing
Integration, Racial. *See* Blacks—Integration

Librarians, Black. *See* **Black librarians**

Librarians, Negro. *See* **Black librarians**

Libraries and Blacks
 See also **Black librarians**
 xx **Black librarians**

Literature
 See also **Black literature**

Marches for Black civil rights. *See* **Blacks—Civil rights**

Minstrels, Black. *See* **Black minstrels**

Minstrels, Negro. *See* **Black minstrels**

Music, American
 See also **Black songs; Spirituals**

Music, Black. *See* **Black music**

Music, Negro. *See* **Black music**

Musicians, Black. *See* **Black musicians**

Musicians, Negro. *See* **Black musicians**

Nationalism, Black. *See* **Black nationalism**

Nationalism, Negro. *See* **Black nationalism**

Negritude. *See* **Blacks—Race identity**

Negro artists. *See* **Black artists**

Negro athletes. *See* **Black athletes**

Negro authors. *See* **Black authors**

Negro folk songs. *See* **Black songs**

Negro folklore. *See* **Black folklore**

Negro librarians. *See* **Black librarians**

Negro literature. *See* **Black literature**

Negro minstrels. *See* **Black minstrels**

Negro music. *See* **Black music**

Negro musicians. *See* **Black musicians**

Negro nationalism. *See* **Black nationalism**

Negro poetry. *See* **Black poetry**

Negro race
 Use for works dealing with anthropological and biological discussions without reference to geographical area. For works on the people and works on ethnic discussions use **Blacks**
 See also **Color of man; Ethnology; Race problems**

Negro spirituals. *See* **Spirituals**

Negro suffrage. *See* **Blacks—Suffrage**

Negroes. *See* **Blacks**

Negroes—Art. *See* **Black art**

Negroes as businessmen. *See* **Black businessmen**

Negroes in art. *See* **Blacks in literature and art**

Poetry—Collections
 See also **Black poetry**

Race awareness
 See also **Blacks—Race identity**

Race problems
 xx **Negro race**

Racial identity. *See* **Blacks—Race identity**

Race identity. *See* **Blacks—Race identity**

Race psychology. *See* **Blacks—Race identity**

Religion
 See also **Blacks—Religion**

Segregation in education
    xx **Blacks—Education**
Separatism, Black. *See* **Black nationalism**
Slavery in the U.S.
    xx **Blacks**
Songs
    See also **Black songs**
Spirituals
    See also **Blues (Songs, etc.)**
    x Black spirituals; Negro spirituals
    xx **Black songs; Music, American**
Suffrage
    See also **Black suffrage**
Witchcraft
    x Black art (Magic)